Endings

Endings

A Sociology of Death and Dying

Michael C. Kearl

New York · Oxford
Oxford University Press
1989

Oxford University Press

Oxford   New York   Toronto
Delhi   Bombay   Calcutta   Madras   Karachi
Petaling Jaya   Singapore   Hong Kong   Tokyo
Nairobi   Dar es Salaam   Cape Town
Melbourne   Auckland

and associated companies in
Berlin   Ibadan

Copyright © 1989 by Oxford University Press, Inc.

Published by Oxford University Press, Inc.,
200 Madison Avenue, New York, New York 10016

Oxford is a registered trademark of Oxford University Press

Library of Congress Cataloging-in-Publication Data
Kearl, Michael C.
Endings: a sociology of death and dying/Michael C. Kearl.
p. cm.   Bibliography: p.   Includes index.
ISBN 0-19-504515-7
1. Death—Social aspects. 2. Death—Cross-cultural studies.
3. Life cycle, Human—Social aspects. I. Title.
HQ1073.K43   1989
306′.9—dc19   88-25579   CIP

1 2 3 4 5 6 7 8 9

Printed in the United States of America
on acid-free paper

A Digest on the Degree of Public Concern about Important State Issues, September 1986, pp. 2–3. Reprinted by permission of the Field Institute.

Adweek (1984). Reprinted with permission of *Adweek* 1984.

Anderson, Jack (1986). Reprinted with permission of United Media.

Arlens, Michael J. (1976). "The Cold, Bright Charms of Immortality" in *The View from Highway 1* by Michael J. Arlens. Copyright © 1974, 1975, 1976 by Michael J. Arlen. Originally published in *The New Yorker*. Reprinted by permission of Farrar, Straus, and Giroux, Inc.

Aronson, M. K., and R. Lipkowitz (1981). Reprinted with permission from the American Geriatrics Society, *Senile Dementia, Alzheimer's Type: The Family and the Health Care Delivery System* by M. K. Aronson and R. Lipkowitz (*Journal of the American Geriatrics Society*, Vol. No. 29 (12), pp. 568–571, 1981.)

Barton, D. (1972). Reprinted by permission of the *Journal of Medical Education*.

Berger, Peter, and Thomas Luckmann (1964). Reprinted with permission of *European Journal of Sociology*.

Berns, Walter (1979). *For Capital Punishment: The Morality of Anger*, April, 1979. Reprinted by permission of Harper's Magazine.

Bishop, Jim (1982). Reprinted by permission of *San Antonio Light*.

Blauner, Robert (1966). Reprinted by permission of *Psychiatry*.

Cohen, Richard (1985). Reprinted by permission of Richard Cohen.

Eringer, Robert (1986). *Secret Agent Man*. From *Rolling Stone*, January 16, 1986. By Straight Arrow Publishers, Inc. © 1986. All rights reserved. Reprinted by permission.

Goldstein, Robert (1984). Published by permission of Transaction, Inc. from "Political Funerals," by Robert Goldstein, *Society*, vol. 21, no. 3 (March/April) 1984. Copyright © 1984 by Transaction, Inc.

Harper's Magazine (1985). *Please Excuse Johnny From Death Ed*, May, 1985. Reprinted by permission of Harper's Magazine.

Harrington, Alan (1977). © 1977 by Alan Harrington. From *The Immortalist*. Published by Celestial Arts, Berkeley, Calif.

Holquist, Michael (1986). Reprinted by permission of *The Key Reporter*.

Kastenbaum, R., S. Peyton, and B. Kastenbaum (1977). *Sex Discrimination after Death*, *Omega* 7:351–359. Reprinted by permission of Pergamon Journals, Inc. © 1977.

Koestler, Arthur (1977). Reprinted with permission from *Psychology Today Magazine*, Copyright © 1977 (APA).

Moody, Raymond (1975). Reprinted by permission of Mockingbird Books, Inc.

National Hospice Organization (1982). Reprinted by permission of The National Hospice Organization.

Pine, Vanderlyn, and Derek Phillips. © 1970 by The Society for the Study of Social Problems. Reprinted from *Social Problems* Vol. 17, no. 3, Winter 1970, pp. 405–417 by permission.

Reuters (1976). Reprinted by permission of Reuters.

Rosenbaum, Ron (1982). *Turn On, Tune In, Drop Dead*, July 1982. Reprinted by permission of Harper's Magazine.

Ruesch, Hans (1951). Reprinted by permission of Hans Ruesch.

San Antonio Light (1977, 1986). Reprinted by permission of *San Antonio Light*.

Sanders, Charles (1966). Reprinted by permission of *Ebony* Magazine © 1966 Johnson Publishing Company.

Schmitt, Raymond, and Wilbert Leoanrd II (1986). Reprinted by permission of The University of Chicago Press.

Seiden, Richard (1979). Reprinted by permission of *Suicide and Life-Threatening Behavior*.

Spilka, Bernard, Larry Stout, Barbara Minton (1977). Reprinted by permission of The Society for the Scientific Study of Religion.

Starobinski, Jean (1986), pp. 16–20. Reprinted with permission from *The New York Review of Books*. Copyright © 1986 Nyrev, Inc.

Turner, Ronny, and Charles Edgley (1975). Reprinted by permission of *Sociology and Social Research*.

Westie, Frank (1973). Reprinted by permission of the American Sociological Association.

For Joanie, Frank and Zachary
And in Memory of Eve and Charles Rankin

Preface

Beware ye as ye pass by,
as ye be now so once was I.
As I be now so must ye be.
Prepare for death and follow me.

> Traditional eighteenth-century
> New England epitaph

You have begun a book that will take at least one twenty-five-thousandth of your life to complete. Why have you chosen to consume your precious time by reading and reflecting on a matter supposedly so morbid, tasteless, and terrifying as death? Is not death, after all, the shatterer of hopes, the foreclosure on ambitions, and the destroyer of enterprises? Does it not mean the terror experienced by those who die and the deep grief felt by those who survive? What more could one possibly want to know about it?

I was raised to think in such ways, and my decision to spend even a larger portion of my life to write this text was prompted by several experiences. One involved a chance conversation with an individual who had been dead for two centuries. It was on a crisp, clear fall day in New Hampshire—one of those picture-postcard days, with the hills brilliantly painted in reds and yellows and the smell of frost in the air. Rejoicing that such a day fell on a Saturday, I ventured out on back roads to explore my new home with several fellow students. We came across an old Yankee cemetery which looked like a perfect setting for our amateur photographic pursuits. There I happened across a tombstone with the inscription cited above. Here lay an individual who, like me, undoubtedly once reveled on days such as this. Unlike the

An old cemetery in Nantucket, Massachusetts. The dead are an integral part of life, reminding the living of the transitoriness of existence. The Bettmann Archive, Inc.

contemporary tombstones upon which are generally etched only the bureaucratic details required to sort us from others, this marker described a unique self: his schooling and occupation, the names of his wife and children, and his immortal aspirations were all detailed in obsolete prose and in old-style lettering. With the limitation of three square feet, why would one's final thoughts for the living be concluded with the injunction to "prepare for death and follow me"? Why should one even want to undergo such preparations, and how would one go about it? Only many years later did it occur to me that death can be thought of not as some unfortunate accident or eventual fate to obsess about or deny, but rather as the finish line of existence, as a point of closure much like the conclusion of one's educational goals or the completion of a major project.

Death has been so convincingly defined by philosophically minded psychiatrists and clinically experienced psychologists that sociologists seem to have little of their own to contribute. Several years ago, sociologist David Unruh (1981), writing for the discipline's major review journal, asked, "Is there a sociology of death?" His answer was an unconvincing affirmative, and his examples of a research tradition were limited and dry: interactions between the dying and the living, widowhood and bereavement, and funerary rituals. Here my intent is to demonstrate that there is such a sociology of death, not simply determined by its subject matter but rather complete with its own methodological strategies and theoretical unities. As will become abundantly evident, death and dying issues are omnipresent, and there is no way a single volume can summarize, let alone simply index, the full scope of the subject matter.

Science is but developed perception. By pulling together information that most of us are routinely exposed to but typically ignore or give passing attention to, such as holiday auto fatality rates or Congress's restoration of citizenship rights to Robert E. Lee in 1976, I seek to sensitize the reader to death's role in everyday life and to search for connections between its manifestations, considering, for instance, the impact of publicized suicides on subsequent fatal accidents.

Sociology is not only a science but an art as well. Of art, Jack Nicholson once said, "My first acting teacher said all art is one thing—a stimulating point of departure. And if you can do that in a piece, you've fulfilled your cultural, sociological obligation as a workman. What you're supposed to do is keep people vitally interested in the world they live in" (Schruers 1986, p. 48). To be developed is a new perspective, one allowing us to stand back and examine social life from a different vantage point. We live in a society in which entrepreneurs market space on an orbiting mausoleum. At supermarket checkouts we are bombarded by tabloid headlines about ghosts and former lives. From our mass media we absorb thousands of death stories, including those from prime-time television meant to entertain us. Our scientists debate whether an asteroid killed the dinosaurs and whether or not a perpetual winter will follow an all-out nuclear exchange. Theologians protest abortion and capital punishment, and yet tens of thousands are killed worldwide each year in the name of religion. And our political leaders spend a majority of the federal budget on military instruments of destruction and on those most likely to die, the elderly. Yet ours is supposedly a death-denying culture, hiding within institutional settings—such as nursing homes and hospitals—the dying process, paying embalmers to make the dead look as if they are just asleep, and giving all kinds of publicity to those who cheat death, whether by surviving with an artificial heart or by living more than one hundred years.

I hope that this book will be an engaging point of departure, a theater of ideas that brings together the research and speculations of anthropology, economics, politics, religion, philosophy, and psychology, as well as sociology.

San Antonio
April 1988

M.C.K.

REFERENCES

Schruers, Fred. 1986. "The Rolling Stone Interview: Jack Nicholson." *Rolling Stone.* August 14, pp. 32–52.
Unruh, David. 1981. "Is There a Sociology of Death?" *Contemporary Sociology* 10/ (4):508–12.

Acknowledgments

Writing about death is a lonely enterprise. People assume that behind it lies some morbid motivation, an unresolved internal conflict, or perhaps a traumatic childhood experience. The subject matter is not one readily amenable to casual discourse, even with one's academic colleagues. On the other hand, having claimed interest in, if not expertise on, the subject has meant being the recipient of many previously unshared thoughts; numerous newspaper clippings and bizarre facts that no one knows what to do with; and such relics from family attics as Haitian voodoo dolls and death masks, Mexican Day of the Dead art, a nineteenth-century embalming kit, tombstones, and even a casket.

There are several individuals without whose support this work would not be possible. My wife, Joanie, tolerated years of death talk and a house full of death artifacts, sacrificed many hours to proofreading and editing, and balanced endings with beginnings by bearing two wonderful sons. Lillian Robinson, our ever-cheerful nanny and housekeeper, helped manage our beginnings, enabling *Endings* to be completed.

Intellectually, this work owes most to individuals I have never met, such as Peter Berger, Kathy Charmaz, Victor Marshall, and Jessica Mitford; and many who are dead, such as Philippe Ariès, Ernest Becker, Emile Durkheim, Karl Mannheim, and Wilbert E. Moore. It is their thoughts that inspired this enterprise, their ideas that I have interwoven and hopefully enriched through juxtaposition and illustration.

Further inspiration and reinforcement came from rich conversations with Bernard Spilka, Edwin Shneidman, Richard Harris, John Donahue, Paul Robertson, Charles White, and Sid Plotkin. Chad Gordon, Charles McConnel, Richard Machalek, and Peter French provided supportive readings to early drafts of selected chapters, bolstering my confidence as I ventured outside sociology into the myriad of academic disciplines addressing the human condition. Insights into the funeral industry were provided by four years of experience as a public member on the Texas State Board of Morticians, where I learned both sides of the industry debate from James Reveley, Herbert Baker, and Grady Baskin. And my knowledge of hospice largely derived from the dedicated staff at St. Benedict's Hospice, where I served on a community advisory committee.

The direction this book ultimately took is largely due to the hundreds of students who passed through my Sociology of Death and Dying classes at Trinity University over the past decade. Their observations and questions, informed by the liberal arts climate of the institution, constantly challenged me to expand the scope of inquiries and to seek connections between disciplinary purviews. A note of thanks also goes to Trinity's faculty development program for supporting a semester's leave to initiate this endeavor.

At Oxford University Press, my thanks go to Susan Rabiner, who first approved the enterprise, and to Valerie Aubry, Niko Pfund, and Ellen Fuchs, who saw it through to completion. The manuscript benefited immensely from the copy-editing of Wendy Keebler.

Finally, there are those special others whose own endings occurred in the course of writing this book, forcing me to leave the realm of intellectualizing to fully feel the sting of death's harsh arrow: my grandparents, Charles and Eve Rankin, and Michael Russell, my best friend. Although sorely missed, they remain very much a part of my life.

Contents

Endings

Chapter 1

Introduction: Death's Revelations of Life

Death and the sun are not to be looked at steadily.
La Rochefoucauld (1613–80), *Maxims*

It has been claimed that one can never look directly at the sun or at one's own death. And yet, throughout human history, both have been the enduring themes of myth and religion, science and magic, curiosity and fear. From our late-twentieth-century vantage point we find that as the sun is understood as being the source of life in the natural order, so death is becoming recognized as the central dynamism underlying the life, vitality, and structure of the social order. Death is the muse of our religions, philosophies, political ideologies, arts, and medical technologies. It sells newspapers and insurance policies, invigorates the plots of our television programs, and—judging from our dependency on fossil fuels—even powers our industries.[1] It is the barometer by which we measure the adequacy of social life, such as when we compare cross-cultural life expectancy rates to gauge social progress or compare national homicide rates to infer the stability of social structures. The nature of the interrelationships between death and life is the subject of this text. In the sense of gestalt, the foreground of life is only possible with the background of death.

We are now in the midst of a virtual renaissance of interest in endings, both publicly and academically. With the lifting of the taboos surrounding the subject of death (the word itself was banned for years from the *Christian Science Monitor;* Feifel 1959, pp. 115–16),[2] formerly obscured relationships among the living, the dying, and the dead are now becoming clearer. Here

Death barometers the quality of life in numerous ways. On the shores of Lake Michigan dead fish indicate a fundamental disequilibrium between the natural order and
the social order of man. Nancy Hays, Monkmeyer Press.

we shall attempt to take advantage of this situation, to sensitize ourselves to
the spectrum of death-related phenomena and thereby provide the background necessary for understanding our values toward such issues as abortion or euthanasia, for framing our fears, and for recognizing the connections between seemingly disparate events. Our goal is to explore how death
contributes to social change and to articulate the ways in which attitudes
toward death are socially generated and serve social functions, especially as a
means of social control.

The traditional goal of death education has been to socialize individuals to an inevitable event in their lives. Increasingly such lessons have become the responsibility of educational institutions, places where a variety of perspectives come to be employed when analyzing any phenomenon. What has transpired is that the centrality of death is coming to be appreciated by nearly every disciplinary purview. Further, as college curriculums increasingly stress coherency and interdisciplinary experiences, the death socializations and fears of individuals have come to be understood within much broader frameworks, including not only those of religion and philosophy but also those of medicine, biology, psychology, economics, politics, demography, and ecology (Steele 1975). This book is an attempt to map the separate contributions of each of these fields to the American experiences of death, recognizing that none singly monopolizes our understandings.

The Omnipresence of Death

Much of the American public begins its workday with news of death. On one June day in 1985, for example, the front-page headlines carried news of the death of Karen Quinlan, a "brain-dead" young woman who had survived for nearly a decade after being disconnected from a respirator, and the location of the skeleton remains of Josef Mengele, an architect and symbol of Nazi atrocities. We struggle to give at least some thought to the ethical implications of both their lives and deaths, at least until the toast is ready for buttering. Checking the medical section for new breakthroughs, we read that the likelihood of a coronary is five times greater during heavy exercise but that those who exercise hard are 40 percent less likely to have a heart attack. Such trade-offs have come to be routine from the oracles of science. While waiting for the bus, we share neighborhood news. "Did you hear about the elderly couple who moved in two doors down? He was going to sell out and finally retire, and they bought the place to fix up. Well, he collapsed in the yard while raking leaves." We think, "What a way to go. How many years of retirement contributions did he forgo?"

Although we live in a society in which most biological processes are privatized and hidden from general public view (or, if not, as is the case for eating, at least obscured by etiquette), births, sexual activities, and deaths—the basic expressions of our biological being—remain the major items of gossip. In fact, if one were to sensitize oneself and record any and all encounters with death themes over the course of a single day, one would be overwhelmed by their omnipresence; they lie within our fantasies and dreams, language and metaphor, jests and news, sports and music. Such instances, however, are rarely given second thought, and few connections are typically made between them. Why, for example, did jokes emerge in the mid-1980s about AIDS and the space shuttle *Challenger*? Were they simply nervous reactions to two devastating events? If so, why were there not similar instances of morbid humor surrounding Legionnaires' disease or the crash of the *Hindenburg*? As we will see, such death encounters are like separate points of a pointilist canvas, and one must stand back to see the entire picture.[3]

Throughout the twentieth century, there has existed a fundamental tension between social science theorists seeking either to minimize or to maximize death's potency in molding the psychologies, philosophies, religions, and politics of individuals and social systems. To a large extent, the minimalists control our times, perhaps reflecting our culture's death-denial orientation. It may also reflect the refusal of many academicians to accept the fact that so much of their disciplinary scopes can be reduced to such a basic, inevitable, and biological phenomenon. In psychology, for example, we rarely find contemporary researchers addressing death's bearing on cognition and motivation. And yet how do we explain the need some individuals have to flirt with death in order to feel alive, whether through hang gliding, winter rock climbing, or parachuting, and why the extent of such flirtations varies from culture to culture. Those psychologists who do discuss death often neglect to fully consider its social aspects and variance. Emile Durkheim's elaborations of the social factors shaping religious thought systems were, in part, reactions against the reductionist interpretations of theorists who perceived death fears as being the source of religion and, hence, of society. In political science, the role of death as a means of mobilizing a collectivity toward united action, such as the sinkings of the *Lusitania* and the *Arizona* which led the United States into two world wars, remains largely unexplicated. According to Robert Blauner (1966), modernization has supposedly meant the emancipation of the living from the control of the dead. Such practices as ancestor worship are assumed to be a part of the *Weltanschauung* of traditional, past-oriented societies, certainly not a feature of the progressive, future-time-oriented milieu of contemporary life. And yet the dead still vote, are rented as companions, are brought before live television audiences, endorse the tickets of American political parties, and are held as hostages in foreign lands.[4] This text will reaffirm death's centrality to our thought systems and activities, to balance out the minimizing theses currently in vogue.

Death as a Mirror of Life

Across cultures and time, death has been woven into the fabric of life. As Huntington and Metcalf observed in *Celebrations of Death,* "life becomes transparent against the background of death" (1979, p. 2). "Life" cannot exist without "death," and vice versa; therefore, death can be understood as an indicator of life. Just as subatomic physicists bombard and shatter the nuclei of atoms in order to reveal their constituent parts and processes, we shall see how death similarly reveals the most central social processes and cultural values. The funeral, for example, is one of the few occasions on which the bonds connecting the individual with the broader society are ritually dramatized and, as is the case in eulogies, the most central beliefs of a people are verbalized and reaffirmed.

Much of what we know of past societies is based on funerary evidence. Just as the natural order during the Jurassic era is ascertained by fossil remains, so life during the First Dynasty of ancient Egypt is reconstructed from the artifacts found in the tomb of Tutankhamen. We can pursue this research strategy further to find out not only who we were but who we are now and to ascertain how social reality "works." By studying the psychology of grief and the sociology of bereavement, for example, we can gain insight into the processes that shape and maintain identity. By analyzing newspaper obituaries over time, inferences can be made about changing attitudes toward age, sex, and race. In fact, the social implications of death are routinely recognized for reasons of political interest. For instance, when the Soviet newspapers *Trud* and *Sovetskaya Rossiya* blamed the Reagan administration for the 1982 Air Florida crash in Washington, D.C., claiming it was caused by the dismissal of air-traffic controllers the previous summer, death was being employed in East-West debates as an indicator of the adequacy of one's political economy (*San Antonio Express-News* 1982).[5] Further, national life expectancy and mortality rates have become the bases of international comparisons of technological development, urbanization, social stratification, humanitarianism, social disorder, and pollution.

Beyond being an indicator of life, death invigorates social systems and challenges their values. Death has mobilized collective action for a myriad of causes, from snail darters to whales, from consumer coalitions promoting changes in funerary practices to support for military causes in places unknown by a majority of the population. Why, for instance, is most of the federal budget allocated to the bureaucracies of death, to those who prepare to kill and to those most likely to die, namely the military and the elderly recipients of Social Security and Medicare support? Should society pay

This macabre seventeenth-century lithograph portrays the
transitoriness of power and the omnipotence of death. The
worms coiled through the skeleton reflect the period's fascination with decomposition. From T. Carey's *The Mirrour
which Flatters not*, published by R. Thale, London, 1639.
Dover Pictorial Archives.

hundreds of thousands of dollars for comatose patients with irreversible
symptoms when hundreds of thousands of young people go to bed hungry?
Is spending hundreds of billions of dollars to perfect and design instruments
for mass death the best way to guarantee peace? And is preventing the man-
made extinction of some rare creature to take precedence over the irrigation
of a desert?

The Iranian handling of the bodies of the eight American commandos who had died accidentally while attempting to rescue fifty-three American hostages illustrates how social rituals involving the dead contribute to the collective integrity and solidarity of political orders. For President Jimmy Carter and the United States, the deaths of the commandos represented American resolve to protect its interests and people abroad against an international injustice, the takeover of a national embassy. When the Iranians publicly displayed the bodies of the commandos and held them hostage as well, the president expressed national outrage by claiming violation of "all principles of humanity and decency" (Stevens 1980). The event dramatized a we-they distinction. As Carter put it, the Iranians "indicated by this inhumane act of displaying these bodies the kind of people with whom we have been dealing to try to secure the freedom of our fellow Americans," in contrast to the "self-sacrificial and heroic attitude" of our own. For the Iranians, the dead symbolized the righteousness of their cause, demonstrated by the ineptness of a major power to challenge it. For both political systems, the deaths simultaneously served to legitimate the ideologies of those in power and to unify public resolve.

It is this power of death to either galvanize or corrode social systems and to either stimulate or neutralize the social participation of their members that is the primary focus of this book.

Cultural, Social, and Individual Perspectives on Death

Individual knowledge and fears of death are conditioned by social environment. For this reason, the logic of this book progresses from the cultural to the social institutional and finally to the individual level of understanding death. To study the attitudes and fears of individuals divorced from their sociocultural milieus would be like analyzing ecological niches by studying animals in zoos. Individual thought always has social origins. As anthropologist Mary Douglas observed, "Classifications, logical operations, and guiding metaphors are given to the individual by society. . . . The sense of a priori rightness of some ideas and the nonsensicality of others are handed out as part of the social environment" (1986, p. 10).

The first layer of death's reality is peeled away in Chapters 2 through 4, which examine its cultural meanings. Cross-cultural comparisons are utilized in order to suspend our own ethnocentrism and to reveal the common forces underlying the tremendous cultural diversity. By examining the Greco-Roman and Judeo-Christian traditions, the *ars moriendi* of western Europe during the Middle Ages, the funerary practices and beliefs of the Puritans and those of Victorian England, as well as the traditional Mexican observances of All Souls' Day, we shall comprehend the scope of death's impact on what Clifford Geertz (1973) calls the "logico-meaningful" dimension of reality. We shall note how the cycles of death and rebirth pertain not only to nature but to the life-course rhythms of cultures, social groups, and individuals as well. And we shall observe how cultural thought systems, in order to make symbolic sense out of death, integrate their theses of mortality into their languages, religions, values, rituals, and conceptions of time, in other terms, into their *cultural death systems*. To explore death's indicator status, Chapter 2 concludes with an analysis of how cemeteries symbolically reflect a culture's basic beliefs and values.

Chapter 3 shifts from an anthropological to a sociological perspective and, beginning with the AIDS epidemic, develops a model of factors that determine death's disruptive potential as well as the social strategies for dampening its effects. In noting how the bubonic plague possibly contributed to the collapse of feudal orders and to the emergence of capitalism in Western cultures, we see how death can also be socially functional. By limiting population growth, strengthening the bonds of social solidarity (recall the collective grief shared in the United States following the explosion of the space shuttle *Challenger*, a sense of unity that would not have existed had the flight been a success), and allowing for the upward mobility of the young, death contributes in many ways to the reinforcement and change of social structure. Turning to the funeral as a ritual strategy for controlling the possible disorder and disillusionment caused by death, it will be demonstrated how societies can harness its power to reaffirm and define their most central values and goals. And by examining one facet of funerary ritual over time, the obituary, we will explore what progress society has made toward eliminating racism and sexism during this century.

Chapter 4 examines the meaning we assign to death as a function of who typically dies, how, where, when, and why. All societies make distinctions between good deaths and bad deaths. Because of the prolongevity revolution, which has made death basically a province of the old and a consequence of our biological limitations, the frustrations that historically surrounded the norm of premature deaths have been replaced by the moral and ethical dilemmas posed by postmature deaths. It is the poor, the disenfranchised, and those most socially marginal who are most likely to die premature, avoidable, man-made deaths, whether by suicide or homicide. We will consider the implications of a black male being six times more likely to be murdered than a white male in the United States, and the reasons why a seventy-year-old Japanese female is six times more likely to commit suicide than her American counterpart.

Chapters 5 through 11 analyze the social institutions that shield people from the anomic terrors of death by providing reasons for living, explanations for mortality, and opportunities for personally transcending death. Simultaneously, they also shape the death fears of any culture, whether by being the actual causes of death or by employing its fears as mechanisms of social control. Historically, the more powerful the institution, the greater the influence of its death ideology on the broader cultural outlook toward life.

We begin with religion, the institution that has traditionally provided the cultural explanations for why death occurs as well as the ritual and hope for those in their final passage. This is the source of such transcendent beliefs as judgment, heaven and hell, purgatory, resurrection, and reincarnation. It is the social sphere in which the potency of such postmortem conceptions in controlling the masses, in directing personal attentions to collective—as opposed to self-serving—goals, was first discovered. Chapter 5 concludes with an analysis of how denominational affiliations and intensity of religious beliefs shape individual attitudes toward some of the major thanatological issues of our times: abortion, euthanasia, capital punishment, and the right of the terminally ill to commit suicide.

With modernization, religion's monopoly over death explanations and consolations was broken. From philosophy, psychology, and the natural sciences emerged new, secular conceptualizations of finitude which would become part of the American death system. In Chapter 6 we consider the psychological paradigms linking death fears with neuroses, sensuality, creativity, and thrill seeking. We examine the tenets of existential philosophy, which address the costs of denying the fundamental anxiety and the possibility that culture is the consequence of death repressions. From the eschatologies of science, such as the Big Bang and evolutionary theories, comes the unsettling idea that the individual's death means nothing, that it is but a random event, without spiritual or moral implications, in a universe that is indifferent toward the human condition. As a result, for the first time in Western history, it is the here and now that is considered paradise and the hereafter that is unknown. And it is the quantity, not the quality, of life that has come to be culturally revered.

Chapter 7 details the relationship between death and work, a connection that has existed ever since the eviction from Eden, when Adam and Eve were made mortal and forced to labor. Despite the social evolution of the workplace, work continues to kill and will continue to do so as long as it is cheaper to pay off the victims' survivors than to incorporate safety features. And no longer is it just the laborer who dies, but also those from areas surrounding the work sites who are now dying from the toxic by-products poisoning the environment. On the other hand, it is work that provides individ-

The weighing of souls by the Archangel Michael. Xylographic
page from *Ars Moriendi*, printed by Johann Weissenburger,
Landshut, 1514, Dover Pictorial Archives.

uals a source of meaning for their lives (hence the terrors of having one's
work self symbolically killed, such as being "axed" or "terminated"), that
keeps them preoccupied and distracted from contemplating their existential
fate, and that provides the opportunity at least for one to be remembered
after death through one's products or one's inclusion in a hall of fame. This
chapter concludes with a study of that multibillion-dollar business that
works directly with the dead: the American funeral industry.

Another social sphere directly responsible for death and its avoidance is the polity. So extensive has the relationship become between modern political systems and the final passage that we find national governments involved in deciding why we die (through declarations of war or controlling carcinogens in the environment), how we die (such as by failing to pass gun-control legislation or by allowing the comatose terminally ill to be disconnected from life-support systems), when we die (such as by determining when a fetus can be legally aborted), who dies (the pogroms of Nazi Germany and the Khmer Rouge in Cambodia come to mind), and where we die (such as through federal support for nursing home care). Chapter 8 concludes with the contemporary politics of abortion and capital punishment.

Chapter 9 focuses on the military establishment, where man challenges nature as the cause of death. In the course of this century, tens of millions have died because of the warfare policies of their leaders. Here we consider why trillions of dollars are being spent perfecting the instruments of mass death, whether it is an impetus built into our genes or into the dynamics of our political economies. In addition to the contemporary military eschatology, namely a nuclear Armageddon, the rise of terrorism around the world is also discussed.

Having detailed a number of social processes directly shaping the American death system, we turn to those avenues by which our culture's thanatological lessons are primarily transmitted: the arts and mass media. As knowledge of death has become increasingly secondhand information, the influence of such media as television, cinema, music, and sports has become increasingly potent. In Chapter 10 we consider such things as who normally gets killed during prime time on television and how giving publicity to a suicide can increase suicide rates and fatal auto accidents.

The final (and perhaps major) social force shaping and embodying our culture's death fears and immortality hopes is the medical establishment, discussed in Chapter 11. Here the forewarnings of death are given (a diagnosis of cancer perhaps causes today the terror that a priest's damnation caused in the past), the actual process of dying is routinized and housed, and the formal pronouncements of death are publicly made. So central is this institution in addressing such cultural values as health, activism, and death defiance that huge resources have been invested within it, exceeding 10 percent of the entire American gross national product. Within the huge secular cathedrals dedicated to battles against death, we find physicians, our culture's high priests on matters of life and death, redefining the very boundaries of life (what obligations are owed to those permanently existing in a nonterminal vegetative state?) and researching ways individuals can survive with artificial hearts or transplanted kidneys.

All of these institutions exist in dynamic relationship with one another; any change occurring within any one comes to affect them all. For example, when the forces of secularism broke religion's monopoly over the management and conceptualizations of death, the death concerns of individuals shifted from fears of postmortem judgment to fears of dying undignified deaths within impersonal institutional settings. Using the methods and research of the sociological discipline, we empirically consider such questions as the impact of the death penalty on state- and national-level homicide rates, the racial and social-class biases determining who actually is executed in this country, the role of religious beliefs in determining suicide rates, the impact of war on the homicide rates of combatant nations, and the class and sexual politics underlying the abortion controversy.

Having portrayed the cultural and social milieus of death, the text concludes with the subjective experiences of those who die and those who survive (Chapter 12). Here we consider death socializations and fears across the life span, psychiatrist Elisabeth Kübler-Ross's studies of emotional phases of the dying process, reports of the near-death experiences of those revived from "clinical death," grief and widowhood, and the emergence of cultural grief experts and social support networks. Unlike the more psychologically oriented texts, however, we will also consider the ways in which these individual experiences of death are socially molded.

The goal of this book is not only to sensitize the reader to the spectrum of death issues but also to stimulate curiosity and new inquiries into thanatological matters. What sense can be made of all of the death information we are bombarded with every day? What parallels can be established between death and all other forms of social endings, whether they be divorces, graduations, job changes, retirements, or farewells between friends? To promote such thinking, each chapter, having overviewed the relevant issues, concludes with a more focused analysis of one of the themes developed.

Conclusion: Beginning with Endings

One thousand years ago, with the approach of the first millennium, there were those in western Europe so convinced that the end was near that they retreated to mountaintops to construct arks in preparation for the Flood. Now there are those who view the approach of the year 2000 with equal trepidation, pointing out the ominous signs of our times: nuclear weapons are proliferating; the environment is being destroyed by acid rain and chemical dumps; industrial technology produces cataclysmic disasters in places such as Bhopal, India; at least one animal species becomes extinct each day; murder and violence have become routine plot devices for obtaining high television ratings; religion legitimizes car bombings and wholesale terrorism; and white American adolescents commit suicide while their black counterparts murder each other at unprecedented rates. Meteorologists speak of the conclusion of the earth's benign climate, ecologists predict the ending of the planet's capacity to support our species, astronomers postulate the existence of a death star causing periodic extinctions of most life forms on the planet, physicists worry about the "nuclear winter" that would follow a nuclear exchange, Rev. Pat Robertson tells his followers that the Bible predicts the beginning of the end of the world during the 1980s, existential philosophers speak of the death of God, and President Ronald Reagan jokes about starting World War III. In many ways, ours is a culture of endings, and here we will track this theme across the social landscape and develop its social implications.

To provide a baseline of your own beliefs while simultaneously introducing the topics of this text, consider the questionnaire that follows. Speculate on the sources of your orientations, values, and fears, and with whom you even discuss such matters of endings.

Taking Inventory

A. Background

Whose death was the first death you remember?

_____ a relative

_____ a friend of the family

_____ a neighbor or acquaintance

_____ a person I did not know

_____ an animal

Do you own a gun?

_____ yes   _____ used to, now don't   _____ no

Do you smoke?

_____ yes   _____ used to, now don't   _____ no

Do you hunt?

_____ yes   _____ used to, now don't   _____ no

How many funerals have you attended in the last five years?   _____

Have you known a person who committed suicide?

_____ yes, knew well

_____ yes, knew somewhat

_____ yes, knew indirectly (a friend of a friend, etc.)

_____ no

Have you known a person who was a victim of murder?

_____ yes, knew well

_____ yes, knew somewhat

_____ yes, knew indirectly (a friend of a friend, etc.)

_____ no

What age do you think you will live to see? _____

You are afraid of dying.

disagree strongly	disagree somewhat	neutral	agree somewhat	agree strongly	don't know	never thought about it
_____	_____	_____	_____	_____	_____	_____

When you die, your wish is that your remains be

_____ buried

_____ cremated

_____ entombed

_____ really don't care

_____ parts used for transplants, the remainder buried or cremated

_____ used for the training of medical students

Do you believe there is some form of life after death?

_____ yes, one retains his or her identity and exists in some conscious state

_____ yes, but personal memories are gone

_____ yes, but not exactly clear in what state

_____ no

_____ really don't know

_____ never really thought about it

Do you believe that after you die you will be in some way aware of the activities of the living?

_____ yes _____ no _____ not sure

What percentage of the federal budget do you think should be spent on the military? _____

What percentage of the federal budget do you think is being spent on the military? _____

Do you believe nuclear weapons will be used in war during your lifetime?

_____ yes, there will be a world war between the superpowers

_____ yes, a few will be exploded in a limited contest between the superpowers

_____ yes, a few will be exploded in a limited contest involving Third World or developing nations

_____ no, nuclear weapons will never be used

Do you favor or oppose the death penalty for persons convicted of murder?

_____ favor _____ oppose _____ don't know

B. For the following questions, mark the response that comes closest to your attitude toward each of the following issues.

There are too many murders on television and in the movies.

disagree strongly	disagree somewhat	neutral	agree somewhat	agree strongly	don't know	never thought about it
_____	_____	_____	_____	_____	_____	_____

Murders on television and in the movies adversely affect young children.

disagree strongly	disagree somewhat	neutral	agree somewhat	agree strongly	don't know	never thought about it
_____	_____	_____	_____	_____	_____	_____

A person has the right to end his or her own life if this person has an incurable disease.

disagree strongly	disagree somewhat	neutral	agree somewhat	agree strongly	don't know	never thought about it
_____	_____	_____	_____	_____	_____	_____

A person has the right to end his or her own life if this person is old, tired of living, and ready to die.

disagree strongly	disagree somewhat	neutral	agree somewhat	agree strongly	don't know	never thought about it
_____	_____	_____	_____	_____	_____	_____

American industry is receiving unfair blame for excessive pollution.

disagree strongly	disagree somewhat	neutral	agree somewhat	agree strongly	don't know	never thought about it
_____	_____	_____	_____	_____	_____	_____

The chemicals in the products we use are slowly killing us all.

disagree strongly	disagree somewhat	neutral	agree somewhat	agree strongly	don't know	never thought about it
_____	_____	_____	_____	_____	_____	_____

When a person has a disease that cannot be cured, physicians should be allowed by law to end the patient's life by some painless means if the patient and his family request it.

disagree strongly	disagree somewhat	neutral	agree somewhat	agree strongly	don't know	never thought about it
_____	_____	_____	_____	_____	_____	_____

The medical advances of the next fifty years will extend the average life span to over one hundred years.

disagree strongly	disagree somewhat	neutral	agree somewhat	agree strongly	don't know	never thought about it
_____	_____	_____	_____	_____	_____	_____

Human immortality is scientifically possible.

disagree strongly	disagree somewhat	neutral	agree somewhat	agree strongly	don't know	never thought about it
_____	_____	_____	_____	_____	_____	_____

Within the next century, average life spans of Americans will exceed one hundred years.

disagree strongly	disagree somewhat	neutral	agree somewhat	agree strongly	don't know	never thought about it
_____	_____	_____	_____	_____	_____	_____

A pregnant woman should have the right to obtain a _legal_ abortion for any reason.

disagree strongly	disagree somewhat	neutral	agree somewhat	agree strongly	don't know	never thought about it
_____	_____	_____	_____	_____	_____	_____

Religion is the best way to cope with the fears of dying.

disagree strongly	disagree somewhat	neutral	agree somewhat	agree strongly	don't know	never thought about it
_____	_____	_____	_____	_____	_____	_____

In general, people are receiving good service from the American funeral industry.

disagree strongly	disagree somewhat	neutral	agree somewhat	agree strongly	don't know	never thought about it
_____	_____	_____	_____	_____	_____	_____

Too little money is spent in this country on terminally ill patients about to die.

disagree strongly	disagree somewhat	neutral	agree somewhat	agree strongly	don't know	never thought about it
_____	_____	_____	_____	_____	_____	_____

The federal government should pay most of the costs of organ transplants.

disagree strongly	disagree somewhat	neutral	agree somewhat	agree strongly	don't know	never thought about it
_____	_____	_____	_____	_____	_____	_____

You worry a lot about being killed in some man-made accident, such as a car crash or a plane crash.

disagree strongly	disagree somewhat	neutral	agree somewhat	agree strongly	don't know	never thought about it
_____	_____	_____	_____	_____	_____	_____

You worry a lot about being killed in some natural calamity, such as a hurricane or earthquake.

disagree strongly	disagree somewhat	neutral	agree somewhat	agree strongly	don't know	never thought about it
_____	_____	_____	_____	_____	_____	_____

You worry a lot about contracting and dying of some disease, such as AIDS, cancer, or Legionnaire's disease.

disagree strongly	disagree somewhat	neutral	agree somewhat	agree strongly	don't know	never thought about it
_____	_____	_____	_____	_____	_____	_____

The death of an individual in a place like Bangladesh or Ethiopia has less social impact than a death in the United States.

disagree strongly	disagree somewhat	neutral	agree somewhat	agree strongly	don't know	never thought about it
_____	_____	_____	_____	_____	_____	_____

Most wildlife will probably disappear in its natural setting during your lifetime.

disagree strongly	disagree somewhat	neutral	agree somewhat	agree strongly	don't know	never thought about it
_____	_____	_____	_____	_____	_____	_____

Something terrible will befall mankind around the year 2000.

disagree strongly	disagree somewhat	neutral	agree somewhat	agree strongly	don't know	never thought about it
_____	_____	_____	_____	_____	_____	_____

NOTES

1. Experiencing the nationwide decline in liberal arts enrollments, an Indiana University social and economic history course was renamed "Black Death." Enrollments went from 15 in 1978 to 125 by 1985 (Kilman 1985).

2. The veil of silence, however, continues to exist in a number of quarters in the United States. The Eagle Forum, a profamily group based in Alton, Illinois, sent out a letter to parents concerning the moral content of schooling. The letter recommended that parents lodge complaints against the curriculum of their schools under the provisions of the 1984 Protection of Pupil Rights Amendments to the General Education Provisions Act if certain subjects are broached. Included in this list of taboo areas are:

> Values clarification; use of moral dilemmas; . . . and survival games including life/death decision exercises;
>
> Death education, including abortion, euthanasia, suicide, use of violence, and discussions of death and dying; . . .
>
> Instruction in nuclear war, nuclear policy, and nuclear classroom games; . . . (*Harper's Magazine* 1985)

3. Academia rarely provides such an overarching perspective, particularly where it concerns the human condition. The so-called social sciences have typically carved up the subject matter into the disciplinary purviews of anthropology, psychology, sociology, economics, and political science, often divorcing themselves from history, art, religion, philosophy, mass media, and literature—subjects often relegated to the humanities—and from biology and ecology—disciplines segregated in the natural sciences. This segregation exists not only in college curriculums or in the distinctive academic methodologies, but physically as well: on college campuses those of one discipline are often housed together, often separated by floors from related disciplines and by buildings from unrelated ones. Here, nevertheless, another attempt is made at least to pull together the varied manifestations of death and to demarcate the full scope of thanatology by using the so-called sociological imagination, focusing on the interrelationships between social history and biographical experiences, between social structure and consciousness.

4. Ballots cast by individuals later discovered to have been dead are acknowledged to have influenced the outcomes of John F. Kennedy's presidential campaign victory in Illinois and the first victory of "Landslide" Lyndon Johnson (Maxwell and Crain 1978; Royko 1971). In California, the Ghost Adoption agency will pick out a spirit to suit specifications and hold a seance during which the entity decides if he or she wants to be adopted (*San Antonio Express-News* 1979). On October 6, 1980, "Speedy," the mummy of a black pauper who had died in the 1920s, was brought onstage on the television program "That's Incredible!" During the 1980 Democratic National Convention, the movie *Open the Gates* was shown to delegates, in which Hubert Humphrey endorsed the Carter-Mondale ticket; the night before the election,

a Democratic advertisement showed clips of Harry Truman rallying for the party cause.

5. The Soviets may still have been smarting from the attention paid by the Western press to their rising mortality rates. Between 1964 and 1975, death rates had risen 38 percent (Cooper 1979) from alcoholism and such common capitalist diseases as coronary heart disease and cancer (*New York Times* 1979). Nearly every other industrialized country, on the other hand, has experienced continuously declining rates since records have been kept (see Chapter 8 herein).

REFERENCES

Blauner, Robert. 1966. "Death and Social Structure." *Psychiatry* 29:378–94.

Cooper, Richard. 1979. "Death Rates Herald the Birth of Soviet Capitalism." *New York Times.* June 26, p. A19.

Douglas, Mary. 1986. *How Institutions Think.* Syracuse, N.Y.: Syracuse University Press.

Feifel, Herman. 1959. "Attitudes toward Death in Some Normal and Mentally Ill Populations." In Herman Feifel, ed., *The Meaning of Death.* New York: McGraw-Hill, pp. 114–30.

Geertz, C. 1973. *The Interpretation of Cultures.* New York: Basic Books.

Harper's Magazine. 1985. "Please Excuse Johnny from Death Ed." May, p. 24.

Huntington, R., and P. Metcalf. 1979. *Celebrations of Death: The Anthropology of Mortuary Ritual.* New York: Vail-Ballou.

Kilman, Scott. 1985. "Facing Declining Enrollment, Instructors of Liberal Arts Jazz Up Their Courses." *Wall Street Journal.* December 26, p. 9.

Maxwell, William E., and Ernest Crain. 1978. *Texas Politics Today.* New York: West.

New York Times. 1979. "Death Rate of Men Up in Soviet Towns." June 11, p. 5.

Royko, Michael. 1971. *Boss: Richard J. Dailey of Chicago.* New York: Dutton.

San Antonio Express-News. 1982. "Soviets Lay Crash Blame on Reagan." January 17, p. 2A.

———. 1979. "Ghosts to Order." June 10, p. 5B.

Steele, Stephen. 1975. "Socialization of Death-Related Behavior: Environmental Factors and Social Organization." Paper presented at the Annual Meeting of the American Sociological Association.

Stevens, W. 1980. "Outrage over Bodies." *New York Times.* April 29, p. 2.

Chapter 2

What Death Means:
Death in Cross-Cultural and
Historical Perspective

 A Murder in the Arctic

"You said the fellow you killed provoked you?"

"So it was."

"He insulted Asiak [an Eskimo wife]?"

"Terribly."

"Presumably he was killed as you tried to defend her from his advances?"
Ernenek [her husband] and Asiak looked at each other and burst out laughing.

"It wasn't so at all," Asiak said at last.

"Here's how it was," said Ernenek. "He kept snubbing all our offers although he was our guest. He scorned even the oldest meat we had."

"You see, Ernenek, many of us white men are not fond of old meat."

"But the worms were fresh!" said Asiak.

"It happens, Asiak, that we are used to foods of a quite different kind."

"So we noticed," Ernenek went on, "and that's why, hoping to offer him at last a thing he might relish, somebody proposed him Asiak to laugh [have sexual intercourse] with."

"Let a woman explain," Asiak broke in. "A woman washed her hair to make it smooth, rubbed tallow into it, greased her face with blubber, and scraped herself clean with a knife, to be polite."

"Yes," cried Ernenek, rising. "She had purposely groomed herself! And what did the white man do? He turned his back to her! That was too much! Should a man let his wife be so insulted? So somebody grabbed the scoundrel by his miserable little shoulders and beat him a few times against the wall—not in order to kill him, just wanting to crack his head a little. It was unfortunate it cracked a lot!"

"Ernenek has done the same to other men," Asiak put in helpfully. "But it was always the wall that went to pieces first."

The white men winced. "Our judges would show no understanding for such an explanation. Offering your wife to other men!"

"Why not? The men like it and Asiak says it's good for her. It makes her eyes sparkle and her cheeks glow."

"Don't you people borrow other men's wives?" Asiak inquired.

"Never mind that! It isn't fitting, that's all."

"Refusing isn't fitting for a man!" Ernenek said indignantly. "Anybody would much rather lend out his wife than something else. Lend out your sled and you'll get it back cracked, lend out your saw and some teeth will be missing, lend out your dogs and they'll come home crawling, tired—but no matter how often you lend out your wife she'll always stay like new."

Ruesch 1951, pp. 87–88. Reprinted by permission of
Harper and Row Publishers Inc., © 1951.

In the frozen North, death came to a man who failed to respect the cultural order of another people. To his own kind, it was murder; to those whose reality was so clumsily rattled, his death was an unfortunate accident, like that of a drunk killed in an auto accident. On the other side of the planet, the University of Melbourne was compelled to respect the sanctity of death: the school was legally forced to relinquish its hundreds of ten-thousand-year-old human bones to Australian aborigines. What for scientists was a link to prehistoric societies was for the native people their cultural and spiritual heritage (Angier 1984). Such are the cultural lessons of death. The meaning of death and the relationship between the dead and the living are culturally relative.

Like the climatologists who so eagerly awaited the close-up photographs of Jupiter and Saturn in order to understand the atmospheric dynamics of earth, we need cross-cultural comparisons in order to comprehend ourselves. "Death" is a socially constructed idea. The fears, hopes, and orientations people have regarding it are not instinctive, but rather are learned from such public symbols as the languages, arts, and religious and funerary rituals of their culture. Every culture has a coherent mortality thesis whose explanations of death are so thoroughly ingrained that they are believed to be right by its members.[1] Any social change is accompanied by modifications of these death meanings and ceremonies. The goal of this discussion is to eventually relate these systems of beliefs about death to specific social processes.

For instance, consider the following historical generalization by Arnold Toynbee: "[O]ne index of pessimism is suicide. In a society where life is rated at so low a value that death is held to be the lesser evil, suicide will be held

In Pieter Vander Aa's *Naaukeurige Versameling* ("Precise Collection"), American Indians are depicted torturing, dismembering, and eating captured Spaniards. To legitimate their occupation of foreign lands and suppression of indigenous cultures, European colonialists often devised stories of cannibalism to demonstrate the depravity of those they brutally subjugated. The University of Texas Rare Books Collection.

to be one of the basic human rights, and the practice of it will be considered respectable" (1980, p. 13). Would there be a rash of suicides if it were scientifically verified that the hereafter was some celestial Disneyland? And what happens to our fears and orientations about death when there occurs a dramatic change in our self-concept, such as when Copernicus dethroned the earth from the center of the cosmos or when Darwin dethroned man from a plane above the animal kingdom? Human history is an anthology of such disruptions and their consequences. In fact, the thesis of this book is that our conceptualizations of death so profoundly shape cultural meaning that any change in the quality of death or in the envisioning of the hereafter is amplified through the entire social order, bringing changes from top to bottom, from the relative power of different social institutions to the language in everyday life.

Another way of looking at culture is as a legacy which living generations have inherited from those of the past. F. Lloyd Warner (1959), for instance, defined human culture as the symbolic organization of the remembered experiences of the dead as it is felt and understood by the living. He adds that the human condition of individual mortality and the comparative immortality of our species and social institutions make most human activities, in essence, an exchange of understanding between the living and the dead.

Cultural Responses to Death

A basic accomplishment of any cultural orientation is its capacity to give symbolic order and meaning to human mortality, assisting the individual with "coming to terms with death [by comprising] a refutation of the meaninglessness of life that death, even longed-for death, appears to proclaim" (Choron 1964, p. 9). This philosophical insight has anthropological implications: "the issue of death throws into relief the most important cultural values by which people live their lives and evaluate their experiences" (Huntington and Metcalf 1979, p. 2). As will be developed in Chapter 6, society can be perceived as a symbolic stage on which individual actors achieve earthly heroism, simultaneously satisfying the human need for self-esteem and attention while providing causes so that its members need not worry about what life means or have the time to reflect on the terrors of death.

Most of us rarely experience the precariousness of social life. We awake in the morning fully confident that the social game board, on which we are but a piece, has not changed. We assume that the props we use in our daily routines are all where we left them, that people will drive on the same side of the road, that clock hands will continue to go clockwise, that a five-dollar bill is worth more than a dime, that we are married to the same person we were the night before, and that the sun will not become a supernova. We are confident that things tomorrow will be as they are today. So normal and natural do these things seem that they have a reality as firm and concrete as the mountains in the distant background.[2] Such is the taken-for-granted quality of society, whose first function is the production of order and meaning. Only an ordered world is a predictable world, and the essence of society is the predictability of its members' actions. And within such a surprise-free world, one has the feeling of a certain invulnerability, the sense that things are controllable (or, at least, predictable) and fair, and trust in the premise that this world remains benevolent to those who observe the rules (Goleman 1985).

But there are times in the course of history when a "reality rip" occurs within the fabric of this cultural canopy of security. A gunman unleashes a barrage of bullets at a local McDonald's, a passenger jet crashes into a shop-

The boundaries between the realms of the living and the dead vary from culture to culture. In the catacombs of the Monreale Monastery in Palermo, Sicily, the living come face-to-face with the mummified remains of monks and laymen. The Bettmann Archive, Inc.

ping mall, a volcano erupts and covers a town with suffocating mud and ash, or a nuclear weapon is detonated overhead. For the survivors, it often seems as if the world itself has died. The rules of life suddenly have no currency in what has become a malevolent world. Fear, rage, or shock normally follow, and many sense the loss of personal worthiness—either because they believe themselves no longer to be worthy of security provided by society or because they blame themselves for the others' deaths. The meaningfulness of one's entire cultural enterprise is discovered to be no more than a sandcastle before the incoming tide.

Death poses the fundamental threat to the order and meaning that social systems erect to shield their members from the anomic terrors of chaos. We, as a species, need a sense of universal purpose and design inherent in the universe and the sense that we are the expression of such a purpose. Psychoanalyst Susanne Langer (1960, p. 287) observed, "Man can adapt himself to anything his imagination can cope with; but he cannot deal with Chaos. Because his characteristic function and highest asset is conception, his greatest fright is to meet what he cannot construe—the 'uncanny,' as it is popularly called." Mythologist Joseph Campbell (1974) hypothesized that myth-making began with the first awareness of mortality, forcing early man to seek purpose, to rationalize the irrational, and to deny death's finality. Many non-modern societies organize much of their social life around the ever-present reality of death, and all cultures have varying recipes for dealing with the challenge.

The flip side of this ability of cultures to shield their members against the terrors of death is their power accrued through threatening an individual's exposure to the unfiltered forces of chaos. When, for example, one receives the evil eye in Greece or a voodoo hex in Haiti, one's greatest fears of the terrors lurking outside the protective canopy of one's culture are exploited. In describing the workings of voodoo, anthropologist Wade Davis observes how one's fate can be sealed by the mind:

For just as an individual's sickness may have a psychosomatic basis, it is possible for a society to generate physical ailments and conditions that have meaning only in the minds of its people. . . . An individual breaks a social or spiritual code, violates a taboo, or for one reason or another believes himself a victim of a putative society. Conditioned since childhood to expect disaster, he then acts out what amounts to a self-fulfilling prophecy. (1985, p. 136)

These fears can be so great that they lead to the overstimulation of the sympathetic adrenal system, causing death; indeed, one can be scared to death.

Ethos, Ritual, and Evolving Traditions

The veil of order and meaning that societies construct against chaos is called the cultural ethos, which, according to anthropologist Clifford Geertz (1973, p. 127), includes "the tone, character, and quality of their life, its moral and aesthetic style and mood; it is the underlying attitude toward themselves and their world that life reflects." It shapes their worldview, "their picture of the way things in sheer actuality are, their concept of nature, of self, of society." The cultural vision of death, the death ethos, similarly affects the behaviors of the living. It determines such things as the militancy of a people, their fears of or hopes for reincarnation and resurrection, their willingness to perform organ transplants or take out life insurance, as well as their attitudes toward capital punishment and abortion. Where postmortem existence is understood to be wretched and drab, hedonism and self-indulgent behaviors often follow. Where the quality of one's postmortem fate varies, such as in cultures in which the religious conceptions of heaven and hell predominate, there can be daily preoccupations with sin. When such preoccupations serve basic social functions, they will be routinely reinforced through ritual exercise, assisting in the internalization of the moral values and ideals of a culture. Such rituals involve the "symbolic fusion of ethos and world view" (Geertz 1973, p. 113), thereby giving cosmic significance and legitimization to the cultural recipes for everyday life.

Each culture must address the eternal search for the meaning of life and death. But what exactly does this mean? In considering the various facets of death ethos cross-culturally, Arnold Toynbee (1980) and others have developed typologies of orientations toward life and death:

- Cultures can be death-accepting, death-denying, or even death-defying. In the death-defying West, the strategies for salvation have historically included activism and asceticism. In the East, the strategies have often been more contemplative and mystical.

- Death may be considered either as the end of existence or as a transition to another state of being or consciousness. For Buddhists and Hindus, the arch-ordeal envisioned is not death but rather the pain of having to undergo another rebirth. It is the end of rebirths that is their goal, not the end of death, which is the goal of Christianity.

- Considering the two previous dimensions, it should be evident that death can be viewed as either sacred or profane, a state or process perceived to be either sacrosanct or polluting for the living.

- Where there is some immortality conception, it can either be personal or collective. In the West, postdeath conceptions typically involve the integrity and continuity of one's personal self. In the East, the ultimate goal is often an undifferentiated and impersonal oneness with the universe.

- Cultures have taken hedonistic and pessimistic orientations toward life in facing the inevitability of death. One can take an "eat, drink, and be merry, for tomorrow we die" approach to life. There is, for instance, some evidence that many members of the American baby-boom generation, realizing that they are the first downwardly mobile generation in American history (Longman 1985), watching their parent and grandparent generations' frugal life-styles ending either in premature death (and, therefore, never enjoying the retirement that was being saved for) or in massive medical bills for various ailments and illnesses (Ruffenach 1985), now spend their savings for self-indulgent life-styles.

- The American notion of life being what is objective and concrete while the hereafter has an illusory quality is far from being universal. The Hindus, for example, handle the problem of death by viewing life as the illusion and the realm between reincarnations as that which is objective. Hence, for many in Eastern cultures, the primary concern is to avoid rebirth by extinguishing one's self-centeredness (thereby, for the Buddhists, being absorbed into an impersonal, collective over-soul), whereas in much of the West, this concern is to obtain as high a quality of personal existence as is possible in the here and now.

- Finally, cultures vary in terms of their understanding of the relationships between the worlds of the living and the dead. For some, the dead are perceived to have an active role in shaping the affairs of the living, involvements that can be either welcomed, tolerated, or vigorously avoided.

The basic research problem for a number of historians and anthropologists is to determine what types of social systems and what kinds of dynamics engender these particular thought systems.

Perhaps the most common of rituals involves the transformations of identity across the life cycle, the so-called rites of passage. As individuals, we face events that bring disorder to our biographies, such as puberty, childhood, graduation, childbirth, old age, and death. The social system tends to transform these events, which are personally unique (e.g., "How could anyone know the agony of *my* fortieth and forty-first years?"), into events that are socially typical ("These terrifying experiences of mine are not unique; others have experienced the 'midlife crisis' as well") and therefore socially meaningful and personally less frightening (even if our problem has no cure, do we not feel better if there is at least a name for it?). These cultural rites of passage assist in such transformations and transitions of self.

Even to argue that there are such people as children, adults, and the elderly is to imply that one passes through a series of ontologically distinct orders of being. As Victor Turner (1967, p. 72) noted among the Ndembu, "One tends to grow up by definite stages, each of which is the death of the previous stage, by a series of deaths and entrances." Arnold van Gennep (1960), one of the first anthropologists to elaborate upon such rituals, saw regeneration as the law of life and of the universe: the energy that is found in any system, whether a personality or a culture, gradually becomes spent and must be routinely renewed. But to be between roles, or in some way outside of them, is to be socially polluting. Late adolescence in America, for example, is problematic because individuals are neither children nor adults; widowhood in our couple-oriented society is problematic because widows belong neither to the world of singles nor to the world of marrieds. Such conditions call for rites to eventually reincorporate the individual back into the group, thereby returning the individual to the customary routines of life.[3]

The biographical transition requiring the greatest amount of ritual is the passage from the world of the living to the world of the dead. Where death is not meaningfully integrated into the cosmos or where it is perceived to be a transition state, it becomes polluting (Douglas 1966).[4] The occasions for death to become polluting for the cultural ethos occur when new ways of looking at the world invalidate all traditional social ideas, such as with the following types of changes.

Changes in the Timing of Death

Death now typically occurs after full, completed lives. As Talcott Parsons and Victor Lidz observed:

> The problem of the *meaning* of death is coming . . . to be concentrated about death occurring as the completion of a normal life cycle. . . . This central, irreducible problem is becoming disentangled from the problem of adjusting to deaths that occur earlier in the life cycle, particularly in infancy and early childhood, which was much more general in the pre-modern period. (1967, p. 137)

As we will see in the chapters to come, this has led to concerns with the quality, as opposed to the quantity, of life as well as to individuals' fears of incompleteness.

Changes in the Quality of Death

With medical and technological innovations, death comes in slow motion to individuals isolated in institutions for the dying. Fears of dying are replacing fears of one's postmortem fate. And moral dilemmas abound regarding maintaining the existence of the brain-dead.

Changes in the Conception of Selfhood

The evolution of conceptions of self has gone from a collectivist to an individualist orientation. In the past, personal extinction did not hold the terror that it does today, as that which was of central importance, namely one's tribe or clan, continued to survive.

Changes in Social Structure

The challenge of death is most extreme within small, primitive societies where famine, disease, or war could lead to the destruction of the entire group. As will be developed in Chapter 3, with the creation of large bureaucratic structures, roles have become more important than their replaceable occupants.

Philippe Ariès, in his historical portrayals (1975, 1981) of death epochs in Western civilization, reveals how cultural shifts in the relationship between individuals and social structure are measured by changes in conceptions of death and in funerary ritual.

Language, Thought, and Symbol

Most of what we know of the world is secondhand knowledge conveyed to us through conversation. But talk is comprised of symbols, of categories that allow the perception of an unambiguous and ordered world that otherwise would be random chaos. In other terms, words sensitize us to what is culturally important (ignoring what is not) and thereby trigger mind-sets that channel our anticipations, perceptions, and cognitions. The principle of linguistic relativity, first put forth by Benjamin Whorf nearly fifty years ago, holds that the structure of a language influences its speakers' perceptions and understandings of reality as well as their behaviors toward it (Whorf 1956). Language thus reflects the way in which we see our environment and everything in it. The importance of an object in a society can be measured by how many words there are for that object. The acquisition of language is the cultural education of one's senses. Words allow generalizations and discriminations, giving priorities and orderings to experiences. Those without language cannot take the perspective of others (and, therefore, intersubjectivity would be impossible), nor can they envision things removed from them in place and time. When an event cannot be categorized and identified, the experience of terror often results. The man with the unknown malady feels a certain relief if the disease at least has a name (see Lindesmith, Strauss, and Denzin 1977; Berger and Luckmann 1967).

Language functions not only to describe but also to create things "out there." Through interactions with others a "reality" emerges that takes on a life of its own, "a reality that confronts the individual as an external and coercive fact" (Berger and Luckmann 1967, p. 58). Hence novel experiences with death, as during a war or an epidemic, produce a new vocabulary (consider "AIDS," "MIAs," and "Holocaust") which, when repeated often in everyday life, ultimately alters the death ethos. In a sense, the use of language is ritual in its most elementary form: words carry implicit values and biases and hence, when used, repeat and reaffirm a fusion between worldview and ethos. The ethos is also affected when these symbols are overused; they become fatigued and lose their meaning, as does a word when it is repeated over and over again.

On matters of death, political systems routinely employ euphemisms rather than state the stark, fatal consequences of some of their functions. When overseeing the slaughter of seven million Pennsylvania chickens to contain a virus, for instance, the federal government said it had "depopulated" the birds. In Nazi Germany, carloads of Jews were assigned to *Sonderbehandlung,* or "special treatment" (Friedrich 1984). When, in 1944, the Germans wanted to obliterate all evidence of their "final solution," the Jewish work crew assigned to the gruesome task was forbidden to use the words "corpse" or "victim" and told to refer to the bodies as *Figuren,* that is, as puppets or dolls (Lewis 1985). American troops in Vietnam "wasted" the enemy, and the CIA "terminates with extreme prejudice" (Friedrich 1984).

We live in a culture in which *dead* is a four-letter word, and four-letter words are often obscene. People don't die. Instead, they get lost ("I lost my wife," "We lost our dog"), they leave ("He has departed this life," "Their grandfather has left them," "She's gone on the final voyage"), or they fall asleep ("She has earned her rest"). Our dislike of saying that someone is dead reveals the profoundness of our death denials (Brown 1945; Rodabough 1980). Despite the euphemisms employed when actual death occurs, mortality does enter into American slang when referring to nonthanatological matters. In the work world, people hustle to beat "deadlines" (or, at least, make efforts to avoid appearing to be simply "killing time") out of fear of being "terminated" or "axed" and ending up in a "dead-end job." In sports, one team must "kill" or "destroy" another in competition to truly establish its supremacy. David Gutmann (1973, p. 50) observed how the "young peo-

Expression	Literal Meaning
die by the hedge	inferior meat
make a die of it	try
dead letter	neglected law
dead from the neck up	stupid
dead set	persistent attempt
dead loss	waste of time
dead nuts on	extremely attached to
dead on	very accurate
deadpan	expressionless
the dead spit of	exactly like
deadly	extremely
on the dead	honestly
dead ass	worthless
deadfall	nightclub
deadhead	nonpaying spectator
deadlights	the eyes
dead one	retired hobo
dead president	paper money
dead soldier	empty bottle

From Partridge 1953, 1963;
Phythian 1976;
Wentworth and Flexner 1975.

ple of the counter-culture now obsessively use the terms 'life' and 'death' to
make political, moral, racial, and even generational distinctions . . . [taking]
away the horror of death by presenting it as an invention of the establishment, a side effect of Con I and Con II." The difficulty of not punning in
any discussion of death is evidence of death's centrality to our language,
hence to our cultural thought systems.

Another reason for our tendency to pun when discussing death is that our
notion of death is so mired in ambiguities. Thanatologist Edwin Shneidman
(1980, p. xviii) observes that the conception of death has become an oxy-
moron, a combination of opposites, in contemporary American society. We
spend hundreds of billions of dollars to devise weapons to kill millions of
people and yet are willing to spend hundreds of thousands of dollars to care
for a single terminally ill, irreversibly comatose individual. We speak of death
when we don't mean it, and when we do mean it we use euphemisms. What
such linguistic tendencies indicate about who we are and what our cultural
ethos is all about will be an underlying concern throughout the chapters that
follow.

Death and Conceptions of Time

Time figures prominently in how a cultural ethos is shaped and, as with physicists' discovery of the space-time continuum, social scientists are slowly
appreciating the full extent to which cultural time systems are interwoven
within cultural thought systems. Physicists, however, don't have to worry
about how time changes meaning. Sociocultural systems are like a musical
score: change the rhythm—such as putting a funeral dirge to a calypso
beat—and you change the meaning of the piece. Cultures differ temporally,
for example, in their general orientation toward the future or the past. Central to this orientation is whether the "golden years" are collectively understood to exist either in the future (hence, time is seen as being progressive
[Nisbet 1979] and evolutionary) or in some golden past (as paradise lost).
This broad temporal distinction determines the role of the dead in everyday
life and the extent to which the behaviors of the living are oriented toward
their ancestors or to their heirs.

Another broad temporal difference between cultures concerns the flow of
time. J. B. Priestley (1964) notes that profane time is passing time, time as
wear and tear, time as entropy and decay, time as eventually ending with
death. The ideal state among aborigine beliefs, on the other hand, is time
"all at once" as opposed to "one thing after another." This sacred time is
the collapsing of the past, present, and future into an eternal now in order
to, in part, allow heroics of the past to be continuously part of the sacred

present. The Last Day, according to contemporary Christian theology, is to be the end of time and, hence, the end of death. With secularization, however, for the first time in history, it is the here and now that is paradise and the hereafter that is unknown.

Mircea Eliade (1963, p. 3) describes "the myth of the destruction of the World, followed by a new Creation and the establishment of the Golden Age." The bliss of beginnings demands the destruction of what was before only to be followed by the progressive degradation of the cosmos. *Cosmogony* (the thesis of the creation or origin of the world or universe) requires *eschatology* (the doctrine of the last or final things). To be seen is how both individuals and social systems go through cycles of death and rebirth. And why not? Is it not the rhythm of nature that in order for there to be the rebirth of spring, there must be the apparent death of winter? Do we not each day go through a mini-death (sleep), only to be resurrected (awaken refreshed) each morning? And are there not times in our lives when we wish to shed some used-up portion of ourselves? Whether cultural time is seen to be cyclical and regenerative or linear and entropic similarly determines the status of the dead in everyday life.

A final temporal variation entails the impact of life expectancy rates and their fluctuations on the cultural ethos. In his "On the Problem of Generations," Karl Mannheim (1952) toyed with some ideas concerning the relationship between social progress and human longevity. For example, what if we all, like butterflies, simultaneously came into existence, grew old together, and died at the same time? Would we not be free to create our own social structure and value systems, free to discard the constraints upon the living dictated by those long deceased? And how might this tempo of change be related to increasing or decreasing life expectancy? Two-thirds of the improvement of our species' life expectancy has been gained since 1900 (Preston 1976). So profound have been the ramifications of this great event that many fail to appreciate the shift or know how to properly culminate full, completed lives. Riley (1983) observed that the point in the life span at which death's punctuation typically comes undoubtedly shapes a culture's meaning of life. Where death normally cuts individuals down suddenly and unexpectedly, where the notion that "life exists in the midst of death" is an everyday fact instead of a metaphor (Riley 1983), death is often viewed as externally caused—an outlook that typically spawns an ethos of fatalism. The more premature the death, the greater the state of social frustration, the greater the need for meaning, and the more frightening the spirit of the deceased (Blauner 1966).

But with the mortality revolution, the lengthening of life spans has been academically linked with a broad range of historical changes: romantic love replacing arranged marriages, prolonged adolescence and greater parental emotional investments in children, the possibility of divorce, the general confinement of bereavement to the elderly, occupational specialization, and the shift from ascribed to achieved roles as the basis of social stratification (Goldscheider 1976, pp. 184–86). Where death occurs upon completed role obligations and full lives, arriving expectedly and in slow motion, as is the case in modern society, the cultural ethos typically features autonomy and self-control. The norm of premature deaths in the past has been superseded by deaths that can either be "on time" or "postmature." Further, as Ivan Illich noted:

With the predominance of serial time, with concern for exact time-measurement and recognition of simultaneity of events, a new framework for the recognition of personal identity is constructed. The person's identity is sought in reference to a sequence of events rather than in the completeness of his life-span. Death ceases to be the end of a whole and becomes an interruption in the sequence. (1975, p. 30)

In general, because of death, there is the feeling of being constrained by time, whether by the historical time our biographies happen to intersect[5] or by the monotony of time many find in the drudgery of their work. Nowadays many individuals attempt to stop time, such as with age-obscuring cosmetics, exercise, and drugs. By having children, we launch another time sequence, one perhaps more in synchronization with natural rhythms.

Death and Social Evolution

Men of all times may well fear death, as Bacon wrote, "as children fear to go in the dark." But they deal with that fear first by imagining something existing in the darkness, and then acting accordingly. (Stannard 1977, p. 10)

Though this book is about the death ethos of contemporary Western societies in general and the United States in particular, it is important to locate some of the sources of our historical legacy. As will be seen, orientations toward death reflect a people's orientation toward life. Where preprogrammed lives are unthinkingly lived by those having minimal conceptions of identity, death is not problematic. Conversely, where identity is itself a personal problem, where the meaning of existence is so frail that the demise of a social member sparks existential doubt among the survivors, death becomes problematic for both the individual and the social system. Baumeister (1986, p. 42) notes that "if awareness of death is thus intimately linked to self-awareness and individuation, then the history of death can provide evidence about the historical evolution of self-awareness and individuality."

As Rousseau perhaps first observed, social evolution was a movement from nature to culture, from human life being governed only by impulse in reaction to the immediate environment to human life being oriented to symbolic matters with the constant awareness of inevitable demise:

His desires do not exceed his physical needs, the only goods he knows in the universe are nourishment, a female and repose; the only evils he fears are pain and hunger. I say pain and not death because an animal will never know what it is to die; and knowledge of death and its terrors is one of the first acquisitions that man has made in moving away from the animal condition. (1964, p. 116)

Deaths of Ancient and Premodern Selves

In graves dating back as far as 60,000 B.C., bodies have been found bound in fetal positions amidst flowers, ivory ornaments, shells, and painted bones. Though it remains a matter of speculation and debate whether such burials were intended to assist in rebirth or to prevent the deceased from returning to disturb the living, it does seem that the idea of some form of postmortem existence emerged with this knowledge of our mortality. But the very idea of postmortem existence, through combating the fears of self-cessation, was to lead to new anxieties.

By the time of ancient Egyptian civilization, the resurrection-based religion of Osiris, which applied the stratification system of the living to the afterlife, had emerged. Immortality became conditional as the idea of judgment was discovered to be a powerful and ingenious tool to enforce obedience. Early Christians added the strategy of forgoing earthly pleasures to ensure salvation. Over time, to allay mounting fears of damnation, Christian rituals were to include preventive therapies, such as baptism to cleanse the soul of original sin. And, as opposed to the ancient Egyptian idea that the soul must be totally without sin to guarantee a desirable passage, Christians only required that the good of the soul outweigh sin in order to avoid divine wrath.

For a number of centuries, however, death fears minimally involved concerns about postmortem judgment. Both life and death were tame. Identities were largely preprogrammed and remained stable throughout life. Similarity and conformity were valued as individuals simply attempted to conform to God's image. As the self was yet to be discovered, the loss of self by death was similarly accepted without question or concern (Ariès 1974, p. 28). One's death was one's own; the dying person organized his or her own pub-

Wooden models of boats ferrying the dead, Egypt twelfth
dynasty, ca. 1900 B.C. The Bettmann Archive, Inc.

lic death ritual, knew its protocol, and remained in control, being deferred
to by the clergy and physicians (Ariès 1974, p. 10). There was a simplicity
to the rituals; they were accepted and carried out without theatrics or emotion. What worried individuals was not having forewarning that their end
was near. But then there were to occur profound changes in identity, in
social structure, and in the quality of death.

The Middle Ages

The idea of death pervaded the late Middle Ages. In part, this was the result of a series of epidemics and plagues that decimated European populations (see Chapter 3). In addition, there was widespread disillusionment with the traditional feudal institutions, which obviously were in a state of decline. Artists and writers symbolized this disintegration with realistic images of death and decomposition in a style known as the *ars moriendi*. Tomb sculpture, for example, featured life-size bodies in advanced stages of decay, replete with snakes and maggots. As their institutions gave way, people were thrown back on themselves as never before, being forced to produce their own meaning and purpose for life. With a cultural ethos out of focus, the death of a person became even more shattering and frightening (Helgeland 1984–85).

In addition, beginning in the twelfth century, attitudes toward death began metamorphosing with the emergence of individualism. In the context of the plagues, individuals not only became conscious of the brevity and fragility of their lives (Ariès 1974, p. 45),[6] understanding existence as a stay of execution, but they also became aware of their own unique selves and in so doing discovered their own deaths. A life was no longer subsumed within the collective destiny of the group (hence the fading of the vendetta system, as kin members were no longer seen to be functionally equivalent; Baumeister 1986) but became viewed as a biography, each moment of which would be judged by Christ after death (Ariès 1981, pp. 103–6). It was at this time that people concerned themselves with their distinguishing characteristics, began writing autobiographies, became interested in drama and in the distinctions between roles and their occupants, and postulated the existence of an internal inner self (Baumeister 1986).

Death, not life, became the natural force that one had to master: "a man insisted upon participating in his own death because he saw in it an exceptional moment—a moment which gave his individuality its definitive form" (Ariès 1975, p. 11). To assist in this mastery, an instructional manual on the art of dying, entitled *Ars Moriendi,* was to be a best-seller for two centuries (Illich 1975, pp. 30–31). With the concurrent rise of the Reformation, salvation once again became conditional upon the quality of one's life, and hell replaced death as the primary fear.

Attitudes toward death continued to evolve slowly. Toward the end of the fifteenth century, death themes began to take on erotic meanings. No longer were there warnings; death now "raped" the living in an era when individuals were taking advantage of newly opened opportunities for social mobility. There can still be found nowadays, however, an ethos of a dying culture

"The Triumph of Death" by Pieter Bruegel the Elder (1525/30–1569) illustrates the horrendous cycles of war and plague associated with feudalism's demise and the Protestant Reformation in sixteenth century Europe. The turmoil culminated in the internecine Thirty Years' War. It would be another three centuries before civilian casualties would once again outnumber those of the military.

whose obsession with morbidity has produced an artistic motif bearing considerable resemblance to that of the *ars moriendi.*

Death in Traditional Mexican Culture

Analogous to the death motifs of the *Ars Moriendi* (albeit without the obsession with putrefaction and decay) is the folk art of traditional Mexican culture. Since Día de los Muertos, the Day of the Dead or All Souls' Day, is still observed throughout Mexico and in portions of the American Southwest, and since Hispanics now comprise the largest influx of immigration into this country, the tradition is leaving its mark on the American death ethos.

Poet Octavio Paz writes that Mexicans are "seduced by death." To the American eye, their culture is steeped with morbidity: there's the life-death drama of the bullfight;[7] the Day of the Dead folk art, replete with skeletons and bloody crucifixes; and the pervasive death themes within the works of such muralists as Orosco, Diego Rivera, and David Alfaro Siqueiros (see Waugh 1955).[8] This death-rich cultural tradition reflects the fusion of Indian and Catholic legacies. The former includes the heritage of human sacrifices practiced by the Mayans and Aztecs.[9] In describing a Mayan priest during his sixteenth-century visit to the New World, Bishop Landa wrote: "Then like a ravenous tiger he plunged in his hand and tore out the living heart." The blood of such sacrifices and ritual suicides was dripped on bits of bark, which were then burned as incense to pacify the deities, for whom it was nectar (Hoelterhoff 1985). Geoffrey Conrad and Arthur Demarest describe the sacrificial rituals spawned by this ethos:

A line of men moves slowly up a steep staircase toward the summit of a pyramid. As each man reaches the top, he is seized and pinioned across an altar. A priest

Day of the Dead folk art. Kemp Davis.

approaches, holding a stone-bladed knife with both hands. Raising the knife above his head and concentrating his strength in the blade, the priest intones a prayer, then plunges the knife downward. The man on the altar dies in a shower of his own blood. His heart is torn out and placed in a bowl. His body is carried to the edge of the steps and dropped. As it rolls and bounces toward the bottom, another man is brought forward and stretched across the altar. Hundreds of people have perished since this ceremony started; hundreds more will die before it ends.

Beside the pyramid stands a rack displaying the skulls of tens of thousands of previous victims. Like the broken bodies accumulating at the foot of the staircase, the skulls are those of captives taken in battle. They have been sacrificed to feed the sun. If the sun is not nourished with the vigorous blood of warriors, he will grow too weak for his daily struggle against the forces of darkness, and the universe will be destroyed. (1984, p. 1)

Ironically, these Indian cultures were almost destroyed by European imperialists: the conquistadors and colonists unintentionally caused a biological pogrom with their Old World parasites and infectious diseases against which the native populations had no defense (Crosby 1986).

On All Souls' Day, which is said to be descended from the Last Supper (which was, of course, a funeral feast), the deceased are honored and revered because *"Están en un lugar mucho mejor que este mundo."* ("They are in a much better place than this world"). By midafternoon families and friends gather to share prayers at family altars, drink wine, and reminisce about the lives of the deceased. Places are often reserved for the departed and their favorite foods cooked. In this way the dead come to life again in the thoughts of the living. Nowadays, this celebration benefits the social and economic institutions of Mexican society; death, in a sense, supports the living. The traditional candy skulls and skeleton cakes are sold. Further, this day actively unites families, friends, and communities, as people travel hundreds of miles to visit the gravesites of relatives. The picnics held after mass in the cemetery bring entire communities together, again demonstrating the social gravity generated by death.

 Spaniards' Distaste for Life Insurance Leaves the Industry There Languishing

When Felix Mansilla tried to take out his first life insurance policy, his wife was aghast. She didn't want to benefit from her husband's death.

 "She thought making a profit would be in bad taste," Mr. Mansilla recalls. Eventually, "she went along for the children's sake," he says.

It's attitudes like this that make selling life insurance to Spaniards a difficult job. Mr. Mansilla knows. Today he's the president of the National Federation of Spanish Insurance Companies.

Public distaste for life insurance has left the industry in Spain more malnourished than in any other major Western European economy. Only nine of every
100 Spaniards have life insurance, for an estimated annual per capita premium
cost of $10.20. That compares to $154 in Western Europe and $230 in the
U.S. . . .

Some examples of what insurance sales people must contend with in Spain:

The mother of a drowned fisherman flatly refused to accept his death benefits from
an insurance company.

A village priest railed against the trade, asking, "Who but God can insure life?"

Last month, the Socialist General Union of Workers denounced Spain's state-con-
trolled telephone company for providing "scandalous" life insurance and pension
coverage for 160 top executives.

Part of the resistance is cultural. Until recently, especially in rural areas,
mourning widows were expected to withdraw from society and dress in black
from head to toe. Any hint that her husband's death had enriched her would
tarnish her reputation.

José Marie Miraza, sales director in Spain for the Dutch insurance company
Nationale-Nederlanden N.V., believes that opposition to life insurance is rooted
in Christian and Islamic beliefs. The Moslems, who ruled much of Spain for
seven centuries, strictly forbade insurance, and the Roman Catholic Church long
took a dim view of it.

Another obstacle may be the national inclination to procrastinate. "The average Spaniard still lives from day to day," complains an insurance executive. "It's
difficult for him to program 20 to 30 years ahead. He believes in fate."

Westley 1984. Reprinted by permission of the
Wall Street Journal, © Dow Jones & Company, Inc. 1984.

Such phenomena, despite their surface appearances, are not necessarily features of a death-accepting culture. In a country historically marked by unsta-
ble, corrupt, authoritarian regimes, it is interesting to note how honoring
the dead has given individuals license to comment on the living. A satirical
magazine published even in the smallest hamlet that owns a print shop,
called *La Calavera* (The Skull), is filled with satirical poetic eulogies of living
members of the community, ranging from the town drunk to the mayor's
wife. The famous skeletal caricatures of Posada served to raise political consciousness in Mexico before the revolution. In sum, it is not simply the case
that life is so miserable that death is preferable. In fact, the festive death rituals are neither positive nor negative but rather "an existential affirmation of
the lives and contributions made by all who have existed . . . [and] the affirmation of life as the means for realizing its promise while preparing to someday die" (Sanchez 1985). They reflect not only Mexico's cultural heritage
but also its fusion with economic and political exigencies.

The Deaths of Early Modern Selves: Puritans and Victorians

The Puritans brought to the New World a new sense of identity growing out of the Reformation and a novel body of eschatological concerns, which together were to provide a cultural legacy of death ambivalence. Theirs was a time of transition from religious certainty to doubt, from science only revealing God's fingerprint on creation to casting doubts on His involvements.

In general, the earliest settlers of the New World were rootless and adventurous young males for whom life in a rugged, untamed, and uncivilized land was cheap. The looseness of New World social fabric, the lack of solidarity among the living, was reflected in the apathy displayed toward their dead, necessitating laws requiring burial to ensure that the bodies would not be left unattended. The Puritans, on the other hand, arrived in close-knit families and communal relationships in which each individual had a unique function. They did not question the inferiority of mortal existence or the innate depravity of man, and they sensed that the Apocalypse and Christ's Second Coming were imminent. But unlike the *contemptus mundi* tradition of the Old World, which saw the inherent superiority of the hereafter to a vile and loathsome here and now, the Puritans also believed that the everyday world was systematic and meaningful, with every detail of nature revealing God's grand design. Man's mission was to live and work with this gift, to pursue "one's calling," and to be happy in both life and death (Stannard 1977). Failure to observe the divine covenant, failure to live a sin-free existence, led to such signs of God's displeasure as violent storms, extended droughts, and military reversals.

Complicating matters for the believers, there was also a belief in predestination, that one's postmortem fate had already been established at birth by an inscrutable God and that what few salvations there were bore no correlation to one's behaviors in life. This belief, coupled with the increased self-consciousness of the times, stimulated Puritans to produce numerous diaries and engage in introspection as strategies for detecting signs of their electedness. However, they also realized that self-deception was a pervasive possibility in a world in which evil and witchcraft were everywhere, hence their unremitting fears of death.

With increasing religious pluralism, urbanization, literacy, and the growing role of science and technology, Christianity began retreating from everyday life. With this fading of the sacred, moral absolutes were to dissolve. No longer was identity taken for granted. Liberated by the Enlightenment, people began to experience a new feeling of possibility and to search for new models of fulfillment. In observing the romanticism spawned in Germany,

Daniel Bell noted that there was a "momentous break with the centuries-old conception of an unbridgeable chasm between the human and the divine. Men now sought to cross that gulf, and as Faust, the first modern, put it, attain 'godlike knowledge,' to 'prove in man the stature of a god,' or else confess his 'kinship with the worm'" (1980, p. 279). There were optimistic attempts to reform society so that these divine individual potentialities could be realized. The late eighteenth century and the first half of the nineteenth were to be an era of political revolutions, experiments with utopian communities, and personality cults. From this context there appeared another period of death preoccupation, one that was to be expressed in the arts, rituals of mourning, and the rise of various spiritualist movements. Like the *Ars Moriendi*, which occurred with the end of feudalism and the discovery of the self, the morbid romanticism[10] of Victorianism corresponded with the end of agrarian life[11] and the discovery of a private self, a self that was not only distinct from but superior to the public self (see Gottlieb 1959, p. 158).

The rise of the private self and the cult of romantic death arose out of the emotional attachments that were replacing the traditional economic bondings of family systems. People became more concerned with others' deaths than with their own (Ariès, 1974, p. 56), realizing that it was only through these significant others that one's true, unique self was made possible.[12] It was also a time when the upper classes became repulsed by the sight of infant bodies littering the roadsides and streams, victims of the infanticide that had reached epidemic proportions in 1800 in England, France, and Germany.[13] As a result, elaborate funerals emerged, featuring

Hearse and four horses, two mourning coaches with fours, twenty-three plumes of rich ostrich-feathers, complete velvet covering for carriages and horses, and an esquire's plume of best feathers; strong elm shell, with tufted mattress, lined and ruffled with superfine cambric, and pillow, full worked glazed cambric winding-sheet, stout outside lead coffin, with inscription plate and solder complete; one-and-a-half-inch oak case, covered with black or crimson velvet, set with three rows round, and lid panelled with best brass nails; stout brass plate of inscription, richly engraved; four pairs of best brass handles and grips, lid ornaments to correspond; use of silk velvet pall; two mutes with gowns, silk hat-bands and gloves; fourteen men as pages, feathermen, and coachmen, with truncheons and wands, silk hat-bands, etc.; use of mourners' fittings; and attendant with silk hat-band etc. (Morley 1971, p. 19).

The relationship between the survivors and the deceased became important, as is evident in the explicit mourning etiquette prescriptions of the Victorians.[14] The dialectic of death was fully appreciated. Taking into account the secularization of the period, Walter Houghton observes:

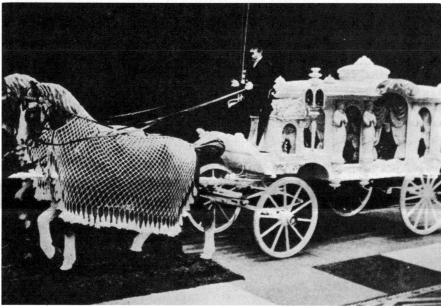

A hand carved draped hearse from about 1898 and an ornate child's hearse from the late nineteenth century. From Robert Habenstein and William Lamers, *The History of American Funeral Directing*, 1955, Milwaukee Bulfin Printers.

The death scenes which fill the Victorian novels are clearly connected with the religious crisis. They are intended to help the reader sustain his faith by dissolving religious doubt in a solution of warm sentiment. When the heart is so strongly moved, the skeptical intellect is silenced; and when feelings of profound love and pity are centered on a beautiful soul who is gone forever, the least religious affirmation, the slightest reference to heaven or angels, or to reunion with those who have gone before (and no decent death bed in any novel was without them) was sufficient to invoke a powerful sense of reassurance. (1957, p. 277)

As was the case during the great plagues of the Middle Ages, this was also a time of dramatic change in mortality patterns. The rapid emigration from the land to poorly prepared urban settings led to massive overcrowding, which, when coupled with poor sanitation, resulted in a virtual cesspool for infectious diseases. Not only did death come prematurely, but its appearance was stratified by social class. In 1830 London, the average age at death for the gentry was estimated to be forty-four years, dropping to twenty-five years for tradesmen, clerks, and their families, and only twenty-two for laborers and their families (Morley 1971, p. 7). In Manchester, England, in 1840, fifty-seven out of one hundred children died before the age of five. But here for the first time, appreciating the conflicts between the individual and society (this was the era of the "noble savage" myth, the notion that one is essentially free of sin, only corrupted by society), the individual was seen to be due in death the dignity and respect that may not have been accorded in life.[15] And grief became a preeminent feeling: "even where there was a cause for grief, it seems that it often became necessary to force it, and it is quite clear that a show of exaggerated grief became a mark of would-be gentry" (Morley 1971, p. 17).

This romanticism persisted until the mid-nineteenth century, when "a brutal revolution in traditional ideas and feelings" (Ariès 1974, p. 85) began to emerge, spawned in the United States by the Civil War and in Europe in the Franco-Prussian War, and finally culminating in the First World War. Death became increasingly privatized and the social scope of grief contracted, undoubtedly concurrent with the shift from *Gemeinschaft* to *Gesellschaft* solidarities—that is, from an era in which the "social gravity" binding a people consisted of intimate bonds between residents of small towns in which individuals knew one another, to the impersonal bonds now linking heterogeneous and yet interdependent strangers within large urban areas. Fears shifted from concern about postmortem judgment to the process of dying (the elderly fear nursing homes more than death itself). And it became the tendency for Western culture to hide the presence of death (Feifel 1959, p. xii), which was replacing sex as the cultural taboo (Gorer 1965).

The Tabooed Deaths of Modern Selves

As recently as the early twentieth century throughout much of the Western world, the death of a man still profoundly altered the space and time of a social group, possibly rippling outward to affect the entire community (Ariès 1981, p. 559). But after the First World War, there was to be a new kind of identity, a new kind of dying, and a new kind of grief. This new self was to emerge out of mass education, mass communication, total war, the considerable differentiation and specialization of the world of work, and the near-total secularization of the everyday world. Instead of the self being understood as a biographical accomplishment, it was to be comprehended as simply the product of broad, abstract social forces. Instead of the self as a whole person having intrinsic worth, the individual became viewed by others as but a means to an end and viewed by the major organizations as but an interchangeable role occupant. Being no longer self-evident who exactly the public self was or what its social contributions were, its death became a forbidden topic. As Philippe Ariès put it (1981, p. 560), "except for the death of statesmen, society has banished death. . . . Society no longer observes a pause; the disappearance of an individual no longer affects its continuity."

For the individual, one consequence of such devaluations of the personal self is alienation. Now that secularization is nearly complete, the moral pluralism of our lives encourages innovation, but at the cost of skepticism and doubt. With the lack of traditional role models resulting from the tremendous pace of social change and with the tremendous complexity of social life, commonsensicality has evaporated, and the individual becomes hostage to experts who prescribe recipes for self-presentational strategies in the world of work, for ways to deal with one's aging parents, for maintaining good health, for experiencing good sex, and for having good deaths.[16] There is no way to evade society's grasp, no Frederick Turner frontier, no Thoreauvian woods to escape to. Ironically, as the self becomes increasingly fragmented (now being "other-directed," people pay experts to tell them who they really are, whether it's their work-self, spouse-self, parent-self, leisure-self, or community-self), the cultural system stresses authenticity and self-actualization. Further, society no longer allows the full self to expire. As we will see in Chapter 3, with death generally confined to the elderly, we die as lesser selves, disengaged from our social roles.

In Ariès's (1974) view, the contemporary era of tabooed death arose, in part, from this cultural tendency to rely on others to define and to organize one's fate. Here it was the attempts of those close to the dying person to conceal the patient's condition in order to spare his or her feelings. The

Myriad products exist to obscure our aging and mortality. Kemp Davis.

patient, on the other hand, became responsible for the management of his or her stigma, taking care that the efforts of normals to ease matters for him or her were seen as effective and appreciated (Goffman 1963). This interpersonal dynamic eventually became culturally amplified, and death itself became denied in order to dampen "the disturbance and the overly strong and unbearable emotion caused by the ugliness of dying and by the very presence of death in the midst of a happy life" (Ariès 1974, p. 87). With the expulsion of death from everyday life, the subjects of death and dying became taboo, topics of disapproval and shame (Gorer 1965).

Being forbidden (Ariès 1974), the actuality or inevitability of death became something to be hidden. Our cultural obsession with youth can be understood as a huge, collective death-denial obsession. Individuals not only hide the deaths of their relatives in nursing homes and hospitals,[17] but they also obscure their own mortality, their own aging process, with hair dyes and face lifts. There are parallels between not informing a dying patient that he or she is going to die and not telling the young about old age; both reveal the extent of our cultural denials. No longer are funerals important social events, nor are cemeteries prominent landmarks of our communities (Rodabough 1980, pp. 22–27).

Without the traditional consolations of religion, death exposes the inauthenticity of our lives and yet still reveals our desire to be divine, to be immortal. Robert Lifton observes,

we are not absolutely convinced of our own immortality, but rather have a need to maintain a sense of immortality in the face of inevitable biological death; and . . . this need represents . . . a compelling urge to maintain an inner sense of continuous symbolic relationship, over time and space, to the various elements of life. (1971, p. 173)

This need to transcend individual biological life is not merely a matter of cultural denial. As will be developed in Chapter 6, it is a need built into our species and a faith on which all cultural meaning systems depend. The crisis of our times, according to Alan Harrington, is that because of the secularization and pluralization of religious thought in an era of materialism, the limitless faith in the progress of science and technology, subconscious fears of nuclear weapons obliterating everything and everyone,[18] and shattered egos with the devaluations of the self, death has simply become absurd:

Death is an imposition on the human race and no longer acceptable. Men and women have all but lost their ability to accommodate themselves to personal extinction; they must now proceed physically to overcome it. In short, to kill death; to put an end to mortality as a certain consequence of being born. . . .

The most imaginative philosophical and religious answers to the "problem of death" have become precisely irrelevant to the fact that we die. Humanity's powers of self-deception seem to be running out. . . . Hence, no therapeutic treatment, however inspirational, can do more than apply a coating of salve to our concern. . . .

Having lost faith, a great many men and women have returned to the old superstitions now cloaked in new disguises. God may have retreated, but the *gods* today are by no means dead. Though disposed to destroy them, we simultaneously bow down to some of the weirdest assortment of deities ever known, such as History, Success and Statistics. We worship purveyors of Luck, Fashion and Publicity. We follow shifting gospels based on journalistic graffiti passing for honest news. We humbly receive the word from makeshift divinities seated at the head of couches, sexual statisticians, psychological testers, poll-takers, various merchants of paranoia, the manipulators of public relations and television personalities—the multiple gods of our quickening century. (Harrington 1977, pp. 1, 15)

Having surveyed what death can mean cross-culturally, we can now pick up the indicator theme of Chapter 1 and consider how one type of artifact can reveal a culture's ethos. Specifically, let us examine the cemetery and see how burial customs and memorials display a culture's model of who its members are and what values they hold.

Cemeteries as Cultural Institutions

> Blest be the man that spares these stones,
> And curst be he that moves my bones
>
> From epitaph of William Shakespeare

What are your feelings when you approach a cemetery? They probably vary depending on the time of day and whether or not you are alone. The point is that it is very hard to be indifferent to these islands of solitude that we have set aside for the dead. We know that for most residents, whose memories have been erased by time, the tombstones are their only claim to fame. Personally, my feelings are summed up by an old Norman Rockwell print that once hung in my grandparents' breakfast nook: an apprehensive young boy is carrying a bottle of milk in the dead of night, tiptoeing past a cemetery. In this chapter I would like to arm the lad with a flashlight and accompany him to see how these cities of the dead truly affect the worlds of the living, how, perhaps of all funerary artifacts, the cemetery is the most sociologically didactic.

Cemeteries are cultural institutions that symbolically dramatize many of the community's basic beliefs and values about what kind of society it is, who its members are, and what they aspire to be. Any change in the social ethos is accordingly reflected in these cultural barometers. As rights of the living came to be defined and contractualized, so have the rights of the dead come to be elaborated—the sanctity of the dead is normally directly related to the sanctity of the living. However, when such is not the case, as when the dead are more revered than the living or when their remains are desecrated,[19] there are dramatic tensions splitting the world of the living, portending social change.

Cemeteries are sacred places where the dead are allowed to remain undisturbed. The word *cemetery* derives from the Greek for "sleeping place." Given the parallels between the evolution of cultural orientations toward death and the developmental schedule of childhood understandings of death (see Chapter 12), as well as Christianity's portrayals of the resurrections that will follow the Second Coming, this etymology should not be surprising. These cities of the dead may, in fact, have been the precursors of the cities of the living.[20] Lewis Mumford speculated:

Early man's respect for the dead . . . perhaps had an even greater role than more practical needs in causing him to seek a fixed meeting place and eventually a continuous settlement. Though food-gathering and hunting do not encourage the permanent occupation of a single site, the dead at least claim that privilege. Long ago the Jews claimed as their patrimony the land where the graves of their forefathers were situated; and that well-attested claim seems a primordial one. The city of the dead antedates the city of the living. In one sense, indeed, the city of the dead is the forerunner of the city of the living. (1961, p. 7)

Attitudes toward the Dead

The impetus to preserve the dead together undoubtedly derived from religious concerns, symbolizing hopes for immortality and reassuring the living that they, too, would not be forgotten (Warner 1959). Christianity's adoption of the African cult of martyrs was based on the assumption of the sacredness of the dead.[21] During the fifth century in western Europe, one writer claimed that "the martyrs will keep guard over us, who live with our bodies, and they will take us into their care when we have forsaken our bodies. Here they prevent us from falling into sinful ways, there they will protect us from the horrors of hell. That is why our ancestors were careful to unite our bodies with the bones of the martyrs" (Ariès 1974, p. 16). Given the collectivist orientation of the times, what was important was not giving each body an identifiable home—though common in Rome, the practice of separate sepulchers and tombstones was only to reoccur around the thirteenth century with the emergence of individualism—but rather that one's remains were as close to those of a saint as possible (Ariès 1975). Later, among Catholics, cemeteries became the places where bodies of the dead would sleep until Judgment Day (RIP: "Requiescat in pace").

Between the tenth and twelfth centuries, the cemetery became a public place, an asylum for the crowded living. In fact, they had become so busy that the church finally had to forbid such activities as gambling and dancing within cemeteries. As urban areas became increasingly overpopulated and spatial needs for transportation systems and market areas reached a premium, the world of the living had to be segregated from the world of the dead. In describing the management of this dilemma in eighteenth-century Paris, Richard Etlin (1985) shows how praxis preceded ideology, how action was to precede its justification. With no room in filled parish cemeteries, the dead came to be housed in necropolises ringing the outskirts of towns. Rationalizations would come later: the developing art of medicine sensitized the population to the health hazards of bodies floating to the surface and of the stench of common graves; religious officials came to view direct contact with the dead as something indecent. Once relocated, freed of the constraints of space and tradition, funeral architecture was to blossom. In the spirit of the Enlightenment, the cemetery became a "space of emulation." As a consequence, "it is no longer Christian redemption that is set against the destructive power of death, but the fame which a man can conquer through his own efforts, inspired by the example of great men of the past, so as to live in the memory of posterity. Eternal life is to be found only in the eternal gratitude of future generations" (Starobinski 1986, p. 18). And so began the cult of memory which was to fuel the nostalgia for the glorious past.

In the New World, which did not have the memories of numerous generations to maintain or extreme class differences to exaggerate, the dead were abandoned in unkept graveyards. Until the 1820s, Philadelphians were buried in temporary vacant lots, eventually covered over by urban growth. In the South, family plots were plowed under with changes in land ownership. According to Stanley French (1975), such neglect of the dead came to an end in the 1830s with the creation of Mount Auburn near Boston. Mount Auburn initiated the "rural cemetery" movement (no longer a "graveyard" or "burial ground," which were the traditional nomenclatures), housing the dead within enclosed, gardenlike settings.[22] As was the case in Paris, utilitarian concerns preceded ideological elaborations. Urban progress was not about to become stymied in deference to these nauseating pockets of death. The sensibilities of the post-Enlightenment era were disgusted by the stench of filled graveyards, noted the virulence of disease in proximity to burial sites, and were offended by disrespect for the dead.

This new cemetery concept was to be duplicated throughout the country, reinforced by the rise of Romanticism, increasing patriotism, and the fact that the founding generation of Americans was expiring. Not only was it to dramatize the cult of memory that was in vogue at the time, but it also served as a vehicle for moral instruction. In "An Address Delivered on the Consecration of the Worcester Rural Cemetery," Levi Lincoln observed in 1838: "The sweetest memorials of the dead are to be found in the admonitions they convey, and the instructions they give, to form the character, and govern the conduct, of the living" (cited in French 1975, p. 78).

Turning to the present, there is no question that cemeteries are still an important institution—we observe National Cemetery Week during the first week in May—and that they continue to reflect changes in the cultural ethos. The contemporary cemetery is laid out in a road-and-block plan similar to that of a real estate development (Blaney 1977, p. 219). With the weakening of the extended family, there has been the concurrent elimination of fences around family plots. Burials three or more bodies deep mirror the high-rise world of the living, as do the increasing entombments within mausoleums, which also symbolize the degree to which modern life is housed within man-made urban environments, totally divorced from the natural order. And the increasing number of pet cemeteries is perhaps indicative of the loneliness of modern life.[23]

A room interior in a hotel for the dead in Canton, China, 1932. The deceased could be visited and fed by relatives who paid a monthly rental of $20, $15, or $10 for first-class, second-class, and third-class accommodations respectively. The Bettmann Archive, Inc.

We are stratified in death as we are in life. In contemporary American society, the location of burial is still determined on the basis of race, ethnicity, religion, and social class. So emotionally charged, in fact, are such segregations that in 1971 an individual who had buried a black domestic servant in his family plot in an all-white Dade City, Florida, cemetery finally succumbed to threats and had to have the remains disinterred and moved to an isolated black cemetery. During the Chinese Cultural Revolution, Red Guard youths closed Peking's cemeteries to foreigners. The Catholic church bans from its cemeteries not only non-Catholics but also apostates, heretics, schismatics, the ex-communicated, suicides, dwellists, Freemasons, Communists, and public sinners. And Mills County, Texas, even has burial by political preference in the Democratic Cemetery. Cemeteries serve as central cultural totems for the living.[24]

The Social Messages of Tombstones

No content analysis of a cemetery would be complete without consideration of the tombstones and their inscriptions. The relative sizes of the stones have

Shakers File Suit to Protect Cemetery

Colonie, N.Y.—The last eight Shakers in the United States filed suit in State Supreme Court in Albany today to bar construction of a new baseball stadium here that they said would desecrate the grave of the founder of their religion, Mother Ann Lee.

But the bulldozers are already at work preparing the ground for the new $1.2 million stadium adjacent to the Shaker Cemetery, about seven miles northwest of Albany. The cemetery, with about 450 graves, is the last physical evidence of the first Shaker community in the United States, which was established here in 1776. . . .

A lawyer for the Shakers, Douglas Ward, argued in court papers that "this undertaking threatens to destroy one of the last remaining Shaker settlements in the United States, an historical site of national significance, as well as permanently degrade the environmental quality and character" of the neighborhood. . . .

In reply, Susan Tatro, a lawyer for the town, and Robert Lyman, a lawyer for the county, said an environmental impact statement was not required because the impact would be minimal. They also asserted that the Shakers did not have standing to bring the suit because they had in effect given up ownership of the cemetery.

"For the last 12 or more years, the cemetery has been designated and maintained by the town of Colonie as an historic site completely at the town's expense," they said.

been taken as indicators of the relative power of males over females, adults over children, and the rich over the poor. In immigrant graveyards, the appearance of inscriptions in English signifies the pace of a nationality's enculturation into American society. The messages and art reflect such things as the emotional bonds between family members and the degree of religious immanence in everyday life. For example, the imminent millennialism sensed by the Puritans and their contempt for mortal existence led to the skull and crossbones being the most persistent tombstone symbol of early New England days (Habenstein and Lamers 1962, p. 201). Over time, with increasing hope in a desirable immortality and Romantic faith in the perfectability of man, there was a concurrent change from skeletal images to portrayals of winged cherubs on the gravestones. The contemporary uniformity of tombstones bearing brief bureaucratic summaries of the identities of those beneath (as opposed to "any revelations of unique selves"; Blaney 1977, p. 220) is evidence of the rationalization and bureaucratization of our

The waning of harsh Puritanical influences and the rise of a
secular New England death ethos are mirrored in the grave-
stone art. Between the seventeenth and eighteenth centuries,
the skull and crossbones motif became more angelic. By the
late eighteenth century, the angel wings were dropped, ultimately giving way to the romanticist urn and willow tree
theme of the nineteenth century. Dover Pictorial Archives.

times.[25] As Baumeister points out, "the homogenization of death resembles the homogenization of other aspects of modern life. Death, too, has lost some of its individualistic features" (1986, p. 94).

There is renewed controversy over whether such constant and expensive reminders of the dead are even necessary.[26] Might there be less need for cemeteries now that most of those who die do so in old age and now that our culture is so future-time-oriented? In the People's Republic of China, the attempt to replace traditional burials with cremation stems from the growing scarcity of land and resources.[27] With the increasing geographic mobility of Americans, can roots ever be put down on land not sanctified by the remains of one's forefathers? A small but significant segment of the population is choosing to leave no funerary memory whatsoever, having their cremated remains scattered over oceans or countryside.[28]

The Political Significance of Cemeteries

With the emergence of the nation-state, cemeteries have assumed considerable political significance as major cultural totems of the living. Political systems have had to take into account the symbolic potency of their dead citizens.[29] In anticipation of a detailed discussion in Chapter 8, let us here consider several examples of how cemeteries dramatize the political concerns of different cultures.

As we have seen, cemeteries—as opposed to the more collectivist connotations of "burial grounds"—are designed to preserve the memories of individuals. To remember those who gave their lives in service to their country, the United States allows only the elite to be buried in its most politically sacred of burial sites, Arlington National Cemetery. Those whose political contributions are unparalleled might be interred within their own cemeteries or mausoleums, as is the case behind the Iron Curtain for Lenin, Tito, Ho Chi Minh, and Mao. And if a historical injustice needs to be rectified, memories of the victims are rescued from oblivion. As part of its atonement for complicity in the slaughter of three million Jews, the Polish government in 1983 agreed to help restore Jewish cemeteries that had been uncared for since World War II.

But what of the infamous or those a society desires collectively to forget? One strategy is to deny individualism in death. West German authorities chose to bury the deceased members of the Baader-Meinhof terrorist group in a collective grave beneath a single stone.[30] Another strategy is to eliminate any reminder whatsoever. To obliterate any vestige of memory of those killed fighting for the Hungarian revolution in 1956, the government buried the

freedom fighters in unmarked sites within an unmarked section of a Budapest cemetery.[31]

Perhaps the most vivid examples of the political significance of cemeteries
occurred during the fortieth-anniversary observances of the ending of World
War II. In 1985, the World War II cohort was entering old age, and their
sacrifices were being ritually reaffirmed as part of the increasing militarism of
the 1980s. Further, there was a need to reaffirm the decaying alliance structure between the United States and its West European allies and to stem the
tide of rising anti-Semitism. To accomplish these ends, President Ronald
Reagan traveled to Europe to use the war cemeteries as his podium for reflections on the past and hopes for the future. But things did not go as planned.

Initially, the plans included the president's participation in memorial services at the huge cemetery at Normandy, where thousands had died establishing a beachhead on the European continent. He was then to preside over
a wreath-laying ceremony of reconciliation at Bitburg, West Germany, the
gravesite of nearly two thousand German soldiers. West German Chancellor
Helmut Kohl complained about not being included at the Normandy
reunion of his present allies, but this came nowhere near the outrage
expressed over the Bitburg visit. The Bitburg cemetery, as was eventually discovered, contained the remains of nearly fifty members of the Waffen SS, the
elite military arm of the Nazi SS. The sacred is easily polluted and made profane. Jewish groups were shocked, especially since the president failed to pay
homage to the millions of victims who had died in Nazi concentration
camps.[32] Jewish spokesman Elie Wiesel, chair of the U.S. Holocaust Memorial Council, said, "The fear of forgetting remains the main obsession of all
those who have passed through the universe of the damned" (Clines 1985).
The national commander of the American Legion said, "We wish to state
that it would not set well with American veterans for the President to lay a
wreath at the graves of Nazi soldiers" (Weinraub 1985). And 257 members
of the House of Representatives signed a letter saying that the planned visit
"threatens to have long and serious repercussions in the United States." A
similar letter was signed by 53 senators, also requesting that Reagan drop the
cemetery trip.

But Chancellor Kohl, perhaps moved by his cemetery reconciliation the
year before with France's president Francois Mitterrand at Verdun, said it
would hurt relations if the president did not go to Bitburg after so much
talk. The president ended up going, but only after a stop at the mass graves
of the Bergen-Belsen concentration camp. The controversy did not subside,
especially after Reagan said that German soldiers buried at Bitburg were victims of the Nazis "just as surely as the victims in the concentration camps"

(Hoffman 1985). Said Rabbi Alexander Schindler, president of the Union of American Hebrew Congregations, "The President has made a terrible statement that brings shame to the American people. It insults not only Jews and others who suffered and perished in the camps, but every American and Allied soldier who gave his life to liberate Europe from the Nazi death grip" (*New York Times* 1985).

In sum, though the United States is supposedly a death-denying culture, funerary artifacts can be as symbolically charged now as ever before.

Conclusion

Culture has been portrayed here as a symbolic canopy that shields its members against the terrors of death by giving meaning to human existence and mortality. This death ethos is routinely reaffirmed through ritual, language, and the cultural conceptions of time. Some societies have worshipped death, and others, like our own, have worshipped life. Neither approach has been particularly successful or healthy: "Societies that cannot cope sanely with death cannot cope with life, because death is part of life, and in fact, gives a certain direction and purpose to life" (Fehrenbach 1984). What death means—whether it is a rite of passage from life or a transition to another form of existence, whether individuals are understood to live in order to die or simply to die because they have lived—is entirely a matter of cultural definition. Whatever the definition, the meaning of life itself follows. If life is typically punctuated prematurely, a cultural fatalism often results. If death normally comes to full, completed lives, the ethos is more likely to feature the values of control and personal efficacy.

These cultural orientations are far from being stable; they fluctuate with changes in the conception of selfhood, in the timing and quality of death, and in the structure of social organization. During times of major social change, death is no longer meaningfully integrated into the cosmos, leading to preoccupations with the morbid and, in the case of contemporary American culture, to heated social controversies over such matters as keeping the hopelessly ill alive, condoning abortions, and practicing capital punishment. A major contribution of cultural historian Philippe Ariès was to give a historical model to the different conceptualizations of death in western Europe, integrating such diverse artifacts as cemeteries, tombstones, and religious dogma.

Death's meaning is very much a sociological problem. The chapters that follow will develop the social and demographic forces that underlie the historic shift from one death system to another, transforming the death fears and immortalist hopes of a people and thereby altering the meaning of their lives.

NOTES

1. In his study of the historical exaggerations of cannibalism, Arens (1979) demonstrates the role of ethnocentrism in biasing the comparative method. To legitimize their occupation of a foreign culture, for instance, European colonialists devised stories of cannibalism to demonstrate the cultural depravity of those often brutally subjugated.

2. Unlike that of the rest of nature's animals, our environment is primarily manmade and symbolic in quality. Instead of being figures on the landscape, we are shapers of it. Society is a human production, and humans are social products. We exist in society just as society exists within us; "reality" is the interplay between self and society, between biography and history (Mills 1959).

3. Further, even though there may be no change in role identity, there still may be need for some periodic ritual reaffirmation of one's biography. Part of the cause of the so-called midlife crisis, beyond one's true understanding of one's finality, is that, unlike the earlier life stages, there is a paucity of ritual. There are no more "firsts," such as graduations, marriages, children, or jobs.

4. To be unpolluted is to be ritually pure. As described by Robert Lifton (1968, p. 45), purity encompasses "such beliefs as self-denial (or even self-surrender) on behalf of a higher cause, the urge to eliminate evil, and ideological single-mindedness. . . . Rather than constituting antagonistic motivations, purity and power are in fact psychologically inseparable. . . . Purity is 'godlike' and 'god given' in the sense of virtue so absolute that it transcends moral frailty, and of influences or 'works' that outlast any individual life."

5. Will we see the Nostradamus Effect? That is, given the collective tragedies forecast for 1986, 1988, and 1992, will there be increased instances of risk taking and suicides among those believing in the prophecies of worldwide drought, massive earthquakes, and a massive confrontation between good and evil?

6. As the fetal positions of early buried individuals bring varied interpretation, so does this obsession with the macabre. Ariès (1981, p. 130) believes these images "do not signify fear of death or of the beyond [but] are a sign of a passionate love for this world and a painful awareness of the failure to which human life is condemned."

7. The running of the bulls through the streets of Pamplona in Spain has led to the goring deaths of more than fifty people since the festival began in 1591.

8. Women and death are inextricably woven together within this death ethos. Death is the temptress but simultaneously is the mother taking her children back into the eternal womb. In José Zorrilla's *Don Juan Tenorio*, a favorite play during the last days of October, the central character ultimately triumphs over death through rebirth when a beautiful virgin intervenes and sees that he repents his sins and is transported to heaven.

Mexicans feel tremendous respect for mothers and death, yet there is a dichotomy. The worst insults in the Spanish language have to do with mothers, and Mexican women are often treated no better than the family dog. The prevailing macho attitude of Mexican males has been hypothesized to be a way of fighting fear—fear of death and of the mystery of creation. *"Chinga tu madre"* becomes a defiant challenge to death as well as a recognition of the sexual nature of the temptress gathering dying souls in her embrace.

9. Recent arguments have been made that pre-Colombian human sacrifices served a nutritional function for the elite, who ritually consumed the sacrifice.

10. There were considerable fears of premature burial, reflected in the English Burial Act of 1900, one of whose statutes specified a time between death pronouncement and interment, and in precautionary letters left at bedsides. Count Karnice-Karnicki invented a contraption that included a breathing tube, warning flag, and ringing bell for those buried prematurely.

11. In 1790, nearly two-thirds of English laborers worked on the land; by 1840, the fraction was one-third (Morley 1971).

12. The interest in seances and ghost photography at the time may well indicate the discovery that the dead continue to serve as significant others for the living. In addition, the idea existed during this era that others may know one's identity better than one knows oneself (a premise of psychoanalytic therapy), and therefore to lose them is, again, to lose a part of oneself.

13. Paul Ehrlich and his associates speculated that "the birth-control movement and Victorian prudery (especially the powerful disapproval of extramarital sexual activity and illegitimacy) were both reactions to infanticide" (1977, p. 192).

14. During the early Victorian period, a twelve-month mourning period was prescribed for those suffering the death of a parent or spouse, nine months in the case of a grandparent's death, six months for a sibling, and three months for an aunt or uncle. By the late period, indicative of changing relationships within the family, the prescribed mourning period for grandparents had declined to six months and to two months for uncles and aunts.

15. The new industrial division of labor produced wealth, and the conspicuousness of this wealth did not end with the living. Wealth, after all, was intimately linked to respectability and salvation. For the lower classes, there arose an obsession to copy the death ceremonies of the upper class as a way of reaffirming the importance of their increasingly problematic identities. According to an 1843 report, of the more than 24 million pounds deposited with savings banks, 6 to 8 million pounds was saved in order to meet funeral expenses. Nowadays, people save not for their physical deaths but for their social deaths, old age.

16. In fact, this self-estrangement has been so thorough that the self is even divorced from its biological being: instead of being our bodies, we have bodies just as we have houses and cars. So ignorant have we become of this body-self that we entrust it to body mechanics, otherwise known as physicians, to decipher its symptoms.

17. Like other biological acts, such as defecating or having sex, dying is indecent in public places.

18. Victor Marshall described this as being "the possibility of death 'out of control,' more capricious and infinitely more terrifying than even the plagues" (1980, p. 60).

19. The degree of anti-Semitism, for instance, can be gauged by the desecration and vandalism of Jewish cemeteries.

20. Not surprisingly, there is controversy on this point. Ariès argues that initially the cities of the dead were beyond the city borders of the living. But with increasing urbanization, the living encroached around the boundaries of the dead. Legitimization was needed. St. Vaast, who died in 540, had selected a tomb outside the city of Amiens, but his pallbearers found his corpse growing increasingly heavy. With the archpriest's appeal to a saint and the clergy's selection of a burial spot within the cathedral, the remains suddenly lightened. By the sixth century, the union of the cemetery and church began (Ariès 1975).

21. Special rights of the dead are still observed. In the Commonwealth of Massachusetts, for instance, gravestones are protected under both criminal and civil law, and their theft is considered a felony.

22. One can develop at great lengths the semiology of this phenomenon. Warner (1959), for instance, saw the cemetery at Newburyport, Massachusetts, as both a city and a garden, signifying the duality of nature and society. The garden is a symbolization of the death-rebirth process. And there are the feminine connotations of inserting the body into Mother Earth followed by the closing.

23. There is even a trade association for pet cemeteries, the National Association of Pet Cemeteries. According to E. C. Jordon, president of the association, what distinguishes pet from human cemeteries (besides the fact that the former must pay real estate taxes) is that people bury people because they have to, but they bury their pets because they want to. The most extravagant memorial was given to a pet fly of the poet Virgil (70–19 B.C.): a mausoleum costing about eight hundred thousand sesterces, approximately one hundred thousand dollars (Wallechinsky and Wallace 1977).

24. Events in San Antonio, Texas, a city comprised of a number of large ethnic groups, demonstrated how politically charged such sacred totems can be. In 1985, a Rev. Callies went before the San Antonio City Council to try to get the city to keep "colored people cemeteries clean and free of debris." Representing the United Cemetery Committee, a group concerned with the care and maintenance of the city's black cemeteries, he proposed the following:

> That the city put into effect the care and maintenance of the black cemeteries.
>
> That these cemeteries be renamed from "Colored People's Cemeteries" to "Loving Care Memorial Park."
>
> That the city install chain-link fences on two streets bordering the cemeteries.
>
> That the city care for the proper positioning and erection of tombstones.

That sunken graves be filled.

That water hydrants be installed.

That grave markers be provided on graves at all times.

That the city provide continuous maintenance of cemeteries on a daily basis.

The city of San Antonio until that time had owned and maintained only eight of the thirty-one cemeteries on its black east side. The sole source of income from these areas was from the opening and closing of graves. The area of the Colored People's Cemetery was comprised of four lots covering approximately six acres. It was estimated that the cost of maintaining this area would be forty to fifty thousand dollars annually. With only about twenty-five interments per year into CPC, only three thousand dollars would be available each year.

In late March, the City Council considered a pair of options for improving some of the private east-side cemeteries, including the Colored People's Cemetery. Under the first plan suggested by the Parks and Recreation Department, the city would spend approximately one hundred sixty thousand dollars during the following fiscal year to bring the cemeteries under city control, righting more than five hundred tombstones and performing the landscaping. The other plan, proposed by a City Council member, was that the gravestones be removed and one large marker erected as a collective memorial for the dead. According to Councilman Van Archer, "That way they could bring those big ol' mowers in there rather than clipping around each stone." Finally, a resolution was passed asking the city manager to include funds in the next budget that would allow for the repair and maintenance of the Colored People's Cemetery.

25. There are, of course, exceptions to this trend toward standardization. One wonders what inferences will be made by future archeologists when they find the thirty-six-ton, exact-size granite replica of a 1982 Mercedes-Benz 240D in the Rosedale Cemetery in Linden, New Jersey. Sculpted in seventeen months from a sixty-ton slab, it was commissioned by the brother of the deceased, who had promised but failed to deliver the real vehicle to his sibling before his death.

26. By their very presence, cemeteries remind us that the meter is running. In fact, the tombstone of Archie Arnold (1920–1982) in the Scipio Cemetery near Fort Wayne, Indiana, is flanked by two parking meters, based on his final request.

27. When considering the 5 million Chinese who are buried each year, an official of the Funeral Management Bureau in Peking observed that the burial of only 1 million people would consume 1647 acres of land and 10.5 million cubic feet of lumber (Burns 1985).

28. Even so, there is still concern for maintaining some form of individualism in death. California law as of January 1984 prohibits the commingling of human remains. Bill Elkin, who had been hired by Bay Area mortuaries to scatter ashes, discovered this when he dumped the ashes of as many as fifty-six hundred people on his property instead of scattering them over the Sierras or over the ocean from his plane.

29. Many do not know that the Union Jack flies over North Carolina. In 1976, England was sold a small plot of land on an island on which were buried British

soldiers who had lost their lives in 1942 in a small coastal boat when it was sunk by a German U-boat torpedo a mile and a half off the coast.

30. In May 1979, the last 48 unidentified bodies of the 913 suicides from the People's Temple mission in Guyana were buried in a common grave.

31. In 1982, cemetery officials posted a notice to the families of the dead that Section 21 was being cleared, in accordance with the law limiting cemetery use to twenty-five years, and that unless families paid for exhumation and buried their relatives elsewhere, the state would truck the remains away for burial in a collective grave. Similar notification of the time limit was not sent to those families who lost members fighting against the revolution (Fenyvesi 1983).

32. The Soviet bloc, not usually known for its pro-Jewish sentiments, commemorated the fortieth anniversary of the liberation of the Ravensbrueck death camp with a ceremony that involved ten thousand people, including top Communist party officials.

REFERENCES

Angier, Natalie. 1984. "Burying Bones of Contention." *Time*. September 10, p. 32.

Arens, W. 1979. *The Man-Eating Myth: Anthropology and Anthropophagy*. New York: Oxford University Press.

Ariès, Philippe. 1974. *Western Attitudes toward Death*. Baltimore: Johns Hopkins University Press.

———. 1975. "Death Inside Out." In Peter Steinfels and Robert Veatch, eds., *Death Inside Out: The Hastings Center Report*. New York: Harper & Row, pp. 9–24.

———. 1981. *The Hour of Our Death*. New York: Alfred A. Knopf.

Baumeister, Roy. 1986. *Identity: Cultural Change and the Struggle for Self*. New York: Oxford University Press.

Bell, Daniel. 1980. *The Winding Passage*. New York: Basic Books.

Berger, Peter, and Thomas Luckmann. 1967. *The Social Construction of Reality*. Garden City, N.Y.: Doubleday Anchor Books.

Blaney, Herbert. 1977. "The Modern Park Cemetery." In Charles O. Jackson, ed., *Passing: The Vision of Death in America*. Westport, Conn.: Greenwood Press, pp. 219–43.

Blauner, Richard. 1966. "Death and Social Structure." *Psychiatry* 29 (November):378–94.

Brown, Arnold. 1945. *The Use of Words*. New York: Macmillan.

Burns, John. 1985. "Cremation Urged in China in Drive to Save Land." *New York Times*. May 23, p. 6.

Campbell, Joseph. 1974. *The Mythic Image*. Princeton, N.J.: Princeton University Press.

Choron, Jacques. 1964. *Death and Modern Man*. New York: Macmillan.

Clines, Francis. 1985. "Reagan's Remarks Stir New Debate." *New York Times*. April 19, pp. 1, 6.

Conrad, Geoffrey, and Arthur Demarest. 1984. *Religion and Empire: The Dynamics of Aztec and Inca Expansionism.* New York and London: Cambridge University Press.

Crosby, Alfred. 1986. *Ecological Imperialism: The Biological Expansion of Europe, 900–1900.* New York and London: Cambridge University Press.

Davis, Wade. 1985. *The Serpent and the Rainbow.* New York: Simon & Schuster.

Douglas, Mary. 1966. *Purity and Danger.* New York: Praeger.

Ehrlich, Paul, Anne Ehrlich, and John Holden. 1977. *Ecoscience: Population, Resources, Environment.* San Francisco: W. H. Freeman.

Eliade, Mircea. 1963. *Myth and Reality.* New York: Harper & Row.

Etlin, Richard. 1985. *The Architecture of Death: The Transformation of the Cemetery in Eighteenth-Century Paris.* Cambridge: MIT Press.

Fehrenbach, T. R. 1984. "'Fear' of Death the Real Enemy." *San Antonio Express-News.* January 8, p. 3J.

Feifel, Herman. 1959. *The Meaning of Death.* New York: McGraw-Hill.

Fenyvesi, Charles, 1983. "Indecent Burial." *New Republic.* January 11, pp. 13–14.

French, Stanley. 1975. "The Cemetery as Cultural Institution: The Establishment of Mount Auburn and the 'Rural Cemetery' Movement." In David Stannard, ed., *Death in America.* Philadelphia: University of Pennsylvania Press, pp. 69–91.

Friedrich, Otto. 1984. "Of Words That Ravage, Pillage, Spoil." *Time.* January 9, p. 76.

Geertz, Clifford. 1973. *The Interpretation of Cultures: Selected Essays.* New York: Basic Books.

Goffman, Erving. 1963. *Stigma: Notes on the Management of a Spoiled Identity.* New York: Prentice-Hall.

Goldscheider, Calvin. 1976. "The Mortality Revolution." In Edwin Shneidman, ed., *Death: Current Perspectives.* Palo Alto, Calif.: Mayfield, pp. 163–89.

Goleman, Daniel. 1985. "Emotional Impact of Disaster: Sense of Benign World Is Lost." *New York Times.* November 26, pp. 17–18.

Gorer, Geoffrey. 1965. *Death, Grief and Mourning.* New York: Doubleday Anchor Books.

Gottlieb, Carla. 1959. "Modern Art and Death." In Herman Feifel, ed., *The Meaning of Death.* New York: McGraw-Hill, pp. 157–88.

Gutmann, David. 1973. "The Premature Gerontocracy: Themes of Aging and Death in the Youth Culture." In Arien Mack, ed., *Death in American Experience.* New York: Schocken Books, pp. 50–82.

Habenstein, Robert, and William Lamers. 1962. *The History of American Funeral Directing.* Milwaukee: Bulfin Printers.

Harrington, Alan. 1977. *The Immortalist.* Millbrae, Calif.: Celestial Arts.

Helgeland, John. 1984–85. "The Symbolism of Death in the Later Middle Ages." *Omega* 15(2):145–60.

Hoelterhoff, Manuela. 1985. "Mayan Treasures: Corn, Blood and Jade." *Wall Street Journal* (June 11):28.

Hoffman, David. 1985. "German Soldiers Called 'Victims.'" *Washington Post.* April 19, pp. A1, A34.

Houghton, Walter. 1957. *The Victorian Frame of Mind, 1830–1870.* New Haven, Conn.: Yale University Press.

Huntington, Richard, and Peter Metcalf. 1979. *Celebrations of Death: The Anthropology of Mortuary Ritual.* Cambridge: Cambridge University Press.

Illich, Ivan. 1975. "The Political Uses of Natural Death." In Peter Steinfels and Robert Veatch, eds., *Death Inside Out: The Hastings Center Report.* New York: Harper & Row, pp. 25–42.

Langer, Susanne. 1960. *Philosophy in a New Key.* Cambridge, Mass.: Harvard University Press.

Lewis, Anthony. 1985. "'Remember, Remember.'" *New York Times.* December 2, p. 23.

Lifton, Robert, ed. 1971. *History and Human Survival.* New York: Vintage.

Lindesmith, Alfred, Anselm Strauss, and Norman Denzin. 1977. *Social Psychology,* 5th ed. New York: Holt, Rinehart and Winston.

Longman, Phillip. 1985. "The Downwardly Mobile Baby Boomers." *Wall Street Journal.* April 12, edit. page.

Mannheim, Karl. 1952. "On the Problem of Generations." In Paul Kecskemeti, ed. and transl., *Essays on the Sociology of Knowledge.* London: Routledge and Kegan Paul, pp. 276–322.

Marshall, Victor. 1980. *Last Chapters: A Sociology of Aging and Dying.* Monterey, Calif.: Brooks/Cole.

Mills, C. Wright. 1959. *The Sociological Imagination.* New York: Oxford University Press.

Morley, John. 1971. *Death, Heaven and the Victorians.* Pittsburgh: University of Pittsburgh Press.

Mumford, Lewis. 1961. *The City in History: Its Origins, Its Transformations, and Its Prospects.* New York: Harcourt Brace Jovanovich.

Nisbet, Robert. 1979. *History of the Idea of Progress.* New York: Basic Books.

New York Times. 1983. "Shakers File Suit to Protect Cemetery." April 18, p. 12.

———. 1985. "Remarks by Reagan Prompt Outcry from Jewish Groups." April 15, p. 4.

Parsons, Talcott, and Victor Lidz. 1967. "Death in American Society." In Edwin Shneidman, ed., *Essays in Self-Destruction.* New York: Science House, pp. 133–40.

Partridge, Eric. 1953. *A Dictionary of Slang and Unconventional English.* New York: Macmillan.

———. 1963. *Slang Today and Yesterday.* New York: Bonanza Books.

Phythian, B. A. 1976. *A Concise Dictionary of English Slang.* London: Hodder and Stoughton.

Preston, S. 1976. *Mortality Patterns in National Populations.* New York: Academic Press.

Priestly, J. B. 1964. *Man and Time.* New York: Dell.

Riley, John. 1983. "Dying and the Meanings of Death: Sociological Inquiries." *Annual Review of Sociology* 9:191–216.

Rodabough, Tillman. 1980. "The Cycle of American Perspectives toward Death." *Journal of the American Studies Association of Texas* 11:22–27.

Rousseau, Jean. 1964. "The Second Discourse." In Roger D. Masters, ed., *The First and Second Discourses.* New York: St. Martin's Press.

Ruesch, Hans. 1951. *Top of the World.* New York: Harper & Row.

Ruffenach, Glenn. 1985. "Reflections on Parents' Retirement Illustrate Fears of Next Generation." *Wall Street Journal.* December 11, p. 33.

Sanchez, Ricardo. 1985. "'Day of the Dead' Is Also about Life." *San Antonio Express-News Star.* November 1, pp. 1–2E.

Shneidman, Edwin. 1980. *Death: Current Perspectives,* 2d ed. Palo Alto, Calif.: Mayfield.

Stannard, David. 1977. *The Puritan Way of Death: A Study in Religion, Culture, and Social Change.* New York: Oxford University Press.

Starobinski, Jean. 1986. "Burying the Dead." *New York Review of Books.* January 16, pp. 16–20.

Toynbee, Arnold. 1980. "Various Ways in Which Human Beings Have Sought to Reconcile Themselves to the Fact of Death." In Edwin Shneidman, ed., *Death: Current Perspectives,* 2d ed. Palo Alto, Calif.: Mayfield, pp. 11–34.

Turner, Victor. 1967. *The Forest of Symbols: Aspects of Ndembu Ritual.* Ithaca, N.Y.: Cornell University Press.

Van Gennep, Arnold. 1960. *The Rites of Passage,* trans. by M. Vizedom and G. Caffee. Chicago: University of Chicago Press.

Wallechinsky, David, and Irving Wallace. 1977. *The People's Almanac Presents the Book of Lists.* Garden City, N.Y.: Doubleday.

Warner, F. Lloyd. 1959. *The Living and the Dead.* New Haven, Conn.: Yale University Press.

Waugh, Julia. 1955. *The Silver Cradle.* Austin: University of Texas Press.

Weinraub, Bernard. 1985. "Reagan Reverses His German Plans; Will Visit a Camp." *New York Times.* April 17, pp. 1, 7.

Wentworth, Harold, and Stuart Flexner. 1975. *A Dictionary of American Slang.* New York: Thomas Y. Crowell.

Westley, Ana. 1984. "Spaniards' Distaste for Life Insurance Leaves the Industry There Languishing." *Wall Street Journal.* March 29, p. 28.

Whorf, Benjamin. 1956. *Language, Thought, and Reality.* New York: John Wiley.

Chapter 3

Death's Impacts on Society

... any man's death, diminishes me, because I am involved
in Mankinde;
And therefore never send to know for whom the bell tolls;
It tolls for thee.

John Donne, *Devotions*

John Donne's famous insight is perhaps even truer now than it was almost four centuries ago. Each individual, of course, makes unique contributions to the social order. One's death means not only the cessation of these contributions but also the partial death of all of those for whom the deceased was a significant other. For example, consider the death of a close friend—a person who applauded your accomplishments, consoled you during your disappointments, and brought out of you a self that you both liked and enjoyed. With the death of this significant other comes the simultaneous destruction of a portion of yourself, a self never again to be reactivated. Further, this person was probably a friend of others. As Stanley Milgram (1977, p. 294) calculated the "small-world" phenomenon, one American is five and a half steps removed from any other American (e.g., a friend of mine has a friend who knows a person whose friend's brother-in-law I know; that is equal to five intermediaries).

Death's impact ripples not only across acquaintance networks and space but across time as well. In 1984, for instance, the eightieth anniversary of the sinking of a wooden excursion steamboat, the *General Slocum,* in the East River of New York City was observed. There was a wreath-laying ceremony attended by relatives of the 1030 victims of the disaster and even by one of its survivors. To this day, there are residents in the New York area who are experts on the sinking, who still debate whether Captain William Van

Over a thousand passengers drowned in the sinking of the *General Slocum*, a wooden excursion boat, in the East River of New York City. In 1984, relatives of the victims attended a wreath-laying ceremony commemorating the eightieth anniversary of the accident. New-York Historical Society.

Schaick was negligent or simply panicked in allowing an on-board fire to lead to the second-worst disaster in the history of American inland passenger shipping (*New York Times* 1984). What was the cumulative effect of so many deaths on succeeding generations? The young were never to have families of their own, never to have the opportunity to make a medical breakthrough or inspire their contemporaries with words or music. The adults were never to continue their roles as parents or grandparents, perhaps never to leave their memory on the consciousness of those now alive.

These were the kinds of impacts John Donne envisioned. However, because of the nature of modern social solidarities, the death of a single individual can have even more far-reaching implications. The death of an American president, for example, can cause prices to fall on stock exchanges around the world, armies to be mobilized, and suicides to increase. In 1985, Leon Klinghoffer, a sixty-nine-year-old wheelchair-bound stroke victim, was gunned down by Palestinians who had hijacked the *Achille Lauro,* an Italian ocean liner on which he was a passenger. His death, in part, led to the collapse of the Italian government, which was perceived to be inept in its management of the crisis. Because of mass-media innovations, we hear of deaths on the other side of the globe; because of our interconnectedness within the world system, we are affected by deaths we would have never known about if they had occurred a century or two ago.

The geneses of the cultural conceptualizations of death surveyed in Chapter 2 did not occur randomly or within some social vacuum. These meaning systems by which a people understands life and death are the products of social negotiations. The substance of these negotiations is shaped by culture's historical encounters with war and plague, the types of death it normally experiences, and the belief systems considered in Chapter 2. These belief systems, in turn, are shaped by the chemistry of institutions constituting a given society; the more culturally powerful its religion is, for instance, the more likely is its worldview to be routinely incorporated into everyday life. All social institutions, from the family to the political economy, must cope with death and dampen its disruptive potential. Death has not only dysfunctional but functional consequences as well. For example, though the death of a leader may lead to initial chaos and crises of power, it can also mean a reaffirmation of collective solidarity in the funeral proceedings and room for upward mobility for those in the hierarchy of power.

This chapter begins with a general analysis of how death affects social systems and individuals alike, first demonstrating its disruptive potential in a case study of the American AIDS epidemic. The discussion will show that such disruptions have not only socially dysfunctional but functional consequences, that social systems have developed social mechanisms for dampening death's forces of chaos and even transforming them into enhanced social solidarities. We will see, for example, how exposures to death can lead to the evolution of new social groups, how relationships within old groups can be reinvigorated, and how death can produce greater social equalities among the living. In conclusion, we consider the funeral ritual as the traditional social mechanism by which death's disruptive energies are dissipated or harnessed.

The Disruptive Potential of Death

Immortal social systems are occupied by mortal individuals. When death removes social actors from their positions of responsibility and interdependency, there is the threat that the bonds of social solidarity will become unglued. For instance, one wonders how many contemporary American families have disintegrated following the deaths of their older members. It is not unusual that the only time siblings, cousins, and different generations come together and interact is at the home of the oldest generation (e.g., the grandparents, the matriarch and/or patriarch of the familial system) during the holidays. With the social and geographical mobility of our times, these individuals have become increasingly separated by age. Many of one's family members may hold values and have life-styles considerably at odds with those of oneself or one's friends: the long-haired, liberal nephew must interact with his John Birch uncle, the physician must interact with the artist, and the churchgoer with the atheist. Where else but in a family could such exchanges occur? One probably would not select such a chemistry of people for one's friends, nor would there be such diversity among one's coworkers. Generally, because of the familial norm of having to tolerate and listen to fellow members, we see in the family the social cohesions that cut across differences in age, occupation, social class, and religion. Consider the consequences of the grandparents' deaths. Perhaps there is no other member who can control the loyalty of all, bring together the diverse elements, or be the object of common caring (if nothing else, an ailing older parent can provide a common task for nearby offspring who otherwise share no activity together). Often schisms appear over the distribution of the estate, signaling the beginning of the disintegration of this most important social unifier.[1]

But perhaps the ability of death to disrupt—and even to destroy—social groups is greatest when a political leader dies, particularly where there is a deteriorating political situation. Such deaths can trigger power struggles between factions, undermine the legitimacy of regimes, and, in a chain reaction, set off other deaths. India, for example, erupted in violence following the assassination of Prime Minister Indira Gandhi in late 1984. Even her critics admitted that she was what had held a fractious country together. Months before her death, she said, "If I die today, every drop of my blood will invigorate the nation." What was invigorated was violence. After Gandhi was slain by a Sikh bodyguard, the country's Hindu majority attacked the small but powerful Sikh minority. By the time of her internationally televised cremation, some seven hundred fifty Indians had died—a sacrifice of one for each million Indians.

The political disruptiveness of the power vacuum caused by a leader's death is further amplified by the potential crises of succession. Particularly when the death comes suddenly and unexpectedly, social systems face the problem of restoring the social order. To survive, they must have established responses. And even when a leader's death comes expectedly and slowly, as in the case of Soviet Premier Leonid Brezhnev, the transition of power is never guaranteed to be smooth:

In the 65 years that it has been in power, the Soviet Communist Party has failed to devise a means of transferring authority from one leader to another that guarantees that the transition will be safe and trouble-free.

In a sense, most Russians have been preparing for the succession to Leonid Brezhnev for at least six years, since the first signs of the heart trouble that his doctors identified as the cause of his death. Yet when the announcement came today, it was far from clear who would take over Mr. Brezhnev's key post as general secretary of the party, or whether any of the candidates in the ruling Politburo had the power to claim the post and hold it. (*New York Times* 1982a)

Fears of the impact of Brezhnev's death were not confined to the Soviet Union but, like a ripple in a pond, affected all. There was, for example, the concern that internal strife within the Soviet Union would lead to further international venturism. Without knowledge of the policies of his successors,[2] Western democracies did not know how much to devote to military as opposed to economic investments.

When his death finally did occur, immediate word was withheld: Soviet television changed its scheduled programs tonight without explanation, setting off rumors that a member of the Politburo had died. On the national network channel, a variety concert in honor of Soviet Police Day was replaced by a film about Lenin and reminiscences of World War II.

Such changes are usual when a member of the leadership dies, but official spokesmen said they had no information about any death in the Politburo. . . . News about the death of a leader is usually delayed for at least a day until an official obituary can be composed and funeral arrangements made. (*New York Times* 1982b)

Even the rumor of a leader dying can rattle the social order.[3] Political systems must respond to such reports, which can further fan the embers of chaos:

Iran denied rumors in European financial circles Wednesday that its supreme leader Ayatollah Ruhollah Khomeini is dead, saying the stories were invented by a U.S.-led "propaganda machine of the superpowers." . . . The news agency said the rumors were aimed at blunting the "great Iranian victories" at the war front with Iraq. (*San Antonio Express-News* 1983)

Death disrupts not only the social bonds of a society but the social atom as well—the individual, for whom death can destroy social motivation and participation. Only when our cultural death-denial system is punctured do we have a glimpse of the chaos posed by death, and for many even this glimpse can destroy the complacency and security they have in the social order. On the first anniversary of the 1984 San Diego McDonald's mass murder of twenty-one people (detailed in Chapter 4), it was obvious that life for the survivors would never be the same. For them, the very fabric of society was ripped when death was let in. Such experiences forever shatter one's ability to suspend doubt, to be shielded from the anomie and terror posed by unexpected death. Following the great earthquakes that hit Mexico City in 1985, killing thousands, there were reports of suicide, serious depression, trauma, and people aimlessly walking the streets. Mass death can lead one to think and act as if the world itself were dying. And what scars are borne by the population of individuals born between 1930 and 1940? In much of Europe, this generation's formative years coincided with World War II. How does the personality structure of these individuals differ from that of their American counterparts because of such exposures to death?

To further explore how death can not only disrupt the social order but fundamentally alter it as well, let us consider the impact of epidemics on social life and social history.

The AIDS Epidemic

For most of human history, the Four Horsemen of the Apocalypse—famine, pestilence, war, and strife—regularly inhibited any population growth. Perhaps more than anything else, the central accomplishment of modernization has been to keep the first two horsemen at bay, consigning them either to mythology or to the Third World. We now believe that mass death is something we can control, that human ingenuity can keep the natural forces that kill us at bay.[4] But this hubris of modernity has perhaps made postindustrial society more vulnerable to natural calamity when it does occur. The ability of disease to alter the modern social order—to bring about suspicion, fear, and irrational behavior—has been most recently apparent with the outbreak of the AIDS epidemic. As AIDS victims came to be considered lepers, the seams of the social fabric unraveled in ways reminiscent of the Black Plague half a millennium earlier.

There are no survivors of this disease, which mutates some one thousand times faster than other known viruses and whose victims double in number every year. AIDS effectively destroys the body's autoimmune system, leaving it vulnerable to the diseases of antiquity, such as leprosy, Pneumocystis carinii pneumonia, and rare carcinomas. The virus suspected of causing the disease has been found in the teardrops, blood, semen, and saliva of its victims by scientists at the National Cancer Institute. Some professionals think it could be transmitted through mosquito bites. AIDS has been portrayed as a Third World anomaly, a disease from such impoverished countries as Haiti, Kenya, Uganda, Zaire, Rwanda, Burundi, and Tanzania. By 1986 there were twenty thousand cases of AIDS reported in the United States, and sample studies based on blood tests indicated that an additional five hundred thou-

Allegoric representation of the Four Horsemen of the Apoc-
alypse: War, Hunger, Plague, and Death. From Albrecht
Durer's *Apocalypse*, Nuremberg 1498. Dover Pictorial
Archives.

sand to one million Americans could be symptomless carriers. The Centers
for Disease Control in Atlanta estimated that one hundred thousand people
could develop advanced stages of the disease by 1990 and more would be
dying annually of this disease than die in automobile accidents. In 1987, Dr.
Otis Bowen, the secretary of Health and Human Services, predicted that the
worldwide AIDS epidemic would become so serious that it eventually would
dwarf such earlier medical disasters as the Black Plague, smallpox, and
typhoid (*New York Times* 1987). At an international AIDS forum in Stockholm, the World Health Organization estimated that one hundred fifty

thousand individuals would develop AIDS just in 1988, doubling the total number of cases worldwide since the epidemic's beginnings in the 1970s.

There has been a historic connection between disease and social status—evident, for example, in the caste taboos on contact across caste lines (McNeill 1976). In the first few years of the AIDS epidemic, the victims of the disease were disproportionately members of some stigmatized or disenfranchised status group. The disease was first observed in homosexual populations in 1981 when several instances of such rare problems as Pneumocystis carinii pneumonia and Kaposi's sarcoma, a rare skin cancer, appeared in California and New York clinics. The carrier populations identified next included Haitians, intravenous drug users, and bisexuals. Though blacks comprised 12.5 percent of the population, they accounted for about a quarter of the reported cases (Boffey 1985). In 1987, 80 percent of the estimated fifty thousand New York City females infected with the virus were either black or Hispanic (Gross 1987), as AIDS became the leading cause of death for women aged twenty-five to twenty-nine in that city.[5] But eventually the victims were to include those without moral or social stigma, particularly the recipients of blood transfusions and infants born to infected mothers (in 1988, it was reported that one of every sixty-one babies born in New York City carried AIDS antibodies, one in forty-three in the Bronx [Lambert 1988]).

The AIDS-related death of movie idol Rock Hudson served to heighten both public consciousness and hysteria regarding the disease. A 1985 New York Times/CBS national survey found that half the American public believed that AIDS could be transmitted through casual contact, despite sci-

AIDS Cases per Million of Population in the United States

All men:	White	333	All women:	White	10
	Black	859		Black	119
	Hispanic	806		Hispanic	80

	White	Black	Hispanic
Heterosexual men who are intravenous drug users	13	289	271
Gay or bisexual men who are not intravenous drug users	276	434	434

Sources: Dr. Roger Bakeman; Centers for Disease Control (from Levine 1987). © Aug. 17, 1987 by U.S. News & World Report. Reprinted by permission.

entific evidence to the contrary (Eckholm 1985). Forty-seven percent thought it was possible to catch the disease by drinking from a glass just used by a patient, 32 percent thought the syndrome could be spread through kissing, and 28 percent said it was possible to become infected from a toilet seat. Thirteen percent said they had changed their personal behavior to avoid getting the disease. The disease bred fear, suspicion, and desperate action often bereft of reason. New York City television technicians refused to work on a scheduled live interview with an AIDS patient; a Kokomo, Indiana, thirteen-year-old hemophiliac was denied permission to attend school after having contracted AIDS from his blood transfusions; and St. Louis morticians refused to embalm the remains of AIDS victims (Wallis 1985). In New York City, where one-third of the reported cases in the country lived in the mid-1980s, ambulance companies refused to transport AIDS patients and funeral homes regularly demanded as much as one thousand dollars extra to handle the bodies of AIDS victims (Firmer 1985). The Episcopal bishop of California issued a pastoral letter in response to fears among Bay Area parishioners that drinking communion wine from a common cup could transmit AIDS (Berger 1985). Newspapers developed regular AIDS sections.

As AIDS fears metamorphosed into homophobia, the virus triggered discriminations and actual violence against homosexuals, erasing a decade of increasing acceptability of gay rights. A civil war even existed among homosexuals: in Hempstead, Long Island, a homeless man killed his lover when, immediately after having sex, his lover had informed him that he had AIDS (Gutis 1987). Sperm banks began rejecting homosexual donors (*San Antonio Express-News* 1985a). There were consumer backlashes against businesses owned or staffed by homosexuals. A Detroit woman who had received a book from a gay-lesbian bookstore called the store asking if the package could be opened without contracting the disease (*Wall Street Journal* 1985). And cruel and tasteless jokes dealing with homosexuality and AIDS proliferated; as in the past, death anxieties are often managed through gallows humor.

The Defense Department announced that it would screen all prospective military recruits for AIDS exposure, later expanding the screenings to those already in uniform. One of the concerns was that the disease could be transmitted during battlefield blood transfusions. The homosexual community saw this as a possible precedent for similar screenings in private industry. And so it was to be: a Dallas-based energy company ordered all of its food-service employees to undergo an AIDS screening test, and insurance companies began screening applicants for symptoms. The House of Representatives approved a measure giving the U.S. surgeon general the power to shut down public bath houses and massage parlors in a much-publicized war on AIDS. Said Rep. William Dannemeyer of California, "it seems only prudent

In June 1983, AIDS victims march against death during the annual Lesbian/Gay Freedom Day Parade in San Francisco. UPI/Bettmann Newsphotos.

that we take all precautions and not make the general population into guinea pigs for determining transmissibility of the AIDS virus" (*San Antonio Express-News* 1985b). In Houston, undercover policemen trailed a victim who had ignored the city health director's order to abstain from sexual relations. Said a police captain of the vice division, "we've got a man who's definitely a threat to society" (*San Antonio Express-News* 1985c). AIDS victims who knowingly spread the deadly disease to strangers could be considered murderers, claimed the chairman of the Bexar County Hospital District in Texas (Smith and Valle 1985) and the prosecutor of a Los Angeles trial involving an AIDS victim accused of selling his blood and engaging in prostitution.

Such discrimination and recriminations culminated in 1986, when the Supreme Court ruled 5–4 that private homosexual acts between consenting adults are not protected by the constitutional right of privacy, thereby upholding the constitutionality of laws in twenty-four states making it a crime to commit sodomy. The following year, the president endorsed the idea of mandatory AIDS tests for those seeking marriage licenses and for immigrants seeking permanent residence in the country (Japan had already adopted a program designed to keep out foreigners found to be carriers of the AIDS virus, and in 1987 the Soviet Union adopted measures requiring the mandatory testing of suspected carriers and prison terms of up to five years for carriers knowingly infecting others). Society seemed bent on assigning a new scarlet letter of the times. Nathaniel Hawthorne's scarlet A was to be retained, but now it was to be attached to those stigmatized by AIDS. Dr. Richard Restak, a well-known neurologist and author of *The Brain,* argued that until more was known, AIDS victims should be quarantined.

The inevitable search for explanations produced a host of speculations. One of the easiest explanations for any misfortune is a conspiracy theory. Political activist Dick Gregory argued that the spread of AIDS was attributed to germ warfare. If AIDS is really the result of homosexual activity, why, he asked, did it not appear in ancient Greece, where homosexuality was common? "How is it in the first three years that 99.9 percent of all the victims are Americans? They have homosexuals all over the world," Gregory observed, and he hinted that Haitian refugees may have been used as guinea pigs (Davidson 1985). Religious fundamentalists claimed that the epidemic was divine justification, God's revenge on sodomites and junkies.[6] And even science was to find reason to criticize the homosexual life-style. Researchers at the National Jewish Center for Immunology and Respiratory Medicine claimed to have evidence that isobutyl nitrate, a recreational drug widely used as an aphrodisiac by homosexuals, increased the risk of contracting AIDS (*New York Times* 1985b). It was not long before *the* contemporary cultural eschatology was applied to the epidemic. The dean of medicine at Brown University, Dr. David S. Greer, claimed that survivors of a nuclear war would suffer from immune system depression, and, like those with acquired immune deficiency syndrome, they would be left susceptible to deadly infections (*Houston Post* 1985). Observed Lance Morrow in a *Time* magazine essay:

In a way, AIDS suits the style of the late 20th century. In possibly overheated fears, it becomes a death-dealing absolute loose in the world. Westerners for some years have consolidated their dreads, reposing them (if that is the word) in the Bomb, in the one overriding horror of nuclear holocaust. . . . Now comes another agent of doomsday, this one actually killing people and doubling the number of its victims every ten months as if to reverse the logic of Thomas Malthus. (1985)

The saddest part of the story, of course, involves the victims of this epidemic. Victims are stigmatized, trust evaporates, and panic rules. The mere diagnosis of the disease can trigger suicides. AIDS sufferers discover that the worst aspect of the disease is the sense of isolation and personal rejection. "It's like wearing the scarlet letter," says a thirty-five-year-old Harvard-educated lawyer who was forced out of a job at a top Texas law firm. "When people do find out, there is a shading, a variation in how they treat me. There is less familiarity. A lot less" (Wallis 1985, p. 45). Victims were frequently discharged by firms concerned with health risks to coworkers and consequently deprived of insurance benefits (Roth 1985). As a result, in 1987, the Supreme Court ruled that people with contagious diseases were covered by a federal law prohibiting discrimination against the handicapped in federally aided programs.

Hopes for a cure are routinely fanned by the culture's warriors against death, the medical researchers (see Chapter 11). There has even been quibbling between researchers of the United States and those of France over who was first to even identify the AIDS virus. In March 1987, an experimental drug called AZT (marketed under the name Retrovere) was approved by the FDA for AIDS victims. The drug had shown some promising results. The problem was that its manufacturer, Burroughs Wellcome, could not initially produce enough to meet the demand for a prescription whose annual cost was between seven and ten thousand dollars.

Some experts believe that the federal government will inevitably have to take a more active role. As the AIDS toll mounts, the cost of caring for patients, which ranges from fifty thousand to one hundred fifty thousand dollars each, will overwhelm local resources. In American society, disasters are gauged not only in death rates but also in costs. The New York City health commissioner estimated that AIDS cost the city one hundred million dollars annually (Barbanel 1985). With the number of cases doubling each year, an administrator of New York City's St. Luke's-Roosevelt Hospital said, "I can already see the whole hospital system coming apart at the edges" (Wallis 1985, p. 47).

Such has been the impact of a disease that, according to 1987 projections by the Centers for Disease Control, will account for nearly 3 percent of all deaths in the early 1990s. In 1987, suicide, pneumonia, and cirrhosis of the liver were far more frequent causes of death than AIDS, whose victims were the same in number as those of emphysema, kidney failure, and murder (Russell 1987). Imagine the social disruption wrought by diseases killing more than forty thousand times the number of Americans currently dying of AIDS. Such massive death rates have occurred numerous times in human history, often fundamentally altering its course.

To grasp the macrosociological dynamics of disease, one must first consider the reciprocal relationship between food and parasite. There must be an equilibrium between the two, or both systems can perish; "outside" disruptions must lead to compensatory change throughout the system in order to minimize overall upheaval.[7] Some microparasites allow the host to survive indefinitely, whereas others kill at once.[8] As the body's immune system is triggered by the destruction of cells, so the social system reacts to the death of its constituent member cells. But like a body weakened by too many diseases, society's regenerative powers can truly be thwarted if the social order goes through cumulative or broad-scale disasters (Cornell 1982). Of one of the first recorded epidemics to hit the West, in 430 B.C. in Attica, Thucydides wrote: "people lacked a fear of gods or law of men. There was none to restrain them . . . they judged it to be the same whether they worshipped them or not." (Cartwright 1972, p. 4).

The epidemics of the Middle Ages not only killed millions (the Black Death of 1347–51 alone may have killed as many as one-third of the world's people), but they hastened the demise of the European feudal order. Class tensions were increasingly aggravated, as the poor died while the rich fled (Renouard 1978). As one Toulouse bourgeois coolly observed in 1561: "the aforesaid contagious disease only attacks poor people . . . let God in his mercy be satisfied with that. . . . The rich protect themselves against it" (Braudel 1981, p. 85). Social duties were either abandoned or conducted at a distance; French parliaments and English courts emigrated, mayors and lawyers fled their posts, and municipal officers forgot their responsibilities. The frayed nerves of society were further agitated by increasing political and ecclesiastical corruption. Offices had to be filled as their holders died, and often only power- and money-seeking individuals could be found (Thompson 1978, p. 21). The church's claims of infallibility were to be challenged because of the high mortality rate of its priests: if the plague was intended only for sinners and its victims included priests, then the priests must be sinners. Further, anticlericism was fueled as the surviving priests fled their congregations and were replaced by the undereducated and unworthy (McNeill 1976, p. 185). To add to the problem, the church abandoned its ordination practices during and shortly after the plague (Ziegler 1969, p. 260). The sacraments performed by the priests were supposed to ward off the anger of God. However, since the priests were not ordained and thus did not carry the blessing of God, how could the sacraments be valid?

In sum, the medieval death system could not provide technological defense, eschatological meaning, or psychological comfort (death was still understood as punishment for man's sins) in the face of mass death (Kastenbaum and Aisenberg 1972). Such impotence seriously undermined the legitimacy and authority of political and religious institutions (Cornell 1982, p. 65). People became demoralized and turned to new forms of meaning, perhaps accounting for the sudden popularity of the flagellant and occult movements (Thompson 1978, p. 23). Some historians see the corruption of the clergy as eventually resulting in the Reformation. Further, as populations shifted, life-styles changed, altering the social texture: manners declined, gaudy fashions became popular, and new symbols emerged (Thompson 1978, p. 21).

The bubonic plague also may have put Western culture on its trajectory toward capitalism. Because of their diminished number and numerous inheritances, many surviving peasants because richer and more powerful. Prices fell as the market became glutted. The switch to wages and rents, already in progress, was accelerated as workers demanded higher wages; labor became a commodity (Ziegler 1969). Landlords rented property in order to pay the labor, and, to attract renters, rents were cut almost in half in some areas (Thompson 1978). As wages increased in urban areas by as much as 50 to 150 percent, governments passed maximum price and wage laws that later led to rebellion, especially among the peasants (Thompson 1978, p. 30).[9]

The Effects of Mass Deaths on the Social Order

Epidemics bring a demoralization of the survivors and a loss of faith in their inherited customs and beliefs. But the causes of death need not be invisible to wrought such doubt. The same applies to mass deaths from pogroms, murder, suicide, or natural calamity. Further, such demoralization is amplified if the population losses occur within the twenty- to sixty-year age bracket, as is the case with AIDS. Those are the years during which society can count on the greatest social commitment and responsibility from its members. Those are the years of critical life experiences, when one learns and passes on the lessons for succeeding generations.

This notion of the differential impacts of death stemming from the chemistry of age groups that happen to be dying brings us to the significance of death from the perspective of demographic transition theory. According to this theory, there are five demographic epochs in the history of human population growth which have a profound bearing on such things as the pace of social change, the rate of cultural evolution, or the relative size of dependent populations. In the earliest period, both birth and death rates are high and approximately equal, about forty per one thousand individuals (Braudel 1981). The population is in equilibrium with its environment. With social evolution, there are declines in death rates which outstrip the changes occurring in birth rates. Here the agrarian procreative tradition—of having large numbers of children to ensure the survival of a few (which was the first form of social security for old age) and to have as many hands helping with the farm as is efficient—is transported to urban centers, to places where improved medicine guarantees less infant death but where having children becomes an economic liability. With a majority of societies in this phase of dramatic population growth rates, some claim that we may be approaching the ecological limits of our species' numbers. Paul Ehrlich, in his 1968 *The Population Bomb,* predicted that the population of the Third World would double in twenty-five years and that the choice is for either a "birth rate solution" or a "death rate solution."[10] The final epoch, only now being approached by a few of the most industrialized countries, is characterized by equal birth and death rates, but this time at a much lower level.

With these points in mind, consider Figure 3.1, which compares the death rates of two developed and two developing countries. Looking at the death rate for males, a Mexican child is over twenty-two times more likely to die than his Netherlands counterpart, and in his thirties he still has a four-fold greater chance of expiring. Comparing the death rates of men aged 15–64, Mexican society loses the skills, energy, and insights of proportionately twice as many men each year as does the Netherlands.

Death comes more frequently in the Third World, from both natural and man-made forces,[11] either demographically retarding the pace of progress because of birth rates massively outstripping death rates and thereby making an increasingly youthful—hence dependent and nonproductive—population, or because too many socially critical individuals are killed within too short a time. In November 1985, for example, ninety-five Colombians were killed, including eleven supreme court judges and thirty-three other judges, after guerrillas seized the Palace of Justice, which housed the country's Supreme Court. Two weeks later, that country was rocked by a volcanic eruption that rivaled the deadliness of Mount Vesuvius's A.D. 79 explosion which destroyed the legendary cities of Pompeii and Herculaneum (Russell 1985). That same year, one of the poorest and most densely populated countries in the world, Bangladesh, was hit by a cyclone, drowning at least ten thousand. Life is cheapened where existence is marginal and where too many compete for too little. In such places death becomes a relatively unshocking routine.

The African drought of the 1980s which left as many as thirty-five million desperately hungry people in its wake, provides another sad illustration, causing "the worst human disaster in the recent history" of the continent, according to a UN report. This report, published by the office of the UN disaster relief coordinator, observed that thirty-six African nations face food shortages and that twenty-seven of them are urgently in need of food aid from abroad. The problems of one country are exported to another, as, for

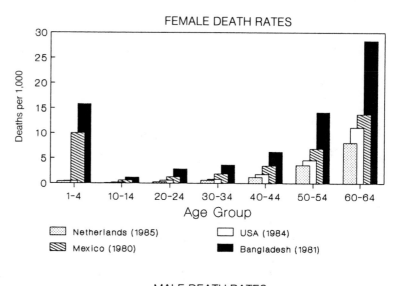

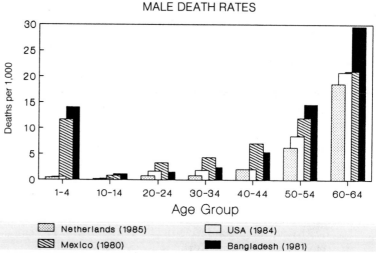

Figure 3.1 Death rates by age, gender, and country. Data source: United Nations Demographic Yearbook, 1986.

instance, when tens of thousands of emaciated Mozambique emigrants, sick with such maladies as pellagra, diarrhea, and cholera, arrived on dusty trails to Zimbabwe (Johnson 1984). Between 20 and 30 percent of those affected by the prolonged drought, floods, cyclones, and civil conflicts were children under the age of five (*San Antonio Express-News* 1984a). In Chad, where life had always been marginal, the drought weakened the very social fabric that formerly had enabled civility to persist in a seemingly inhospitable land: in families the men ate first, the women second, and then the children; cousins were no longer welcome when they came to share the scarce food; and parents simply let their sick children die so there would be more to eat (Kamm 1985). And in Uganda, a country already bled by the barbarous regime of Idi Amin and by the civil war that followed, the drought further contributed to disregard for human rights and civility. Observed one Catholic priest, "Death has become an everyday story. Children aren't afraid of dead bodies any longer. They've seen too many" (Lescaze 1985).

The Effects of Individual Deaths on the Social Order

As we have seen, entire social systems can be destroyed or fundamentally altered if there are too many deaths of socially critical individuals. But such events are rare when compared to the times smaller groups are shattered by the deaths of a few individuals, necessitating tremendous readjustments for the living.

Survivors of a cyclone that decimated the population of Manpura Island, Pakistan, in November of 1970. Some 25,000 of the island's 30,000 inhabitants perished in the storm which may have claimed over half-a-million lives. UPI/Bettmann Newsphotos.

How many remember why for nearly two decades the United States fared so poorly in the Winter Olympics? In the mid-1960s a plane carrying a sizable portion of the U.S. team crashed, killing not only a competitive team but a future generation of coaches and mentors as well. Consider the ramifications of the death of a thirty-year-old parent: for the surviving spouse, there is the expansion of the parenting role and the sole responsibility for breadwinning; for the children, an accelerated maturity might be demanded as they must now shoulder certain "adult" responsibilities; and for the grandparents, aunts, and uncles of the children, there may be the assumption of a number of parenting duties. The smaller the group and the more unique the contributions of individuals, the greater the ramifications of a single death.

The disruptive potential of death for any social group is not only a function of the proportion of its members who happen to die or of the critical roles performed by those lost, but it is also a function of the nature of the group's social solidarity, the types of bonds linking individuals. In *Gemeinschaft* societies, such as the small towns and rural cultures of the nineteenth century where people knew one another intimately, individuals often have unique, important, and irreplaceable functions. Such deaths cannot be ignored. They must be marked by a communitywide outpouring of grief for genuine social losses and a collective reaffirmation of shared values in order to assist the stricken group to reestablish and reintegrate itself.

But with increasing social complexity and the concurrent devaluations of the individual (discussed in Chapter 2), the deaths of typical individuals can be disregarded. In *Gesellschaft* societies such as our own, which are characterized by impersonal associations among total strangers, social organizations have "a permanence and autonomy that makes them effectively independent of the individuals who carry out the roles within them" (Blauner 1966, p. 393). Here an individual's death is not the loss of a whole, unique person but rather the loss of a role occupant who can be simply replaced, as

Table 3.1 The Costs of Death
The amount of social rearrangements occasioned by an individual's death for the society as a whole, for the family and friends of the deceased, and for the dying person (− little; + some; ++ considerable).

Social unit	Modern	Primitive
Society	−	++
Family	−	+
Friends	+	−
Individual	++	−

The family of Vaclav and Katerina Venigr at the funeral of their son, Joseph. Few deaths have the emotional impact of the loss of one's child. Otto Hanus, Institute of Texan Cultures, San Antonio, Texas.

is the case in bureaucracies, where offices and functions are impersonal and transferable.[12] Thus, with individual lives being in less direct and less total involvement with others, individual deaths have become less damaging to the network of social relationships. As we will see, such changes have had a detrimental effect on our self-esteem; at home, at work, and even at play, we realize how easily replaceable we have become.

There is another way to conceptualize how this historic change in social solidarity has altered the disruptions unleashed by death. Imagine that any one death generates a finite amount of grief that must be socially dissipated. In *Gemeinschaft* societies, where individualism is minimal and personal identifications are with the group as opposed to the self, this grief was spread out over a large network (see Table 3.1). The "grief work" that had to be done was collectively shouldered. And the dying individual knew that the primary social unit, the clan or tribe, would certainly continue despite his or her demise. In modern *Gesellschaft* societies, on the other hand, the brunt of death is borne not by the collectivity but rather by the dying individual and a few of his or her immediate associates. In sum, "it seems that, when social integration is dominant and social values are accepted automatically, the awareness of death is limited. But when social disorganization is prevalent and individualism intensifies, the consciousness of death becomes stronger" (Bardis 1981, p. 1). As we will see in Chapter 12, the dying and the immediate survivors are now left to their own resources to deal with the terrors of death; society no longer has to be bothered.

The Social Functions of Death

Describing death's disruptiveness is not meant to imply that death is always dysfunctional. Even in the case of the Black Plague, death can be socially functional as well. Death threatens community continuity but, in so doing, contributes to the strengthening of the social structure. As the preindustrial slash-and-burn technique enriched the soil for the following year's crops, so the death of one generation enriches the opportunities of the succeeding ones. Blauner points out that death's sword is double-edged: "The very sharpness of its disintegrating potential demands adaptations that can bring higher levels of cohesion and continuity" (1966, p. 394).

Without death, the Malthusian nightmare[13] would shortly be realized and social change would be improbable. As the African drought may now be demonstrating, there is a limit to the ability of the earth to support human population. Only death checks the high birth rates observed throughout the developing world. "Death may be even more important in contributing to cultural growth and flexibility than in supporting genetic change" (Parsons, Fox, and Lidz 1973, p. 3) by stemming sociocultural entropy (Parsons and Lidz 1967).[14] For example, is it not in the interest of the political order that racist attitudes be buried with their carriers and not passed on as a legacy to younger generations? Further, because of the accelerating pace of social change, many individuals now outlive their traditional institutional life-course recipes (contemporary "old age," for example, has been characterized as being a "roleless role") and predicate their lives on values and principles long forgotten. In other words, death allows collective forgetting and the ecstasy of fresh beginnings.[15]

Death also facilitates collective remembering, thereby contributing a continuity between a society's past, present, and future. Most social systems, for instance, have an established folklore about the "good old days," the "golden years," and a "paradise lost"—myths portraying the superior qualities of earlier times and generations. With death, such mythologies are allowed to flourish, in part because of the normal psychological processes that lead to idealizations of the deceased (see Chapter 12). The dead, in effect, remain social players, invested with the ideal-type attributes of the living and serving as their flawless role models. As Sandra Bertman observed:

The dead do not leave us: They are too powerful, too influential, too meaningful to depart. They give us direction by institutionalizing our history and culture; they clarify our relationship to country and cause. They immortalize our sentiments and visions in poetry, music, and art. The dead come to inform us of tasks yet to be completed, of struggles to be continued, of purposes to be enjoined, of lessons they have learned. (1979, p. 151)

Related to death's control over population growth are its democratic aspects (Hocking 1957, p. 12): because of death, hierarchical societies can capture the loyalties and commitments of the young by giving them upward mobility as vacancies occur at the higher rungs. Implicit within the stages of the life course is a temporally structured mobility plan (Becker and Strauss 1968; Berger and Pullberg 1965): each year of school is predicated upon the previous year's training and anticipates the following; high school is a stepping stone to college; the college diploma is the license for advanced training; education is assumed to lead to work, where one "moves up" through a hierarchy of achievement levels; and so on. "The mobility ethos, by contrast with values that are bound to the family or a subculture, is one of the few norms continuously reaffirmed in the life of the individual and thus taking on for him the character of massive reality" (Berger and Luckman 1964, p. 340). But such mobility cannot continue indefinitely. We cannot forever be reeducating the old or denying the young the promise of eventually occupying positions of social authority.

Certainly the threat of death operates to ensure social order; it is the ultimate mechanism by which societies can establish the conformity of the populace. Even the crime underworld has its oaths and rules, which, if violated, would mean death. Further, death demands attention. Fatal accidents and public executions attract bystanders like decomposing matter attracts flies. If it is not death per se which is the featured attraction, then it is its probability. The crowds attracted to races involving aircraft, cars, motorcycles, and hydroplanes are reminiscent of the audiences for the contests of life and death in the Coliseum of ancient Rome. Such is the sacral power of death. From the earliest of recorded times we have evidence of death's constituent role in achieving the proper social and emotional intensity required for integrative rituals. Fowl, sheep, goats, bulls, and people have all been subject to sacrifice either to appease the gods or to symbolize a culture's resolution of the tensions between life and death.[16]

Further, death's power as a social magnet can create new social solidarities or enhance old ones. Death gives priorities and focuses attention on social problems. It also invigorates social bonds. For this reason, many wars and crusades were initiated out of internal strife. For the economically depressed and politically turbulent United States of the 1930s, World War II brought rebirth to a dying economy. The mass death at Pearl Harbor on December 7, 1941, made hawks out of isolationists, and the casualties of the European and Asian campaigns brought a rarely seen unity and resolve to the American people, with dramatic declines of homicide and suicide rates.

This peculiar ability of death to enhance social integration is worth further attention. Some social groups are able to successfully harness the power released by the deaths of their members to amplify the solidarities among the living. For example, there is the Texas Aggie Memorial Day on April 21: every year since 1883, in hundreds of places around the world, alumni of Texas A&M have gathered for a roll call (the Muster) of those who have died during the previous year. In addition, when a student of that university dies, a notice is posted, and on the first Monday evening following the death all the lights are turned off at exactly ten P.M. and the cadets congregate to hear the Silver Taps. Or consider the state funerals of national leaders: such events are among the few mandatory occasions when enemies and friends must come together and ritually interact. Sometimes the strategy backfires. In the final months of World War II the city of Dresden was firebombed, supposedly to destroy Nazi morale. The attack was devastating; a beautiful historic city was reduced to ashes, and more than eighty thousand were killed. To the dismay of strategists, the effect was the reverse of what was expected: it fortified German resolve.

The appearance of death (whether in the form of a public execution or a cockfight), the sharing of death (combatants watching their friends die, the attachments formed between families in hospital emergency wards) or grief (the Widow-to-Widow program or the SIDS groups), or concern over some portended death (the Save the Whale coalitions, for example) bring together individuals who otherwise might never have been socially joined. In this sense, death does serve the social function of intensifying and expanding relations among the living.

Case Study 1: The Space Shuttle Challenger

On January 28, 1986, the American space shuttle *Challenger* exploded approximately seventy seconds after launch. The seven crew members, including the first American teacher in space, were killed.

This disaster followed a year of rising doubts about technological safety. In 1985, more than two thousand people had died in commercial airline crashes, the greatest number killed in any year. But of all these disasters, including the crash a month earlier of a leased jet carrying 240 American troops home from Europe for Christmas, it was the space shuttle tragedy that commanded the greatest amount of media attention and enforced the greatest amount of uniform national grief. A Los Angeles radio announcer was fired for airing a *Challenger* joke, and Americans were told that they would remember what they were doing when they heard the news just as they remembered the day Pearl Harbor was bombed and when John F. Kennedy was assassinated (von Hoffman 1986).

There were a number of reasons for such attention. First, the country watched on live television as seven smiling individuals—a cross-section of our society, with two women, a black, and a Japanese-American—garbed in their Buck Rogers uniforms, walked to their spacecraft and only moments later were collectively consumed in a huge fireball high over the Florida skies. Even the constantly repeated reruns of the disaster were terrifying. Second, as opposed to most of the earlier flights of the space shuttle, the public had some prior knowledge of, and hence some empathy for those killed, particularly Christa McAuliffe of New Hampshire, who had been selected from thousands of applicants as a vehicle through which American children could be stimulated by and encouraged to participate in the American space program. To make matters worse, so complete was the astronauts' destruction that there were no corpses to base a funeral service on.[17] Finally, in addition to these more apparent reasons for collective grief, the attention focused on this accidental death stemmed from even deeper symbolic sources. In a number of ways, a space shuttle is the technological symbol—better, totem—of the United States. With a price tag of more than a billion dollars, it truly is a piece of collective property that everyone obviously must contribute to. It is quite probably the most complex machine ever created, created by probably the most elaborate division of labor organized to create a single product. To see such a symbol of ourselves explode accidentally like some huge fireworks display was simply too much to take.

With hindsight, we can perceive a trail of ominous signs. The previous flight two short weeks earlier had been the most delayed flight for both launch and reentry. If the delays were not caused by such man-made flaws as errant technology, it was the weather that conspired against our conquering the heavens. And like the need for religion to obscure any signs of its man-made origins, most people do not want to see their technological devices broken down into their simpler, and sometimes flawed, component parts. The day before the *Challenger* launch, the news had included visual images of workers struggling to remove the handle of the spacecraft. A bolt had frozen and had to be drilled out for the door to even be opened.

A Lockheed employee shields his eyes as he watches the space shuttle Challenger explode in mid-air seconds after lift-off at the Kennedy Space Center in Cape Canaveral, Florida. A crew of seven died in the tragedy on January 28, 1986, including teacher astronaut Christa McAuliffe. UPI/Bettmann Newsphotos.

The disaster also punctured what can only be called the American tech-nological hubris, a hubris that also underlay the president's so-called Star Wars initiative. Had our machines become so complex that reliability was no longer possible? If the United States could not even guarantee the proper functioning of a spacecraft that carried human passengers, how much faith could be placed in a technology that had the even more awesome task of selecting and destroying thousands of ICBMs and their decoys in the event of an all-out nuclear exchange? In a *New York Times* editorial, Tom Wicker wrote:

> In a larger sense, however, a kind of catharsis might be derived from the burning spectacle, if the human consequence were to be a tempering of pride in Man's achieve-ments, a sobering view of his limits, a greater reluctance to climb Mt. Everest for no other reason than that "it was there." Not as a procedural guide to space exploration or Star Wars or arms control but as a brake on Man himself, his vanity, ambition and audacity, the Challenger's fate might prove instructive. (1986)

In observing the spate of *Challenger* jokes that arose in conjunction with the limitless hyperbole of the American press and the scores of wreath-layings around the country, editorialist Nicholas von Hoffman (1986) noted certain similarities with the underground humor of the Soviet Union spawned by the monotonous propaganda of the "party-line press." Media demands for orthodoxy seem to be correlated with sharp political humor. Perhaps, accord-ing to von Hoffman, the ease with which these deaths were used to mobilize American sentiments is evidence of the extent to which the adversarial rela-tionship between the press and the White House had evaporated.

Case Study 2: The Hunting Ritual

Another example of how death can create and reinforce social solidarity is hunting, a ritual engaged in by an estimated 20 million Americans. It should not be surprising how differently the social sciences view this particular activ-ity. Psychologists, for instance, talk of it as a socially acceptable means for venting homicidal tendencies, a release from stress or routine, or the orgasmic thrill[18] of the kill (Copp 1975). Although many hunters will testify that their satisfactions come from the hunt and not the actual kill, it is cer-tainly the possibility of death, an animal's death, that makes this activity more exciting than stalking a creature in order to photograph it. And news-papers are more likely to feature photographs of hunters lifting the heads of dead deer than they are to display images of the animal in life.

It seems through death, through stalking prey as one's ancestors had done many years earlier (albeit not with scopes, walkie-talkies, or high-powered

Deer hunters display their bounty at a hunting lodge in Bingham, Maine. Culver Pictures.

rifles),[19] one learns to respect nature and to realize one's place within the ecological system.[20] According to philosopher Ortega y Gasset, it is in this venatic ritual that one can become the symbol of courage, endurance, and skill. If that is overstated, then hunting is at least typically a ritual by which males reaffirm their solidarities. And in portions of the rural West, being allowed to go on the hunt is a rite of passage for young males, some of whom are still "blooded" from their first kill.[21]

And finally, hunting is a status ritual as well. One aristocratic pursuit, for example, is the fox hunt. And even within this select group there is a stratification system. Junior members must stay in the back of the pack, always allowing the right-of-way to those who have "earned the colors of the hunt," which often requires three years of participation and an invitation from the master (Perlez 1985). In the domain of leisure there are stratified types of guns, types of game, and regions within which one attempts to make a kill. The French peasants, before the Revolution, were forbidden to hunt by the ancien régime.

The attempt to limit commerical use of wild game began around the turn of the century following hunting excesses that have become part of American legend. But such prohibitions are unique neither to America nor to this age. As long ago as the 15th century, selling or buying deer meat was illegal in England, a country so keen on protecting the sport of kings that under the Normans, poachers were blinded or maimed. In the 16th century, Andrew Boorde, writing about venison, warned, "I do advertise every man . . . not to kill, and so to eat of it, except it be lawfully for it is a meat for great men." (Dooley 1980)

Even if the native game is gone, exotic game ranches have sprung up to cater to the hunter's need. According to a 1980 survey of the Texas Parks and Wildlife Department, 357 Texas landowners had stocked exotic big game mostly for hunting purposes. At the YO ranch near Mountain Home, Texas, hunters in 1984 paid up to fifteen hundred dollars just for the privilege of stalking and shooting.

The Social Shock Absorbers of Death

To minimize death's disruptiveness—even possibly taking advantage of its functionality—social systems have evolved ways to dampen its shock. Later we will consider the specific institutional strategies, such as the ideological attempts of religions to redirect death fears, but here we deal with the general structural mechanics.

One of the easiest methods is to reduce the social identity of those most likely to die, either by making them lesser persons or by minimizing their social spheres of influence. The chapters that follow will show the positive correlation between social class and life expectancy—how rich outlive poor, how whites outlive blacks, and how urbanites outlive their rural counterparts. Philippe Ariès, in *Centuries of Childhood* (1962), reported that extremely high infant mortality rates in western Europe before the seventeenth century produced a situation in which children were essentially nonpersons before the age of five.[22] Their deaths received the funerary attention that would today be given to dead pets. Similarly, the contemporary "death lepers," the elderly, are systematically disengaged from their social roles before they expire. Not only are they retired from work, but they are increasingly segregated from the rest of society, first in retirement communities and old-age organizations and ultimately in nursing homes and hospitals.

Secondly, social systems can simply hide the dying and grieving processes. In contemporary American society, we pay individuals to manage the deaths of our relatives impersonally within institutional settings and then pay others to embalm their remains. As described by Blauner:

This separation of the handling of illness and death from the family minimizes the average person's exposure to death and its disruption of the social process. When the

dying are segregated among specialists for whom contact with death has become routine and even somewhat impersonal, neither their presence while alive nor as corpses
interferes greatly with the mainstream of life. (1966, p. 379)

Furthermore, those bereaved now must grieve in private and are expected to
resume their work roles within days.

Third, social systems have increasingly been able to eliminate premature
death. Minimizing the death risks—such as through warning of the health
dangers of cigarettes, lowering highway speed limits, and using antibiotics
to control infectious diseases—increases the predictability of death, confining it to the old. Rarely needed are the historical cultural explanations for
sudden, premature deaths, as death often comes to those who have completed their life projects. Many of the old never expected to live as long as
they have and, when faced with the chronic, degenerative diseases of
advanced age (and even the discriminations of an ageist society), are now put
in the position of seeing death as preferable to a continued existence. And
for the survivors of elderly victims of Huntington's or Alzheimer's disease,
their deaths may actually be viewed as a blessing.

 Birthrights Up for Auction as Investments in London

"May I ask you for your bids on this absolute reversion to three-quarters of this
trust fund receivable on the death of a gentleman who will be 81 this month.
Who'll give me a start?"

Guy Enriquez has begun another of his firm's little-known monthly auctions
in which people make hard-headed bets on the life expectancy of other people's
relatives. The assembled bidders were there to buy the inheritances coming-some-
day-to heirs who, for various reasons, prefer immediate cash to waiting for it.

. . . Foster & Cranfield have been selling reversionary interests since 1843.

Hershey 1978.

Finally, the changing nature of social roles has also contributed to society's
ability to dampen the effects of death. Historically, there has been the shift
from particularistic to universalistic, from ascribed to achieved roles. This
means that individuals are rarely known as entire selves but rather as role
functionaries. This creates an analytical distinction between the individual
and the role, unlike the case in which the two are so thoroughly fused that
the death of the individual means the death of the role. Instead, roles rarely
can be held indefinitely by their incumbents but rather must be ritually surrendered. With the bureaucratic structure of contemporary societies, such
ritual surrenderings are part of the institutionalized rules of succession. In

the case of the elderly, they are disengaged from many of their social roles to minimize the disruptions caused by their deaths. Further, given the accelerating pace of social change, many of these roles themselves have become obsolete before their occupants have grown old. And many of the principles and values on which the old predicated their lives have already been forgotten.

Reinforcing Social Bonds: Funerary Rituals

Most apparent of all the social shock absorbers of death is the funeral. The ritual disposal of the dead and social reintegration of the affected living are two of the few cultural universals known. But the cross-cultural variations in funerary observances are incredible. One can depart New Orleans–style, complete with marching brass bands and humorous graveside eulogies, or one can be the focal point of political protests, as when thousands march in the funeral processions of victims of political oppression. Huntington and Metcalf observe: "Funerals are the occasion for avoiding people or holding parties, for fighting or having sexual orgies, for weeping or laughing, in a thousand different combinations. . . . But it is not a random reaction; always it is meaningful and expressive" (1979, p. 1).

Perhaps weddings are overrated as social events. It is at funerals that you meet the widest spectrum of people, where you see how many lives can be touched by a single individual. The funeral is the finished picture of a person, providing a ritual occasion when one reflects on the successes and shortcomings of a concluded biography. It also marks the endeavors of a generation: only the generation of the deceased can provide the frame of reference needed to grasp the principles to which one's biography was dedicated. Finally, funerals are the greatest source of social change (Boulding 1985).

There seems to be a human need for ritual. In probably no instance is this need greater than in the case of death, when individuals undergo the rites of separation from the world of the living, of transition from the living to the dead, and finally of reincorporation into the world of the dead. Concurrently, there is the need to ritually assist the survivors of death through their period of grief and back into the everyday routines of society. Death is polluting, and the funeral is also a purification ritual.[23] Here the failure of a ceremony to appropriately capture the meaning of mortality and to dramatize the change that has overtaken the living and the dead can lead to confusion, anger, and frustration.

Rituals are not mere reflectors of cultural values; they also participate in their structuring. The complexity of funerary rituals reflects the complex and often contradictory emotions occasioned by death: the love for the deceased

Leaving the San Fernando Cathedral (far left), a funeral procession moves along the Main Plaza in San Antonio, Texas. Incarnate Word College, San Antonio, Texas.

and the loathing of the corpse; the desire to preserve bonds with the dead and the need to break them; the sense of aloneness and vulnerability occasioned by the death of preceding generations and the simultaneous joy at one's consequential upward mobility; and, in the case of the long, painful, dehumanizing death of an older family member, the sense of relief that the suffering is over and the guilt at being glad that the end has arrived. The variety of funerary rituals even within one society reflects the basic cultural distinctions made by the living, mirrored in the diverse rituals for individuals on the basis of their age, sex, ethnicity, religion, social class, cause of death, and length of residency. For instance, in Chapter 4 we will see how different types of death vary in terms of their social disruptiveness, thereby altering the ritual accordingly. The death by natural causes of an octogenarian, for example, does not require the large attendance nor does it entail the extreme emotions occasioned by the accidental death of a thirty-year-old. As Binford observed, "the form and structure which characterize the mortuary practices of any society are conditioned by the form and complexity of the organizational characteristics of the society itself" (1971, p. 23). Funerals have the clearly apparent, manifest (Mandelbaum 1959) functions of disposing of the body, aiding the bereaved and giving them reorientation to the world of the living, and publicly acknowledging and commemorating the dead while reaffirming the viability of the group.

Although for some cultures and religious groups funerary ritual is explicitly directed for the dead, it is always a rite of passage for the principal survivors, a mechanism for restoring the rent in the social fabric caused by death. Fifteen hundred years ago, St. Augustine wrote: "Wherefore all these last offices and ceremonies that concern the dead, the careful funeral arrangements, and the equipment of the tomb, and the pomp of obsequies, are rather the solace of the living than the comfort of the dead." And as anthropologist Bronislaw Malinowski noted, death "threatens the very cohesion and solidarity of the group. . . [and the funeral] counteracts the centrifugal forces of fear, dismay, demoralization, and provides the most powerful means of reintegration of the group's shaken solidarity and of reestablishment" (1948, p. 53). Bereavement is a shared experience, ideally captured by a funeral's framework of supportive relationships (Irion 1976, p. 36). Without such ritual, individuals may be unable to function in their roles if overwhelmed by grief, incapacitated by fear, or unable to develop new relationships to replace the old.

The scope of funerary ritual often extends far beyond the basic funeral ceremony. First, there may be the ritual of dying itself, the actual separation of self from society. This, for instance, includes the traditional deathbed scene, complete with life reviews and final words (see Chapter 12), or the contemporary segregation of the dying from the living (Chapter 4), where much of the survivors' grief work is completed before the slow-motion expiration of one of their members (Chapter 12). For those diagnosed as lepers in twelfth-century Europe, this rite of separation featured a service similar to the requiem mass. It was followed by the reading of the rules of isolation, with the guarantee that one's basic needs would continue to be met: "this separation is only corporeal. . . . God will never forsake you" (Musto 1987).

Following the ritual of separation come a number of rites of transition for both the deceased and the bereaved. There is the first pronouncement of death, typically limited to only the physician. Even though a death may be common knowledge among nurses and hospital staff, it is the physician who tells the family and signs the death certificate. Further, it is family members who have the right to be the first to be publicly informed that a death has occurred, which is why we often hear on news broadcasts that "the names of the victims in the fatal auto accident are being withheld pending notification of next of kin."[24]

From the immediate family, the news spreads outward—like ripples in a pond—from friends and more distant relatives to employers, fraternal orders, and other organizations the deceased belonged to (Sudnow 1967, pp. 153–68). If one is not immediately informed of the death of a significant other, there may be feelings of being not only slighted but also hurt, as one then feels alone in dealing with one's grief. Various bureaucracies must also be informed—such as Social Security, insurance agencies, and voters' registration—as the deceased is no longer entitled to the benefits of the living. Finally, the community is informed of the loss of one of its members. In some small communities, this news is still personally conveyed: a courier delivers to the various merchants and shops handbills on which there is a brief obituary and the time of funeral services. In larger, more urban areas, such news appears in the death notices section of their newspapers' vital statistics page.

The next phase of funeralization involves the preparation of the dead. In a number of cultures the body is cleansed and prepared by the next of kin. Nowadays in American society, however, this ritual has generally been surrendered to experts, namely the staffs of funeral establishments, perhaps symbolizing the extent to which we rely on experts to manage the affairs of both the living and the dead. But there is ritual involved in the delivery of the deceased's remains from the place of death to the establishment where they are prepared for the public funerary observances. In many states, the "first call"—that is, when a mortuary establishment takes possession of the body from the hospital or city morgue—must be supervised by a licensed funeral director and not simply conducted by some assistant or driver.

The following transition phase often involves the body lying in state for a period of public viewing. This may be in the form of the traditional Irish wake, as described below, or the hours of public visitation to a funeral home's "slumber room" or "funeral parlor" (see Chapter 8 for details on how the funeral industry manages funerary ritual). Whatever the form, this is the time when personal farewells can be addressed to the dead and when the bereavement roles of the survivors are first formally recognized. In contemporary American culture, there is some debate about the necessity for such public viewings. Critics of the funeral industry, for instance, see this practice as contributing to the use of embalming services, which, in turn, is the "foot in the door" for such other things as elaborate caskets, matching funeral apparel, and the like. Industry proponents, on the other hand, argue the therapeutic benefits of seeing the remains and the need to reaffirm, not disguise, the reality of death. Kraeer, for instance, claims that of the eight hundred bereavement cases he studied, of those survivors without any services for their deceased, more than one-third suffered from social withdrawal, fear, depression, and chronic anger—the "signs of arrested progress in grief recovery" (1981, p. 254). Twenty-two percent of those who had exposure to at least some minimal kind of formalized funeral rites were unsuccessful in

The Irish Wake

The more I attend Irish wakes, the less I think of them. The well-dressed clay in the fancy box belies the belief that the soul has fled to judgment. Wakes do nothing for the dead; they console the living.

Every one I attend leaves a scar inside my chest. My father told me that, in the old days before embalming, the dead lay on cakes of ice. The mourners sat up all night around the casket. When the ice melted, it made a crackling sound and the corpse shifted a little.

This was enough to send the men into the kitchen for a swig of whiskey. This went on for three nights. Then, to the accompaniment of shrieks and tears from the widow and children, the lid was slowly lowered.

The immediate family went into the first coach. There was always a silent struggle to come in second. Whether it was her brother and family, or his, was a mark of distinction. This was followed by a low-gear trip to the church. Everybody counted the cortege to see how many true friends he had.

The solemn high mass, the many blessings with holy water of the facade in the box, was interrupted by a priestly homily on what a good man he was—if anyone could find something good to say about him.

The mourners rode to the cemetery, each with a heavy fear in his heart: "Someday this is going to happen to me, and I don't want to think about it." In the old days, the sufferers had to stand by the open hole, watching the casket as it was lowered on creaky ropes.

They stopped that bit. These days, everybody is asked to depart before the casket disappears. These days, nobody sits up all night at a wake. The "viewings" are from 2 to 5 p.m. and from 8 to 10 p.m. All of them are highly charged with emotion.

The widow cries on cue whenever a new mourner enters the funeral home. Flowers are stacked around the casket—things he cannot smell or see. The more elaborate the standing flowers, the more important the donor is.

Bishop 1982. From "My Brother John Is Gone."
San Antonio Light. November 10, p. 4c. © 1982.
Reprinted by permission.

their reorientations, while only 12 percent of those who had been part of a full funeral service had problems in their adjustments. "Full-service funerals," Kraeer writes, "help to clean out the wound and treat it so that healing may occur" (1981, p. 255).

This brings us to the funeral service itself, which is complete with its own set of ritual activities for individuals to publicly acknowledge and express their feelings. This is the culminating rite of transition and heralds the period of incorporation of the deceased into the world of the dead and the reincorporation of the bereaved into the world of the living.

The service involves such issues as who is officially bereaved and how the extent of bereavement translates into proximity with the deceased. The barber of the deceased, for example, is normally expected to have greater distance from the casket (having lesser legitimacy in occupying the bereavement role) than is the case for the deceased's widow and children. What religious, military, or fraternal rituals are to be observed? Are there to be eulogies, and, if so, by whom and when? Assuming that there is a casket containing the deceased at the service, what pallbearers will remove it following the service? Following the procession to the cemetery,[25] a similar set of ritual options arises at the graveside service.

For Indian Hindus, reincarnation beliefs contribute to another form of funeral ritual. If married, the deceased is typically cremated (unmarried persons may be buried) at a ceremony presided over by the eldest son (in addition to a priest), following the preparations of the body and the chanting of mantras. The ashes are collected for depositing in one of India's holy rivers, and the family observes a ten-day period of ritual impurity, until the soul of the deceased is assumed to have incorporated itself into another body. Traditional Okinawan Buddhists, two or three years following a death, can be found removing any remains from the bones and giving them a ritual washing. The bones are then placed in a burial urn, where they remain for thirty-three years before they are taken out to be placed on a high platform to join the bones of other ancestors.

The postdeposition rituals in the two examples above are illustrations of what have been called "brown" or "secondary" funerals (Hertz 1960; see also Huntington and Metcalf 1979). Often, such funerals signify the conclusion of the bereavement role for the survivors and are the last time the bereaved can legitimately grieve in public. The second period of Jewish mourning custom, for instance, the *shloshim*, occurs thirty days after the burial and concludes the mourning period for all but the spouse, mother, and father. The *avelut*, which concludes their mourning, occurs one year after the burial. These secondary funerals can also indicate the completed passage of the deceased from the limbo between the worlds of the living and of the dead. Often, such funerals observe the dead collectively, such as the anniversary observances many cities have for their firemen or policemen who died in the line of duty during the previous year.

There are also less obvious, "latent" functions (Mandelbaum 1959) served by funerals. Symbolically dramatized in funerary ritual are reaffirmations of the extended kinship system. The restrictions and obligations of survivors (such as their dress, demeanor, food taboos, and social intercourse) serve to identify and demonstrate family cohesion. Also dramatized are the economic and reciprocal social obligations that extend from the family to the com-

The cremation of a Hindu in Benares, India. As is custom, the next of kin lights the funeral pyre as the mourners look on. The Bettmann Archive, Inc.

munity and from the community to the broader society. In other words, the social bonds of the living are acted out, remembered, and reinforced in the minds of community members (Mandelbaum 1959). Not surprisingly, such functions have political significance. When, in 1982, 16,500 aborted fetuses were found in a container at the home of a Los Angeles man who ran a medical laboratory, three years of heated debate over their disposal followed. Antiabortionists sought permission to hold funeral services for the fetuses, claiming they were humans whose social membership had to be ritually reaffirmed, while a prochoice group, represented by the American Civil Liberties Union, argued that the remains were unwanted biological tissue and should be cremated without ceremony (*New York Times* 1985a).

Also reaffirmed in funerals are the social roles of the living. Claiming that the deceased was a winner in his or her roles reaffirms the system itself by having produced the opportunities for such a person to even create meaning. Why do we not speak ill of the dead? They are the roles they play, and to speak ill of them is to speak ill of ourselves. In the homosexual community,

Mourners gather at a funeral in Newville, Pennsylvania. David Strickler, Monkmeyer Press.

as the list of AIDS victims grows there is the sense that the traditional rituals are insufficient. When another member of New York City's People with AIDS Coalition dies, white helium balloons are released from St. Peter's Episcopal Church in Greenwich Village. Ashes of one partner are sometimes mixed with those of the other who predeceased him and then are dispersed in a place meaningful for the couple. And increasingly, the rainbow flag, the symbol of the annual Gay Pride Parade, is displayed on coffins (Dullea 1987).

Sociologist Emile Durkheim, interested in the dynamic tension between the autonomy of the individual and the individual's identification with society, studied such phenomena as the mourning obligations of various categories of kin. He turned the relationship between belief and ritual 180 degrees: ritual is essentially brought about by sociological factors, and men create the eschatology to rationalize their ritual behavior at mourning. "Men do not weep for the dead because they fear them; they fear them because they weep for them." Durkheim's student, Radcliffe-Brown, pushed this notion one step farther, portraying funerary ceremonies—events that certainly do not allow indifference—as rituals designed to create, not alleviate, anxieties. His overarching interest was the relationship between publicly displayed sentiments and social integration. Following his mentor, Radcliffe-Brown claimed that emotion does not causally affect such expressions as weeping. Instead, by ritually weeping, the wailer comes to feel the culturally appropriate sentiment: "ceremonial customs are the means by which the society acts upon its individual members and keeps alive in their minds a certain system of sentiments. Without the ceremonial those sentiments would not exist, and without them the social organization in its actual form could not exist" (1964, p. 324). So, although there may be some innate experience of genuine grief, how that grief is expressed and understood is culturally shaped. Also culturally standardized are the reactions of others to those expressing legitimate grief.

This brings us to the concern some experts have expressed about the contemporary paucity of funeral ritual. Geoffrey Gorer (1965), for example, proclaims that "we must give back to death—natural death—its parade and publicity, readmit grief and mourning." To illustrate what we have lost as a culture, let us consider just one facet of funerary ritual, the eulogy. The traditional funeral was a time when a biography was wrapped up and reviewed for its lessons. Below is a eulogy from the turn of the century, appearing in a Swedish-language newspaper from Springfield, Massachusetts.

 A Memorial to Gabriel Carlson

It is with a feeling of sadness and pain that I write at this time. This is because I have the sorrowful duty to bid adieu to our highly beloved chairman as he entered the grave's silent rest home on April 22. Since among this paper's readers he had many friends, I will recount something about him. Gabriel Carlson was born in the Kansas congregation Vasa Lan, Finland, on the 6th of April, 1861. He was a Finn but he could not speak Finnish, he was, of course, a "Swedish Finn," which is the same as Swedish, for the Swedish Finns have the same origin as the Swedes.

In Carlson's region in Finland during the time he grew up, there were no schools, therefore he missed any schooling background. But in spite of this he has in this country in the mechanical field made unheard of advances and he was not only a mechanic, but an inventor. He has through his many and important inventions not only left behind a fortune for his family but has attained for himself an important name in this country and in Europe.

At the age of 20 he came to the U.S.A. and first went to Texas where he for a very small salary worked on the railroad. After a short stay there he traveled to Minneapolis, Minnesota, where he stayed for 13 years. There he worked partly in a milk room and partly in a factory where they made "confectionery." It was while working in this place that his "inventing genius" was awakened and he invented a candy machine that brought him a fortune and gave many Swedes work.

The most fortunate thing that happened to Carlson in Minneapolis was not his inventions but that in the Tabernacle through the preaching of Ang. Skogkbargh he was brought to God. This fortunate occurrence was for the rest of his life very dear to him, and he often spoke of it. The Sunday before his death he spoke of his salvation and that he had been a Christian for 24 years. He said it was not only his salvation, and that he was a happy child of God, but it had helped him in his daily life. He often said, "If the Lord had not taken me in hand, I would never have come up as I did, it was He who blessed me." He said to me that his first and even the most important invention came to him one morning when he was walking to Sunday school, like a revelation from God. He therefore felt he was in debt to God for everything he was and owned and he was always afraid to take away from God what belonged to Him. I have often heard him pray by himself and in public asking God to keep him from becoming selfish. "When I had little" he would often say, "it was easy to give His share to the Lord, but now since I have gotten so much, of what a strife and struggle." Brother Carlson was unusually generous. Many people, both in Springfield and in other places, will remain forever grateful to him. He had a big heart and a generous hand for the needy and therefore he knew well the worth of the promise, "The one who concerns himself for the poor, God will help on the day of misfortune."

This fall when were out together I said to him, "You scatter money here and there, how will it go in the long run?" He answered smiling, "Yes, the more I give to the Lord, the more I get." He believed firmly that it paid off to give to the Lord, and he did not come to shame with that belief.

It is now 14 years in May since he came to Springfield with two empty hands, and his inventing capacity. He was able to interest some financial men to form a company, and a factory for the manufacturing of candy machines was started. Only six men were employed at first, but through Carlson's inventions and his ability as a leader it has grown so before the hard times came some 300 were employed. From that small start it has become the biggest factory of its kind in the world, and these machines are sold the world over.

During these 14 years Carlson has been an active and a very much respected member of our congregation and we say with deep sorrow, "You are missed for your place stands empty." Empty in the S.S., empty in the young people's groups, empty on the board and empty in our church. . . . Brother Carlson was never absent from a "preaching" meeting and what was more was always present at a prayer meeting, no matter what the weather was.

Friday morning the 17th of April, brother Carlson left his home as usual to go to work. He said goodbye to his family and said he would not have time to come home for lunch but would come for supper, but he never returned alive to his home, for at two p.m. while he was working on a machine in his own invention room, his coat caught in a cog of the machine. Instantly he was dragged into the machine. It stopped at once and workers pulled him loose, but his whole left side was horribly mangled, several ribs and part of his lung were crushed. He was taken at once to the hospital, and the doctors did everything to try to save his life but in vain. When he on Friday evening awakened after the operation I went to his room and he smiled and said, "I am so content, so content—oh how great it is to be a Christian." Later he said, "I am so happy, so happy that all my sins are forgiven." The news of the tragic accident spread like wildfire through the community and especially among our congregation, so when we all gathered for a meeting the whole congregation prayed with tears to God to spare their beloved brother and let him work still a while amongst them. On Saturday morning I hurried again to the hospital and I said, "Brother Carlson, we prayed for you last night when we gathered." "I could feel that, I was so happy, so happy last night, I felt you were praying for me," he answered. Since he had much pain and he was able to talk with difficulty I stayed only a short time. It was with indescribable sorrow that I left his room for I had the feeling I would not be able to talk to him again in this life. When I returned in the afternoon he was unconscious. His wife and oldest daughter and some of the sisters of our congregation and I were by his side during his last night on earth. When his beloved wife, with whom he had lived happily for 20 years, said in his ear, "Jesus Christ God's son's blood cleanses us of our sins," he answered weakly, "Yes." Just before he closed his eyes for good, his wife said, "Dear Papa, say a word before you leave us," and he said, "See God's Lamb." He went to sleep at 5:35 just as the sun was rising on Easter morning, while I inwardly prayed the good Lord to carry him over "death's river." His wife cried, "Go in peace beloved husband," and his older daughter, Hilda, said, "Goodbye Papa, go to Heaven."

So died our dear chairman, who had been to the congregation here and to Swedes in general such a great help. He has left an empty space among us, that no one can fill. He is missed over our whole field in the East. He was a trustee in the Eastern Mission Association as well as for our dear children's home in Cromwell, Conn. He did what he could and has gone to get his reward from his Savior. We did so want to keep him, but it was God's wish to take him away at life's high point. Why, we will find out when we get Home. Here we must console ourselves with the knowledge that "all the Lord's ways are righteous and truth." . . .

G. N. Jegnell, Springfield, Mass., April 30, 1908.

There are a number of possible reasons for the declining use of eulogies in contemporary American funeral services. Undoubtedly it is part of the cultural shift toward minimalist funerals. Typically, it is the old who die, and, as we saw in Chapter 2, their deaths do not cause the social frustrations requiring the rituals that must be performed for those who die prematurely.

Further, since it is the old who must receive such eulogies, often the deceased has long since outlived his or her useful role, has already been depersonalized in some institutional setting, and has outlived most of those who could even present such a biographical summary. Another reason may be a cultural aversion to anything ritualistic or repetitive. But the decline could also be one more symptom of our supposed cultural ethos of death denial and one more piece of evidence that we no longer know individuals as whole persons in our bureaucratic, urbanized, and depersonalizing society.

Obituaries: Death as a Measure of Life[26]

One facet of funerary ritual is the obituary. Like the eulogy, it is where a biography is summed up and the individual's contributions to the social order are recalled. This chapter concludes by exploring the inferences about the living that can be derived from these postmortem synopses. In particular, let us consider what progress our society has made toward eliminating the major biases (namely sexism, racism, and ageism) that have historically limited the social opportunities of certain groups. This is no small question, particularly in light of the recent political and legal efforts of women, minorities, and elderly persons to end the discriminations that block their opportunities to serve society. Have things gotten better, and, if so, for whom and at what pace?

From what funerary evidence could we ascertain that discrimination against, say, blacks was waning? Where the worlds of blacks and whites are rigidly segregated, we find separate communities for both the living and the dead; cemeteries and funeral parlors are no more integrated than the homes and service establishments of the living. Another, even simpler strategy for quantifying discrimination would be to analyze the obituaries devoted to blacks in newspapers and magazines. Such an analysis has been conducted in the case of sexism. Psychologists Kastenbaum, Peyton, and Kastenbaum (1977), for instance, demonstrated how sexual stratification was reflected in the relative length and proportion of newspaper obituaries for females as opposed to males. They concluded that within the short term following one's demise, the American death system "has more the function of confirming and perpetuating than of re-evaluating existing values" and that "obituaries might be regarded as more conservative representations of social values" (p. 356).

Analyzing obituaries for evidence of ageism poses greater difficulties of interpretation. As elaborated on in Chapter 4, forces exist in modern society that diminish the status of the old. Many of the elderly are disengaged or retired from their socially significant roles in order to minimize the social disruptions occasioned by their inevitable deaths. So, although longer biographies would seem to require greater summary expositions and although the elderly's proportion of all deaths increases with modernization, because of the diminished social impacts of older persons' deaths we might not find the increase in obituary space given to their biographies that we would expect.

With these points in mind, let us see what lessons are imbedded within a longitudinal sample of obituaries. For this exploratory analysis, a random sample of 2209 obituaries from 1923 to 1979 was collected from two national news magazines, *Time* and *Newsweek*. These magazines were chosen because of the size of their readership and their likelihood to reveal—or possibly to shape—national, as opposed to regional, discriminatory biases. In other words, while local obituaries are the social register of the middle class (Gerbner 1980), national obituaries are the register of the national elite. A twenty-item questionnaire was devised as the basis for the content analyses, which included such measures as age at death, sex, race, institution of recognition, cause of death, work status at death (retired or working), presence or absence of photographs of the deceased, and inches of column space devoted to the person.

Table 3.2 summarizes the characteristics of our obituary sample, both in total and over four time periods: the period between the international wars (1923–38), the war years (1939–53), the era of postwar confidence (1954–64), and finally the era of Vietnam, Watergate, and stagflation (1965–79). Over these four historical periods, the proportion of obituaries given to those dying before old age declined by nearly one-third (from 34.3 percent before World War II to 23.2 percent since 1965), while those of individuals eighty years old and older increased by an identical amount.

According to these obituaries, it appears that the effect of the civil rights and feminist movements has been slight: though the proportion of obituaries for blacks nearly doubled over the four time periods, the latest proportion still remains nearly one-tenth that of their proportion of the living. The proportion of obituaries for females is actually less in the most recent period than in the first. The decline of female obituaries during wartime is not so surprising given the increases in male fatalities, but why between 1954 and 1964 did this proportion bottom out? Perhaps working women were not to be reinforced as a cultural image during this era of the procreative ethic. Such questions of the living posed by the dead will be a continuing theme of this book.

The bottom section of Table 3.2 indicates that the publicity given the biography of a deceased individual derives not only from such ascribed characteristics as sex and race but from the type of role within which the deceased excelled. Sociologists see individuals in terms of the roles they play and rec-

Table 3.2 Percentages of Obituary Measures over Four Time Periods

		1923–38 (n = 668)	1939–53 (n = 476)	1954–64 (n = 484)	1965–79 (n = 581)	TOTAL
Age	0–59	34.3%	25.8%	19.0%	23.2%	26.0%
	60–69	23.7	23.7	26.1	23.5	24.2
	70–79	22.8	27.1	31.3	27.4	26.9
	80+	19.2	23.5	23.6	25.9	22.9
Sex	Male	83.3	85.7	90.0	85.9	86.2
	Female	16.7	14.3	9.1	14.1	13.8
Race	White	95.2	96.8	93.1	92.4	94.4
	Hispanic	1.7	0.9	1.7	2.4	1.7
	Asian	1.1	0.6	2.3	1.5	1.4
	Black	0.8	1.1	1.3	1.5	1.1
	Other	1.2	0.6	1.6	2.2	1.4
Institution of Recognition	Arts	13.3	21.7	26.7	33.7	23.3
	Business	19.5	18.6	22.6	20.2	20.2
	Public office	6.2	8.6	9.9	7.3	7.8
	Military	6.0	10.3	7.2	6.2	7.3
	Family relation	12.1	3.8	1.0	4.4	5.8
	Sports	5.0	4.9	6.2	5.1	5.3
	Nobility, high society	6.2	5.7	4.3	2.7	4.8
	Sciences	2.4	4.6	4.3	4.4	3.8
	Religion	3.6	4.9	2.9	2.4	3.4
	Education	3.8	3.4	2.5	2.4	3.0
	Medicine	1.7	2.5	2.1	1.3	1.8
	Legal	2.0	0.8	0.6	0.5	1.1
	Other	10.8	6.6	5.4	5.4	7.4

ognize that these roles are shaped by broad sociocultural forces. Over the fifty-six years considered, individuals involved with the arts and business received more than 40 percent of all obituaries. The 250 percent increase in the percentage of obituaries for those in the arts is striking, perhaps indicating a dramatic increase in the centrality of leisure consumption to everyday life and the need to escape (observe that the greatest percentage increases occurred during the periods of war and social fragmentation). Another reason for the postwar decline of female representation was that being related to a famous person, by marriage or biological connection, no longer guaranteed one's place in the pages of *Time* or *Newsweek,* as it had during the 1920s and 1930s.

Table 3.3 explores this institutional arena of fame further. In the first column it is apparent from the variance in mean obituary lengths that the institution of one's fame contributes to the length of one's memory. Could this be a rough measure of overall institutional import, with law (whose obituaries' mean is 3.74), for example, being more significant than sports (mean 2.75) and religion (mean 2.73)? Institutional importance, as measured by length of obituaries, is negatively related to the length of obituaries given to females and older individuals and is positively related to those given to non-whites.[27] The likelihood of females receiving an obituary is significantly increased if they achieved distinction in the arts, were connected with the social elite, or were related to another famous person. Nearly 14 percent of obituaries for elected public officials and for those in high society were for nonwhites, as were one-third of those linked to unions. These were the only institutional categories in which the proportion of obituaries for nonwhite approached or exceeded their numerical proportion in life. Further, consid-erable discrepancies were also observed in the mean ages of death and the percentage of obituaries allocated to those eighty and older. The sample shows that union members and sports stars die young, whereas those involved with religion, education, and medicine live the longest.

At this point you are probably wondering exactly what fame means, at least as it is being measured here. It certainly involves personal accomplishment, in addition to age, race, and institutional arena. But fame also has to do with the way one's biography happens to intersect social history. Take, for exam-ple, the ability to achieve fame within the military. Undoubtedly, to receive

Table 3.3 Characteristics of Obituaries from Differing Institutional Spheres

Institutional sphere	Mean obituary length[a]	Percent female	Percent nonwhite	Mean age at death (s.d.)	Percentage of obits 80+
Arts	3.12	22.0%	4.0%	66.19 (14.6)	20.4
Business	2.95	2.5	2.1	69.22 (11.8)	18.6
Elected public office	3.15	1.8	13.7	69.14 (13.9)	21.6
Military	3.15	4.4	7.7	65.88 (18.6)	26.3
Familial relation	2.36	64.0	4.8	60.21 (25.2)	28.7
Sports	2.75	1.8	4.6	59.20 (18.2)	13.6
Nobility, high society	2.87	40.8	13.7	65.74 (23.1)	28.3
Religion	2.73	5.4	6.9	75.50 (16.2)	47.9
Education	3.11	6.1	4.6	71.53 (16.1)	30.3
Medical	3.20	7.5	2.5	70.52 (14.5)	26.3
Technology	3.07	0	0	72.17 (14.3)	27.6
Legal	3.74	0	0	69.65 (9.0)	13.6
Union	4.33	0	33.3	53.00 (19.9)	66.7
MEANS	3.00	13.8	5.6	67.39 (16.3)	22.9

[a]The comparison of raw mean obituary lengths proved misleading as the range was one-quarter of an inch to over eight hundred inches of column space, with the mean being less than two. To control for the effect of decade (obituaries have gotten longer over time) and for editorial differences between the magazines, the obituaries were recoded for length into quintiles by magazine and by decade (thus, mean length = 3.0).

an obituary in a national magazine, one must have achieved a high rank during a war (racism and sexism enter into the analysis). This is a cohort effect: one born in 1915 could not achieve fame as a general in either world war as his biography fails to "correctly" intersect social history. Further, consider two hypothetical, equally important World War I soldiers born in 1890; one dies in 1973 and receives a shorter obituary than the other, who dies in 1983. Does the difference mean that stature increases with age (particularly if one is the last veteran to die), or is it a measure of the antiwar climate of the early 1970s and the increasing militarism of the 1980s, that is, a measure of the historical climate during which one dies?

From the right-hand column of Table 3.4, it is evident that different generations do not receive equally long obituaries. In other words, some generations apparently found greater historical opportunities for fame (such as those born in 1870–79 or 1890–95) than others.[28] Returning to the issues of sexism and racism, consider the proportion of obituaries dedicated to females and nonwhites laid out by eleven periods of birth (called cohorts). As opposed to the modest historical decline in female obituary representation that we saw in Table 3.2, here the trend is curvilinear. Of the obituaries given those born during World War I or later, nearly one in five were for females. Further, among generations born since the mid-1920s, the percentage of obituaries devoted to nonwhites more closely resembles their demographic composition (11 percent by the 1980s), although they are also more likely to die younger and therefore appear in our sample.

We have explored how death can possibly be used to measure the stratifications of life through obituary analyses. Though the approach is intuitively appealing, as many questions were raised as were answered. Specifically, one

Table 3.4 Obituary Characteristics of Different Birth Cohorts

Year of birth	Percent female	Percent nonwhite	Mean obituary Length of cohort
before 1860	19.6%	4.3%	2.97
1860–69	11.7	3.6	3.01
1870–79	13.1	2.6	3.21
1880–89	11.1	5.2	2.90
1890–95	11.2	5.9	3.26
1896–1900	14.4	6.7	3.00
1901–10	13.5	6.0	2.89
1911–15	9.2	13.0	3.11
1916–25	18.1	10.8	2.88
1926–39	24.1	11.7	2.83
after 1940	17.0	13.7	2.82

must take into account the historic period in which death occurs as well as the cohort of the deceased before making any inferences about how age, sex, or race affects these immediate postmortem biographies. From the dead we see how thoroughly interwoven biography is with social history. But it is this methodological limitation that makes obituary analyses so theoretically fertile. For example, in Table 3.4, it is evident that some generations are considered more "successful" than others—at least in terms of our mean obituary lengths for different cohorts.[29]

Conclusion

For both society and the individual, death is the proverbial double-edged sword, bringing disruption and yet enhancing social solidarities, cutting short personal aspirations but also allowing the upward mobility of younger cohorts. In considering some of the social consequences of the AIDS epidemic, we saw how fear of the disease has led to the diminishing of social trust and the stigmatization of its victims. But the disease has also led to increased social solidarity and the reaffirmation of traditional values. People who had previously never met have come together to fight the disease and to reduce the suffering of its victims; conservative Christian groups view the lethal malady as a major legitimization of their monogamous values and heterosexual life-styles, reversing the diminishing religious significance of the sex act while simultaneously retarding the perceived growing evils of secular humanism.

One of modern society's major accomplishments is its ability to minimize the disruptive potential of death: deadly situations are either banned, predicted, or routinized, and the individual's opportunity even to be exposed to the deaths of others has been all but eliminated. By socially disengaging and depersonalizing those most likely to die, by making social roles more important than their incumbents, by establishing rules of succession, and by routinizing the death trajectory within hidden, institutionalized settings, cultural denials can be maintained. Nevertheless, the reality we live in was largely shaped not only by the dead but by the way in which they died. The nonflammable pajamas American infants must wear, the speed at which we can drive, the personal invasions of privacy at airport terminals, and the chemical additives in the foods we eat all exist because of others' deaths.

On the other hand, because of our growing interdependency on others and our worldwide systems of communication, the potential social disruption caused by a single individual's death has never been greater, and modern society's vulnerability to death has, in fact, been increased. A single death caused by terrorism, for example, can lead to the mobilization of the military, the loss of confidence in a political regime, or the loss of personal freedoms. Because death is not expected, most of the premature deaths that do occur (e.g., automobile fatalities, swimming accidents, or deaths caused by terrorism) are considered newsworthy.

Death's ability to disrupt the social order while simultaneously revealing the central values of a culture and the major bonds among its members is perhaps most evident in the funeral. This ritual not only serves as a rite of passage for the survivors and the dead, but it also reaffirms the cultural ethos and the entire social order. So potent are these reaffirmations that, as later chapters will show, both political and religious systems routinely attempt to manipulate their form.

NOTES

1. In early human societies, attempts to cope with death may have contributed significantly to the evolution of patriarchy. Consider the situation in which the infant mortality rate exceeded 70 percent and female life spans were not much more than twenty-five years, in part because of the high death rates associated with childbirth complications. For the tribe or clan to even survive, women had to be bearing and nursing children all the time, creating the sexual division of labor. Further, as Gerda Lerner contends (1986), since warlike tribes often killed their male prisoners and enslaved the conquered women and children, female subordination became not only the basis of class distinctions but the first basis of property itself.

2. Within three years, five senior members of the aging Soviet leadership had died, nearly the last of the Politburo Bolsheviks (*San Antonio Express-News* 1984b). When founding generations die out, there is no longer a living compass to direct and oversee their blueprint for change.

3. In the Soviet Union, the very absence of a leader from a state ceremony can provoke such rumors. When the ashes of Defense Minister Dmitri F. Ustinov were lodged in the Kremlin wall, the ceremony was marked by the absence of the Soviet leader, Konstantin U. Chernenko. Diplomats and Kremlin watchers recalled that nonattendance at such ceremonies in the past had signaled failing health for Soviet leaders (Mydans 1984).

4. We have generally forgotten that more individuals died of the "Spanish influenza" of 1918–19 than were killed during World War I.

5. By the late 1980s, the director of the World Health Organization's AIDS program declared that a third stage of the global epidemic had been reached: prejudice about race, religion, social class, and nationality was spreading as fast as the AIDS virus itself (Altman 1987).

6. Critics on the political right also blamed the victims. They criticized the surgeon general's declaration that AIDS was the nation's "number one health priority" and charged that the allocation of $26 million in 1983 was too much, more than the

combined total spent for the less stigmatizing Legionnaires' disease and toxic shock syndrome (Krauthammer 1983).

7. McNeill (1976) notes that in childhood diseases there is a social history of the microbes that have shaped the human condition. When humans left the disease-ridden tropics, we realized an immediate improvement of health and vigor. But temperate ecological balances are more easily disrupted, which is why biological variety is reduced in these latitudes and food chains are shortened.

8. By analogy, over history humans have proven to be parasites of the natural order, a cancer of the ecosystem. But runaway population explosions have been followed by corrections. With the dispersion of humans away from the tropics, there was the historically rapid depletion of big-game resources. Within a few hundred years, however, animal domestication allowed population density to increase ten to twenty times (Braudel 1981).

9. Kastenbaum and Aisenberg (1972, p. 196) observed, "Moreover, it was during these very years of heightened vulnerability and suffering that the Inquisition began to use torture and death as official instruments of administrative policy."

10. Ehrlich offered three scenarios for the coming "famine decades." The first ends in a limited nuclear war with 100 million dead Americans. The second forecasts famine sweeping across developing nations in Asia, Africa, and South America. Mexico, the last noncommunist state in Latin America, falls to Maoist rebels, while the United States faces riots, martial law, and clouds of "killer smog." In the final scenario, the United States finally wakes up to the population problem after famine has already claimed 500 million lives.

11. Francesco Simeoni, the Italian prosecutor of the mining company whose dam collapse in 1985 killed nearly two hundred people, observed, "This is not India or some third world country. This is a civilized country and a disaster like this should never have happened" (Dionne 1985).

12. Observe, however, the immortality options bureaucracies are creating nowadays—annual awards banquets, professional halls of fame, and having one's name preserved on some document that is saved on microfiche.

13. Malthus warned in 1798 that population increases geometrically until an inevitable famine or other disaster occurs.

14. Wilbert E. Moore notes: "We thus encounter the paradox that life expectancies are low and social succession high precisely in the underdeveloped areas of the world where the social order is commonly supposed to be traditional and relatively unchanging" (1963, p. 26).

15. Anthropologist Mircea Eliade (1959) saw entire cultures going through rhythms of death and rebirth. In all probability, this universally observed cycle was derived from observing the natural rhythms of the seasons and of sleep: as the death of winter is required for nature's rebirth in spring, so must death/sleeping be required for the rebirth/restored experiences of individuals. Over time, there is the sense of the progressive degradation of the cosmos (the contemporary, scientific portrayal of this process is the model of entropy; Chapter 6); with age there comes both material and spiritual pollution. Bureaucracies proliferate with increasing numbers of

superfluous roles clogging efficiency, causing a sociological equivalent of arteriosclerosis. Important symbols become fatigued from repeated ritual enactments (much as the constant repetition of a word destroys its meaning, so repeated historical reenactments erase the memory), losing their meaning in the process.

16. One school of anthropological thought claims that there was a nutritional motivation to the ritual human sacrifices of the Mayans. Death still has nutritional value for the economy, as it does create jobs.

17. Months later, when remains of the astronauts were finally located and identified, there was confusion and some controversy over a second memorial service.

18. The noun *venery*, interestingly, means both the act or sport of hunting and sexual intercourse.

19. I would be remiss to ignore the role of the gun and all that it stands for. According to Berkowitz and LePage (1967), the mere sight of a weapon can be a conditioned stimulus that evokes aggressive thoughts and behaviors. "Happiness is a warm gun," John Lennon sang satirically; he, of course, was later slain by a "Saturday-night special."

The hunting lobby has effectively killed gun control in the United States. Noted thanatologist Edwin Shneidman observed: "Our recent inability to amend our gun laws in the wake of a series of catastrophic assassinations has been a national disaster and a grisly international joke, spotlighting our irrational tie to our essentially anti-intellectual legends of romanticized homicide. Our romanticization of killing in peacetime and being killed in wartime is only one of the tragic paradoxes that result from our anachronistic values" (1973, p. 69).

20. It could reasonably be argued that hunting is a seasonal ritual as well. The death of summer is the time for the death of the season's abundance.

21. This rite-of-passage role of hunting is evident every fall in the advice columns of the sports section, often reading like the following: "But if you are buying for the come-of-age individual a first gun, make that gun a .22 rifle. It is extremely important these days to get a gun in the hands of youngsters; it can help introduce youngsters to the fun of hunting, and to help them understand why hunting as a game management tool is of ultra-importance" (Maly 1979).

22. Often names were not even given until a child survived the period of highest infant mortality. To avoid excessive emotional attachments to such shortlived creatures, early New England Puritan parents would send their children to relatives or friends, ostensibly for discipline (Stannard 1975, p. 19). Later chapters will develop the implications for preindustrial personality structures of having been raised by a mother with minimal emotional investment.

23. James Frazer (1934) saw mortuary ritual as being motivated out of fear of the soul of the deceased, an attempt of the living to control the power of the ghosts of the dead. The origin of tombstones derived from the piling of heavy stones on graves to prevent the spirit of the deceased from rising. What is culturally polluting is to be within a rite of passage, to be somewhere between the established social categories such as being neither of the world of the living nor of the world of dead or, in the case of recently bereaved females, being neither married nor single. In this sense,

funerals serve to depollute the deceased and the principal survivors. Further, they serve as a way of controlling the power of the dead.

24. Consider NASA's silence following the space shuttle *Challenger* disaster when, weeks later, salvage operations located part of the crew compartment which contained human remains. A member of one of the families, who asked not to be identified, said, "We were asked not to say anything until NASA confirmed what they had found. But they said they had identified some but not others" (Schmidt 1986).

25. Some political funerals have no bodies but rather feature protesters carrying an empty coffin to dramatize their grievances. This assumes that the remains are not going to a crematorium. However, as was the case in the funeral services for former Vice-President Nelson Rockefeller, there can be graveside services for cremated remains.

26. The discussion in this section draws on and sometimes quotes directly from Kearl (1986–87).

27. The correlation (Pearson's r) between these mean institutional lengths and the percentage of female obituaries is -0.54, while that between institutional length and percentage nonwhite is 0.56 and with age of death is -0.28.

28. The shorter mean lengths of the more recent birth cohorts undoubtedly derive in part from the fact that these individuals died well before old age.

29. Whether it is an effect of our methodology (no cohort was born and allowed to die in extreme old age within the fifty-six-year span of the present study) or of the social opportunities historically opening up to a particular generation when it comes of age is not clear.

REFERENCES

Altman, Lawrence. 1987. "Key World Health Official Warns of Epidemic of Prejudice on AIDS." *New York Times*. June 3, pp. 1, 13.

Ariès, Philippe. 1962. *Centuries of Childhood*. New York: Vintage Books.

Barbanel, Josh. 1985. "AIDS Cases Seen Costing New York $100 Million." *New York Times*. October 18, p. 11.

Bardis, Panos. 1981. *History of Thanatology*. Washington, D.C.: University Press of America.

Becker, H. S., and A. Strauss. 1968. "Careers, Personality, and Adult Socialization." In B. Neugarten, ed., *Middle Age and Aging: A Reader in Social Psychology*. Chicago: University of Chicago Press, pp. 311–20.

Berger, Joseph. 1985. "Communion-Cup Fear Addressed." *New York Times*. September 13, p. 16.

Berger, Peter, and S. Pullberg. 1965. "Reification and the Sociological Critique of Consciousness." *History and Theory* 4:196–211.

Berger, Peter, and Thomas Luckmann. 1964. "Social Mobility and Personal Identity." *European Journal of Sociology* 5:331–44.

Berkowitz, L., and A. LePage. 1967. "Weapons as Aggression-Eliciting Stimuli." *Journal of Personality and Social Psychology* 7:202–7.

Bertman, Sandra. 1979. "Communicating with the Dead: An Ongoing Experience as Expressed in Art, Literature, and Song." In Robert Kastenbaum, ed., *Between Life and Death*. New York: Springer, pp. 124–55.

Binford, Lewis. 1971. "Mortuary Practices: Their Study and Their Potential." *American Antiquity* 36(3):6–29.

Bishop, Jim. 1982. "My Brother John Is Gone." *San Antonio Light*. November 10, p. 4C.

Blauner, Robert. 1966. "Death and Social Structure." *Psychiatry* 29:378–94.

Boffey, Philip. 1985. "Expert Calls AIDS Rate among Blacks High." *New York Times*. October 23, sec. II, p. 4.

Boulding, Kenneth. 1985. Public lecture, Trinity University, February 12.

Braudel, Fernand. 1981. *Civilization and Capitalism, 15th–18th Century. Vol. I: The Structures of Everyday Life*. New York: Harper & Row.

Cartwright, Frederick. 1972. *Disease and History*. New York: Thomas Y. Crowell.

Copp, John. 1975. "Why Hunters Like to Hunt." *Psychology Today* 9 (December):60–62.

Cornell, James. 1982. *The Great International Disaster Book*, 3d ed. New York: Charles Scribner's Sons.

Davidson, Bruce. 1985. "AIDS Germ Warfare, Needs Media Probe, Gregory Says." *San Antonio Express-News*. October 9, p. 10A.

Dionne, E. J. Jr., 1985. "Italian Town Begins to Bury Its Dead." *New York Times*. July 23, p. 5.

Dooley, Susan. 1980. "Pass the Buck." *New Republic*. November 29, p. 11.

Dullea, Georgia. 1987. "New Rituals Ease Grief as AIDS Toll Increases." *New York Times*. May 11, p. 18.

Eckholm, Erik. 1985. "Poll Finds Many AIDS Fears That the Experts Say Are Groundless." *New York Times*. September 12, p. 9.

Ehrlich, Paul. 1968. *The Population Bomb*. New York: Ballantine.

Eliade, Mircea. 1959. *Cosmos and History: The Myth of the Eternal Return*, trans. by Willard Trask. New York: Harper & Row.

Firmer, Sara. 1985. "Fear of AIDS Grows among Heterosexuals." *New York Times*. August 30, p. 1.

Frazer, James. 1934. *The Fear of the Dead in Primitive Religion*, Vol. II. London: Macmillan.

Gerbner, G. 1980. "Death in Prime Time: Notes on the Symbolic Functions of Dying in the Mass Media." *Annals* 447:64–70.

Gorer, Geoffrey. 1965. *Death, Grief and Mourning*. New York: Doubleday Anchor Books.

Gross, Jane. 1987. "The Bleak and Lonely Lives of Women Who Carry AIDS." *New York Times*. August 27, pp. 1, 14.

Gutis, Philip. 1987. "AIDS Cited in Killing of Sex Partner." *New York Times*. March 4, p. 16.

Hershey, Robert Jr. 1978. "Birthrights Up for Auction as Investments in London." *New York Times*. March 6, pp. D1, D5.

Hertz, Robert. 1960. *Death and the Right Hand,* trans. by R. Needham and C. Need-
    ham, intro. by E. E. Evans-Pritchard. New York: Free Press.

Hocking, William. 1957. *The Meaning of Immortality in Human Experience.* New
    York: Harper.

Houston Post. 1985. "Fallout: AIDS-like Reactions?" September 22, p. 17A.

Huntington, Richard, and Peter Metcalf. 1979. *Celebrations of Death: The Anthropol-
    ogy of Mortuary Ritual.* Cambridge: Cambridge University Press.

Irion, Paul. 1976. "The Funeral and the Bereaved." In Vanderlyn et al., eds., *Acute
    Grief and the Funeral.* Springfield, Ill.: Charles C. Thomas.

Johnson, Marguerite. 1984. "Death Haunts a Parched Land." *Time.* July 16, p. 46.

Kamm, Henry. 1985. "Drought Weakens Age-Old Social Fabric in Chad." *New York
    Times.* February 4, p. 3.

Kastenbaum, Robert, and Ruth Aisenberg. 1972. *The Psychology of Death.* New York:
    Springer.

Kastenbaum, R., S. Peyton, and B. Kastenbaum. 1977. "Sex Discrimination after
    Death." *Omega* 7:351–59.

Kearl, Michael. 1986–87. "Death as a Measure of Life: A Research Note on the Kas-
    tenbaum-Spilka Strategy of Obituary Analyses." *Omega* 17(1):65–78.

Kraeer, R. Jay. 1981. "The Therapeutic Value of the Funeral in Post-Funeral Coun-
    seling." In Otto Margolis et al., eds., *Acute Grief: Counseling the Bereaved.*
    New York: Columbia University Press.

Lambert, Bruce. 1988. "One in 61 Babies in New York City Has AIDS Antibodies,
    Study Says." *New York Times.* January 13, pp. 1, 13.

Lerner, Gerda. 1986. *The Creation of Patriarchy.* New York: Oxford University Press.

Lescaze, Lee. 1985. "Luckless Land: Idi Amin May Be Gone, but Ruinous Violence
    Continues in Uganda." *Wall Street Journal.* July 24, pp. 1, 12.

Levine, Art. 1987. "The Uneven Odds." *U.S. News & World Report.* August 17, pp.
    31–33.

McNeill, William. 1976. *Plagues and Peoples.* Garden City, N.Y.: Anchor Press/
    Doubleday.

Malinowski, Bronislaw. 1948. *Magic, Science and Religion, and Other Essays.* Glencoe,
    Ill.: Free Press.

Maly, Fred. 1979. "The Dos and Don'ts of Gun Shopping." *San Antonio Light.*
    December 19, p. 8F.

Mandelbaum, David. 1959. "Social Uses of Funeral Rites." In Herman Feifel, ed.,
    The Meaning of Death. New York: McGraw-Hill, pp. 189–217.

Milgram, Stanley. 1977. "The Small World Problem." In Stanley Milgram, *The Indi-
    vidual in a Social World: Essays and Experiments.* Reading, Mass.: Addison-
    Wesley, pp. 281–95.

Moore, Wilbert. 1963. *Man, Time, and Society.* New York: John Wiley.

Morrow, Lance, 1985. "The Start of a Plague Mentality." *Time.* September 23,
    p. 92.

Musto, David. 1987. "AIDS and Panic: Enemies Within." *Wall Street Journal.* April
    28, p. 28.

Mydans, Seth. 1984. "Chernenko Fails to Attend Rites for Defense Chief." *New York Times.* December 25, p. 1.

New York Times. 1982a. "Uncertain Succession a Soviet Weakness." November 11, p. 1.

———. 1982b. "Switch to Beethoven on Soviet TV Hints at a Death in the Politburo." November 11, p. 8.

———. 1984. "80 Years Later, New York Steamboat Disaster Is Still Debated." June 11, p. 18.

———. 1985a. "Burial of 16,500 Fetuses Is Ordered after 3 Years." August 29, p. 14.

———. 1985b. "Drug Is Linked to Risk of Contracting AIDS." September 13, p. 16.

———. 1987. "Bowen Expects AIDS to Dwarf Black Plague." January 30, p. 8.

Parsons, Talcott, R. C. Fox, and Victor Lidz. 1973. "The 'Gift of Life' and Its Reciprocation." In A. Mack, ed., *Death in American Experience.* New York: Schocken Books, pp. 1–49.

Parsons, Talcott, and Victor Lidz. 1967. "Death in American Society." In Edwin Shneidman, ed., *Essays in Self-Destruction.* New York: Science House, pp. 133–40.

Perlez, Jane. 1985. "Sport of Nobility: Common Event in Genesee Valley." *New York Times.* December 2, p. 16.

Radcliffe-Brown, A. R. 1964. *The Andaman Islanders.* New York: Free Press.

Renouard, Yves. 1978. "The Black Death as a Major Event in World History." In William Bowsky, ed., *The Black Death: Turning Point in History.* Huntington, N.Y.: Robert E. Krieger.

Roth, Terence. 1985. "Many Firms Fire AIDS Victims, Citing Health Risk to Co-Workers." *Wall Street Journal.* August 12, p. 19.

Russell, Cheryl. 1987. "Fear of AIDS May Re-create the Virtuous 50's." *Wall Street Journal.* March 30, p. 16.

Russell, George, 1985. "Colombia's Mortal Agony." *Time.* November 25, pp. 46–52.

San Antonio Express-News. 1983. "Iran Denies Rumors of Khomeini's Death." February 10, p. 10A.

———. 1984a. "UN: Drought Cause of Landmark Disaster." October 30, p. 3A.

———. 1984b. "Dmitri F. Ustinov, U.S.S.R. Defense Minister, Dead at 76." December 22, p. 3A.

———. 1985a. "Sperm Banks Reject Gays." September 23, p. 19.

———. 1985b. "War against AIDS Bans Bath Houses." October 3, pp. 1, 17.

———. 1985c. "Undercover Officers Follow AIDS Victim." October 3, p. 19A.

Schmidt, William. 1986. "Families of 2 Astronauts Say Their Remains Are Identified." *New York Times.* March 26, p. 11.

Shneidman, Edwin. 1973. *Deaths of Man.* New York: Quadrangle/New York Times.

Smith, Mark, and Isabel Valle. 1985. "AIDS Spreaders Called Murderers." *San Antonio Express-News.* October 13, pp. 1A, 13A.

Stannard, David. 1975. "Death and the Puritan Child." In David Stannard, ed., *Death in America*. Philadelphia: University of Pennsylvania Press, pp. 9–29.

Sudnow, David. 1967. *Passing On: The Social Organization of Dying*. Englewood Cliffs, N.J.: Prentice-Hall.

Thompson, James. 1978. "The Plague and World War: Parallels and Comparisons." In William Bowsky, ed., *The Black Death: Turning Point in History*. Huntington, N.Y.: Robert E. Krieger.

Von Hoffman, Nicholas. 1986. "Shuttle Jokes." *New Republic*. March 24, p. 14.

Wall Street Journal. 1985. "As Fear of AIDS Spreads, People Change Ways They Live and Work." October 10, p. 33.

Wallis, Claudia. 1985. "AIDS: A Growing Threat." *Time*. August 12, pp. 40–47.

Wicker, Tom. 1986. "An Awful Event." *New York Times*. January 31, p. 27.

Ziegler, Phillip. 1969. *The Black Death*. New York: John Day.

Chapter 4

How We Die:
The Social Stratification of Death

Some deaths are better than others. That sounds like a curious thing to say, but if you knew you had to die and had a choice in the matter, would you rather die of old age or be a random victim of a serial murderer?[1] Would you rather die at seventy-five or thirteen? And if one must, as a soldier, die in battle, is it better to die by leaping on a live grenade to save one's companions or to be shot in the back attempting to flee? How one dies not only has bearing on how one culminates one's biography (thereby giving meaning to the whole), but it also shapes the quality of grief of significant others. The death trajectory can be the time when one demands the most of others, and at issue is the utility of their sacrifices. The way in which death typically punctuates life has profound personal, social, and cultural consequences. For any cultural ethos to make sense, good lives must end in good deaths.

But it is not just the type of death that affects how people live their lives, the ability of a family or polity to rebound from the death of a leader, or whether a culture becomes fatalist or hedonistic in its outlook. We must also take into account the social position of those who die, for society tends to depersonalize those most likely to expire. Further, we must consider when death occurs, whether it often strikes suddenly and unexpectedly or comes in slow motion with considerable forewarning. And we must consider where death most often occurs, for people prefer to be in familiar places in which they have control.

"Good" Deaths

If death must be premature, history teaches us how dying at the right time enhances our prospects for immortality: Alexander the Great dying at the height of his conquests, Thomas Benton dying the day after his completion of a mural for the Missouri state capitol, or George Patton dying at the end of World War II.[2] Some premature deaths are good because the death itself means something: the willingness of Nathan Hale to die for his country, Ché Guevara dying for his principles, or those who sacrifice themselves to save others. Next are those deaths that occur "on time," following full and completed lives, and with the survivors-to-be fully prepared. For example, consider Hubert Humphrey, who continued to perform his public duty despite painful cancer and therapy and was able to give his public farewells and receive acknowledgments and thanks for his lifetime of contributions. Bing Crosby almost saw his three score and ten years of life and died doing what he loved most, playing golf.

And then there are deaths that strike us as being "bad." Consider, for example, the premature death of Freddy Prinze, the Chicano actor who achieved too much too soon and did not receive the psychiatric care he needed. Then there are the drug-related deaths of rock stars Elvis Presley and Jimi Hendrix, the collective suicides of the followers of Rev. Jim Jones's People's Temple in the jungles of Guyana, or all the women who have died from pregnancy-related causes. Postmature deaths can be bad as well. There is the slow-motion expiration of an eighty-year-old man, who earlier in life had been active in his work and community, a loving family man, who because of diabetes develops gangrene in his leg. His health deteriorates dramatically, but despite the expectations of his physicians, his will to live refuses to be extinguished. The leg is amputated, and, bedridden, he slips in and out of consciousness for a period of years. No longer does this man have control over his life and death, his existence now maintained in an institution where the convenience of the staff, not the residents, determines the quality of care. His battle exhausts the resources and emotions of his family, and eventually his wife, too, falls seriously ill. This type of postmature death is not only considered by most to be bad but is becoming increasingly commonplace.

 Activist Takes Own Life

Paris—A 73-year-old founding member of the Association for the Right to Die with Dignity, Marguerite Liegeois, killed herself last week after having sent a letter to the association's members explaining she was in declining health and "the only way to a dignified and upright death is to voluntarily interrupt life," the association said today. It did not disclose the manner of suicide.

New York Times 1985b. Copyright © 1985
by the New York Times Company. Reprinted by permission.

The ability of a society to allocate as many good deaths as possible to its members is a measure of its cultural adequacy. Deaths become good when they serve the needs of the dying, their survivors, and the social order. They are not necessarily easy deaths but rather allow individuals to die in character, at their own pace, and in their own style (Dempsey 1975, p. 231). The British, for example, attempted to put a halt to the hunger strikes of imprisoned Northern Ireland Catholics, fearing that their deaths would become politically good for the opposition side. But if good deaths and death fears are unequally distributed among the various stratified groups, there would arise basic questions about the adequacy of the entire cultural order to provide dignity and meaningful existences to all its social groups. Fears of irrational death, for example, are thought to be possible sources of violence, fear of any risk taking, alienation, anomie, and social withdrawal.

The Social Implications of Death's Timing and Location

Sociologists are increasingly appreciating time's role in shaping the everyday experiences of individuals as well as in determining the very essence of social order. It is because of death that we have the sense of time's passing and the need to prioritize our actions. Certainly for the dying, time becomes "the ultimate scarcity" (Moore 1963). Further, the time at which death normally occurs in the life span and how long it typically takes for people to die shape both cultural meaning systems and individuals' fears.

Whereas the ethos of preindustrial societies was shaped by the prevalence of unanticipated and premature deaths (it was, for instance, considered foolish not to have saved for one's funeral expenses by one's late teens or not to recognize that "one's time had come"), people nowadays generally die at the conclusion of full, completed lives. Death has been dropped from our conscious consideration when making plans. For example, those planning to enlarge their families rarely consider the possibility of the woman dying during pregnancy.[3] However, the occurrence of postmature deaths is now altering our value systems. With modernization, deaths are anticipated, and the period of liminality between life and death, which traditionally followed physiological extinction (which was why, as developed in Chapter 2, "secondary" funerals were conducted months after death occurred), now precedes it. Today, people normally die slow-motion deaths from chronic ailments and thereby often die socially, as when institutionalized in a nursing home, before expiring biologically.[4] To die "on time," on the other hand, is to synchronize the social and biological deaths, ideally allowing one's affairs to be put in order, being permitted to say what one must to the survivors-to-be and to complete unfinished business. But beyond when it occurs in the life cycle, there are other temporal facets of good deaths and bad.

Perhaps all the cultural emphasis given in contemporary society to the quantity rather than the quality of life is evidence of a reduction in the influence of religion and philosophy in mitigating death fears. As the moral worthiness of one's existence no longer has a culturally agreed-upon basis for ascertainment or automatically translates into the quality of one's postmortem existence, all that can be focused on is life's quantity—which is a matter of life-style moderation and "proper" utilization of medical services (see Chapter 11). Kalish and Reynolds (1974) report that people want to live to an older age than they expect to live, and, interestingly, there is some correlation with social class. They found that 65 percent of blacks interviewed desired to live past the age of ninety, compared with 25 to 28 percent of Japanese-, Mexican-, and Anglo-Americans. Slightly more than half of the blacks and Anglos, about one-half the Japanese, but only one-third of the Mexican-Americans favored allowing people to die if they want to, though all proportions declined with age of respondent.

The timing of death is a frequent plot device in police and detective stories. The timing of a murder, for example, establishes the boundaries of alibis and the whereabouts of people. The time of death of former U.S. vice-president and New York governor Nelson Rockefeller stimulated some questions about the quality of his demise. Rockefeller died in the room of a young female staff member, who reported his death more than an hour after it occurred, as later established by a coroner. The question was raised regarding whether this public figure had expired in the course of some illicit activity.

Perhaps one of the most striking findings concerning death's timing was detected by Phillips and Feldman (1973), who found by chance that death could be postponed for social reasons. As the story goes, Phillips wanted to demonstrate equiprobability in a statistics course. He had his students plot the months of death of more than thirteen hundred famous deceased Americans, expecting that there would be roughly one hundred ten deaths per month. But such a pattern was not discovered. Instead, they replotted the data in terms of individuals' months of birth, looking at monthly death rates before and after anniversary months. They found a relationship between birthdays and time of death, with lower than statistically expected death rates in the month before the birth month (a "death dip") and greater than statistically expected rates for the month following (a "death peak"). Phillips (1972) postulated that famous persons manage their time of death in order to receive the public attention and expressions of respect that typically come with their birthdays. Kunz and Summers (1979–80) detected a similar pattern among nonfamous residents of Salt Lake City: fewer than 10 percent of the 747 deaths studied occurred in the three months before the individuals' birthdays, while nearly half occurred during the following three-month period. Perhaps Mormon families are likely to treat family members as dignitaries. Nevertheless, the link between self and society may be more profound than ever realized.

Finally, there is the timing of the death trajectory. Death can either come quickly or, too frequently nowadays, in slow motion. These slow-motion deaths, often of the elderly, tax the dying and their families and caregivers alike. Keleman claims "this society is programming its members to die quickly" (1974, pp. 80–81). Many elderly people consider sudden death and slow death to be equally tragic. In many ways, a sudden and unexpected death has greater impact on the survivors than on the deceased.

The Elderly

We are in the midst of an "aging revolution," a revolution so profound that its very omnipresence hides the scope of its character. Two-thirds of the improvement of our species' longevity since prehistoric times has occurred since 1900 (Preston 1976); many older persons have lived longer than their parents by twenty years or more. Perhaps it would take the teleporting of a William Shakespeare to the present, from London to Leisure City or Orlando, for us to fully appreciate the change. To the Renaissance mind suddenly transplanted to Orlando, the sea of gray hair would undoubtedly rival the jet airplane overhead in shock value; longevity was an exceptional experience, as most died in childbirth, epidemics, and accidents, and war (*Science* 1980). However, there is some question about whether the additional quantity of life has come at the price of quality.

Death has become the province of the elderly, with more than 80 percent of all deaths in the United States occurring to individuals over sixty-five years of age.[5] In many ways the American "problems" of old age are bound up with the "problems" of dying. The old are culture's "shock absorbers of death" (Hochschild 1973, p. 85), and, in a number of ways, they are our culture's "death lepers." Their susceptibility to any changes in the environment has also made them an indicator of any death threat. How hot was it? It was so hot that fourteen older persons died from the heat. How virulent was the recent flu epidemic? The city was recording twenty elderly deaths a day from it over the period of a week. And how bad was the pollution? During December 1952, a low-lying fog carried coal gas over London and killed approximately four thousand, again mostly elderly people. Like the coal-miner's caged canaries, the elderly's death rate shows us how bad things have gotten.[6]

Curiously, though thanatology and gerontology have emerged concurrently as academic subject matters, the American Gerontology Society has rarely addressed this subject of death. Between 1967 and 1980, of the more than twenty-six hundred articles appearing in print in the *Gerontologist* and the *Journal of Gerontology*, fewer than forty (1.5 percent) dealt with any aspect of death. Perhaps this silence is bound up with the same denial system that allows the cosmetics industry to flourish: by dying gray hair and having face-lifts we can hide our aging, hence our deaths.

The predominant theory of social gerontology remains disengagement theory (Cumming and Henry 1961), which portrays a mutual parting of the ways between society and its older members. For the social system, disengagement represents not only a way of dampening death's impact but also a mechanism for providing upward mobility for the young within hierarchical organizations and for withdrawing from the scene those with obsolete skills and values. For the individual, it is supposedly a way to shed diminishing commitments that accompany diminishing energies. In actuality, disengagement is a series of minideaths: loss of work role and organizational memberships, deaths of friends and spouse (which mean the end of one's particular selves that only they brought out), loss of driver's license (the death of independent mobility), and so on.

But it is helplessness, not death, that is the elderly's chief fear. Author Malcolm Cowley described this dread in the following way: "It is the fear of being as dependent as a young child while not being loved as a child is loved but merely being kept alive against one's will. And there's a temporal irony to their life experiences. Retrospective time seems to pass with increasing rapidity as one ages. When you're as old as me, you'll learn that time devours you (1980, p. 57). And yet, for the old, the ongoing experience of time often takes an eternity, for there is nothing meaningful to do (Kalish 1976, p. 487).

 Gov. Lamm Asserts Elderly, If Very Ill,
Have "Duty to Die"

Denver—Elderly people who are terminally ill have a "duty to die and get out of the way" instead of trying to prolong their lives by artificial means, said Gov. Richard D. Lamm of Colorado.

People who die without having life artificially extended are similar to "leaves falling off a tree and forming humus for the other plants to grow up," the Governor told a meeting of the Colorado Health Lawyers Association at St. Joseph's Hospital.

"You've got a duty to die and get out of the way," said the 48-year-old Governor. "Let the other society, our kids, build a reasonable life."

Some groups of the elderly immediately denounced Mr. Lamm for the statements. . . . Mr. Lamm, when asked, said he did not have any particular age in mind for the terminally ill to "get out of the way" and that the decision should be made by the ill person in consultation with doctors and family members.

The Governor said that the cost of treatment that allows some terminally ill people to live longer was ruining the nation's economic health.

Steven Mehlman, a spokesman for the American Association of Retired Persons in Washington, D.C., said cutting off treatment to the terminally ill was no way to stem the rising cost of hospital care. "It is not the elderly's fault," Mr. Mehlman said. "We're the victims of health care inflation, not the cause."

New York Times 1984a. Copyright © 1984
by the New York Times Company. Reprinted by permission.

Alzheimer's disease, in many ways, has come to epitomize the "bad" death of the disengaged elderly. Alzheimer's is a lethal form of senility, an incurable mental deterioration that over a prolonged period sees the realm of forgetfulness expand from minor details to obliviousness of one's identity and the identity of family members. The disease kills approximately one hundred thousand a year in the United States, striking an estimated 20 percent of those eighty years of age and older. In 1985, the National Institute on Aging estimated that there were 2 million cases of Alzheimer's disease in the United States. Given present estimates of increases in the numbers of older individuals, Alzheimer's will affect 2.6 million persons in the year 2000, and its victims will exceed 4.8 million by 2030.

The 2 million Alzheimer's victims die a number of social deaths long before physically expiring. "A diagnosis of Alzheimer's disease today carries with it a sentence of eventual mental emptiness," according to a government guide for health practitioners (Boffey 1985). Some victims become violent and abusive; most are confused, anxious, and unable even to dress themselves. Few nursing facilities will accept Alzheimer's patients, having little time or staff to deal with their constant needs, and fewer still are the services available for patients or their families. Government insurance programs do not pay for their extended periods of care. In sum, the total burden of care is generally placed on family members, compounding the tragedy. Imagine awakening in the morning with your spouse of forty years asking who you are. Family caretakers often are shunned by friends in the later stages of the disease, producing a new form of widowhood: living with a spouse who is socially dead.[7]

On the other hand, proximity to death can bring certain satisfactions as well. John Powys observes in *The Art of Growing Old* that "the one supreme advantage that Old Age possesses over Middle Age and Youth is its nearness to Death. The very thing that makes it seem pitiable to those less threatened and therefore less enlightened ages of man is the thing that deepens, heightens and thickens out its felicity" (1944, p. 203). Before her death, Clare Boothe Luce discussed the satisfactions of having outlived her enemies. The old find the ways in which death organizes life. If we were all immortal, all projects could be delayed or worked on indefinitely, as there would be no pressure for completion. Further, there might be no need for priorities.

Where the Old Die: Institutions of Dying

The myth of the elephant burial ground, that secret place where pachyderms go to die, is nourished in our society because our old, too, typically expire within settings divorced from everyday life. The "problem" of old age—accentuating the word *problem* because the biological inevitability of growing old and dying has little or no cultural recipe for doing it correctly, and therefore it is socially problematic—has been institutionalized in retirement communities, adult day-care centers, nursing homes, and hospitals. More than four out of every five elderly people die hidden away from everyday life in institutional settings, spending their final days in a nursing home or hospital (Lerner 1970, p. 5). There they are at the mercy of the staff, compelled to conform to rules and regulations that may be contrary to their own needs and desires, dying socially while waiting for the end to come.

Chapter 11 will develop the role of the medical establishment in overseeing and managing the timing and form of the final passage, and Chapter 12 will consider the reactions of individuals to dying and bereavement. But this chapter gives brief focus to the nursing home, a place feared more than death by the elderly and an industry that has, along with funeral homes, been the subject of considerable investigation, by both congressional researchers and mass-media muckrakers. Despite two decades of exposés, the problems continue.

It would be nice if there were some Shangri-la where those who must face the end of their lives could go, or at least if it were possible to die in one's home, surrounded by one's family, friends, and memory-laden possessions. For a number of reasons, even the latter option eludes a majority of dying Americans:

- Because of the greater infirmities of advanced years and more people surviving to experience them, chronic old-age disabilities often require frequent, if not full-time care.
- The contemporary family has contracted in size, meaning fewer siblings to share the caregiving burden of elderly family members. Further, there is a different form

of solidarity among family members. The family has transformed from a unit of production to a unit of consumption, with emotions serving as the glue between members. With secularization, religion's power to obligate the young to care for their old has weakened. Since so many older persons exhaust their resources, they no longer have the resources to control the loyalty of their young.

- It has become an American custom to institutionalize those who are unable to live independently and whose families have exhausted other resources for care.

- For caregivers, there are economies of scale for managing many residents. Professional staff time is expensive and scarce, and it is therefore more efficient if, say, a physician walks from room to adjacent room as opposed to driving from one personal dwelling to another. (Inflation in energy costs since 1973 has added to this cost as well.)

Spurred by the infusion of Medicare and Medicaid money, the approximately twenty-three thousand nursing homes in the United States became a booming private industry, doubling in patient capacity between 1966 and 1974 (Jacoby 1974). More than 80 percent of institutional homes are commercial nursing homes, in which there is the inherent conflict between profit and service. This sets the stage for a potential atmosphere of alienation, conflict, and neglect. According to Senator Frank Moss, "people off the street, paid the minimum wage, who have no training and who are grossly overworked, provide 90 percent of this work in nursing homes" (Butler 1975). Frustrated by their thankless task of hand-feeding the feeble, cleaning bedpans, and often getting insulted by angry and aggressive patients, nursing aides can face further hostility with each other when accusations of patient mistreatment are made.

Who are the 1.3 million elderly residents of the twenty-three thousand nursing homes in this country? Seventy percent are women. Some 96 percent are white, 60 to 80 percent are poor, and the average age is seventy-eight. Some 85 percent who enter die there; one-third of those admitted die within the first year, and another third live one to three years.

 Aged in Nursing Home Barred Abortion Aid

Sparta, Ill.—Seventy-one residents of the Randolph County Nursing Home have received letters from the Illinois Department of Public Aid notifying them they are no longer eligible for abortions financed by public funds.

"They won't pay us what we need to operate on for the public aid residents and they waste time and postage for things like this," Thomas Behnen, nursing home administrator, said.

Social death in a Miami Beach nursing home. Paul S. Conklin, Monkmeyer Press.

At their worst, these facilities are depersonalization machines, staffed by caregivers at the bottom of the professional health-care ladder. Residents must face an existence of regimentation and impersonal care. Instances of patient abuse and neglect abound: the old are physically beaten and their possessions stolen, bed sores remain untreated, and the incontinent are left to sit or lie in their own excrement. The victimized remain silent, not reporting the mistreatment for fear of retaliation. A 1975 special Senate subcommittee claimed that nursing homes were the most dangerous places to be in terms of fire safety. Physicians seldom conduct regular rounds, and all too often there is no emergency medical equipment. Rehabilitation (speech, occupational therapy, or physical therapy) is rare.

During the early 1980s, there was movement to relax or repeal many of the federal rules governing nursing home services, patient rights, and staff qualifications at long-term facilities. A 1982 proposal of the Reagan administration dropped the requirement for annual nursing home inspections, replacing it with a flexible policy based on past compliance with health and safety rules. Four years later, however, a study by the National Academy of Sciences called for stronger federal regulations, claiming that many of the 1.3 million residents in homes that receive Medicaid and Medicare funds "have their rights ignored or violated, and may even be subject to physical abuse" (Pear 1986). A 1986 Senate report found that more than one-third of the nation's skilled nursing homes failed to meet basic federal health and safety standards and claimed that many "more closely resemble 19th-century asylums than modern health-care facilities" (*San Antonio Light* 1986).

In a number of ways the symbol of nursing home abuse came to be, in the 1980s, the Autumn Hills establishment of Texas City, Texas, near Galveston. There, according to charges of the prosecution, at least eight and as many as sixty elderly people had died because of substandard care resulting from management's greed. In Texas, as in thirty-three other states, the method of compensating nursing homes for their services was on the basis of a daily rate per patient rather than for actual services rendered—a system that potentially encourages cost-cutting and neglect (King 1983). The state maintained that these individuals were knowingly starved, deprived of medication, or allowed to lie in their own filth. Two times murder indictments were brought against the home, and twice they failed to reach trial. On the third attempt, the corporation and its owner, its president, a director of nurses, a nursing consultant, and an administrator were on trial for murder—"murder by omission," according to Special Prosecutor David Marks. According to state investigations, staffing reports were falsified to obtain more money while the number of nurses on duty was substandard. Lapses in patient care were covered up by patient charts, which had either not been kept up (one patient listed as weighing 132 only weighed 96 pounds) or falsified. Of the ninety-nine charts reviewed, doctors' orders were not being followed in seventy-one and there were sixty-two medication errors. The thirty-five deaths recorded in a ninety-day period indicated more than twice the death rate of comparable facilities (King 1983). Following a six-month-long trial and seven days of impasse in jury deliberations, the state district judge declared a mistrial.

In sum, things have not changed greatly since Edith Stern's observation more than forty years ago: "Unlike some primitive tribes, we do not kill off our aged and infirm. We bury them alive in institutions. To save our faces, we call the institutions homes—a travesty on the word. I have seen dozens of such homes in the last six months—desolate places peopled with blank-faced men and women, one home so like the other that each visit seemed a recurrent nightmare" (Stern 1947).

Premature Death: The Greatest Inequality of All

> If the rich could hire other people to die for them,
> the poor could make a wonderful living.
>
> Yiddish proverb

The much-ballyhooed reductions in mortality from the late 1960s through 1980 mostly occurred among older people. While, for example, those between seventy-five and seventy-nine gained four years of additional life expectancy, the corresponding gain for fifteen-year-olds was less than one year (Preston 1984). In other words, even though there were fewer children and half again as many older people in 1980 than there were in 1968, scarce social resources apparently were disproportionately allocated to those most likely to die. Further, those who died the premature bad deaths were most likely to be the most disenfranchised groups in the American social hierarchy.

In a 1985 study of childhood mortality rates in Boston, a city where medical care is generally available to all, there was a strong inverse correlation with income: black or poor children were seen to have considerably higher chances of dying than those from white or wealthier families. Were the death rates to be equal, then 282 of the 760 actual deaths (37 percent) studied among the poorer families would not have occurred. Prolongevity in the United States is not equal opportunity. The life expectancy of Native Americans is still less than fifty years. Black men have the highest death rates from accidents and violence of any statistical group, and their suicide rates have risen at a much faster pace than for their white counterparts (Barron 1984). Though blacks make up some 12 percent of the U.S. population, they comprised more than one-third of all American casualties in Vietnam. The infant mortality rate of nonwhites is double that of whites (1.9 vs. 1.0),[8] the greatest discrepancy in forty years. And, as evidenced in Table 4.1, even their benefits from the war against the contemporary symbol of death, cancer, are likewise prorated. A 1985 report released by Health and Human Services

Table 4.1 Five-Year Relative Survival Rates for Ten Types of Cancer

	Percent white	Percent black
Endometrium (uterine lining)	81	44
Breast (females only)	68	51
Cervix	64	61
Prostate	63	55
Bladder	61	35
Colon	49	37
Rectum	45	30
Stomach	13	13
Lung	10	7
Pancreas	1	2

Source: U.S. Department of Health and Human Services 1980.

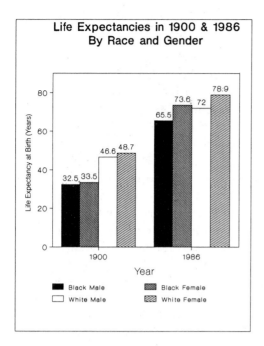

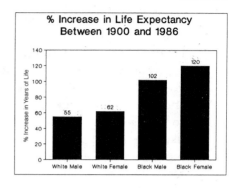

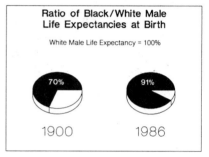

Figure 4.1 Life expectancy.

Secretary Margaret Heckler, based on an eighteen-month study of minority groups' health, called such disparities in death rates a "tragic dilemma" (Davidson 1985).

As shown in Figure 4.1, the life expectancy differences between whites and nonwhites has diminished since 1900. At the turn of the century, white males lived 43 percent longer than black males (whose life expectancy at birth was but thirty-two and a half years), and white females lived 45 percent longer than black females. But over the following eighty-two years, blacks at birth could expect to live more than twice as long as their great-grandparents, diminishing the longevity gap with their white counterparts to 10 percent or less. Social progress, at least by this indicator, has been considerable. Nevertheless, the life expectancy differences between the races has produced political ramifications, evident in the Social Security complaints of black males, whose life expectancy at birth has yet to exceed sixty-five, the age at which one can retire with full benefits, and yet from whose earnings full deductions are taken.

Ironically, there may be a selective survival to advanced age of the elderly disadvantaged. According to Markides and Machalek (1982), "Black Americans, for example, experience higher mortality rates than whites at every age up to approximately age 75, after which point they are expected to live longer than whites." Markides and Machalek note that this pattern, in part, "may be a factor contributing to the low rates of institutionalization in nursing homes of elderly blacks, Native Americans and other disadvantaged populations . . . [and also their] low suicide rates in old age."

Life expectancy is a function not only of race and social class but of gender as well. Though throughout the animal kingdom the female is generally the longer lived, such has not always been the case in human populations. Until about 1800 in much of Europe, more than 1 percent of live births were accompanied by the death of the mother. The average woman gave birth about six times during her lifetime; therefore, she ran about an 8 percent chance of dying in childbirth (Shorter 1982). Nowadays, according to the World Health Organization, in developing countries one-quarter of all deaths of women of childbearing age occur during pregnancy or childbirth—some 99 percent of the five hundred thousand women who so died worldwide in 1986 (Brooke 1987).[9] Death remains intimately involved with procreation and, hence, the sex act. And the connection between death and sex is now even more multifaceted; as was evidenced in the discussion on AIDS and as will be developed in an analysis of the popularity of the death-sex motifs of the James Bond films, such fusions between these two biological processes remain very much a part of our consciousness. As Michel Foucault noted, "Sex is worth dying for. . . . Sex is indeed imbued with the death instinct" (cited in Morrow 1987).

With improvements in maternal care and in the ability to manage childbirth complications,[10] the greater life allowance of males evaporated. During the twentieth century, the life expectancy advantage of females has increased: white females had 5 percent greater life expectancy than white males in 1900 and 10 percent greater in 1986; black females had a 3 percent life expectancy advantage over black males in 1900 and 12 percent in 1986. There is growing evidence that differences in death and sickness rates between men and women "are related more to their behaviors and roles in society than to their biological inheritance" (Lewis and Lewis 1977). Nevertheless, such advances have not meant a greater female immunity to death. As the remainder of this discussion will show, sexism figures prominently in the social distribution of death and grief. For example, given the current seven-year advantage females have over males at birth coupled with the typical practice of women marrying older men, the American woman is practically guaranteed having to bear the burden of the death of her spouse.

"Bad" Deaths

For much of human history there has been concern with how to die well. In the fourteenth and fifteenth centuries in western Europe, for example, Ariès (1974, p. 38) reports that it was believed that the moment of death would give one's "biography its final meaning, its conclusion." Robert Fulton writes in *Death and Identity* that "Death asks us for our identity. Confronted with death, man is compelled to provide in some form a response to the question, 'Who am I?'" (1976, p. 3). How we die reveals not only the essence of personal values and principles but also the adequacy of social arrangements for ensuring that good lives can be lived. If too many social actors take their own lives at the time of their greatest social contributions, for example, or if too many are victims of internal violence, then their funerals become the springboards of major social change.

Most social systems cannot handle equivocal death. For a variety of reasons, there is a social obsession to explain the causes.[11] We have a need to explain not only why we die but what caused the demise of generations past. Egyptian mummies, for example, now undergo the scrutiny of the most modern scientific instruments to ascertain what killed the pharaohs three thousand years ago. If the causes of death are not understood, fears are intensified and doubts about the adequacy of social arrangements to prevent death are generated. Take, for instance, the mysterious death of Jason Findley, a clean-living New Jersey high school honors student who had planned to attend West Point the following fall. Jason went into a bedroom of his grandmother's house to call a girlfriend. Four minutes later, a cousin entered the room to find him dead, the phone receiver next to his ear. What killed the seventeen-year-old? Need others worry about the cause of his demise? The autopsy revealed a hemorrhage in his inner ear, and reconstructions of that night revealed that there had been a thunderstorm. Was he killed by an electrical surge or by an acoustic shock, an inaudible high-pitched sound capable of stopping the heart? Months later no one knew (Llorente 1985). If death cannot be avoided, it must at least be explained so as to seem manageable.[12] One consequence of the attempts to minimize the number of equivocal deaths is categorizing the forms of death.

In the United States, the 140 possible causes of every death are classified on death certificates into one of the following modes: natural causes, accidental, suicide, and homicide (abbreviated as NASH). This standard NASH classification system, however, fails in being able to place a given death in one of the mutually exclusive categories. As Shneidman observes,

it emphasizes relatively trivial elements in the death of human beings while omitting altogether the psychological role they may have played in their own demise. The

NASH classification, Cartesian and apsychological in spirit, implies that human beings are biological machines to which things happen, rather than vital, introspective, unique individuals who often unconsciously play a decisive role in their own fate. (1980a, p. 154)

For example, given the estimate that some 20 percent of single-occupant auto fatalities are in actuality suicides, what differences in classification would there be if the victim was a Catholic as opposed to being a Protestant? How does one categorize a voodoo death? And what if—and such cases are not that unusual—for sexual pleasure someone masturbates with a rope around his neck while standing on a chair and accidentally falls, hanging himself? Is this a suicide or an accident?

Though we will employ the NASH system as a means for considering how people die prematurely, for each mode we need to consider not only the personal intentionality underlying the death but its social context as well. As illustrated by the studies of people who seem to postpone their deaths for social occasions, when one dies, as well as how, is profoundly shaped by one's relationship to the social order. Death is, in fact, a dual process simultaneously involving the dying and the surviving. The quality of grief, for example, is shaped by the quality of death; the nature of pathological relationships within a family perhaps conditions whether a family member dies of anorexia nervosa, a hang-gliding accident, a drug overdose, or execution for killing someone else.

Suicide

Life for military dependents is not easy. Family members must tolerate frequent moves, constant readjustments, and low pay. Danny Holley, a thirteen-year-old living at Fort Ord, helped buy food for his sister and two brothers by collecting cans for a penny apiece. One day he told his mother, "If there was one less mouth to feed, things would be better." Then he hanged himself (*New York Times* 1984c).

In the space of less than two months in 1985, nine young Indian males on the Wind River Reservation in central Wyoming committed suicide. Since the beginning of the year there had been nearly fifty suicide attempts.

Such suicides illustrate why, at least in American society, this form of death has invidious connotations, stigmatizing victim and survivors alike. Was life in the military and on reservations so bad that death was truly preferable? Suicides continue to provide a burden for the survivors long after they have been committed.

No one really knows why people commit suicide, and perhaps the person least aware is the victim at the moment of the decision. In the United States,

A young boy contemplates a suicide leap as a group of anxious firemen move a safety net into place. Nancy Hays, Monkmeyer Press.

an individual takes his or her own life every twenty minutes, some twenty-seven thousand lives a year. Between 1970 and 1980, there were two hundred eighty-seven thousand suicides, three-quarters of whom were males. During this period, the suicide rate for men fifteen to twenty-four years of age increased by 50 percent, while the rate for similarly aged young women increased by less than 5 percent. Among those twenty-five to thirty-four, the rate for males increased nearly 30 percent, while the female rate declined by nearly 20 percent (*San Antonio Express-News* 1985). By 1987, suicide had become the fifth leading cause of premature death, accounting for over six-hundred and fifty-thousand years of potential life lost each year (*San Antonio Light* 1987). Across cultures and times, suicide has been either one of the most stigmatizing or the most honored of all death forms.

The Bible mentions several suicides without any connotation of condemnation. Saul "took a sword, and fell upon it," and Ahithophel "put his household in order, and hanged himself." In the West, the stigma attached to this act can be dated to St. Augustus, who, fearing excessive martyrdom and the penchant for suicide, used a theological deterrent against its practice. Later, St. Thomas Aquinas was to portray suicide as a mortal sin usurping God's power over life and death. But with Rousseau, in his emphasis of the natural state of man (inspiring the myth of the noble savage), sin was transferred from man to society. So where do we look for causes, to the individual or to the social environment?

So great is this riddle of self-destruction that most disciplines of the human sciences have proffered explanations ranging from theories of hormonal imbalances to cultural alienation. Here we will consider the spectrum of theories of self-destruction and then focus attention on the suicides of the American young and old.

Theories of Suicide

As with all theories of human behavior, scientists have located the cause of self-destructive behavior both within the individual and without, as either a personal or a social pathology. At the biochemical level of explanation, it has been found that brain-damaged individuals, young children, and animals can commit suicide without symbolizing any unconscious conflict. Metabolic disorders, biochemical deficiencies, and neurophysiological dysfunctions have precipitated violence without awareness (Haywood 1984). For instance, some persons suffering from depression, schizophrenia, alcoholism, or personality disorder were discovered to have abnormally low serotonin level, which is the critical, common factor in deciding whether or not suicide is attempted (Greenberg 1982). Marie Asberg, a psychiatrist at the Karolinska Institute in Stockholm, found that among patients hospitalized for suicide attempts, those with low levels of serotonin (5-hydroxyindoleacetic acid) were ten times more likely to have died from suicide after one year than those with higher amounts (Goleman 1985).

Historically preceding the theories of biochemical imbalances were the paradigms of psychic force imbalances. Again, the causes of suicide are seen to be rooted in the individual, but here psychological factors are the focus. Sigmund Freud, who viewed suicide as murder turned 180 degrees around, saw its genesis arising from the unconscious, in that part of the self that bears the residue of primeval ancestors. Characterized by a duality of motivation, the check-and-balance relationship between eros, the life force, and thanatos, the death force, is altered. Unconscious feelings of hostility, guilt, or dependency held toward some significant other, for example, are directed toward that person held within oneself (the introjected image). Suicides are ambivalent and dyadic; they reflect contradictory feelings and attitudes toward one's relationships with others.

Recognizing that suicides vary in their timing and intentionality, Edwin Shneidman (1980b) recommends that all forms of self-destructive behavior be considered as suicide substitutes and partial deaths. To publicly insult one's superior at work in his or her presence can be seen as the suicide of one's work self. To seriously abuse alcohol, tobacco,[13] or other drugs is to indirectly destroy oneself, not only biologically but socially as well, as one either alienates or withdraws from significant others and surrenders one's social commitments. In conceptualizing such partial suicides, Shneidman employs the notion of "subintentioned death": "there are many deaths that are neither clearly suicidal nor clearly accidental or natural but are deaths in which the decedent has played some covert or unconscious role in 'permitting' his death to occur, sort of 'accidentally,' or by 'inviting' homicide, or, by unconsciously disregarding what could be life-extending medical regimen, and thus dying sooner than 'necessary'" (p. 425).

Among many disturbed individuals observed by psychiatrists and psychologists, suicides were preceded by the feelings of hopelessness, helplessness, alienation, preoccupation with trivia, cynicism, the inability to control moods, irregular and destructive health behavior patterns, absence of creative dreaming, unbearable loss or threat, and the availability of the means to kill oneself (Haywood 1984). Some survivors of suicide attempts expressed not so much the desire for death as that they sought to shed old, used-up selves. Clinical findings show that the actual period of high lethality is of relatively short duration, that there is generally always ambivalence. In analyzing the trends in methods for committing suicide over the past twenty-five years, Jeffrey Boyd (1983) found that only the rate of suicide by firearms has risen continuously.

Coast Court Rules Insane Person
May Not Be Held to Be a Suicide

San Diego—In a ruling that could affect numerous insurance policies, a state appeals court has ruled that an insane person cannot be said to have committed suicide. The court said such a person "cannot form the intent to take his own life."

In the opinion issued by the Court of Appeals for the Fourth District, Justice Gerald Brown wrote: "If a person is insane, he cannot form the intent to take his own life. Insane persons cannot commit suicide."

The ruling came in an appeal of a civil suit filed by Alice M. Searle against the Allstate Life Insurance Company, which refused to pay her claim on a life insurance policy held by her late husband, Martin. He apparently killed himself about 10 months after he took out the policy, which had a clause barring payment if a suicide occurred within two years of the policy's taking effect.... Many life insurance policies include clauses that forbid payment to policy holders who kill themselves. The ruling, if left intact after an expected appeal to the California Supreme Court, apparently would invalidate such clauses in cases where the deceased is found to have been insane.

New York Times 1979. Copyright © 1979
by the New York Times Company. Reprinted by permission.

Suicides become somewhat more of a sociological phenomenon when we consider the copycat instances. David Phillips demonstrated in 1974 how suicides increase in the month of highly publicized suicide stories. In subsequent research, he suggested that such stories even increased motor vehicle fatalities, citing a 31 percent increase in California auto deaths on the third day following publicized suicides. How can television news stories trigger such imitations? And what personal or social pathology makes one receptive to such suggestions? When we consider the victims who lack meaning in their lives or who suffer from alienation or social disengagement, we are no longer so clearly in the realm of biochemical explanation but, rather, are dealing with higher-order processes involving the fit between individual and society.

There is considerable cultural and historical variation in reactions toward suicidal behavior, and in a number of instances suicides have been celebrated. There is a Greco-Roman tradition of heroic suicides, but it was a right reserved for the entitled. The Greeks required their would-be suicides to first secure permission from the Senate. Their slaves, however, did not have this right; they were assumed to be commodities, and their deaths would be equivalent to the destruction of the master's property. In Northern Ireland IRA hunger strikers in British prisons committed slow-motion suicides that

Suicide Note Left by a Young
College Professor

To all who love me
Whoever you are,
I regret the agony
I cause you
By choosing this way.
Another way
Would have been easier for you
But harder for me.
Tonight I am being totally selfish
I find pleasure
In becoming what I want to be
I only hope this releases you
From your bonds to me
So that this, too, forces you
To become what you want to be
I am too tired and too old.

---

generated a climate of even greater hate. In Japanese culture, the traditional hara-kiri suicide was perceived as a noble way to end dishonor, and the militaristic suicides of kamikaze pilots were revered as entailing the greatest personal sacrifice.[14]

Evident in Table 4.2 is the considerable variation in suicide rates throughout the world. There is no obvious correlation between the rates by which individuals relinquish their lives and the level of economic development or nature of political system: the lowest rate is found in Egypt (0.3 percent per 100,000 of the population), where life remains hard and 90 percent live beneath the middle class; near the other end of the scale is Sweden, which takes care of its citizens from womb to tomb and yet suffers a suicide rate of 18.6 per 100,000. And why would the United Kingdom have half the rate of its former colonies?

In general, we see that men are more likely to commit suicide than women and that the rate of suicides for both sexes increases with age. In Israel, for example, if we take the fifteen-to-twenty-four-year suicide rate for men and divide it by the rate for similarly aged women, we obtain a ratio of 9.0. In other words, young men are nine times more likely to commit suicide than young women. Among those sixty-five years of age and older, the ratio declines to 1.5, meaning that men have a suicide rate "only" 50 percent greater than women, reflecting the much greater increase in the suicide propensity of females relative to males with age. In old age, suicide is more equal-opportunity, except in Denmark, Sweden, Switzerland, and the United States, where the sex ratio of rates in old age is greater than it is for those aged fifteen to twenty-four. In these countries, old age seems to pose a greater burden for males than for females.

By examining these suicide rates across the life cycle for both men and women, we have a crude indicator of the stresses associated with each life stage for different nationalities. Consider the difficulties of cultural life-course pathways in middle age relative to early adulthood. Dividing rates for those forty-five to sixty-four by those for people twenty-five to forty-four years of age, we see the greatest transition problems in Norway for men (where the rate increases 57 percent) and in the United Kingdom (90 percent increase), West Germany (83 percent), and the Netherlands (81 percent) for women.

During a career spent demarcating and elaborating upon the sociological discipline, Emile Durkheim applied his sociological method to this riddle of suicide variability. In an era when psychological paradigms were used to locate the motivating dynamics with the personality structure of the victim, Durkheim demonstrated that rates correlated with social phenomena, that

Table 4.2 Suicide Rates for Selected Countries, 1980 (per 100,000)

	Male				Female				
	15–24	25–44	45–64	65+	15–24	25–44	45–64	65+	Total
Austria	28.8	40.0	58.1	77.2	6.7	12.7	21.8	31.1	35.5
Switzerland	31.0	39.2	50.6	59.4	13.2	16.3	24.3	22.2	32.5
Denmark	16.3	51.4	71.2	67.7	7.7	25.5	41.1	32.4	29.9
W. Germany	19.0	30.1	40.8	60.4	5.6	12.1	22.0	26.6	27.8
Sweden	16.9	35.3	39.4	42.7	5.8	13.6	19.6	13.2	27.7
France	14.0	25.5	36.2	62.3	5.2	9.1	14.9	21.3	22.9
Japan	16.6	26.8	32.9	51.3	8.2	11.9	16.3	44.4	21.4
Poland	19.5	31.8	34.9	24.7	4.3	4.6	6.3	5.8	19.3
USA	20.0	24.0	25.3	38.0	4.7	8.9	10.5	7.4	18.9
Canada	27.8	30.3	30.2	28.6	5.7	10.1	12.8	8.7	17.2
Australia	17.6	23.1	23.1	25.3	4.5	8.1	8.6	7.9	15.2
Norway	20.4	19.2	30.3	25.0	3.3	8.0	13.0	7.5	14.2
Netherlands	6.2	13.4	20.7	27.8	2.7	9.8	17.7	18.0	10.8
Israel	10.8	9.4	12.9	23.4	1.2	4.3	6.6	15.9	9.6
UK	6.4	14.1	16.6	19.3	3.0	6.0	11.4	12.3	9.1
Ireland	6.2	11.1	12.1	4.3	2.5	4.8	8.4	3.6	6.6

Source: U.S. Department of Commerce Bureau of the Census, *Statistical Abstract of the United States 1982–83*, National Data Book and Guide to Sources, 103d ed., p. 81.

Protestants were more prone than Catholics, alienated urbanites more than rural inhabitants, and single individuals more than married ones.

From a Durkheimian perspective, instances of self-destruction have come to be understood as the result of imbalances in the relations between individuals and their social system. If the causal antecedents were less social and more psychological or physiological in origin, one would expect relatively uniform distributions of suicides across various social groups. But such is not the case. Suicide rates vary not only by country but by sex, age, religion, marital status, and ethnicity as well. Durkheim claimed that such differences can be best understood as an indication of either excessive or insufficient social participation and/or regulation, or of a radical disruption in the nature of one's ties.

Durkheim suggested that varying levels of integration and regulation could produce four distinct types of suicide: egoistic, anomic, altruistic, and fatalistic (Durkheim 1951). Egoistic suicides, the most prevalent form in the United States (Shneidman 1973), result from too little social integration, such as the suicide of an unmarried retired male. Conversely, excessive integration can produce altruistic suicides, as in the case of Japanese hara-kiri, in which the dishonored ritually disembowel themselves, or the Indian suttee, in which widows throw themselves on their husbands' funeral pyres. Too little regulation or the shattering of one's accustomed relationships can lead to anomic suicides, such as from the normlessness following economic collapse or as reflected by the deaths of poor men suddenly enriched or the wealthy suddenly impoverished (Ellner 1977; Pierce 1967; Stack 1978). On the other hand, where there exists excessive regulation in conjunction with high personal need to control one's environment, fatalistic suicides can result, as when one's goal commitments become blocked and feelings of desperation and helplessness result (Peck 1980–81). Admittedly, such forms are ideal types, and in reality it is virtually impossible to separate or attribute an isolated motive to suicidal behavior.

As exceptionally logical and "clean" as Durkheim's typology may seem, an examination of the gender, age, and ethnic differences in suicide rates reveals some difficulties in employing the paradigm. For instance, in the case of childhood and adolescent suicides, one could infer the cause to be anomic (social disorganization of home life following divorce), excessive egoism (inability to participate in the adult order), or even fatalism (as when a young black faces excessive and often contradictory regulation from both the black community and dominant white institutions). Why, in the seventy-to-seventy-four-year-old age group of Americans, do white men commit suicide at a rate nearly three times higher than nonwhite men and nearly five times higher than women the same age? And why do black youths seem more

Bodies lay strewn about a vat containing Kool-Aid laced with cyanide at the Jonestown commune of the Peoples Temple cult in Guyana. The earlier death of Representative Leo Ryan (D-California) signalled the start of the mass murder–suicides which left 913 Peoples Temple cultists dead. UPI/Bettmann Newsphotos.

Rev. Jones on Suicide

The date was May 31, 1977, Memorial Day. The place—San Francisco's Golden Gate Bridge, the world's number one location for suicide. Several concerned Bay Area residents had joined together as an ad hoc committee to promote the idea of a suicide deterrent for the bridge. One speaker at this anti-suicide rally was Jimmy Jones, who eighteen months later would lead over 900 members of his People's Temple to their own suicides in the jungles of Guyana. His remarks, in part:

"It is entirely fitting that on Memorial Day we are here on account of the hundreds of people who are not casualties of war, but casualties of society. For, in the final analysis, we have to bear collective responsibility for those individuals who could not find a place to go with their burdens, who came to that place of total helplessness, total despondency, where they took their own lives here on this beautiful bridge, this Golden Gate bridge, a symbol of human ingenuity, technological genius but social failure. . . .

"In his mind, the person who takes his life is a reflection on all of us. Many of the over 600 who have taken their lives here were very young. Indeed, some were teenagers—people who had great abilities, talents, even genius, whose lives were barely begun, yet for various reasons they found themselves with no recourse, no way out of personal problems, aggravated by the terrible alienation and loneliness of a society that often seems to have no time, no desire to reach out to people who need help. . . .

"Basic human values, basic decency, kindness, cooperation are less and less evident. Economic pressures and psychological pressures mount. More and more individuals feel unhappiness—and helplessness—in their acquisitiveness for pleasure and accumulation in this selfish society. They turn to artificial stimulants, they lose touch with themselves. Their problems, their insecurities mount, and become despondency. The suicides of society cause us to reflect on the terrible trend. . . . And so this week my son said to me, 'For the first time, Dad, I felt like committing suicide.' He said, 'I want to tell you what was on my mind. Maybe it might cause people to care if I jumped off the bridge while you were speaking.' We worked our way through that, but I think that perhaps we should all identify closely with that kind of personal experience, because at one time or other we have all felt the alienation and despair."

Seiden 1979, pp. 116–19. Reprinted by permission
of *Suicide and Life-Threatening Behavior* © 1979.

inclined to kill each other while white youths seem more intent on killing themselves?

In American society, the suicides of two age groups—the old and the young—have attracted the most attention in recent years. To further develop the possible social factors underlying these premature deaths, let us consider in greater detail the self-destructive behaviors of these two socially marginal groups.

Suicides of the Old

Each year between five thousand and eight thousand elderly Americans take their own lives—a number undoubtedly quite conservative given the biases in so recording their cause of death. Between 1948 and 1981, the suicide rate of the American elderly declined 39 percent from a rate of 28.1 to 17.1 suicides per 100,000 individuals sixty-five years of age and older. However, as the 1980s progressed, suicides of the old began increasing. In 1982, the rate rose to 18.3 and increased again to 19.2 the following year (Gottschalk 1986). The National Center for Health Statistics reports that in 1981 there were 28.4 reported suicides for every 100,000 men from sixty-five to seventy-four years old.[15] The rate rose to 41.4 among men seventy-five to eighty-four years old. And for men over eighty-five, the figure jumped to 50.2, 155 percent greater than the rate for men fifteen to twenty-four years of age. Undoubtedly, the true suicide rate of the elderly, particularly elderly white males, is much higher.

For some elderly individuals, suicide is preferable to loneliness, chronic illness, and dependency. Death pacts are becoming more common as the elderly seek alternatives to their painful, slow-motion deaths. Further, there is also indication, given the memberships of such groups as Britain's Exit, that propensity may be positively correlated with education, that with greater

---

 ### Elderly Taking Death into Their Own Hands

Wylie Boyle sent his housekeeper on ahead to the post office that wintry Saturday morning in Paducah, Texas, early this year. Then, as he had every day, the 86-year-old retired insurance salesman went to visit his wife, Avis, at Richards Memorial Hospital.

Mrs. Boyle, 84, suffered from Alzheimer's disease, a progressive, irreversible deterioration of the brain that, over time, can turn simple chores into impossible ones and loved ones into strangers.

That morning a nurse heard a strange sound when she passed by the hospital room, as if an oxygen tank has been overturned. She pushed open the door. There was Mrs. Boyle, a small red stain growing larger on the front of her nightgown.

Boyle, himself with failing eyesight, was sitting in a bedside chair. He had a .38-caliber pistol in his hand. Before anyone could move, he shot himself in the heart. The couple died in seconds.

San Antonio Express-News 1984b. Reprinted by permission of The Associated Press, © 1984.

---

education one is more aware of one's ambiguous role in life (Welsome 1983). As all lives must end, do you prefer to die as a nonperson, forgotten in a nursing home and totally stripped of dignity and independence? Or would you rather take your own life if you see no reason for living? Many of the elderly take a variety of high-powered medicines and are warned of the fatal consequences of too many pills. What if someone with an irreversibly deteriorating condition is found dead in bed some morning? Many doctors will simply investigate no further and list the cause of death as "natural" (Malcolm 1984). If the social system does not wish to improve the lot of the elderly, how long before it will sanction suicide as a solution?

The 1983 suicides of Arthur Koestler and his wife provided an interesting testimonial. Koestler, a noted intellectual, novelist, and anticommunist, belonged to Exit, a British organization founded in 1935 and dedicated to the right to die with dignity. Koestler had written in a publication of the group that, unlike animals, human beings do not expire "peacefully and without fuss in old age." In his 1981 preface to *A Guide to Self-Deliverance,* he wrote, "There is only one prospect worse than being chained to an intolerable existence: the nightmare of a botched attempt to end it" (cited in Blake 1983). Koestler suffered from leukemia and Parkinson's disease. His wife had no known ailments, but, as described by their close friend Melvin Lasky, "their marriage was almost impossibly close; her devotion to him was like no other wife's I have ever seen" (Pace 1983). They were found sitting together dead, both having swallowed the *Guide's* prescribed dosage of poison.

Increasingly, we hear stories in which elderly persons shoot their ailing spouses and then fatally shoot themselves. One spouse who did not commit suicide was seventy-six-year-old Roswell Gilbert, who killed his seventy-three-year-old wife as "an act of love." She suffered from Alzheimer's disease and a painful case of osteoporosis. In May 1985, a Fort Lauderdale, Florida, jury convicted Gilbert of first-degree murder. Though the governor and state cabinet were asked to grant clemency, they were concerned with what that would mean in a state where more than 2 million are older than sixty-five years. Such cases put us in a moral catch-22. Certainly society cannot condone such mercy killings, but common sense tells us that such acts are civilized and humane.

It was in this context that Betty Rollin published in 1985 a controversial book entitled *Last Wish,* in which she describes how she and her husband helped her terminally ill mother to commit suicide. Ida Rollin, at the age of seventy-three, was diagnosed as having ovarian cancer in 1981. After two bouts with chemotherapy, during which she lost her hair, was unable to eat because of an intestinal blockage, and lost control of her bowels, she told her

Woman Gets Suspended Term for Aiding in Sister's Suicide

A 72-year-old woman pleaded no contest to voluntary manslaughter in the death of her ailing sister, who begged for her assistance in committing suicide, and a judge gave her a six-year suspended sentence. If the case had gone to trial, it could have set a legal precedent in North Carolina on the issue of mercy killing.

daughter that she wanted to die. At the time, Rollin said, the doctors gave her mother six months to live. The daughter and her husband phoned physicians across the country, attempting to find out what pills would enable her mother to commit suicide painlessly and with dignity. After considerable searching they found one. Ida swallowed the pills in the presence of her daughter and son-in-law while lying in bed in her Manhattan apartment on October 17, 1983 (Klemesrud 1985).

Rollin toured the country promoting her book, appearing on a number of radio and television call-in shows. Needless to say, some approved of her actions, but religious fundamentalists vehemently objected, saying that the timing of death should be God's decision alone. People felt guilty if they had similarly assisted in the deaths of their parents, and others felt guilty if they had not. This seems to be evidence of basic moral doubt on such issues. Undoubtedly, its resolution would be the result of more mass-media expositions of such cases as that of Karen Ann Quinlan, as well as academic expositions such as this book. Further, religious legitimization would have to be given as well as scientific evidence of lesser pain and greater satisfaction accruing to those who have some control over their ends.

Dorris Porter argues in *Common-Sense Suicide* that the old should have the right to commit suicide. Robert Butler, former head of the National Institute on Aging, said: "It's tragic and shameful that the situation of the elderly in this country is so bad that suicide is even considered an option" (cited in Portwood 1978).

Teen Suicides

Adolescence is a difficult time of considerable body change, of looking into a mirror and trying to recognize oneself. On the springboard of early adulthood, the future holds many insecurities while the present features hyper-regulations that may be felt to control one's destiny. Most studies of childhood and adolescent suicides attribute self-destructive behavior to an inability to cope with stressful situations, to the angry and impulsive behavior often evident at this life stage, and to a belief in the nonfinality of death

(Toolan 1975; Jacobziner 1965). It is also a stage of life in which the fatalistic types of suicides may occur (Maris 1969).

Since 1959, there has been a 300 percent increase in the suicide rate of American teenagers. Self-destructive behaviors in this age group become even more striking when one appreciates that for every actual suicide there are anywhere from fifty to two hundred attempts. Herbert Hendlin observes in *Suicide in America* that the United States now leads the world in the suicide rate of its young men and that its young women are not far behind. Although, according to the international data presented earlier, this is not quite the case, suicide is the third leading cause of death (following accidents and homicides) among individuals aged fifteen to nineteen. Interestingly, though the increase was steady over time, it was not until the suicides of teenagers from the upper middle class were reported that the media belatedly picked up on the "epidemic."[16]

In American culture, the unexpected suicide of a well-off individual generates considerable anxiety. And considerable anxiety has been generated within the past decade. Consider the 1982–84 suicide epidemic involving older adolescents from the affluent suburbs of Dallas, New York, Houston, and Chicago. Within a seventeen-month period between 1979 and 1980, twenty-eight teenagers took their own lives in Chicago's North Shore. In 1983, at least six teenagers in Plano, an affluent white-collar Dallas suburb of 93,000, had taken their lives. That town's suicide rate for every 10,000 fifteen- to nineteen-year-olds was 8, nearly ten times greater than the national average of 0.85. There parents sponsored awareness programs, listened to discussions by experts, dialed suicide hotlines, and began having new and different dialogues with their children. In Putnam Valley, New York, parents and teachers filled a junior high auditorium to discuss why a fourteen-year-old student had hung himself and how to prevent such an occurrence again. But there was a contagion effect. Such is the social disruptiveness of this type of suicide. Had these adolescent suicides occurred among the lower classes, they would barely be newsworthy. But these deaths of those with the most to look forward to in American society shook the very core of the culture and seemed to be a slap in the face of its value system.

Some claimed that these deaths were the result of a certain fear of success, that achievement or the possibility of happiness may mean giving up the past, the most secure part of the self. Or it could be the case that these children of affluence were deprived of the challenges essential for maturity. George Hendry (1984), emeritus professor of theology at the Princeton Theological Seminary, wrote: "we leave our young people, who are on the threshold of maturity, unprepared for the negative elements in life, the sufferings and tragedies, the ambiguities, irrationalities and futilities. And the encounter, when it comes, may shake the foundations of their being and threaten their will to live." Others pointed to adolescent stress and disappointments, whether academic or social. And television, as generally seems to be the case, shared in the blame, supposedly leading children to expect quick answers while undermining their tolerance of frustration.

Longitudinally, there is considerable correlation between the suicide rate of fifteen to twenty-four-year-olds with the rates of divorce, unemployment, and declining church attendance. While such relations can always be spurious, there is evidence of some causal connection. Between 1954 and 1978, the number of divorces per 1000 married women rose from 9.5 to 21.9; the unemployment rate for those aged sixteen to twenty-four climbed from 10.6 percent in 1954 to 18.0 percent in 1982 (the rate of underemployment was probably even higher); and the weekly church attendance rate for those aged eighteen to twenty-nine fell from 48 percent in 1954 to 28 percent in 1973. As these rates for divorce, unemployment, and church attendance have leveled off or reversed since the late 1970s, so, too, has the rate of young suicides (Stack 1986).

Another correlation was noted by psychologist Lee Salk (1985), who observed that the threefold increase in adolescent suicides between the mid-1950s and mid-1980s corresponded with a 50 percent decline in infant mortality. When comparing the birth certificates of fifty-two Rhode Island adolescent suicide victims with a matched sample of youths born in the same hospitals at the same time, Salk and his associates found ten risk factors that the victims were three times more likely than the control group to have in common, including respiratory distress following birth, absence of prenatal care during the first half of the mother's pregnancy, and chronic illness (such as hypertension or kidney disease) in the mother. Salk argues that the increasing rate of teenage suicides may simply be the result of natural selection weeding out the less fit.

Homicide

On one summer day in 1984, James Oliver Huberty entered a San Diego McDonald's wearing camouflage trousers and carrying a 12-gauge shotgun, a 9-millimeter semiautomatic pistol, and what appeared to be a 9-millimeter Uzi semiautomatic rifle with armor-piercing bullets. One witness said that Huberty yelled that he had "killed many in Vietnam and he wanted to kill more." He did. Before being killed himself, Huberty had murdered twenty-one individuals and wounded nineteen others (Cummings 1984). The fast-food establishment, attempting to avoid stigma, was razed.

The initial shock was followed by collective wonder at such senseless

slaughter. As has been the case with other murderers of notoriety, a biographical autopsy was conducted by the mass media.[17] If an individual—often a
later-born son, with a rebellious personality instilled from an authoritarian
family, alienated, possibly sexually dysfunctional, and having a weak superego—senses that the end is near, and if he wants to strike out against society
so as to make others feel as he does himself, perhaps nothing can stop him.

An American's chances of being murdered are greater now than they have
been in many decades. Homicide rates increased more than 122 percent
between 1963 and 1980, making this form of man-made death a national
public health problem. An MIT study based on 1970 homicide rates showed
that Americans living in large metropolitan areas had a greater risk of being
murdered than an American World War II soldier had of being killed in
combat (Koch 1985). One out of ten thousand will die violently each year,
one every twenty-three minutes (Meredith 1984). The odds of an American
being murdered over his or her lifetime is one chance in 133: black men have
a 1-in-21 chance of being murdered,[18] white men a 1-in-131 chance, black
women a 1-in-104 chance, and white women a 1-in-369 chance (New York
Times 1985c). In other words, black men are six times more likely to be murdered than white men (eight times more likely among twenty-five- to thirty-
four-year-olds; Davidson 1985), and black women three times more likely
than their white counterparts. In 1986, according to the FBI's Uniform
Crime Reports, blacks constituted 44.2 percent of all homicide victims,
though comprising less than 12 percent of the total population (Muldor
1988).

Victimization has been not only a matter of race but also a matter of age.
For fifteen- to twenty-four-year-olds, deaths from homicides increased four-
fold between 1950 and 1980 (Brody 1988). In Los Angeles during 1987,
gang warfare claimed four times the number of lives as were lost in the sec-
tarian conflicts of Northern Ireland. Instead of the switchblades of West Side
Story, the estimated seventy thousand members of that city's six hundred
street gangs now prefer Uzi submachine guns and Chinese replications of
the Soviet AK-47 assault rifles (San Antonio Light 1988).

Such truculence in recent times has systematically violated each of the lay-
ers of reality connecting the self with the broader society. First, there has
been the violation of the private spheres of self, the murders occurring at
home (40 percent of the total) at the hands of either robbers or misfits such
as Charles Manson. With the Huberty assassination and terrorism have come
the violations of the community sphere; the taken-for-granted security of
shopping malls and other public spaces has been shattered for many when
violated by homicide.

Finally, death has come to the broad public sphere, as illustrated by the

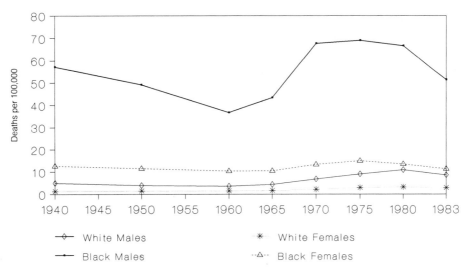

Figure 4.2 Attributes of American murder victims, 1940–1983. Data source: U.S. Bureau of Census, 1987.

Tylenol poisonings of 1982, once again demonstrating how greater social interdependencies make more individuals vulnerable to the whims of any psychopath. The poisoning of random capsules in Chicago and the copycat tamperings elsewhere made America's leading painkiller the object of near hysterical fear, disrupting the public trust and confidence in the entire social order. Earlier, in the 1970s, this collective vulnerability was revealed in a series of aircraft hijackings. Whereas historically approximately one-third of homicides involved intimates (family members or lovers), another third occurred between acquaintances (friends, coworkers), and the final third was between strangers, the recent increases have primarily been in the latter category (Meredith 1984, p. 44). In fact, an estimated four thousand Americans are killed annually in apparently motiveless murders (Lindsey 1984).[19]

Not many species murder their own kind. So where do we look for the reasons? To the psyches of individuals or to the nefarious forces within society? Most killings occur on the spur of the moment, often during a quarrel, which would seem to indicate that personality and situational factors are at work. But nearly four out of five countries reporting their homicide rates to the United Nations are lower, in some cases much lower, than the United States, giving evidence of sociocultural origins. In New York City alone, for instance, there are twice as many homicides annually as in all of Japan (Lamm 1987, p. 34). Countries with higher rates include Mexico, Nicaragua, and South Africa. There is little question that the general availability of

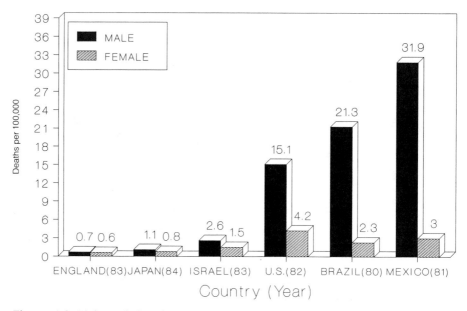

Figure 4.3 Male and female homicide rates for selected countries. Data source: United Nations, 1987.

firearms is one factor shaping this homicidal ethos of American culture: handguns were involved in the murders of 11,522 Americans in 1980, compared with 77 in Japan, 23 in Israel, 8 in Britain and Canada, and only 4 in Australia (Raskin 1985).[20] Another factor probably involves our tradition of violence.

As is evident in Figure 4.3, the United States, indeed, has a violent culture. Not even its leaders are immune: from Washington through Reagan, ten of the thirty-nine chief executives had been attacked by armed assailants, and four of them died.[21] In the week following John Hinkley's attempt to assassinate Reagan, there was a 300 percent increase in the number of death threats received by the White House. This ethos of violence and death is built into "Wild West" legends, with their famous shoot-outs at high noon when men "talked with their guns." But in actuality, according to historian Roger McGrath (1985), frontier violence was quantitatively and qualitatively different from the violence patterns of today. In his analysis of Bodie, Colorado, a notorious boomtown nearly a century ago, McGrath found a higher homicide rate but lower rates of robberies, burglary, juvenile crime, and rape than is the case today. Generally, violence occurred between willing combatants or was directed toward things, such as stagecoaches and trains, and did not affect women, the old, the young, or the infirm (1985, p. 26). In other words, the mythology of the Old West may be but a projection of the present. Violence, quite simply, has become a culturally acceptable option for dealing with frustrations. When, in the winter of 1985, a Goddard, Kansas, junior high school student could no longer take the abuses of his classmates or the indifference of his school's administrators, he went to school armed and began a search-and-destroy mission, Rambo-style. One can now even "murder" one's friends for fun: throughout the country by the mid-1980s, there emerged Photon franchises where individuals could shoot at each other with laser beams in a science-fiction environment.

Not only have murders become more prevalent, but they have also become more brutal in form and mindless in motive. Observing the indifferent and indiscriminate murders by young black men (although blacks comprise only 12 percent of the U.S. population, they commit approximately one-half of all homicides; Levin and Fox 1985, p. 51), a retired black New York homicide detective remarked: "It appears that they don't have any idea of the consequences of taking someone's life. When you get a guy to 'fess up as to why he did it, you get very shoddy answers: 'He took my coat.' 'He took my dollar.' 'He stepped on my girlfriend's foot'" (Stengel 1985, p. 33). Perhaps

The vigilantes get their man: After an eight-hour gunfight, a sheriff's posse surrounds wounded Wells Fargo bandit John Sontag at Sampson's Flats, California, in the late 1800s. Brown Brothers.

Table 4.3 Homicide Rates for the Fifty Largest U.S. Standard Metropolitan Statistical Areas (1980)

Rank	City	Rate	Rank	City	Rate
				Rates per 100,000	
1	Miami	34.3	27	Washington D.C.	10.7
2	Houston	28.1	28	San Francisco–Oakland	10.6
3	New Orleans	25.5	29	Phoenix	10.4
4	LA–Long Beach	23.7	30	San Diego	10.0
5	New York City	20.5	31	Sacramento	9.7
6	Memphis	19.8	32	Greensboro–Winston Salem–	9.5
7	Birmingham	19.7		High Point	
8	Dallas–Ft. Worth	19.3	33	Tampa–St. Petersburg	9.1
9	St. Louis	18.0	34	Denver–Boulder	9.0
10	Ft. Lauderdale–Hollywood	17.7	35	Buffalo	8.6
11	San Antonio	17.4	36	San Jose	7.9
11	Cleveland	17.4	37	Anaheim–Santa Ana–	7.1
13	Detroit	17.1		Garden Grove	
14	Chicago	16.8	38	Hartford	6.8
15	Atlanta	15.9	39	Cincinnati	6.6
16	Kansas City	15.5	40	Portland, Ore.	6.4
17	Riverside–San Bernardino–	14.2	41	Milwaukee	6.3
	Ontario		41	Seattle–Everett	6.3
18	Nashville–Davidson	14.1	43	Providence–Warwick–Pawtucket	5.9
19	Baltimore	13.0	44	Boston	5.1
20	Dayton	12.8	45	Salt Lake City	4.9
20	Philadelphia	12.8	46	Pittsburgh	4.8
22	Oklahoma City	12.7	47	Rochester	4.6
23	Louisville	11.9	48	Nassau–Suffolk	4.4
24	Indianapolis	11.3	49	Minneapolis–St. Paul	3.9
25	Newark	10.9	50	Columbus	1.8
26	Norfolk–Va. Beach–Portsmouth	10.9			

Source: Statistical Resources Branch, Division of Vital Statistics, National Center for Health Statistics.

all of the unemployment, drugs, antichild sentiment, poverty, and relative inequities of the society have produced a new individual, one whose tremendous self-hatred is projected onto others like oneself (only 10 percent of the single-victim homicides in the United States are committed across racial lines; Levin and Fox 1985, p. 51) and whose only sense of self-importance is derived from controlling their deaths. As Alvin Poussaint notes, "Violence can be a potent drug for the oppressed person. Reacting to the futility of his life, the individual derives an ultimate sense of power when he holds the fate of another human being in his hands" (1972, p. 72).

From this cultural climate a new kind of killer has emerged, the mass killer, whose name is often more widely known than those of recent vice-presidents. They conduct their evil across cities and states, selecting as their victims random individuals, toward whom they hold no animosity, or they remain in their communities to bask in the attention given to their crimes. Between the mid-1970s and mid-1980s, law enforcement officials reported more than thirty cases in which a single killer had murdered six or more individuals; between 1979 and 1983, there were at least seventeen men who had killed a minimum of ten individuals each and at least nine who had killed more than twenty (Lindsey 1984). Some, like James Huberty, James Whitman (an ex-marine who, in 1966, killed fourteen people from a University of Texas tower after murdering his mother and wife), Richard Speck (who shot and stabbed eight student nurses to death in Chicago in 1966), and Patrick Henry Sherrill (a disgruntled Oklahoma postal worker who, having discovered in 1986 that he was about to be terminated, vented his frustrations on his work colleagues, killing fourteen), have one murderous frenzy. Others, like Theodore Bundy (an intelligent and good-looking man in his mid-twenties who traveled coast to coast bludgeoning coeds to death during the mid-

Having just escaped from the Marin County Hall of Justice, a wild-eyed William Arthur Christmas, a San Quentin convict, holds a revolver to the head of a hostage on August 8, 1970. Deputy District Attorney Gary Thomas (far right) and Maria Graham (second from right) were critically wounded in an ensuing shootout that left three dead. UPI/Bettman Newsphotos.

1970s), John Wayne Gacy (a Chicago homosexual accused in 1980 of killing thirty-three young boys), and Juan Corona (a California farm contractor who killed more than twenty-five migrant workers over a period of years), are serial killers.

The aberrance of these individuals has stimulated a rich literature of psychiatric speculation and case histories, focusing on such things as neurological disorders, childhood symptomatologies, family background, the influence of artificial food coloring and flavorings, and the sexual aspects of violent acts. Particularly frustrating, however, has been the general inability of experts to detect any common denominators underlying the personality profiles of these killers. Whereas 45 percent of homicide arrestees are under the age of twenty-five, 85 percent of the mass murderers Levin and Fox (1985, p. 59) identified are older; 80 percent are white; and only one-quarter of their crimes occur in the South, where more than 42 percent of the nation's homicides are normally committed. Often being quite intelligent, and apparently random in their violence, these mass murderers are extremely difficult to apprehend.

Anthropologist Elliott Leyton (1986) claims that the phenomenon involves more social-psychological dynamics. He argues that these serial killers suffer from profound status frustration, directing their violence toward representatives of the social class that either excludes them or threatens their status. During the early phases of capitalism, they often were new members of the middle class who punished "the lower orders who threatened their morbid sensitivity to their class position" (1986, p. 277). Nowadays, their vengeance is directed against those perceived to be frustrating their aspirations for upward mobility, such as lower-middle-class men seeking upper-middle-class respectability.

In sum, the realization that a kindly neighbor, friendly work acquaintance, or even the president of the city's Jaycees can potentially lose control and become one of these contemporary Dr. Jekyll–Mr. Hydes has done much to dissolve the bonds of trust between community members.

Accidental Death

Accidental death is no less sociological than suicide or homicide even if we consider those deaths over which individuals have no control, such as natural disasters. Only cancer, heart disease, and stroke kill more Americans than accidents. For those one to thirty-eight years of age, accidents are the leading cause of death (*New York Times* 1984c) and account for 60 percent of all adolescent deaths (Goleman 1987). And yet such endings perhaps remain the most equivocal of all. In plotting these deaths on Shneidman's scale of subintentionality, fewer would be scored as "no personal control" than might be suspected. In addition, as we will see, the ability to socially control and predict such deaths contributes to the fueling of a culture's death denials while simultaneously enhancing the confidence its members have in its basic institutions.

Consider the spectrum of deaths categorized as accidental: a rock climber loses his footing and falls one thousand feet; a private plane stalls out following the failure of its engine; a contaminated can of salmon kills a family of three; a young swimmer drowns; an older driver hits and kills a jaywalker; a grizzly bear mauls a camper. Certainly each of these is theoretically preventable: the climber may have known the mountain exceeded his skills; the maintenance of the aircraft's engine could have been double-checked; the child in the water could have received better adult supervision; the contaminated can could have been recalled by its packers; the skills and vision of the older driver could have been tested by the state license examiners; rangers, observing the scarcity of food for the park's bears, could have closed the campsites. Having less apparent intentionality than either homicide or suicide, this broad category of death is less stigmatizing for survivors. But the rate of such fatal accidents varies considerably, providing evidence of social factors underlying their occurrence.

 The States Where It Is Safest to Live

The safest state in which to live is New Jersey—and the most dangerous is Wyoming. This is revealed in figures recently released by the National Safety Council, which says New Jersey residents are involved in fewer accidents than people in any other state.

Generally speaking, says the council, the Northeast is the safest part of the country. In the South and Midwest, people are more likely to die in accidents on the road, at home and at work. . . . While an average of 40.2 people out of every 100,000 died accidentally in the U.S. in 1982, only 10.9 died by accident in New Jersey. In Wyoming, however, the accident rate is 89.2 for 100,000.

Accidental death rates after New Jersey are: New York, 26.3; Rhode Island, 28.5; Delaware, 28.7; Maryland, 30.0; New Hampshire, 30.7; Hawaii and Ohio, 31.6; Minnesota, 31.8 and Illinois, 32.0. The nine most dangerous states after Wyoming are: New Mexico, 68.2; Nevada, 64.8; Montana, 61.9; Georgia, 60.5; South Dakota, 59.9; Mississippi, 59.3; Idaho, 57.6; Oklahoma, 56.4; and Louisiana, 53.9.

One major accomplishment of modernization has been to minimize accidental deaths (between 1913 and 1982, the American accidental death rate
per 100,000 individuals declined 52 percent, from 81.6 to 38.9), particularly those occurring as a result of acts of nature. Warnings of the National
Weather Service have unquestionably reduced the death toll from tornadoes,
hurricanes, and dramatic shifts in the weather. The ability of the Chinese to
predict the 1975 earthquake in the Haicheng area saved the lives of thousands; their failure to predict the massive Tangshan quake the following year
led to the deaths of more than eight hundred thousand. Here enters the
political significance of controlling accidental deaths (see Chapter 8). Modern political systems go through elaborate rituals to prevent their occurrence,
assisting the death repressions of the citizenry by fireproofing infant sleep-
wear, requiring health warnings to be affixed to cigarette packages, overseeing the purity of pharmaceuticals, monitoring planes in the air, and mandat-
ing the use of seat belts in private automobiles.[22] Fearing that such disasters
could reveal regime inadequacies, the Soviet Union does not report Russian
air disasters or deaths from natural disasters, although it assiduously details
those of the United States.

While accidental deaths caused by nature have decreased, those caused by
people have separate historical cycles of rise and fall following the introduction of each technological innovation. As recently as 1984, one hundred
Americans died from telephone-related injuries (Llorente 1985). Auto fatalities, for example, first rose during the period of product introduction, but
with the institutionalization of safety procedures, from seat belts to speed
limits, the death rates eventually declined.[23] In 1925, there were 18.2 deaths
per 100 million vehicle miles; in 1950, the rate had dropped to 7.59; by
1984, it had declined to 2.68.[24] One of the most dramatic instances involves
the collective accidental deaths occurring during airline disasters, the worst
of which was in 1977 when two 747s collided on a runway in the Canary
Islands, killing 583. And 1985 was the year of the jumbo jet crashes: 329
perished when an Air-India 747 crashed into the sea off the Irish coast; 520
died when a Japan Air Lines Boeing 747 crashed into a mountain near
Tokyo; and in Dallas, a Lockheed L-1011 missed landing at the airport during a violent thunderstorm, killing 130. Nearly two thousand people were
killed that year in scheduled airline flights worldwide, almost doubling the
number of the previous year and more than in any other single year.[25]

Sociologist David Phillips has established a reputation for demonstrating
relationships between fatal accidents and other forms of premature death.
Examining motor vehicle fatalities in the state of California between 1966
and 1973, he found a 9 percent increase in the week following publicized
suicide stories, after controlling for the days of the week (Saturday, followed

Table 4.4 Compliance with Seat-Belt Laws

	Date of law	Usage before law	Usage shortly after	Usage Feb. 1986
New York	Dec. 1984	16%	70%	46%
New Jersey	Mar. 1985	18	70	45
Michigan	July 1985	26	59	44
Illinois	July 1985	16	40	29
Nebraska	Sept. 1985	26	46	53

Source: U.S. Department of Transportation and state highway departments (Wong 1986).

by Sunday and Friday, has the highest rate of fatal auto accidents), the month, and whether there is a holiday weekend (Phillips 1977). In fact, Phillips discovered that not only did auto deaths increase by 31 percent three days after such suicide stories, but their numbers multiplied with greater media coverage. He also found that the type of suicide publicized correlated with the type of auto accident: the ratio of single- to multiple-vehicle accidents increased after a story of a straight suicide but decreased when the story described a suicide following a murder. On the other hand, multiple-vehicle accidents involving passenger deaths, as well as deaths from both noncommercial and commercial plane crashes (Phillips 1980),[26] became more frequent following these murder-suicide stories and less frequent when the story was of a pure suicide (Phillips 1979). Such accidental deaths imply that suggestion has a role in triggering their occurrence.

In addition, we need to take into account the fact that many individuals simply refuse to take advantage of lifesaving information and technology or enjoy flirting with life-threatening situations, such as by climbing the facades of buildings, hang gliding, crossing the Atlantic alone in small crafts, or skiing out of control. Table 4.4 shows how the passage of mandatory automobile seat-belt laws—supposedly based on findings indicating diminished rates of death and injury when belts are used properly—has failed to produce universal compliance. Despite national rituals of accidental death avoidance, personal factors will still lead individuals to flirt with deadly situations.

Conclusion

This chapter gave a glimpse of the relationship between how death typically punctuates the lives of society's members and the resultant ethos toward life-and-death matters. With modernization, as death has basically been confined to the elderly, there has been a shift in the focus of the death ethos from premature to postmature demises. Instead of an *Ars Moriendi* for coping with externally caused, premature, and uncontrollable deaths, there has arisen the death-with-dignity movement with recipes for personal control over "on-time," controllable, good deaths.

However, without the traditional solaces, the social frustrations surrounding the increasingly rare deaths of children have been heightened, particularly for those dying of terminal diseases. Their deaths evoke one of the few instances of communitywide outpourings of sentiment. For those denied a "full life," we allow wishes to be granted, extravagant trips to be taken, and special camps to be provided. One terminally ill Hispanic youth wanted to dance on television with the Solid Gold Dancers. His dream came true following considerable newspaper publicity of his story in his native Dallas. Such privileges are not granted to terminally ill adults. Between 1982 and 1985, there were similar tales of thirty-seven children (eighteen males and nineteen females, ranging in age from five to nineteen, median age 12.6) reported in nineteen stories in the *New York Times* and the *Houston Post*. In the early 1980s there emerged such groups as the Sunshine Kids, Young Fighters, and A Child's Wish Come True. Camp Good Days and Special Times began in 1980 to provide camping experiences and support groups for children with cancer. By 1985, A Child's Wish Come True, Inc., had helped more than three hundred chronically ill children realize their dreams, whether attending a professional football game or visiting Disneyland.

Of those other deaths that do occur prematurely, there has been a historic increase in the proportion over which the victim has some control: as opposed to dying prematurely because of disease or attack by some predatory creature, individuals now are killed by homicide, technology-related accidents, or suicide. These are the causes of more than three-quarters of all deaths of those fifteen to twenty-four years of age in the United States and are the reasons why this age group is the only one experiencing an increase in mortality since 1960 (Goleman 1987). In fact, American teenagers are as likely to die before their twentieth birthday now as they were in the 1940s and 1950s (Brody 1988). As is often the case, because of human nature, it is often the victim who is blamed. However, social research is discovering that it may be the social system that is at fault, that homicides are spawned by a culture of violence, and that suicides result from a social system that fails to give certain of its members a meaning to exist. No longer is death perceived to be the "great leveler" but rather is understood as some class-linked probability.

When considering the comparatively lower suicide rates of American blacks compared to whites, Jules Henry observed that "the culture of the very poor is a *flight from death*" (1965, p. 33). Without hope for the upward mobility of oneself or one's children, the temporal focus is on the here and now as individuals "concentrate on those experiences which give [them] continual and vivid reassurance that [they are] alive—heightened perhaps and smoothed by drugs or aicohol" (Henry 1965, p. 33). Although bearing surface similarities to hedonism, such life-styles are not devoted to living for pleasure but rather simply fleeing from death. The upper classes, too, flee from death, such as by consuming the latest elixirs from science or, in the case of pop superstar Michael Jackson, sleeping in a glass, coffinlike, oxygen-enriched, $125,000 hyperbaric chamber. But upper-class deaths are something abstract, natural, unintended, and in the future.

One theme emerging from these analyses of the timing and forms of death is Shneidman's notion of subintentioned death. Such deaths cannot be conceptualized as having a single underlying dimension of suicidal tendencies (e.g., cigarette smokers are more cowardly in managing their suicidal tendencies than are wrist slashers). What about those filling society's high-mortality occupations, such as the test pilots portrayed in Tom Wolfe's *The Right Stuff* or those who flirt with death by mountain climbing, hang gliding, or parachuting? Certainly in addition to conceptualizing, say, a subintended "accidental" death in terms of a suicidal proclivity, we need to consider the varying degrees to which individuals may need to feel alive by putting themselves in dangerous, possibly deadly, situations. Perhaps this additional psychological need underlies part of society's embracing of the automobile; simply attempting to make a left turn during rush hour can provide all of this kind of stimulation that many Americans need.[27]

But, again, most deaths occur to those who have lived full lives. Because of the historical recency of this allotment of time, the elderly can be perceived as pioneers in time, exploring the temporal limits of their biochemistry. Those now old are trailblazing a new stage of the life cycle whose mythology portrays it as the time one "earns" for individualism, self-actualization, and fulfillment. Retirement and leisure have become the cultural consolations for those who must die. Instead of exploring the West in covered wagons, this generation of older persons is exploring the end of time in retirement communities, senior centers, old-age groups (such as the American Association of Retired Persons), and nursing homes, with the physician acting as trail-guide (Kearl 1985).

Thus far, we have considered how the cultural orientation toward life and death is shaped by who dies and how they die, as well as where and when. The chapters that follow will develop the institutional action systems that also contribute to the death meaning system. Death fears, for example, are a function not only of the deaths one normally encounters but also of one's death understandings as shaped by religious depictions of the hereafter or political portrayals of the lethal intentions of a political regime's adversaries.

NOTES

1. The early Greeks appreciated this distinction between good deaths and bad deaths, incorporating it into their lexicon: *thanatos* (natural death due to old age) and *ker* (the spirit of violent death and death by disease).

2. One wonders about the even greater immortal stature Winston Churchill or Dwight Eisenhower would have achieved had they died two decades earlier than they did.

3. According to a 1985 study at the Centers for Disease Control, the death rate from pregnancy-related causes among women thirty-five and older was halved between 1974–78 and 1982. Although women of this age still have three times the likelihood of dying, this scientific finding removes death from the planning concerns of even the older parents.

4. Consider the Karen Ann Quinlan story and the considerable press attention given it. For every Karen Ann, how many elderly patients are there, existing in the contemporary limbo between the worlds of the living and the dead? But her death was ironic in that it was both premature, because of her young age, and yet postmature, in that she had been socially dead for a decade.

5. Fewer people are dying before the age of sixty-five, according to the federal Centers for Disease Control. Monitoring what they call "years of potential life lost" by Americans who die before their sixty-fifth birthdays, health researchers found the total number of years lost because of early death dropped 3 percent from 1982 to 1983, from 9.43 million years to 9.17 million (*New York Times* 1985a). In 1960, 55 percent of all male deaths in the United States occurred among those sixty-five years of age and older (Blauner 1966).

6. To puruse this indicator status farther, the great number of elderly dying in nursing home fires indicates our real concerns about the place of the old, and their victimization by crime rates is a measure of the degree of community cohesion.

7. Huntington's disease, described by one victim's spouse as like having Alzheimer's and cancer, is certainly another form of bad death. With developments in genetic deciphering, individuals can now be tested to see if they will develop and die of the disease. The ambivalence of high-risk persons toward being tested is a modern analogy of the Puritans' obsession with (and fears of) discovering whether or not they were among the elect.

8. South Dakota, the state with the lowest white infant mortality rate (0.8), has the highest nonwhite rate (1.9).

9. In Bangladesh, one study found that when a mother dies in childbirth her infant has a 95 percent chance of dying within a year (Brooke 1987).

10. Edward Shorter describes how this decrease in maternal death was largely an urban phenomenon, where the rates declined sooner and faster. In London, for

instance, the rate dropped from 24 per 1000 births in the late sixteenth century to 12 per 1000 by the late eighteenth and to 4 per 1000 by the 1830s (1982, p. 99).

11. Even after more than two decades, the cause of Marilyn Monroe's 1962 death still remains controversial. In 1985, the Los Angeles police attempted to quell allegations that she had been murdered by releasing a once-confidential report. Another rumor still persisting holds that there was a huge cover-up, as then–Attorney General Robert Kennedy had supposedly been with her at the time of her death.

12. Following the Soviet nuclear reactor disaster in Chernobyl, there surfaced considerable fears of radiation poisoning. Such death fears are interesting, particularly in light of the fact that no one in the United States has ever died as a result of the operation of a commercial nuclear power plant, while tens of thousands annually perish on the nation's highways. Observed Professor Norman Rasmussen of MIT, "People hate to contemplate dying in strange ways. This makes a thing like radiation seem all the more menacing" (Wilford 1986).

13. The sex differences in mortality rates may be a result of preventable, man-made causes, specifically the use of tobacco. Gus Miller and Dean Gerstein, in studying eight thousand residents of Erie County, Pennsylvania, found that 90 percent of the sex difference observed in death rates can be ascribed to smoking. The other 10 percent difference was partially a result of homicides and accidents (*Science 83* 1983).

14. Before taking off, the Japanese kamikaze pilots attended their own funerals. Garbed in burial robes, they chanted, " . . . and thus for the Emperor I will not die at home." In the air, it became a battle between the fliers who fought to die and boat gunners who fought to live. Curiously, a certain form of immortality was given to these victims of altruistic suicide. American cameras caught their sacrifices on film, giving them at least celluloid immortality.

15. This compares with the total American civilian suicide rate of 11.9 per 100,000 population in 1980, 12.0 in 1981, 12.2 in 1982, and 12.4 in 1983.

16. Actually, 1977 was the peak year of suicides for those aged fifteen to twenty-four, when the rate was 13.3 per 100,000 individuals in that age category. In 1980, it was 12.3, and in 1983 the rate dropped to 11.9, according to the National Center for Health Statistics.

17. Medical autopsies are conducted as well. A University of Florida researcher has been conducting experiments on the brains of executed prisoners, without the permission of the prisoners or their families, to determine whether childhood head traumas are related to later aggressive behavior (*Seattle Times/Post Intelligencer* 1985).

18. In the fifteen years between 1965 and 1980, the homicide rates for young white males tripled, from 4.9 per 100,000 to more than 15.5. Nevertheless, four out of ten homicide victims in the United States are black (Stengel 1985). Homicide is the leading cause of death among American black males between the ages of fifteen and twenty-four (to thirty-nine years by some estimates; Meredith 1984). For a black man who dies between the ages of twenty and twenty-four, the chance that his life ended in homicide is greater than 1 in 3 (*New York Times* 1984d).

19. Richard Ramirez, the accused "night stalker" who terrified Californians during

the mid-1980s by randomly killing as many as twenty individuals, told a prison guard, "I love to kill people. I love watching people die" (Chambers 1986).

20. Of the thirty-three thousand Americans killed by handguns in 1982, according to the National Center for Health Statistics, 50 percent were classified as suicides, 42 percent were homicides, and only about 5 percent were listed as unintentional or accidental. In the fifteen-to-thirty-four age group, guns were the second leading cause of death following traffic accidents. For all ages, firearms are involved in two-thirds of all homicides and about three-fifths of all suicides (Eilers 1986). And this trend has been increasing: in 1961, 52.5 percent of murders and nonnegligent manslaughters were committed with firearms, climbing to 65.4 percent in 1970 and 67.9 percent by 1974.

21. Andrew Jackson (1835, attacked by a psychotic who thought himself to be King Richard III of England); Abraham Lincoln (1865, killed by actor John Wilkes Booth, a Southern sympathizer); James Garfield (1881, shot by a radical member of the Republican party and died two months later); William McKinley (1901, killed by an anarchist); Theodore Roosevelt (1912, wounded in the chest by a man claiming to be guided by McKinley's ghost); Franklin Delano Roosevelt (1933, a barrage of bullets killed his companion, Chicago mayor Anton Cermak, in an open car); Harry S. Truman (1950, Puerto Rican nationalists gunned their way into Blair House, where Truman was staying); John F. Kennedy (1963, killed by Lee Harvey Oswald, a suspected pro-Castro radical); Gerald Ford (1975, shot at in two separate incidents within one week, first by a female Charles Manson cult member and then by a female political activist and midlife sufferer); and Ronald Reagan (1981, wounded by John Hinkley).

22. Kastenbaum and Aisenberg observe: "Excessive concern with accidental death must be equivalent to insufficient concern with natural death. . . . It is the inevitability of death that is at the root of our behavior. . . . What simpler way to repress the consciousness of his own mortality than by concentrating on those who die in 'unlucky' accidents in avoidable situations?" (1972, pp. 240–41).

23. The number of people who died in motor vehicle accidents declined in 1983, helping to reduce the death rate for all accidents in the United States to the lowest level in seventy years, according to the National Safety Council. The accidental death rate in 1983 was 38.9 per 100,000, 4 percent lower than the 1982 rate. In 1913, the first year the council tabulated these statistics, the rate was 81.6 per 100,000 (*New York Times* 1984c). Nevertheless, auto accidents are the fifth leading cause of death (U.S. Public Health Service 1974).

24. During the first five years of the 55-mph speed limit (1975–80), the death rate actually increased from 3.45 to 3.50 deaths per 100 million vehicle miles. And the fatality rate on the interstates in 1984 was less than a third that on other roads (1.2 vs. 3.72) (Mancuso 1986). Nevertheless, auto accidents still killed 45,700 people in 1985, according to the National Safety Council.

25. Ironically, the year that saw the greatest death toll in commercial aviation also brought the discovery of the wreck of the supposedly unsinkable *Titanic*, one of the great symbols of collective accidental death. For weeks, photos of the ship in its

watery grave of seventy-three years filled the news. It would take the simultaneous destruction of four 747s to equal the death toll of this famous accident.

26. In his study of plane crashes, Phillips limited himself to those murder-suicide stories occurring in the United States between 1968 and 1973, where there was one murderer acting alone killing two or more victims, where both the suicide casualty and his murdered victims died within two days, and where the story was covered on the front page of the *New York Times* or *Los Angeles Times* and/or on the ABC, CBS, or NBC evening news.

27. Pursuing this logic further, consider the relationship between the American teenager and the automobile. Is there any relationship among their high auto fatality rate, their tendency to experiment with illegal substances, and their relatively high rate of suicide attempts?

REFERENCES

Ariès, Phillippe. 1974. *Western Attitudes toward Death: From the Middle Ages to the Present.* Baltimore: Johns Hopkins University Press.

Barron, James. 1984. "Black Men as Breadwinners Losing Ground, Study Says." *New York Times.* August 1, p. 6.

Blake, Patricia. 1983. "Going Gentle into That Good Night." *Time.* March 21, p. 85.

Blauner, R. 1966. "Death and Social Structure." *Psychiatry* 29:378–94.

Boffey, Philip. 1985. "Alzheimer's Disease: Families Are Bitter." *New York Times.* May 7, pp. C1, C6.

Boyd, Jeffrey. 1983. "The Increasing Rate of Suicide by Firearms." *New England Journal of Medicine* 308(15):872–74.

Brody, Jane. 1988. "Trip across Adolescence Is Just as Risky as Ever." *New York Times.* March 3, p. 14.

Brooke, James. 1987. "3d World Worry: Fatal Childbirth." *New York Times.* February 14, p. 4.

Butler, Robert. 1975. *Why Survive? Being Old in America.* New York and Evanston, Ill.: Harper & Row.

Chambers, Marcia. 1986. "Suspect is Quoted: I Love to Watch People Die." *New York Times.* May 9, p. 11.

Cowley, Malcolm. 1980. *The View from Eighty.* New York: Viking Press.

Cumming, Elaine, and W. Henry. 1961. *Growing Old.* New York: Basic Books.

Cummings, Judith. 1984. "Neighbors Term Mass Slayer a Quiet but Hotheaded Loner." *New York Times.* July 20, pp. 1, 7.

Davidson, Joe. 1985. "U.S. Study Cites 'Distressing Disparity' in Health Conditions for Blacks, Whites." *Wall Street Journal.* October 15, p. 5.

Dempsey, David. 1975. *The Way We Die: An Investigation of Death and Dying in America Today.* New York: McGraw-Hill.

Durkheim, Emile. 1951. *Suicide.* Glencoe, Ill.: Free Press.

Eilers, Robert. 1986. "People Who Die Because a Gun Is Available." *New York Times.* August 4, p. 16.

Ellner, Melvyn. 1977. "Research on International Suicide." *International Journal of Social Psychiatry* 23:187–94.

Fulton, Robert. 1976. *Death and Identity*. Bowie, Md.: Charles Press.

Goleman, Daniel. 1985. "Clues to Suicide: A Brain Chemical Is Implicated." *New York Times*. October 8, pp. 17, 18.

———. 1987. "Teen-Age Risk-Taking: Rise in Deaths Prompts New Research Effort." *New York Times*. November 24, pp. 13, 16.

Gottschalk, Earl Jr. 1986. "After Years of Decline, Suicide Rate Is Rising among Elderly in U.S." *Wall Street Journal*. July 30, pp. 1, 7.

Greenberg, J. 1982. "Suicide Linked to Brain Chemical Deficit." *Science News* 121(22):355.

Haywood, Charles. 1984. "Suicide as an Act of Violence Is on the Rise." *New York Times*. November 28, p. 24 (letter to ed.).

Hendlin, Herbert. 1982. *Suicide in America*. New York: W. W. Norton.

Hendry, George. 1984. "Possible Reasons for Teen-Age Suicide." *New York Times*. November 16, p. 31.

Henry, Jules. 1965. "White People's Time, Colored People's Time: Of Hope, Achievement, and Time in the Lower Class." *Trans-action* 2(3):31–34.

Hochschild, Arlie. 1973. *The Unexpected Community*. Englewood Cliffs, N.J.: Prentice-Hall.

Jacoby, Susan. 1974. "Waiting for the End: On Nursing Homes." *New York Times Magazine*. March 31, pp. 13–15, 76–93.

Jacobziner, H. 1965. "Attempted Suicides in Adolescence." *Journal of the American Medical Association* 191:7–11.

Kalish, Richard. 1976. "Death and Dying in a Social Context." In Richard Binstock and Ethel Shanas, eds., *Handbook of Aging and the Social Sciences*. New York: Van Nostrand Reinhold, pp. 483–507.

Kalish, R., and D. Reynolds. 1974. *Death and Ethnicity: A Psychocultural Study*. Los Angeles: University of Southern California Press.

Kastenbaum, Robert, and Ruth Aisenberg. 1972. *The Psychology of Death*. New York: Springer.

Kearl, Michael. 1985. "The Aged as Pioneers in Time: On Temporal Discontinuities, Biographical Closure, and the Medicalization of Old Age." In Charles Gaitz, George Niederehe, and Nancy Wilson, eds., *Aging 2000: Our Health Care Destiny, Vol. II: Psychosocial and Policy Issues*. New York: Springer-Verlag, pp. 43–59.

Keleman, Stanley. 1974. *Living Your Dying*. New York: Random House.

King, Wayne. 1983. "Deaths Laid to Nursing Home Pose Aid Payment Questions." *New York Times*. April 4, pp. 1, 11.

Klemesrud, Judy. 1985. "Daughter's Story: Aiding Mother's Suicide." *New York Times*. September 9, p. 17.

Koch, Edward. 1985. "Death and Justice." *New Republic*. April 15, pp. 12–15.

Kunz, P. R., and J. Summers. 1979–80. "A Time to Die: A Study of the Relationships of Birthdays and Time of Death." *Omega* 10(4):281–89.

Lamm, Richard. 1987. "The Uncompetitive Society." *Dartmouth Alumni Magazine.*
    May, pp. 32–36.

Lerner, M. 1970. "When, Why and Where People Die." In O. G. Brim, H. E. Free-
    man and N. A. Scotch, eds., *The Dying Patient.* New York: Russell Sage
    Foundation.

Levin, Jack, and James Fox. 1985. *Mass Murder: America's Growing Menace.* New
    York and London: Plenum Press.

Lewis, Charles, and Mary An Lewis. 1977. "The Potential Impact of Sexual Equality
    on Health." *New England Journal of Medicine* 297(16):863–69.

Leyton, Elliot. 1986. *Compulsive Killers: The Story of Modern Multiple Murder.* New
    York: Washington Mews Books, New York University Press.

Lindsey, Robert. 1984. "Officials Cite a Rise in Killers Who Roam U.S. for Victims."
    New York Times. January 21, p. 1.

Llorente, Elisabeth. 1985. "Jersey Student's Sudden Death Baffles Forensic Investi-
    gators." *New York Times.* September 11, p. 17.

McGrath, Roger. 1985. "The Myth of Frontier Violence." *Harper's.* February, pp.
    26–28.

Malcolm, Andrew. 1984. "Some Elderly Choose Suicide over Lonely, Dependent
    Life." *New York Times.* September 24, pp. 1, 13.

Mancuso, James. 1986. "Highway Death Rate Has Been Declining since 1925." *New
    York Times.* January 14, p. 26.

Maris, R. W. 1969. *Social Forces in Urban Suicide.* Homewood, Ill.: Dorsey Press.

Markides, K., and R. Machalek. 1982. "Selective Survival, Aging and Society." Paper
    presented at the World Congress of Sociology, Mexico City, August.

Meredith, Nikki. 1984. "The Murder Epidemic." *Science 84.* 5(10):42–48.

Moore, Wilbert E. 1963. *Man, Time and Society.* New York: John Wiley.

Morrow, Lance. 1987. "Kennedy Going on Nixon." *Time.* May 18, p. 90.

Muldor, Christopher. 1988. "Do Black Crime Victims Matter?" *Wall Street Journal.*
    May 9, p. 16.

New York Times. 1978. "Aged in Nursing Home Barred Abortion Aid." April 14.

———. 1979. "Coast Court Rules Insane Person May Not be Held to Be a Suicide."
    September 4, p. A25.

———. 1982. "Woman Gets Suspended Term for Aiding in Sister's Suicide." May
    26, p. 12.

———. 1984a. "Governor Lamm Asserts Elderly, If Very Ill, Have 'Duty to Die.'"
    March 29, p. 12.

———. 1984b. "Boy's Suicide by Hanging at Army Base Shocks Coast Community."
    August 30, p. 8.

———. 1984c. "Accidental Death Rate Drops." October 16, p. 7.

———. 1984d. "Violent Death Rate of 50,000 a Year Cited as U.S. Health Con-
    cern." November 28, p. 14.

———. 1985a. "Americans' Deaths under the Age of 65 Lessen, Centers Say." Jan-
    uary 24, p. 11.

———. 1985b. "Activist Takes Own Life." February 28, p. 20.

————. 1985c. "Odds of Being Murdered Are 1 in 133, Study Says." May 6, p. 11.

Pace Eric. 1983. "Arthur Koestler and Wife Suicides in London." *New York Times.* March 4, pp. 1, 13.

Pear, Robert. 1986. "Stiffer Rules for Nursing Homes Proposed in U.S.-Sponsored Study." *New York Times.* February 24, pp. 1, 9.

Peck, Dennis. 1980–81. "Towards A Theory of Suicide: The Case for Modern Fatalism." *Omega* 11(1):1–14.

Phillips, David. 1972. "Deathday and Birthday: An Unexpected Connection." In J. Tanur, ed., *Statistics: Guide to the Unknown.* San Francisco: Holden-Day, pp. 52–65.

————. 1977. "Motor Vehicle Fatalities Increase Just After Stories about Murder and Suicide." *Science* 196:1464–5.

————. 1979. "Suicide, Motor Vehicle Fatalities, and the Mass Media: Evidence toward a Theory of Suggestion." *American Journal of Sociology* 84(5):1150–74.

————. 1980. "Airplane Accidents, Murder, and the Mass Media: Towards a Theory of Imitation and Suggestion." *Social Forces* 58(4):1001–24.

Phillips, David, and K. Feldman. 1973. "A Dip in Deaths before Ceremonial Occasions: Some New Relationships between Social Integration and Mortality." *American Sociological Review* 38:678–96.

Pierce, A. 1967. "The Economic Cycle and the Social Suicide Rate." *American Sociological Review* 32(3):457–62.

Portwood, Doris. 1978. "A Right to Suicide?" *Psychology Today.* January, pp. 66–76.

Poussaint, Alvin. 1972. *Why Blacks Kill Blacks.* New York: Emerson Hall.

Powys, John. 1944. *The Art of Growing Old.* London: Jonathan Cape.

Preston, Samuel H. 1976. *Mortality Patterns in National Populations.* New York: Academic Press.

————. 1984. "Children and the Elderly in the U.S." *Scientific American* 251(6):44–49.

Raskin, Julius. 1985. "We're Killing One Another at a Great Rate." *New York Times.* April 9, p. 26.

Rollin, Betty. 1985. *Last Wish.* New York: Linden Press/Simon & Schuster.

Salk, Lee, et al. 1985. "Relationship of Maternal and Perinatal Conditions to Eventual Adolescent Suicide." *Lancet* (March 16).

San Antonio Express-News. 1984a. "The States Where It Is Safest to Live." April 15, p. 2 of *San Antonio Star* supplement.

————. 1984b. "Elderly Taking Death into Their Own Hands." November 11, p. 1L.

————. 1985. "Experts: Suicide Serious Public Health Problem." June 21, p. 13A.

San Antonio Light. 1986. "Report Targets Nursing Homes." May 21, p. A3.

————. 1987. "Suicide Is No. 5 Cause of Premature Death." August 21, p. A1.

————. 1988. "L.A. Has Become Gang-Infested 'Hell.'" April 17, p. A11.

Science. 1980. "Shadow of Death over Aging." 207(4438):1419.

Science 83. 1983. "Update." December 4(10):14.

Seattle Times/Post Intelligencer. 1985. "Brains of Men Executed in Fla. Being Studied." October 6, p. A8.

Seiden, Richard. 1979. "Rev. Jones on Suicide." *Suicide and Life-Threatening Behavior* 9(2):116–19.

Shneidman, Edward. 1973. "Suicide." *Encyclopedia Britannica.* New York: Encyclopaedia Britannica. pp. 383–85.

———. 1980a. "The Death Certificate." In Edwin Shneidman, ed., *Death: Current Perspectives.* Palo Alto, Calif.:Mayfield, pp. 148–56.

———. 1980b. "Suicide." In Edwin Shneidman, ed., *Death: Current Perspectives.* Palo Alto, Calif.: Mayfield, pp. 416–34.

Shorter, Edward. 1982. *A History of Women's Bodies.* New York: Basic Books.

Stack, Steven. 1978. "Suicide a Comparative Analysis." *Social Forces* 57(2):644–53.

———. 1986. "A Leveling Off in Young Suicides." *Wall Street Journal.* May 28, p. 30.

Stengel, Richard. 1985. "When Brother Kills Brother." *Time.* September 16, pp. 32–36.

Stern, Edith. 1947. "Buried Alive." *Women's Home Companion.*

Toolan, J. 1975. "Suicide in Children and Adolescents." *American Journal of Psychotherapy* 29:339–44.

United Nations. 1987. *1985 Demographic Yearbook.* New York: Publishing Division of the United Nations.

U.S. Department of Commerce Bureau of the Census. 1983. *Statistical Abstract of the United States 1982–83,* National Data Book and Guide to Sources, 103rd Edition:81.

———. 1986. *Statistical Abstract of the United States: 1987.* Washington, D.C.: Superintendent of Documents.

U.S. Department of Health and Human Services. 1980. *Cancer Patient Survival Experience* (June).

U.S. Public Health Service. 1974. *Vital Statistics of the U.S. 1970,* Vol. 2. Washington, D.C.: U.S. Government Printing Office.

Welsome, Eileen. 1983. "Death Pacts Rising among the Elderly." *San Antonio Express-News.* October 16, p. 1F.

Wilford, John. 1986. "Technology Missteps: Atomic Difference." *New York Times.* May 5, p. 8.

Wong, Jan. 1986. "Despite Recent Laws, Many Motorists Are Still Casual about Wearing Seat Belts." *Wall Street Journal.* March 7, p. 19.

Chapter 5

Death and Religion

Reverend Miller concluded the funeral service with assurances of Rose's inevitable resurrection and her entry into heaven. He had been with the elderly bedridden woman until her final breath. It was to him she had confided her fears of dying, and it was he who had administered the final blessings. And so another biography was concluded. The congregation filed out to the burial site in the churchyard. The shadow of the crucifix swept over the consecrated ground as she was laid to rest in the company of her ancestors.

Images such as these come to mind when thinking of religion's relationships with death. Politics is normally thought to be the institution of the living, and in contemporary secular societies religion is the institution associated with the dead. Some have argued that without death there is no need for religion. Anthropologist Bronislaw Malinowski, for instance, claimed that "death, which of all human events is the most upsetting and disorganizing to man's calculations, is perhaps the main source of religious belief" (1972, p. 71). Regardless of its origins, religion was to nearly monopolize knowledge about death and the hereafter for most of human history; it was to be the institution that managed the death watch and funerary ritual, oversaw the cemetery, and structured the bereavement roles of survivors. However, with secularization, medical innovations, and the predominance of natural deaths in old age, religion's control over matters of the dying and the dead has seemingly weakened. Religion now shares its responsibility for defining and managing death with medicine, science, and philosophy. Such dramatic social change, coupled with dramatically changing technologies and novel ethical dilemmas, is producing new relationships between religion and death.

For instance, members of fundamentalist sects occasionally refuse medical treatment in life-threatening situations, leading to court-ordered interventions to save their lives. Religion, too, played a role in the Jonestown story,

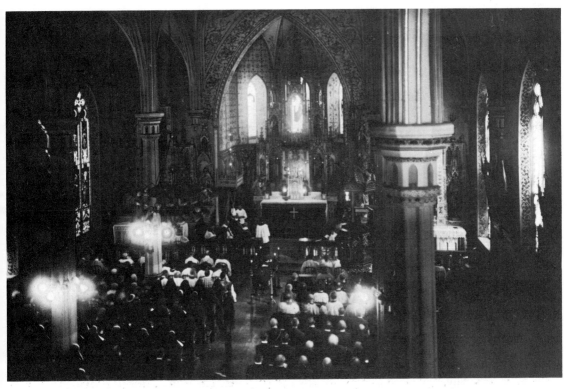

A Catholic mass for the deceased. Incarnate Word College, San Antonio, Texas.

enhancing the power of Rev. Jim Jones to persuade nearly a thousand people to flee the perceived conspiracies of secular society and finally to take their own lives in a commune deep within the jungles of Guyana. The kamikaze-style car bombs causing so much havoc in the Middle East are the weapons of individuals willing to die for Islam. Religious groups have come out in public opposition to nuclear proliferation, abortion, euthanasia, and capital punishment. Roman Catholic nuns were threatened by the Vatican with expulsion from their orders for their stand on abortion in publicly supporting Catholics for a Free Choice. Perhaps as many as 40 percent of hospices operate out of religious hospitals. And the Mormons baptize the dead, procreate to provide bodies for spirits caught in preexistence, and theologically reinforce the physical fitness ethos (abstinence from tobacco products, caffeine, and alcohol) to minimize premature deaths.

This chapter will appraise the contributions of religion, both as a thought system and as a system of institutionalized action, to the American death ethos. We begin with an overview of what, exactly, institutional thought systems are and then turn to some of the ways in which religious knowledge addresses the problem of mortality.[1] Certainly there is no way so vast a topic can be adequately summarized, so the focus here—given this text's theme of endings—will be on the temporal frames of reference provided by this institution. Second, we will explore one facet of the social psychology of religion and observe the ways in which religiosity affects the attitudes of Americans toward some of today's major death issues: abortion, capital punishment, suicide, and euthanasia. Finally, we explore several ways in which contemporary religious groups are involved in both the cause and the prevention of death.

An Institutional Approach to Death

Institutions shield people from the anomic terrors of death. Peter Berger and Thomas Luckmann claim that "the integration of death within the paramount reality of social existence is . . . of the greatest importance for *any* institutional order. This legitimation of death is, consequently, one of the greatest fruits of symbolic universes" (1966, p. 101). Here and in the chapters to follow, the goal is to see how institutions contribute to the construction of a symbolic universe, how the reality that people take for granted is socially generated and personally internalized. These institutions provide the legitimizations and sanctions ensuring that social reality remains convincing and that individuals' participations are appreciated and their efforts remembered.

The institutional analyses begin with religion for several reasons. First, religion has historically monopolized death meaning systems and ritual. This is, after all, the institution that has brought us the conceptions of salvation and reincarnation, heaven and hell, the symbol of the cross, resurrection, and the ritual of extreme unction. It is also the source of miracles. At the Santa Chiara cathedral in Naples, faithful Catholics annually gather to pray and witness the liquefaction of the "venerated blood of San Gennaro," their patron saint. San Gennaro was an early Christian bishop whom the Romans beheaded in A.D. 305. His venerated blood rarely fails to liquefy during the three days of ceremony, and it is taken as a sign of better times to come (*San Antonio Light* 1987). Second, religion provides an ideal-type illustration of how institutions create and maintain death anxieties and transcendence hopes as mechanisms of social control. Members of many generations in the West have lived with the complete certainty that they would have to face some postmortem judgment. One's every action was assumed observed, and one was accountable for each and every biographical moment—perhaps the greatest Hawthorne effect (the phenomenon where people act differently

Lucifer reigning over the souls of sinners. Illustration by
John Baptist Medina for John Milton's *Paradise Lost*, London, 1688. Dover Pictorial Archives.

when they know they are being watched) ever produced. Finally, it has been
the death-related ideologies, rituals, and attitudes of members of the institution of religion that have yielded the greatest amount of social research. It
is from the insights and methodologies of these studies that we can begin to
address the contributions of the other social institutions to the American
death ethos.

To begin with, let us consider exactly what institutions are and how their
relationships with death can be approached. We start with the proposition

that most of what we know is secondhand knowledge. Not only is what I "know" (or what I think I know) something I have learned from others, but the very way in which I perceive the novel and unknown is shaped by the interpretive templates instilled in me by my society. For instance, a dream about a dead relative might, in one culture, mean the attempt of that spirit to give warning; in another culture, the dream might be understood as a signal of some neurosis or guilt or as nothing more than some random nocturnal neural firings. The social worlds of everyday life are groupings of individuals bound together by networks of communication and universes of discourse, each producing a distinctive constellation of consciousness. Institutions are carriers of this consciousness, acting as both cognitive blinders (perception, for instance, is highly selective) and stabilizers of experience (Berger, Berger, and Kellner 1973).

Consider, as an example, the social act of driving a car. Driving is an institutionalized activity. As such, it involves a set of rules for one's own activities and expectations for the behaviors of others. Driving also entails a particular style of awareness or field of consciousness: one is sensitized to stop lights and traffic signs and not to cloud formations or air temperature. In fact, driving is so routinized for the veteran that its activities become automatic. The actor in this given role does not contemplate actions that do not exist, hence is shocked when the norms are violated, as when someone drives in the wrong direction on a freeway, people get out of their cars at a stop light, or erroneous directions are given on highway signs. Institutionalization involves this type of habitualization, which carries the psychic gain of minimizing doubt and narrowing the scope of possible action. In other words, institutions allow us to "know" about things of which we have no knowledge.

Institutions "work" cognitively in much the same way as the act of driving. They give us the templates by which to focus our attention and make sense of the social world. This social world, stripped of its veil of taken-for-grantedness, becomes quite complex. When exposed, we see how precarious our working assumptions of life really are and how important it is for society to minimize nihilistic doubt. As meaning-craving animals—social creatures who subsist on symbols and labels to even understand themselves—humans cannot live with this kind of uncertainty for long. They are thus responsive to the ideologies of their culture which intellectually address this doubt, and they immerse themselves within the socially prescribed activities that allow them to forget it (or, as when obeying all the rules of the road while driving, to think that they are somehow safe from the dangers that lurk).

In part, the sociological strategy of this book is to link the structures of consciousness with particular institutional processes. For instance, in the case of religion, we will see how religious affiliation and intensity of religious beliefs are highly predictive of Americans' attitudes toward abortion, suicide, and euthanasia, three of the most controversial death issues of our times.

Also to be analyzed is the role of each institution in actually causing or preventing death through its own death rituals. Besides being cognitive-knowledge systems, institutions are also systems of social action. Institutional goals enter the personal motivations of people, eliminating boredom and keeping people busy along canalized routes of behavior. Organized religions hold considerable sway over political, social, and economic activities. One can, for instance, analyze the activities of different denominations in the areas of capital punishment or nuclear politics, or evaluate how Islam fundamentalism can move individuals to actually welcome their own martyrdom.

The overarching concern will be to see how the relative power of these various institutions to define and structure the activities and thoughts of individuals produces distinctive cultural understandings of death. Because each institution entails different ways of perceiving the social world, it is the metaphors of the most powerful institution that penetrate all cultural levels of meaning.

Religion's Legitimizations of Death

> Institutions are powerful to the extent they help man to face what cannot be cured but must be endured.
>
> (Duncan 1968, p. 218)

A malnourished child dies in the arms of his mother, his bloated little body, covered with flies, baking under the relentless African sun. Beneath the shadow of a smoldering volcano, an exhausted father frantically searches for his family and friends buried in a sea of mud triggered by a surprise eruption. There is no despair or agony comparable to what this woman and man experience. And yet thousands of times each day around the world, such tragedies are routine. For many of the survivors, often the only consolation is simply that it is "God's way," part of some grand, incomprehensible design. As the family is the institution devoted to the emotional needs of the individual, as the economic order is devoted to the work instinct, so religion is the institution dedicated to spiritual needs.

Death is the marginal situation[2] *par excellence* (Berger 1969b, p. 23), revealing the innate precariousness of social life and the threat of anomic terror that lies just beneath its surface, beneath its assumptions of order and

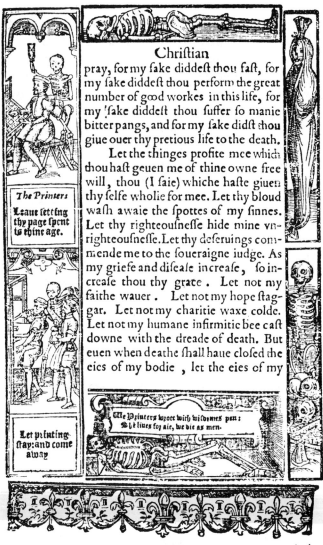

A prayer for the dead from *A Book of Christian Prayers*, printed in London in 1590. Dover Pictorial Archives.

meaningfulness. No cultural ethos can survive unless it provides a way to render death sensible or understandable, unless death can be legitimized. If death is perceived to be the absolute end, then life's meaning would be precarious. It would be a futile existence if, no matter how one lived on earth or what good deeds one achieved, the conclusion is always the same: nothingness. Such would be perhaps the ultimate form of cognitive dissonance. Religion has traditionally been the institution responsible for making sense of such marginal situations, for addressing "the problem of how to bear the end of life" (Becker 1973, p. 12).

Within the Judeo-Christian tradition of the Western world, death's legitimization has largely been the domain of the Christian church (as Judaism lacked a detailed eschatology; Choron 1964).[3] Under its influence, death and faith were to become inseparable. "Whether the theme is immortality, resurrection or a host of others, Christianity has been proclaimed by its followers as the avenue to victory over death" (Spilka, Stout, and Minton 1977, p. 1)—demonstrated, for instance, in 1987, when television evangelist Oral Roberts claimed that God had used him to resurrect a person who had died during his sermon. Under the protection of this traditional sacred canopy (Berger 1969b), "man could stand secure in the knowledge that death was a personal matter between God and himself. The very purposefulness of his death placed him at the center of existence and elevated him above all other creatures as the principal subject of creation" (Fulton 1965, p. 3). Ironically, with the exception of Jesus's death, the Bible deals little with the anticipations of death, the experiences of dying, or the possibility of any afterlife existence (Gatch 1980).[4]

 Whatsoever thy hand findeth to do, do it with thy might; for there is no work, no device, nor wisdom, in the grave whither thou goest.

Ecclesiastes 9:10.

Being special creatures, we tend to attribute cosmic significance to our activities and are prone to view supernatural forces at work in our affairs, particularly those that produce the unintended consequences of our actions. Traditional Chinese folklore, for instance, holds that natural calamity indicates the loss of the "mandate of heaven," portending the decline of dynasties (Mathews 1976). Knowing the potency of variable reinforcements in shaping our behaviors and beliefs—the "slot-machine effect," if you will—imagine the reinforcements to this ancient belief when, in 1976, a massive earthquake killed hundreds of thousands of Chinese in Tangshan, and then, shortly thereafter, Chairman Mao Tse-tung died. The realm of such external influences is the sacred cosmos. Juxtaposed against the "profane," commonplace world of everyday life, the "sacred" entails the experience of the mysterious, extraordinary, and uncontrollable forces that act against chaos and underlie the affairs of nature and man (Douglas 1966).[5] William May notes that "long before there were official gods, religion meant most simply 'alertness' or 'attentiveness'" (1973, p. 100) toward the sacred. He further observed that "destructive power and death, not life, is the object of awe" (p. 101).

It would seem easy to argue that religion is no more than a symbolic pacifier for death and dying. Indeed, three-quarters of all Americans frankly declare that religion would become more important to them if they had only six months to live (Baum 1982). Our need for answers to the whys of suffering and death attracts us to numerous religious explanations, or "theodicies," much like moths drawn to the light of a candle. As William James (1897) stated, "we believe all that we can and would believe everything if only we could." And contrary to the Marxist "opiate of the masses" depiction, this need for theodicy is not solely to be found among those at the bottom of the social heap. Meredith McGuire, for instance, found that it is the educated, and not just the poor and uneducated, who are attracted to the scores of faith-healing groups in the United States (1982).[6]

But does having the answers and an abundance of faith actually diminish the anxieties posed by death? How do we even go about measuring such notions as death fears and religiosity? Answering this question has proven to be no small task for researchers seeking to scientifically test theories concerning religion's impact on individuals' death orientations and dying experiences. For instance, the seemingly straightforward concepts of religiosity and fear of death turn out to be complex notions and have been statistically demonstrated to be multidimensional phenomena. In the case of the latter, Leming's Death Fear Scale (1985, pp. 159–60) includes eight dimensions of death anxiety, stemming from concerns with the deaths of self and others as well as concerns with the process of dying and the state of being dead. These include the specific fears of (1) dependency, (2) pain in the dying process, (3) indignity of the dying process, (4) isolation and separation in the dying process, (5) leaving loved ones, (6) afterlife concerns, (7) the finality of death, and (8) the fate of the body.

Nevertheless, Spilka, Hood, and Gorsuch (1985, pp. 131–32), in reviewing thirty-six published research investigations addressing the relationship between individuals' religion and/or belief in life after death with their death fears, observed that twenty-four—or two-thirds—found increasing faith to be correlated with diminished anxieties (seven studies failed to detect any relationship; three reported greater faith being associated with greater anxieties). In another study, this time of 276 clerics from fourteen different religions, Spilka, Spangler, and Rea (1983) found clergy to be satisfied with the effectiveness of the aid their theology and religion provided in working with the dying and their families. However, the overall level of death anxiety among these clerics was fairly high, particularly among the more educated.

There are obvious limits to this pacifier metaphor for religion's functions. It fails to take into account religion's role in keeping us from being oblivious to human suffering. It fails to take into account the considerable tests religion requires in exchange for its possible solace of explanation. For instance, as Toynbee noted, "When the belief in personal immortality is associated with a belief in a judgment after death—a judgment that will consign the dead to either eternal bliss or eternal torment—the price of a human being's belief in the survival of his personality after his death is anxiety during his lifetime" (1976, p. 36). All religions demand behavior that is not self-serving, whose purpose is something higher than oneself—in other words, religion commands morality. Individuals' need for meaning can be as strong or even stronger than the need for happiness, and in return there is often the demand for some form of religious masochism (Berger 1969a, p. 58). To demonstrate their faith and willingness to sacrifice self for it, for example, the Holy Ghost People of Appalachia drink strychnine, handle fire, and pick up poisonous snakes (Watterlond 1983).[7]

One leitmotif shared by many religious theodicies is that death is a price to be paid, whether as a toll of the original sin, as the precondition for rebirth or oneness with God, or as the cost for being able to reproduce. With the loss of Paradise, part of Adam and Eve's retribution was death, producing, according to Alan Harrington, a never-ending stream of self-recrimination and supplication:

We must have done something wrong; otherwise there wouldn't be death. This reasoning has led the races of mankind to make a cruel and foolish, and sometimes beautiful spectacle of themselves courting a higher authority which exists only in their own heads. Imagine how mystifying our behaviors would seem to a task force of interplanetary explorers from Alpha Centauri, especially if they had no idea of death. From their viewpoint, gazing down on us from the windows of their saucers, members of the strange colony below would seem periodically to go mad, with the outbreaks taking both weirdly personal and ceremonial forms.

Consider the neurotic circus we put on. Earth people are forever falling into agonized postures, extending their arms in supplication and knocking their heads on the ground. They gather regularly listening to one of their number talk, or speak in unison, ring bells, blow mournful horns, light candles and fall down. . . . In these states, are the inhabitants suffering or enjoying themselves? Does some sort of gain result? . . .

This vaudeville of despair, performed so far as we know before no audience but the players themselves, might be judged a terrible waste of time and energy. But until now it has served to ward off mass-suicide. In our tragic and also stupid situation, the worship of imaginary forces has been essential. Without false gods to console and torment us, the haphazard nature of existence could not have been borne. (1977, pp. 45–46)

Religion, Time, and Death

Consider the variety of ways in which religion involves time. There are the escapes from daily routines during Holy Week or the Sabbath, the religious rituals marking the various phases of one's biography (e.g., the baptismals following birth, the transitions into adulthood such as bar mitzvahs, marriage ceremonies, and the funeralizations following death), and the saints associated with each day of the Catholic calendar. During the mid-1980s, when Pope John Paul II beatified a seventeenth-century American Indian woman and canonized ninety-three Korean martyrs who had died for their faith between 1839 and 1867, he rescued from oblivion the memories of these individuals and made them role models for present and future generations. It is interesting to note that the English word *secular* is a temporal concept as well, coming from the Latin *saeculum,* meaning a generation, an age, or the spirit of an age.

Max Weber found in the religions of the world permutations of four distinct types of time-based death consolations: the promise of compensation in this world, the promise of compensation in a beyond, dualism (entailing man's two natures: the spiritual, which is not mortal, and the physical, which is), and the doctrine of karma (which involves the sum of actions throughout one's cycle of reincarnations). Each of these types provides the believer with a temporal orientation transcending that which is normally experienced in everyday life. The eschatological themes found in Christianity—the notions of judgment, immortality (whether in heaven or hell), the end of the world, and the resurrection of the dead—are "the driving force of [a] salvific history radically oriented toward the future. Eschatology is thus not just one more element of Christianity, but the very key to understanding the Christian faith" (Gutierrez 1973, p. 162).

Religious belief and ritual are thus largely temporal (Brandon 1951). Religious time is set up against profane time—time as wear and tear, time as decay, time as death. Such a time frame of ultimate existence and of moral truths must be of a different realm, and this is the sacred. Not only does this otherworldly orientation to time make death a transition instead of an ending, but it also allows religions to conceptualize and integrate the net sum of human activities. Our separate endeavors, as well as those of our ancestors and successors, are but unrelated, discrete events—much like the separate notes of music—unless there is some overarching frame of reference to integrate them into some harmonic whole. Part of religion's role is to establish this broader temporal perspective on everyday life, to provide the sense of coherency and comprehensibility to both personal and social experiences,

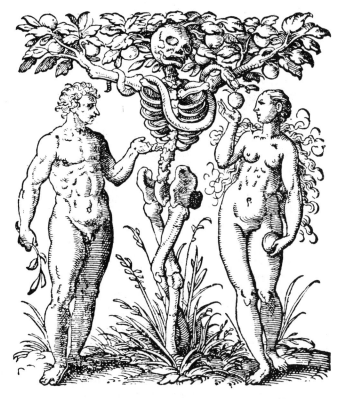

The Tree of Knowledge and Death. Woodcut by Jost
Amman from Jacob Rueff's *De conceptu et generatione hom-
inis*, printed in Frankfurt in 1587. Dover Pictorial Archives.

and to place generations now alive in context with those dead and those yet
to be born.

The Continuity of Generations

Of all creatures, humans are unique in their need for a sense of overarching
coherency and meaning in their lives. To accomplish this, the totality of discrete biographical episodes both experienced and anticipated by the individual must be transcended. As Meerloo (1970, p. 47) suggests, only children
live in the present, while the mature live simultaneously in the past, present,
and future. The very sense of identity, of self-comprehensibility, is thus
dependent on such experiences of temporal continuity. Michael Novak

writes that "it seems better to imagine religion as the telling of a story with one's life" (1971, p. 45).

Just as individuals need a sense of order in their biographical experiences, there are both personal and social needs for individuals to transcend their own lives and to understand their own biographies within the context of those of their ancestors and successors. The experience of community, for instance, has a retrospective aspect, involving "a tradition carried from generation to generation . . . [wherein] the living acknowledge the work of the dead as living on in themselves forever" (Michels 1949, p. 160). As stated by Bertrand Russell, it is "making part of one's life part of the whole stream and not a mere stagnant puddle without any overflow into the future" (cited in Shneidman 1973, pp. 47–48). The symbolic representations of such continuity are deeply woven into the fabric of religious symbolism (Bellah 1964), inculcating a trust in the continuities of life, of one's people, of one's works for others, and allowing one to see them comprising a long chain of meaningful being (Baum 1982).

One way humans have attempted to participate in this sacred time is by replicating the activities of their ancestors. What is sacred is the order that links our activities with an overarching meaning. Sacred time is the collapse of the past and the future into an eternal now so that the heroics of our ancestors and our descendants are forever part of the present. To accurately repeat the rituals of one's ancestors, as in a traditional ceremonial dance, is to participate in sacred time. In this sense, the expeditions of Thor Heyerdahl and the duplication of the voyages of the *Godspeed* (the ship carrying tradesmen and farmers to Jamestown in 1607) and the *Mayflower*, while being scientific and historical enterprises, may also be religious rituals. In addition to religious ceremony, religious artifacts also play a role in the linkage of generations. To further achieve this sense of continuity (the experience Alex Halley captured in *Roots*), Catholics often pass down through generations of family members such things as baptismal robes, confirmation veils, and coffin crucifixes, and Jews pass down the talit, tefillin, kiddish cup, and menorah.

To even establish such intergenerational continuities requires that the identities of the dead be remembered. And, again, religion has been a major institutional source of such recollections. Jews, for instance, have the Chevra Kevod Hamet (society to honor the dead). Churches maintain records of baptisms, marriages, and funerals. And Bibles are often the place where family genealogical records are maintained. But in the United States it is perhaps the Mormon church that has gone to the greatest lengths to preserve the memories of the deceased. Believing that you must "seek after your dead" to ensure a reunion with them in the Celestial Kingdom, not only must your own dead be recalled, but (since "no human can be less closely related to

Draped with a prayer shawl, the casket of Rabbi Moshe Feinstein, one of the world's leading authorities on Jewish religious law, makes its way through a funeral procession of 200,000 Orthodox Jews in Jerusalem. Reuters/Bettmann Newsphotos.

any other human than approximately fiftieth cousin") those of everyone else as well. The Genealogical Society of Utah houses this "family of men" within a nuclear bomb-proof archive deep inside the Wasatch Mountains which contains the world's largest genealogical data base.

Beliefs in Longevity and Life after Death

Of all religious ideas concerning time, certainly the belief in some form of life after death must be one of the foremost. In the past millennium, generally anxiety centered not on whether immortality was to be had but in what form. The extent of such preoccupation and fear about whether or not one's fate was eternal torment within some Dantean nightmare or an endless cycle of rebirths remains a matter of historical speculation (Stannard 1977). Also a matter of speculation—albeit one that taxes the secular imagination—are the sociological consequences of a society of people running around with the constant, nagging obsession that each moment of their lives is being judged

and that any slip-up could result in unbelievable terror. Anyway, with secularization, moral relativity, and the diminution of sin, it seems that this anxiety has metamorphosed into the question of whether our postmortem fate
is existential nothingness or some form of postdeath existence.[8] Desire for
the latter translated in the late 1970s into the popular reception given Raymond Moody's *Life after Life*. The book's thesis was supposed scientific support for some form of existence after death, based on testimonies of those
who had been "clinically dead" before being resuscitated (see Chapter 12).

In the 1970s, Glenn Vernon and his associates surveyed American college
students from various regions of the country to ascertain their death orientations. Though the sample was not random and cannot be taken as being
representative of any larger group, the results are suggestive of religion's role
in shaping postdeath beliefs. From the considerable denominational variations in responses to the six questions in Table 5.1, there seems little question that religion does shape assumptions of the hereafter as well as its attendant fears. Mormons and Catholics are most likely to desire life after death,
to expect afterlife reunions with loved ones, and to believe in the efficacy of
religious observances on behalf of the dead. Further, members of these two
religious groups are also the most likely to radically change their manners of
living with the discovery that life after death did not exist.

To obtain a more representative picture of religion's impact on beliefs in
an afterlife, Kearl and Harris (1981–82) analyzed two years (1978 and 1980)
of the National Opinion Research Center's (NORC) General Social Science
surveys. Based on the nearly three thousand individuals in these surveys, it
can be inferred that more than 70 percent of the American public eighteen
years of age and older believe in some form of life after death. The likelihood
of believing varies according to the intensity of individuals' religious beliefs,
though not as greatly as one might suspect: 84 percent of those "strongly
religious" believed in life after death, as opposed to 68 percent of those less
strongly religious. Even for those reporting no religious beliefs, more than
38 percent indicated belief in life after death.[9] There was no association
between age and afterlife beliefs, indicating that proximity to death does not
necessarily heighten immortalist hopes. And, contrary to the Marxist prediction that this form of "false consciousness" should be inversely related to
one's position in the social hierarchy, no relationship could be detected
between immortalist beliefs and income or education. Of those from house-
holds earning more than twenty-thousand dollars a year, 73 percent were
believers in life after death, compared with 70 percent of those making less
than ten thousand dollars. Sixty-nine percent of those having less than a high
school degree were believers, as were 74 percent of those with high school

Table 5.1 The Impact of Religious Affiliation on Orientations toward Death among American College Students

1. How frequently do you think of your own death?
2. If you knew positively that there was no life after death in store for you, do you think that your manner of living in the present would be changed?
3. Do you have a strong wish to live after death?
4. Does the question of a future life worry you considerably?
5. Do you feel that religious observances by the living can somehow benefit the state of those already dead?
6. Do you anticipate reunion with your loved ones in an afterlife?

QUESTION	1 Frequently and very	2 Large change	3 Yes	4 No	5 Yes	6 Yes	 Total
Independent	20.0%	9.4%	20.0%	75.3%	11.8%	16.5%	85
Catholic	16.5	30.6	61.6	62.7	65.7	52.8	466
Methodist	13.1	17.1	50.2	74.0	11.9	40.9	269
Presbyterian	20.0	8.6	45.7	85.7	8.6	42.9	35
Episcopalian	12.0	21.9	37.0	74.0	13.7	28.8	73
Congregational	10.6	12.5	43.8	78.4	7.2	34.1	208
Lutheran	12.0	19.0	63.8	63.8	8.6	51.7	58
Baptist	22.1	21.0	59.7	59.7	13.3	52.5	181
Mormon	9.5	46.6	88.4	80.7	67.6	90.2	275
"Protestant"	14.0	16.3	44.2	69.8	18.6	34.9	41
Jewish	16.7	22.0	52.7	62.0	38.0	34.7	150

Source: From Vernon 1979.

degrees and 71 percent of those with at least some education beyond high school.

As opposed to nonbelievers in life after death, America's immortalists are

- less likely to subscribe to the right of individuals or society to take lives, whether by suicide, abortion, or euthanasia;
- more likely to disapprove of premarital sex, homosexuality, and the legalization of marijuana;
- more likely to support making divorces tougher to obtain;
- slightly more likely to be satisfied with family and work and to report being happy;
- more likely to belong to three or more organizations;
- slightly more likely to be politically conservative; and
- slightly more likely to hold a "great deal" of confidence in medical and religious authorities.

Though the Bible is less than clear about the nature of postmortem existence, it is quite explicit about the extreme life spans lived by the early believ-

Table 5.2 Supercentenarians in Genesis

	Age (in years)	Scripture reference
Adam	930	Gen. 5:5
Seth	912	Gen. 5:8
Enosh	905	Gen. 5:11
Kenan	910	Gen. 5:14
Mahalalel	895	Gen. 5:17
Jared	962	Gen. 5:20
Enoch	365	Gen. 5:23
Methuselah	969	Gen. 5:27
Lamech	777	Gen. 5:31
Noah	950	Gen. 9:29
Shem	600	Gen. 11:10–11
Arpachshad	438	Gen. 11:12–13
Shelah	433	Gen. 11:14–15
Eber	464	Gen. 11:16–17
Peleg	239	Gen. 11:18–19
Reu	239	Gen. 11:21–22
Serug	230	Gen. 11:22–23
Nahor	148	Gen. 11:24–25
Jerah	205	Gen. 11:32
Sarah	127	Gen. 23:1
Abraham	175	Gen. 25:7
Ishmael	137	Gen. 25:17
Isaac	180	Gen. 35:28
Jacob	147	Gen. 47:28
Joseph	110	Gen. 50:26

ers (see Table 5.2). This correlation between moral worthiness and longevity was echoed in the obituary analysis of Chapter 3, where it was found that the longest-lived members of all institutional groups were members of the clergy. Such connections between morality and longevity were historically made by a number of traditional cultures where, because of the rarity of old age, those who did survive to advanced age were seen to have made such an accomplishment because of their moral superiority. The fact that so many churches remain controlled by gerontocracies is evidence that this attribution is still made.

Religion as a Cause and Preventer of Death

We have considered some of religion's ideological orientations toward death as well as its social and psychological influences. For example, as if in exchange for one's restraint of selfish egoism in working for the benefit of others, religions provide temporal extensions of one's self, whether it be the bliss of eternal existence in some paradise or the end of painful reincarnations with one's absorption into a collective oversoul. But religions contribute to the cultural death ethos in even more direct ways by determining who dies and how.

On the societal level, religions supposedly serve as the basis of moral order and social harmony, preventing a social jungle in which murder and suicide would be routine. But organized religions have also legitimized violence and death. Islamic law, for instance, carries such penalties as stoning for adultery and execution for heresy. Few wars match the ferocity of those conducted for a holy cause. It was in the name of religion that Christians fought Muslims during the Crusades, that Catholics fought Protestants during the Thirty-Year War, and that torture was perfected during the Spanish Inquisition. Today, it is in the name of religion that Christian troops kill Druse militiamen in Beirut, that Catholics and Protestants create widows in Northern Ireland, and that bombings and shootings occur in India between Hindus and Sikhs.[10] The rise of Muslim fundamentalism in some Arab countries, perhaps reflecting disappointments with transplanted "satanic" Western ideals and institutions, has the potential of producing both civil and international war.

Though speculations are numerous, it seems that religion becomes the instrument of death when it attracts the socially downtrodden and disenfranchised or when there exists no consensus on a common language, culture, and ethic. In Lebanon, years of poverty and second-class treatment of Shiites by the dominant Christians and Sunnis have produced unbridled hatred and deadly terrorism. Between 1983 and 1984, the Islamic Jihad (Islamic Holy War) claimed reponsibility for the deaths of 315 individuals, including the suicidal bombing of marine barracks in Beirut, which produced more American military casualties in a single day than since the height of the Vietnam War (Barnes 1985). A new twist was added to the bloody strife in South Africa when approximately ten thousand South African Muslims called for a holy war against apartheid; for the first time, Islamic religious fervor was added to the demands for the end to apartheid. And, as illustrated by the tens of thousands of deaths following Ayatollah Khomeini's revolution in Iran, when religious movements are successful they can often turn to the political right and become oppressive (Maloney 1984). Khomeini and his holy men were to maintain a *jihad,* or holy war, with Iraq throughout the 1980s as a means of remaining in power. The ayatollah pronounced: "War is a divine blessing. It is a gift bestowed upon us by God. The thunder of cannon rejuvenates the soul" (Anderson 1986).

Two apprehensive Muslim girls stand guard armed with a machine gun and rocket launcher in a street in Lebanon. Said Elatab, Unicef.

With the approach of the year 2000, coupled with international fears of a nuclear holocaust, chiliastic beliefs were bound to surface. Pat Robertson, a popular television evangelist ("The 700 Club") and candidate for the Republican presidential nomination in 1988, told his followers that the Bible predicts a nuclear war and the beginning of the end of the world during the 1980s. So potent were these millennial concerns—the ultimate of endings— that they were to enter the 1984 U.S. presidential campaign. Scores of national religious authorities petitioned the candidates to denounce the "Armageddon ideology," a belief of some fundamentalists that the Soviet Union fits biblical prophecies as being the source of evil and that nuclear war is God's means of punishing the wicked (*San Antonio Express-News* 1984b).

In the West, however, religion's role in cultural conflicts has generally been to prevent war rather than to cause it. A number of religious groups played an active role in protesting American involvement in the Vietnam War and nowadays condemn any use of nuclear weapons. In a 1984 address, Pope John Paul II spoke against what he saw as the emerging "culture of death," citing the nuclear arms buildup, abortion, drugs, and terrorism as evidence (*San Antonio Express-News* 1984a).[11] The following year, American Catholic bishops linked their antiabortion crusade to other human rights issues, including nuclear disarmament, capital punishment, poverty, euthanasia, equal rights, and racism. Seeking a "consistent ethic of life," the bishops argued that these "different issues are linked at the level of moral principle because they involve the intrinsic dignity of human life and our obligation to protect and nurture this great gift" (Berger 1985). Conservative Protestant groups similarly perceive contemporary death issues as being part of some coherent secular conspiracy. Labeling this profane ideology "secular humanism," these religious groups see its precepts encompassing the denial of God's existence, failure to interpret the Bible literally, and support of moral relativism, sexual permissiveness, abortion, and suicide (Mackay-Smith 1985).

The chapters that follow will review in greater detail the involvements of religious groups with each of the contemporary death debates. To conclude the discussion here, let us first gauge the actual potency of religious affiliation and intensity of belief in shaping individuals' attitudes toward some of the major ending controversies in the United States: capital punishment, suicide, euthanasia, and abortion. Finally, we will address individualism and materialism, two of the secular factors that theologians have identified as being responsible for the weakening of religion's death legitimizations and for the rise of the "culture of death" that Pope John Paul II sensed.

Religious Attitudes toward Contemporary Death Issues

During the 1970s and 1980s, various religious groups were to mount well-publicized campaigns against abortion, capital punishment, and society's right to allow the suicide or passive euthanasia deaths of the terminally ill. As is evident in Table 5.3, the relationship between the official positions and activities of different church organizations and the personal value orientations of their members is imperfect. In general, when compared with those professing no religion, religion increases one's likelihood to favor capital punishment and to oppose abortion and the moral right of the incurably ill to either take their own lives or have them painlessly ended by a physician.

Beginning with the capital punishment controversy (see Chapter 8), Protestants and Catholics are nearly indistinguishable from each other and from society as a whole in supporting by a 7-to-3 margin the right of the state to execute its citizens. On only this issue do Baptists resemble those with no religion, both groups being the least likely to favor the practice. Presbyterians and Jews, two of the otherwise more liberal theological groups in the United States, were the most likely to support capital punishment, as were those Protestants and Catholics with weak to moderate religiosity.

Differences between Protestants and Catholics regarding abortion were also negligible in 1984, although evangelical members were twice as likely (42 percent vs. 21 percent) as mainline parishioners to favor a ban on all abortions. Those of non-Catholic or non-Protestant orientations (Jewish, "other," and "none") were twice as likely to favor a woman's right to an abortion upon demand. Although the intensity of religious belief produced a greater change in the abortion attitudes of Catholics (34 percent of those weak or moderately religious agreeing to the right to an abortion on demand as opposed to 12 percent of those claiming to be strongly religious, for a difference of 22 percent) than was the case for Protestants (16 percent difference) in 1978, by 1984 the opposite was the case. The abortion controversy of the 1980s was to polarize the Protestant community more than the Catholic.

Between 1978 and 1985, society as a whole became more aware and supportive of the right-to-die and death-with-dignity movements that stemmed from the increasing ability to technologically prolong life and the dying process (see Chapters 4 and 11). Over these seven years, there was an increase of 8 percent of the American public believing that it was acceptable for the incurably ill to end their lives by suicide or euthanasia. But the acceptance of such activities was generally suppressed by religion, particularly for the strongly religious. And whereas Jews and those claiming to have no religion saw little difference between how the lives of the incurably ill were ended

Table 5.3 The Impact of Religion on Individuals' Attitudes toward Contemporary Death Issues

	Favor capital punishment		Believe suicide ok if one has an incurable disease[a]		Agree desired euthanasia by physician ok[b]		Agree women have right to abortion on demand[c]	
	1978	1984	1978	1985	1978	1985	1978	1984
TOTAL	66%	70%	38%	44%	58%	64%	32%	37%
Protestant	71	70	35	39	55	61	30	35
Baptist	66	65	27	33	51	58	24	27
Methodist	75	73	42	43	60	66	38	42
Lutheran	72	81	43	35	68	63	32	47
Presbyterian	87	76	42	63	64	70	42	53
Catholic	72	71	31	41	56	62	25	32
Jewish	79	96	79	81	72	78	62	74
No religion	65	66	78	83	79	85	67	61
Religiosity								
Protestants								
strong	69	66	19	25	38	49	20	24
weak–moderate	72	73	46	50	67	71	36	46
Catholics								
strong	67	65	18	27	39	51	12	27
weak–moderate	75	75	39	51	69	69	34	37
Jews								
strong	83	92	92	56	83	67	67	46
weak–moderate	76	79	71	90	65	80	59	100

[a]Specifically, response to the question, "Do you think a person has the right to end his or her own life if this person has an incurable disease?

[b]Responses to the question, "When a person has a disease that cannot be cured, do you think doctors should be allowed by law to end the patient's life by some painless means if the patient and his family request it?"

[c]Responses to the question, "Please tell me whether or not *you* think it should be possible for a pregnant woman to obtain a *legal* abortion if the woman wants it for any reason."

Source: Computed from National Opinion Research Center 1985.

(approximately 80 percent in 1985 believed suicide or euthanasia was "ok"), members of most denominations made the distinction that physician control was preferable.

Individualism and Materialism: The Desacralization of Death

Individualism, the nemesis of religious belief, entails the "release of the individual from the ties and constraints of community" (Nisbet 1970, p. 372). The individuated actor, detached from enduring and significant relationships, rarely feels the traditional institutional restraints that governed the thoughts, hopes, fears, and behaviors of earlier generations. On the other hand, also no longer restrained are one's darker impulses, as was the case in the small towns and villages where people knew and helped one another.[12] It has been suggested that on a macro level, the resultant excesses of egoism (the preoccupation with individual self-interest) will destroy the moral fabric of society. On the individual level, such excesses of freedom are hypothesized to lead to moral relativism and anomie.

The heresy of individuated consciousness is the fact that it means choice (the original meaning of *haeresis;* Berger 1969a, p. 45), which is the original sin, the cost of partaking from the tree of knowledge (Harrington 1977, p. 18). Without the cosmically legitimized frames of reference and recipes for passing through the life cycle, the individual is now perceived to be the victim of neuroses (Fromm 1941), alienation, chronic anxiety, and profound existential doubt.[13] Whether one looks at the impact of individualism on a large scale, such as the destruction of the environment in the pursuit of self-interest, or views it from a more micro level, where the individual places self-determination or self-interest above responsibility for others, individualism detrimentally affects society.

For numerous reasons, individualism—whose roots (and criticisms) date back to the Reformation and the emergence of industrialism—has proliferated tremendously in the past century. Observing the cultural climate now promoting its growth, Robert Bellah writes:

At every level, people learn patterns of reward and advancement that focus on their own individual achievement. Career patterns take the middle class out of the place in which they were born—frequently far from their family and relatives. They go to universities, where many of them learn that the things they were taught in Sunday school are not necessarily true.

Our society makes it harder and harder to maintain tight-knit families, small-town environments and other social contexts that can provide support, reinforcement and a moral meaning for individuals—contexts in which they can see that everybody is working for the common good.

Psychology has played a role in this. The language of therapy tends to emphasize almost exclusively the needs, interests, feelings and wishes of the individual and not those of the broader society. Even commitments to others and to community are evaluated in terms of their payoff in personal gratification. . . . Today there's a deep sense in our culture that if you don't reach the pinnacle of radical freedom and control, you haven't validated yourself. . . .

Another part of the picture is that the balance between doubt and belief has gone awry. Doubt makes sense only if one also believes. If you don't believe anything, then the doubt is just nihilism. . . . When the high intellectual culture becomes one of criticism, dissent and doubt, it doesn't play the role of what Walter Lippmann called

The Goddess Heresy. From a satiric anti-Reformation hand-bill designed by Anton Eisen, Paderborn, Germany, late six-teenth century. Dover Pictorial Archives.

"the public philosophy, which gives people confidence that there's something out there they can count on. (1984, pp. 69–70)

The ideal-type individualist has an identity in a continuous state of flux. This person is highly educated, a liberal favoring the rights of all social groups (without moral certainty, who is to say what is right?), agnostic, and a consumer of various identity markets (such as psychiatrists, marriage or job counselors, EST, and t-group therapies). In the attempt to live a pleasurable and enjoyable life, the individualist develops an orientation to death that justifies narcissism. Life is only valued so long as one has mastery over it and derives pleasure from it. Death becomes merely a technicality to terminate a life deemed not worth living anyway. This ethos is seen by the religiously inclined to have led to the following cultural manifestations of death themes:

- the high rates of suicide and homicide, particularly among the most socially disenfranchised;
- the existentialists' proclamation of the death of God;
- the death-with-dignity and right-to-die movements;
- legalization of abortions;
- the acceptability of suicide under certain conditions, such as for the terminally ill;
- the acceptability of passive euthanasia for the comatose; and
- mass-media pornography of death.

The legitimacy given to the value of self-determination provides a new orientation to death, one with a greater emphasis on personal control. Death is no longer accepted with passive resignation and mystical trust. In a society that views this world as the net totality of existence and in a desire to break from Christian tradition, death has become an alien intruder, disrupting the satisfactions of the here and now. The individualist fears death as it is no longer shared within a communal context, and it takes on a more personal meaning where the individual suffers alone the indignity, pain, and loss of mastery along with the fear of what lies ahead. Existential anxiety perhaps increases with education; the more sophisticated we become, the more unnatural death becomes and the more ingenious become our rationalizations to explain it away (Harrington 1977). The individualist seeks to spare others the burden of care and spare himself or herself the indignity of the loss of mastery. Since individualism, with its greater propensity toward narcissism, prompts us to seek pleasure and to avoid pain and indignity at all costs, death is the final degradation—an object of fear, silence, and denial (Mount 1983).

Ironically, at the time of greater personal autonomy, there has been the concomitant social tendency to no longer hold individuals accountable for their actions, thereby diluting the concept of personal sin. Pope John Paul II noted in his 1984 "Reconciliation and Penance" that "this usage contrasts social sin and personal sin, not without ambiguity, in a way that leads more or less unconsciously to the watering down and almost abolition of personal sin, with the recognition only of social guilt and responsibility." Blamed is not the "moral conscience of the individual but rather . . . some vague entity or anonymous collectivity, such as the situation, the system, society, structures or institutions" (Dionne 1984).

The cultural focus on the body—our material, individual selves—as opposed to the soul—which is all that is not part of us but rather the extension of society—has led to the weakening of the moral order, yielding moral doubt and a diminished spirit of sacrifice. In John Paul II's fifth encyclical of 1986, "The Lord and Giver of Life," Marxism and other forms of philosophical materialism are called "the signs and symptoms of death" as they spell the loss of God and of all signs of sinfulness:

Materialism, as a system of thought, in all its forms, means the acceptance of death as the definitive end of human existence. Everything that is material is corruptible, and therefore the human body (insofar as it is "animal") is mortal. If man in his essence is only "flesh," death remains for him an impassable frontier, a limit. Hence one can understand how it can be said that human life is nothing but an "existence in order to die."

It must be added that on the horizon of contemporary civilization—especially in the form that is most developed in the technical and scientific sense—the signs and symptoms of death have become particularly present and frequent. One has only to think of the arms race and of its inherent danger of nuclear self-destruction. Moreover, everyone has become more and more aware of the grave situation of vast areas of our planet, marked by death-dealing poverty and famine. It is a question of problems that are not only economic but also and above all ethical. But on the horizon of our era there are gathering even darker "signs of death": A custom has become widely established—in some places it threatens to become almost an institution—of taking the lives of human beings even before they are born, or before they reach the natural point of death. . . .

Does there not rise up a new and more or less conscious plea to the life-giving Spirit from the dark shades of materialistic civilization, and especially from those increasing signs of death in the sociological and historical picture in which that civilization has been constructed? (*New York Times* 1986)

To methodologically test some of these assertions about the relationship between individualism and the ideology of death that John Paul II feared was emerging, Kearl and Harris (1981–82) examined the results of national opinion surveys to see whether increasing individualism makes people more likely to favor permissive orientations toward suicide, abortion, and the right to die. They found statistical evidence for an underlying logic by which persons integrate the issues involving the right of individuals to control the form and timing of the final rite of passage. Specifically, the following items, presented in order from most to least likely in receiving a positive response, were found to produce a scale:[14]

1. Should it be possible for a pregnant woman to obtain a legal abortion if the woman's health is seriously endangered by the pregnancy?
2. Should it be possible for a pregnant woman to obtain a legal abortion if there is a strong chance of a serious defect in the baby?

3. When a person has a disease that cannot be cured, do you think doctors should be allowed by law to end the patient's life by some painless means if the patient and his or her family request it?

4. Do you think a person has the right to end his or her own life if this person has an incurable disease?

5. Do you think a person has the right to end his or her own life if this person has dishonored his or her family?

In other words, with increasing permissiveness (or a greater number of "agree" responses on this scale), one first accepts abortion, then the right to die, and finally suicide. The more restrictive one's orientation to this ideology, the more likely health factors legitimize the death and the rite of passage is controlled by the medical institution.

The notion of individualism is a multifaceted concept and was difficult to nail down. To measure it, sets of variables were selected from two large national surveys[15] that were thought to represent potential indicators of some of its aspects, such as holding permissive orientations toward the social rights of various social groups, tolerance for behavioral deviance (specifically, attitudes toward legalizing marijuana), being anomic or alienated, and having hazy conceptions of life after death. These measures were then entered as independent variables into a statistical regression in which the death ideology scale was the dependent variable. To be assured that measures of individualism had a true influence, Kearl and Harris controlled for other important variables that would be related to a tolerant death orientation in "modern," urban, industrial society, including high education, low religiosity, youthfulness, and having been divorced. In less statistical terms, a number of background variables and measures of individualism were turned loose against the death ideology scale to see exactly what correlated with it.

As it turned out, the strongest predictors of individuals' death ideologies were found to be religion and education. Catholics, believers in life after death, the least educated, and the most intensely religious were the most restrictive in terms of their position on the death scale, being less likely to approve of suicide, the right to die, and abortion. But the indicators of individualism involving social liberalism and anomie were found to contribute to the ideology as well. Those most permissive in their death ideologies were those who

- approved of homosexuals' rights;

- disagreed with the statement, "It is much better for everyone involved if the man is the achiever outside the home and the woman takes care of the home and family";

- approved of "a married woman earning money in business or industry if she has a husband capable of supporting her";
- agreed with the statement, "Most public officials are not really interested in the problems of the average man"; and
- had been divorced.

The authors asked, "What other concepts or variable can unite such diverse things as intensity of religious belief, education, divorce, attitudes toward marijuana legalization, homosexuality, race, feminist issues, immortality outlooks, and anomie?" (Kearl and Harris 1981–82, p. 279). In sum, there is statistical evidence of an ideology of death that is the antithesis of the "consistent ethic of life" proposed by American Catholic bishops in 1985.

Conclusion

Of all the social institutions, religion has traditionally had the most direct and influential impact on the language, logic, and temporalities of the cultural death ethos. This institution has inspired some of the greatest thoughts, works of art, and noble sacrifices known to our species, but it also has underlain the motives of some of the greatest atrocities ever perpetrated against humanity. It was to appease the religiously envisioned deities that Aztec priests tore out the hearts of their sacrificial victims, and it is in the name of religion that violence is committed against nonbelievers in Northern Ireland, Iran, and Lebanon.

From the theoretical perspective of functionalists, it is religion that provides the basis of moral solidarity for a society. Religion is the best-tested instrument for reminding people of their larger duties and obligations, for establishing moral codes, for instilling the voice of conscience, and for warning of any social infringements occurring to the spiritual values of a culture or the personal dignity of individuals. The recent rise of fundamentalist Islam in the Middle East can thus be perceived as a reaction against the moral depravity of the materialistic West, and the religious foundations of the anti-abortion, anti-capital-punishment, and anti-nuclear-proliferation movements illustrate religions' role in providing a cultural check and balance against the technologically (as opposed to humanistically or morally) driven forces of change. Conflict theorists, on the other hand, typically approach religion as a tool by which the social elite maintain their social power, such as by diverting the motivations of the subjugated from the here and now to the hereafter. They note, for example, that "the Catholic church cultivated fear of death in the times of the plagues in order to advance its own control over individual life and over the secular, political domain as well" (Marshall 1980, p. 48). Regardless of one's theoretical perspective on religion, to study this institution is to study the basic tensions within the relationships between individuals and their society.

Through time, these relationships between self and society have undergone constant change, producing greater complexities of both social structure and identity with concurrent modifications of postlife conceptualizations. With the exception of the Egyptians (who left the legacy of the nondemocratic quality of a culture's immortality machinery, evidenced by the fact that it is generally only the elite who were preserved well enough to survive to the present time), early societies generally did not develop an eschatology of rewards and punishment after death (Bellah 1964). The ancient Greeks and Romans, for example, were resigned to the idea of the dead's universal consignment to some shadowy world or eternal void. But this other realm was to be transformed with the emergence of individualism into a stratified hereafter, with attendant fears of the eternal torment of the nonelect (Stannard 1973, p.1307). In other words, religion was the institution that discovered an incredibly potent means by which death could be used as a mechanism of social control. As opposed to the secular tactic of killing the deviant, religion's strategy was to create a hereafter and to correlate one's fate in this unobservable realm with one's actions in life. A new fusion was thus created between social control and personal motivations, between the objective and the subjective domains of experience: individualism coupled with the idea of postmortem judgment meant one was accountable for each moment of one's biography. But by the twentieth century, when individualism became complete and religion had considerably diminished in everyday life, there occurred another great theological transition: whereas before it was the hereafter that held the promises denied in earthly existence, for the first time in history it was the here and now that was considered paradise and the hereafter that was unknown. Without the theological deterrents against excessive egoism and rewards for self-sacrifice, other secular institutions have stepped in to fill the void. Chapter 6 considers the two broad secular alternatives to religious eschatology and theodicy, the humanistic and naturalistic paradigms for death.

This certainly does not conclude the story of religion, for its influence is felt throughout American society. We will see below, for instance, the contests between clergy and funeral directors over funerary rituals, the sacred themes implicit within America's civil religion, and churches' involvements with medical ethics and nuclear disarmament. With cases of people having been technologically resurrected from death and reporting similar stories of some form of postdeath existence, will science, when it ultimately reaches its zenith of insight, only find itself next to religion, which was originally there?

NOTES

1. I specify "religious knowledge" as opposed to church-oriented religion because religious institutions are not universal; it is not just members of churches, sects, or cults who provide the consolations for our transcendent concerns, define the status of the dead, manage the eschatology of any given culture, or control the moral order. Religion, in the sense used here, is but the set of cultural symbols and ideas that address the meaning of human existence and the nature of the unknown.

2. Thomas O'Dea (1966) develops three facets of this marginal state of the human condition. First, marginality involves *uncertainty,* as much of human action often does not lead to predictable outcomes. Second, there is our relative *powerlessness* in many situations; natural disasters, suffering, and death, for instance, are events over which we often have no control. And, finally, there is the problem of *scarcity,* the fact that there exist tremendous inequalities of wealth, power, and prestige.

3. Milton Gatch writes of this point: "The Greek notion seems to have been that immortality was earned through one's contribution to the state and that the locus of immortality was in the collective memory of the state. The Hebrew understanding is at once more primitive and more organic. Personality and identity are terms which attach not to the person but to the People; thus, when one dies, personality and iden-tity are not disrupted, for the People continues" (1980, p. 37).

4. Gustavo Gutierrez (1973, p. 162) notes that although the traditional theologi-cal expositions on the "last things" were an "appendix not too closely related to the central themes," since the nineteenth century such eschatological themes have con-tinuously gained in importance.

5. On speaking of the ways society makes itself felt and experienced as "religious," Emile Durkheim wrote: "We speak a language that we did not make; we use instru-ments that we did not invent; we invoke rights that we did not found; a treasury of knowledge is transmitted to each generation that it did not gather itself, etc. . . . Since they exercise over us a pressure of which we are conscious, we are forced to localize them outside ourselves, just as we do for the objective causes of our senses" (1961, pp. 242–43).

6. A University of Pennsylvania Cancer Center study found among patients who underwent unorthodox treatments for cancer that 79 percent had some college edu-cation and 42 percent had no evidence of the disease or only localized tumors at the time of the interviews (*San Antonio Express-News* 1984c).

7. Such ritual is derived from a literal reading of the last few verses of the Gospel of Mark and other passages in the 1611 English translation of the King James version of the Bible. Following Jesus's resurrection and before his ascent, he pronounces: "They shall take up serpents; and if they drink any deadly thing, it shall not hurt them; they shall lay hands on the sick, and they shall recover" (Mark 16:18).

8. It might be noted that some denominations provide more secularized versions

of immortality—or, if not immortality, at least the means of having one's memory perpetuated. "Acknowledging that 'you can't take it with you,' the Episcopal Church is trying to make it easier for its members to 'send it on ahead' in their wills, as one priest jokingly put it" (Vecsey 1978). Like colleges, hospitals, and art galleries, Episcopal clergy and financial officers are now seeking bequests from older members to generate income.

9. As Vernon found, denomination seems to have a greater effect on whether or not one believes in life after death than does the intensity of one's religious beliefs. For instance, in the NORC samples, 85 percent of "strongly religious" Protestants held postlife beliefs, as opposed to 70 percent of those "not very" religious; 78 percent of "very religious" Catholics so believe, as do 64 percent of the "not verys." For Jews, on the other hand, weaker faith is correlated with a greater likelihood of believing in some form of postdeath existence.

10. Indian leader Indira Gandhi's assassination may have occurred as a reaction to her ordering a military crackdown and occupation of the Golden Temple at Amritsar, the holiest shrine of the Sikh minority. The disturbance that brought military intervention involved a thanksgiving service by temple priests which was interrupted by militants advocating a separate Sikh country and attacking governmental policy. At least six hundred people, possibly a thousand, were killed in the resulting battle (Smith 1984).

11. There was considerable precedence for such ideological linkages. In 1970, for instance, Pope Paul VI had equated euthanasia with abortion in declaring absolute respect for man from conception to death.

12. A 1974 national survey conducted by the Center for Policy Research revealed that between 1964 and 1974, the portion of the American public certain of God's existence dropped by 8 percent to 69 percent, while during the same period the percentage "definitely believing" in the existence of the devil increased by 11 percent to 48 percent total, with another 20 percent considering the devil's existence probable (*San Francisco Chronicle* 1974).

13. Stark, Doyle, and Rushing (1983), for instance, demonstrated that church membership significantly dampened the likelihood of suicide, even when taking employment status, education, and age into account.

14. These items were coded as "yes" = 1, "no" and "don't know" = 0. Together they formed a Guttman scale with a coefficient of reproducibility of 0.94. This means that if one agrees with question 4, then one also agrees with questions 1 through 3; if one disagrees with question 2, then one will also disagree with questions 3 through 5.

15. The data sets used were the 1977 and 1978 General Social Surveys of the National Opinion Research Center.

REFERENCES

Anderson, Jack. 1986. "Bloody War Helps Iran's Leaders Keep Control." *San Antonio Express-News*. October 5, p. 5M.

Barnes, John. 1985. "Shiites: At the Cutting Edge of Islamic Revolution." *U.S. News & World Report.* July 1, pp. 25–29.

Baum, Rainer. 1982. "A Revised Interpretive Approach to the Religious Significance of Death in Western Societies." *Sociological Analysis* 43(4):327–50.

Becker, Ernest. 1973. *The Denial of Death.* New York: Free Press.

Bellah, Robert. 1964. "Religious Evolution." *American Sociological Review* 29:358–74.

——— 1985. "A Conversation with Robert Bellah, 'Individualism Has Been Allowed to Run Rampant,'" interviewed by Alvin Sanoff. *U.S. News & World Report.* May 27, pp. 69–70.

Berger, Joseph. 1985. "Bishops Tie Abortion Fight to Rights Issues." *New York Times.* November 15, p. 15.

Berger, Peter. 1969a. *A Rumour of Angels: Modern Society and the Rediscovery of the Supernatural.* Garden City, N.Y.: Doubleday.

——— 1969b. *The Sacred Canopy: Elements of a Sociological Theory of Religion.* Garden City, N.Y.: Doubleday/Anchor.

Berger, Peter, Brigitte Berger, and Hansfried Kellner. 1973. *The Homeless Mind: Modernization and Consciousness.* New York: Random House.

Berger, Peter, and Thomas Luckmann. 1966. *The Social Construction of Reality.* Garden City, N.Y.: Doubleday.

Brandon, S. G. F. 1951. *Time and Mankind.* London: Hutchinson.

Choron, Jacques. 1964. *Modern Man and Mortality.* New York: Macmillan.

Dionne, E. J. Jr. 1984. "Pope Says Sin 'Lies with Individuals.'" *New York Times.* December 12, p. 3.

Douglas, Mary. 1966. *Purity and Danger.* New York: Praeger.

Duncan, Hugh D. 1968. *Symbols in Soceity.* New York: Oxford University Press.

Durkheim, Emile. 1961. *The Elementary Forms of the Religious Life,* trans. by J. Swain. Glencoe, Ill.: Free Press.

Fromm, Erich. 1941. *Escape from Freedom.* New York: Farrar and Rinehart.

Fulton, Robert. 1965. *Death and Identity.* New York: John Wiley.

Gatch, Milton. 1980. "The Biblical Tradition." In Edwin Shneidman, ed. *Death: Current Perspectives,* 2d ed. Palo Alto, Calif.: Mayfield, pp. 35–45.

Gutierrez, Gustavo. 1973. *A Theology of Liberation: History, Politics and Salvation.* Maryknoll, N.Y.: Orbis Books.

Harrington, Alan. 1977. *The Immortalist.* Millbrae, Calif.: Celestial Arts.

James, William. 1897. *The Will to Believe and Other Essays in Popular Philosophy.* New York and London: Longman Green.

Kearl, Michael, and Richard Harris. 1981–82. "Individualism and the Emerging 'Modern' Ideology of Death." *Omega* 12(3): 269–80.

Leming, Michael. 1985. "Religion and Death Attitudes." In Michael Leming and George Dickinson, eds., *Understanding Dying, Death, and Bereavement.* New York: Holt, Rinehart and Winston, chap. 6.

McGuire, Meredith. 1982. *Pentecostal Catholics.* Philadelphia: Temple University Press.

Mackay-Smith, Anne. 1985. "Schools Are Becoming the Battleground in the Fight against Secular Humanism." *Wall Street Journal.* August 6, p. 35.

Malinowski, Bronislaw. 1972. "The Role of Magic and Religion." In W. A. Lessa and E. Z. Vogt, eds., *Reader in Comparative Religion.* New York: Harper & Row, pp. 63–72.

Maloney, Lawrence. 1984. "Plague of Religious Wars around the Globe." *U.S. News & World Report.* June 25, pp. 24–26.

Marshall, Victor. 1980. *Last Chapters: A Sociology of Aging and Dying.* Monterey, Calif.: Brooks/Cole.

Mathews, Jay. 1976. "'Will of Heaven' Idea Still Stirs China." *San Francisco Chronicle.* July 31, p. 9.

May, William. 1973. "The Sacral Power of Death in Contemporary Experience." In Arien Mack, ed., *Death in American Experience.* New York: Schocken Books, pp. 97–122.

Meerloo, J. 1970. *Along the Fourth Dimension.* New York: John Day.

Michels, Roberto. 1949. *First Lectures in Political Sociology.* New York: Harper & Row.

Mount, Eric. 1983. "Individualism and Our Fears of Death." *Death Education* 7:25–31.

National Opinion Research Center. 1985. *General Social Surveys, 1972–1985: Cumulative Codebook.* Chicago: National Opinion Research Center, University of Chicago.

New York Times. 1986. "Excerpts from Pope's Encyclical, 'The Lord and Giver of Life.'" May 32, p. 4.

Nisbet, Robert. 1970. *The Social Bond.* New York: Alfred A. Knopf.

North San Antonio Times. 1984. "Jews forming society to honor the dead" (Nov. 8):6.

Novak, Michael. 1971. "Religion as Autobiography." In Michael Novak, *Ascent of the Mountain, Flight of the Dove.* New York: Harper & Row.

O'Dea, Thomas. 1966. *The Sociology of Religion.* Englewood Cliffs, N.J.: Prentice-Hall.

San Antonio Express-News. 1984a. "Pope Urges: Combat 'Culture of Death.'" April 15, p. 12A.

——— 1984b. "Religious Leaders Battle in Bible, Politics Debate." October 14, p. 9A.

——— 1984c. "Studies: Educated Drawn to Faith-Healing." November 25, p. 11B

San Antonio Light (UPI). 1987. "'Blood' of Saint Beheaded in Year 305 Liquefies after Prayer." September 20, p. A21.

San Francisco Chronicle. 1974. "The Devil Is Gaining." April 4, p. 21.

Shneidman, Edwin. 1973. *Deaths of Man.* New York: Quadrangle/New York Times Books.

Smith, William. 1984. "The Roots of Violence." *Time.* July 2, pp. 35–36.

Spilka, Bernard, Ralph Hood Jr., and Richard Gorsuch. 1985. *The Psychology of Religion: An Empirical Approach.* Englewood Cliffs, N.J.: Prentice-Hall.

Spilka, Bernard, John Spangler, and M. Priscilla Rea. 1983. "Religion and Death: The Clerical Perspective." *Journal of Religion and Health* 20(4):299–306.

Spilka, Bernard, Larry Stout, and Barbara Minton. 1977. "Death and Personal Faith: A Psychometic Investigation." *Journal for the Scientific Study of Religion* 16(2):169–78.

Stannard, David. 1973. "Death and Dying in Puritan New England." *American Historical Review* 78 (December):1305–30.

———— 1977. *The Puritan Way of Death: A Study in Religion, Culture, and Social Change.* New York: Oxford University Press.

Stark, Rodney, Daniel Doyle, and Jess Rushing. 1983. "Beyond Durkehim: Religion and Suicide." *Journal for the Scientific Study of Religion* 22(2):120–31.

Toynbee, Arnold. 1976. "Various Ways in Which Human Beings Have Sought to Reconcile Themselves to the Fact of Death." In Edwin Shneidman, ed., *Death: Current Perspectives.* Palo Alto, Calif.: Mayfield, pp. 13–44.

Vecsey, George. 1978. "Episcopal Church Is Seeking More Funds from Bequests." *New York Times.* March 7, p. 18.

Vernon, Glenn. 1979. "Death and Religious Affiliation: Some Research Findings." In Glenn Vernon, *A Time to Die.* Washington, D.C.: University Press of America, pp. 65–77.

Watterlond, Michael. 1983. "The Holy Ghost People." *Science 83* 4(4):50–57.

Chapter 6

Secular Perspectives on Death

In 1975, a middle-aged woman named Sarah Jane Moore attempted to assassinate President Gerald Ford in San Francisco. The act appeared to have neither ideological nor personal motivation. Had such behavior occurred a few centuries earlier, when religion monopolized such explanatory schemes, we may have been satisfied with the deduction that "the devil made her do it." But no longer is such an interpretation deemed adequate. Instead, our cultural ethos perceives human action in scientific and psychological terms. Accordingly, Moore's uncontrollable urge stemmed either from some midlife hormonal imbalance, some flaw in her personality structure, mental illness, or her alienation from American society.

As developed in Chapter 5, religion was the traditional guardian of meaning, and believing individuals, beneath the sacred canopy that sheltered them from chaos (Berger 1967), were assured that their life and death were acts of divine will. "The very purposefulness of his death placed him at the center of existence and elevated him above all other creatures as the principal subject of creation" (Fulton 1966, p. 3). But this cosmic ethnocentrism was to be shattered by Copernicus, Darwin, and Einstein, who cumulatively removed mankind from the center of the cosmos, from exclusive status above and apart from the animal kingdom, and from God's frame of reference. With secularization and the permeation of the scientific perspective, the modern cultural ethos had to incorporate the possibility that the cosmos was not divinely constructed around man, but rather that it was the product of random chance and that human affairs were governed by the same natural forces controlling the impulses and fates of animals. Further, with humanity's historically increasing complicity in nearly all forms of premature and mass death, no longer could "bad" deaths be blamed on sacred forces or angry gods.[1]

Stripped of divinity, *Homo sapiens* was eventually to be viewed in terms of a Dr. Jekyll–Mr. Hyde tension between two conflicting selves, the biological and the symbolic. The biological self, the relative of the ape, is the creature-self that kills, eats, defecates, and dies; it is the self whose fate is largely pre-determined and whose behaviors are programmed drives. The symbolic self, on the other hand, is the essence of free will, infinite in its desires and constrained only by imagination. The former is mortal, the latter immortal, in outlook. And one self cannot predominate without a sacrifice to the other.

Exactly which of these selves is more relevant for viewing human destiny has been a matter of centuries-old debate, as has been the way by which to conceptualize their tension: it underlies the religious distinction made between body and soul, the philosophical debate over whether fate is shaped by determinism or free will, the nature-nurture controversy in anthropology, the noble savage–civilized beast dichotomy of Romantic literature, and the psychic tension between the ego and the id in shaping personality systems. From this controversy, there emerged two broad strategies for viewing the human condition: the objective-scientific and the subjective-philosophical. The former focuses on the material factors determining human behavior. In recent years, for example, there has emerged one strain of scientific thought called sociobiology (Wilson 1975), which reduces human behavior and consciousness to biochemical processes. Whereas historically the forces of determinism were viewed in religious terms—as in the theologies of predestination or fate—featuring tensions between good and evil, today these forces are seen to reside in the interworkings of thousands of genes and in the ways they collectively react to hostile environments.

Even though reason and objectivity were to be the hallmarks of post-Renaissance Western thought, during the twentieth century there has been a resurgence of interest in subjective experiences. The objective, measurable, material world "out there" was discovered often to have little to do with the personal, subjective worlds that are differentially experienced by social actors. Beliefs, for example, were found to have considerable resiliency against disconfirming evidence, which is why most newspapers still carry astrology columns. Out of such insights emerged the subjectively inclined paradigms of psychology and philosophy, which were to join those of science to replace the evaporating consolations of religious explanations. Each of these two secular orientations toward the human condition came with convincing (if not comforting) eschatologies, leaving indelible marks on the American death ethos.

Endings of Symbolic Selves: Philosophical and Social Science Views

In her final moments of existence, a time of supposed insight into life's ultimate meanings, Gertrude Stein is reported to have asked, "What, then, is the answer?" Pausing, she then queried, "But what is the question?" While the full meaning of Stein's epilogue could preoccupy philosophy students for years to come, it may well involve the one question that has haunted the human animal since the first glimmer of self-consciousness: "Why must I die?" Man is the only species aware of its own inevitable demise, and the implications of this insight have long been pursued by theologians, philosophers, anthropologists, psychologists, and humanist thinkers. College curriculums and entire sections of bookstores are filled with the thoughts of intellectuals attempting to map death's role in shaping the origin of cultures, the structure of personalities, and the genesis of religious thought, and with speculations of whether social structure is the cause of violence or perhaps is a suppressor of some instinctive predisposition toward aggression. But it is not just because of the influence of these individuals on the actively searching and questioning members of a society that we consider their contribution to the American death ethos. In addition, it is because so many of their ideas have leaked into the popular thought system—such as through the transcendent themes of cinema's *Star Wars* trilogy, the advice of popular self-improvement books, or the immortalization rituals for sports superstars—that we focus on these academic attempts to make death meaningful.

The search for meaning—the inquiry into why we exist, how we exist, and why death occurs—is no longer constrained by religious dogma or confined to religious seminaries. In coffee houses, college classrooms, and government-sponsored think tanks, the search is pursued for its own sake, for its own philosophical merits. But advances in technology and scientific understanding have made such questions practical issues as well. We now find physicians, lawyers, and ethicists making decisions about when a fetus becomes a nonabortable person entitled to citizenship rights, determining whether death occurs with the cessation of heartbeat or brain activity, weighing the quality of life of those existing in a nonterminal vegetative state, and debating whether the soul leaves the body at death.[2]

Our understandings of life and death no longer fit neatly within some Aristotelian logic where they are simply mutually exclusive, antithetic ideas. Beyond the modern conceptualization of a life-death continuum, the humanities and social sciences are appreciating the interdependencies between the polar extremes: for there to be life, there must be death, and vice versa; the very possibility, let alone meaning, of one is conditioned by the

Hospitals Turn to Philosophers on Life Issues

Several New York teaching hospitals are using philosophers in their day-to-day operations to help their medical staffs make better decisions affecting the life and death of patients.

John D. Arras, a philosopher recently appointed to the clinical staff of Montefiore Hospital and Medical Center in the North Bronx, said the intent was to have philosophers help physicians make judgments about life and death with a deeper insight into the "meaning of life" and into the complex and conflicting moral and ethical questions that are involved. In some instances, they give advice on specific cases, and in other instances, they are consulted by physicians on general problems they confront in their practices.

Typically, the philosophers are called into a case by medical staff members who are confused or troubled, and they give advice based on ethical literature and legal precedents. They do not go along on medical rounds and they rarely talk to patients or their families. Often they pose questions to the doctors rather than provide answers.

The philosophers, for example, give advice on when or whether a terminally ill patient or a deformed or brain-damaged infant should be allowed to die, or who should be admitted to an overcrowded intensive care unit, or under what circumstances a patient can refuse exotic life-support technology. But the philosophers only offer advice and never make any actual decisions.

Sullivan 1982. Copyright © 1982
by the New York Times Company. Reprinted by permission.

other. From these academic sources, two influential intellectual traditions have emerged that detail fully what this means, how this dialectic works: existential philosophy and psychoanalytic thought.

The Search for Meaning

> death is the external limit of my possibilities and not a possibility of my own. I shall be dead for others, not for myself; it is the Other who is mortal in my being.
>
> de Beauvoir 1972, p. 441

Why did Freddy Prinze, a gifted and popular Hispanic comedian, who in his twenty-one years had seemed to accomplish so much and who had apparently so much to look forward to, choose to commit suicide? Why did the estranged husband murder his in-laws, wife, and children before taking his own life? And what drove the Nazis to commit their atrocities? Rationality must be imposed on such instances of disorder. Humans must have protection from the potential meaninglessness of life that is posed by such deaths. As Nietzsche said, "He who has a 'why' to live can bear with almost any 'how.'" These "whys" are detectable in the myths of all cultures, which attempt to ensure that their members do not die meaningless deaths. But not any "why" will do. Doubt and anxiety increase with education; with greater sophistication, the more "unnatural" we become, and the more ingenious the cultural rationalizations must be to explain death away (Harrington 1977, p. 35).

Death Fears

When viewing an obituary page and coming across such statements as "She took pride in maintaining her home" or "He was known as a conscientious worker," one is often humbled by the brevity in which a long life can be summarized and its probable insignificance in the grand scheme of history. I remember the same feeling when being handed a small box containing the ashes of my beloved grandfather from the crematorium. Is existence no more than building a sandcastle before an incoming tide?

"Death asks us for our identity," notes Robert Fulton. "Confronted with death, we are compelled to provide in some form a response to the question, 'Who am I?' . . . Death challenges the very meaning of life, or self, and social structure" (1965, p. 3), such as by trivializing our opportunities for heroics. This is why, in part, the suicide of a close friend is so shattering: one is forced to review not only the biographical events leading up to the friend's demise but also one's own life, which, when analyzed from the perspective of a detached observer, may have all the significance of the emperor's new clothes. As Sartre (1956) observed, death reveals our inauthenticity by exposing the ultimate banality of many of our concerns, such as keeping up with the Joneses, being seen on television by acquaintances, or having the largest collection of beer cans in the state.

Perhaps the clearest social example of this fear of meaninglessness in contemporary society is the status of those most likely to die, the elderly. There is nothing inherently problematical about the biological inevitability of growing old. But old age has become the marginal condition of social life. Americans go to great lengths to obscure their own aging, such as through the use of cosmetics and hair dyes, and their own aged, who are segregated in old-age communities or relegated to nursing homes (see Chapter 4). As evident in Table 6.1, when a nationwide survey of Americans eighteen years of age and older was conducted in 1974, only 2 percent of the public viewed their sixties and seventies as the best time of life, while more than one-third

Table 6.1 The Perceived Best and Worst Years of Life

	Best Years of Life		Worst Years of Life	
	18–64	65+	18–64	65+
Teens	16%	7%	20%	10%
20s	33	17	5	7
30s	24	22	3	5
40s	13	17	3	3
50s	3	8	6	4
60s	1	6	12	14
70s	—	2	21	21
Other	1	2	6	7
Wouldn't choose any	7	15	17	22
Not sure	2	4	7	7

Source: Harris 1975.

saw those years as the worst. If, indeed, the basis of society is the production of identities and the maintenance of self-esteem, this parabolic feature of the "good" years across the life cycle, in which everything is "downhill" from the thirties on, must be explained and legitimized within "the context of the most general frame of reference conceivable" (Berger and Luckmann 1967, p. 99), if the taken-for-granted intelligibility of society is to be believed. If there is no "cash-in" value for maturity, for years of social participation and social experience, why grow old? In concluding his Pulitzer-winning analysis of old age in America, Robert Butler hypothesizes:

After one has lived a life of meaning, death may lose much of its terror. For what we fear most is not really death but a meaningless and absurd life. I believe most human beings can accept the basic fairness of each generation's taking its turn on the face of the planet if they are not cheated out of the full measure of their own turn. The tragedy of old age in America is that we have made absurdity all but inevitable. We have cheated ourselves. (1975, p. 422)

What comes to mind is a statement by existential philosopher Albert Camus, who claimed that there "is but one truly serious philosophical problem and that is suicide. Judging whether life is or is not worth living amounts to answering the fundamental question of philosophy" (1955, p. 4).

An additional facet of this threat of meaninglessness posed by death is the possibility that oblivion is the fate for all, regardless of how one lives. The reward for both sinners and saints, for hedonists and self-sacrificers alike, is simply nothingness. Such insight is particularly disconcerting for the contemporary individualist as described in Chapter 5. French philosopher

Stages of a Woman's Life from the Cradle to the Grave. Nineteenth century, Library of Congress.

Jacques Choron (1964) argued that consciousness of death is not tolerable for this secular, modern self, and went on to develop the difficulties Western philosophy has faced since the Renaissance in giving meaning to life in the shadow of death. Instead of fear of death per se, Choron claimed that the anxiety involved the fear of self-extinction. For him, "endurance" beyond death and time is the essential precondition for social life and its activities to have meaning.

   A third anxiety occasioned by the prospect of death is the fear of being forgotten or ignored. How many are able to name the deeds, or even recall the names, of great-great- or great-grandparents? Based on a decade's worth of informal sampling of college undergraduates, it generally seems that most family ancestors are forgotten after approximately seventy years following their deaths.[3] Of the 100 billion or so humans who have ever existed, we have perhaps only the names of 6 or 7 billion (Shoumatoff 1985). Ernest Becker goes beyond Choron's fear of extinction, portraying death fears as the dread of "extinction with insignificance" (1975, p. 51). The job of any culture thus becomes a sacred and religious one: to ensure the perpetuation of its members and to give them the sense of connection with their future and past (Lifton 1968, p. xiii). This need for "an assurance of eternal survival for his

Stages of a Man's Life from the Cradle to the Grave. Nineteenth century, Library of Congress.

self" may also, however, comprise part of man's irrational nature. Attempts to transcend oneself through heroism may lie at the root of human evil (Becker 1975). Being a "loser" in life, John Hinkley sought immortality through infamy by trying to kill the president of the United States. For others, the desire to be heroic has led to making others lesser persons. As Arthur Miller observed in his play *Incident at Vichy* (1964), "everybody needs his Jew." Hannah Arendt (1964) coined the phrase "banality of evil" to describe Adolf Eichmann, the bureaucrat who sent millions of Jews to the gas chambers without even a moment of remorse. And the primitive ritual human sacrifice is another extension of this logic of "death for more life."

Finally, the prospect of endings spawns fears that one has somehow not been self-fulfilled. In *Death and the Creative Life,* Lisl Goodman argues that contemporary death fears are but fears of being incomplete, of not having realized one's potential. In comparing her interviews with twenty scientists and twenty artists with seven hundred ordinary people regarding the fulfillment of life and their death anticipations and fears, Goodman speculated that perhaps death acceptance is easier for the intrinsically motivated, those for whom work is an end in itself, than it is for the extrinsically motivated, those for whom work is but a means to another end (1981, p. 128).[4] This brings to mind an observation of Gardner Murphy, who claimed that "the struggle for fulfillment of selfhood may be compensatory for a lost immortality" (1959, p. 326).

Managing the Fundamental Anxiety

Though religion came to be viewed as some outdated psychotherapy for death fears, the secular rationalizations still inherited the fundamental anxiety it historically had addressed. What was to replace the typical, traditional loss-of-paradise rationalizations that portrayed death as the price for some primal transgression (such as the original sin); a misunderstood, lost, or forgotten message from on high; or an improper response to some divine command (we were given a test and failed, as in the Pandora's box myth) (Harrington 1977, pp. 46–47)? Do we even need such tortured, self-condemning explanations? Perhaps not. Epicurus, acknowledging that the fear of death is the master of all other fears in life, nevertheless claimed that death can mean nothing to us as it can never be experienced, and that to be obsessively concerned about death in life is a perversion.[5] To tackle such questions, the instruction of Plato's *Phaedo*—which taught that the pursuit of philosophy is but a practice of dying—was to be reemployed by existentialists.

Existential philosophers have generally placed death at the center of their thinking, seeing it as determining the very boundaries of life. Otto Rank, for instance, speculated that the fear of death is the fundamental component of human anxiety and that immortality beliefs have been one response to that anxiety.[6] Taking the subjective experiences of individuals as the "primary reality" for analysis, existentialists developed over the past century the contention that a conscious awareness of one's own mortality is a prerequisite for personal development and for the ability to construct a life meaning. André Gide (1970 [1958]) observes how man only realizes his authenticity with the release from social constraints, which normally only occurs with the approach of death. Most modern individuals, however, rarely have such intensified life experiences prompted by the awareness of their inevitable demise because they either deny or circumvent death. As a consequence of this failure to confront death directly, existentialists claim that reality itself is avoided, and the psychic energy devoted to our denials could alternatively be spent fueling our bids for self-actualization and providing the sense of urgency required to accomplish socially meaningful tasks (Charmaz 1980, pp. 43–51).

There are a number of reasons why the full significance of death continues to be denied despite the liberating potentials of its acceptance. In part, this has to do with the overwhelming terror of total demise and the psychotic

consequences of dwelling fully on the subject. Also involved is the afore-
mentioned tension between our biological and our symbolic social selves,
which has intensified with the evolution of civilization (Freud 1962 [1930]).
Perceiving ourselves to be special, divine creatures, we refuse to accept the
fate of other creatures in nature, who merely play the simultaneous roles of
predator and prey within some niche of the food chain. On the other hand,
death also reveals the inauthenticity and meaninglessness of many of our
social endeavors—an insight societies have a vested interest in their members
not considering. Working for a letter grade, for instance, holds little motivation for a terminally ill student, and hence the loss of the instructor's control over the activities and loyalties of that pupil. In addition, confounding
our ability to accept our own deaths are our conflicting desires for separate-
ness, individuality, and independence on the one hand, and for union, connectedness, and dependence on the other.[7] Ernest Becker writes that "on the
one hand the creature is impelled by a powerful desire to identify with the
cosmic process, to merge himself with the rest of nature. On the other hand
he wants to be unique, to stand out as something different and apart. . . .
The urge to immortality is not a simple reflex of the death-anxiety, but a
reaching out by one's whole being toward life" (1973, pp. 151–52).[8] However, this "reaching out" comes at the cost of either losing or learning too
much about oneself. According to psychoanalytic theory, which is "a study
in human self-limitation and in the terrifying costs of that limitation"
(Becker 1973, p. 51), a considerable portion of psychological illness is
caused by an excessive fear of self-knowledge. Thus, to avoid our inevitable
oblivion, we repress our fears of self-extinction, extinction with insignificance, and being somehow incomplete.

   This notion of repression is a product of psychoanalytic theory. According
to this secular tradition of thought, the management of death fears involves
the additional tension between the conscious and unconscious minds.
Believing that only a small portion of the mind was given to consciousness,
Freud gave considerable attention to the role played by the unconscious in
shaping our irrationalities, impulses, contradictory feelings, and inherent
ambivalence toward death. The sexual energy (the libido) and homicidal
urges (thanatos) deriving from the id—the beast within us which has no reality orientation and therefore considers itself immortal—must constantly be
harnessed by the ego and superego (through such defense mechanisms as
repression, regression, projection, and sublimation) so as to be channeled
into socially acceptable behaviors, or else, as the reality-oriented ego is aware
of, one might risk destroying oneself. From this perspective, psychosexual
development involves the resolution of certain death wishes; though civilization supposedly has engendered in us a disdain for killing, much as domes-

tication has bred out the killer from the dog, the beast remains within our irrational subconscious, ready to resurface on the battlefield, in a domestic squabble, or perhaps in the stadium of a British soccer match. The first of these homicidal urges normally experienced by males, according to Freud, supposedly derive from the hereditary encodement of some archetypical conflict between sons and tyrannical fathers: the Oedipal complex.[9] And clinical experience finds that those most preoccupied with thoughts of death are the most socially marginal, namely children, the elderly, and the psychologically disturbed:

Death themes and fantasies are prominent in psychopathology. Ideas of death are recurrent in some neurotic patients and in the hallucinations of many psychotic patients. There are the stupor of the catatonic patient, likened to a death state and the delusions of immortality in certain schizophrenics. It may well be that the schizophrenic denial of reality functions, in some way, as a magical holding back, if not undoing, of the possibility of death. If living leads inevitably to death, then death can be fended off by not living. (Feifel 1959, p. 115)

Culture as a Consequence of Death Denial

Arthur Koestler, noted author and founder of Exit, wrote before his own suicide: "If the word death were absent from our vocabulary, our great works of literature would have remained unwritten, pyramids and cathedrals would not exist, nor works of religious art—and all art is of religious or magic origin. The pathology and creativity of the human mind are two sides of the same medal, coined by the same mintmaster" (1977, p. 52).

One function of society is the production of identities and the providing of bases for self-esteem. As Ernest Becker (1973) observed in his Pulitzer-winning book, *The Denial of Death,* society is a symbolic stage for individual actors to achieve earthly heroism, simultaneously satisfying the human need for self-esteem and providing causes so that its members need not worry about what life means or have the time to reflect on the terrors of death. In his *Notes from the Underground,* Dostoyevski observes:

Perhaps the only goal toward which mankind is striving on earth consists of nothing but the continuity of the process of achieving—in other words, of life itself, and not the goal proper, which, naturally, must be nothing but two times two is four—in other words, a formula; and two times two, gentlemen, is no longer life, but the beginning of death. (1974 [1864], p. 38)

The contemporary crisis of religion, according to Becker (1973, p. 7), is that so many no longer see the institution offering any valid heroic opportunities.

A man saw a ball of gold in the sky;
He climbed for it,
And eventually he achieved it—
It was clay.

Now this is the strange part:
When the man went to the earth
And looked again,
Lo, there was the ball of gold.
Now this is the strange part:
It was a ball of gold.
Aye, by the heavens, it was a ball of gold.

Stephen Crane 1964. Reprinted by permission
of Harper & Row Publishers, Inc.

The sense of temporal connectedness with past and future generations that religion provides is no longer a concern for those sensing an existential meaninglessness to their lives and suspecting that they will probably be forgotten.

In this "incessant process of attaining," invidious comparisons are inevitably made. Given the arbitrariness of social reality, we are creatures of comparison, contrasting our present selves with our former selves and with the biographies of significant others when they were in a comparable life phase.[10] We ritually contrast our biographies with those of others at school reunions, Christmas card exchanges, and professional meetings, comparing promotion rates at work, material possessions, family development, and the like—in other words, our claims to being special. Such preoccupations derive from our psychological need for attention. With maturity, this pursuit of attention (Derber 1979) extends beyond our coordinates in space—pets and young children put on a show only for an immediate audience—and time. The "postself" involves one's concerns with the attention to be given oneself in history (Schmitt and Leonard 1986). R. D. Laing asks, "Who is not engaged in trying to impress, to leave a mark, to engrave his image on others and on the world—graven images held more dear than life itself?" (1967, p. 48).[11]

From this logic, the social structure becomes essentially a vehicle for transcendence, a mechanism for producing conceptions against chaos, and history becomes but the succession of immortality ideologies and opportunities.[12] Professional sports, for instance, "facilitates the postself by providing occasions, settings, and processes through which its participants can be remembered, eulogized, and endeared" (Schmitt and Leonard 1986, p.

1090). Social roles provide the structure and meaning around which a culture orients its life endeavors, and these must be assumed eternal lest immortality beliefs lead to an indifference to the affairs of the world. Such a sense of immortality, Robert Lifton noted, "is much more than a mere denial of death; it is part of the compelling, life-enhancing imagery binding each individual person to significant groups and events removed from him in place and time" (1968, p. 7). Even the "gospel of love for humanity and the relief of human suffering as the true purpose of existence," Dostoyevski believed, would be impossible without "the concurrent and supporting belief in immortality" (cited in Choron 1964, p. 16).[13]

Cultural Options for Symbolic Immortality

According to Franz Kafka, "Man cannot live without a continuous confidence in something indestructible within himself" (cited in Choron 1964, p. 15).[14] Five cultural strategies have been identified by which such psychological needs for indestructibility have been addressed (Morgenthau 1967; Schneidman 1973; Lifton 1979; Kalish 1985): the biological, religious, creative, natural, and mystic modes. The biological mode involves one's genetic immortality, which provides a sense of continuity with one's ancestors and descendants. Bertrand Russell, in discussing this aspect of parenthood, writes: " . . . there is an egoistic element, which is very dangerous: the hope that one's children may succeed where one has failed, that they may carry on one's work when death or senility puts an end to one's efforts, and, in any case, that they will supply a biologic escape from death, making one's own life part of the whole stream, and not a mere stagnant puddle without any overflow into the future" (cited in Shneidman 1973, pp. 47–48). The religious mode, detailed in Chapter 5, entails the eternal life of the believer, whether obtained through resurrection, reincarnation, metempsychosis, or some other form of rebirth. A deceased individual can also avoid oblivion by remaining in the memories of others through his or her works (Hartshorne 1964, pp. 157–58). Observes Sandra Bertman:

The dead do not leave us: They are too powerful, too influential, too meaningful to depart. They give us direction by institutionalizing our history and culture; they clarify our relationship to country and cause. They immortalize our sentiments and visions in poetry, music, and art. The dead come to inform us of tasks yet to be completed, of struggles to be continued, of purposes to be enjoined, of lessons they have learned. We need the dead to release us from obligations, to open new potential, to give us belongingness and strength to continue with our lives. (1979, p. 151)

Of this artistic mode of immortality, W. H. Auden said in accepting his 1967
National Medal for Literature:

> To believe in the value of art is to believe that it is possible to make an object, be it
> an epic or a two-line epigram, which will remain permanently on hand in the
> world. . . . In the meantime, and whatever is going to happen, we must try to live as
> E. M. Forster recommends that we should: "The people I respect must behave as if
> they were immortal and as if society were eternal. Both assumptions are false. But
> both must be accepted as true if we are to go on working and eating and loving, and
> are able to keep open a few breathing holes for the human spirit." (cited in Laing
> 1967, p. 49)

The natural mode of symbolic immortality involves the continuance of the
natural world beyond the individual's lifetime. In a sense, the ecology movement can be seen as an immortality attempt of many individuals whose
efforts lead to the preservation of some natural habitat or species of life.
Finally, there is the mystic mode, whereby transcendence is achieved through
altered states of consciousness. It is a variant of this that comprises the "pop
thanatology" of American society, a topic considered in the section that
follows.

 A Chance of a Lifetime or Longer

Houston—All men dream of immortality, but what, thought Corky Anderson,
a part-time drummer and sign painter in Estancia, New Mexico, of the ordinary
fellow who has no chance at it?

What of the plain Joes and Janes of the world who are neither generals nor
movie stars nor captains of industry, those whose scribbled poems are never published, whose great ideas are never patented, whose large and luminous thoughts
on the nature of man, or maybe just a good recipe for barbecued spareribs, are
never graven in stone for posterity?

What these people need, Mr. Anderson decided not long ago over a beer at the
Blue Ribbon Bar with a few friends, is a time capsule. So he and his fellow seers
have founded a new enterprise, Timewaves Inc., to provide a spot where just
plain anybody can have a shot at immortality—or at least another hundred years.

To this end, Mr. Anderson and his partners, who include his girlfriend, an
Albuquerque lawyer and a local title insurance agent who is big in the Rotary
Club, have acquired a plot of land in a trailer park along State Road 41 in Estan-
cia, Pop. 837.

They intend to turn the plot of cracked earth and dry weeds into a repository
for those ordinary bits and pieces that illuminate the life of Everyman—your
dog's paw prints, that autographed picture of Annette Funicello, Aunt Trudy's

recipe for trifle, X-rays of an old football injury, whatever strikes the individual fancy. . . .

The subscriber sends the item to Timewaves, which will copy it onto microfilm and bury the film in a time capsule in the trailer park. Arrangements can also be made to have the objects themselves interred. A century from next year, in 2085, somebody is to dig up the capsule and thumb through to the echoes of a century past. The cost for microfilming is $7 a page.

King 1984. Copyright © 1984
by the New York Times Company. Reprinted by permission.

Modern science has added to these traditional strategies (or hopes) for death transcendence such options as organ transplants (at least a portion of one's self remains alive), sperm banks (allowing for the genetic immortality of deceased donors), and artificial hearts.[15]

The Continuing Fascination with the Paranormal and the Occult

In addition to these "high-brow" secular reasonings, we must note the continuing public attention given to supposed evidence of a hereafter: the events associated with seances, the communications of spiritualists and Ouija boards, stories and photographs of ghosts (e.g., Gettings 1978) and haunted houses, tales of déjà vu and former lives, and the fact that during the mid-1980s more than 40 percent of adult Americans claimed to have had contact with the dead (*Harper's Magazine* 1987).[16] For many, these, too, provide the bases of personal ideologies by which to cope with the fundamental anxiety.

By the late 1980s, Americans were paying hundreds of dollars per hour to psychics "channeling" advice from alleged spiritual entities. Such rituals were but part of the "New Age" philosophy. In 1987, the spiritual experiences of actress Shirley MacLaine were dramatized in a two-part prime-time television broadcast on a major network. The nation's top paperback publisher, Bantam Books, increased its number of New Age–type books tenfold since the late 1970s, its fastest-growing line of nonfiction books (Levine 1987). A Gallup survey of the American public indicated that one in four believed in reincarnation, and a survey conducted by the University of Chicago's National Opinion Research Center revealed two-thirds of Americans claiming to have had a psychic experience (Levine 1987).

Though denigrated for the quality of their journalism, such periodicals as *National Enquirer* and *Star* are among the top twenty U.S. magazines in terms of circulation. Their success derives to a considerable extent from reporting stories supposedly documenting the nonfinality of death and ways to avert death. The frequent themes of the immortality pulps include encounters with the dead, miracle medical breakthroughs, life-after-death experiences, and stories of reincarnation.

Over the years, considerable popularity has been given to the Bridey Murphey genre. In the 1950s, Cinni Morrow, in a deep hypnotic trance, described in a deep brogue her former life as an Irish girl, Bridey Murphey, who was born in 1798 and was eventually murdered in 1864 in a German wood. Though the story was to be discounted because no record existed of the people she named or the geographical landmarks she cited, it was to be followed by numerous others. Other books discussing reincarnation, such as those by Seth Speaks (in its seventh printing in 1977) and Edgar Cayce (whose *Edgar Cayce on Reincarnation* was in its sixteenth printing in 1975), continue to sell briskly.

Focusing on the Vitality of Endings

A major contribution of philosophy and the social sciences to the American death ethos has been to shift the cultural focus away from individuals' anxieties over their postmortem fates, concentrating instead on how approaching endings are actually experienced. Consider the qualitative difference between "Monday time" and "Friday time," the pressures to culminate activities with the approach of a deadline, and the intensity of the final minutes of a sporting contest. The contention is that there are analogies between these sensations and death itself and that it is only the approach of death that gives life its vitality.

A maxim of existential thinking is that one cannot fully live unless the inevitability of one's own demise is faced. In part, this implies that once death is unfearfully accepted, then one no longer fears to embrace the challenges constantly posed by life; one must die a number of symbolic deaths (Koestenbaum 1971) if one is to continue growing and become self-actualized. Further, it is only because of temporal limits that one even has a temporal orientation (Moore 1963), hence any reason for priorities and self-review. Finally, there may be nothing more to fear in endings than the knowledge they reveal about ourselves.

The approach toward any temporal limit, whether death or some bureaucratic deadline, can trigger some of the most "real" and exhilarating experiences of life.[17] There can be a certain sense of ecstasy in knowing one's finiteness, as Susan Sontag observed: "It sounds very banal, but having cancer does put things into perspective. It's fantastic knowing you're going to die; it really makes having priorities and trying to follow them very real to you" (cited in Charmaz 1980, p. 45).

Perhaps the most individualizing experiences occur just before the conclu-

KEY TO IMMORTALITY℠

Carry the Key

Plan to be an organ and tissue donor

For more information
call 214/688-2609

 Coalition on Organ and Tissue Donor Awareness of the Dallas/Fort Worth Metroplex

3701 Junius Street, P O Box E004, Dallas, Texas 75246, **214/688-2609**

Promising to unlock the door to eternal life, this advertisement encourages the donation of organs and tissue after death as a means of transcending one's end. © Transplant Services, University of Texas Southwestern Medical Center, Dallas.

sion of one's life or role career. Individuals in exit trajectories no longer need to conform to the triviality or to the norms of the status hierarchy. One can say what one likes, for there is nothing to lose. Further, there is the assumption that endings occasion special insight, which undoubtedly derives from the legacy of the deathbed scene:

Parents with superimposed specter of their daughter. From
Fred Gettings, *Ghosts in Photography*, Harmony Books, 1978.

There was a time when the deathbed was kind of proscenium, from which the personage could issue one last dramatic utterance, full of the compacted significance of his life. Last words were to sound as if all of the individual's earthly time had been sharpened to that point: he could now etch the grand summation (Morrow 1984).

Approaching conclusions are generally the only social occasion when individuals are compelled to derive a sense of coherency and meaningfulness from their encounters with time. The middle-age awareness of one's own mortality, as will be seen in Chapter 12, is a time of introspection, taking stock, and life reviews (Neugarten 1970; Butler 1963). Task deadlines and annual self-evaluations can thus be seen as artificial attempts of work supervisors to capture the life-review processes observed among those on death trajectories (Kearl 1980).

Whether one considers music resolutions, the denouements of literature and drama, or the conclusions of human biographies, any failure to culminate "correctly" risks losing the overall meaningfulness of the social product (McKee 1980–81; Kearl 1980).[18] The problem of our times, according to this perspective, is the apparent lack of cultural consensus over exactly how endings—whether of work, the family, or life itself—should be ideally conducted (Hagestad and Smyer 1982), perhaps accounting for the expanding political-legal involvements in status terminations. We do know that "good" endings require personal control and the minimization of degradation. As a consequence, we are witnessing the emergence of our own *Ars Moriendi,* the death-awareness movement (which includes the right-to-die and hospice movements described in Chapter 11 as well as the public's receptivity to Kübler-Ross's 1969 stages of the death process discussed in Chapter 12) simultaneously with increased sensitivities toward political lame-duckism, the proliferation of divorce experts, and the debates over mandatory retirement.

Endings of Biological Selves: Perspectives of Natural Science

Having considered such topics as religious eschatologies and psychoanalytic perspectives on mortality, it is easy to lose sight of what has been perhaps the most profound source of ending metaphors and lessons of death: the natural order. Since the earliest of times, it has been nature that kills and the workings of the natural order (or, at least, our understandings of them) that have shaped our fears of death, our conceptualizations of the evanescence and precariousness of life, and our notions of regeneration. For instance, the Darwinian notion of the survival of the fittest has shaped not only how we view the contests within the animal kingdom, where death is a necessary part of the process of evolution, but also how we view social theory and political ideology: the earth being inherited by the strong (and by those with the genes of the strong) and not the weak. In many ways, society is a structure erected against the onslaughts of nature, and perhaps our oversight of this is indicative of the successes of modern society in obscuring natural death.

Through scientific observation, we are the recipients of increasingly detailed stories of death on the individual level and on the species level, as well as on the cosmic level, as revealed through studies of the changing bio-chemistry accompanying death, the extinctions of animals, and the astro-nomical recordings of supernovas. In fact, it is from science that we learn that what we actually see of each other is death: the outer skin, hair, and fingernails are but the dead remains of the living tissue beneath.

In many ways, humans have gone to remarkable lengths to hide as much of their biological selves as possible. And what cannot be hidden is routin-ized and covered with etiquette. In contemporary America, we cover as much of our bodies as we can (women less so than men, indicating the power order), and we defecate, procreate, and die in private (the Trobrianders sur-round eating with as much shame as excretion; Malinowski 1949). Within the memories of older Americans, our animal status was even adjudicated in the so-called *Scopes* monkey trial. With urbanization and modernization, the contemporary individual often loses sight of nature's thanatological lessons; the cycle of death is now either distorted in zoological settings or presented in the carefully edited video footages of "Wild Kingdom" and Disney productions.

Nevertheless, according to this perspective, it is the material factors of our biochemistry and our environments that ultimately shape the nature and fate of *Homo sapiens*. The subjective experiences and meaning systems of the for-mer humanistic perspectives are here seen to exist as but tangential phenom-ena; consciousness plays only a peripheral role in determining how death affects the course of human behavior.

Endings and Immortalities in Nature

A herd of wildebeests flees the watering hole with the approach of the car-nivores, only to slow down with the sacrifice of one of their own numbers. Scores of pilot whales swim onto shore, stranding themselves on the beach and defying all efforts to save them from certain death. Such dramas have shaped the content of human ritual and belief, with natural death becoming a powerful symbol and metaphor for human existence: from the logic of the seasons—from the bounty of summer, the death of winter, and the rebirth of spring—came the first eschatologies and cosmogonies; following a kill, the carnivore is satiated, just as the gods are after some ritual sacrifice; and as the principle of survival of the fittest operates in the natural order, so, according to some, do laissez-faire dynamics work in the economic order.

As a dead animal is often the first death experience for American children, it was undoubtedly from nature that *Homo sapiens* received their first thana-tological instruction. One initial impulse probably included fear; the nor-

The death of a Thomson gazelle. L. L. Rue, Monkmeyer Press.

mally curious adult chimpanzee has been observed to flee in horror from even a death mask of another chimp. But human hunters had to be pragmatic, observing the omnipresent dramas of life and death all around them. They learned that death comes to the weak, the defenseless, or the overly brash; that larger animals live longer than smaller animals; later, that each food source subsists on lower levels and is prey of higher ones; and that, in a sense, each death is a contribution to the whole. In fact, the very emergence of language, and hence of culture, may have stemmed from the hunter's need to plan and coordinate with others in order to kill large game. Being not particularly fast, without the benefit of claws or fangs, and having left the relative safety of the forests for the savannas, our ancestors had to cooperate and plan, developing strategies, alliances, and leaders. Eventually, humans became the only creatures that intentionally killed their own kind for reasons of religious or political ideology.[19] In addition, this creature of symbols was to realize how quickly his culture could dissolve back into nature, like the forest overgrowing unkept structures, if it was not routinely reinforced, for "beneath the veneer of civilization there lurks the barbarian, and beneath the barbarian the savage, and beneath the lowermost trace of culture there lies exposed a solid core of animal appetite" (Clark 1953).

With the refinements of scientific observation, new lessons on death have come at an increasingly rapid pace. Where population pressures of their prey become excessive, for example, African hyenas and English foxes have been seen killing more than they could possibly eat. "Murder" is not uncommon. Calculations of the number of lifetime heartbeats among mammals and birds have indicated a global constant, as if there is a natural allotment of lifetime. We have come to learn of the interdependencies of all life forms within all-encompassing yet fragile ecosystems into which natural selection has incorporated great resiliency,[20] and of how the elimination of one life form can disrupt the entire system and the elimination of too many can destroy it.[21] In general, death is an unremarkable event in nature. To die of "natural causes" is not to expire in old age, as is the case in modern human societies, but to typically die young (probably much more than 90 percent of all animals die before maturity). Natural death, according to the scientific perspective, is mostly a random event, an event without meaning.

Scientific observers have also detected a logic to existence in nature that bears certain similarity with the insights of those studying existence in symbolic cultures. Analogous to the existentialist focus on our transcendence urges and the psychoanalytic focus on our sexuality, evolutionary biology contends that the ultimate motive (albeit an unconscious one) is biological transcendence. Natural selection favors creatures that maximize not only their own reproduction but also that of their close kin, genetically encoding such disparate behaviors as cooperation, conflict, self-deception, and infanticide.[22] When viewing the immortalist motives described above, these observers would claim that through fame individuals can afford to ensure the financial well-being and hence the survival of their grandchildren, who, in turn, will keep their memory (their symbolic immortality) alive after death. In other words, perhaps we are unconsciously driven genetically toward transcendence, and all of its symbolic forms are mere epiphenomena of the biological mode. In fact, those who ignore such innate urges may face premature extinction. A study by Evelyn Talbott of ninety-eight women suggests that married women over the age of fifty who have never had children may face an increased risk of dying suddenly of heart disease (*New York Times* 1986).

In addition, like religion, the modern scientific perspective provides humans with a sense of interconnectedness with the cosmos. Astronomer Carl Sagan (1985), for instance, points out that we are made from the material borne by stars and that we share a nearly identical biochemistry with all other life forms. With each breath, we take in scores of the same oxygen molecules breathed by Christ. But unlike religion, science does not portray the universe as existing for our benefit. Osborn Segerberg notes:

> Science includes physics but leaves metaphysics to philosophy, adheres to the natural and leaves the supernatural to religion. While science uses logic and intuition, it is not based on them; while it relies on faith (in an orderly universe, for example), it does not use faith. (1974, p. xvii)

According to this thought system, there are no sacred truths, only probabilities.

The Eschatologies of Science: Man versus Nature

Whereas theologians and philosophers have pondered beginnings and endings for a few thousand years, science has provided in just one century the most detailed and complex cosmology ever envisioned. To conclude this chapter on secular perspectives toward endings and death, let us consider how nature kills man, such as by earthquakes and drought, as well as how man is killing nature, such as when the ecological balances of the past are disrupted by human activity and population growth. Natural death has motivated scientific and technological innovation, seeking to predict, if not control, the forces that kill us.

On Man Killing Nature

When the first colonists of North America arrived across the Bering Strait during the Pleistocene ice age some twelve thousand years ago, they found the last two fertile continents untouched by *Homo sapiens*. North America teemed with such large mammals as mammoths, mastodons, three-ton ground sloths, bear-sized beavers, saber-toothed cats, camels, and armadillolike glyptodons the size of automobiles. But this Eden was not to last. These Stone Age descendants of Ukrainian hunters may have conducted one of the largest mass exterminations of big animals ever recorded. Within one thousand years, the time it took the Clovis people to spread from Alaska to Tierra del Fuego, North and South America lost nearly three-quarters of their genera of big animals (Diamond 1987, p. 84).

In *The Doomsday Book of Animals,* David Day provides more recent examples of man's capacity to induce species' holocausts. For example, as late as 1860, it could be argued that the passenger pigeon was the most successful bird on earth, comprising nearly 40 percent of the entire North American bird population. Though diminished by 1870 through relentless hunting, a single flock a mile wide and 320 miles long, containing an estimated 2 billion birds, passed over Cincinnati. The last surviving pigeon, Martha, born

Slaughtered for the hide. From *Harper's Weekly*, December 12, 1874.

in captivity, died in the Cincinnati Zoo on September 1, 1974. Scientists estimate that man is responsible for the extinction of anywhere from one to thirty species a day (Gruson 1985; Wilson 1986). At this rate, which is four hundred times that of nature, one million species—nearly 10 percent of the known number—may be extinct by the beginning of the next century (Schneider 1985).

Such extinctions are caused by the growth of human populations and the fact that we are running out of biological room. As the world population surpassed 5 billion in 1986, overfishing, overcutting, overclearing, overdamming, overfertilizing, overgrazing, and overpolluting had become commonplace. And with industrialization and the transition from self-subsistence to market economies, the slaughter of nature is further accelerated by the following lethal logic. First, there is the mechanization that leads to incredible new efficiencies in extracting fish from the seas, minerals from beneath the ground, and timber from above. The initial bounties lead to lower prices which, in turn, require even larger economies of scale only obtainable through ever larger and ever more efficient methods of fishing, harvesting, and farming.[23] The economic costs of remaining competitive further fuel the extractive frenzy as state-of-the-art trawlers, loggers, tractors, and harvesters put their owners further into debt. But ultimately, nature gives out as it is no longer able to regenerate itself.

Between 1970 and the mid-1980s, the fish catch per person fell by 13 percent worldwide (Peterson 1985), and several popular species were nearly pushed to the brink of extinction. In Africa, the deserts annually expand thousands of square miles as a rapidly growing human population strips indigenous vegetation for fuel (wood remains the chief energy source for many inhabitants) and to make room for profitable crops or livestock. Here the removal of ground cover leads to a greater runoff of rain, reducing evaporation into the clouds and thereby contributing to the severity of the region's routine droughts. Each year, the tropical forests—already only 60 percent of their original cover—are felled and bulldozed at a rate equal to the area of the Netherlands and Switzerland combined (Wilson 1986). The fragile soil that had been naturally and routinely enriched by the decomposing biomass of the jungle is quickly depleted when planted with cash crops. The land is then poisoned by fertilizers, used to extract a few more harvests in the name of short-term economic profit. Even where there is plenty of productive land, the clearings continue because of flaws in social organization. Catherine Caufield (1985) notes that the tropical rain forests in Brazil, Colombia, El Salvador, and Indonesia are cut as a means to deflect pressure for land reform: 4.5 percent of Brazil's landowners own 81 percent of the land, and in El Salvador two thousand families own 40 percent.

Another example of nature being intentionally killed in the name of human greed is the plight of the African elephant and rhino. As economic systems begin to die, man resorts to elements from nature as his basis for exchange: gold, silver, petroleum, and ivory. When the market value of rhino horns exceeded ten times the per-ounce value of silver, in one year the number of black rhinos in the Tanzanian Ngorongoro Crater declined from seventy-six to twenty-six because of poaching. Pathetically, as their numbers decline, the value of their parts inflates, encouraging further exploitation.

As will be further developed in Chapter 7, even in the most developed societies the slaughter of nature continues. Though the destruction is less intentional and direct, the consequences are even more insidious. Acid rain, for instance, is killing Germany's fabled Black Forest[24] just as it has killed hundreds of lakes in the American Northeast and Canadian Southeast. Plutonium, the deadliest substance known, has been detected in the drinking water of New York City. And, because of the accumulation of carbon dioxide (which is no longer absorbed by the dying forests), methane, chlorofluorocarbons, and other man-made gases in the atmosphere, a greenhouse effect is forecasted. With predictions of average temperatures worldwide increasing by as much as 9 degrees Fahrenheit by the year 2100, the consequences would be catastrophic, making dustbowls of the food-producing regions of North America, Western Europe, and Russia (*New York Times* 1985b).

With the remnants of species increasingly likely to be preserved only in zoos, research institutes, and parks, matters of cost and utility enter. Civilization's encroachment upon the natural order has been so thorough that not all species can be saved. Despite a cost-benefit analysis, a ritual in which the benefits of economic expansion are weighed against the costs of losing a species of animal, an extinction may be legitimized even though we have little, if any, idea about the species' worth. So the creatures saved are those having utility. Consider, for instance, the perspective of zoos. To garner public support, animal collections must attract audiences. The most popular animals are often those that are cute, furry, and large-eyed. Consequently, with time, Darwin's thesis of the survival of the fittest may have to be modified to the survival of the cutest. Also saved will be those creatures that enhance our own longevity, such as the proverbial guinea pig, which serves as a model for experiments with vaccines and drug treatments.

Considering the points above, one wonders about the intensity of effort devoted to endangered species. For example, less than thirty California condors are left, and it is estimated that it will cost more than 2 million dollars to save a creature whose niche, which included feeding on dead mastodons, has all but disappeared. Perhaps such actions are best understood as another contemporary ritual of death defiance, challenging instead of simply celebrating (as was the case in the past) the natural processes that kill us.

In sum, the human species is painfully discovering that it is not immune to the biological law that once a species' population exceeds the carrying capacity of its habitat, then a "die-back" or population crash occurs as checks and balances come into play (Peterson 1985). Whereas the self-concept of preindustrial man incorporated a sense of being a part of the natural order, a creature that contributes to its regeneration, modern science now brings the perspective that we are a species of death, destroying the ecosystem of which we are a part. And if we are no longer to rely on the brutal regulation of our numbers through disease and famine, then we must create and honor our own artificial means of voluntary control, or the result can only be war.

A grieving Pedro Casalins stands on the site of his former home. Casalins's family was killed in a mudslide triggered by volcanic activity near Armero, Columbia, in November, 1985. The Bettmann Archive, Inc.

On Nature Killing Man

Nature shapes human deaths not only figuratively but literally as well. Hurricanes, tornadoes, tidal waves, fires, volcanoes, blizzards, poisonous foods, attacks by wild animals, and disease are all part of nature's arsenal to remind us of our cosmic insignificance. During the 1970s, there was a 50 percent increase in the recorded number of natural disasters over the previous decade and a fivefold increase in the number of deaths (which were more than 114,000 a year) caused by these events (Eckholm 1984). For the survivors of such natural calamities, there is psychological as well as physical devastation. Feelings of security, trust, and invulnerability are shattered, as well as the sense that the world is comprehensible, predictable, and meaningful (Janoff-Bulman 1982). In other words, the crucial cultural assumptions become undermined, and the world becomes perceived as a malevolent place where life has no meaning (Horowitz 1986).

In many ways, social structure is erected against the deadly onslaughts of the natural order, and social evolution supposedly means the minimization of such accidental deaths. There is a certain grim irony to the fact that the greatest devastation has occurred in those societies least able to cope: the developing countries of Africa, Asia, and Latin America.[25] Typhoons, for example, kill thousands in places like Bangladesh, and earthquakes decimate similar numbers in China, Mexico, and Chile. There may be a greater ability of highly interdependent and modern societies to absorb the shock of natural disasters and to instill in the minds of their members a sense of immunity to the onslaughts of nature. On the other hand, societies may have evolved to be "modern" by virtue of not having had to absorb as many natural disruptions. Even when natural disaster befalls a supposedly developed society, the social and political consequences can be considerable. Poorly run governments often neglect public dikes and waterworks, leading to floods and droughts. The Italian earthquake of the early 1980s obliterated entire villages, burying countless thousands in the wreckage. Delayed by impassable roads, bad weather, and bureaucratic ineptitude, rescue workers took forty-eight hours or more to reach the most isolated hamlets. Many who died of shock and exposure might have lived had help been more efficient. This did little to buttress the waning confidence the populace had in their government. Further, corrupt governments are often exposed when supposedly financed safety designs are revealed never to have been incorporated. Such was the case in the 1985 Mexican earthquake, in which much of the greatest structural damage occurred to government-contracted buildings.

Table 6.2 Natural Disasters and Loss of Life Worldwide, 1947–67

	Occurrences	Fatalities
Floods	209	173,170
Typhoons, hurricanes, cyclones	148	101,985
Earthquakes	86	56,100
Tornadoes (including simultaneous swarms)	66	3,395
Gales and thunderstorms	32	20,940
Snowstorms	27	3,520
Heat waves	16	4,675
Cold waves	13	3,370
Volcanic eruptions	13	7,220
Landslides	13	2,880
Rainstorms	10	1,100
Avalanches	9	3,680
Tidal waves (alone)	5	3,180
Fogs	3	3,550
Sand and dust storms	2	10

Source: Cornell 1982, p. 4. Table 1 from *The Great International Disaster Book*, Third Edition. © 1982, James Cornell. Reprinted with permission of Charles Scribner's Sons. Imprint of Macmillan Publishing Company.

These incidents from the recent past pale in comparison to the natural disasters that brought death to entire cities and civilizations. Though occurring nearly two thousand years ago, the disappearance of Pompeii beneath the lava and ash of Mount Vesuvius still captures our imaginations and fears. A few centuries earlier, one of the most promising civilizations of the New World, a culture from the Cauca Valley in Colombia and Ecuador whose survivors may have spawned the Mayan, Inca, and Aztec empires, was similarly snuffed out by a volcanic eruption. And in the Old World, a similar fate may have befallen the advanced predecessors of the classical Greeks, the Minoans, inspiring the Atlantis mythology.[26] So profound were these cataclysms that their impacts reverberated for centuries in folklore, legend, and religion.

 The Ten Deadliest Volcanic Eruptions

Mont Pelee, Martinique. May 8, 1902. More than 30,000 killed in the seaport of Saint-Pierre; sixteen of the eighteen ships in the harbor were destroyed.

Mount Vesuvius, Italy. August 24, A.D. 79. At least 20,000 killed in the cities of Pompeii and Herculaneum, many buried by ash and cinders.

Mount Etna, Sicily. March 25, 1669. Eruption sent lava over fourteen cities and towns, killing 20,000.

Tambora, Java. April 5, 1815. Thirty-six cubic miles of volcanic matter spewed into the sky; 10,000 to 20,000 died.

Laki, Iceland. June–August 1783. Lava covered twenty villages, and an estimated 10,000 died of eventual starvation.

Mount Kelut, Indonesia. May 1919. Water, ash, and lava inundated 104 towns, leaving 5000 dead.

Mount Vesuvius, Italy. December 16, 1631. Lava and mud flows covered fifteen villages, killing 4000.

Galunggung, Java. October 8 and 12, 1822. Explosions and eruptions destroyed one-hundred villages and killed 4000.

Mount Lamington, New Guinea. January 15–20, 1951. Earthquakes and a superheated liquid cloud killed between 3000 and 5000.

New York Times 1985a. Copyright © 1985 by the New York Times Company. Reprinted by permission.

When researching cross-cultural myths, sacred texts, classical literature, and legends, Immanuel Velikovsky claimed to have discovered a number of intriguing similarities. For instance, paralleling the biblical story of the sun standing still in the sky, the *Manuscript Quiché* of the Mayas and the Mexican *Annals of Cuauhtitlan* refer to the moon remaining stationary. The tale of the world turning red (Exodus 7:20–24) is matched by the Finnish epos of *Kaleuala,* which describes the world sprinkled with red milk, and the Altai Tatars' story of when "blood turns the whole world red" (Velikovsky 1950, p. 50). And likewise, the biblical reports of darkness (Exodus 19:22) are echoed in the folklore of Sudanese tribes, the epos of the Finns, the Babylonian *Epic of Gilgamesh,* and the Iranian book *Anugita.* In his controversial *Worlds in Collision,* Velikovsky, a physicist, argued that human traditions uniformly record overwhelming natural disasters[27] and postulated that a worldwide catastrophe occurred approximately 1500 B.C., producing a synchronized history of ancient cosmologies. Specifically, he believed that the proto-planet of Venus passed in close proximity to the earth, causing monumental geological stress. As a consequence, early mankind was obsessed with the behavior of heavenly bodies, identifying its gods with the planets.[28]

One of the great scientific ending stories is the mass extinction of dinosaurs. Among the most successful of creatures, having flourished for more than 160 million years, the largest ever to roam the earth, they suddenly vanished some 65 million years ago. Speculation remained unfounded until the 1970s, when Walter Alvarez, a geologist, found unusually high concentrations of iridium within a layer of clay marking the break between the Cretaceous and Tertiary periods, the time of the great lizards' disappearance as well as that of about half the genera. Because iridium is a thousand times more abundant in extraterrestrial matter than it is on the earth, Alvarez and his father, Nobel-laureate physicist Luís Alvarez, advanced the theory that a meteorite was responsible for the extinction of dinosaurs and most species of plants and animals. In 1985, University of Chicago chemists reported that carbon in the Cretaceous sediment exceeded by ten thousand times that in previous and proceeding periods, indicating worldwide fires that consumed the oxygen of the atmosphere and may have put enough soot in the air to block photosynthesis, thereby killing the food chain from the bottom up (Wolbach, Lewis, and Anders 1985).

If one such cataclysmic event was not enough, John Sepkoski and David Raup, two University of Chicago paleontologists, reported that there were other mass extinctions, periodically destroying upwards of 75 percent of all species every 26 million years (1983).[29] One theory accounting for such regularity is the postulated existence of a dwarf binary sister of our sun. This death star, called Nemesis (after the Greek goddess who persecutes the excessively rich and powerful),[30] is hypothesized to reach its perigee every 26 million years, when it shakes loose and hurls a hail of comets from the Oort cloud on the fringe of our solar system. Some of these collide with the earth, filling its atmosphere with dust that blots out the sun for months, leading to global death (Molander 1984; *Science News* 1984; Wilford 1984).[31]

Public dissemination of this new theory of what killed the dinosaurs interestingly coincided with the release of scientific studies predicting a worldwide "nuclear winter" following a nuclear war (see Chapter 9). Humans and dinosaurs, both existing atop their respective food chains and seemingly impervious to any challenge to their dominance in the animal kingdom, are and were helpless before the forces of natural chaos. Why else would the extinction of dinosaurs 65 million years ago, which is not exactly recent news, become *Time* magazine's cover story of May 6, 1985?

Finally, science has given us the ultimate of cosmologies, the birth and death of the entire universe. There are two rival theses about the ultimate fate of the universe, both originating from the Big Bang theory. One thesis, derived from the Second Law of Thermodynamics, sees the universe as open, expanding for eternity and slowly sinking into a thermal equilibrium that is "heat death." In other words, the death of the universe is predestined and inevitable; in 100 billion years the energy needed to sustain life anywhere in the universe would be so dispersed as to be unusable. Death is nothing more than entropic disorder, and life is nothing more than entropy reduction.

The other thesis portrays a closed universe, with gravity eventually halting the outward expansion and then producing the collapsing of the cosmos and ultimately yielding another future rebirth but without the fossil remnants of the prior order. In sum, humans mean very little in the cosmic scheme of things. As Somerset Maugham wrote in *Of Human Bondage:*

On the earth, satellite of a star speeding through space, living things had arisen under the influence of conditions which were part of the planet's history; and as there had been a beginning of life upon it, so under the influence of other conditions, there would be an end: man, no more significant than other forms of life, had come not as the climax of creation but as a physical reaction to the environment. . . . There was no meaning in life, and man by living served no end. It was immaterial whether he was born or not born, whether he lived or ceased to live. Life was insignificant and death without consequences. (1952, pp. 653–55)

It might be noted that such scientific metaphors of endings derive not only from the macroscopic world but from the microscopic as well. Research in quantum mechanics has demonstrated the death of matter and the simultaneous birth of energy, that is, the interchangeability of the two, symbolized in Einstein's famous equation, $E = mc^2$:

Before atoms were well understood it was believed they were hard and changeless— a concept that gave people a scientific toe-hold on immortality. . . . [The] atoms we borrowed from the environment gave us specks of permanent reality; each one of us, for example, breathing hundreds of oxygen molecules breathed by Christ. With Einstein, came quantum mechanics which "hinted that reality might depend to some extent on the perception of the observer." Some subnuclear events see "virtual particles" born and die in less time than it would take light to cross the diameter of an atomic nucleus. One bewildering outcome of quantum theory has led some scientists to speculate that the entire universe, including the time in which it exists, may have been created by a spontaneous quantum fluctuation—a twitch in the nothingness that preceded it. Could a twitch in the opposite direction convert the universe back into nonexistence? (Browne 1980)

Such scientific speculation seems to have brought us full circle to the perspective of religious creationists who speak of the universe being miraculously created out of nothing.

Conclusion

George Orwell once said of modern intellectuals: "For 200 years we had sawed and sawed and sawed at the branch we were sitting on. And in the end, much more suddenly than anyone had foreseen, our efforts were rewarded—and down we came. But unfortunately there had been a little mistake. The thing at the bottom was not a bed of roses after all; it was a cesspool filled with barbed wire" (cited by Bellah 1985). In this chapter, we have considered those who have sawed on the branch of religion, who have attempted to provide secular alternatives to the religious perspectives on death. One group, the humanists, still attempts to maintain the religious premise that death has meaning; the other group, those in the natural sciences, has simply dismissed the issue altogether, portraying an individual's death as a random, routine event that holds little more cosmic significance than the demise of an ant.

From existential and psychoanalytic thought derives the proposition that the fear of death is the primary motive underlying all human behavior, including aggression, and that culture is the consequence of transcending these fears through life-extending symbols and structures. From this perspective, history is seen to be the succession of "immortality ideologies" and social structure as a complex of stages or arenas, on which one can perform one's heroics (in roles allowing for interpersonal comparisons) in the hopes that some form of temporal transcendence can be accomplished.

Existential philosophers also have sensitized us to how death leads to alterations in the way conventional time is experienced and how social endings reveal the essence of any enterprise. In the case of life's final phase, whose ending quality has itself been culturally labeled a social problem, Simone de Beauvoir wrote:

> It is the meaning that men attribute to their life, it is their entire system of values that define the meaning and value of old age. The reverse applies: by the way in which a society behaves toward its old people it uncovers the naked, and often carefully hidden, truth about its real principles and aims. (1972, p. 87)

And with death being the central metaphor for all role conclusions, any shift in its timing and form will affect the meanings of other exiting experiences. Our culture is now cultivating models for good endings. The media, for example, have become selective in their culminary images, addressing such things as good divorces, good retirements, and good deaths. This cultural attention to good endings has come to influence historical revisionisms as well. For example, in his recent biography of George Washington, Wills (1984) argues that two of the three great moments that seemed for his contemporaries to sum up his life—the resignation of his commission as commander in chief, his sponsorship of the new Constitution in 1787, and his surrender of the presidency by a farewell address—involved knowing how to quit. Further, it was revealed that the father of our country had told his physicians to let him die (*Palo Alto Times* 1976).

Whereas the attention given to the ending of our symbolic selves has led to untested speculations concerning the primacy of death fears and transcendence motives, from the natural sciences has come the notion that death means nothing. Modern scientific theodicy fails to incorporate a model of man's origins *and* destination. As Frederick Hoffman wrote: "To equate evil with disease, discomfort, or 'remediable circumstance' is to remove from human psychology the sanction of man's complicity in the development of a moral sense" (1959, p. 135). With the reduction of religious mitigations against death and science's ability to postpone it, emphasis has shifted to the quantity, not the quality, of life spans; premature death has become but a matter of bad luck, without any moral or spiritual implications.

However, there is a point at which perhaps contemporary science and the humanities converge. Scientific research suggests that the unique, defining characteristic of humans is neither physiological nor morphological. The work of Jane Goodall and other behavioral biologists indicates that humans are also not unique in their ability to make tools, use symbols, or create norms and culture. But only the human organism is aware of the existence of its predecessors and successors. Only the behavior of humans is influenced by generations removed in space and time, to whom many of our activities and their products are directed. These differences, combined with the unique awareness of our own mortality, are what set the parameters of the human condition. We are the only creatures who conceptualize, anticipate, fear, celebrate, and transcend the endings of ourselves and others.

This urge to bridge the lives of the dead with those of the present has inspired not only religion but both philosophy and science as well. In fact, the success of the Soviet Union's space program stems, to a considerable extent, from the ideas of one philosopher, Nikolai Fyodorov, which influenced a scientific genius, Konstantin Tsiolkovsky, to seek ways to bring about a mass resurrection. Fyodorov, considered by many to be the most erudite individual in the waning years of tsarist Russia (his followers included Dostoyevski, Tolstoy, and Pasternak), believed that the ecosystem of humans was the entire cosmos, which was an organic whole wherein "the biggest difference between the life of rocks and the life of human beings is that they live at different velocities in time and at different degrees of consciousness in space" (Holquist 1986). His "philosophy of the common task" held that since humans had the highest state of consciousness and all that is living is interconnected, humanity's responsibility was to regulate and bring order to nature throughout the universe. Our efforts to kill each other are wasteful and should be redirected toward the enemies of chaos and chance, which are the causes of the entropy and death of both the self and the cosmos.

Fyodorov was to profoundly influence Tsiolkovsky, who, more than a century ago in working to achieve his mentor's dreams, devised aerodynamic tests for air frames, solved the problem of rocket flight in a uniform gravitation field, calculated the amount of fuel needed to overcome the earth's gravitational pull, invented the gyroscope to stabilize rockets in space, and built a centrifuge to test the effects of rapid acceleration on living organisms. This story prompted its chronicler, Walter McDougall, to speculate on the day when science "will have reached the absolute limits in its quest for the origins, extent, composition, and fate of the material universe. When that day arrives, the technolocratic pump may cavitate, the human heart have a meltdown, and science become again a branch of moral philosophy" (1985, p. 459).

NOTES

1. As the end of personal life gives special insight, so perhaps does the death of entire social orders. Existential and psychoanalytic thought did not emerge from some sociocultural vacuum. Evolving over the course of two world wars, during the obsolescence of *gemeinschaft* social order, the ending of Alvin Toffler's (1980) second historical wave, the approach of the millennium, in the context of growing fears over nuclear war, overpopulation, and ecological disaster, perhaps societies as well have

their coda syndromes. Harold Innis describes the creative surges spawned by the collapse of cultures: "With a weakening of protection of organized force, scholars put forth greater efforts and in a sense the flowering of the culture comes before its collapse. Minerva's owl begins its flight in the gathering dusk not only from classical Greece but in turn from Alexandria, from Rome, from Constantinople, from the publican cities of Italy, from France, from Holland, and from Germany" (1951, p. 5). But it has been the unprecedented numbers—the scores of millions—of man-made deaths during the twentieth century that have truly sparked reflections into our innermost drives and capacities for evil.

2. An example of the last is the case of James Kidd, an itinerant miner who disappeared in 1946 and willed an estate of half a million dollars to scientific research that could prove that the soul leaves the body after death. The trial, conducted in 1967, generated eight hundred thousand pages of transcripts. Three groups were petitioners in the case: well-funded parapsychological foundations, trance mediums, and medical research centers. The judge decided in favor of one of the medical research centers, the Barrow Neurological Institute. The Supreme Court overturned the decision and called for a retrial. Ultimately, the estate was granted to one of the parapsychological institutes, the American Society for Psychic Research (French 1987).

3. One pernicious implication of social class is the enhancement of one's prospects for being remembered. Queen Elizabeth II, as an extreme example, knows a seventy-three-generation pedigree.

4. Certain differences were, however, detected among the elite. Scientists appeared to have a greatly expanded time perspective and were more future-oriented than the artists. They were also more consciously preoccupied with death. Artists were more likely to view death within themselves, whereas the scientists saw death as an external force. Such preoccupations were not related to fears of death.

5. In his Commentary 124–27, Epicurus wrote: "As the true understanding of the nature of the gods relieves us from fear in this life, so the knowledge that consciousness ceases at death relieves us from fear with regard to a subsequent life. Moreover, since death will not be terrible when it comes, there is no reason why its anticipation should disturb us" (Bailey 1979, p. 331).

6. As will be developed, such transcendent beliefs come in various guises, achieved not only through religiously based beliefs in life after death but through other symbolic modes as well. Existentialism is typically linked with the absence of belief in life after death. In France, where the influence of existentialism has perhaps been greatest, the proportion of believers in life after death declined from 58 percent to 35 percent between 1948 and 1968 (Segerberg 1974, p. 22).

7. Otto Rank (1950; 1975) viewed human development as a longitudinal series of alternations between these conflicting desires.

8. Pursuing this logic, Peter Koestenbaum writes: "To believe in immortality does not mean to have overcome the primal anxiety about our own death; it means that we have decided to make a strenuous effort—both psychologically and intellectually—to lead an existence which works constantly at convincing ourselves that the anxiety about our death is unfounded and can be overcome" (1971, p. 10).

9. If true, one wonders about the psychic stamp upon the identities of those baby-boomer males born in the late 1940s who, because their fathers left for the Korean War at the time when such patricidal thoughts were being harbored, think they have won the contest. Nevertheless, it is from this framework that one typically approaches such questions as the adulthood impacts of having encountered mass death as a child, whether because of war, terrorism, or natural calamity. And there are numerous adults on psychoanalytic couches who, as children, perhaps harbored a death wish toward a grandparent who that day had admonished them for some misdeed, only to have the grandparent die that night of some massive coronary. The guilt ensuing from this coincidence of a magical style of thinking has the potential of haunting someone for decades.

10. Such activities historically increase when the bases of social comparisons shift from "tradition-directedness" and "inner-directedness," to the "other-directedness" that characterizes modern life (Riesman 1961).

11. Death does not nullify personality, for example, "as long as it has the character of deliberate martyrdom, freely accepted or even consciously sought" (Borkenau 1965, p. 53).

12. Kathy Charmaz observes the big irony in perceiving culture as the consequence of repressed death: "While animals use the death instinct to die, human beings use it aggressively to build civilization and make history in their efforts to fight death. Paradoxically, civilization turns the human being against itself" (1980, p. 59). Daniel Bell comes to a similar conclusion by means of a different logic: "the modern hubris is the refusal to accept limits and to continually reach out; and the modern word is *beyond*—to go always beyond, beyond morality, beyond tragedy, beyond culture. It is in this sense that modern culture is anti-institutional and antinomian, driven by 'unyielding rage' to apocalyptic anger" (1980, pp. 279–80).

13. Consider the irony of the fact that the Soviet Union, the first society to ever proclaim the finality of death, still needs to make a cult figure out of the embalmed remains of Lenin.

14. Frederick Hoffman claims that "as the belief in immortality (which is eternity individualized) becomes less and less certain, more attention is paid to time, and time achieves a spatial quality" (1959, p. 136).

15. Americans' hopes for the actuality of self surviving biological extinction are decreasingly satisfied through religious faith but, instead, require scientific proof. One century's worth of attempts to garner evidence of the survival of human personality after death has been documented (Lescarboura 1920). Even Thomas Edison wrote of people dying and their bodies being deserted by a swarm of highly charged energies that goes into space and enters another cycle of life. In a 1920 *Scientific American* interview, he said: "I have been thinking for some time of a machine or apparatus which could be operated by personalities which have passed onto other existence or sphere. . . . I am inclined to believe that our personality hereafter does affect matter. If we can evolve an instrument so delicate as to be affected by our personality as it survives in the next life, such an instrument ought to record something" (cited in Stevenson 1977).

16. This is not to deny that serious intellectual attention has been directed toward such phenomena (see, for example, C. J. Ducasse 1961 and H. H. Price 1965). Here, however, the focus is on the "pop" psychological and thanatological stories disseminated by the popular press.

17. Stanley Keleman (1974) argues that the human organism has a sense of excitement about dying that is similar to the excitement of facing the unknown, that perhaps there is an in-built genetic program for dying which is an integral part of its total developmental agenda.

18. As Mead (1926) and later Duncan (1962) observed, endings distinguish the essence of aesthetic experience from all other acts through their power "to capture the enjoyment that belongs to the consummation, the outcome, of an undertaking and to give to the implements, the objects that are instrumental in the undertaking, and to the acts that compose it something of the joy and satisfaction that suffuse its successful accomplishment" (Mead 1926, p. 384). Only in conclusions are the connections between means and ends realized, the "clash of interests and impulses resolved" (Duncan 1962, p. 82), when "we contemplate, and abide, and rest in our presentations" (Mead 1926, p. 385). This aesthetic potential is not simply a province of the arts but exists as well in the culmination of role biographies.

19. Musing on our bestial origins is not confined to academic circles, being a source of considerable public fascination. We study the animal kingdom and observe the large numbers of closely related species (i.e., the numerous kinds of finches, dogs, and cats) and yet note that humans have no evolutionary peer group. Where are the near- or proto-humans? Some would claim that humans have killed off all contenders, that the closely related contemporaries of the human species went the way of many other extinct mammals when encroached upon by expanding human populations. Others observe that apes in general are following the path of extinction, evidenced by the shrinking number of their similar species.

20. In studies of wolves, for instance, the pack concentrates its killing in a different area of its territory each year, allowing the prey population to recover elsewhere. While this may appear to anthropomorphizing human observers to be adaptive decision making—some, such as Peter Kropotkin (author of the 1903 book *Mutual Aid: A Factor of Evolution*), going so far as to claim that nature is governed by the noble principle of reciprocal altruism—it simply is the result of the wolves concentrating their hunt where the returns are the greatest.

21. Ninety percent of all life forms known to have existed have, indeed, perished. As much of our understanding of civilizations past derives from funerary artifacts, so do the fossilized remains of creatures contribute to our reconstructions of species long extinct. From them we find that the number of species simultaneously alive has remained roughly constant over the past 280 million years.

22. Perhaps it was a legacy of the Romanticists' virtuous conception of nature juxtaposed against the supposed evils of human society, but it was not until the 1970s that reports of infanticide in the animal kingdom began coming in from the field. Sociobiologists claim that such murders occur when, for instance, a new male langur takes over a troop. The new dominant male kills unweaned infants in order to bring

the mothers into estrus sooner, enabling him to more rapidly sire his own offspring (Burke 1984).

23. Even the rituals of death contribute to the decimation of the natural order. In India, the Hindu tradition of cremation is depleting forests and polluting water systems. Each cremation consumes enough wood to provide six months' worth of cooking fuel for the average family. And with increasing prices of fire wood, families are forced to throw their partially burned dead into the Ganges, which further contaminates a river used for washing and drinking (*New York Times* 1988).

24. We are haunted by the old German maxim that when the trees die, so do the people.

25. The human tendency is to continue to blame the victims for their fate. The increase in casualties has been blamed on such factors as deforestation and erosion, which reduce the land's resilience in the face of climatic extremes; people moving to disaster-prone areas because of poverty; and the excessive rates of human population growth (Eckholm 1984).

26. According to Daniel Stanley and Harison Sheng, this eruption on the Greek island of Santorini may have produced the inexplicable phenomena described in Exodus. Each volcano has its own identifiable ash, and glass fragments identical with those produced by the Santorini blast were found deep in the soil of the Nile delta near Port Said (Wilford 1985).

27. Though recorded, like most terrifying events, this one is largely forgotten because of collective amnesia.

28. In ancient Mexican sources, Venus is referred to as "the star that smokes." Human sacrifices were brought to Venus by the Mayas and, until the nineteenth century, by the Pawnee Indians when the planet appeared especially bright (Velikovsky 1983, p. 41).

29. In the United States alone, there are eleven confirmed sites where large asteroids have landed. In Canada, there are twenty definite impacted sites. If the Nemesis hypothesis is correct, the next doomsday is due in 14 million years.

30. It is intriguing to note that Latin roots of the word *disaster* are "evil star" (Mollander 1984).

31. To add to nature's lethal arsenal of events to worry about is the death of stars. A supernova within thirty light years of the earth could end life instantly, its energy falling on the surface of the earth equivalent to that of one hundred thousand to one million hydrogen bombs. These are relatively rare events, occurring in our galaxy once every fifty to one hundred years. But even so, some ten to twenty supernovas are expected within a sixty-light-year radius of the earth before the death of the sun.

REFERENCES

Arendt, Hannah. 1964. *Eichmann in Jerusalem: A Report on the Banality of Evil.* New
    York: Viking.
Bailey, Cyril. 1979. *Epicurus: The Extant Remains.* Westport, Conn.: Hyperion Press.

Becker, Ernest. 1973. *The Denial of Death.* New York: Free Press.

———. 1975. *Escape from Evil.* New York: Free Press.

Bell, Daniel. 1980. *The Winding Passage.* New York: Basic Books.

Bellah, Robert, 1985. "A Conversation with Robert Bellah, 'Individualism Has Been Allowed to Run Rampant," interviewed by Alvin Sanoff. *U.S. News & World Report.* May 27, pp. 69–70.

Berger, Peter. 1967. *The Sacred Canopy.* Garden City, N.Y.: Doubleday.

Berger, Peter, and Thomas Luckmann. 1966. *The Social Construction of Reality.* Garden City, N.Y.: Doubleday Anchor Books.

Bertman, Sandra. 1979. "Communicating with the Dead: An Ongoing Experience as Expressed in Art, Literature, and Song." In Robert Kastenbaum, ed., *Between Life and Death.* New York: Springer, pp. 124–155.

Borkenau, Franz. 1965. "The Concept of Death." In Robert Fulton, ed., *Death and Identity.* New York: John Wiley, pp. 42–56.

Browne, Malcolm. 1980. "Reality: A Grand Illusion?" *New York Times.* February 26, p. C2.

Burke, Barbara. 1984. "Infanticide: Why Does It Happen in Monkeys, Mice, and Men?" *Science 84.* May, pp. 26–31.

Butler, Robert. 1963. "The Life Review: An Interpretation of Reminiscence in the Aged." *Psychiatry* 26:65–76.

———. 1975. *Why Survive? Being Old in America.* New York: Harper & Row.

Camus, Albert. 1955. *The Myth of Sisyphus and Other Essays.* New York: Alfred A. Knopf.

Caufield, Catherine. 1985. "A Reporter at Large." *New Yorker.* January 14, pp. 41–101.

Charmaz, Kathy. 1980. *The Social Reality of Death.* Reading, Mass.: Addison-Wesley.

Choron, Jacques. 1964. *Death and Modern Man.* New York: Collier Books.

Clark, Grahame. 1953. *From Savagery to Civilization.* New York: Henry Schuman.

Cornell, James. 1982. *The Great International Disaster Book,* 3d ed. New York: Charles Scribner's Sons.

Crane, Stephen. 1964. *Poems of Stephen Crane,* selected by Gerald McDonald. New York: Thomas Y. Crowell.

Day, David. 1981. *The Doomsday Book of Animals.* New York: Viking Press.

De Beauvoir, Simone. 1972. *The Coming of Age.* New York: G. P. Putnam's Sons.

Derber, Charles. 1979. *The Pursuit of Attention.* New York: Oxford University Press.

Diamond, Jared. 1987. "The American Blitzkrieg: A Mammoth Undertaking." *Discover* 8(6):82–88.

Dostoyevski, Fyodor. 1974 [1864]. *Notes from Underground.* Trans. by Mirra Ginsburg. New York: Bantam.

Ducasse, C. J. 1961. *A Critical Examination of the Belief in a Life after Death.* Springfield, Ill.: Charles C. Thomas.

Duncan, Hugh. 1962. *Communication and the Social Order.* New York: Bedminister Press.

Eckholm, Erik. 1984. "Fatal Natural Disasters on Rise." *New York Times.* July 31, pp. 15, 16.

Feifel, Herman. 1959. "Attitudes toward Death in Some Normal and Mentally Ill Populations." In Herman Feifel, ed., *The Meaning of Death.* New York: McGraw-Hill, pp. 114–30.

French, Peter. 1987. "The Ghosts' Day in Court." Lennox Philosophy Lecture, Trinity University.

Freud, Sigmund. 1962 [1930]. *Civilization and Its Discontents.* New York: W. W. Norton.

Fulton, Robert, ed. 1965. *Death and Identity.* New York: John Wiley.

Gettings, Fred. 1978. *Ghosts in Photographs: The Extraordinary Story of Spirit Photography.* New York: Harmony Books.

Gide, André. 1970 [1958]. *The Immoralist.* Trans. by Richard Howard. New York: Vintage Books.

Goodman, Lisl. 1981. *Death and the Creative Life.* New York: Springer.

Gruson, Kerry. 1985. "Effort to Save a Species Leads to Brief Cheer, Then Gloom." *New York Times.* October 7, p. 9.

Hagestad, Gunhild, and Michael Smyer. 1982. "Dissolving Long-Term Relationships: Patterns of Divorcing in Middle Age." In S. Duck, ed., *Personal Relationships 4: Dissolving Personal Relationships.* New York: Academic Press, pp. 155–88.

Harper's Magazine. 1987. "Harper's Index." March, p. 15.

Harrington, Alan. 1977. *The Immortalist.* Millbrae, Calif.: Celestial Arts.

Harris, Louis. 1975. *The Myth and Reality of Old Age in America.* Washington, D.C.: National Council on Aging.

Hartshorne, Charles. 1964. *The Divine Relativity: A Social Conception of God.* New Haven, Conn.: Yale University Press.

Hoffman, Frederick. 1959. "Mortality and Modern Literature." In Herman Feifel, ed., *The Meanings of Death.* New York: McGraw-Hill, pp. 133–56.

Holquist, Michael. 1986. "The Philosophical Bases of Soviet Space Exploration." *Key Reporter* 51(2):2–4.

Horowitz, Mardi. 1986. *Stress Response Syndromes.* New York: Jason Aronson.

Innis, Harold. 1951. *The Bias of Communication.* Toronto: University of Toronto Press.

Janoff-Bulman, Ronnie. 1982. "Adaptive Strategies for Victims vs. Observer." *Journal of Personality* 50(2):180–92.

Kalish, Richard. 1985. *Death, Grief, and Caring Relationships.* Belmont, Calif.: Brooks/Cole.

Kearl, Michael. 1980. "Time, Identity, and the Spiritual Needs of the Elderly." *Sociological Analysis* 41:172–80.

Keleman, Stanley. 1974. *Living Your Dying.* New York: Random House.

King, Wayne. 1984. "A Chance of a Lifetime or Longer." *New York Times.* May 14, p. 8.

Koestenbaum, Peter. 1971. *The Vitality of Death: Essays in Existential Psychology and Philosophy*. Westport, Conn.: Greenwood.

Koestler, Arthur. 1977. "Cosmic Consciousness." *Psychology Today*. April, pp. 53–54, 104.

Kübler-Ross, Elisabeth. 1969. *On Death and Dying*. New York: Macmillan.

Laing, R. D. 1967. *The Politics of Experience*. New York: Ballantine Books.

Lescarboura, A. C. 1920. "Edison's Views on Life and Death." *Scientific American* 123 (Oct. 30):446.

Levine, Art. 1987. "Mystics on Main Street." *U.S. News & World Report*. February 9, pp. 67–69.

Lifton, Robert. 1968. *Revolutionary Immortality: Mao Tse-Tung and the Chinese Cultural Revolution*. New York: Random House.

———. 1979. *The Broken Connection*. New York: Simon & Schuster.

McDougall, Walter. 1985. *The Heavens and the Earth: A Political History of the Space Age*. New York: Basic Books.

McKee, Patrick. 1980–81. "Consummation: A Concept for Gerontological Theory." *International Journal of Aging and Human Development* 4:239–44.

Malinowski, Bronislaw. 1949. *Sex and Repression in Savage Society*. London: Lund Humphries.

Maugham, Somerset. 1952. *Of Human Bondage*. New York: Random House.

Mead, George. 1926. "The Nature of Aesthetic Experience." *International Journal of Ethics* 36:382–93.

Molander, Roger. 1984. "Only 14 Million Years until Doomsday." *New York Times*. May 12, p. 23.

Moore, Wilbert. 1963. *Man, Time, and Society*. New York: John Wiley.

Morgenthau, H. 1967. *The Modern Vision of Death*. Richmond, Va.: Knox.

Morrow, Lance, 1984. "A Dying Art: The Classy Exit Line." *Time*. January 16, p. 76.

Murphy, Gardner. 1959. "Discussion." In Herman Feifel, ed., *The Meaning of Death*. New York: McGraw-Hill, pp. 317–40.

Neugarten, Bernice. 1970. "Dynamics of Transition of Middle Age to Old Age." *Journal of Geriatric Psychiatry* 4:71–87.

New York Times. 1985a. "Volcanoes: The 10 Worst." November 15, p. 4.

———. 1985b. "Action Is Urged to Avert Global Climate Shift." December 11, p. 13.

———. 1986. "Research Links Motherhood to Lower Heart Attack Risk." November 20, p. 13.

———. 1988. "Curbing Cremation Fuel Needed." March 8, p. 18.

Palo Alto Times. 1976. "George Washington Told His Doctors to Let Him Die." February 16, p. 1.

Peterson, Russell. 1985. "Human Species Threaten the Earth's Ability to Support Life." *New York Times*. January 3, p. 18 (letters to ed.).

Price, H. H. 1965. "Survival and the Idea of 'Another World.'" In J. R. Smythies, ed., *Brain and Mind: Modern Concepts of the Nature of Mind.* New York: Humanities Press, pp. 1–33.

Rank, Otto. 1950. *Psychology and the Soul.* Philadelphia: University of Pennsylvania Press.

———. 1975. *Art and Artist, Creative Urge, and Personality Development.* New York: Agathon.

Reisman, David. 1961. *The Lonely Crowd.* New Haven, Conn.: Yale University Press.

Sagan, Carl. 1985. *Cosmos.* Westminster, Md.: Ballantine.

Sartre, Jean-Paul. 1956. *Being and Nothingness.* New York: Philosophical Library.

Schmitt, Raymond, and Wilbert Leonard II. 1986. "Immortalizing the Self through Sport." *American Journal of Sociology* 91(5):1088–1111.

Schneider, Keith. 1985. "U.S. Opposes Plan for Storing Genes." *New York Times.* November 28, pp. 1, 11.

Science News. 1984. "Nemesis: Searching for the Sun's Deadly Companion Star." September 1, p. 134.

Segerberg, Osborn. 1974. *The Immortality Factor.* New York: E. P. Dutton.

Sepkoski, J. John, and David Raup. 1983. "Mass Extinctions In the Fossil Record." *Science* 219(4589):1240–41.

Shneidman, Edwin. 1973. *Deaths of Man.* New York: Quadrangle/New York Times.

Shoumatoff, Alex. 1985. *The Mountain of Names: A History of the Human Family.* Simon & Schuster.

Sullivan, Ronald. 1982. "Hospitals Turn to Philosophers on Life Issues." *New York Times.* March 19, p. 1.

Toffler, Alvin. 1980. *The Third Wave.* New York: Morrow.

Velikovsky, Immanuel. 1950. *Worlds in Collision.* New York: Macmillan.

———. 1983. *Stargazers and Gravediggers: Memoirs to Worlds in Collision.* New York: William Morrow.

Wilford, John N. 1984. "Search for Nemesis Intensifies Debate over Extinctions." *New York Times.* December 18, pp. 25, 28.

———. 1985. "New Find Is Linked to Events of Exodus." *New York Times.* December 24, pp. 15, 19.

Wills, Garry. 1984. *Cincinnatus George Washington and the Enlightenment.* Garden City, N.Y.: Doubleday.

Wilson, Edward. 1975. *Sociobiology: The New Synthesis.* Cambridge, Mass.: Harvard University Press.

———. 1986. "Rain Forests in Decline." *San Antonio Express-News.* November 17, p. 10A.

Wolbach, Wendy, Roy Lewis, and Edward Anders. 1985. "Cretaceous Extinctions: Evidence for Wildfires and Search for Meteoric Material." *Science.* October 11, pp. 167–69.

Chapter 7

Death and Work

Well now John Henry was a little boy
Settin' on his mammy's knee
You know he picked up a hammer and a little bit of steel
He said, "This hammer gonna be the death of me, lord lord
Hammer gonna be the death of me." . . .

Well now John Henry picked up a thirty-pound hammer
By that steam drill he did stand
Well he beat that steam drill three chests and down
And he laid down his hammer and he died, lord lord
He laid down his hammer and he died.

When God foreclosed on Eden, Adam and Eve were not only made mortal but they were forced to work as well. This connection between death and work has remained ever since in the West. It is evident in our folk culture, as in the song "John Henry," and in the very metaphors by which we understand contemporary work activities. In the attempt to "bury" competitors, supervisors establish "deadlines" that must be observed if workers are to avoid being "terminated," "axed," or forever consigned to "dead-end" jobs; companies adopt a "poison pill" defense against hostile takeover attempts. Also evident in "John Henry" is how work invests life with meaning, not only because of this possible price of death but also by virtue of its ability to provide symbolic immortality for those who do good work. In fact, as opposed to all other animals who leave just the skeletal or fossilized imprints of themselves, only humans leave remnants of what they have created.

Chapters 5 and 6 considered the institutional ways death has been dealt with on an ideological level by religious and secular intellectuals. Here the focus is on the first of several institutions whose activities lead, both directly and indirectly, to the increasingly "unnatural" lives and deaths of their social members.[1] We will develop how social evolution has altered the nature of labor's lethality and its immortality potential. We will explore how, for example, economic life has led to the death of nature, how work-related mortality is socially stratified, and how lethal products continue to be produced. To conclude, a case study will be made of those whose work routinely involves the dead—morticians and embalmers—and how their industry contributes to the American cultural ethos of death denial.

The Centrality of Work to Self and Society

Perhaps more than any other institution, the type of work predominating in a particular culture shapes the personality structures of its individuals, the metaphors of their thoughts, the limits of their aspirations, and the organization of their social systems. Peter Berger (1964, p. 211) observes that to be human and to work appear as inextricably intertwined notions. To work means to transform the natural order: only through such modifications can the world be made into an arena for human conduct, human meanings, and human society. Some theorists go so far as to argue that working provides the archetype for all of one's experiences of reality, with all other provinces of meaning being but its modifications (Schutz 1973; see also Berger, Berger, and Kellner 1973). Through working, the self integrates its present, past, and future into a specific dimension of time and realizes itself as a totality in its working acts. Yet ironically, the very labels for work bear connotations of suffering, as in the Latin *labor,* Spanish *trabajo,* and French *travail* (Berger 1964, p. 212). Apparently there remains a residue of this distress. University of Manitoba researchers reported that the risk of men dying of a heart attack was greatest on the first day of the work week. In their long-term follow-up study of nearly four thousand men, they found that thirty-eight had died of sudden heart attacks on Monday, whereas only fifteen died on Friday. Further, for men with no history of heart disease, Monday was particularly dangerous, averaging 8.2 heart attack deaths for Tuesday through Sunday and nearly three times as many on Monday (Rabkin, Mathewson, and Tate 1980).

Since earliest times, working has been imbued with religious significance because of its mimicking of creation. The Protestant work ethic, as Max Weber (1958) noted, is one such example of how labor can be invested with religious significance. The Puritans viewed work as a purgative means toward salvation, and the Russians have also incorporated work into their ideological answer to death.[2] However, with the mechanization and bureaucratization of work, one's traditional relationship with one's product is typically lost. In part, this entails the loss of one's transcendent opportunities through craftsmanship, which involves the idea that quality enhances the prospects of a product surviving its producer. Take, for example, the gargoyles fashioned by the Italian-American stone carvers adorning the National Cathedral in Washington, D.C. Not only can the old artisans look up and see the creations of their predecessors and of their own youth, but they also can abide in the satisfaction of knowing that their works will survive hundreds—if not thousands—of years. Such satisfactions are easy to understand but nowadays increasingly difficult for most to attain.[3]

Even the act of consuming mass-produced products has religious connotations. In her analysis of the origins of mass consumption in late-nineteenth-century France, Rosalind Williams (1982, p. 6) observed that one of the Latin sources of the word *consumption* in Romance languages, *consummare*, is from *cum summa*, "to make the sum" or "to sum up." In a materialistic society, the meaning of labor is summed up through the acquisition of goods. And as was the function of religion in preindustrial times (Durkheim 1961), it is now within the economic sphere that central social beliefs are reaffirmed, social solidarity is provided, and individuals are linked with the broader social order. For instance, in the shopping mall—the postwar palaces where the "sacramentalism of consumption" is conducted—consumers are reminded of the glories of materialism, rub elbows with fellow community members, and, considering the spectrum of international product lines, come in direct contact with the world system.

What men and women had once hoped to inherit from their parents, they now expected to buy for themselves. What were once bought at the dictate of need, were now bought at the dictate of fashion. What were once bought for life, might now be bought several times over. (McKendrick, Brewer, and Plumb 1982, p. 1)

The Evolution of Work and the Changing Nature of Death

There are a number of ways to abstract work's history in order to reveal the changes in the interdependencies of self and social structures. Alvin Toffler (1980) demarcates three distinctive epochs, each precipitated by major technological innovations in the workplace. In the first and earliest period, life's game was against nature, and the rhythms of work with the land was determined by the movements of the sun and seasons. One's variety of work allowed near self-sufficiency but was also all-consuming; one often worked the same land and in the same manner as one's ancestors and, like them, labored until dropping dead. With energy coming from such renewable sources as muscle power and the burning of wood, and with the logic of the seasons, the cosmos must have seemed governed by a general law of death and rebirth.[4]

One difference between preindustrial and postindustrial workers is the degree the latter are removed from the natural order, from the natural logic of births and deaths. This is still evident in the different life worlds of contemporary farm and urban workers. On television there was featured a boy with his prized swine entry at a regional stock show. When asked if his pet's fate at the slaughterhouse bothered him, he replied, "I guess it's the name of the game." This is not so apparent to the urban resident, whose carnivorous appetites are met at a supermarket where all creatures are similarly packaged, bereft of feather, hoof, and hide. Modern urbanites can no more grasp the source of much of their food than they can dispose of the remains of a dead pet.

With industrialism, the game of work became a game against fabricated nature, a world where the machine predominates and the rhythms of life are mechanically paced and bureaucratically organized. With energy deriving from the machine instead of directly from nature, entropy came to replace the principle of regeneration in cultural eschatologies and cosmogonies: the cosmos no longer was seen to renew itself, as nature does in the spring, but rather it wears out and falls apart, like an old machine. In fact, considering the machine's reliance on fossil fuels, namely coal and oil, industrialism can be seen as being dependent on death. Instead of individuals meshing their lives to the eternal rhythms of nature, they are prefitted to serve the immortal essence of the corporation.[5] And though the concurrent rise of individualism had meant personal accountability for salvation, with the technology of mass production one lost the ability to be personally remembered through one's products as their creation had become a collective enterprise. Further, capitalism's cultural repudiation of the past in its incessant quest for the novelty of change (Bell 1976) has brought about not only the obsolescence of craftsmanship but also the intentional obsolescence of products.[6] Throughout the developed world we see the destruction of the past in order to install a more disposable present.

With postindustrialism, Toffler's Third Wave (1980) of human history, the work product has become even more ephemeral. The nature of work now often involves the exchange of services, a game between persons. Given the prevalent nature of work, which is either the management or manipulation of information, little survives in an era of computer erasures and paper shredders. What legacy is the future grandparent to leave of his or her working self for the heirs? A memo? A job rating? Concurrently, work has become even more essential to the identity of individuals, evidenced by the postwar attempts of minorities, women, and the elderly to obtain equal opportunity in the workplace. Who one is is what one does. To lose one's work has become a form of symbolic death.

Known as "breaker boys," these children sorting coal in a mine in the 1890s worked long hours for low wages under dangerous and unhealthy conditions. Brown Brothers.

Death on the Job

Work's lethal potential has, like its transcendent opportunities, been altered by technological and social evolution. In preindustrial contexts, workers' deaths were primarily conspiracies of nature. Man the hunter, for example, was also man the hunted. There were the parasitic infections of the field workers, such as the schistosomes from the flooded rice fields which invaded human bloodstreams and created a debilitated and short-lived peasantry, who were handicapped for sustained work, for resisting military attack, or for throwing off political domination and economic exploitation. Historian William McNeill (1976, p. 45) posited that such infections of agricultural field workers may have played a central role in the erection of social hierarchies in the early river-valley civilizations, the legacies of which are maintained to this day.[7] The old extractive industries, such as mining, fishing, and logging, were and continue to be notorious killers. In this century, for example, some 103,000 people have been killed in mine accidents in the United States. Death and coal have always gone together (Serrin 1979), as have death and the high seas (commercial fishing has the highest fatality rate of any industry). Whereas in ordinary occupations the job-related death rate was 12 per 100,000 in 1975, it averaged 122 in the hazardous occupations and was 268 for lumbermen (Barth and Hunt 1980, p. 6). As evident in Table 7.1, these blue-collar industries have about 5.5 times more deaths than expected by chance.

In industrial times, death from work increasingly came from man-made, not natural, origins. The primitive technology that characterized early industrialization killed and maimed thousands, including women and children fatigued from monotonous work and exhausting hours. Observed Karl Marx, "The raising of wages leads to *overwork* among the workers. The more they want to earn, the more they must sacrifice their time and perform slave labor in which their freedom is totally alienated. . . . Thus, even in the state of society which is the most favorable to the worker, the inevitable result for the worker is overwork and premature death, reduction to a machine, enslavement to capital" (1964, pp. 71, 73). Such work-related deaths contributed, in part, to the rise of unions and to adversarial relationships between labor and management. Conflicts between these two groups led to deadly violence. In 1877, federal U.S. troops had to be employed to put

Table 7.1 Occupational Injury and Illness Fatalities and Employment for Employers with 11 or More Employees, by Industry Division[9]

	1981				
	Average annual employment (in thousands)	Percentage of work force	Fatalities	Percentage of total	Ratio of fatality % by % of workforce
Agriculture, forestry, fishing	845	1%	130	3%	3.0
Mining	1,047	2	500	11	5.5
Construction	2,982	5	800	18	3.6
Manufacturing	19,507	31	990	23	.7
Transportation and public utilities	4,677	7	750	17	2.4
Wholesale and retail trade	15,475	24	730	17	.7
Finance, insurance, real estate	4,183	7	120	3	.4
Services	14,265	23	350	8	.3
Total private sector	62,263	100%	4,370	100%	

Source: U.S. Department of Labor, mailing from Dallas in 1984.

This 1882 woodcut depicts a sick child beset by polluted air emanating from Standard Oil's Hunter's Point refinery plant. The Bettmann Archive, Inc.

down a violent national railroad strike, and eleven members of the Irish terrorist society Molly Maguires were hung for killing mine officials. In 1892, at the Carnegie steel mills in Homestead, Pennsylvania, seven guards and eleven strikers and spectators were killed in another strike.

During the course of this century, increasing bureaucratic coordination was to produce greater rationality, efficiency, and safety in the workplace. In rationalizing the work environment, all potential situations are identified and given appropriate action routines, thereby supposedly eliminating all idiosyncratic events. But fatal accidents continue to occur, as Chris Wright (1986) discovered in studying the British offshore oil industry, one of the newest industries but also the one with the worst safety record. Though on the surface it would seem that the victims of this industry died because of hazardous working conditions or personal carelessness, Wright locates the causes of accidents within the work organization itself. The practice of subcontracting, for instance, which allows main contractors to distance themselves from labor disputes, led to ignorance of safety routines and confusion over the location of legitimate authority and decision making. Most victims were subcontracted personnel. Others died in attempting to deal with abnormal tasks through established routine or attempting to meet the organizational demands for a speedup in their activity.

It was not until the mid-1980s that the federal government first compiled occupational death rates in the United States. Examining death certificates from all fifty states and the District of Columbia for the period of 1980 to 1984, the National Institute for Occupational Safety and Health found the overall annual fatality rate in the workplace to be 9 deaths per 100,000 workers. The most lethal occupation was mining, with 30.1 annual deaths per 100,000 workers, followed by construction (23.1 deaths per 100,000); agriculture, forestry, and fishing (20.3); and transportation, communication, and public utilities (19.5). The least lethal occupation was wholesale trade, with just one death per 100,000 individuals. Although males comprised only 52 percent of the work force, they made up 95 percent of all deaths.[8] And the fatality rate of workers sixty-five years of age and older (18 deaths per 100,000) was four times greater than that of those sixteen to nineteen years of age (whose rate was 4 per 100,000) (New York Times 1987).

Thus, contrary to evolutionary, progressive stereotypes of the workplace, work still kills. Accidental deaths caused by cave-ins, rough seas, and falling timber are being superseded by deaths caused by organizational blunders and such hidden, slow-motion hazards as radiation, chemical poisoning, and stress. The executive director of the Occupational Safety and Health Administration (OSHA), Eula Bingham, noted that "A particular American form of suicide is holding a steady job" (Lens 1979). With postindustrialism, not only has death not been eliminated from the workplace (there were 3740 work-related deaths in the United States in 1984 in private workplaces with eleven or more employees, a 21 percent increase over the previous year [Wall Street Journal 1985b]; between 1980 and 1984, 32,342 Americans died at work [New York Times 1987]), but, as we will see, it now invisibly emanates to surrounding neighborhoods and counties, as in the case of radiation, or even to neighboring countries, as in the case of acid rain.

Daniel Berman observes in Death on the Job (1979) that some one hundred twenty thousand deaths are directly attributable to dangerous working conditions. He claims that capitalism kills and that we all pay the burial costs, as it is cheaper for companies to kill than to improve working conditions.[10] When, for example, the Staco thermometer plant in Poultney, Vermont, was twice cited in 1975 by the state's occupational safety agency for mercury overexposures, inadequate engineering devices to control exposures, and insufficient availability of medical personnel, it was first fined eight hundred dollars and later fined seventy-five dollars (Trost 1985, p. 14). No license to

Death by High Technology

A Michigan man who died last summer was the first worker killed by a robot in this country, and his death suggests the need for new approaches to factory safety, a Federal safety expert said today.

. . . The 34-year-old victim, working with automated die-casting machinery last July, was pinned between the back of a robot and a steel pole, the national Centers for Disease Control reported today. The worker suffered a heart attack, lapsed into a coma and died five days later.

The Atlanta-based federal health agency noted that more than 6,200 robots were in use nationwide.

New York Times 1985a. Copyright © 1985
by the New York Times Company. Reprinted by permission.

do business was lost, and no one went to jail.[11] Until 1986, the Nuclear Regulatory Commission had not proposed for nearly thirty years any major revision to its radiation exposure limits for workers, even though improved knowledge indicated that certain types of radioactive materials were more carcinogenic than previously thought. Even company medicine evolved to serve not the worker, as one might expect, but to protect the companies' interests in lawsuits.[12]

A mid-1970s federal study conducted by the Institute of Occupational Safety and Health reported that one out of four workers is exposed to some substance thought to be capable of causing death. Fewer than 5 percent of the workplaces in the sites surveyed were found to have industrial-hygiene services, active plans to prevent or reduce the exposure of employees to hazardous substances and to such physical conditions as radiation and excessive noise (Burnham 1977). Based on his participation in a 1980 congressional study of workers impaired by chemicals, Edward Bergin estimated that nearly 2 million Americans are disabled by worksite gases, chemicals, and dust (Bergin and Grandon 1984). He said that "the amazing thing we found is that only one out of 20 people suffering from occupational diseases received anything from the state workers' compensation system which is supposed to take care of work-related injuries and diseases. When we looked closely at the compensation system, we found that while it may pay for a broken leg on the job, it is designed not to pay for occupational diseases" (Anderson 1984). And it has been estimated that half of us die of cardiovascular diseases, which are all stress-related (*U.S. News & World Report* 1979).

Of the 66,000 or so chemicals generated by American industry, 90 percent are classified by the Environmental Protection Agency as being potentially hazardous to human health (Magnuson 1985), and 575 are deemed dangerous in large doses by the federal government. Although scientists believe that between 1500 and 2000 of these are carcinogenic, only 17 are federally regulated in the workplace.[13] Hundreds of thousands of workers are exposed to such toxins as asbestos (90 percent with no protective equipment), benzene, cutting oil, mercury, and coal dust. According to an Environmental Protection Agency study, at least 6928 accidents involving toxic chemicals occurred in the United States between 1980 and 1984. Spills and emissions totaled 420 million pounds of chemicals, killing 139 and injuring at least 1478 persons (Diamond 1985a).[14] Even in the new white-collar, high-tech industries of California's Silicon Valley, workers involved in the manufacture of semiconductors are bringing legal suit because of acid burns, poisonings, hair loss, and lung irritations (Sanger 1984). Appeals to Washington for remedial action and compensation are rarely acted upon, as the federal government is itself a major culprit. The latest tally by the Environmental Protection Agency found that carcinogens from 343 military bases, weapons plants, and other federal facilities are major polluters of the public environment (Taylor 1985).

As mentioned, death has emanated from the workplace to the surrounding environment. Each year there are 300 million tons of toxic waste generated (Stoler 1985), and communities are discovering their soil and water being contaminated by lead, mercury, arsenic, dioxin, vinyl chloride, and PCB. The General Accounting Office predicts that more than 378,000 of these waste sites may require corrective action. Of the 1246 hazardous waste dumps surveyed by a congressional committee in 1985 (of the more than 17,000 identified by the EPA [Shabecoff 1983]), half were polluting nearby groundwater (Magnuson 1985). So great had the toxic-waste problem become by 1980 that the U.S. surgeon general called it "an environmental emergency" (Magnuson 1985). Thus, in a number of ways, economic life has come at the cost of death.

Finally, it should be noted that work can kill not only the individual and the environment but one's chances for genetic immortality as well. The National Peach Council in 1977 made the suggestion to the federal government that only older workers who do not want children and persons who would like to get around religious bans against birth control be allowed to handle a pesticide known to cause sterility.

Putting a Price on Human Life

It is not just the worker—who has one chance in ten thousand of dying on the job—who must face the deadly consequences of work. Also killed or dying are consumers, individuals living in proximity to the workplace, and entire ecosystems. The search for short-term profitability has brought about long-term death. A 1984 report of the Council on Economic Priorities, for example, revealed that cancer deaths increased 265 percent from 1950 to 1975 in rural counties with large concentrations of chemical and petroleum industries. Over the same time period, cancer deaths increased 148 percent in the seventy-one industrialized urban counties studied, amounting to about 1134 per 100,000 people (*San Antonio Express-News* 1984a).

 City on the Spot: Give Up Jobs or Risk Health

Listen to the anguish of Tacoma as residents struggle with an issue that has nationwide implications: What cancer risk is acceptable to keep 575 people working in a copper smelter that is releasing arsenic into the air? . . .

Most of the time "the arsenic danger was accepted as a condition of employment," reports Chuck O'Donahue, a smelter worker for 21 years and business agent of United Steelworkers Local 25. A respiratory-cancer rate among smelter workers 2½ times normal was seen as balanced by a payroll now up to 22 million dollars a year. . . .

ASARCO has spent more than 40 million dollars on pollution control. Even unionists believe the company is doing everything it can to protect employees from arsenic exposure. The smelter "is as safe as it can be made," says Mike Wright, an industrial hygienist with the United Steelworkers Union. "Now the smelter should do for the community what it did for the workers." . . .

Studies show that the lung-cancer rate in this city of 160,000 is below the national average. Children attending school 100 yards from the smelter have been found to display no detrimental health effects, though there are abnormally high levels of arsenic in their hair and urine. But arsenic cancers have a long latency period—up to 50 years.

"Arsenic may be a quiet killer like asbestos," says Brad Smith, an insurance man with three children. A *Tacoma News Tribune* poll found two-thirds of the people questioned believed the smelter to be a health hazard.

Chrysler 1983. Reprinted by permission
of *U.S. News and World Report* © 1983.

Given the nature of the U.S. political economy, such numbers of work-related deaths have forced a cost-benefit analysis to be applied to death. Was it more profitable to pay the death benefits and keep things as they were or to build greater safety and pollution controls into the work setting? Columnist Bill Keller (1984) noted that the "value of human life has eluded poets, theologians and philosophers for centuries, but the Government has an answer. Rather, several answers." In their accountants' measurements of the economic benefits of proposed regulations that might reduce accidental deaths, the Occupational Safety and Health Administration calculated a life to be worth $3.5 million, the Federal Aviation Administration placed the smaller value of $650,000 per life, and the Environmental Protection Agency estimated the range to be between $400,000 and $7 million (Keller 1984). In deriving such appraisals, government economists now try to compute from a person's behavior what value he or she puts on his or her own life, the latest variant of blaming the victim. If, for instance, one person accepts a job that doubles his or her risk of death for one thousand dollars more a year while another accepts the same risk for two hundred dollars more, then the former is estimated to value his or her life five times as much.

In 1984, the White House budget office told the Labor Department to devalue the life of a worker from $3.5 million to $1 million for the purposes of writing a safety regulation aimed at construction workers. Opponents viewed this action as an attempt to scuttle pending safety and environmental regulations affecting millions. Representative David Obey of Wisconsin said: "If the administration establishes that federal regulatory protection cannot be provided unless the costs of providing that protection do not exceed the value of the lives that will be saved and if it then insists upon placing a very low value on a worker's life, few regulatory protections will be found to be affordable" (*San Antonio Express-News* 1984b).

Industries have found that what is affordable is simply to expose less valuable persons to work's lethal situations. And here we return to the issues of social stratification.

The Stratification of Mortality in the Workplace

Death rates are stratified along the dimensions of social class. A U.S. government report, *Work in America,* reported in 1973: "Satisfaction with work appears to be the best predictor of longevity—better than known medical or genetic factors—and various aspects of work account for much, if not most, of the factors associated with heart disease." But work satisfaction is a positive function of occupational status. In a 1985 Harvard Medical School study of southern Florida, blue-collar workers were found to be 40 percent more likely to die of heart disease than white-collar workers, even when controlling for such factors as smoking, exercise, and neighborhood of residence (*New York Times* 1985c).

Following the Three-Mile Island and other nuclear mishaps, ads promising lucrative jobs began appearing in the newspapers of some of the most economically depressed areas of the country. Wanted were what the media came to call "nuclear sponges," individuals willing to risk their lives and genes to clean the lethal waste generated in the name of economic life. Who took

Table 7.2 Comparing the Death Rates of Harlem with the
Rest of New York City

	Death Rates per 100,000		
	Harlem	City Avg.	Harlem/city ratio
Infant mortality	43	19	2.26
Cirrhosis of liver	127	30	4.23
Murder, suicide, accidents	134	61	2.20

Source: Sterne 1978. Copyright © 1978 by the New York Times Company.
Reprinted by permission.

these jobs? The lower classes, of course, which brings us to the social stratification of death in the workplace. Is death equal-opportunity?

Even those who do not fit into capitalism's needs, such as minorities and
members of America's underclass, can face premature deaths. Not only does
their not working mean fewer resources for medical care, but, as evident in
Table 7.2, insufficient diets of poor mothers lead to higher infant mortality
rates, boredom and alienation yield more alcohol and drug-related deaths,
and a culture of violence and misery produces an abundance of suicides and
accidents.

On the other hand, major corporations have for years invested heavily in
the health of their corporate executives. Talented personnel are a crucial
resource, and, after years spent grooming them, companies want to extend
the career life expectancy of their human capital investments. To accomplish
this, management's perquisites include athletic facilities, spa memberships,
and resort privileges. But by the mid-1980s, corporate concerns for physical
health were extended to all employees, with many companies sponsoring
programs in which workers could exercise at company expense, employee
wellness programs, and therapy for substance abusers. However, the motivations behind this apparent democratization of concern generally did not
stem from humanitarian philosophy but rather from lower insurance costs,
increased productivity, and lower absenteeism and turnover. Further, during
this period, the number of persons entering the labor market was half that
of a decade earlier (when "baby-boomers" and women flooded entry-level
positions).

But the higher-status professions may not be immune to work's lethal
potential. Consider the health threats posed even for the high-status occupations, such as the cumulative detrimental effects of stress and the implications of blocked career aspirations possibly leading to the high incidence
of suicides among some medical specialties or the job-produced carcinomas
of older dentists. In a University of Oregon study, physicians, dentists,

police officers, and lawyers were found to be three times as likely as non-professional white-collar workers to commit suicide (Grollman 1971). One in 31 physician deaths is now attributable to suicide, and from 36 to 77 of every 100,000 physicians annually die by their own hand. Occupational level or socioeconomic status by itself does not predict suicide or suicide rate: "clergymen have a prestige score of 87 but a suicide rate of 10.6, while dentists have a prestige score of 90 and a suicide rate of 45.6. At the lower end of the occupational prestige scale, mine operatives and laborers have a prestige score of 15 but a suicide rate of 41.7; on the other hand, machinery operatives score 24 on prestige and have a suicide rate of 15.7" (Maris 1981, p. 146).

The Stratification of Mortality in the World System

The potential for work to spawn death was best illustrated not during the early days of technology and safety regulations but rather during the waning weeks of 1984. In the working-class district of Tlalnepantla in Mexico City during November, eighty thousand barrels of gas exploded at a depot of the state oil company Pemex, destroying about three hundred houses and killing a reported four hundred persons. Local residents said bulldozers buried hundreds more. Most victims had been killed by more than a dozen blasts at the liquefied petroleum gas facility that showered flames and debris onto homes and buildings. Three weeks later, in Bhopal, India, toxic gas leaking from an American-owned (Union Carbide) insecticide plant killed two thousand, including children in the womb, and impaired the lungs and eyes of more than two hundred thousand more. As described by one observer:

Hundreds died in their beds, most of them children and old people weakened by hunger and frailty. Thousands more awoke to a nightmare of near suffocation, blindness and chaos. . . . By the thousands, they stumbled into the streets, choking, vomiting, sobbing burning tears, joining human stampedes fleeing the torment of mist that seemed to float everywhere. Some were run down by cars and trucks in the panic. . . . "The whole city became a big gas chamber," said Indira Iyenger, an official of Mother Teresa's Missionaries of Charity. (McFadden 1984)

According to another witness, the streets of Bhopal were littered with the corpses of dogs, cats, water buffalo, cows, and birds killed by the gas, methyl isocyanate. Most of the victims were children and old people who were overwhelmed by the gas and suffocated (Hazarika 1984a). One year later, survivors were detected by the Industrial Toxicology Research Center to be suffering damage to their chromosomes and immune systems, increasing their vulnerability to infection and their likelihood of producing children with

Residents of Bhopal stand in front of the Union Carbide factory gate on December 14, 1984. Earlier in the month, deadly gas that was to be converted into harmless pesticide leaked from the plant, causing widespread death and illness. UPI/Bettmann Newsphotos.

genetic defects (*New York Times* 1985b). Human progress reveals human frailties, especially when culture fails to keep pace with technological innovation that yields greater interdependencies.

Union Carbide had been required by Indian law to design, engineer, build, and operate its Bhopal insecticide plant with local labor, materials, machines, and staff unless the company could prove to the Indian authorities that such resources were unavailable (Diamond 1985b). The company followed the law and opened its plant in 1977. This formula of high technology coupled with a low-technology cultural system was obviously an explosive mixture, apparent even to an Indian journalist who had asserted during the preceding two years that safety standards at the plant were inadequate and that a catastrophic leak could result (Hazarika 1984b). On the night of the disaster, a supervisor had detected a leakage but, believing it was simply water, postponed action until after his tea break. "Internal leaks never bothered us," said one employee (Diamond 1985a).

With the developed nations' exploitation of the developing nations' cheaper labor and resources, such mishaps will undoubtedly continue to occur. Profitability further derives from not having to incorporate the safety procedures or pollution devices required in the United States; only perhaps with postindustrialism does a social system begin to design jobs to fit people instead of industrialism's tendency to design people to fit jobs. In Cubatao, Brazil, industrial pollution from international firms is so severe—more than a thousand tons generated daily, breaking the first pollution meters from overload—that military rulers label it a national security zone while residents call it *O Vale da Morte*, "The Valley of Death." Babies are born without brains, bones, or limbs. Such is the cost of maintaining that country's greatest source of income—tax receipts (Cramer 1985).

Products That Kill

Work's contribution to the cultural death ethos is not limited to the lethality of the workplace or its by-products. When we think of certain cars (Pintos), drugs (thalidomide), foods (a nationally distributed batch of canned meat infected with salmonella), what comes to mind are symbols of the potential deadliness of some our supposedly safe products and—in this era of mass production and mass consumption—of our collective vulnerability to them. Many sense an increasing "unnaturalness" of our fabricated goods and feel that we may all be collectively killing ourselves with their use, much like the Romans of antiquity drinking tainted waters from lead pipes.

Some industries continue to manufacture products knowing full well their lethal potential and, during the mid-1980s, no longer worrying so much about zealous federal regulation (between 1984 and late 1987, the Consumer Product Safety Commission did not issue a single product-safety regulation; Saddler 1987). For example, in 1983 it was revealed that Dow Chemical knew as early as the mid-1960s about evidence that dioxin exposure might cause people to become seriously ill and even die but that the company withheld its concern from the government and continued to sell herbicides contaminated by dioxin to the U.S. Army (*New York Times* 1983). Two years later, officials of Eli Lilly failed to disclose the overseas deaths of twenty-eight people who had used the new arthritis drug Oraflex at the time when the company was seeking approval to sell the drug in the United States (Shenon 1985a). Also that year, the Food and Drug Administration charged

Japan Air Lines' Head Begs Forgiveness for 520 Deaths

The president of Japan Air Lines faced the relatives of victims of the world's worst single-plane disaster and bowed low and long.

He turned to a wall covered with wooden tablets bearing the victims' names. He bowed again. Then, in a voice that sometimes quavered, Yasumoto Takagi asked for forgiveness and accepted responsibility.

The ceremony today marked the final memorial service sponsored by the airline for the 520 people who died in the Japan Air Lines crash [two months earlier].

On Tuesday 3,271 people attended a service in Osaka. Today, about 1,400 people—some 700 family members, 693 airline employees and other guests—crowded into Hibiya Public Hall.

For Mr. Takagi and his employees, the service marked the culmination of a two-month exercise in accountability. Since the night of Aug. 12, the airline has mobilized its staff, from the president on down, to offer the gestures of apology and regret that Japanese require at such times.

In the days after the accident, when family members had to travel to a small mountain village to identify the bodies, airline staff stayed with them, paying all food, drink and clean clothes. Even after most of the bodies were identified, the airline assigned two staff members to each family to attend to needs as varied as arranging for funerals or blocking intrusive reporters.

J.A.L. set up a scholarship fund to pay for the education of children who lost parents in the crash. It spent $1.5 million on the two elaborate memorial services. The airline dispatched executives to every victim's funeral—although some were turned away. And Mr. Takagi has pledged to resign soon as a gesture of responsibility.

that SmithKline Beckman had suppressed information that Selacryn, a blood-pressure drug, was linked to thirty-six deaths and more than five hundred cases of liver and kidney failure (Shenon 1985b).

One industry in particular, though, has been singled out as the major producer of death, and yet its products continue to be sold and its workings subsidized by the federal government: the 16-billion-dollar tobacco industry. More than 60 million American adults now smoke the highly addictive "coffin nails," committing what former secretary of HEW Joseph Califano called "slow-motion suicide." Since 1930, per capita cigarette consumption of Americans aged fourteen and older increased from about fourteen hundred to more than thirty-five hundred.[15] As recently as the late 1970s, the federal government, through a series of guaranteed loans and grants from the

Jacob Balde's seventeenth-century anti-smoking pamphlet, *Die Truckene Trunckenheit* (The Dry Drunkenness) enlists a death-figure to encourage abstinence. Printed by Michael Endter, Nuremberg, 1658. Dover Pictorial Archives.

Department of Agriculture, spent 80 million dollars a year to support the growing of tobacco and its price (Lyons 1978).

Experts estimate that cigarette smoking is the major single cause of cancer mortality, contributing to 30 percent of all cancer deaths and responsible for 83 percent of male lung cancers, the most lethal form and prevalent kind of cancer afflicting the American male (Clapp 1984). The U.S. Public Health Service revealed that cigarette smokers, when compared to nonsmokers, have twice the risk of heart attacks, bladder cancer, and strokes; four times the risk of cancer of the esophagus; seven times the risk of death from emphysema or chronic bronchitis; eight times the risk of cancer of the larynx; and twenty-five times the risk of lung cancer. Smoking is also linked to deaths attributed to digestive system disease, accidental fires, and the stillbirths and miscarriages of infants of smoking mothers. Former surgeon general Dr. Julius B. Richmond estimated that thirty deaths every hour in the United States are attributable to cigarette smoking. The Office of Technology Assessment estimated that the treatment of smoking-related diseases annually cost the country between 12 and 35 billion dollars and that those diseases killed 139,000 Americans in 1982 alone (Molotsky 1985a, p. 12). Other government estimates place the annual number of premature deaths caused by cigarettes at 350,000 (Bean 1986), or about 17 percent of all deaths.

Cigarette-related deaths are not uniform across social groups but reveal once again the underlying stratifications of culture. For example, smoking disproportionately harms black Americans, who have the highest rates of smoking-related diseases—coronary heart disease and lung cancer—of any population group. Black men have a lung cancer rate 40 percent higher than that of white men, and black women have a 36 percent higher rate of coronary heart disease than white women (Eckholm 1985). With increasing numbers of women smoking, their lung cancer rate has multiplied five times since 1955; equal opportunity in the workplace has occurred with equal opportunity of dying from this cause. Further, the longevity of younger generations is affected as well, as increasing numbers of children born to smoking mothers are suffering long-term irreversible effects.

In the mid-1980s, the surgeon general of the United States claimed that cigarette smoking at work posed a greater health threat to workers than workplace hazards. For those in hazardous working environments, such as the asbestos industry, whose lung cancer rate for nonsmokers is ten times greater than for other workers, cigarette smoking multiplies the danger, increasing the cancer risk by a factor of eighty-seven. In Table 7.3, there is some evidence that even the possibility of smoking is inversely related to the occupational status of one's job or profession.

Table 7.3 Smoking on the Job
Percentage of smokers in each occupation, according to a survey of
47,481 randomly selected people nationwide, conducted by the
National Center for Health Statistics from 1978 to 1980.

	Percentage of workers who smoke
Men: highest rates	
Painting, construction, maintenance	55.1%
Truck drivers	53.6
Construction laborers (except carpenter aides)	53.0
Carpenters	50.8
Auto mechanics	50.5
Guards, watchmen	50.5
Janitors, sextons	49.8
Assemblers	48.7
Electricians	48.3
Sales representatives, wholesale trade	48.1
Women: highest rates	
Waitresses	51.1
Cashiers	44.2
Assemblers	42.9
Nurses aides, orderlies, attendants	41.0
Machine operators	41.0
Practical nurses	40.3
Packers (except meat and produce)	40.0
Manufacturing examiners, inspectors	39.3
Managers, administrators	38.0
Hairdressers, cosmetologists	37.5
Women: lowest rates	
Elementary schoolteachers	19.8
Food service	24.6
Secondary school teachers	24.8
Bank tellers	25.7
Sewers, stitchers	25.8
Registered nurses	27.2
Men: lowest rates	
Electrical, electronic engineers	16.2
Lawyers	21.9
Secondary school teachers	24.9
Accountants	26.8
Real estate agents, brokers	27.8
Farmers	28.1

Source: U.S. Surgeon General, cited in Molotsky 1985b.

And yet smokers continue to be assigned to perhaps the safest areas of aircraft, the tail sections, and are allowed to pollute public areas even though nonsmokers suffer the effects of passive smoking.[16] Many mass media depend heavily on the hundreds of millions of dollars spent in advertising this product, dwarfing the amounts spent educating the public about its negative effects.[17] Further, tobacco sales have been a stable source of government revenue for years, now yielding about 4.6 billion dollars. The total combined investment in "smoking education" by the three major voluntary health organizations—the American Cancer Society and the heart and lung groups—was 1 percent of that spent on advertising (Gitlitz 1985). Despite appeals by state medical societies and the National Advisory Council on Drug Abuse to ban cigarette advertisements, they continue, because of the power of the tobacco industry to overwhelm the media. In a randomly chosen issue of a major newspaper that published a four-and-a-half-inch editorial on the harmfulness of cigarettes, an advertisement for Merit cigarettes occupied two pages, and another for Kent covered nearly an entire page (Gitlitz 1985).

Federal agencies spent even less. When it was reported that the U.S. government was spending 5 million dollars a year on research for a "safe" cigarette (compared to the nearly 1.5 billion dollars the industry spends on advertising), David Fishel, a spokesman for R. J. Reynolds, was asked if his company was also looking for such a cigarette. "I don't know anything about it. We don't know of anything that makes a cigarette unsafe, so how could we be working toward a safer cigarette?" (Cohen 1985). Dr. Sidney Wolfe, director of the Health Research Group, noted that if the federal government could spend "$250 million to combat a nonexistent disease, swine flu, it should spend at least that much on smoking" (Lyons 1978).

The industry has come to adopt its own right-to-die ideology, viewing the likes of the American Cancer Society as authoritarians trying "to remake their lives." Victor Weingarten, executive director of the National Commission on Smoking and Public Policy, claimed that rather than trying to limit freedom of choice, the commission hoped to "restore the individual's freedom to choose," which for years had been dominated by heavy cigarette advertising and lobbying (Brody 1978). Such attempts to provide education on evil may, however, backfire. Dr. Peter Borne, when addressing in 1977 the American Medical Association's Ad Hoc Committee on Smoking Research, said: "If our behavior research shows that a high percentage of cigarette smokers began the habit in a rejection of authority then we must be sure that the imposition of Government authority will not do more to increase their dependence rather than encourage them to quit" (*New York Times* 1977).

The industry now finds the Third World as its new growth market, where sophisticated promotions are freely made on television and radio to the relatively unsophisticated public. Per capita cigarette consumption, for example, quadrupled in Indonesia from 1973 to 1981 and increased 8 percent annually in Kenya. Governments benefit as well: tobacco is Zimbabwe's largest cash crop; Brazil collects 75 percent of the retail price of cigarettes in taxes. In Bangladesh, according to a 1981 study published in the British medical journal *The Lancet,* people spend about 20 percent of their incomes on tobacco. In these countries not only is the product more expensive, but it is more lethal as well. A 1979 study by Oak Ridge National Laboratory in Tennessee found that the Benson & Hedges Special Filter cigarette had 17 milligrams of tar in the United States, 22.3 in Kenya, 29.7 in Malaysia, and 31.1 in South Africa (Mufson 1985).

Death and Immortality of Working Identities

> It would seem to be a cultural theme in America that individuals justify their lives by asking themselves whether or not their having lived "made a difference." They mean by this a positive, *lasting* difference to other individuals, the community, and, among those with more grandiose hopes, the society and even mankind.
>
> Westie 1973, p. 19

In February 1985, six pioneer inventors were inducted into the National Inventors Hall of Fame in Arlington, Virginia. These inventors, credited with originating air conditioning, the artificial heart, phototypesetting, tape recording, and Teflon, joined fifty-three others. One year later, seven recently discovered asteroids were named for the seven astronauts who had died in the explosion of the space shuttle *Challenger.* Work, like religion, provides immortality for the elect. Art galleries and libraries are filled with works of the dead. Gutzon Borglum is immortalized by his Mount Rushmore Memorial, Leonardo da Vinci by the *Mona Lisa,* Thomas Edison by the incandescent bulb, and Henry Ford by the automobile bearing his name. The Hartford, Connecticut, law firm of Day, Berry, and Howard sports the name of three deceased partners, and the memories of scientists live on in the names of the astronomical bodies, plants, and animals they either discovered or hybridized. Work gives individuals the major opportunity to "leave one's mark."

As is evident in Table 7.4, corresponding with the rapid differentiation of the workplace has been a proliferation of heavens. Memories of the work elite

Table 7.4 Halls of Fame

	Year established
American Association of Nurserymen	1965
Art Directors	
Automotive	1939
Black Academy of Arts and Letters	1970
Black Filmmakers	1973
Business	
Hall of Fame of Distinguished Band Conductors	1980
Hall of Fame for Great Americans	1900
Hall of Fame for U.S. Business Leadership	1975
National Auctioneers Association	1968
National Auto Auction Association	
National Aviation	
National Cowboy Hall of Fame and Western Heritage Center	1955
National Inventors	1934
National Women's	1969
Pickle Packers International	1955
Television Academy	
Theater	
United Methodist Church, Board of Global Ministries, Health and Welfare Ministries Division	
Veterans of Foreign Wars of the U.S.	
Womens Hall of Fame	

are maintained in a host of halls of fame, for everyone from pickle packers to auctioneers. If one fails to gain the highest forms of work-related immortality, such as through induction into a hall of fame or through one's works, there are still other possible means for being remembered. In particular, there are the numerous "Who's Who" compilations (e.g., *Who's Who among Elementary School Principals, Who's Who in Commerce and Industry, Who's Who in Rock,* and *Who's Who in Science in Europe*). And, for academicians, if one fails to make this compilation, one can at least make the card catalogue. Even better, one's ideas can be celebrated in school texts—one's name is at least remembered and perhaps even quizzed on.

Though there has been an increase in the number of individuals, many believe that modernization has brought a concurrent increase in the number of opportunities to "leave one's mark," whether through leaving a musical score on others' lips, ideas in their minds, or inventions that survive their creators.[18] Such personal needs to be remembered only come with the extreme individualism of modern societies; there was no time to worry about such things when survival was a daily unknown. Further, such needs probably intensify the higher one is in the social hierarchy: "The higher the posi-

tion the more the constraint to justify one's existence. People in higher rank-
ing occupations, particularly the professions, rarely, except facetiously,
justify the pursuit of their occupations with the remark, 'It's a living'" (Westie 1973, p. 19).

But nowadays, when there are so many ways to be remembered—photographs, books, movies, occupational awards and citations, financial contributions—and so many seeking recognition, these expectations for professional immortality are typically not met. As if in exchange for its diminishing
of transcendent opportunities, postindustrialism has increased the opportunities for rebirth experiences in the workplace. As Seymour Sarason observes
in *Work, Aging, and Social Change,* we are now witnessing the obsolescence
of the single-career imperative. With specialization and rapid obsolescence,
one must now plan or expect a series of careers. This comes with considerable
disruption. Such a conflict arises when the heightened expectations and
desires for job fulfillment engendered by a highly educated society clash with
the realities too often found in work: boredom, sense of personal stagnation,
disillusionment, and frustration in dealing with increasingly bureaucratized
organizational structures.

Sarason chronicles the biographies of several individuals who sought a radical career change, who, in effect, committed career suicides to shed used-up
selves and to begin anew. Given work's centrality to identity, such changes
did not occur casually; it was necessary for each to confront questions about
the meaning of work and, by extension, face existential questions about the
meaning of life. Like the approach toward one's own demise, this process of
self-examination led to rearrangements of priorities and a redefinition of
work. As such, these individuals' ventures into new work and life roles had
the character of a spiritual quest.[19]

Career Endings

Because the conclusions of most modern work careers are no longer punctuated by death, but rather by the institutionalization of retirement, individuals must either determine and shape their own rite of leavetaking or accept
the bureaucratic timetables and rituals of separation. The individual, as
author of his or her own work biography, now has some control over how
he or she is to be remembered by the quality of his or her culminating behaviors. Individuals now recognize opportunities in the ways careers can be concluded and that, as in any other social situation involving choice, invidious
comparisons are being drawn and ending strategies rank-ordered in terms of
their desirability: it is better to give a two-week notice than to receive a pink

slip, better to end "on an upbeat" than to disappear "over the hill," better to be premature than postmature when departing,[20] and better for Richard Nixon to take control over his own premature exit than to be bureaucratically terminated. Our considerations here will be limited to those individuals concluding their work histories, in other words the "old," and not those who, whether because of termination or personal mobility, leave one job for another.

Within the modern work sphere, the individual must now consider when his or her "time has come." The possibility for "Albert Schweitzerism," remaining in role until one's death and all the while accruing increasing prestige, is limited for all but a few occupations. In part, this is because of the rapid evolution (and obsolescence) of knowledge and skills required to compete effectively in an ageist marketplace in which the rationalities of efficiency and profit require the price-measured values of commodities and services to be stripped of other values, particularly those deriving from age-reward hierarchies (Cottrell 1960, p. 108).

It is worth noting one pernicious implication of social class that derives from this perspective. Berger and Luckmann (1964) have argued that the materialistic basis of class-consciousness has weakened, and substituted in its place has been the orientation toward mobility: the higher one's class, the greater the mobility expectation and the longer one's career "peaking" can be postponed (one peaks educationally in graduate or professional school as opposed to high school or college; one peaks occupationally at a higher rung and at a later time than one who, for example, "gets stuck" in middle management). The higher one's class, then, the more likely one can exit when one realizes mobility has run out.[21]

The spectrum of economic exit systems, of forms by which work-role careers are concluded, can be projected on a continuum of personal control over one's own passage. An exit may be totally volitional—a move for a better job, retiring in order to enjoy the "good years"—or involuntary, with such endings as retirement because of poor health or mandatory limits falling somewhere in between. The stigma associated with involuntary exits, particularly in the case of personal role failure, has received elaboration by Ball (1976), who developed the organizational strategies of degradation, shutting out, and cooling out as means for removing the unwanted. As epitomized by professional football and baseball, either one's involuntary role termination can be publicly dramatized with the ritual destruction of identity (Garfinkel 1956), by treating one as a "dead man" or nonperson (Ball 1976), or it can be privately altered in a routinized consolation process (Goffman 1952).[22] Hence volitional endings can possibly entail organizational embarrassment (such as quitting because of an injustice and then "blowing the whistle" as one's "parting shots"), just as involuntary endings can produce personal embarrassment (Harris and Eitzen 1978).[23] Such tensions underlie the contemporary need for ending ideologies for the older worker. Old, loyal, lifelong workers cannot be embarrassed through degradation ceremonies. The clash between meritocracy and seniority, between embarrassment and pride, saving face or dissolving it, are increasing bureaucratic dilemmas.[24] Such ending ideologies must, for the social system, reinforce social integration and reaffirm collective values, while they address for the individual the personality needs for intellectual order and provide insight that one's sacrifices have not been meaningless.

For a variety of reasons, then, work careers must be ended, whether because of the push of younger generations or the pull of other alternatives. The dynamics, however, have altered considerably as a result of life expectancy increases in conjunction with economic pressures toward maintaining or diminishing one's temporal license within work roles.[25] But regardless of what factors precipitate the role exit, individual efforts to control the form, and hence the meaning, of one's own exit trajectory are inevitably shaped by structural factors.[26] For example, the "lame duck" phenomenon observed in the American presidency derives from the eleven-week transition period before the election victor becomes legitimized as the new role incumbent. Nevertheless, some endings are better than others. And it is the central contention here that the social system is coming to recognize and celebrate those who excel in their role performances until the very end, despite age (the George Burns phenomenon), physical disability (the public death of Hubert Humphrey), or diminished expectations and accountabilities.

Managers of the Dead: The American Funeral Industry

When we think of death and work, certainly one connection that comes to mind are those we pay to transport, sanitize, reconstruct, clothe, and dispose of the dead, employees of the 7-billion-dollar-a-year American funeral industry. Over the past two decades, this industry has received considerable criticism. Allegations that its practitioners have taken unwarranted advantage of those in the throes of grief have led to congressional hearings, new trade practices rules from the Federal Trade Commission, and undercover sting operations staged by various consumer groups. This section will consider not only these complaints but also some of the underlying sociocultural reasons why they even occur.

Welcome, 1962: A funeral parlor welcomes mourners with an elaborate funeral display. James Van Der Zee.

The Staged Funerary Performance

One enters a funeral home ill prepared; this is not a department store or a dentist's office, places for which one has prior experience and knows "the game." One does not take a number or push a cart down aisles. Nor does one see samples of the quality of work done. Instead, one enters at the mercy of a receptionist, who announces to the staff that another performance is to begin and to "get into role." The prospective customer, unfortunately, knows neither the cues nor the script. He or she is then introduced to the funeral director. As Turner and Edgley note, "the change of titles from 'undertaker' to 'funeral director' has been perhaps the largest single clue to the dramaturgical functions the industry now sees itself as performing. He is indeed a 'director,' controlling a dramatic production" (1975, p. 84).

To make the drama more interesting, recall that this new player is not one-self. Often a significant other's death has just occurred, and one has begun feeling the most awesome of emotions, grief (see Chapter 12). Experiencing feelings that perhaps have never been felt before and entering the bereave-ment role, for which one may have no performance expectations, one meets the person who "knows" about such things, the funeral director. The new widow or widower is then led to a private "counseling" room, a diploma-filled office looking much like that of any health-care professional. Like the operating room of a hospital or the kitchen of a restaurant, one never sees the "backstage" to the service performance, as that would detract from the intended professional impression being fostered "onstage" (Turner and Edgley 1975, p. 380).[27]

Having offered the well-rehearsed condolences, the funeral director offers education about the typical way death is managed. One does not even think, for example, of transporting the remains in the back of one's car or con-structing a casket oneself. Instead, this person is concerned with such things as the inclusion of the proper religious rituals, the need to rehearse entrance and exit cues, who sits where, and the timing of eulogies. The professional supremacy of this "expert"—and one's own ignorance on the matter—is further reaffirmed by the specialized technical language used. By law, the cus-tomer must receive an itemized list of funerary services to be selected from, including the embalming process, dressing and cosmetology, pallbearers' limo, use of stateroom, and preparation of the death certificate and burial permits. Overseeing the myriad of choices, one also notes that there is a unit pricing system, a package deal, at a discount price. Often, not knowing what the services or products even are, the bereaved consumer accepts the "full-service" treatment.

In the confines of the office, death can be abstracted and given distance. The funeral director, in a professional-looking business suit, does not bring to mind the dirty work of draining blood or digging graves. But after a calm-ing talk with this understanding maven of death, one is led out of the office and taken to the casket room, a totally alien place filled with the parapher-nalia of death. One is often left alone in this room, supposedly to allow pri-vate, unpressured decision making. In actuality, one is being socialized to the industry's conception of death management.

One learns that burial occurs in a coffin equipped with an exhaust-pipe-like "burper valve" (so the casket does not explode in a depressurized aircraft compartment)—not in a body bag or burial shroud. As one funeral director

The Language of Death in the Funeral Profession

Frontstage Labelings

baby or infant, *not* stillborn
casket, *not* coffin
case, patient, *or* Mr. Smith, *not* corpse
cemetery *or* memorial park, *not* graveyard
cremains, *not* ashes
deceased *or* departed, *not* dead person
estate, *not* grave plot
funeral director, *not* undertaker
interment, *not* burial
inurnment, *not* potting
memory picture, *not* last look
monument, *not* tombstone
preparation room, *not* embalming room
professional car, *not* hearse
slumber room, *not* laying-out room
service, *not* funeral
slumber robe, *not* shroud
space, *not* grave
vital statistics form, *not* death certificate

Bailey 1983.

Backstage Labelings

coffins: tin cans, containers, stovepipes
restorations: pickling, curing the ham

Turner and Edgley 1975, p. 383. Reprinted by
permission of *Sociology and Social Research* © 1975.

---

put it, "you don't want to bury your mother like Rover, do you?" Another, when asked about the difference between two similar-appearing units having a thousand-dollar price difference, replied, "The difference, ma'am, is like between a Cadillac and a Ford." One also learns that there exist funerary attire and footwear—the dead are not dressed in gunny sacks or hospital garb to meet their maker. And one learns that color coordination of casket and deceased's clothing is a consideration—and if the dead gets dressed up, then he'd better look good too, as others are obviously going to see him. Casket display rooms are masterpieces of implicit psychology, taking into account the counterclockwise direction most people go when entering a new space,[28] the juxtaposition and spacing of differently priced (and colored) models, and the effects of lighting. Even though federal law requires the equivalent display of the three least expensive units, there are ways to guarantee that they are not purchased. Certainly the easiest way is to present the cheapest in tasteless color. Another, pioneered by a San Antonio establishment, charges ten dollars for their "charity casket." Although the wholesale price of this simple wooden coffin is $117, by pricing it as they do, they know it will not sell, making an automatic "bump up" to the next higher unit (Reveley 1980).

Attempts to Professionalize a Lower-Middle-Class Occupation

Funeral directing is one of the few state-recognized professions that provide upward mobility for those who, by chance of birth, are often thwarted in their attempts to achieve professional respect. This status has been hard won, deriving from more than a century of attempts in the United States to expand and to legitimize this occupational purview. Cross-culturally, it is often the lower classes that were typically assigned to handling the dead, such as the Eta of Japan or the Untouchables in India. But the "Dismal Trade" of eighteenth-century England was to evolve into a host of thanatological specialists seeking social recognition and status: embalmers, restorers, morticians, and some even calling themselves "grief experts."[29]

To give the industry and its product historical legitimization, the National Funeral Directors Association commissioned Robert Habenstein and William Lamers (1955). Their book, *The History of American Funeral Directing*, reviews the history of funeral practice in Western civilization from ancient Egypt on, and it was required reading for years in mortuary colleges. The American tradition, however, was considerably less glamorous than the mummies entombed in the Great Pyramids.

Though undertaking existed as a late-seventeenth-century occupation in England, because of its upper-class caterings it was not transplanted into the more egalitarian New World (Habenstein and Lamers 1955, p. 226).[30] Instead, the American funeral industry was to undergo its own evolution. Following the growth and prosperity of commerce coupled with the absence of uniform religious regulation of funerals, sideline activities of a number of occupations were to become a specialized trade. One line of its ancestry goes back to early-nineteenth-century cabinet and furniture retailers, who found the manufacture and sale of caskets to be a profitable side venture. Having the supplies and paraphernalia on hand, the early undertakers were eventually able to best the potential rivals for the trade: "inviters to funerals," sextons, liverymen (who were having a difficult time meeting the rental demand for funeral carriages), carpenters, town health officials, and "layers-out of the dead" (often nurses or midwives). Before the Civil War broke out, undertaking had taken on the characteristics of a service occupation with a set of tasks and functions organized into a pattern of behavior toward the dead that basically included the laying out, the coffining, and the transporting of the body to the grave. Around these central functions, certain auxiliary services, such as the furnishing of paraphernalia of mourning, i.e., clothing, emblems, remembrances, etc., were, to a more or lesser degree, included. (Habenstein and Lamers 1955, p. 249)

The Civil War was to add another function to the industry—the preservation of human remains—legitimizing the occupation as a professional guardian of public health.[31] In the two earlier decades, the medical profession had explored means for chemically preserving anatomical specimens and for sanitizing corpses to arrest epidemics. The fluids and methods for their injection were improved upon and employed to ship soldiers' remains home. President Lincoln's funeral procession from Washington, D.C., to Springfield, Illinois, advertised the new embalming craft (Pine 1978, p. 274). Public acceptance of embalming was to grow, despite the guarded fact that Lincoln's remains eventually did turn black and had to be covered with powders. Later, medical practitioners, such as surgeon-embalmers and chemists, were to conduct training schools in the new preservation techniques for the suppliers of coffins and funeral transportation before surrendering the function to them. Further, with urbanization and its concomitant contraction of private residences, embalming and the laying out of the dead moved from the home to the funeral parlor (DeSpelder and Strickland 1983, p. 169).

In many states around the turn of the century, there appeared state laws regulating embalming, occurring within a few years of the industry's incorporating itself on the state level and creating national trade associations.[32] These state regulations reflected not only the public sanitation concerns arising out of the public health movement of the time but also the professional aspirations of the occupation (Federal Trade Commission 1978). This professional image was to be further shaped by trade publications, such as *The Casket,* and by later laws that gave further monopoly over the care of the dead. In a number of states, for example, there are "first call" rules which say that only licensed personnel can pick up remains from a hospital or morgue. Further, the historical attempts of funeral directors to obtain professional role distance from their traditional task of corpse care has produced state laws ensuring their monopoly over the directive aspects: though there is nothing unique in selling funerary merchandise, these statutes often require that the contract for funeral goods and services be signed only by a licensed funeral director, not an embalmer or salesperson. And, like physicians, both funeral directors and embalmers generally have to pass state examinations for licensure upon successful completion of professional educational requirements and a period of apprenticeship (or "interning"). They had become special people: until the mid-1970s, physicians, butchers, and undertakers were exempt from jury duty in Texas, as these groups were supposedly desensitized to blood.

Industry critics claim that the professional image of funeral directing is a sham and has no clinically proven therapeutic value. Charmaz (1980, p. 194) observed that the professional appearance of funeral directors is largely borrowed from both the theological and the medical professions. In many states, little more than a high school degree coupled with mortuary education and apprenticeship—both generally monitored by a state agency such as a state board of morticians[33]—is required for one to become a licensed funeral director or embalmer. In the state of Texas, there is a statewide examination system involving both paper-and-pencil and practical demonstration. Further, there is a conscious attempt of the death industry to reify, to convince us of, the existence of "the traditional American funeral." What this is was described by Jessica Mitford in her stinging 1963 criticism of the industry, *The American Way of Death,* and her 1977 reevaluation:

the funeral men mean the full treatment: display of the embalmed and beautified corpse reposing on an innerspring or foam-rubber mattress in an elegant "casket"; "visitation" of the deceased in the mortuary "slumber room"; an open-casket ceremony at which the mourners parade around for a last look; a burial vault that allegedly affords "eternal protection"; elaborate "floral tributes" from family and friends; a "final resting place" in a "memorial park" or mausoleum. (1977, p. 190)

Van Pine, on the other hand, claims that the funeral industry contains the "underlying systematic body of theory and knowledge, professional authority, sanction of the community, a regulative code of ethics, subcultures, and financial rewards" to qualify as a profession (1975, p. 147). It certainly is the case that they have tried to project a professional image, ever since embalming-fluid preparers started calling themselves professors (Habenstein and Lamers 1955, p. 340);[34] and they truly perceive themselves to be professionals, as evidenced in the title of one of their trade publications, *The Professional Mortician.* Partly because of the cultural denial of death and tendency to avoid all funerary matters, the public ignorance of funerary matters produced a knowledge vacuum that industry people were more than willing to fill. Funeral directors assert in books, magazine articles, and interviews that they have the right and even the responsibility to try to change the funeral arrangements made by either the deceased or the family if the mortician feels those decisions were made without full appreciation of the importance of funeral rituals (Severo 1978). Wrote Howard C. Raether and Robert C. Slater in *The Funeral Director and His Role as a Counselor,* "we not only have a *right,* but the time has arrived when we can say we have a responsibility to do so" (1975, p. 67). Nevertheless, many note the inherent incompatibilities of simultaneously being a counselor and an aggressive salesperson.

In a recent Gallup poll of 1500 randomly selected Americans, whereas clergymen rated 63 in honesty and ethical standards, physicians 50, and professors 45, funeral directors rated 30, ahead of lawyers, U.S. senators, business executives, and state officeholders. One wonders about the public complaints against this industry and all of the attendant charges of abuses. First, the Federal Trade Commission found during its five years of research that only one thousand complaints were registered for the 10 million deaths that occurred. Second, the institution most profiting from the dying/death process is now the medical institution, as will be detailed in Chapter 12. How much of this public outcry is actually linked to class issues, such as the public perception that the non-upper-middle-class industry personnel cannot be trusted to monitor their own? How much is linked to the American death orientation whereby the industry is the cultural scapegoat for failed immortality?

Though we will probably never know the answers to these questions, we do know that a number of groups received considerable publicity for mounting their attacks on the industry. Certainly the Consumer's Union, Gray Panthers, Memorial Societies, and the Federal Trade Commission benefited, their credibility enhanced by revelations of "horror stories" on the sensitive matter of death. The 1984 FTC funeral regulations[35] resulted from the public having to fight hard to avoid being charged for facilities and services not utilized, such as chapel, visitation room, public lounges, and parking facilities. Public testimonies revealed individuals being charged seventy-five dollars for "body deodorants," money billed for clergy who never attended services, bodies removed from institutions without authorization and not being released to families desiring another mortuary, embalmings without family permission, and people paying as much as four thousand dollars for a casket supposedly constructed of expensive wood but being, in fact, a simple varnished three-ply. A striking 58 percent of funeral homes studied by the FTC committed at least one abuse of billing against the bereaved. With the adoption of the FTC trade regulations, the Catholic church's entry into the business, and Colorado's elimination of its state board of morticians and licensure requirements for embalmers and funeral directors, there are indications that the industry is undergoing a period of deprofessionalization.

The Structure of the Industry

As a business, the funeral home is the safest, with its failure rate of 10.9 per 10,000 establishments as the lowest of all businesses. The reasons for this are

predictable sales (normally 1 death a year for every 110 residents in the typical market area), comfortable profit margins (a 10 percent pretax profit on
approximately four hundred thousand dollars is average), and limited competition (one cannot just break into the business with an advertising assault
and expect immediate sales; Jacobs 1985). In addition, as Pine and Phillips
observed, the industry profits

because people increasingly lack both the ceremonial and social mechanisms and
arrangements that once existed to help them cope with death, monetary expenditures
have taken on added importance as a means for allowing the bereaved to express (both
to themselves and others) their sentiments for the deceased. For with so few modes
of expression remaining to the bereaved, funeral expenditures serve as evidence of
their concern for both the dead and the conventional standards of decency in their
community of residence. (1970, p. 416)[36]

Social status is operative throughout life, and its power does not necessarily diminish at death. Pine and Phillips (1978) give reasonable support to the
hypothesis that the single most important influence on the magnitude of
funeral expenditures is one's location within the status hierarchy. And
funeral homes are stratified along the lines of the living, catering to particular
ethnicities, social classes, and religions. Further, their products and services
continue to evolve, limited only by what the public is willing to spend and
for what. The New Williamsburg Company of Arlington, Virginia, sells
designer caskets. Some feature Laura Ashley–like floral fabrics, and a teak
model looks like a Danish-modern coffee table. Milwaukee funeral directors
Arthur Reid Jr. and Carl Yandell are selling caskets that look like luxury cars:
one can tour eternally in a Mark V Continental, a Mercedes-Benz converti-
ble, or a Cadillac Seville. These models come with chrome grille, hood orna-
ment, parking lights, and padded interiors, all for $5,000 to $7,400. When
the time comes for these vehicles-for-eternity to be lowered into the ground,
there is still the ritual throwing on of dirt. But one can use the Gordon Leak-
Proof Earth Dispenser. With it, according to an industry ad, "No grasping
of a handful of dirt, no soiled fingers. Simple, dignified, beautiful, reverent!
The modern way!" (Mitford 1963, p. 76). Mourners in Louisiana can ride
past a seven-by-five-foot window at the Pointe Coupee Funeral Home and
view the deceased without even leaving their cars. And, for $39,500, one can
even purchase a solar-powered tombstone, encased in bulletproof glass, featuring a video system from which the deceased presents his or her epitaph
and thoughts for perpetuity (*People Magazine* 1977).

When certain morticians offered cut-rate funerals, the industry counterat-
tacked vigorously. One maverick mortician from Texas, testifying to Congress and speaking out against the industry on a number of popular televi-

Now You Can Be Driven towards Your Heavenly Reward
in the "Cadillac of Motor Homes"

And you can do it with lots of company. The Airstream Inc. "funeral coach" has discreet compartments in the rear for the casket and up to 20 baskets of flowers, and commodious quarters up front for the bereaved, the pallbearers and the minister, plus the funeral functionaries—up to 19 or 20 people. . . .

"Funeral directors are really excited about this," says Karl Croel, director of sales and marketing. The coaches cost $85,000, while the going price of a hearse is about $40,000. But a couple of standard funeral limousines can cost another $60,000, so the funeral coaches look economical. Airstream says it has received 13 orders.

In addition to sparing families the pain of separation en route to the cemetery, and maybe saving money for funeral directors, the funeral coach has another virtue: It could ease the traffic tie-ups that result from caravans of mourners traveling to a burial.

Dolan 1981. Reprinted by permission
of the Wall Street Journal, © Dow Jones & Company, Inc., 1981.

---

sion talk shows, returned home to receive telephoned death threats and to find a coffin manufacturer refusing to do any more business with him. A few years later, he found a group of investors willing to finance a funeral home franchise, called United Dignity, specializing in simple dignified funerals. *Mortuary Management Magazine* blasted the enterprise in an article entitled "There Could Be a McDonald's in Funeral Service";

One can only imagine the number of gullible and disgruntled American funeral directors and critics of the American funeral, lining up to become potential franchise holders. . . . [For the price] they will probably get a lot of advice, one used cremation retort with a book of matches, plans on how to remodel a long closed fast food joint for the use as a funeral home, plus discount availabilities for the purchase of Wisconsin sap sucking pine coffins. (The no-frills type that all Americans love, of course.) . . .

Coupons clipped from the local newspaper advertising will also be a very special component of any United Dignity franchise holder.

Just like McDonald's or Wendy's, potential customers would be asked to watch their local newspaper supplements for the "specials." (Fisher 1983)

The industry, however, faces a peculiar structural dilemma: though the number of deaths in the United States has doubled since 1900, the number of funeral establishments is nearly five times as great. According to Pine's (1981) study of 945 establishments for the National Funeral Directors Association, more than half survive on fewer than one hundred services a year.[37] Since 1960, there has been a 17 percent drop in the national total of funeral homes; mortuaries can only expand by taking away their competitors' market share. Related industries are suffering as well: during 1967–68, there were 650 casket companies nationwide, posting sales of just under $300 million. Today, the total number of casket makers is down to 410, including Simmons caskets, which, with Simmons Universal (the makers of beds and mattresses), is part of Simmons USA, which, in turn, is owned by Gulf and Western Industries. In 1965, limousine manufacturers produced 4880 hearses and related vehicles; by the mid-1980s, the annual sales of hearses averaged only 800, an 83 percent plunge in two decades. And consider the relationship of florists with the industry. In an article for funeral directors, the president of the Florists' Telegraph Delivery Association wrote:

Your highest duty is creation. It is surely a function that is guided by the Great Creator, for in your hands has been placed the responsibility of creating a living Memory Picture. . . . [There is] the attitude in some places that the present high standards of funeral service are unnecessary. Being close to the funeral directors in their daily work, FTD florists feel that this attitude is dangerous and strikes at the very roots of our civilization. (reported in Mitford 1963, p. 113)

Certainly, the embalmed body is the cornerstone of this industry. Without it there would be no need for a slumber room, elaborate coffin, or funerary apparel.[38] Without it, one's burial might cost no more than one thousand dollars rather than the customary three thousand dollars or more (see Table 7.5). Despite the fact that the National Disease Control Center in Atlanta has found no health reasons for embalming (with the exception of a few com-

Table 7.5a Cost of Typical Traditional Funeral

Staff and overhead charges (includes cost of staff on call, arranging for clergy and burial, obtaining and filing death certificate)	$ 906
Transporting from place of death to funeral home	70
Embalming	135
Makeup and dressing of body and placement in casket	60
Mid-priced metal casket	2200
Use of viewing room for one day	40
Use of funeral chapel	60
Staff at chapel	166
Setting up floral arrangements	49
Use of hearse to cemetery	100
Use of two limousines for family	200
Register book	10
TOTAL	$3996

Note: Price does not include such common expenses as flowers, clergy fees, organist, cemetery plot, burial cost, and tombstone, which are usually not provided by funeral home. They would cost approximately $1900.

Table 7.5b Cost of Typical Cremation

Staff and overhead charges	$518
Transporting from (local) place of death	70
Preparing the body for relative to identify	60
Cardboard container for the body	60
Hearse to the crematorium	100
Cremation	120
TOTAL	$928

Note: Price does not include cost of memorial service, urn, or scattering of ashes. Those expenses would amount to a minimum of $170. Burial of the ashes would add about $400.

Source: Wall Street Journal 1985a.

municable diseases), the practice continues for a majority of deaths. Attempts to discourage embalming, such as through cremation or refrigeration, have naturally met considerable industry resistance. Writes the chairman of the board of Pierce Mortuary Colleges (which is owned by Pierce Chemicals, a major producer of embalming fluids):

Cremation is not a new or modern method of disposal of dead human bodies. We're not sure when this method was first used—or where. The words "Funeral Pyre" are words that go back a long time, but the connotation isn't always good because in many cases, the human body was still alive when the fire was lighted. Joan of Arc is a good example and it was a means of punishment for many others. . . . Very recently, the newspapers and magazines are full of complaints from so called cremations where several bodies are cremated at the same time and the families are not sure that the remains they receive are from their loved ones. (Pierce 1983)

In many instances, funeral directors fostered the impression with consumers that the embalming practice is required by law. In Texas, a law was passed that a body cannot be cremated for forty-eight hours after death; as most establishments do not have refrigeration units, many homes invoked their own rule that a body must be embalmed after two days. Then there were reports circulated that heart pacemakers had exploded during cremation.

Nevertheless, cremations increased in frequency, particularly in urban areas with high rates of geographic mobility. On the West Coast, for example, more than a third of deaths are cremated. And the Catholic church, a longtime supporter of the traditional means of disposition, in the late 1970s removed its objections to cremation. But the industry was not about to accept defeat; new services and disposal rituals were to emerge for the cremated remains. The California Neptune Society offers to scatter the ashes in the Pacific Ocean. And in 1985, a group of Florida undertakers unveiled plans to place ashes in earth orbit. In the world's first commercial space venture, the Celestis Group signed a contract with Spaces Services Inc.[39] to place 1900 miles in space a satellite containing 13,000 capsules, each holding the ashes of a person reduced to three-eighths by one and a quarter-inch in size (Biddle 1985). This orbiting mausoleum, expected to last for some 63 million years, will be coated with a reflective material—so that it can be seen by relatives on earth—and will be inscribed with all the names. The venture was approved by the Transportation Department and received the blessings of the Reagan administration as a "creative response" to the president's urging of more commercialization of space (*San Antonio Light* 1985).

Conclusion

Next to one's family, work provides the central preoccupation in life for most social members. Of all the social institutions considered in this book, it is work that most directly plugs the individual into the broader society and most directly shapes the styles of consciousness by which "reality" is apprehended. As action normally precedes ideology, it may well be the case that the historical musings of theologians and philosophers about death have been considerably influenced by changes occurring with this, the major arena of social action. In any event, so central is work to modern identities that to lose one's job is to die a symbolic death (hence the death metaphors in work parlance, such as "getting axed" or "being terminated"). Sociologist M. Harvey Brenner (1977) found that for each percentage increase in the American unemployment rate, there is a 4.1 percent increase in suicides, a 5.7 percent increase in homicides, and a 1.9 percent increase in deaths from heart disease, cirrhosis of the liver, and stress-related disorders (cited in Brody 1982). And witnessing the fears of some work-oriented individuals that they will die shortly after retiring, work can be seen as instilling vitality to life and giving meaning to existence.

In this chapter, we have seen how work kills, not only figuratively but literally as well. Industrial evolution has not totally eliminated the risks of death in the workplace. Rather, it has altered the form by which economic activity kills, often invisibly and cumulatively over the course of many years. The contemporary John Henrys do not typically die of exhaustion or cave-ins but rather of black-lung disease, asbestos-related cancers, chemical poisonings, and stress. And death is not equal-opportunity. Exposures to work's lethal potential are, as has probably been the case throughout history, generally stratified along the lines of social class.[40] Further, with capitalism's accent on profit, many of the most hazardous occupations have been exported abroad.

On the other hand, it is through work that one's memory is most likely to be preserved. Traditionally, immortality through work has always been the privilege of a limited few. In preindustrial times, the options were largely restricted to those in government, the aristocracy, soldiers, priests, and a handful of artistic and literary geniuses. But nowadays, because there are so many more arenas in which one can possibly leave a mark, perhaps a greater percentage of individuals have at least some chance of attaining a degree of "local immortality,"[41] even though the opportunities for gaining "cosmopolitan immortality" may be even more restricted today than in the past.

Finally, we considered a case study of the funeral industry, one occupation dedicated to the maintenance of the culture's death denials, as evidenced by its attempts to continue embalming the dead so as to create a "living memorial" for the deceased. The tendency of lower-class families to provide their members in death the dignity (and the immortality that a tombstone provides) that they did not receive in life has contributed to the growth of a multibillion-dollar industry whose practices have received considerable criticism in recent decades, leading to federal interventions on behalf of dead and bereaved citizens.

The two chapters that follow take up the polity and the military, two institutions that oversee society's death occupations (such as the police, armed forces, executioners, and munitions workers) and legitimize their deadly activities.

NOTES

1. Both theoretical Marxists and functionalists conceptualize society to be an integrated whole. As opposed to the latter group, which focuses attention on the role of value integration in achieving this sense of totality (hence their traditional concentration on religion), conflict theorists are more likely to see cultural integration occurring around the economic mode of production.

2. Peter Berger and Thomas Luckmann argue that upward mobility within the hierarchical organizations of work has become a form of secular salvation. Such mobility is no longer a means to an end but has become, for many, the end in itself (1964).

3. Perhaps religion has been the only institution that has provided projects, such as the construction of the great cathedrals of Europe, spanning the lives of several generations. Today different generations rarely find themselves engaged in a common enterprise.

4. This is a logic captured by the major religions of the world, which came into existence during this First Wave (Toffler 1981; Eliade 1959).

5. Corporations are recognized by the courts as an "immortal being" as they outlive their founding generation.

6. It used to be the case that through working each generation left a residue, like the great coral reefs, a portion of which later generations tended to preserve. But with impermanence and planned obsolescence, contemporary products are no longer intended to survive their producers. The bearing of this understanding on contemporary worker pride can only be speculated.

7. Profound urban-rural inequities in life expectancy remain in China and India. According to a 1986 report of the Congressional Joint Economic Committee, rural residents live twelve years less than urban folk in China, and in India the gap is eight years.

8. It is worth noting that 42 percent of women who died on the job were victims of homicide, compared with 11 percent for males. However, the annual odds are 2 in 100,000 that a male worker will be murdered at work (*Wall Street Journal* 1987b).

9. According to the National Institute for Occupational Safety and Health, there were considerable state-by-state variations between 1980 and 1984 in the death rates within these industry divisions (rates do not include deaths caused by illness, such as heart attacks):

	Avg. no. of deaths	Rate per 100,000 workers	Construction industry rate	Manufacturing rate
Arizona	64	7.4	15.5	3.4
Arkansas	80	13.8	30.8	6.3
Colorado	134	12.4	30.0	6.7
Kansas	98	13.2	28.1	5.1
Louisiana	190	14.8	19.3	17.7
Mississippi	107	18.0	30.4	9.3
Missouri	112	7.0	19.1	3.1
New Mexico	52	15.8	23.0	16.4
Oklahoma	102	11.2	24.8	10.1
Tennessee	129	9.4	22.9	3.5
Texas	792	15.6	29.6	9.4
U.S. TOTAL	7,000	9.7	23.0	4.2

San Antonio Light 1987. © 1987 by San Antonio Light. Reprinted by permission.

10. The Karen Silkwood legend—a laboratory analyst for a nuclear-fuel fabrication company mysteriously died in an auto accident while she was gathering evidence of alleged plant safety violations—grows out of this insight.

11. Three former executives of a film-recovery plant were found guilty of murder in a landmark 1985 trial stemming from the death of a worker who inhaled cyanide on the job. Cook County Circuit Judge Ronald Banks said, "They [the defendants] knew the workers were becoming nauseated and vomiting. They [the workers] complained." This was perhaps the first time American corporate officials had been con-

victed of murder in the job-related death of an employee (*Austin American-Statesman* 1985). Two years earlier, however, the Supreme Court let stand a ruling that protected Manville Corporation—the leading U.S. asbestos maker, which had filed for protection from its creditors under chapter 11 of the federal bankruptcy law—from suits by victims of asbestos-related diseases that would amount to more than 2 billion dollars over the next twenty years (*San Antonio Express-News* 1983).

12. It is the victim who is typically blamed, as industrial medicine and psychiatry normally locate the causes of worker accidents and disease in the personality characteristics of the workers and not in the workplace environment. Not until May 1980, with a rule announced by the Labor Department, were workers for the first time able to obtain their on-the-job medical records, including details of their exposure to dangerous substances.

13. Also discovered was the fact that 163 chemicals that are neurotoxins often bring about subtle symptoms that are little understood, and yet 20 million people work with one or more of them. Often these substances come home with the worker, contaminating the family laundry, bathroom, furniture, air, and food.

14. The storage of chemicals contributed to 36.2 percent of the deaths and injuries, valve and pipe problems 16.8 percent, problems in the production process 12.8 percent, and human error 12.8 percent. In more than 40 percent of the mishaps the cause was unknown (Diamond 1985a).

15. The peak year was 1963, when the average American aged fourteen and older smoked 3900 cigarettes.

16. During the 1980s, the battles between smokers and nonsmokers have been heating up. Cities and states have banned smoking in most public buildings, and a myriad of no-smoking signs has sprouted up across office desks and store doors.

17. In late 1985, the American Medical Association called for a complete ban on the advertising and promotion of all tobacco products. The tobacco industry was joined by the American Civil Liberties Union in opposition. A spokesman for the latter said, "The First Amendment does not permit a prohibition on truthful advertising of products that may lawfully be distributed and sold" (Boffey 1985).

18. One wonders what life would be like if there was no one interested in maintaining, or even respecting, the work legacies of preceding generations. The European aristocracy may be the only Western group able to account for ten or twenty generations of their ancestors' doings.

19. The rebirth metaphor in the workplace is also used on a corporate scale. The Navistar advertisings of 1986, for example, included the line, "The rebirth of International Harvester."

20. For example, in the workplace, one can become socially "dead" upon prematurely announcing a forthcoming leave, which is perhaps why Supreme Court Justice Potter told none of his colleagues of his intended retirement until the day before his formal announcement. No one gives you any information, as you no longer have a future with the group.

21. A number of structural factors impinge upon individual efforts to control the timing and form of work exits. As conceptualized by the emergent model of age strat-

ification in social gerontology, the dynamics derive from the dialectic between cohorts of aging individuals and a continuously changing set of age-appropriate roles (Riley 1976). Individuals and roles are taken to be analytically distinct, the former linked with the latter via the social processes of socialization and allocation. With modernization, such roles have become increasingly age-stratified, and the paradigm sensitizes one to the crises of succession and to the interaction between the developmental tasks faced by similarly aged individuals and the particular slice of social history within which they age, directing attention to cohorts and to generational conflicts (Mannheim 1952; Ryder 1972; Bengtson and Cutler 1976). For example, the social consequences of "cohort bulges," the existence of a relatively large generation whose very size strains the ability of various institutions (through which it ages) to allocate rights and opportunities (e.g., larger classroom sizes, lesser probability to be class president or cheerleader, greater competition for college seats, and greater pressures on the housing market when the cohort reaches maturity, thereby fueling inflation) has been linked to such phenomena as the American antiwar protests of the late 1960s and early 1970s as well as the rise of nazism in Germany during the 1930s (see Jones 1980). Further, other factors may be involved in producing the surpluses or deficiencies in the number of people in relation to the availability of statuses and roles. In the Soviet Union there appears to be a reluctance on the part of the older generation, with its historical association with the Revolution, in transferring political power to the younger, less ideologically pure generations; some American oil companies are having to invest heavily to retain older executives who, as a cohort, worked their way up the corporate ladder and therefore had the field experiences and the total organizational picture, unlike the younger, more specialized generations whose career experiences have been componentiated; and finally, there are the organizational needs to experiment with new chemistries of individuals comprising research and work teams in order to ascertain relative effectiveness and efficiencies.

22. To illustrate the extent to which terminations have been institutionalized, consider the following document handed out to the management of Datapoint Corporation, a Southwest U.S. computer company:

Termination Notification
It is imperative that we ensure a clearly communicated, consistent message to all affected individuals. To ensure this Human Relations has prepared the following "out-processing" format that management is directed to adhere to.

Exit Interview
Statement of intent: In an effort to make this company a more cost efficient and better managed organization, certain changes are required. Of immediate concern will be the need for a corporate wide reevaluation of manpower requirements. After a thorough review of this department/unit, the decision has been made to restructure, consolidate and where appropriate eliminate or reassign areas of responsibility. Conse-

quently, effective today, Friday, 5 August, 1983, we have reassigned or where appropriate, eliminated your area of responsibility. This action has resulted in the need for a reduction in force, and accordingly, you are being released from the company today. Your final paycheck includes _____weeks severance pay (refer to Severance Pay Procedure, Attachment C). You will also be provided the following: . . .

Do you have any questions concerning your termination or the conditions of separation? (Managers need to be as empathetic as possible, but firm.)

Summary to Management Group
It is vital that you stress, if asked, that " . . . there is no recall provision in a Reduction in Force . . . " decision. Although this is an unpleasant task, we expect that it will be handled in a professional, yet sensitive manner. . . .

---

23. A 1987 survey of Richmond, Virginia, entrepreneurs by *Richmond Surroundings* magazine found 58 percent of men and 39 percent of women claiming failure to be their greatest fear, far surpassing their fears of death (*Wall Street Journal* 1987b).

24. For example, the worker may be laid off because of organizational hardships and not personal inadequacies; hence, one is "RIFed" (reduction in force), not fired. Another termination strategy to minimize personal embarrassment includes the corporate buy-out programs.

25. One national survey of workers aged thirty to forty-nine earning $25,000 to $65,000 a year found they left for another firm on the average of every thirty-one months and changed jobs within their own company every twenty-one months.

26. Perhaps the most detailed explication of exiting processes is to be found in Glaser and Strauss's *Status Passage* (1971), in which the social quality and personal desirability of an ending are conceptualized to be functions of the interactions between institutional properties (e.g., whether the passage is scheduled, prescribed, inevitable, reversible, legitimate, collective, and of programmed duration) and individual orientations (e.g., clarity of passage signs, its personal significance, whether or not the passage is voluntary, and the locus of control).

27. As graphically described by Turner and Edgley, in the embalming room the corpse is not only embalmed but also "washed, shaved, sprayed with disinfectant, sliced, pierced, creamed, powdered, waxed, stitched, painted, manicured, dressed, and positioned in a casket. Through the use of other chemicals the flesh is softened, stretched, shrunk, restored, colored, and even replaced" (1975, p. 381).

28. Wilber Krieger's *Mortuary Management*, a late-1940s industry text, suggests placing the cheapest units to the left of the door of the casket display room so that when one enters, the door blocks the view. The book also describes how the prospective customer can be tunneled to the more expensive items.

29. Many of the morticians I know are a little too outgoing, a little too loud. It started me thinking about what it must be like to always be around grieving people, to always be sympathetic and understanding to the recently bereaved. How upset does one get over the death of total strangers?

30. In fact, a number of cultures find it immoral to use death as a means of enrich-

ment. In the 1970s, for example, Mozambique banned private funeral parlors and private coffin manufacturing when nationalizing the funeral industry.

31. It is interesting to note that Thomas H. Holmes, the self-proclaimed "father of modern embalming," gave instructions that upon his own death, which came in 1900, he *not* be embalmed, trusting no embalmer's work but his own. During the Civil War, Holmes had obtained a government contract to embalm the bodies of dead Union soldiers. He restricted his clientele to officers, figuring their families could afford his hundred-dollar fee.

32. In 1882, the first national association, the Funeral Directors National Association of the United States, was formed. Twelve years later, Virginia became the first state to pass a law regulating embalming, and by the turn of the century twenty-three additional states had followed suit (Federal Trade Commission 1978).

33. In the case of embalming, for at least the state of Texas, law even dictates the number of bodies that must be embalmed (sixty over a twelve-month period, five of which must be completed on one's own) and the monthly case reports that must be submitted. Over the past three years of practical embalming testings, only one person has ever failed the test. In general, state boards of morticians oversee the examination and licensing of embalmers and funeral directors, manage the apprenticeships of these two occupations, grant reciprocity, approve the course of instruction at mortuary colleges, provide information to the consumers of the state, and seek injunctions against funeral establishments, embalmers, or funeral directors found violating the law, as well as handling all complaints against the industry by the public.

34. To preserve the dignity of the profession, an Abilene, Texas, funeral home sued the phone company for listing it in the Yellow Pages under "Frozen Foods."

35. As of April 30, 1984 (it was to be January 1, but the Funeral Directors of America was able to obtain a court injunction), the public must be informed exactly what is to be included in funeral costs during first meetings and before contract negotiations, dissolving the "packaged funerals" that can include costly and unwanted items. Before this ruling, only six states—New Jersey, Connecticut, Florida, Colorado, Arizona, and Texas—required presale price disclosure. Further, prices must be given over the phone when requested.

36. It is interesting that the Code of Professional Practices of the National Funeral Directors Association (1965) states: "[the funeral director] . . . shall provide the necessary services and merchandise in keeping with the wishes *and finances* of the family."

37. Specifically, Pine (1981) found the following breakdown:

Services per year	Establishments within range	Average services annually
0–99	50%	62
100–199	31	140
200–299	10	233
300–499	7	382
500+	2	764

38. Bill Pierce, chairman of Pierce Chemicals, wrote: "Some of us will conform to the new era in Funeral Service and these people will provide the very finest of Funeral Service to the public they have ever had. They will do it within the structure of rules and regulations that are designed to produce this type of modern Funeral Service. It will have all the aspects of modern science in body preservation and disinfection regardless of the cause of death and the circumstances. This is where all Funeral Service must start. Without this type of initial attention, all of the other facets of funeral service will fail because without the dead body being present in a proper viewable condition, which means 'professional embalming' there is no need for the other parts of the funeral service" (Pierce 1985).

39. Space Services is a Houston-based company whose president, Donald K. Slayton, is one of the original seven American astronauts.

40. This is not to deny that some high-risk professions, such as space travel and test flying, are reserved for high-status professionals. The higher one's position within occupational hierarchies, the more likely one is to have personal control over one's own death, as opposed to being unknowingly killed.

41. I am indebted to my colleague Richard Machalek for the concept.

REFERENCES

Anderson, Jack. 1984. "U.S. Official Hits at Bureaucracy." *San Antonio Express-News.* March 14, p. 17A.

Austin American-Statesman. 1985. "Executives Convicted in Poisoning Death of Worker on the Job." June 15.

Bailey, William. 1983. *Euphemisms and Other Double-Talk.* New York: Doubleday.

Ball, D. 1976. "Failure in Sport." *American Sociological Review* 41:726–39.

Barth, Peter, and H. Allan Hunt. 1980. *Workers' Compensation and Work-related Illnesses and Diseases.* Cambridge, Mass.: MIT Press.

Bean, Ed. 1986. "Tobacco Industry's Court Victories Fail to Slow Product-Liability Suits." *Wall Street Journal.* January 30, p. 29.

Bell, Daniel. 1976. *The Cultural Contradictions of Capitalism.* New York: Basic Books.

Bengtson, Vern, and Neil Cutler. 1976. "Generations and Intergenerational Relations: Perspectives on Age Groups and Social Change." In Robert Binstock and Ethel Shanas, eds., *Handbook of Aging and the Social Sciences.* New York: Van Nostrand Reinhold, pp. 130–59.

Berger, Peter. 1964. "Some General Observations on the Problems of Work." In Peter Berger, ed., *The Human Shape of Work: Studies in the Sociology of Occupations.* New York: Macmillan.

Berger, Peter, Brigitte Berger, and Hansfried Kellner. 1973. *The Homeless Mind: Modernization and Consciousness.* New York: Random House.

Berger, Peter, and T. Luckmann. 1964. "Social Mobility and Personal Identity." *European Journal of Sociology* 5:331–44.

Bergin, Edward, and Ronald Grandon. 1984. *The American Survival Guide: How to Survive in Your Toxic Environment.* New York: Pierson.

Berman, Daniel. 1979. *Death on the Job*. New York: W. W. Norton.

Biddle, Wayne. 1985. "Space Entrepreneurs in Florida Are Plotting an Orbit for the Departed." *New York Times*. January 25, p. 11.

Boffey, Philip. 1985. "A.M.A. Votes to Seek Total Ban on Advertising Tobacco Products." *New York Times*. December 11, pp. 1, 32.

Brenner, M. Harvey. 1977. "Health Costs and Benefits of Economic Policy." *International Journal of Health Services* 7(4):581–623.

Brody, Jane. 1978. "Massive Drive Urged to Combat Smoking." *New York Times*. February 1, p. A10.

———. 1982. "Unemployment: Consequences and Damages." *New York Times*. November 30, pp. 17–18.

Burnham, David. 1977. "1 in 4 Americans Exposed to Hazards on Job, Study Says." *New York Times*. October 3, pp. 1, 22.

Charmaz, Kathy. 1980. *The Social Reality of Death*. Reading, Mass.: Addison-Wesley.

Chira, Susan. 1985. "Japan Airlines' Head Begs Forgiveness for 520 Deaths." *New York Times*. October 25, p. 4.

Chrysler, K. 1983. "City on the Spot: Give Up Jobs or Risk Health." *U.S. News & World Report*. November 14, p. 71.

Clapp, Marjorie. 1984. "Scientist: Lung Cancer Victims Need Right to Sue." *San Antonio Express-News* June 19, p. 8A.

Cohen, Richard. 1985. "Tobaco Industry Ignores Truth. *San Antonio Express-News*. June 30, p. 2M.

Cottrell, Fred. 1960. "The Technological and Societal Basis of Aging." In Clark Tibbitts, ed., *Handbook of Social Gerontology: Societal Aspects of Aging*. Chicago: University of Chicago Press, pp. 92–119.

Cramer, Richard. 1985. "The Valley of Death." *Rolling Stone*. October 24, pp. 28–34, 84–86.

DeSpelder, Lynne, and Albert Strickland. 1983. *The Last Dance: Encountering Death and Dying*. Palo Alto, Calif.: Mayfield.

Diamond, Stuart. 1985a. "U.S. Toxic Mishaps in Chemicals Put at 6,928 in 5 Years." *New York Times*. October 3, pp. 1, 13.

———. 1985b. "The Bhopal Disaster: How It Happened." *New York Times*. January 28, pp. 1, 6.

Dolan, Carrie. 1981. "Funeral Party Can Now Get $85,000 Ride." *Wall Street Journal*. September 9, p. 31.

Durkheim, Emile. 1961. *The Elementary Forms of the Religious Life*. Glencoe, Ill.: Free Press.

Eckholm, Erik. 1985. "Report Says Smoking Causes Heavy Health Damage to Blacks." *New York Times*. August 12, p. A7.

Eliade, Mircea. 1959. *Cosmos and History: The Myth of the Eternal Return*. New York: Harper & Row.

Federal Trade Commission. 1978. *Funeral Industry Practices*. Washington, D.C.: Bureau of Consumer Protection.

Fisher, Tom. 1983. "There Could Be a McDonald's in Funeral Service." *Mortuary Management Magazine*. January, pp. 46–47, 58.

Garfinkel, Harold. 1956. "Conditions of Successful Degradation Ceremonies." *American Journal of Sociology* 61(4):420–24.

Gitlitz, George. 1985. "Drop Cigarette Advertising." *New York Times*. May 11, p. 21.

Goffman, Erving. 1952. "Cooling the Mark Out: Some Adaptations to Failure." *Psychiatry* 15:451–63.

Grollman, Earl. 1971. *Suicide: Prevention, Intervention, Postvention*. Boston: Beacon Press.

Habenstein, Robert, and William Lamers. 1955. *The History of American Funeral Directing*. Milwaukee: Bulfin.

Harris, D., and D. Eitzen. 1978. "The Consequences of Failure in Sport." *Urban Life* 7:177–88.

Hazarika, Sanjoy. 1984a. "Gas Leak in India Is Said to Kill 410 and Injure 12,000." *New York Times*. December 4, p. 1.

———. 1984b. "Indian Journalist Warned 2 Years Ago of Danger of Gas Leak." *New York Times*. December 11, p. 5.

Jacobs, Sanford. 1985. "The Most Likely to Survive—A Funeral Home or a Florist?" *Wall Street Journal*. September 16, p. 25.

Jones, Landon. 1980. *Great Expectations: America and the Baby Boom Generation*. New York: Coward, McCann and Geoghegan.

Keller, Bill. 1984. "What Is the Audited Value of Life?" *New York Times*. October 26, p. 8.

Lens, Sidney. 1979. "Dead on the Job: Steady Work Can Be a Suicide Trip." *Progressive* 43 (November):50.

Lyons, Richard. 1978. "Califano in Drive to End Smoking: Calls Habit 'Slow-Motion Suicide.'" *New York Times*. January 12, p. A14.

McFadden, Robert. 1984. "Disaster in India Agony Questions." *New York Times*. December 10, p. 1.

McKendrick, Neil, John Brewer, and J. H. Plumb. 1982. *The Birth of a Consumer Society: The Commercialization of Eighteenth-Century England*. Bloomington: Indiana University Press.

McNeill, William. 1976. *Plagues and Peoples*. Garden City, N.Y.: Anchor Press/ Doubleday.

Magnuson, Ed. 1985. "A Problem That Cannot Be Buried." *Time*. October 14, pp. 76–77.

Mannheim, Karl. 1952. "The Problem of Generation." In P. Kecskemeti, ed., *Essays on the Sociology of Knowledge*. London: Routledge and Kegan Paul, pp. 276–322.

Maris, Ronald. 1981. *Pathways to Suicide*. Baltimore: Johns Hopkins University Press.

Marx, Karl. 1964. *Early Writings*. Trans. and ed. by T. B. Bottomore. New York: McGraw-Hill.

Mitford, Jessica. 1963. *The American Way of Death*. New York: Simon & Schuster.
———. 1977. "The Funeral Salesman." *McCall's*. November, pp. 190–92, 312–20.
Molotsky, Irvin. 1985a. "Smokers' Illnesses Cost Billions, Report Asserts." *New York Times*. September 16, p. 12.
———. 1985b. "U.S. Cites Broad Smoking Risk." *New York Times*. December 20, p. 10.
Mufson, Steve. 1985. "Cigarette Companies Develop Third World as a Growth Market." *Wall Street Journal*. July 5, pp. 1, 8.
National Funeral Directors Association (NFDA). The Code of Professional Practices for Funeral Directors. Adopted 1965.
New York Times. 1977. "Antismoking Drives Seen as a Spur to Smoking." September 11, p. A22.
———. 1983. "Files Show Dioxin Makers Knew of Hazards." July 6, pp. 1, 10.
———. 1985a. "Death by Robot Brings Call for Improved Safety." March 22, p. 8.
———. 1985b. "Immune System Flaws Are Found at Bhopal." October 30, p. 7.
———. 1985c. "Heart Study Disputes Notion." November 11, p. 16.
———. 1987. "Miners and Construction Workers Are Found to Hold Riskiest Jobs." July 27, p. 9.
People Magazine. 1977. "With His Talking Tombstone, John Dilks Gives Everyone a Chance to Have the Last Word." November 7, p. 89.
Pierce, W. H. 1983. "Cremation Has Its Problems Also." *Professional Mortician* 39:2.
———. 1985. "Editorial Comment." *ProfessionalMortician* 46:10.
Pine, Vanderlyn. 1975. *Caretakers of the Dead: The American Funeral Director*. New York: Irvington.
———. 1978. "The Care of the Dead: A Historical Portrait." In Robert Fulton, ed., *Death and Dying: Challenge and Change*. Reading, Mass.: Addison-Wesley, pp. 272–78.
———. 1981. "Summary of NFDA Report." *Funeral Service "Insider"* (October 5).
Pine, Vanderlyn, and Derek Phillips. 1970. "The Cost of Dying: A Sociological Analysis of Funeral Expenditures." *Social Problems* 17:405–17.
Rabkin, Simon W., Francis Mathewson, and Robert Tate. 1980. "Chronobiology of Cardiac Sudden Death in Men." *Journal of the American Medical Association* 244 (September 19):1357–58.
Raether, Howard, and Robert Slater. 1975. *The Funeral Director and His Role as a Counselor*. National Funeral Directors Association.
Reveley, James. 1980. Public lecture at Trinity University, September 22.
Riley, Matilda. 1976. "Age Strata in Social Systems." In R. Binstock and E. Shanas, eds., *Handbook of Aging and the Social Sciences*. New York: Van Nostrand Reinhold, pp. 189–217.
Ryder, Norman. 1972. "Notes on the Concept of a Population." In M. Riley, M. Johnson, and A. Foner, ed., *Aging and Society, Vol. III: A Sociology of Age Stratification*. New York: Russell Sage, pp. 91–111.

Saddler, Jeanne. 1987. "Consumer Safety Agency's Role Is Questioned amid Charges over Its Chairman's Leadership." *Wall Street Journal.* September 23, p. 66.

San Antonio Express-News. 1983. "N.Y. Asbestos Disease Victims Cannot Sue." February 23, p. 13A.

———. 1984a. "Study Claims Disease Up in Industrialized Rural Countries." October 15, p. 2B.

———. 1984b. "Budget Office: Reduce Value of Worker's Life." October 24, p. 5A.

San Antonio Light. 1985. "Rocket Ride Offers Shot at Eternity." February 13, pp. A1, A16.

———. 1987. "Texas Leads Nation in Job Deaths." October 18, p. D2.

Sanger, David. 1984. "Worries over Toxins Grow in Silicon Valley." *New York Times.* November 10, pp. 1, 32.

Sarason, Seymour. 1977. *Work, Aging, and Social Change: Professionals and the One Life–One Career Imperative.* New York: Free Press.

Schutz, Alfred. 1973. *Collected Papers I: The Problem of Social Reality.* The Hague: Martinus Nijhoff.

Serrin, William. 1979. "The Life and Death of Woman Who Won Right to Be a Miner." *New York Times.* November 8, pp. 1, A16.

Severo, Richard. 1978. "Funeral Industry Is Striving to Improve Its Image in Face of Charges of Deception and Abuses of the Public." *New York Times.* April 25, p. 20.

Shabecoff, Philip. 1983. "E.P.A. Puts 133 More Sites on Hazardous Waste List." *New York Times.* September 2, p. 11.

Shenon, Philip. 1985a. "Report Says Eli Lilly Failed to Tell of 28 Deaths in Oraflex Case." *New York Times.* August 27, p. 12.

———. 1985b. "Drug Case Divided Officials at F.D.A. and Justice Department." *New York Times.* September 19, pp. 1, 14.

Sterne, Michael. 1978. "In Last Decade, Leaders Say, Harlem's Dreams Have Died." *New York Times.* March 1, pp. 1, 13.

Stoler, Peter. 1985. "Turning to New Technologies." *Time.* October 14, p. 90.

Taylor, Ronald. 1985. "Look Who's Polluting the Countryside Now—Uncle Sam." *U.S. News & World Report.* March 4, pp. 85–86.

Toffler, Alvin. 1980. *The Third Wave.* New York: Morrow.

Trost, Cathy. 1985. "Safety Lapse: Mercury Exposure of Workers Ignites Vermont Controversy." *Wall Street Journal.* September 24, pp. 1, 14.

Turner, Ronny, and Charles Edgley. 1975. "Death as Theatre: A Dramaturgical Analysis of the American Funeral." *Sociology and Social Research* 60(4):377–92.

U.S. News & World Report. 1979. "Is Your Job Dangerous to Your Health?" Interview with Dr. Jeanne Stellman. February 5, p. 39.

Wall Street Journal. 1985a. "Cost of Traditional Funeral." June 24, p. 29.

———. 1985b. "Illness, Injury Rate in Workplace Rose in '84, Study Finds." November 14, p. 10.

———. 1987a. "What's News." July 23, p. 1.

———. 1987b. "Murder on the Job." October 6, p. 1.

Weber, Max. 1958. *The Protestant Ethic and the Spirit of Capitalism.* New York: Charles Scribner's Sons.

Westie, Frank. 1973. "Academic Expectation for Professional Immortality: A Study of Legitimation." *American Sociologist* 8(1):19–32.

Williams, Rosalind. 1982. *Dream Worlds: Mass Consumption in Late Nineteenth-Century France.* Berkeley: University of California Press.

Wright, Chris. 1986. "Routine Deaths: Fatal Accidents in the Oil Industry." *Sociological Review* 34(2):265–89.

Chapter 8

The Politics of Death[1]

There has never been a time when
a democracy has not committed suicide.

John Adams

In 1974, two Japanese burial teams arrived in Indonesia to exhume seventeen hundred bodies of soldiers, buried there three decades earlier, for reburial in Japan (*San Francisco Chronicle* 1974). Five years later, U.S. soldiers engaged in a similar activity in the Canal Zone; a little-publicized detail of the transfer of the Panama Canal was the pullout of the American dead as well as the living (*U.S. News & World Report* 1979). Can these be considered rational activities for two advanced industrialized countries of the East and the West? And did the U.S. Congress have nothing better to do during the 1970s than argue the restoration of citizenship to Robert E. Lee (Dewar 1975) and Eugene V. Debs (*San Francisco Chronicle* 1976)? Such events suggest the political significance of the dead, even in modern societies. With the emergence of the modern state and the citizenship role, one retains membership not only in a religious system but in a political order as well.

Death poses the greatest challenge to any political regime, and the dead continue to exert considerable effect on the political affairs of the living. However, given that death also invigorates social systems and their value frameworks, polities have long realized the utility of death for both social change and political consolidation. This chapter begins by considering the relationships contemporary nations have with their dead and dying citizens. Political decisions and activities play an increasing role in determining not only who dies but how and when. We see how, with social evolution, the number of premature deaths in a country has become increasingly politicized, understood as being either politically avoidable or evidence of political

Members of the Chinese People's Liberation Army file past the body of Chairman Mao Tse-Tung to pay their last respects. UPI/Bettmann Photos.

inadequacy. Finally, we consider two of the most heated debates in the American politics of death, the issues of abortion and capital punishment.

Death and Power

The relationship between death and political systems has been intimate since the inception of secular authority. This should not be surprising. Are not death and taxes the two great certainties of life? Given the centrality of death to cultural value systems as well as religion's historical demonstration of the power accruing to those monopolizing its meanings and fears, the ability to harness death is the key to political power. Death is routinely employed by political regimes to invigorate collective solidarity and to stimulate unified action, as demonstrated by events in the United States following the Japanese attack on Pearl Harbor. The dead themselves can symbolize a social

Table 8.1 Political Killings of the Twentieth Century

	Totals, in millions	Averages, per 10,000 population
Deaths by government	119.4	349
Communist	95.2	477
Other nonfree	20.3	495
Partially free	3.1	48
Free	0.8	22
Deaths by war	35.7	22
International	29.7	17
Civil	6.0	26

Source: Rummel 1986. Reprinted by permission of the *Wall Street Journal,* © Dow Jones & Company, Inc. 1986.

order, evidenced by the embalmed remains enshrined in mausoleums in Moscow and Peking. When they are eulogized as martyrs, the dead legitimize the policies of the political elite. And as illustrated by the state funerals for Kennedy, de Gaulle, Churchill, Mao, and Tito, only the dead have the power to bring together the leaders of the world community.[2]

Historically, political systems have sought to monopolize violent death, whether by legitimizing deadly force, as is the case in war, or by controlling its illegitimate use, as by executing murderers.[3] According to the *Twentieth Century Book of the Dead,* more than a hundred million deaths have been caused by governments just since 1900 (Elliot 1972). As evident in Table 8.1 (which excludes executions for criminal acts), less than a quarter of this carnage has occurred because of war. More than 119 million, according to the calculations of R. J. Rummel (1986), have died as the result of pogroms, torture (practiced by one-third of the nations of the world since 1980), famines resulting from political decisions, and privations suffered in slave-labor camps. The U.S. government is far from being innocent of such deeds. In 1984, for example, a CIA document was made public that revealed how the agency instructed Nicaraguan rebels in strategies for gaining popular support, including advice on such matters as political assassinations. The booklet, entitled "Psychological Operations in Guerrilla Warfare," said, in part:

If "it becomes necessary" to shoot a citizen who is "trying to leave the town," guerrillas should explain that "he was an enemy of the people" who would have "alerted the enemy" so that the Sandinistas could "carry out acts of reprisals, such as rapes, pillage, destruction, captures, etc."

The final lesson in the armed propaganda chapter, titled "Selective Use of Violence," involves "neutralizing" selected public officials. The lesson stresses that "it is absolutely necessary to gather together the population affected, so that they will be present and take part in the act."

After the official is publicly "neutralized," guerrillas should offer "extensive explanation" of "why it was necessary for the good of the people" and then "choose carefully" the person "who will replace the target." (Brinkley 1984)

In sum, death has been the instrument routinely used to demarcate the moral boundaries of life and to reaffirm the authority of political orders.

With modernization, political systems have also become collective instruments for controlling all nonviolent forms of death and for managing cultural death fears as well. Given the contemporary political involvements with abortion, suicide prevention, warnings about contaminated food and the risks of smoking, and murder, it should be evident that polities have become responsible for preventing most forms of premature, man-made death.[4] But political responsibility now includes protection from death by the natural order as well. Following an earthquake (the prediction itself is a political responsibility, much like the weather), for example, we no longer appeal to God, as Job did, but rather call Washington for relief. Even the contemporary manifestations of cultural death fears have become politicized, including not only the politically sponsored radioactive mushroom clouds but also fears of cancer and gray hair. When we witness the defense budgets of nations being dwarfed by federal expenditures devoted to those most likely to die—the sick and the old—we can detect a more subtle yet profound involvement with death by modern political economies (see Chapter 11). With modernization, political systems have an ever-increasing influence in determining who dies, how they die, where, and when.

Politicizing Death

As argued in Chapter 2, a basic task of any social system is to give symbolic order and meaning to human mortality, assisting people in "coming to terms with death [through] a refutation of the meaninglessness of life that death, even longed-for death, appears to proclaim" (Choron 1963, p. 9). Traditionally, this task was a province of religious knowledge systems (Berger 1969). Though typically unable to control or predict the social disruptiveness of death, religious regimes at least provided explanations and mitigated anomic terrors. However, with secularization, the innovations of science and technology, and the rise of the nation-state as the most encompassing and powerful of all social institutions, the problem of death has become a political matter.

So extensive has become the relationship between modern political systems and mortality that premature death is rarely understood as being something "natural" or divinely ordained. Rather, such death is assumed to be either intentional or politically avoidable (such as by not heeding government warnings on the risks of smoking or driving without a seat belt). In fact, the U.S. federal government is involved in:

- *Why we die,* whether through declarations of war or through attempts to control carcinogens and enforce safety in the workplace. Even more concretely, in May 1984, a federal district judge ruled that radioactive fallout from the aboveground nuclear tests in the 1950s caused at least nine Utah residents to die of cancer and that the government was guilty of negligence (Peterson 1984). The greater the number of deaths caused by some controllable factor, the more likely social attention and social action results. Before the 1980 MGM hotel fire in Las Vegas, the public was lulled with deaths in ones or twos, even though there were twelve thousand hotel fires each year claiming one hundred sixty lives. After 1980, national safety legislation, in effect, made the possibilities for such fires to occur against the law.

- *How we die,* as by failing to pass gun-control legislation, declaring war,[5] raising interstate highway speed limits, or financing the care of the socially dead in nursing homes and other institutions. With the high technology associated with science and modernization, the state has become responsible for predicting and preventing (if not controlling) death by nature as well, as illustrated by federal expenditures for earthquake and tornado alerts[6] as well as the Centers for Disease Control in Atlanta.

- *When we die,* not only directly, as by determining when a fetus can be legally aborted or a convict executed, but indirectly as well. There is a decrease in suicides and homicides when mobilizing for war (Marshall 1981) or during times of presidential elections (Boor 1981).

- *Who dies,* whether through purges, conscription practices, or abortion subsidy.

In terms of van Gennep's (1960) stages of a rite of passage (the rites of separation, liminality, and reincorporation), the illustrations above demonstrate the polity's role with the rite of separation. But it by no means ends here. In the United States, the death benefits paid by Social Security and the years of Federal Trade Commission hearings on funeral abuse are examples of political involvement in the rite of transition as well.[7] So are the protracted American attempts to locate MIAs in Vietnam and Cambodia, which reveal how a modern state must give ritual attention to members stuck in limbo between the worlds of the living and the dead—a need faced by preindustrial cultures, as seen in Chapter 2. And, like the rites of reincorporation of traditional societies, there are political purgatories (Robert E. Lee had to wait until the bicentennial year to have his citizenship restored) and hells for sinners: former Korean president Syngman Rhee was denied burial in his own country, and former Liberian president William Tolbert must share a common grave with twenty-seven others (*Time* 1980). The man without a country is denied political transcendence and absorption into the sacred.

Because the dead (and dying) are so remote from everyday life, their potency as political symbols actually increases with modernization. As Edelman noted, "psychological distance from symbols that evoke perceptions and emotions heightens their potency rather than reducing it" (1964, p. 11). And so the death of an American businessman at the hands of terrorists in a distant land or the plight of a dying young girl in need of a liver transplant can be all that is required to provoke a response from the highest political authorities.

Bestowing Immortality on Citizens

Janowitz (1980) detected a peculiar bias within the sociology of citizenship literature, a preoccupation with the entitlements of the role (as well as the barriers in obtaining equal rights and privileges) instead of with the associated accountabilities entailed. In death we can see the reverse side of the citizenship role, the possible consequences of fulfilling the obligations and bearing the expected sacrifices of good citizens, whether by volunteering for an ill-fated hostage rescue attempt or, as in the case of the unsuspecting victims of domestic testings of germ or nuclear warfare, by accepting the status of pawns in international politics. The study of political reactions to death reveals another facet of citizenship rarely addressed by sociologists or social psychologists: the psychological gains that accrue through participation in the largest and most interdependent of all human groups, the modern nation-state. State membership provides the individual with not only spatial transcendence (such as pride in seeing the American flag on Mars or the sense of self-importance derived when extensions of the state intercede on one's behalf when one is kidnapped in a foreign land) but temporal transcendence as well. As Durkheim's student, Robert Hertz, observed before his own death for a political cause in the trenches of World War I, "Indeed, society imparts its own character of permanence to individuals who compose it: because it feels itself immortal and wants to be so, it cannot normally believe that its members, above all those in whom it incarnates itself and with whom it identifies itself, should be fated to die" (1965, p. 77). The state, like religion, confers immortality on each of its elect.

In the beginning of 1981, national newsmagazines carried two seemingly unrelated stories: President Ronald Reagan, in his inaugural address, referred to Martin A. Treptow, an obscure hero of World War I,[8] and Pope John Paul II beatified a seventeenth-century Native American female. Analogous to the stages of canonization in the Catholic church (venerable, beatified, and canonized), the American polity rescues from oblivion the memories of certain individuals and confers differing degrees of public veneration. At the lowest level, as in the case of Treptow, a public reference is made to the individual, the president may observe a birth anniversary by sending a wreath, or a federal building may be named after the person. The second level places the polity in more direct contact with the symbol; an individuals' likeness may be placed on currency or postage stamps,[9] or the states may make birthdays of favorite sons a regional holy day. At the highest level of public veneration, national "holy days" are observed, whether through presidential proclamation (the Presidential Proclamation Days are coming to resemble the saint-saturated calendar of the pre–Vatican II Catholic church) or public holiday. In the Communist bloc, this type of devotion to the dead resembles that given to the relics of saints before the church insisted that these observances be directed toward itself (Ariès 1981). Here the dead symbolize the entire political order, evidenced by the embalmed remains enshrined in Moscow, Peking, and Hanoi mausoleums. When the Soviet gerontocracy reviews May Day parades from atop Lenin's tomb, the role of the dead in providing political legitimacy and continuity is perhaps most obvious. The recent controversy in the United States about making Martin Luther King's birthday a national holiday is thus an argument about elevating him to a higher beatified status. The removal of Stalin's remains from public view is an example of *de*canonization.

In sum, polities are like religions in their tendency and need to provide immortality options. Hannah Arendt observed that perhaps the very origins of democracy derived from the transcendence desires of Athenian warriors in the Trojan campaigns:

. . . men's life together in the form of the *polis* seemed to assure that the most futile of human activities, action and speech, and the least tangible and most ephemeral of man-made "products," the deeds and stories which are their outcome, would become imperishable. The *polis* was supposed to multiply the occasions to win "immortal fame," that is, to multiply the chances for everyone to distinguish himself, to show in deed and word who he was in his unique distinctiveness. (1959, p. 176–77)

The preservation of mountains of congressional hearings transcripts is but a contemporary option for such "immortal fame."

The Dead in Political Life

> Political forms thus come to symbolize what large masses of men need to
> believe about the state to reassure themselves. It is the needs, the hopes, and
> the anxieties of men that determine the meanings.
>
> Edelman 1964, p. 2

With the rise of the nation-state as the most encompassing of all social
groups and with its expanding influence over the final rite of passage, "there
is much more problematic relation between political authority and ultimate
meaning than had ever been thought before" (Bellah and Hammond 1980,
p. x). The resolution of this problem can be found in the symbolic treatment
of the dead by political systems. As noted by U.S. congressman Ray Roberts
of the Subcommittee on Cemeteries and Burial Benefits, "the quality of a
civilization is revealed in the way it reveres its dead" (U.S. House 1978a, p.
5). By extending immortality to their citizenry, polities create a sense of continuity with past and future generations while simultaneously addressing the
transcendence anxieties of individuals who must have both a sense of uniqueness and a sense of place in the cosmic scheme of things. However, as the
following illustrations suggest, tensions between these two functions can
emerge, leading either to the extinction or recasting of one's memory, of the
dead becoming an antiregime symbol.

Rousseau's notion of civil religion allows unique insights into such political aspects of the dead. In the United States, political eulogies and the
themes of sacrifice and rebirth are central components of civil religion. They
can be seen in the maintenance of national cemeteries and tombs for
unknown soldiers, in the ritual observances of Memorial Day (begun in 1866
as an undifferentiated tribute to both northern and southern Civil War
dead), and in Veteran's Day and the 1979 recommendation of the President's Commission on the Holocaust to create a national memorial and
museum for the Nazi's World War II victims . Instead of the cross, there is
the flag draping the coffins of veterans; for Good Friday, there is Pearl Harbor
Day; the patron saints of the civil calendar are either the birth or death anni-
versaries of past leaders. Polities, like religions, maintain sacred sites, such as
Arlington National Cemetery, for sacred remains. For political immortality,
there is the eternal flame at Kennedy's tomb and Mount Rushmore. The
tomb of Lenin serves as the cathedral of the Soviet state. Polities can use
death as an occasion for national atonement: on December 24, 1978, China
held a large memorial observance in Peking for two of the most prominent
victims of Mao's purges, Peng Teh-huai and Tao Chu. And finally, polities
can employ the dead to establish reconciliations with each other: to thaw

tensions with Japan, Moscow in 1986 no longer required passports or visas for Japanese wishing to visit family graves on the northern islands the Russians had claimed following World War II.

Case 1: Individualizing Death
In June 1980, the Veterans Administration began to remove 627 bodies of unknown Civil War soldiers from their individual sites in the Grafton, West Virginia, National Cemetery to place them in a mass grave with an imposing headstone bearing the inscription, "Now We Are One." With 55 of the 109 national cemeteries filled (U.S. House 1979, p. 263) and with the World War II cohort reaching old age, a similar plan was advanced to make sacred sites for new burials. Because the unknown Civil War dead had been buried anonymously, and because the space was badly needed, it was expected that such a move would be accomplished with little fuss. It was not. People were outraged, and objections arose from two specific groups: veterans and amateur historians.

The protests of veterans illustrated the importance placed on the political guarantees for individuality after death and how the dead symbolize the temporal extension from the present into the past and future. The contention of a former soldier that "he would not want his own grave disturbed years from now to make room for other veterans" (*Washington Post* 1980) is a plea for political support of his own transcendence. The logic of his argument is that if the individuality of the Civil War dead is erased by a common burial, his own individuality, too, may be lost to posterity. He will fear death less if he is assured that he will at least be remembered. He expects from others one hundred years hence the honor he now pays to a dead soldier. He wants to believe that what is defined as important to the nation will not change, that offering one's life in the service of one's country will merit consideration and honor from a grateful nation forever.

Aficionados of the War between the States perceived the reburial controversy in a different light. Disinterment of the Civil War soldiers from individual locations and reburial in a common grave meant the degradation of the sacred past. Because criminals or victims of mass disease are often buried together, the connotation is a dishonorable one. A letter to the editor of the *Washington Post* asked, "Are we now to say to these nameless heroes that their valor on the battlefields of Gettysburg and Shiloh, Antietam and Chancellorsville and countless other sites where the Blue and Gray clashed was for nought?" (Talbot 1980). The removal of these bodies from their graves was regarded by Civil War buffs as an infringement on the rights of the dead soldiers (Hutchens 1980). As part of the sacred past of the United States, the Civil War has taken on an aura of inviolability. Those who fought and died in that war are regarded as martyrs as surely as any who died for their religious faith.[10] The fact that the reburials provoked controversy and meant different things to different people is evidence of the abstractness and generalizability of the dead as a symbolic form. Political stability often is achieved through such shallow symbolic consensus (Cobb and Elder 1972).

Case 2: Collective Remembering and Forgetting
It is not just the Soviet encyclopedia that requires continuous revision. When the past needs reinterpretation to legitimize the activities or ideologies of the present, certain personages must be resurrected and biographies reviewed. An example is the Chinese veneration given to Peng Teh-huai and Tao Chu in the late 1970s, two individuals dishonored a decade earlier during the Cultural Revolution but whose efforts were to be reappreciated by the Hua regime in the midst of the trial of the Gang of Four (Butterfield 1978).

On the other hand, there may be political need for the past to be forgotten, which leads to the dead being deindividuated and ignored. To forget the 1956 Hungarian Revolution, the Moscow-controlled government in Budapest bulldozed the cemetery plots of the revolutionary leaders it hanged— including that of the former prime minister, Imre Nagy, who had urged democratization (Liptak 1985). In early 1981, the funeral of Hitler's successor, Grand Admiral Karl Doenitz, was attended by the "men of Germany's past" who sought to turn the funeral into "a final grasp at justifying their part of history" (Vinocur 1981, p. 5). The old soldiers were angered by the underrepresentation of the state; the Defense Ministry had refused to send a representative or to allow members of the armed forces to attend in uniform. A century after the American Civil War, the federal government saw fit to restore citizenship rights to two southerners, Robert E. Lee and Jefferson Davis, and to declare a third, Dr. Samuel Mudd, innocent of complicity in Lincoln's assassination. In restoring all rights of citizenship to Davis, President Carter proclaimed, "Our nation needs to clear away the guilts and enmities and recriminations of the past, to finally set at rest the divisions that threaten to destroy our nation and to discredit the great principles on which it was founded" (*Washington Post* 1978).

Case 3: The Dead as Symbols of Political Legitimacy
When a visitor to Moscow in the 1930s asked a Russian Communist, "Why did you embalm Lenin?" he was told, "Because we don't believe in the immortality of the soul" (Kolakowski 1983, p. 33). Because Lenin identified himself so completely with the party, its leadership position, and the state he created, his death occasioned a succession crisis that remains to this day. Realizing this, a "god-building" enterprise was initiated. From this came a

A Letter to the Editor

This week marks the 70th anniversary of the 20th century's first act of genocide: the massacre of 1.5 million Armenians by Ottoman Turkey. Even today, Turkey has never admitted its guilt. Why must the U.S. connive at that ugly denial?

In 1923, when the genocide ended, almost one-half of the world's Armenian population had been slaughtered on its ancestral land, which it had inhabited for more than 3,000 years.

. . . President Reagan, in not wanting "to harm relations with an important ally," opposes a pending Congressional resolution memorializing the Armenian martyrs. And in 1983, he said of the 1915–1923 genocide, "There's virtually no one alive today who was living" at that time. Defense Secretary Caspar W. Weinberger has spoken of the "so-called Armenian genocide resolution."

. . . Henry Morgenthau Sr., Ambassador to Turkey from 1913 to 1916, wrote of "sadistic orgies" and "race extermination" in his frantic cables to Washington. Maj. Gen. James Harbord, upon returning from the Armenian areas in 1919, called it the "most colossal crime of all the ages."

. . . It was on April 24, 1915, that the carnage began, after an edict by Interior Minister Talaat Pasha to "destroy completely all Armenians living in Turkey." Community leaders were hanged and all Armenian males were taken away and bludgeoned to death. Women, children and the elderly were rounded up in all towns and villages and marched hundreds of miles to the sun-scorched deserts of Syria. Few made it. Those surviving starvation or thirst were raped, disembowelled, drowned, buried alive or hauled into harems. Women's breasts were cut off and babies were speared; mothers, clutching their children, threw themselves into rivers. The waters ran red.

To help the human wrecks of this mass murder, in 1919 Congress, with State Dept. cooperation, aided Near East Relief, an American organization.

I know why Turkey denies the genocide. But how can we explain why there are only some 35,000 Armenians now left in Turkey out of a pre-1915 population of more than two million? And why does Turkey now find it necessary to systematically destroy all traces of Armenian culture—monuments, churches, artifacts—in its eastern provinces?

Avakian 1985.

cult of the dead, blatantly modeled on Christian martyrology, to legitimize communist ideology as the "religion of mankind." Party officials took advantage of the traditional belief that the absence of decay indicated the sanctity of holy men and went to considerable lengths to ensure that Lenin's remains were perfectly preserved in order that they, too, would be the object of "religious" pilgrimages and veneration (Emmons 1985, p. 25). Devotionals included such slogans as "Lenin is more alive than all the living." And

Khrushchev established the custom of giving the immortalized Lenin a party card (no. 1) every time new cards were issued (Kolakowski 1983, p. 34). As Emmons observed, "Lenin is the father of his country, a prophet, and the Messiah all rolled into one" (1985, p. 19).

Sacred political immanence was also invested in the remains of Eva Perón, which were held in saintlike regard by many of her Argentine countrymen. She died of cancer in 1952 at the age of thirty-three, and her corpse took six months to preserve at the hands of Dr. Pedro Ara, a Spanish pathologist. In 1955, when Juan Perón was overthrown, Eva's remains were kidnapped by anti-Peronists and stored for fifteen years in a packing case marked "Radio Sets." With the changing of the political tide, the new regime returned the almost perfectly preserved body to the exiled Perón in Madrid. Within two years of his return to power in 1972, Perón died, and his embalmed remains were joined with Eva's. Anti-Peronists are again in power, and Eva has been buried, this time in an officially marked crypt.

Case 4: Political Funerals
The dead can be used to mount an offensive on the legitimacy of a regime. Political authorities can be haunted by the victims of their own terror, as Macbeth was by Duncan, or by those whose immortality cannot be subverted by the regime in power.[11]

In Northern Ireland, El Salvador, the Philippines, South Africa, Iran, Argentina, and Poland, we witness the potency of the dead as antiregime symbols. The events of Northern Ireland redemonstrate the problem of martyring one's opposition. When the eighth IRA hunger striker succumbed to his slow-motion suicide, violence was ignited, and British policy was discredited further. In 1979, twenty thousand Salvadorans participated in a funeral procession for seventeen people slain by police and soldiers during a peaceful demonstration outside the Metropolitan Cathedral in San Salvador (Riding 1979). Chanting antigovernment slogans and carrying banners as well as flowers, this collective demonstration not only coalesced around the dead but was even tolerated by a threatened regime because of the license conferred by death. Also in the Philippines, the mass outpouring of grief for the slain opposition leader Benigno Aquino had to be permitted by the repressive regime of Ferdinand Marcos. Ayatollah Khomeini of Iran consolidated his power in exile during December 1978 by calling for a day of mourning for anti-Shah demonstrators killed during the preceding year (Gage 1978). And in Argentina, the "Mothers of Plaza de Mayo" maintain the memories of the thousands who have disappeared during the antiterrorism campaign of the military junta by contesting the wills of those the government has not acknowledged to be dead (Chavez 1984).

The self-immolation of a Buddhist monk: Cross-legged and stoic, a young Vietnamese monk burns to death on a Saigon sidewalk in 1963 in protest against the Ngo Dinh Diem regime. It was the sixth such suicide in four months. For the Diem regime, these suicides were a source of international embarrassment. For a passing bicyclist, however, it was an event barely worth noticing. UPI/Bettmann Newsphotos.

A crowd of two hundred fifty thousand Polish mourners, one of the largest gatherings in that country since World War II, attended the funeral of Rev. Jerzy Popieluszko, a Solidarity priest who apparently had been beaten by authorities, tied up, and thrown into a reservoir. As one observer noted,

Popieluszko's abductors may have arrogantly assumed that the fragmented opposition would be too weak to forcefully respond to his death. Instead, the tragedy had provided the nation with a new symbol of courage. In their shock and grief, many Poles recalled some of the last words spoken by their martyred priest. "A Christian's duty is to stand by the truth, even if truth carries with it a high price. Please God, let us retain our dignity throughout each day of our lives." (Kohan 1984)

Robert Goldstein has called such mortuary protest ceremonies in repressive regimes "political funerals," observing "the similarities between the use of political funerals in contemporary authoritarian regimes and their wide-

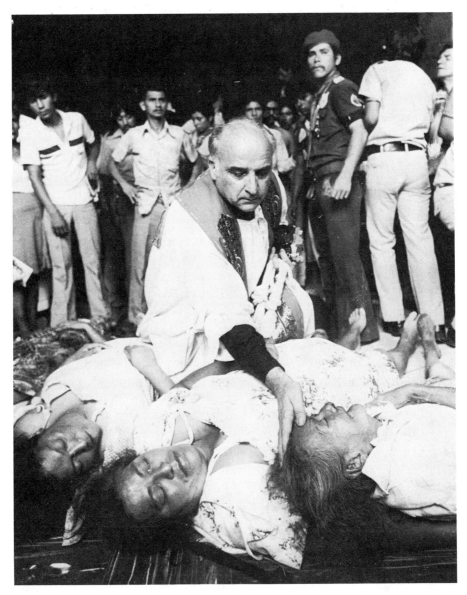

On March 30, 1980, in El Salvador, a priest gives last rites to victims after bombings and gunfire abruptly halted an emotional funeral mass for assassinated Archbishop Oscar A. Romero. UPI/Bettmann Newsphotos.

spread use in Europe between 1815 and 1914, . . . where modernization coincides with highly repressive political systems" (1984, pp. 14–15). When, in its 1985 invocation of emergency powers, the South African government banned mass funerals for blacks, it was the last straw for the international community. Such political funerals were nearly the only lawful form of black assembly, but their frequency—more than five hundred had been killed the previous year—and size had proven too great a threat to the minority white regime (Cowell 1985).[12]

The immortality of past patriots can prove troublesome to new regimes. Such persons cannot be consigned to the Stygian status of the infamous—the Hitlers, John Wilkes Booths, and Lee Harvey Oswalds—wherein their memory is preserved as an antithesis of the ideal citizen, nor can they be venerated as martyrs. For example, the remains of Poland's virulently anticommunist wartime hero, General Wladyslaw Sikorski, were to have been repatriated from Britain. Polish authorities had developed elaborate plans for a reburial ceremony on the anniversary of Sikorski's death and the consecration of the Krakow cathedral. A national competition would determine the design of his sarcophagus, which was to be placed in the cathedral to lie with the remains of other Polish heroes. The refusal of the British Home Office to return the remains was undoubtedly applauded by the one hundred thousand Polish émigrés living in Britain. However, it ironically produced a coalition of the Polish Catholic church with the communist regime, which had recently forgiven Sikorski for his political views (Simmons 1981).[13] Revealed here is not only the politics of immortality but also how the dead dramatize the polity's relationship to everyday life, even the peculiar relationship of church and state in one communist country.

Death and the Political Order

Of what propaganda value are the reports of extreme longevity coming from the Soviet Georgian province? Do Third World despots pay attention to the international report card issued for human rights? And what are the political implications if some groups are found to have lower life expectancies than others?

Such indicators as national life expectancies are now internationally read and understood to be box scores of a polity's social stability (disproportionate death rates of young adults, for example, are indicative of internal oppression), social stratification (the disproportionately greater mortality rates of minorities, whether by suicide, capital punishment, homicides, alcoholism, or infant mortality rates, evince flaws in a polity's ability to provide a uniform quality of life to all), degree of cultural humanitarianism, and technological development. To ignore these indicators of death is to defy all standards of human decency, hence the international outrage when, in the midst of a massive pogrom, the defense minister of the Soviet-sponsored Cambodian government reported in Moscow during October 1979 that "no one is dying of hunger in our country" and that reports of the mass starvation of Cambodians were an invention of "Western and Peking propaganda." Such are the reasons why the politics of death has increasingly entered into American class politics. Take, for instance, the case of Social Security entitlements, in which individuals contribute to the program throughout their working careers with the promise of full benefits upon reaching the age of sixty-five. What if, because of a person's ethnicity or location within the stratification order, he or she cannot even expect to reach that age, as is the case of the black male? For these persons, there are no rebates, no reduced tax schedule, and no earlier age for qualification. Or consider the implications of the striking link between the health problems of poor children in the United States and those of poor children in developing countries. When measured by infant mortality rates, children in the Morrisania section of the Bronx (21 deaths for each 1000 births) and those in the Avalon Park section of Chicago (55 per 1000) have more in common than anyone would have imagined with children in more than thirty of the poorest developing countries of the world (Lyons 1985).

Table 8.2 gives a sampling of countries and the type of statistics that policymakers and propagandists alike employ to gauge the adequacy of regimes. Such data, of course, are always suspect; both politics and the quality of information gathering affect their accuracy. Nevertheless, on the surface it appears that life expectancies increase and infant mortality rates decline where economic development, as measured by GNP per capita, is the greatest: male life expectancies, for example, are in the thirties or forties where per capita GNP is less than a few hundred dollars a year. However, the relationships are far from perfect: the correlation coefficient (r) of the measure of economic development with male life expectancy is .53, with female life expectancy is .57, and with infant mortality rates is $-.68$. Given its per capita GNP, the infant mortality rate of the United States should be approaching zero, certainly not greater than the rate in Taiwan. And female life expectancy at birth in North Korea should be sixty-one years, not the seventy-six years observed. Politics, in addition to economic development and demographic transition theory (described in Chapter 2), are involved in the discrepancies.

The maintenance of such political box scores proved to be a statistical source of embarrassment for the Soviet Union. Although virtually every

Table 8.2 The Political Box Score

	Life expectancy at birth		1986 Infant mortality rate (per 1000)	1984 GNP per capita (in 1983 dollars)
	Male	Female		
Afghanistan (1979)	42	40	180	NA
Argentina (1980)	67	74	34	2024
Bangladesh (1981)	51	49	138	128
Brazil (1980)	64	69	63	1505
Canada (1981)	73	81	8	13100
China (1982)	67	69	38	302
Cuba (1981)	72	74	17	NA
Ethiopia (1984)	49	51	120	111
France (1975)	71	79	10	9510
E. Germany (1983)	69	75	11	9769
W. Germany (1981)	72	79	8	11020
India (1981)	55	57	99	258
Italy	73	80	9	6330
Japan (1980)	75	80	6	10410
Mozambique (1980)	43	46	150	403
N. Korea	66	72	34	1133
S. Korea (1980)	65	72	27	1963
Mexico (1980)	66	72	46	1795
Netherlands (1981)	73	80	8	9338
Peru (1981)	59	63	91	1021
Poland (1984)	66	74	21	6159
Sudan (1983)	50	54	105	291
United Kingdom (1981)	72	78	10	8270
USSR (1984)	63	73	27	7266
USA (1980)	71	79	11	15380

Source: U.S. Bureau of the Census, *Statistical Abstract of the United States: 1988*, 108th ed., 1987 pp. 800, 805.

advanced industrialized country has witnessed continuously falling death rates, the Soviet Union recorded its low point in 1964. Betwen 1964 and 1984, the life expectancy of a newborn Russian male declined by nearly four years, from 66.0 to 62.5. Life expectancy for Russian women likewise decreased, though not as dramatically: in 1964, it was 74.0 years, and now it is 73.5 (Sullivan 1984). In an editorial reply to a *New York Times* argument that this increase was caused by alcoholism, motor vehicle accidents, or the delayed effects of World War II, one physician responded by noting that the Soviet Union was experiencing "a spreading epidemic of the most common diseases of capitalist societies—coronary heart disease and cancer . . . [caused by] increasing industrialization, increased pollution, smoking, hypertension and elevated cholesterol levels" (Cooper 1979). Dr. Murray Feshbach, a research professor of demographics at Georgetown University, also cited food shortages, noting that a diet based on imported American grain was deficient in lysine, an essential amino acid (Sullivan 1984). In sum, the country with the greatest nuclear arsenal in the world more closely resembles—by our measures—Argentina and Brazil than the developed industrialized nations of Europe. The Soviets have opted for one way of managing such embarrassing information: Moscow no longer publishes statistics on longevity.

Death and Social Development

Throughout the developing world, death comes prematurely not only because of nonmodern life-styles, sanitation, and medicine, but because of political instability as well. In other words, demographic transition theory obscures a number of political factors at work in the twentieth century. It does not account for the Vietnamese and Haitians who died when their boats capsized during attempts to escape the political oppression of their homelands. Nor does it describe the routinization of political murders in Lebanon, Cambodia, Ethiopia, El Salvador, and Afghanistan.

Indeed, this is not to deny the potency of nature in affecting mortality rates. It seems that, in addition to problems of social development, nature strikes more viciously where social systems are most vulnerable. Typhoons decimate tens of thousands in Bangladesh, and mammoth earthquakes strike Central and South American countries. In Africa, drought and associated famines are thrusting millions into a prehistoric standard of living. In Mozambique in 1984, rain had not fallen in many parts of the country, and many of the population suffered blindness as a result of vitamin A deficiency and were sick with pellagra, diarrhea, cholera, and other starvation diseases. A UN report of June 1984 showed that 1.5 million of the 13.4 million residents are totally dependent on foreign-relief supplies. Money becomes useless where there is no food. Ide Oumarou of Niger, departing chairman of the Council of Ministers of the Organization of African Unity, said in February 1985 that Africa was "going through one of the darkest periods of her history. . . . Africa, which gives an image of a continent where life and joy should be prevalent, is suffering from the sober reality of death, massive death, violent death" (*New York Times* 1985a).

Throughout much of the Third World, death remains so commonplace that life is cheapened. When Pope John Paul II visited Zaire in 1980, nine people were trampled to death trying to gain admission to the papal mass. "Death is so, so common here," explained a Flemish surgeon at Mama Yemo Hospital. "Our cemeteries are full. Sometimes we have two out of five infants die at birth. We are not Calcutta, but we are similar." The radio and newspapers ignored the deaths, and why not? "There are so many deaths in a day. Except for some of the well-to-do, there is not customarily a mass for one death. Instead, every Friday night, all the parishes have special prayers for the dead, and all the names are read of the dead for one week. With the volume, that is the best we can do," said Rev. Maurice Delabaere, a Jesuit priest (Jaynes 1980).

In Argentina, people simply disappeared as thousands, possibly tens of thousands, fell victim to state-directed terror. During seven years of military dictatorship during the 1970s and early 1980s, military officers were involved in the kidnapping, torture, and murder of at least nine thousand *desaparecidos* (Chelala 1984). In El Salvador, according to a former Salvadoran military official, death squads, or the Union of White Warriors as it called itself, were formally sanctioned purveyors of terrorism. He claimed that government officials routinely ordered police and soldiers to stay out of areas where political murders were about to take place and that assassins were assisted in seeking refuge in Guatemala. The minister of defense, Eugenio Casanova, was said to have personally directed a cover-up in the slayings of four American churchwomen in 1980 (Kinzer 1984).

To be a member of the underclass in the underdeveloped or developing countries is to be one of the untouchables of the world community. For them, human rights are meaningless as life is so cheap. Take, for instance, the native Indians of Guatemala who fought on the losing side of a guerrilla war. Although the Guatemalan army promised to improve the social conditions of these descendants of the Mayans, life remains little better than when the conquistadors arrived in the fifteenth century. There the government was unofficially understood to have identified more than one hundred thousand Indian children who lost at least one parent in the preceding four years (LeMoyne 1985). Given such lessons by the elite, murder became a way of resolving political grievances, personal quarrels, or financial disagreements. Landowners in these partly feudal societies continue to employ force as a means of intimidating peasants and eradicating those who propose change in the social order, such as Marxists and workers in agrarian reform, labor leaders, teachers, politicians seen as too liberal, or any kind of social reformer. "The target is anybody with an idea in his head," says a U.S. diplomat (*U.S. News & World Report* 1984). There were also a few people with ideas in their heads in the Philippines. In 1984, the warning by the defense minister of communist insurgency and a "serious upsurge" in rebel activities led to the deaths of two thousand civilians and military personnel. The promise of the death of old social orders often leads to the death of proponents and opponents alike.

Between 1975 and 1979, the idea of pogrom achieved new terror under

Pol Pot. After the United States stopped bombing Cambodia (including the accidental B-52 bombing of Neak Luong) the Khmer Rouge took over in April 1975. Whole populations were driven from urban centers as the Khmer Rouge claimed they were beginning Year Zero. They killed anyone suspected of being a doctor, a teacher, or an intellectual (Lewis 1984). Perhaps as many as two million Cambodians met death in one of the greatest demoderniza-tion orgies of the twentieth century. Cities were emptied, money abolished, machinery destroyed, and intellectuals segregated from others. Some were forced to work on dams and other irrigation works, surrounded by people dying of hunger, dysentery, and beatings. One killing ground, at the Kokoh Monastery in the Pati District of Takeo Province, displays a vintage twen-tieth-century pyramid built not of Nile stone but rather of thousands of human skulls (Campbell 1983).

Genocide

> Our fate is a warning to all.
>
> Inscription at the site of the Maidanek death camp in Warsaw

In the winter of 1985, survivors of Auschwitz gathered at the site of the Pol-ish concentration camp to observe the fortieth anniversary of their rescue. It was the Russians who had liberated them, a handful of the hundreds of thou-sands who had perished and been incinerated there. The week before the lib-eration, the camp's roster had numbered sixty-six thousand; when the Rus-sians entered, there were only six thousand.

There is a point at which the status of death as a political indicator loses all meaning. Perhaps our ability to even comprehend the agony and suffering of one or two acquaintances is limited, and even less if the victims are strang-ers. Only if the deceased were some significant other do we understand how the ripple of grief from one death can alter the lives of family, friends, reli-gious congregations, and coworkers. Empathy for large numbers is another matter. Who knows the extent to which the continuation of the cold war stems from the inability to grasp how the loss of thirty or more million dur-ing the last world war can fuel the Soviet xenophobia. Another example would be the Cambodian pogrom, which, if translated into American terms, would be the equivalent to eighty million or more persons being terminated at the whim of some third party. That would be news. And yet when this mass death was occurring, the death of Morris the cat, of TV commercial fame, received more press in the American news media.

With these points in mind, consider what the systematic and institution-alized destruction of more than six million Jews during the nazi Holocaust means. The very word *Holocaust* (note the capitalization) is the metaphor applied to all forms of megadeath, as in "nuclear holocaust." Unfortunately, such usage dilutes the full meaning of what transpired under the Nazis, much as the constant repetition of any word renders it meaningless. The political intention was to destroy not only life but the genetic immortality of a people as well.

In the 1930s, the Jews provided the German people with the scapegoats they needed to explain the disastrous legacy of Versailles and to kindle the flames of nationalism and the pseudo–social Darwinist ideology of Aryan supremacy. As the decade progressed and German-occupied territory grew, in minds such as Himmler's the problem was one of ridding an infection from the body politic. But how does one go about extinguishing an estimated eleven million individuals? Immigration and enslavement were not fast enough; there was only the "final solution."

At first, the logistics of executing a pogrom involved such strategies as the digging of huge trenches. Then the condemned were forced into them row by row. Individuals were shot while standing or lying on the remains of victims who preceded them. In Yugoslavia's most notorious nazi death camp, Jasenovac, the Croatians managed the Jewish question in the same manner as the Germans. Recalls Jossip Erlich, one of the survivors: "The first killings that I saw were soon after we arrived at Jasenovac. All the Serbian and Jewish women who came to the camp with me, and the smallest children who were too young for forced labor, were killed and we were made to watch. Some were machine-gunned. Others were killed with clubs. Most were executed with knives, their throats and bellies ripped open. Some were buried alive. It was simple slaughter" (*San Antonio Express-News* 1984). A documented account, called the *Black Book,* compiled by the Yugoslav Federation of Jewish Communities, quotes other camp survivors: "They cut off ears and noses"; "The guard, Jozo, boasted of taking delight in killing 10 to 20 children every evening"; "The prisoner was put on an anvil and struck with hammers." Such glee of the murderers in conducting their business is a common theme in the memories of the survivors.

But such methods proved too inefficient, and perhaps too gruesome,[14] given the scale of the task. Death became mechanized. Newly patented crematoriums were installed that could incinerate bodies in fifteen minutes. The death industries came to be located in proximity to both slave labor camps and rail systems. Rail lines were used not only to "resettle" Jews, the old and infirm, and other minorities, but also to ship out the by-products of these factories: clothing, women's hair, gold and false teeth. Even soap was made from human fat. When the trainloads of victims arrived at these slaughterhouses, individuals were separated into two groups: the strong, who would

Lessons from the Holocaust

Beside, if I have learned anything about the literature of the Holocaust, it is that it does not offer answers. Auschwitz negates all answers.

Take the wartime ghetto of Lodz, the second largest in Poland, as it appears in this chronicle. How can one explain its multifaceted agony, or the passivity and blindness of its inhabitants, or the apparent complicity in its fate of some of its leaders? Why was there no revolt, as there was at Warsaw, at Bialystok, at Vilna? Why was there no attempt to organize resistance or escape? Whose fault was it? That of Mordecai Chaim Rumkowski, the head of the ghetto, alone? Or of his oppressive ghetto police?

. . . The Nazis' aim was to make the Jewish universe shrink—from town to neighborhood, from neighborhood to street, from street to house, from house to room, from room to garret, from garret to cattle car, from cattle car to gas chamber. And they did the same to the individual—separated from his or her community, then from his or her family, then from his or her identity, eventually becoming a work permit, then a number, until the number itself was turned to ashes.

. . . Perhaps this was the ultimate purpose of these diaries and eyewitness accounts—to make man distrust himself. Perhaps this was why, in a world where mass murder was conceived and organized, systematically planned and scientifically perfected, the victims felt the need to put into words their anguish, their suffering and their despair.

. . . The disorder seems total: Children are like old men and women; adults— stripped of authority, impotent, vulnerable—conduct themselves like children.

Elie Wiesel (1984, p. 1), reviewing The Chronicle of the Lodz Ghetto.
Copyright © 1984 by the New York Times Company.
Reprinted by permission.

---

be engaged in slave labor, and all others, who would immediately be disposed of. The latter—including the old, young, sick, and women with children—were told they were to be deloused and showered. They were then locked in the gas chambers.

A number of facets of Ernest Becker's denials of death are discussed in Chapter 6. In the case of the Holocaust, although there was ample proof of the horrors being perpetrated, the Jews, the German people, and even the Allies refused to believe that such carnage was occurring. In fact, some Jews on the Eastern Front, upon hearing of the existence of the "resettlement camps," found life so unbearable that they even paid to be resettled there. Today, some deny that such crimes were even committed, claiming that the film documentaries and survivor stories are Zionist or communist propaganda. One wonders about the implications of such denials and their differ-

Part of the genocide machinery of the Third Reich. Cremation ovens in German con-centration camps brought industrial efficiency to the destruction of human life. Rails leading to the ovens expedited the transportation of corpses to furnaces and the removal of the ashes from the recesses below. The Bettmann Archive, Inc.

ence from the normal collective forgettings (such as the fate of the American Indian).

Although the nazi Holocaust is perhaps the best known, historical instances of genocidal massacres were so numerous that Hannah Arendt argued (1969, p. 288) that they were the order of the day in antiquity. And though one postwar theme of international affairs has focused on human rights, such crimes against collectivities have continued against the hunters and gatherers of the world (such as the Indians of Latin America and East Africa and the aborigines of Tasmania), those subjugated by colonial powers, and minority racial, religious, political, and ethnic groups not yet having achieved a stable accommodation within pluralistic societies—especially dur-ing periods of decolonialization. Leo Kuper, in fact, argues that "the sover-eign territorial state claims, as an integral part of its sovereignty, the right to commit genocide, or engage in genocidal massacres, against peoples under its rule, and that the United Nations, for all practical purposes, defends this right" (1981, p. 161; see also Horowitz 1982).

The Deaths of Kings and Modern Leaders

Political adequacy is gauged not only by the state-sponsored demise of common people but by the deaths of their leaders as well. Too many political assassinations—as in Haiti, between 1806 and 1986, when twenty-eight presidents, presidents-elect, and former presidents were murdered (Bell 1979, p. 31)—are barometers of social chaos. The inability of regimes to protect the lives of their principals is indicative of either impotence, instability, illegitimacy, or ignorance—in short, some major flaw in the structure of power.

Historically,[15] one strategy to alter the course of political events was simply to kill those in power. Political history was undeniably altered by the murders of Julius Caesar, Charles I of England, Louis XVI of France, Czar Nicholas of Russia, Archduke Francis Ferdinand, and Presidents Lincoln and Kennedy. Of the 107 emperors of the Byzantine Empire between A.D. 395 and 1453, only 34 died of natural causes: 23 were assassinated, 18 were mutilated and dethroned, 12 died in prison, and 8 were killed in war (Bell 1979, p. 25). Until the Reformation in western Europe, most regicide was a matter of secret political intrigue and the usurpation of power, rarely a challenge to the legitimacy of kingship.[16] As Michael Walzer observed, "It is no doubt a central feature of kingship that kings are so prone to be killed" (1974, p. 1). Thereafter, however, there appeared public regicide, being legitimized as either the biblical solution for managing tyrants or the Enlightenment-inspired renunciation of the supposedly divinely ordained authority of monarchies. As the unimaginable freedoms of rulers to kill others became constrained and as the structural opportunities to gain political power through murder evaporated in democratic societies, political assassinations became a less rational policy for conspirators and more likely to be viewed as the work of maniacs.

Industrialization was not attended by increased civility in the West. According to art historian David Rapoport, during the so-called Golden Age of Assassination between 1880 and 1940, one major European minister or head of state was murdered every eighteen months. Observed Rapoport, so politically disruptive was the carnage that a 1907 British journal, *The Spectator,* "prophesied that if this end-of-the-century madness did not stop, somebody would kill an Austrian prince and trigger the greatest war in history" (cited in Shurkin 1988).

Murder, however, is not the only form of death that leads to political instability. Two political scientists, Richard Betts and Samuel Huntington (1985), looked at the extent to which the deaths of long-term authoritarian leaders lead to political turmoil because of the lack of established rules of

An international audience shared the grief of the Kennedy family as it watched the televised funeral of the late President John F. Kennedy, assassinated in Dallas on November 22, 1963. National Archives.

succession and the transfer of legitimate power. They found in a sample of twenty-two countries, where such leaders had ruled for ten years or more and had died in office, that the greatest amount of postdeath instability occurred where there were high levels of social organization (e.g., autonomous labor unions and political parties), where economic development and literacy were greatest, and where the deceased ruler had been in power for more than a quarter of a century.

The Politics of Death in the United States

There are two forms of politically sanctioned intentional death whose private rituals have become the topics of renewed controversy in the United States during the 1970s and 1980s: abortion and capital punishment. This chapter concludes with an examination of each of these debates in turn and considers why they should simultaneously resurface to haunt the body politic.

The Abortion Controversy

American women have among the highest rates of unplanned pregnancies and abortions of all industrialized countries. In 1983, more than half of all pregnancies in the United States were unplanned, compared with 31.8 percent in Great Britain and 17 percent in the Netherlands. By the late 1980s, for every one hundred women there were an estimated seventy-six induced abortions in the United States, more than double, for instance, the Canadian rate of thirty-six (Kolata 1988). To legitimize so frequent a practice of ending potential life, a new ideology was in order.

At what point of development does the human organism become a person, a social member in full standing? In the West until a few centuries ago, personhood was not conferred until the infant survived to the age of several years. So great was infant mortality that the naming of small children was postponed, and their deaths did not receive funerary attention. Because of recent medical advances and insight, however, citizenship rights are now being extended to the womb. Death certificates, for example, must be filed if death occurs during the third trimester of pregnancy. But when, exactly, does biological matter become a human being? The Catholic church has argued that "ensoulment" occurs at the moment of conception.[17] The Minnesota Supreme Court ruled in a 1985 case involving the death of an eight-and-a-half-month-old fetus in an auto accident that the man accused in the accident could not be charged with the death because it was not a human being that died, as the victim had not yet been born. Such issues of timing underscore the contemporary abortion controversy.

And then there are the matters of morality. In terms of our political box scores of regime righteousness, what can be inferred from reports that in the "godless" Soviet state there are 2.08 abortions for every child born as opposed to 0.4 abortions for every American child born? Or that in the Soviet Union an eight-minute abortion is available for 5 rubles ($7.50), whereas in the United States the average abortion costs $213 (*New York Times* 1988)?

The abortion history not only involves central moral, religious, and social values but has also been shaped by racism, feminism, and class dynamics. By 1983, there were more than 1.25 million abortions performed annually in the United States, representing the termination of nearly one-third of all the nation's pregnancies. Among minority females in 1983, there were 497 abortions for every 1000 live births—65 percent more than the 302 abortions per 1000 live births by white females (*New York Times* 1987). A powerful political coalition, with perhaps as many as ten million followers, emerged to promote antiabortion legislation. As Philadelphia surgeon Dr. C. Everett Koop, the antiabortion activist who was to serve as President Reagan's surgeon general, observed, "Nothing like it has separated our society since the days of slavery" (Isaacson 1981).

Abortion is not a new phenomenon in the United States. J. C. Mohr claims that before 1840 most abortions were performed on the unmarried and desperate of the "poor and unfortunate classes," but thereafter their numbers increased and included upper- and middle-class white, native-born Protestants (1978, p. 11). Moral crusaders, often physicians, first appeared in the country during the 1850s, with their efforts leading to state legislations criminalizing the procedure during the first decade following the Civil War. Mohr claims that the antiabortion movement of physicians stemmed not simply from the morality of the procedure but also from elitist fears of a drop in the birth rates of society's "better" classes (by 1870, approximately one abortion was performed for every five live births) occurring at the time when physicians sought professional recognition and a monopoly on health. By the beginning of the twentieth century, all states had criminalized abortions, and a formerly indifferent public attitude had shifted to one of firm opposition; abortion was not only illegal but immoral as well. And so it remained until the moral waters were churned by events of the 1960s and 1970s.

Beginning in the late 1960s, there was an unprecedented increase in female participation in the labor force and a corresponding growth in feminist awareness. With the spread of contraceptives, women were to realize a new control over their reproductive capacities, a freedom from the shackles of unwanted pregnancies. It was in this context in 1973 that the Supreme Court made two decisions that struck down the antiabortion statutes of Texas and Georgia. In *Roe* v. *Wade,* an unborn child was deemed not to be a person within the meaning and protection of the term *person* as stated in the Fourteenth Amendment. Basing its ruling on a woman's right to privacy, the Court said that a decision to have an abortion during the first three months of pregnancy must be left to the woman and her doctor. In *Doe* v. *Bolton,* the Court struck down restrictions on the facilities that can be used to perform abortions; this form of death need not be legitimately confined to hospital settings.

Such legitimizations for death by making the victims essentially nonpersons[18] provoked considerable religious response. Dr. Russell Nelson, a member of the Council of the Twelve, the governing body of the Church of Jesus Christ of Latter-day Saints, said that the loss of life from "the evils of war" was "dwarfed by the war on the defenseless" (*New York Times* 1985b). Bishop John J. O'Connor of Scranton, Pennsylvania, claimed in a television interview, "I always compare the killing of 4,000 babies a day in the United States, unborn babies, to the Holocaust. Now Hitler tried to solve a problem, the Jewish question. So kill them, shove them in the ovens, burn them. Well, we claim that unborn babies are a problem, so kill them. To me, it really is precisely the same" (Goldman 1984).[19]

 Aborted Fetuses Buried on Coast

A three-year legal dispute over how to dispose of 16,433 aborted fetuses found in a steel bin ended as the fetuses were given a nonreligious burial with a eulogy written by President Reagan.

Antiabortionists gathered to pray before the fetuses, in six coffin-like boxes, were buried in three unmarked graves.

The battle over whether the fetuses could be turned over to a religious organization went to the United States Supreme Court. It upheld lower court decisions that East Los Angeles could either bury or cremate the fetuses but not arrange or participate in any religious services. . . .

"I am confident that your memorial service will touch many others as you proclaim the inviolability of human life at every stage of development," Mr. Reagan said in a eulogy read by a Los Angeles County Supervisor, Mike Antonovich. "From these innocent dead, let us take increased devotion to the cause of restoring the rights to the unborn."

New York Times 1985c. Copyright © 1985
by the New York Times Company. Reprinted by permission.

With Ronald Reagan's election as president, the prolife movement allied itself firmly with the Republican party, thereby knitting the religious right into the GOP fabric (Gailey 1986a). Not about to alienate this new constituency, the Reagan administration made it clear on numerous occasions that it intended to have the Court review and overthrow its 1973 decision.[20] In opposing abortion, the president initially referred to the procedure as "taking the life of a living human being" and later called it "murder" (Gailey 1986b).[21]

The controversy was to spawn a number of questions. Should abortion curbs be decided by legislators or judges? Can states require minors to obtain parental consent before an abortion? Can a twenty-four-hour "cooling-off" period be required before performing an abortion? Can the government direct physicians to warn women of the risks and consequences of an abortion? What if a female is carrying octuplets and all are doomed unless some are aborted so that the remainder can survive to birth? And must women in their second trimester of pregnancy be required to have an abortion in a hospital? (Gest 1982.) These are all interesting issues, but they perhaps obscure the fundamental underlying class dynamics. We are now within the conservative period of a historical cycle of public permissiveness and legal restrictiveness toward the abortion issue. Attitudes swing with the rise and fall of a fifty-year cycle of economic good times (associated with a general liberalism of public attitudes) and economic bad times (associated with revived conservativism).[22] There is also a historical correlation with the high and low periods of immigration.

A century after their initial support, medical groups were opposing curbs in the abortion law. When attempting to urge the Supreme Court to declare unconstitutional an Akron, Ohio, city ordinance requiring hospital abortions for women past their third month of pregnancy, forbidding abortions for those under the age of fifteen without parental consent, and requiring physicians to read their patients an account of the procedure's dangers, the American Medical Association, the American College of Obstetricians and Gynecologists, the Nurses Association of the American College of Obstetricians and Gynecologists, and the American Academy of Pediatrics argued in 1982 that such measures "interfere significantly with a woman's ability to exercise her constitutional right to decide whether or not to terminate her pregnancy" (Greenhouse 1982). The moral relativity of scientific medicine once again clashed with the moral certainty of religion, a contest to which we will return in Chapter 11.

The effect of class differences on attitudes toward the abortion issue is not simply limited to fears of the upper classes breeding themselves out of existence while the lower classes proliferate. Kristin Luker (1984) found that class is the single most important predictor of one's attitude toward abortion. Luker's study showed the typical profile of a prolife activist as a nonworking, undereducated mother: 20 percent had six or more children, 63 percent did not work, and 40 percent either never went to college or never completed it. For Luker, the spate of abortion-clinic bombings is but one facet of the ongoing class conflict in American society. But it is in the courts and legislatures that the final social decisions are made.

Capital Punishment

Let us consider now the reinvigorated debate over the clearest relationship between the state and death: the intentional execution of its citizens. In 1985, according to Amnesty International, there were 1125 documented executions throughout the world. Whether or not the state has the legitimate right to take life and, if so, whose life and for what reasons is certainly a basis of international comparison, an indicator of political domination, and a gauge of national moralities. Generally, the greater the amount of legitimate violence in a culture, the more likely this form of ritual murder is sanctioned and performed.

Since 1900, more than seven thousand people have been executed in the United States. Following a period of high execution rates during the Great Depression, executions declined considerably with the conclusion of World War II, even though homicide rates (6.4 per 100,000 in 1946) remained fairly constant: eighty-two were executed in 1950, forty-nine in 1959, and only two in 1967. The sociopolitical climate—engendered by the civil rights movement, the Great Society, the *Miranda* decision, and Vietnam—was liberalized, apparently dulling the American appetite for this ultimate form of retribution. At least recently, public support for the abortion of fetuses has been out of sync with support for the execution of adult criminals. A year before *Roe* v. *Wade*, the Supreme Court legitimized the moratorium on capital punishment when, in the case of *Furman* v. *Georgia*, it ruled that the arbitrary way in which death sentences were being awarded violated the Eighth Amendment's prohibition of "cruel and unusual punishments."[23] The sentences against 629 people on death rows were vacated, and the states attempted to satisfy the Court's criticisms (Goodman 1984).

Several states succeeded, particularly given the changing political tides following the dramatic increases in the level of cultural violence and homicide (see Chapter 4). In 1976, the justices decided that the death penalty could be applied if the law guided and restricted the sentencing so that judge and jury took into consideration the aggravating and mitigating factors in each case. The decade-long moratorium was over. Starting with the well-publicized firing-squad execution of Gary Gilmore in 1977, states slowly began to reemploy the death sentence: there were two executions in 1979, one in 1981, two in 1982, five in 1983 (the year the Supreme Court held that a Texas inmate could be executed even though a constitutional challenge to his murder conviction was still technically pending), twenty-one in 1984, and three in the first ten days of 1985. With more than a record number of fifteen hundred convicted murderers on death rows in the thirty-eight states that permit capital punishment, and with this figure growing by about two hundred fifty a year, the rate of executions is expected to keep accelerating for several years at least (Goodman 1984). So many were scheduled to die in Texas that the state prison director asked the courts in 1985 to avoid scheduling more than one execution a day (Reinhold 1985a). According to the nationwide surveys of the National Opinion Research Corporation and Gallup, the moratorium was over in the minds of Americans as well: in 1966, some 42 percent of the American adult public favored capital punishment for persons convicted of murder; in 1978, it was approved by 62 percent; and by 1985, 72 percent of all Americans supported the death penalty, and of these proponents, three-quarters believe it acts as a deterrent (Gallup 1985).

Instead of entering into the debate about the morality of capital punishment, let us first consider the major issues of the controversy and then address the quantifiable questions: who gets executed, how, for what types of behavior, and toward what kinds of victims.

 ### Gilmore's Cell for Sale

Provo, Utah—An old Utah County Jail cell occupied by convicted murderer Gary Gilmore, who died before a firing squad in 1977, is up for sale.

Dave and Afton Fitzen, who operate a demolition company in American Fork, acquired the cell when dismantling the old jail shortly after Gilmore's execution. Fitzen has kept the cell in a shed in Lehi, a community south of here.

"We sure aren't doing this to glamorize Gilmore, but we are trying to get some money for the work we did," Mrs. Fitzen said. "While Gilmore was in jail, he did some drawings and carved on the cell and all that is still there. Some of the words are pretty dirty and the drawings are of cartoon characters. . . . Some people might not look on this too good, but you have to admit the entire thing really is a part of Utah's history," she said.

San Antonio Express-News 1983. Reprinted by permission of The Associated Press © 1983.

An electric chair in Richmond, Virginia. UPI/Bettmann
Newsphotos.

The Execution Ritual

Capital punishment is a public ritual of retribution, generally reserved to one
or few individuals in order to maximize personal humiliation.[24] Historically,
who gets executed and how was a function not only of the nature of the
transgression but also of the social class, sex, age, religion, and citizenship of
the transgressor. In England, the axe was used infrequently, being reserved
for treason and, therefore, a form of punishment used almost exclusively for
the nobility (Cooper 1974).[25] Burning at the stake was reserved for women,
while disemboweling and quartering were meted out to male counterfeiters.

To this day, considerable publicity is given to the deeds and legal proceedings of the accused as well as to the mode of execution. In China, the condemned are paraded before large public gatherings before being driven away to be shot. Further, the contemporary American version of the ritual requires the individuals being executed to be "mentally competent" at the time of death in order that they appreciate the ceremony, understanding that they are about to be killed and why.[26]

Might there be a social need for this kind of ritual revenge that dates back to our barbaric origins? Does not the continuing search for nazi war criminals to bring them to justice, even after four decades, serve to solidify social conscience? And what happens when social systems have no options through which such anger can be vented? Walter Berns, in addressing these questions, writes:

When men are not saddened when someone else suffers, or angry when someone else suffers unjustly, the implication is that they do not care for anyone other than themselves or that they lack some quality that befits a man. . . . [The perpetrators of terrible crimes] have done more than inflict an injury on an isolated individual; they have violated the foundations of trust and friendship, the necessary elements of a moral community, the only community worth living in . . . whose members are expected freely to obey the laws and, unlike those in tyranny, are trusted to obey the laws. . . . Punishment arises out of the demand for justice, and justice is demanded by angry, morally indignant men; its purpose is to satisfy that moral indignation and thereby promote the law abidingness that, it is assumed, accompanies it. (1979, pp. 16–18).

But where does one draw the line? What if the murderer

- was a drunken driver?
- heard the voice of God commanding him to kill his neighbors?
- was guided by some radical ideology, as was the case of the Zebra killers of the Bay Area?
- was paid $100,000 to kill?
- was fifteen years of age or younger at the time the crime was committed?[27]

Are all of these conditions equally deserving of death? Probably not. Society gauges not only the consequences of deviant behavior but the underlying motivations as well when determining punishment. And here we enter into the objections of critics of the death penalty.

The two institutions that oversee the final rite of passage—religion and medicine—came to be drawn into this controversy together in opposition. Both institutions had supported the measure at points of their history. Medieval philosopher St. Thomas Aquinas made a classic defense of the penalty: "If a man be dangerous and infectious to the community, on account of some sin, it is praiseworthy and advantageous that he be killed in order to safeguard the common good" (Goodman 1983). Two French physicians, including Joseph-Ignace Guillotin, developed the French instrument for decapitation, and Louis Pasteur advocated using condemned prisoners for medical experiments. At the beginning of the century, Dr. Richard Strong tested a plague vaccine on forty-two condemned prisoners with permission of the governor of the Philippines before becoming a Harvard professor and dean of tropical medicine (Altman 1980). Recently, the Catholic church has become allied with most mainstream Protestant denominations and with Jewish theologians in opposing the wave of executions. In 1980, by a vote of 145 to 31, Catholic bishops in the United States resolved that the penalty should be eliminated as "a manifestation of our belief in the unique worth and dignity of each person from the moment of conception, a creature made in the image and likeness of God" and that abolition "is most consistent with the example of Jesus, who both taught and practiced the forgiveness of injustice and who came to 'give His life as a ransom for many'" (Goodman 1983, p. 1). The medical institution was also dragged into the controversy when several states legalized death by drugs, wherein physicians would participate by prescribing, preparing, or injecting the lethal solution; supervising others doing it; monitoring the continuous injection to the prisoner; and examining and pronouncing the prisoner dead (Altman 1980). The Hippocratic oath has come to be perceived as legitimizing some deaths but not others.

To summarize specific criticisms, opponents point out the punishment's failure as a deterrent, the risks of error, the preclusion of any chance for rehabilitation, the capriciousness of the law, the legitimization of vengeance and hatred, and the tendency to discriminate against minorities. First, there is no conclusive proof either for or against the deterrence function (see Kobbervig, Inverarity, and Lauderdale 1982). The longitudinal study by Archer and Gartner (1984) of 110 countries show quite convincingly that where the death penalty has been abolished, homicide rates have declined. David Phillips (1980), examining twenty-two publicized executions in London between 1858 and 1921, detected a 35.7 percent decline in the frequency of homicides in the two weeks following the punishment. Hans Zeisel (1976), too, detected a reduction of homicides following executions, but this reduction only occurred for the first three days and was compensated for by an increase over the remainder of the week following the ritual. When South Dakota, in 1939, adopted and used the death penalty, the homicide rate dropped 20 percent over the following decade. But, again, over the same period of time, North Dakota, which did not have the penalty, experienced a 40 percent decline. Yet since the resumption of executions in Florida, the number of felonies has gone down. A similar reduction has taken place nationwide. It is generally agreed that there are too many other possible reasons for the decline, notably the overall drop in the number of men between the ages of nineteen and twenty-nine, the most homicide-prone group. But the debate continues, kept alive by a 1975 analysis by Isaac Ehrlich, a University of Chicago econometrician, who concluded that each additional execution from 1933 to 1967 might have prevented at least one and perhaps as many as eight murders (1975a, 1975b). According to a 1985 study by Hugo Bedau and Michael Radelet, since the turn of the century, 343 people were wrongly convicted of crimes punishable by death, 25 of whom were executed (Margolick 1985). Mistakes continue to be made. In 1983, there were two cases in Massachusetts and one in New York where individuals convicted of first-degree murder turned out to be innocent. The acceptability of this rate of improper executions is a matter of debate. There are those who say one innocent death is too many. On the other hand, there are those who find the rate—if true—to be acceptable. New York's Mayor Edward Koch observed: "If government functioned only when the possibility of error didn't exist, government wouldn't function at all" (1985, p. 14). Death-penalty advocate Professor Ernest van den Haag of Fordham University adds:

All human activities—building houses, driving a car, playing golf or football—cause innocent people to suffer wrongful death, but we don't give them up because on the whole we feel there's a net gain. Here, a net gain in justice is being done. (Margolick 1985)

On the other hand, those supporting the abolition of the death penalty point not only to the evil of executing even one innocent individual but to the fact that most civilized nations have abandoned the traditional concept of *lex talionis,* the law of retaliation, in exchange for sound reason. The homicide rate is nearly twice as high in those thirty-eight states retaining the death penalty than in those having abolished the practice, and in the former there are inconsistencies in when and how often the penalty is even to be applied (Stark 1986). In Florida, which had executed more individuals between 1977 and 1986 than any other state, Ernest Dobbert was electrocuted even though a jury had voted 10 to 2 against the death penalty—the judge, exercising a prerogative given the judiciary in only two other states, overrode the jury and sentenced him to death (Lowenstein 1986). What are the lessons of such public rituals? George Bernard Shaw wrote: "It is the deed that teaches, not the name we give it. Murder and capital punishment are not opposites that cancel one another out but similars that breed their kind" (cited in Stark 1986). But perhaps the most serious of charges concerns the social inequities of punishment, which are measurable.

Who Is Executed, Where, and Why

There is a hidden bias in our culture that execution is a political activity of either the less developed or the totalitarian regimes. In fact, among the industrialized countries of the world, the United States is joined only by the Soviet Union,[28] South Africa, and Japan as regular users of capital punishment. Despite the increasing terrorism and violence through the West in recent years, most polities have repealed the death penalty.[29] In Western European countries, criminal homicide rates are from 20 to 50 percent lower than in the United States. Iran currently holds the international record for numbers of individuals executed annually. In Eastern Europe, only Albania has officially eliminated capital punishment from its statutes.

Though individuals have traditionally been executed for murder and treason,[30] other reasons have included counterfeiting, adultery, failure to observe the sabbath, witchcraft, and involvement with narcotics. During the period of English industrialization, more than two hundred capital offenses were created, including stealing turnips and cutting down trees. Between 1930 and 1965, 455 men, mostly southern blacks, were executed for rape in the United States. But not all murderers, adulterers, witches, turnip stealers, or rapists faced capital punishment. While a combination of psychological and sociological factors produced the misdeeds, purely social dynamics were to determine the punishments. And the most severe of these punishments were not, and are not, equally administered.

Of the more than thirty-five thousand Americans imprisoned for murder during the mid-1980s, only fifteen hundred—less than 3 percent—were consigned to death row. Of the twenty thousand or so homicides committed a year in the United States, fewer than one hundred fifty murderers will be given the death sentence. These one hundred fifty are most typically the poor; more than 90 percent cannot afford to hire a lawyer at the time of their trial (Conyers 1985). Though the first five postmoratorium executions from 1977 to 1982 were of whites, blacks increasingly became those gassed, hung, or lethally injected. Between 1983 and January 1985, eleven of thirty persons executed were black—a proportion three times that of their representation in the total population. Regional differences came into play as well: by early 1985, two of the thirty-five executions in the United States since 1977 had occurred outside the South. The inequalities of who actually gets executed in the United States were becoming overly transparent, dramatized in Virginia's 1985 execution of Morris Mason. Mason was a retarded black man who had been diagnosed three times by the state as a paranoid schizophrenic. He had pleaded with the state himself to be put back into custody before he committed more rape and murder. This ultimate punishment was

A crowd gathers to watch the hanging of two black men on "Hangman's day in Wharton, Texas," February 26, 1910. Wharton County Historical Museum, Wharton, Texas.

clearly not being reserved for those indisputably responsible for the most terrible crimes (Wicker 1985).

A study of sentencings by Samuel Gross and Robert Mauro of Stanford (Joyce 1984) showed that the murderers of whites were more likely to receive the death penalty than those murdering blacks. Their data, in part, are shown in Table 8.3. If we divide the percentage of white homicides leading to death-penalty sentencings by those of black-victim homicides, observe in the right-hand column that not only do the ratios not equal one, but in Mississippi one is ten times more likely to receive the death penalty if the victim is white as opposed to being black. Further, observing the variations of this ratio across states (is, for example, Virginia twice as egalitarian as Mississippi?), there is little question that the death penalty is not meted out equivalently across the thirty-seven states that sanction executions.

Consider the following data from the execution capital of the United States, the state of Florida, where between 1973 and 1977 there were 4863 individuals convicted of murder, of whom 131 were sentenced to death.[31] If we divide the number of murderers not receiving the death sentence by the

Table 8.3 Race and the Death Penalty

	White Victims			Black Victims			White/ black ratio
	Homicides	Death Penalty	Percent	Homicides	Death Penalty	Percent	
Florida	1803	114	6.3%	1683	14	0.8%	7.9
Georgia	773	67	8.7	1345	12	0.9	9.7
Illinois	1214	35	3.0	1866	10	0.5	6.0
Oklahoma	581	40	6.9	252	3	1.2	5.7
N. Carolina	850	21	2.5	966	4	0.4	6.2
Mississippi	208	17	8.2	639	5	0.8	10.2
Virginia	646	15	2.3	742	4	0.5	4.6
Arkansas	396	13	3.3	398	2	0.5	6.6

Source: Joyce 1984, p. 8.

number of those receiving it, we observe that the odds of not receiving the death penalty are 36.1 to 1; in other words, a convicted murderer is thirty-six times more likely to get a life sentence than the death penalty.

Now, in an egalitarian society, one would suppose that the odds would not change given the racial characteristics of either victim or murderer. However, in Florida, we can see from the column totals of Table 8.4 that the odds against the death sentence are eleven times higher when the victim is black as opposed to white. However, black murderers are 40 percent more likely not to receive the death penalty than are white murderers.

With this data set, we can go beyond the Gross-Mauro analysis, as we can take into account not only the race of the victim but also that of the offender. Considering the Table 8.4 entries in terms of offender's race, we see that the odds of a black murderer escaping the death sentence are 40 percent greater than for whites. However, this apparently greater immunity of black murderers to capital punishment stems from the attributes of their victims, whom society seems to place less value on. A white killing a black is nearly

Table 8.4 Odds of Convicted Murders Not Receiving the Death Sentence in the State of Florida

	Black victim	White victim	TOTAL ODDS
White offender	111	28.8	30.3
Black offender	210	5	43.2
TOTAL	220	19.3	36.1

four times more likely not to receive the death sentence than if a white had been the victim. The odds of a black murderer avoiding execution are forty-two times greater when the victim was black as opposed to white. The inherent racism of American society is reflected in the fact that the murder of a white is ten times more likely to produce the death sentence than the murder of a black. In fact, between 1977 and 1986, not a single white was executed for murdering a black person (Zwisohn 1986).

Looking at the data in terms of the victim's race, when a black is murdered, the odds of a black offender not receiving the death sentence are nearly twice that of whites. The law, it seems, is less severe when there is racial homogeneity of offender and victim. But the penalty of racial heterogeneity increases when the victim is white: the odds of white offenders not receiving the death sentence approach six times those of blacks.

Conclusion

This chapter developed the profound interrelationships between death and political orders. Of all twentieth-century institutions, it is the state which has most effectively exploited the power of death as a means of social control. In many developing and totalitarian regimes, where the maintenance of power is the political end in and of itself, this control has come in its most blatant forms, such as through pogroms, calculated privations, and state-directed terror. In the advanced developed nations, this control derives from the emergence of state accountability for maintaining the systems of cultural death denials and for providing the social opportunities for remembering the dead in ways reminiscent of traditional religion.

Political decisions and activities play an increasing role in determining not only who dies but how and when. Even natural deaths are expected to be, if not controlled, then at least predicted by political orders. With the predominance of on-time and postmature deaths in modern cultures, the state has assumed responsibility for nearly all forms of premature death. In fact, so politicized has death become that mortality indicators—such as life expectancy, infant mortality, execution, and homicide rates—have become the bases of international comparisons by which the adequacy of political economies are invidiously gauged.

This chapter began by asking whether nations are acting rationally when they perform rituals for their dead citizens. To approach this question, consider the story of Mr. Carpenter, a homeless man who had been living on the streets for twenty-two years, who was found frozen to death in a park across the street from the White House in December 1984. Not only was this a potential political embarrassment in the capital of the land of plenty, but it turned out that the victim was a decorated World War II hero. Ultimately, he was buried with full honors at Arlington National Cemetery.

Evidenced by the memorials given to Mr. Carpenter and unknown soldiers, the sacrifices of individuals for political causes must be remembered or the very legitimacy and meaningfulness of political orders are threatened. If the dead and their deeds are forgotten or ignored, the sense of immortality of the political order evaporates, and individuals will seek to apply their commitments to other immortality outlets.[32] This is why the personification of evil, the devil, in C. S. Lewis's *The Screwtape Letters,* advises his nephew and disciple to corrupt men by cultivating in them a disdain for the past. This is perhaps what underlies the observation by John Adams of the suicidal tendencies of democracies. Also, de Tocqueville warned: "Thus not only does democracy make every man forget his ancestors, but it hides his descendants and separates his contemporaries from him; it throws him back forever upon himself alone and threatens in the end to confine him entirely with the solitude of his own heart" (1945, p. 106).

Political systems are indeed rational when they perform reburial rituals and restore citizenship rights posthumously. As we have shown, this symbolic potency of the dead derives, in part, from the relationship of the contemporary state to ultimate meaning: the scope of its involvement in all phases of the final rite of passage, its need for a collective sense of continuity with past and future generations, and its ability to address the transcendence needs of people who desire both a sense of uniqueness and a sense of place in the cosmic scheme of things. From such a perspective, a wide range of seemingly disparate, even macabre, events coalesce and make sense.

NOTES

1. Portions of this chapter draw on and often quote directly from Kearl and Rinaldi 1983.

2. President Jimmy Carter committed an international faux pas by being the only major world leader absent at the Yugoslavian state funeral for Marshall Tito.

3. Why do governments maintain records of how citizens die? In nineteenth-century England, the state assumed the estates of those who either committed suicide or were murdered.

4. One manifestation of the recent public health interest in homicide is the formation of the Violence Epidemiology Branch at the federal Centers for Disease Control in Atlanta. "One of the main missions of the CDC is to prevent premature and unnecessary death," says Mark Rosenberg, chief of the newly formed unit. "Violence is every bit a public health issue for me and my successors in the century as smallpox, tuberculosis, and syphilis were for my predecessors in the last two centuries," says

U.S. Surgeon General C. Everett Koop. "Violence in American public and private life has indeed assumed the proportions of an epidemic" (Meredith 1984, p. 43).

5. Polities, like religions, also need their martyrs to promote among their members a willingness to self-sacrifice, even if it means suicide. The Japanese kamikaze pilots are prime examples of this extreme form of political subservience. They attended their own funerals before takeoff. Garbed in burial robes, these pilots proclaimed, "And thus for the emperor I will not die at home." The parallels between political and religious symbols of sacrifice and death "for higher principles" and their rituals of collective remembrance (both have their holy days) are not accidental.

6. For instance, if family and home are lost to hurricane winds, one no longer accepts one's fate like Job but, instead, demands compensation from Washington.

7. Sometimes this involvement is awkward, however. The Social Security office in Vallejo, California, sent out in 1985 the following message: "We want to talk to you about a notification in our office that you are deceased. Please let us know if you are" (*San Antonio Express-News* 1985).

8. In Treptow's bloodied diary, the following passage was found: "America must win this war. Therefore, I will work, I will save, I will sacrifice, I will endure, I will fight cheerfully and do my utmost as if the issue of the whole struggle depended on me alone" (*Time* 1981).

9. Since 1866, the likeness of a living person has been banned from U.S. postage stamps and currency. This is not, however, the norm internationally.

10. The tomb of Vietnam's Unknown Soldier remained empty until 1984, supposedly because of the advanced techniques for identifying bodies. Ironically, this meant that for nearly a decade there were no sacred remains from this unsacred war. There almost never were, given Public Law 93-43, which required that 80 percent of the remains of an unknown for that tomb had to be intact and that laboratory analysis had reasonably concluded that death had occurred between August 1964 and March 1973 (U.S. House 1978b).

11. When the dead are intentionally forgotten, their memories become spirits that haunt the political order. The uninvestigated deaths in El Salvador, for example, led to new antiregime solidarities, including groups never before organized; outraged Salvadoran women created the Committee of Mothers and Relatives of Political Prisoners, Disappeared and Murdered.

12. In South Africa's announcement of the restrictions on funerals, the government said that the presiding minister "shall not at such a ceremony in any manner defend, attack, criticize, propagate or discuss any form of government, any principle or policy of a government of a state, any boycott action, the existence of a state of emergency or any action by a force or a member of force" (Cowell 1985, p. 6)

13. Before the imposition of martial law in late 1981, "the search for an authentic political life in Poland since the independent Solidarity labor union was established" led to further use of the dead. For the first time, on November 11, the sixty-third anniversary of its rebirth as an independent nation following World War I, a communist president laid a wreath at Poland's Tomb of the Unknown Soldier, and the

memory of Marshall Jozef Pilsudski (leader of Poland's authoritarian military regime between 1926 and 1935) was honored (Darnton 1981).

14. Himmler, when inspecting for the first time the method of trench machine-gunning, had brain material scattered on both his face and clothing. Looking pale and shaken, he was assisted from the pit. It was not long afterward that the Auschwitz model for death became disseminated.

15. J. Bower Bell (1979, p. 24) observes the relative absence of assassination in Chinese history.

16. E. L. Withers observed: "Thrones exist to be taken; kings reign to be deposed; and like a rattle of drums, the fall of kings punctuates the drama of history" (1964, p. viii).

17. This timing has not always been the case. In the thirteenth century, Thomas Aquinas and his contemporary theologians calculated that the soul joined the body at the fortieth day of pregnancy. Four centuries later, Torreblanca taught that abortion before ensoulment would be acceptable if the mother was in danger of death or of losing her reputation. Though church law considered abortions to be wrong, for many years penalties differed depending on whether the abortion occurred before or after the entry of the soul (*Time* 1984).

18. Precisely when in the womb a fetus's personhood status is socially recognized continues to be defined. Since 1974, for instance, the Public Health Law of New York State (Section 4164) has required an additional attending physician to be present whenever an unborn child of twenty weeks' gestation is aborted. If the legally aborted infant should survive, all legal rights immediately accrue to the child (Washburn 1984). Ironically, over the period that legalized abortions have been conducted, citizenship rights have been extended to increasingly premature fetuses.

19. We might parenthetically note that Hitler outlawed abortions in order to win the population war.

20. Ironically, White House attempts to curb abortions could increase the country's embarrassingly high infant mortality figures, as unwanted pregnancies often produce high-risk babies. Studies by Michael Grossman and others at the National Bureau of Economic Research concluded that the availability of abortion has been "the single most important factor in reducing the neonatal mortality rate" among blacks over the previous two decades (Otten 1985).

21. Reagan's prolife ideology also extended to the rights of severely deformed infants. In 1983, the president had initiated a regulation with a directive to the attorney general and the secretary of Health and Human Services that required hospitals receiving federal funds to post notices saying, "Discriminatory failure to feed and care for handicapped infants in this facility is prohibited by Federal law." In addition, the poster asked that anyone having knowledge of the denial of "customary medical care" to handicapped infants call the federal government on a toll-free telephone number (Pear, 1983). The following year, however, the administration had to back down from its attempt to force hospitals to maintain the lives of seriously deformed infants.

22. For a description of this economic cycle, see Kearl and Hermes 1984.

23. This issue of "cruel and unusual" death is not confined to death row inmates. Even the manner of killing animals is capable of producing emotional reaction and public controversy. In San Antonio, Texas, for example, the most heated controversy of the late winter of 1986 was over how unwanted pets at the animal control facility were being destroyed. It began with pickets in front of the facility, charging that the current practice of gassing the animals with carbon monoxide from an old automobile engine was inhumane. Then the most viewed local news program showed footage of the animals dying slow, painful deaths. After days of deliberation, the city council settled on a compromise whereby large, unruly animals would be killed in an updated gas chamber while smaller animals would receive injections of sodium pentobarbital.

24. There are notable exceptions to this individualization. In 1568, all inhabitants of the Netherlands were sentenced to death as heretics by the Inquisition, condemning three million (Horwitz 1973, p. 24). During the reign of Henry VIII in England, it is reported that seventy-two thousand people were hanged and many more beheaded.

25. Before murder was understood as a crime against the political order, execution often was preceded by publicly shaming and torturing the accused deviant (*Time* 1983).

26. The Supreme Court made this ruling in 1986 in the case of *Ford* v. *Wainwright*, involving a Florida prisoner who, the defense argued, had slowly gone insane during his incarceration. The same month, however, Georgia executed a retarded man, Jerome Bowden, who was judged to know the difference between right and wrong.

27. Twenty-nine states permit the execution of juveniles, including Indiana, which explicitly allows executions of children as young as ten years of age. The Senate has never ratified two international agreements forbidding the executions of individuals younger than eighteen (Reinhold 1985b).

28. Lenin advocated the death penalty as a weapon in the class struggle, and on June 21, 1918, the new Soviet state passed its first formal death sentence, on Admiral Aleksei M. Shchastny, commander of the Red Baltic Fleet, who had turned against the revolutionaries (Schemann, 1983).

29. Early in 1980, the Parliamentary Assembly of the twenty-one-member Council of Europe condemned capital punishment in peacetime as inhumane and also recommended that the European Convention on Human Rights be amended to make the death penalty illegal. However, Belgium, Cyprus, France, Greece, Ireland, and Liechtenstein still have capital punishment on the books. Only France still carries it out.

30. The Rosenbergs were the last in the United States to be executed for treason, following a highly publicized and controversial trial conducted in the midst of McCarthyism.

31. The author would like to thank Professor James A. Davis of Harvard University, who, using the results of a *New York Times* article of March 11, 1979, produced the following analyses.

32. In the Soviet Union, a visitation to a World War II memorial is a typical part

of the itinerary of a marriage ceremony. Thus, the procreative activities of couples provide for both the personal genetic immortality of each spouse and the collective political immortality of the state. The individualism of the United States now requires the inclusion of individual names on such collective monuments, as evidenced by the Vietnam War Memorial.

REFERENCES

Altman, Lawrence. 1980. "The Doctor's World: The Ethics of Execution by Drugs." *New York Times.* March 4, p. C3.

Archer, Dane, and Rosemary Gartner. 1984. *Violence and Crime in Cross-National Perspective.* New Havern, Conn.: Yale University Press.

Arendt, Hannah. 1959. *The Human Condition.* New York: Doubleday.

———. 1969. *Eichmann in Jerusalem.* New York: Viking Press.

Ariès, Philippe. 1981. *The Hour of Our Death.* New York: Vintage Books.

Avakian, Florence. 1985. "The Armenian Dead." *New York Times.* April 27, p. 17.

Bell, J. Bower. 1979. *Assassin!* New York: St. Martin's Press.

Bellah, Robert, and Phillip Hammond. 1980. *Varieties of Civil Religion.* New York: Harper & Row.

Berger, Peter. 1969. *The Sacred Canopy: Elements of a Sociological Theory of Religion.* Garden City, N.Y.: Doubleday/Anchor.

Berns, Walter. 1979. "For Capital Punishment: The Morality of Anger." *Harper's Magazine.* April, pp. 15–20.

Betts, Richard, and Samuel Huntington. 1985. "Dead Dictators and Rioting Mobs: Does the Demise of Authoritarian Rulers Lead to Political Instability?" *International Security* 10(3):112–46.

Boor, M. 1981. "Effects of United States Presidential Elections on Suicides and Other Causes of Death." *American Sociological Review* 46(5):616–18.

Brinkley, Joel. 1984. "C.I.A. Primer Tells Nicaraguan Rebels How to Kill." *New York Times.* October 17, pp. 1, 12.

Bruck, David. 1984. "Executing Juveniles for Crime." *New York Times.* June 16, p. 17.

Butterfield, Fox. 1978. "Two Victims of Mao's Purges Honored at Big Memorial Service in Peking." *New York Times.* December 25, p. 1.

Campbell, Colin. 1983. "Pol Pot's Bitter Legacy Weighs on Cambodia." *New York Times.* April 5, pp. 1, 7.

Chavez, Lydia. 1984. "Argentina Detailing Army's 'Dirty War.'" *New York Times.* September 21, p. 3.

Chelala, Cesar. 1984. "Argentines Await Antiterror Action." *New York Times.* October 5, p. 31.

Choron, Jacques. 1963. *Death and Western Thought.* New York: Collier Books.

Cobb, R., and C. Elder. 1972. "Individual Orientations in the Study of Political Symbolism." *Social Science Quarterly* 53 (June):79–96.

Conyers, John Jr. 1985. "The Death Penalty Lottery." *New York Times.* July 1, p. 23.

Cooper, David. 1974. *The Lesson of the Scaffold: The Public Execution Controversy in Victorian England.* Athens: Ohio University Press.

Cooper, Richard. 1979. "Death Rates Herald the Birth of Soviet Capitalism." *New York Times.* June 26, p. A19.

Cowell, Alan. 1985. "South Africa Bans Mass Funerals for the Victims of Black Unrest." *New York Times.* August 1, pp. 1, 6.

Darnton, John. 1981. "Poland Rehabilitates a Date, Celebrating Its 1918 Rebirth." *New York Times.* November 12, p. 1.

De Tocqueville, Alexis. 1945. *Democracy in America,* Vol.2, ed. by Phillips Bradley. New York: Alfred A. Knopf.

Dewar, Helen. 1975. "Restoration of Lee Citizenship Likely." *Washington Post.* April 29, p. C1.

Edelman, Murray. 1964. *The Symbolic Uses of Politics.* Urbana: University of Illinois Press.

Ehrlich, I. 1975a. "Deterrence: Evidence and Inference." *Yale Law Journal* 85:209–27.

———. 1975b. "The Deterrent Effect of Capital Punishment: A Question of Life and Death." *American Economic Review* 65:397–417.

Elliot, Gil. 1972. *The Twentieth Century Book of the Dead.* New York: Ballantine Books.

Emmons, Terence, 1985. "The Man and the Cult." *Stanford Alumni Magazine* (Spring):19–26.

Gage, Nicholas. 1978. "Iranians Observe Day of Mourning for Dead in Revolt." *New York Times.* December 19, p. 3.

Gailey, Phil. 1986a. "Abortion Knits Religious Right into G.O.P. Fabric." *New York Times.* June 19, p. 12.

———. 1986b. "Reagan Calls Abortion 'Murder' and Bars a Test." *New York Times.* June 24, p. 9.

Gallup, George. 1985. "Lots of Support for Death Penalty." *San Francisco Chronicle.* February 8, p. 1.

Gest, Ted. 1982. "What the Supreme Court Heard on Abortion." *U.S. News & World Report.* December 13, p. 83.

Goldman, Ari. 1984. "Bishop Defends a Holocaust Analogy." *New York Times.* March 14, p. 17.

Goldstein, Robert. 1984. "Political Funerals." *Society* 21(3):13–17.

Goodman, Walter. 1983. "Religious Alliance against Executions Grows." *New York Times.* December 7, pp. 1, 12.

———. 1984. "Pace of Executions in U.S. Quickens." *New York Times.* December 12, p. 12.

Greenhouse, Linda. 1982. "Medical Groups Opposing Curbs in Abortion Law." *New York Times.* August 31, pp. 1, 8.

Hertz, Robert. 1965. *Death and the Right Hand.* London: Black.

Horowitz, Irving Louis. 1982. *Taking Lives: Genocide and State Power*, 3d ed. New Brunswick, N.J.: Transaction Books.

Horwitz, Elinor. 1973. *Capital Punishment, U.S.A.* Philadelphia: J. B. Lippincott.

Hutchens, Lynn. 1980. "Let Them Rest in Peace." *Washington Post.* July 7, p. A14 (letter to ed.).

Isaacson, Walter. 1981. "The Battle over Abortion." *Time.* April 6, pp. 20–28.

Janowitz, M. 1980. "Observations on the Sociology of Citizenship: Obligations and Rights." *Social Forces* 59(1):1–24.

Jaynes, Gregory. 1980. "Pope Sadly Quits Zaire after the Death of 9." *New York Times.* May 6, p. A3.

Joyce, Fay. 1984. "Courts Study Link between Victim's Race and Imposition of Death Penalty." *New York Times.* January 5, p. 8.

Kearl, Michael, and Michael Hermes. 1984. "Grandparents, Grandchildren and the Kondratieff Wave: Some Thoughts on 'Period Effects' in Intergenerational Analyses." *International Journal of Aging and Human Development* 19(4):257–65.

Kearl, Michael, and Anoel Rinaldi. 1983. "The Political Uses of the Dead as Symbols in Contemporary Civil Religions." *Social Forces* 61(3):693–708.

Kinzer, Stephen. 1984. "Death Squads in El Salvador: Ex-Aide Accuses Colleagues." *New York Times.* March 3, pp. 1, 4.

Kobbervig, Wayne, James Inverarity, and Pat Lauderdale. 1982. "Deterrence and the Death Penalty: A Comment on Phillips." *American Journal of Sociology* 88(1):161–64.

Koch, Edward. 1985. "Death and Justice." *New Republic.* April 15, pp. 12–15.

Kohan, John. 1984. "A Nation Mourns a Martyred Priest." *Time.* November 12, pp. 58–59.

Kolakowski, Leszek. 1983. "The Mummy's Tomb." *New Republic.* July 4, pp. 33–34.

Kolata, Gina. 1988. "Study Finds Rate of Abortion High." *New York Times.* June 2, p. 11.

Kuper, Leo. 1981. *Genocide: Its Political Use in the Twentieth Century.* New Haven and London: Yale University Press.

LeMoyne, James. 1985. "For the Mayas, One More Calamity." *New York Times.* January 10, p. 4.

Lewis, Anthony. 1984. "We Must Remember." *New York Times.* December 13, p. 31.

Liptak, Bela. 1985. "Searching for the Grave of Imre Nagy." *Wall Street Journal.* October 9, p. 31.

Lowenstein, Roger. 1986. "Overriding the Jury, Some Florida Judges Impose Death Penalty." *Wall Street Journal.* January 6, pp. 1, 10.

Luker, Kristin. 1984. *Abortion and the Politics of Motherhood.* Berkeley: University of California Press.

Lyons, Charles. 1985. "Ways to Reduce Infant Mortality." *New York Times.* March 26, p. 26.

Margolick, David. 1985. "25 Wrongfully Executed in U.S., Study Finds." *New York Times.* November 14, p. 13.

Marshall, J. R. 1981. "Political Integration and the Effect of War on Suicide: United States, 1933–76." *Social Forces* 59(3):771–78.

Meredith, Nikki. 1984. "The Murder Epidemic." *Science 84* 5(10):43–48.

Mohr, J. C. 1978. *Abortion in America.* Oxford University Press.

New York Times. 1985a. "Around the World." February 26, p. 5.

———. 1985b. "A Mormon Leader Describes Abortion as 'War on Unborn.'" April 8, p. 9.

———. 1985c. "Aborted Fetuses Buried on Coast." October 8, p. 8.

———. 1987. "U.S. Decrease in Abortions Reported for First Time since '69." August 25, p. 9.

———. 1988. "Life Beyond the Kremlin." May 30, p. 5.

Otten, Alan. 1985. "Slowing Drop in Infant Death Rate Fuels Debate on U.S. Spending for Child, Maternal Programs." *Wall Street Journal.* July 23, p. 60.

Peterson, Iver. 1984. "U.S. Ruled Negligent in A-Tests Followed by Nine Cancer Deaths." *New York Times.* May 11, p. 1.

Phillips, David. 1980. "The Deterrent Effect of Capital Punishment: New Evidence on an Old Controversy." *American Journal of Sociology* 86(1):139–48.

Reinhold, Robert. 1985a. "Pace of Executions Rising since '83 Court Ruling." *New York Times.* August 19, p. 7.

———. 1985b. "Execution for Juveniles: New Focus on Old Issue." September 10, p. 8.

Riding, Alan. 1979. "20,000 in Sal Salvador Mourn Slain Demonstrators." *New York Times.* May 11, p. 3.

Rummel, R. J. 1986. "War Isn't This Century's Biggest Killer." *Wall Street Journal.* July 7, p. 10.

San Antonio Express-News. 1983. "Gilmore's Cell for Sale." January 20, p. 7G.

———. 1984. "Death Camp Survivor Recalls Horrors under 'Balkan Butcher.'" November 25, p. 5C.

———. 1985. "Social Security: Call If You're Dead." September 1, p. 20A.

San Francisco Chronicle. 1974. "Japan to Rebury 1700 Soldiers." November 30, p. 7.

———. 1976. "Senate OKs Citizenship for Eugene Debs." July 1, p. 9.

Schmemann, Serge. 1983. "In Soviet, No Debates Rage around Capital Punishment." *New York Times.* August 3, pp. 1, 4.

Shurkin, Joel. 1988. "Modern Terrorists Are 'Anemic.'" *Stanford Observer.* February, p. 6.

Simmons, Michael. 1981. "Britain Refuses to Give General's Ashes to Poland." *Washington Post.* June 26, p. A27.

Stark, Irwin. 1986. "The Intolerable Horror of Legalized Killing." *New York Times.* August 25, p. 19.

Sullivan, Walter. 1984. "Loss of Life Span in Soviet Is Seen." *New York Times.* October 20, p. 10.

Talbot, R. E. 1980. "Let Them Rest in Peace." *Washington Post.* July 7, p. A14 (letter to ed.).

Time. 1980. "After the Takeover, Revenge." April 28, p. 34.

———. 1981. "A Real Hero." February 2, p. 15.

———. 1983. "Revenge Is The Mother of Invention." January 24, p. 36.

———. 1984. "The Catholic View." September 24, p. 20.

U.S. House of Representatives. 1978a. Hearings of the Subcommittee on Cemeteries and Burial Benefits of the Committee on Veterans' Affairs. "Disposition of Cemeteries in the Panama Canal Zone Where American Veterans Are Buried." March 1, p. 5.

———. 1978b. Hearings of the Subcommitte on Cemeteries and Burial Benefits of the Committee on Veteran's Affairs. "The National Cemetery System and Related Matters." March 14, pp. 31–32.

U.S. News & World Report. 1979. "A Billion Dollars to Give Away Panama Canal?" March 19, p. 46.

———. 1984. "Why Death Squads Still Spread Terror." February 27, p. 30.

Van Gennep, Arnold. 1960. *The Rites of Passage,* trans. by M. Vizedom and G. Caffee. Chicago: University of Chicago Press.

Vinocur, John. 1981. "War Veterans Come to Bury, and to Praise, Doenitz." *New York Times.* January 7, p. 2.

Walzer, Michael, ed. 1974. *Regicide and Revolution: Speeches at the Trial of Louis XVI,* trans. by Marian Rothstein. London: Cambridge University Press.

Washburn, A. Lawrence Jr. 1984. *New York Times.* March 16, p. 26 (letter to ed.).

Washington Post. 1978. "Carter: The Civil War Is Over." October 18, p. A12.

———. 1980. "VA Emptying Graves to Gain Room." June 27, p. A2.

Wicker, Tom. 1985. "An Uncertain Penalty." *New York Times.* June 28, p. 25.

Wiesel, Elie. 1984. "All Was Lost, yet Something Was Preserved." *New York Times Book Review.* August 19, pp. 1, 23.

Withers, E. L. 1964. *Royal Blood: Gory Path to the Throne.* Garden City, N.Y.: Doubleday.

Zeisel, H. 1976. "The Deterrent Effect of the Death Penalty: Facts v. Faith." In P. B. Kurland, ed., *The Supreme Court Review.* Chicago: University of Chicago Press, pp. 317–43.

Zwisohn, Van. 1986. "It's Time to Kill the Death Penalty." *New York Times.* March 13, p. 27.

Chapter 9

Death and the Military Experience

The backfiring of a passing auto triggered the veteran's dream. The recurrent nightmare was so vivid that he could once again smell the stench of smoke and death. Tonight he was contending with the enemy's artillery. With a scream, he hit the foxhole and then looked up to see his distressed wife peering down from the bed. Four houses down, a little girl also dreamed. It was the only time she remembered the brutal murder of her family and friends when the soldiers emerged from a Southeast Asian jungle.

Never before have so many dreamed such dreams. This military century has seen tens of millions die because of the warfare policies of their leaders. In any given year, there is an average of nearly twenty wars being fought worldwide, as the nations of this planet spend more than a trillion dollars producing instruments of death. The best minds of the world—talent that could be applied to the problems of hunger, poverty, energy, or peace—are employed to design such new means of destruction as MIRVs, particle beams, neutron bombs, and deadly biological agents. And because of their innovativeness, there is a new nightmare that haunts civilization like nothing before: the mushroom cloud.

The advent of nuclear weapons marks a totally new chapter in human history. At our disposal is the ultimate ending, a technology that brings death not only to the human race but to the entire natural order as well. But we all know the story—or at least we think we do. For more than forty years the threat has been a leitmotif of our arts, a facet of our denials and anxieties, a subject of scientific inquiries, and a basis of foreign policy. But before detailing the role this threat plays in modern political systems, let's back up a bit and first consider the human propensity to wage war. Running through Western history are two intellectual theses of human truculence: one portrays the individual as the root cause, and the other blames the social system. After considering each of these theories of war's inevitability, we turn to the impact of technological innovations on the strategies for war and the course of political events. We will observe how, for example, the individual warrior has been transformed from a chivalric hero into either an impersonal cog of some huge war machine or a terrorist, and how military preparations do not occur within some specialized appendage of the social order but rather now involve entire political economies whose very welfare depends on the threat of war.

War and the Individual

One central facet underlying the nature-nurture debate of the human condition concerns the inherent pugnacity of our species. During the mid-1970s, considerable attention was given to the "discovery" of the Tasadays, a stone-age people whose vocabulary was bereft of any ideas concerning war or violence. In the wake of the Vietnam War and Watergate, many Americans found hope that perhaps military misadventures stemmed not from themselves but rather from their flawed social institutions. But at the time of this writing, during the mid-1980s, military chic was back "in," evidenced by the enormous popularity of the *Rambo* movies; the expanding market of such paramilitary literature as *Soldier of Fortune* magazine; the proliferation of war toys, whose sales increased more than 600 percent between 1982 and 1987 (*San Antonio Express-News* 1987); and applicants exceeding the available positions in the volunteer army. In the woods of Alabama and elsewhere, people spend considerable sums of money to train in paramilitary camps, learning how "to kill others using sticks, hands, feet, knives, rope and firearms of all descriptions" (Smith 1985). And a spate of books has emerged on the human attraction to war and killing (Holmes 1985; Dyer 1985). So what is the natural propensity?

Many have proposed instinctual theories of violence. Ethologist Konrad Lorenz (1966), for instance, suggested that humans and animals inherited an "aggressive instinct" from their evolutionary past. Sigmund Freud (1959) saw man as a fighting creature whose warlike tendency lies beneath the veneer of civilization, a theme echoed by William James: "Our ancestors have bred pugnacity into our bone and marrow, and thousands of years of peace won't breed it out of us. The popular imagination fairly fattens on the thought of wars. Let public opinion once reach a certain fighting pitch, and no ruler can withstand it" (James 1964). Another noted psychiatrist, Karl Menninger, wrote of "some great impulse" toward self-destruction that lurks in the hearts of men and of nations. What is the nuclear arms race, he asks, if not a global "suicide club" (Farney 1985)?

Sociobiologists have also located war's cause within the individual, portraying violence as a means for males to obtain higher status and hence greater reproductive success. In Napoleon Chagnon's study of the Yanomamo, a particularly belligerent South American people, it was found that those men who had killed at least once (which was an estimated 44 percent of those aged twenty-five years and older) had more than twice the number of wives and children than those who had not killed. Some particularly successful warriors had as many as six wives (Chagnon 1988).

Of all man-made realities, war is a social event that so overwhelms the participants that they can neither fully recall nor describe their experiences of battle. For most, the actual encounters with boredom, chaos, and fear are best forgotten; as Stanley Baldwin, former British prime minister, observed, "War would end if the dead could return." On the other hand, the mythology of glory, excitement, and new surroundings has been a potent historical lure for prospective recruits seeking to escape the monotony of the farm or urban unemployment. And the situation of war still provides the individual one of the greatest sources of comradery, of opportunities for heroism, and of intense life-and-death experiences. When placed in the midst of battlefield action, soldiers report an intense feeling of being alive; future time collapses as one lives for the next heartbeat and not for one's country or mother.[1]

Transforming Civilians into Warriors

A nation at war charges its military institution with the responsibility of forcing enemy capitulation and acceptance of its terms. The discharge of this responsibility generally involves inflicting and suffering large numbers of casualties. The shaping of a populace's attitudes toward death thus becomes a necessity, particularly for those civilians who are put in uniform and told to cast aside all rules of civility, to no longer reflect on their actions but rather to rely on their instilled reflexes.

Though man is perhaps the most violent animal on earth, he must be socialized to kill effectively, even in self-defense. During the Korean War, for instance, the military was forced to turn to psychiatrists for help because of the incredibly high proportion of soldiers who could not pull the trigger in combat (Berger 1977, p. 89). The soldier must also be trained to die when ordered to, prompting Montesquieu to write that "a rational army would run away." To thus prepare the civilian for the alien context of war and death, the individual must be socialized to a new system of beliefs and action.

In basic training, the civilian self must first be ritually destroyed. The younger the individual, the easier this is, which is why the more malleable

A kamikaze pilot on a suicidal plunge toward a U.S. warship on June 27, 1945. UPI/
Bettmann Newsphotos.

eighteen-year-old is drafted before a thirty-year-old.[2] All identity props of
one's former self are stripped: hair is cut, distinctive clothing is replaced by
standard military garb, and behavior becomes impersonalized as it is constrained to regimented activity. The insecurities engendered by this alien
reality leave the individual more responsive to assertive leadership and more
dependent on the orientation of the new peer group. When the metamor-
phosis is complete, one senses belonging to a new reality system that is highly
theatrical:

Dying and killing seem easy when they are part of a ritual, ceremonial, dramatic performance or game. There is need for some kind of make-believe in order to face death
unflinchingly. To our real, naked selves there is not a thing on earth or in heaven
worth dying for. It is only when we see ourselves as actors in a staged (and therefore
unreal) performance that death loses its frightfulness and finality and becomes an act
of make-believe and a theatrical gesture. . . . Uniforms, flags, emblems, parades,
music and elaborate etiquette and ritual are designed to separate the soldier from his

"Those who may try to attack will come up against shattering resistance. Let them not put their pig's snout into the Soviet Kitchen garden." Stalin. Russian World War II propaganda poster. Imperial War Museum, London.

flesh-and-blood self and mask the overwhelming reality of life and death. (Hoffer 1951, pp. 64–65)

"Killing" is a primary concern of the military, but because of civilian socializations, the military uses such euphemisms as "eliminate," "neutralize," and "whack him," in the manner of killing a rat with a stick. Further, the enemy has to be depersonalized, made easier to kill, as many civilians retain favorable (or at least not definitely unfavorable) images of the enemy.[3] Cultural differences, West versus East, probably made this job easier in Vietnam than was the case in World War II, where some of the enemies shared common cultural traditions and backgrounds. Korean and Vietnamese "enemies" were Asians. They were referred to as "slopes," "gooks," "slants," and "zips"—not a human reference in the lot. The military referred to "hitting" or "zapping" them, not killing them. They were pictured as being vastly inferior, requiring opiates and bugles to summon the courage for attack. And they attacked in "hordes," "herds," and "flocks," and their dead were counted like cattle in a slaughterhouse pen before being disposed of in "body dumps."[4]

Verdunkeln! Der Feind sieht Dein Licht! ("Black out! The
Enemy sees Your Lights!"), Nazi war propaganda poster.
Imperial War Museum, London.

Not only are the victims deprived of their individuality, but so, too, are
the killers. History is filled with atrocities committed by unthinking warriors
exercising their instilled lethal instincts. On March 16, 1968, a group of
American soldiers massacred between four hundred fifty and five hundred
men, women, and children at the village of My Lai, located in what was
South Vietnam. This group of soldiers was from Charlie Company, 1st Batal-
lion 20th Infantry of the American Division. They had suffered a lot of casualties in this area during the previous month and were really "pumped up"

Navy Gunners Have Difficulty Sinking Coffin

A crewman aboard the USS Farragut who witnessed the sinking of a coffin by gunfire last month said it "was the worst thing I've ever seen in the Navy."

A Navy honor guard was ordered to fire M-14 rifles at the coffin of a Korean war veteran who was buried at sea July 14 when the coffin would not sink, Navy officials confirmed.

Navy officials said the shooting was orderly and justified in light of the unusual incident. But several crewmen on the guided missile destroyer said a small boat should have been lowered to accomplish the task. Instead, the ship reversed engines to keep the coffin in sight and three riflemen fired more than 200 rounds of ammunition into it until they blew out the bottom, crewmen said.

"It never did sink while we were there," said one crewman who asked not to be identified. "The body was coming out of the casket when we left. It was gross."

Vice Admiral John D. Johnson, commander of Surface Forces Atlantic, said that no violation of regulations have been uncovered. The Navy said the deceased was an ex-enlisted man who had requested burial at sea—a request that the Navy grants its veterans at no charge.

San Antonio Express-News 1980. Reprinted by
permission of The Associated Press © 1980.

---

for any forthcoming battle. Suddenly, in a rice field, the soldiers saw a Vietnamese farmer approaching, yelling "G.I. Number One, G. I. Number One." One of the sergeants gave the order to shoot the farmer; not even the animals were spared. Throughout the village, fires were burning, and soldiers were running wild committing such crimes as looting, raping, and killing. These seemed to be young people who had gone completely mad. In the court-martial of Lieut. William Calley that followed, the defendant had the following explanation: "I was ordered to go in there and destroy the enemy. That was my job that day. That was the mission I was given. I did not sit down and think in terms of men, women and children. They were all classified the same" (Hammer 1971, p. 257).

Honoring the Fallen Warrior: Lessons of Vietnam

A critical component of military theatrics is the ritual attention that must be given to those who actually die in the course of battle. Although much of military ceremony involves the deindividualization of warriors and the depersonalization of their victims, one's own dead must be reinvested with individuality and their sacrifices honored. In part, this entails making every possible attempt to recover the remains and attending them with the greatest pomp and circumstance possible.[5]

The victims of America's only major military loss provided a serious symbolic crisis for the military institution. As mentioned in Chapter 8, the Tomb of the Unknown Soldier for the Vietnam War remained empty until 1984. Unlike any other war, there emerged the POW/MIA issue, leading President Reagan to make the recovery of unaccounted-for Americans "the highest national priority" even though American involvements in Vietnam had concluded a decade earlier.[6] On November 11, 1982, the seven-million-dollar Vietnam War Monument was consecrated, and a final roll call of the war's 57,939 dead was conducted in the National Cathedral as Washington finally honored them as part of a five-day "National Salute to Vietnam Veterans" ritual.

Controversy over the delayed observances and ritual acknowledgments of this unpopular war were inevitable, ultimately focusing on the monument itself. The structure sits in a gradual V-shaped depression—critics say a "pit" or "sinkhole"—in the earth. On its polished black marble, names are inscribed in chronological order in terms of date of death.[7] The first major debate centered on the conception itself. According to Tom Wolfe (1982), the design became bound up in the politics of art; the ambiguity of the lesson from Vietnam seemed to have led to an ambiguity of design: "in the purging of bourgeoisie art, not even an American flag was to be found in the vicinity of this latest expression of modernism." Three months after the monument's dedication, the government's Fine Arts Commission voted to place a bronze statue of three combat soldiers and a flag by the side of the memorial.

The second debate was over some of the twenty-four thousand victims whose names were not included. The government argued that those included had to have died not only between prescribed times but also within designated combat zones. "These veterans have been done an injustice," said Senator Don Nickles, an Oklahoma Republican who took up their cause. "Just because of an arbitrary line, they're not on the memorial" (Shenon 1985). Replied a Defense Department spokesman, "You've got to draw the line somewhere" (*San Antonio Express-News* 1985a). Complicating matters was the fact that there was only room for about five hundred additional names. Eventually, the Pentagon reviewed three hundred cases and added ninety-six names in 1985, most of whom were flight personnel killed in crash landings and takeoffs.

But the Wall, as it is often referred to by veterans, became truly sacred and attracted so many that the granite walkway was extended by six feet. Letters are left for dead sons, photographs are left for dead fathers, and medallions

The Memorial Day ritual of wreath laying at the Tomb of the Unknowns, 1988. UPI/Bettmann Newsphotos.

and flowers are left for fallen comrades. Around the country, similar memorials were erected during the mid-1980s, inscribed with the names of city sons who gave their lives for a cause that still was not understood.

Desocializing the Warrior: The Myth of the Violent Veteran

The transformation of warriors back into civilians poses numerous threats to a grateful—but wary—social order. Like animals with the taste of human blood, the combat soldier who has routinely taken the lives of others returns to be viewed as a different person. He has forbidden knowledge, and his lethal skills can always be turned against the social order, as dramatized in the myth of the violent veteran.[8] He also has a significantly higher likelihood of dying a violent death.

Often, warring nations have experienced dramatic increases in postwar violence. In their analysis of international longitudinal data, Archer and Gartner (1976) found postwar increases in homicide rates among combatant nations, particularly those victorious and suffering the greatest numbers of battle deaths. In other words, homicides are most likely to occur where killing is legitimized by the state. Homicide rates doubled in the United States during the Vietnam War. Violence is not only externalized, but it is also directed against oneself: within their first five years of returning to civilian life, Vietnam veterans were nearly twice as likely to commit suicide as men of the same age group who avoided the war (72 percent higher than veterans who served elsewhere) and 53 percent more likely to die in traffic accidents (Hearst, Newman, and Hulley 1986; Franklin 1987).

The veteran also suffers from a problem of trust, a building block on which all of social life is erected. The everyday, taken-for-granted reality of civilian life ignores much; civility assumes the nonlethal intentions of others. In war, however, all such assumptions evaporate: one cannot trust the ground one walks on, the air one breathes, nor can one expect with full assuredness that tomorrow will come again.[9] There are flashbacks of companions dying, and one develops fears of close attachments after so many have died (28 percent of Vietnam veterans previously married were divorced within six months of returning home). One social ritual to ease reentry into civilian life is to publicly receive a hero's welcome, to be embraced by society and—as in the case of World War II veterans—be given preferential treatment in allocations of jobs, housing, and educational opportunities. However, such was not to be the case for the Vietnam warriors, who received no hero's welcome until after a decade had passed following the war's conclusion. So extensive and lingering were the psychological scars from war experiences that they were labeled the Vietnam syndrome.[10]

War and Social Structure

One of the deepest imprints in Western imagination is the Trojan War, the prototype of all struggles between East and West (Campbell 1985). Another Greek legacy to the West were the theories of war's inevitability. But instead of locating its origins within man, war was seen to be a constituent feature of the external forces that shape individual lives. In Homer's *Iliad*, mortals were but puppets to please the Olympian hierarchy, and war was what amused the gods most. Plato advanced a cyclical theory of the state's periods of prosperity, corruption, and decline—with political maneuvering leading to oligarchy and tyranny, and finally to war and the overthrow of the old order.

During the Middle Ages, a period of religious hegemony over the thinking and activities of everyday Western life, the Catholic church could never completely suppress warfare, though it did for a time limit human slaughter to the interim between Monday mornings and Wednesday evenings. As war could not be prevented, it was refined under Christian guidelines and governed by the laws or codes of chivalry. According to these codes, if one's morality was superior to another's, then, with determination, one would ultimately overcome one's enemies. In 1095, less than a century after the Peace of God and the Truce of God (which limited war to certain groups of persons during specific periods of time), the church proclaimed the First Crusade. A new legitimization was given, one employing the metaphor of bloodletting for the health of the social body,[11] evident in the following observation of Francis Bacon:

No body can be healthful without exercise, neither natural body nor politic; and certainly to a kingdom or estate, a just and honorable war is the rue exercise. A civil war, indeed, is like the heat of a fever; but a foreign war is like the heat of exercise, and serveth to keep the body in health; for in a slothful peace, both courages will effeminate and manners corrupt. But howsoever it be for happiness, without all question, for greatness will maketh, to be still for the most part in arms. (Bacon 1910, p. 83)

In Shakespeare's time, though war was not liked, it remained a necessary evil as the periods without it were viewed to be synonymous with times of social and political unrest. A contemporary, Thomas Fenne, wrote in his 1590 *Fennes Frutes:*

Warre bringeth ruine, ruine bringeth povertie, poverties procureth peace, and peace in time increaseth riches, riches causeth statelinesse, statelinesse increaseth envie, envie in the end procureth deadly mallice, mortall mallice proclaimeth open warre and battaile: and from warre againe as before is rehearsed. (cited in Gist 1947, p. 192)

Shakespeare did not avoid this popular pessimism, and he has the Archbishop of York in *2 Henry IV* saying:

> We are all diseas'd;
> And, with our surfeiting, and wanton hours,
> Have brought ourselves into a burning fever,
> And we must bleed for it: . . .
>   awhile like fearful war,
> To diet rank minds, sick of happiness;
> And purge the obstructions, which begin to stop
> Our very veins of life. (Act II, Scene 1, 585)

From the sixteenth and seventeenth centuries on, the wars of religion were to be transformed into wars of nationality (Toynbee 1950, p. 4). To protect "national interests," each state had to maintain a balance of power with other states.[12] Military buildups were justified by the presuppositions of the others' expenditures.[13] And when wars did break out, they reflected the changes (or desire for changes) in the relative power of the different national groups and ultimately created national boundaries. The Napoleonic era remains a vivid memory, so profound was its exploitation of modern nationalism in expanding the scale of war. The French, politically awakened to the principles of liberty and equality by the Revolution, were willing to be conscripted and fight with élan for their ideals and government against the hostile and frightened monarchies of Europe. In 1793, the entire civilian population of France had mobilized for war, and eventually they were to overrun most of Europe by means of the *levée en masse*. Never before had the world seen anything approaching the scale of mass war as when, in 1812, Napoleon entered Russia with half a million soldiers and a thousand cannons; never before had there been anything approaching the scale of mass slaughter, with four million deaths having been generated by the time of Napoleon's surrender at Waterloo (Dyer 1985).

With industrialization, technological innovation, and the strategy of mass war, the obsolescence of the heroic warrior was complete. Soldiers became mere cogs of some huge, impersonal, industrialized killing machine. During the American Civil War, the attempt to combine the Napoleonic tactics of charging in mass formations with the new factory-assembled instruments of death—breech-loading rifles (propelling bullets ten times farther than the muskets used by Napoleon's troops), land mines, and hand-cranked Gatling guns (which fired 350 rounds a minute)—was to kill more Americans than two world wars and the Korean and Vietnam conflicts combined (Dyer, 1985, pp. 77–79). In fact, more than 2 percent of the nation's 1860 population perished in the War between the States, which would mean nearly five million casualties nowadays.

By the late nineteenth century, Darwin's theory of natural selection and Marx's notion of history as the evolution of class struggle were to affect the way we see ourselves, sensitizing us to the degree to which our "progress" as a species and as a nation was the result of conflict. These ideas were to become incorporated into the political ethos of the pre-world-war time, classically illustrated in Theodore Roosevelt's "strenuous life" speech, given in Chicago on Appomattox Day in 1899:

I preach to you, then, my countrymen, that our country calls not for the life of ease, but for the life of strenuous endeavor. The twentieth century looms before us big with the fate of many nations. If we stand idly by, if we seek merely swollen, slothful ease, and ignoble peace, if we shrink from the hard contests where men must win at hazard of their lives and at the risk of all they hold dear, then the bolder and stronger peoples will pass us by and will win for themselves the domination of the world.

More recently, cultural-materialist theorists have combined Marxist economics with ecological dynamics to postulate that war results from struggles over
scarce resources, whether it be food or oil, and from the inabilities of environments to support their populations. In examining hostilities in preindustrial cultures, for instance, Marvin Harris (1979, p. 91) notes how village
populations are kept in check as warfare leads to female infanticide and the
dispersion of enemy populations. Females are abused and neglected as a premium is placed on the social production of aggressive male combatants. And
with the dispersion of populations, no-man's-lands expand on the fringes of
hunting areas, increasing the habitats and densities of game animals.

Two world wars have not done much to alter the inevitability thesis. In
the late 1960s, in the midst of the Vietnam War, one book appearing on
college campuses that was to generate considerable debate was *A Report from
Iron Mountain* (1967). This work detailed the hypothetical implications of
international peace, according to a collection of minds assembled by the
Hudson Institute. They explored the rather disconcerting assumption that
the basis of social solidarity is the fear of some external threat. In other
words, without the threat of death—particularly the threat of military
aggression—society would become unraveled. Further, if worldwide peace
were to be declared tomorrow, the unemployment rate would rival that of
the Great Depression.

Military conflict historically evolved from ritual warfare, a drama in which
victory in battle was the only goal, to purposive warfare, which aimed at
acquiring territory or power. This shift from symbolic to material gain, from
personal to collective impetus toward war, was accelerated by the forces of
technological innovation and nationalism. By the beginning of the twentieth
century, urbanization, mass education, and mass media increasingly allowed
people to be more aware of what bound them together and how different
they were from those of other nations.

Technology and the Art of Killing

In 1899 and again in 1907, diplomats of Europe and America came together
at the Hague to attempt to establish humane codes of war, particularly to
protect the rights of noncombatants. A third convention was to be conducted in 1916, but that was canceled because of war. New technologies had
made obsolete the rules of war (Moyers 1984).

The course of military history has routinely been altered with innovations
in killing, each change eventually producing new strategies, new defenses,
and new atrocities—the tossed stone replaced by the spear, the spear by an
arrow, the bow by the long bow and crossbow, the crossbow by the musket,

the musket by the cannon and bored rifle, and so on. Each innovation was to impose a logic of its own upon the course of conflict. According to Marshall McLuhan (1968), war is an involuntary quest for identity that follows every new technological age. So great has been the pace of technological change during the past century that such "involuntary quests" have routinized human slaughter with the newest instruments of war.[14]

During the 1980s, there was little observation of the centennial anniversary of the patenting of the machine gun. Wrote its inventor, Hiram Maxim: "In 1882 I was in Vienna, where I met an American whom I had known in the States. He said: 'Hang your chemistry and electricity! If you want to make a pile of money, invent something that will enable these Europeans to cut each others' throats with greater facility'" (Browne 1985). He did, producing a machine that could fire ten bullets each second.

The machine gun was first used by the Europeans to subdue rebellion in their colonial empires. In 1893, it was first employed for large-scale slaughter when fifty British security guards of the Rhodesian Charter Company used four Maxims against five thousand attacking Zulus, killing three thousand. Two decades later, during World War I, Europeans turned their Maxims on each other. Mechanized firepower reduced the individual soldier to an interchangeable part in the increasingly impersonal technology of war. Personal courage became irrelevant for gunners who simply unleashed a stream of bullets against a mass of individuals. In the battle of the Somme alone, more than a million soldiers were mowed down like wheat before a harvester-thresher. Both the machine gunner and his enemy were depersonalized. Instead of observing the chivalric ideal of standing up and showing oneself to one's opponent, the gunner simply tended his machine. No longer did the warrior select one particular representative of the enemy and then concentrate on that target (Moyers 1984). Eventually, both sides were driven into the trenches, eventually to be overrun by rats grown to the size of dogs, having gorged themselves on human flesh.

To solve the problem of the trenches and alter the stalemates achieved because of the machine gun, the tank evolved, "land ships" as they were first called, which could traverse the zone between trenches called "no man's land." Also, the Germans were to introduce the use of poisonous gas, wafting clouds of death over Allied lines.[15] With the submarine, the lines of battle were extended beyond the land-based armies. The sinking of the passenger ship *Lusitania* by a U-boat in 1915 was to erase forever the distinction between civilian and soldier.[16] And then there were attacks from the air (the first coming from Zeppelins over London in 1915), fulfilling H. G. Wells's prophecy that aerial warfare would lead to enraged populations demanding vengeance and "in spasms of patriotic passion, bombing would ripple

"In the arts of death, man outdoes nature, herself, and produces by chemistry and machinery all of the slaughter that does plague, pestilence and famine" (George Bernard Shaw). A baby wails amidst the ruins of South Station in Shanghai, China. Hundreds were killed when Japanese bombs destroyed three trains packed with refugees on September 17, 1937. UPI/Bettmann Newsphotos.

around the globe until 'universal guerrilla war' consumed mankind" (Sherry 1981). With combatants in tanks, gas masks, submarines, and aircraft, the warrior's depersonalization had become complete. With attacks being conducted from beneath the sea or from thousands of feet in the air, no longer could there be any Achilles or Hector. War economies had to be created to support the millions of men on the front, employing women and the aged to replace the missing men back home. War had become total, involving civilians and military populations alike in its maintenance and victimization. George Bernard Shaw was prompted to write, "in the arts of death, man outdoes nature, herself, and produces by chemistry and machinery all of the slaughter that does plague, pestilence and famine. Man outdoes nature" (cited by Moyers 1984).

Shaw, however, was only reflecting on the "arts of death" produced during World War I. Two decades later, even greater ingenuity was applied as the world once again became consumed in war. There were, of course, improvements on old technological themes—faster and larger aircraft, more indestructible tanks, and more devastating artillery—but there were also new developments. Alfred Nobel, the Swedish chemist who invented dynamite, foresaw germ warfare as being the logical conclusion to conflict. Indeed, during World War II, the Japanese subjected prisoners to lethal experiments, exposing them to such agents as tetanus, anthrax, and bubonic plague.[17] American scientists, too, toyed with the idea of using poisons, not biological substances but rather a radioactive form of the element strontium. In a secret 1943 letter, physicist J. Robert Oppenheimer advised his colleague Enrico Fermi to delay work on the atom bomb until "we can poison food sufficient to kill half a million men" (*San Antonio Express-News* 1985b).

But the doomsday weaponry went the route of nuclear, instead of biological or chemical, technology.[18] The pace of evolution of atomic weaponry was staggering. The first nuclear device was detonated before dawn on July 16, 1945, in central New Mexico. Within two months, similar atomic bombs were dropped on Hiroshima and Nagasaki, despite the appeals of their creators to President Truman that the first bomb be used as a demonstration, perhaps at night thirty thousand feet over Tokyo Bay, where it would cause no damage.[19]

The conclusion of World War II did little to retard the technological impetus of or social investments in this ultimate weapon. In 1952, the first hydrogen bomb was tested, causing the total disappearance of the Pacific island of Elugelab. Instead of deriving its energy from the fission of uranium 235, this device achieved one thousand times the power through fusing together hydrogen isotopes. The sixty-two-ton weapon was, with time, made smaller and lighter, allowing its placement on missiles. It was then that President Eisenhower's secretary of defense, John Foster Dulles, presented the impression that the United States would instigate nuclear war if there were any communist encroachment on the free world.

The accelerating pace of innovations has continued. We are now witnessing the development of nuclear weapons that refine the spectrum of radiation wavelengths emitted and the focus of the energy released (power increases by making the radiation more coherent and with shorter wavelengths). In the late 1960s and early 1970s, x-ray warheads were developed to knock out enemy warheads with the enhanced radiation of the x-ray portion of the electromagnetic spectrum. By the late 1970s, scientists had produced the neutron bomb, designed to kill enemy troops with radiation and spare most buildings and industry. Moral outrage resulted. Would the relatively low yield of this weapon encourage its use? Critics called it the ultimate capitalist weapon. During the mid-1980s, work continued on x-ray lasers and particle-

Ground zero of the Nagasaki atomic blast, taken on September 13, 1945. UPI/Bettmann Newsphotos.

beam weapons, which channel the power of a nuclear explosion into beams of radiation that could destroy missiles thousands of miles away. To knock out computers and communication systems and to destroy the delicate circuitry aboard enemy missiles, electromagnetic pulse bombs and microwave weapons were being conceived. And also receiving serious study were such futuristic-sounding devices as gamma-ray lasers, antimatter bombs, and brain bombs (humans suffer confusion and disorientation when subjected to long wavelength radiation) (Broad 1985).

The advent of nuclear weapons has fundamentally altered both the nature of war and the relationship of the military with the rest of society. As Albert Einstein observed, "the atomic bomb has changed everything except the nature of man." According to Leon Wieseltier:

The real distinction between conventional weapons and nuclear weapons is that the latter are not instruments of intention. They are, instead, makers of it. Conventional weapons are mere things, manipulated by men; the men must be understood, therefore, and not the things. In the world of conventional weapons, military facts are broken down into political facts, into the ideas and interests that motivate the elite. But nuclear weapons are systems. The production, deployment, and support of these weapons generates a corresponding social system—an organization of knowledge that leads to an organization of the economy that leads to an organization of society. E. P. Thompson [British social historian and one of the foremost intellectuals in the peace movement] calls it EXTERMINISM, the "order whose institutional base is the weapons-system, and the entire economic, scientific, political, and ideological support-system to that weapons-system—the social system which researches, chooses it, produces it, polices it, justifies it, and maintains it in being." (1983, p. 10)

By the mid-1980s, the rough nuclear parity between East and West as well as the recognition of the suicidal consequences of a nuclear exchange led to renewed interest in lethal chemicals. Western strategists came to believe that the Soviet Union's preferred weapon in a West European war would be chemical arms, and a "chemical gap" was cited: the Soviet Union supposedly had four to eighteen times the weapons tonnage of the United States, four times the number of storage sites, twenty times the number of decontamination vehicles, and nine to ten times the number of military personnel trained and equipped to fight a chemical war (O'Boyle 1986). In 1985, Congress renounced the U.S. moratorium on production of chemical weapons after the Reagan administration had requested more than a billion dollars for chemical warfare programs.[20]

The Political Economies of War

Military needs have come to be bureaucratically interwoven with industrial, academic, scientific, technical, private, and public interests. In the United States, a million dollars is spent every ninety seconds on this institution, which now consumes roughly 60 percent of the federal discretionary budget. In his farewell address in 1961, President Eisenhower warned of the dangers of such an alliance between military and corporate interests and labeled the union the "military-industrial complex." He foresaw the dependence on federal funding leading to the corruption of science and claimed that "public policy could itself become the captive of a scientific-technological elite." And of the expanding peacetime defense industry, he said, "Only an alert and knowledgeable citizenry can compel the proper meshing of the huge industrial and military machinery of defense with our peaceful methods and goals so that security and liberty may prosper together (Weiss 1986, p. 14)."

In sum, Eisenhower cautioned that there were domestic forces at work that would maintain arms expenditures even if the Soviet Union were to become an ally. His premonition has come true. Because of inevitable bureaucratic growth and the residues of past crisis, powerful unchecked factions have emerged which threaten the political balance between the multitude of interests. By focusing on external threats and military security, the political order gets away with postponing domestic reforms—for example, women's rights in Israel (Brozan 1986) or minority rights in the United States during the first half of this century—thereby maintaining the status quo of the elite structure. And in a strange way, the United States and the Soviet Union have become economically dependent on each other's existence.

As evident in Table 9.1, the military demands for monies and personnel represent sizable sacrifices (some may say "libations") that must be made to the political order. In a number of developing countries, particularly in Central and South America, the military has simply taken control of the political levers of power, using its instruments for violence to quell any opposition. Under Argentina's three military juntas of the 1970s, for example, antisubversive campaigns resulted in the disappearance of at least nine thousand citizens (Chavez 1984).

Worldwide, more than a trillion dollars is spent each year on armaments. At a time of severe economic crisis, particularly among the lesser-developed countries, the arming game continues. In 1984, the foreign minister of India linked world poverty to the spending on arms, noting that by reducing global military spending the world's industrialized countries would be able to "augment the presently decreasing levels" of economic assistance to developing countries (Feron 1984). Why has this not occurred? The answer, in part, involves money and power.

The United States is the major arms dealer of the world, often arming others in order to arm itself. The United States accounts for nearly half the total worldwide armaments trade, an important source of revenue at a time of huge trade deficits. According to the Congressional Research Service, the U.S. share of military sales agreements with nonindustrialized nations rose from 32 percent to 39 percent just from 1982 to 1983, while the Soviet's share declined from 27 percent to 17 percent (*New York Times* 1984a).

Numerous are the occupational groups and political constituencies that share (and depend on) the hundreds of billions of dollars spent on the military in the United States each year. Forty-four states, for example, have some part in the manufacturing of the B-1 bomber, on which more was spent in 1984 than the steel industry spent on all research and development (Lamm 1987). In 1984, the ten largest weapons makers realized a 25 percent return on equity, nearly double the 12.8 percent average return for all other manufacturing corporations (Gerth 1985a). (See Table 9.3.) General Dynamics, one of the ten contractors, paid no federal taxes between 1972 and 1984 (its

Table 9.1 The Costs of Arming the Earth

	Cost in per capita dollars (1983 U.S. Dollars) 1984	Percent of GNP 1984	Forces per 1000 population 1984	For each health dollar, amount spent for military 1982	Number of military personnel for each physician 1982
Algeria	63	2.7	7.9	1.74	25.8
Argentina	74	3.7	5.8	3.11	3.1
China					
Mainland	23	7.5	4.0	6.25	6.9
Taiwan	196	6.6	24.7	2.91	21.6
Cuba	155	5.9	29.7	1.70	1.3
Egypt	104	13.5	9.8	1.68	7.7
France	394	4.1	10.4	0.65	5.1
Germany					
East	619	6.3	14.4	1.13	4.6
West	360	3.3	8.0	1.93	3.4
Iran	251	7.2	7.6	6.41	14.8
Iraq	944	42.5	52.5	NA	44.4
Israel	1721	27.1	50.6	8.26	16.3
Japan	102	1.0	2.0	0.21	1.5
Korea					
North	256	22.6	39.9	5.83	NA
South	106	5.4	14.3	23.06	21.2
Nigeria	12	1.7	1.4	3.90	16.0
Qatar	3184 (1980)	NA	21.5	NA	30.0
Saudi Arabia	1990	21.3	8.8	4.63	13.7
Sweden	340	3.1	8.3	0.37	3.7
Syria	405	22.4	39.6	33.48	52.8
UK	436	5.3	6.0	0.96	3.5
USA	765	6.3	9.5	1.43	4.7
USSR	914	12.6	16.4	3.54	3.5

Sources: 1984 data from the U.S. Bureau of the Census, *Statistical Abstract of the United States: 1988*, 108th ed., pp. 826–27; 1982 data from Sivard 1985, pp. 35–37.

Table 9.2 The Spoils of Winning the MX Missile Contract

	Contract amount	Plant locations
Martin Marietta	$380 million	Denver, Vandenberg Air Force Base (CA)
Rockwell International, Autonetics Division	$236 million	Anaheim (CA)
Northrop	$187 million	Fullerton (CA) and Norwood (MA)
Rockwell International	$184 million	Canoga Park (CA)
Morton Thiokol	$149 million	Brigham City (UT)
Boeing	$133 million	Seattle (WA)

Source: New York Times 1982.

Table 9.3 Profits of the Ten Largest Weapons Makers

	Profits as % of equity[a]	1984 Profits (in millions)	Sales to U.S. Govt.
Lockheed	42%	$572	85%
General Dynamics	30	382	86
Northrop	29	167	84
Martin Marietta	28	176	76
Boeing	26	787	42
Grumman	24	108	82
Rockwell International	21	496	63
Raytheon	18	340	49
Litton	16	277	41
McDonnell Douglas	16	325	69

[a]Equity: paid-in capital plus retained earnings.
Source: Gerth 1985b.

pretax profits in 1984 were $683.6 million). At the University of Kansas, one of twenty-four universities receiving Army funding for biotechnology investigation, researchers work on cloning dengue, a severe infectious disease, while at Molecular Genetics Inc., genetic engineers are developing a fast-breeding hybrid of the Rift Valley fever virus, an exotic killer exclusively found in sub-Saharan Africa (Richards and Carrington 1986).

In 1982, President Reagan unilaterally discontinued negotiations for a comprehensive test ban of nuclear weapons, echoing the military's claims of a "testing gap" with the Soviet Union. In fact, as of the beginning of 1985, the United States had conducted some two hundred more nuclear tests than the Soviet Union had (approximately 760 tests compared to 560; Schlesinger 1985). In addition, the president proposed the Strategic Defense Initiative, popularly known as "Star Wars," which could become the most costly federal project ever, one hundred times more costly than the Manhattan Project and ten times the cost of the American space program during the 1960s (Wellborn 1985). Pure scientific research in physics, lasers, metallurgy, artificial intelligence, and dozens of other areas began giving way to direct military uses. The irony is that this attempt to develop a defense system against intercontinental ballistic missiles probably makes war between the Soviet Union and the United States even more likely, according to analysts for Congress's Office of Technology Assessment (Mohr 1985). Further, the feasibility of such a complex system even working has received serious doubt.[21]

With the vast sums of money at stake, weapons systems have developed powerful political constituencies comprised of technocrats, scientists, physicists, mathematicians, engineers, software writers, assemblers—in fact, entire spectrums of white- and blue-collar workers—as well as entire geographic areas whose economies are bolstered by military expenditures.[22] Seventy percent of American programs in research and development and testing and evaluation are now defense-related, and nearly 40 percent of all U.S. engineers and scientists are currently involved in military projects (Lamm 1987). During the 1980s, the media was rife with stories of continued fundings for weapons that did not work and inflated expenditures for products and parts—bolts costing scores of dollars, toilets costing hundreds, and weapons manuals bearing a $1000-per-page charge (Gerth 1985a). Technological sophistication has seen 2 billion dollars (1983) purchase 6735 tanks in 1953 but only 701 tanks thirty years later; 7 billion dollars (1983) bought 6300 fighter planes in 1951, whereas it now costs 11 billion dollars to build just 322 (Isaacson 1983).[23]

In sum, the military impetus is inherent in American society, fueled by exaggerations of adversaries' capacities and by a coalition of interests that have grown dependent on military support. There is a certain madness to the enterprise, as Lewis Mumford observed one year following the first detonation of a thermonuclear device:

Madmen govern our affairs in the name of order and security. The chief madmen claim the titles of general, admiral, senator, scientist, administrator, Secretary of State, even President. And the fatal symptom of their madness is this: they have been carrying through a series of acts which will lead eventually to the destruction of mankind, under the solemn conviction that they are normal responsible people, living sane lives, and working for reasonable ends. Soberly, day after day, the madmen continue to go through the undeviating motions of madness: motions so stereotyped, so commonplace, that they seem the normal motions of normal men, not the mass compulsion of people bent on total death. (Mumford 1946)

Star Wars—the most ambitious, costly, and controversial of all politically sponsored scientific and technological enterprises—is perhaps the epitome of Eisenhower's worst fears.[23] With the increasing pluralization and complexity of military issues (such as how to knock out thousands of incoming missiles and recognize the real warheads from among thousands of decoys), the ignorance of the general population is magnified. This collective nescience leads toward the further delegation of power to elected officials, who in turn defer to the numerous, unelected experts of the military-scientific-academic-industrial elite. As John Kenneth Galbraith notes:

Here we have delegated power on which our very survival depends. It is an astonishing thing we have done; no modern legislature would contemplate surrendering to the executive the right to decide upon and to levy taxes. Death and taxes, one notes, have long been united as the two great certainties of mankind; we would not dream of surrendering power on taxes; we do it quite casually on death. (1982)

Violating the Conventions: Terrorism

Between 1968 and 1985, Americans were attacked in seventy-two countries by another military form, one evolving not out of political-industrial interests or wars of nationalism but rather from ideological or religious forces. Increasingly around the world, we see not two organized rival groups on a battlefield but rather lone individuals or small groups of terrorists attacking the vulnerable spots of the powerful. They attack the taken-for-granted structures of everyday life, bringing death where it is least expected. Buses, aircraft, and even a cruise ship[24] have been commandeered and passengers killed. Car bombs have been detonated on city streets next to crowded restaurants and foreign embassies. Machine guns have opened up and hand grenades have been thrown upon unsuspecting civilians in airports, supermarkets, and cafés. No longer is any place "sacred," off limits to violence; no longer are distinctions made between military and civilian populations, as all have come to be considered fair game. As one retired CIA official observed, "the *purpose* of terrorism [is] *not* to kill, maim, or destroy, but to *terrorize,* to frighten, to anger, to provoke irrational responses. Terrorism gains more from the responses than it gains from the actions themselves" (Eringer 1986). It first gains from the publicity it receives in what has become an information war. Alexander and Finger note, "The media are the terrorist's best friend. The terrorist's act by itself is nothing, publicity is all" (1977, p. 167). And secondly, it gains from the possible overreactions of the states victimized, specifically, at that point where the threat of random death so disrupts the social confidence that people are willing to sacrifice their liberties in exchange for eliminating their fears.

Despite popular conceptions that terrorism is somehow new, history is filled with even bloodier episodes of terrorist activities. Before the twentieth century, most terrorism was religious in nature. The three best known of these religious terrorist groups were the Jewish Zealots of Roman Judea, the Moslem Assassins of the old Ottoman Empire, and the Indian Thugs. The Zealots, active for more than seventy years, were the only terrorist group to have spawned a popular uprising, but that, according to historian David Rapoport, led to the mass suicide of the Masada, the destruction of the Second Temple, the death of half the Jewish population, and the two-thousand-year Diaspora. Rapoport estimated that the Thugs may have killed thirty thousand people a year over the span of anywhere from three to twenty-five centuries (cited in Shurkin 1988).

Although the word *terrorism* has assumed considerable negative connotations during the 1970s and 1980s, it should be appreciated that one man's "terrorist" is another's "freedom fighter." The French became terrorists under the German occupation of World War II; the Lebanese became terrorists under the Israeli occupation of the early 1980s. Some of the activities of the CIA's Political Action Staff, the "dirty tricks" department, were terrorist to American adversaries. Terrorism against the British, for example, allowed Israel to come into existence.

In part, the contemporary threats of so few individuals owes to the evolution of the instruments of war as well as to the increasing vulnerability of modern societies. A single individual can now be armed not only with a machine gun but with a car bomb or even a nuclear weapon.[25] Concurrent with this development of lethal weaponry, there has been in modern, postindustrial societies the increasing assumptions of the civility of one's fellow man, enhancing the vulnerability of the unsuspecting. Even the mob had its code of ethics that included the immunity of noncombatants, especially innocent children and women. But the terrorists of the past two decades have come to see all members of a particular nationality, ethnicity, or religious group as legitimate targets for random attack. Further, the incredible interdependency of modern societies has also contributed to their greater vulnerability: millions can be thrown into darkness with the destruction of a few power lines just as they can all be endangered by the poisoning of a city reservoir.

The Military Eschatology: Nuclear Armageddon

> For they are demonic spirits . . . who go abroad to the kings of the whole world, to assemble them for battle on the great day of God the Almighty . . . at the place which is called in Hebrew Armageddon.
>
> Revelation 16:14, 16

The contemporary eschatology that perhaps most haunts the human species derives from the military institution. Through scientific and technological innovations, we have harnessed forces so great that not only can entire civilizations be obliterated, but the very order of nature, of life itself, can be exterminated. Armageddon, in other words, has become a technological possibility, a military option. According to a 1984 report of the National Research Council, so much smoke and debris from cities devastated by a nuclear exchange would be cast into the atmosphere that sunlight would be blotted out. A nuclear winter would result as average temperatures plummet as much as forty to seventy degrees Fahrenheit. A drop of only five to ten degrees, according to Dr. Mark Harwell, an associate director of Cornell University's Ecosystems Research Center, could "essentially eliminate agri-

Statements of the 2d Reagan-Mondale Debate
on Foreign Policy, October 21, 1984

Q. Mr. President, I'd like to pick up this Armageddon theme. You've been quoted as saying that you do believe deep down that we are heading for some kind of biblical Armageddon. Your Pentagon and your Secretary of Defense have plans for the United States to fight and prevail in a nuclear war. Do you feel we are now heading, perhaps, for some kind of nuclear Armageddon? And do you feel that this country and the world could survive that kind of calamity?

Reagan: Mr. Kalb, I think what has been hailed as something I'm supposedly, as President, discussing as principle is the result of just some philosophical discussions with people who are interested in the same things. And that is the prophecies down through the years, the biblical prophecies of what would portend the coming of Armageddon and so forth. And the fact that a number of theologians for the last decade or more have believed that this was true, that the prophecies are coming together that portend that.

(New York Times 1984c).

---

culture production in the Northern Hemisphere" (*New York Times* 1985a). As a result, the International Council of Scientific Union concluded in 1985 that those surviving the explosions and fallout of a nuclear war would ultimately die of starvation.[26] Undoubtedly, as Robert Lifton (1967) discovered when interviewing the survivors of Hiroshima, those remaining would identify so thoroughly with the dead that they would feel dead themselves.

In late 1943, the USS *Iowa* left its American port secretly carrying the president of the United States, the Army chief of staff, and many of the president's aides and military command to a historic rendezvous with Stalin and Churchill in the Middle East. On the second day, a warning blared as a torpedo homed in on the vessel and barely missed sending the president and his entourage to the bottom of the sea. The weapon, as it turned out, had not been fired from a Nazi U-boat but rather from an American destroyer (Newton 1984). Such stories of human error, of the inability of people to responsibly manage new, complex systems, fuel the fears of possibly how our collective suicide will be initiated.[27] Nuclear war is simply too irrational an alternative for the superpowers to intentionally conduct, but, with increasing reliance on computers and sophisticated technologies, the possibility of accidents increases tremendously. Observed David Frisch, a physicist and participant in the Trinity test of the first atomic bomb: "Our escape from the large costs of conventional defenses into nuclear fantasies can best be described as a religious belief with a creed and rituals that extol nuclear superiority. For

Table 9.4 A Nuclear Balance Sheet: The Two Sides' Arsenals

United States	Soviet Union
STRATEGIC FORCES	
1025 ballistic missiles with total of 2125 warheads	1398 ballistic missiles with total of 6420 warheads
36 submarines with 640 missiles with a total of 5728 warheads	62 submarines with 924 missiles with a total of 2688 warheads
263 B-52 bombers (98 of which carry 12 air-launched cruise missiles each) with a total of 3072 warheads	173 bombers (25 with 10 air-launched cruise missiles each) with a total of 792 warheads
61 FB-111 bombers with a total of 366 warheads	
EUROPEAN THEATER FORCES	
About 90 Pershing 2's with 1 warhead each	270 SS-20's with 3 warheads each; 171 others aimed at Asia but could be moved to European theater
128 ground-launched cruise missiles with 1 warhead each	
(*The allies:* Britain has 64 missiles with up to 3 warheads each on 4 submarines. France has 18 land-based missiles with 1 warhead each and 176 warheads on 6 submarines.)	
222 bombers with a total of about 850 warheads	884 bombers with a total of 3536 bombs
1417 tactical fighter bombers with a total of 3140 bombs. (*The allies:* Britain has 25 bombers with 2 bombs each; France has 28 bombers with 1 bomb each.)	2500 tactical fighter bombers with a total of 4800 bombs.

Sources: Pentagon publications, International Institute for Strategic Studies, Arms Control Association, Center for Defense Information. (*New York Times* 1985b) Copyright © 1985 by the New York Times Company. Reprinted by permission.

example, the U.S. space defense initiatives proposal props up faith by promises of salvation" (Maverick 1985). Another scenario of the contemporary military eschatology foresees the first nuclear war not between the United States and the Soviet Union but rather between such traditionally hostile nations as India and Pakistan, Iran and Iraq, or Israel and Libya (Rosenberg 1984). By early 1987, there were eight countries producing nuclear weapons, three countries suspected of having them, and more than thirty additional countries expected to have nuclear capability before the year 2000.

As we saw in the case of religion, we have a tendency to honor and pray to the forces that kill us. In the late 1970s, the Japanese reacted with anger and disbelief when the atomic bombing of Hiroshima was reenacted—com-

Ringed by naval warships, an enormous mushroom cloud provides a stark and violent contrast to the palm trees and straw huts of the Bikini Islands during an atomic test in 1946. The Bettmann Archive, Inc.

plete with an imitation mushroom cloud—at a Confederate Air Force show in Texas. One Japanese diplomat likened his country's dismay to the American reaction if Japanese veterans were to restage the Bataan death march. American Catholic bishops declared in 1983: "After the passage of nearly four decades and a concomitant growth in our understanding of the ever growing horror of nuclear war, we must shape the climate of opinion which will make it possible for our country to express profound sorrow over the atomic bombings in 1945. Without that sorrow there is no possibility of finding a way to repudiate future use of nuclear weapons" (cited in Boyer 1985, p. 26). Such sorrow has never come. And the United States remains the only country to have killed individuals with a nuclear weapon.[28]

Conclusion

The nightmares associated with the approaching millennium are not of the Deluge but rather of humanity purging earth of all life without any assistance from nature or the Almighty. As seen in this chapter, instead of addressing the problems of an increasingly populated, hungry, and troubled world, governments have chosen to spend trillions of dollars designing and perfecting the means by which to kill each other's citizens. And despite the fact that nuclear weapons have made war totally irrational, entire political economies continue to be organized around their development, production, deployment, and justification.

The United States legitimizes its military buildup not only in the name of self-defense but also to ensure peace and human rights. And yet it was not until 1986 that the United States approved the 1948 genocide treaty,[29] which makes the mass killing of an ethnic, racial, or religious group an international crime and calls on the signers to punish those responsible for any pogrom. The accord, called the Convention on the Prevention and Punishment of the Crime of Genocide, had already been signed by ninety-six nations, including France (1950), the Soviet Union and West Germany (1954), and Britain (1970). Further, although the Western allies make the Soviet Union the scapegoat for the proliferation of nuclear weapons, it has been the export of their own technology and fuel that has given Israel, South Africa, India, and Pakistan the capability of building their own bombs (Subak 1984).

Some think that with the advent of nuclear weapons, peace will be forever safeguarded, as their use would mean not only collective suicide but the death of the entire natural order. However, though other military innovations have held similar promises, there never has been a weapon developed that has not been utilized. As Arnold Toynbee observed in *A Study of History*, when people prepared for war there was war.

NOTES

1. Reflecting on his experiences as a journalist on the front in World War II, Andy Rooney observed that we normally live at 50 percent, and only in war does that experience total 100 percent (ABC News 1987).

2. Perhaps the seemingly greater scars of the Vietnam veterans were a result, in part, of their lesser maturity. The average age of a U.S. recruit for World War II was twenty-six years versus nineteen years for Vietnam.

3. Interestingly, for many warriors, the hatred for those able to remain at home is greater than for the enemy (Dyer 1985).

4. In the early days of the Vietnam conflict, one indicator of field success was measured in terms of the body count. In 1965, after political demands for results, the remains of Viet Cong victims were brought out of the battlefields by American helicopters to prove the count. Soldiers got the "numbers," whatever was required and whoever had to be killed.

5. Ironically, such attention is not guaranteed to those who survive. The National Association of Radiation Survivors, a veterans' group comprised of those exposed to life-threatening doses of nuclear radiation while occupying Hiroshima and Nagasaki, Japan, found that the Veterans Administration had destroyed thousands of documents it had been subpoenaed to produce in a lawsuit. Needing expensive legal assistance to press their claims, the group found that it faced a ten-dollar limit on lawyers' fees—a restriction set by a Civil War–era law (Lindsey 1987).

6. Rosenthal (1985, p. 17) notes that 78,751 American soldiers were missing or unaccounted for following World War II, and another 8177 MIAs were produced by the Korean War, yet neither prompted the widespread protests and demands for government inquiries as did the 2477 men categorized as MIAs following Vietnam.

7. The leftover chunks of stone were to have the sacred immanence of the whole, like the relics of the cross. Granite Industries of Vermont capitalized on this as it began selling these stones for $250 each.

8. An eleven-month study of television programs conducted between 1974 and 1975 found twenty episodes involving the violence of the returning Vietnam veteran. But the myth is not without foundation. A 1973 survey of the U.S. Bureau of Prisons found nearly one-third of the men imprisoned had histories of military service.

9. As discussed in Chapter 6, the approach of endings unleashes a host of new dynamics, and those in exit are "no longer themselves." In Vietnam, this phenomenon became the stuff of the myth of "buying it short" (Herr 1978). Raw recruits, "breathing in" before submerging into the warrior role, immediately learned the countdown game until they could "breathe out" with discharge. In the field, many soldiers wore ETS dates (estimated time of severance) on their helmets to show not only their role seniority but also their time left in an undesirable role. To "be short" meant to have little time left in the field and was associated with the aberration of survival skills and ironic deaths. So potent became the self-fulfilling nature of this myth that the military withdrew those frontline combatants who were short to support roles at unscheduled times in an attempt to thwart this ending dynamic.

10. This is not to deny the existence of painful lifelong wounds inflicted during other wars. Exposures to mustard gas during World War I continue to catch up with and kill a generation of warriors. From World War II have emerged various death clubs. The Atomic Veterans, for example, come from the quarter of a million men exposed to the radiation of nuclear testings; this is an organization devoted to discovering why its members are dying prematurely.

11. The biological metaphors for understanding war continue to be employed. In *The Pursuit of Power* (1982), historian William McNeill equates the study of the organization of military power to the study of macroparasitism among human populations.

12. See Sue Mansfield (1982) for a development of how each civilization develops a characteristic rationale and style of battle that reflects its view of the self, the social order, and the cosmos. Nevertheless, it still primarily boils down to the preservation of national interests.

13. The more powerful the military, the greater its ability to convince the broader society of a "worst-case scenario" of the abilities and intentions of its adversaries.

14. In the United States, there is a tendency to collectively remember or be aware of only such applications of the enemy, such as Hitler's testing of the war plane against the innocent civilians of Guernica, Spain. But Americans, too, have let their innovations generate atrocities. In the early days of the Korean War, for example, the commander of the British 7th Squadron, Sir Scott Mount Crief, had never seen 16-inch guns fire and wanted to know their destructive power. The U.S. admiral aboard the USS *New Jersey*, the flagship of the 7th Fleet, obliged. The fleet sailed to the west coast of Korea, and Crief was put into a helicopter, which flew sixteen to eighteen miles inland, to watch as the *New Jersey* fired a nine-gun salvo, totally demolishing a small Korean town.

15. During World War I, chemical weapons caused approximately one million casualties, including ninety thousand deaths. A British officer made the following vivid description of the horrors of a chemical weapons attack: "Try to imagine the . . . troops as they saw the vast cloud of greenish-yellow gas spring out of the ground and slowly move downwind toward them, the vapor clinging to the earth, seeking out every hole and hollow. . . . First wonder, then fear; then as the first fringes of the cloud enveloped them and left them choking and agonized in the fight for breath—panic" (Adelman 1985). Despite the international sense of atrocity regarding such weapons, their use has continued to the present day. Italy used gas in Ethiopia in 1936; Japan in China in 1937; Egypt in Yemen in 1963–67; the Soviet Union in Laos, Cambodia, and Afghanistan in the late 1970s and early 1980s; and Iran against Iraq in the mid-1980s (*New Republic* 1984).

16. It is worth noting that with the evolution of "total war," attacks on ships—total social systems unto themselves and the source of the "ship of state" metaphor—have been used to justify American military involvements: the sinking of the *Maine* signaled the start of the Spanish American War, the sinking of the *Lusitania* eroded American isolationism and led to entry into World War I, the Japanese attack on Pearl Harbor forced the country into World War II, and the firing on the USS *Turner Joy* in the Gulf of Tonkin was used to legitimize a vast buildup in the Vietnam War.

17. It was recently revealed that high-level Americans covered up these experiments, agreeing not to prosecute Japanese for this war crime in exchange for the research results acquired (reminiscent of the Nazis who were to be employed by NASA). Underlying this deal was American and English fear of falling behind the Soviet Union, Germany, and Japan in biological warfare research. If these Japanese were to be tried, Russia would inevitably ask for the results (*New Republic* 1984).

18. However, in late 1983, the U.S. Senate approved funds for the resumption of production of nerve gas weapons, which had been halted by President Nixon in 1969. In 1984, President Reagan requested 1.126 billion dollars for chemical warfare pro-

grams, and the following year Congress renounced the U.S. moratorium on their production.

19. The Japanese detonations may not have been designed to end the war as was publicly advertised but, according to some historians, were rather a warning for the Soviet Union (see Werth 1964, pp. 1027–45). William Leahy, a five-star admiral and chief of staff to President Truman, claimed that "the use of this barbarous weapon . . . was of no material assistance in our war against Japan. The Japanese were already defeated" (Maverick 1985).

20. President Nixon had terminated the production of these weapons in 1969, saying that the country would abide by the Geneva protocol of 1925 banning the first use of poison gas. Though President Ford eventually signed the protocol (Tolchin 1983), the treaty was not ratified by the Senate until the mid-1980s.

21. However, public relations demonstrations suggest anything is possible. Within one week in September of 1985, a "weapons grade" chemical laser destroyed a stationary Titan 2 intercontinental nuclear missile, and an antisatellite missile, fired from an F-15 jet, directly hit the target satellite.

22. However, during the 1980s, a number of professional groups have emerged addressing the ethical issues of performing defense work, such as the Center for Economic Conversion, Peacework Alternatives, High Technology Professionals for Peace, Computer Professionals for Social Responsibility, and the Union of Concerned Scientists (Ansberry 1986).

23. According to a study by the Congressional Budget Office, new fighter planes typically cost two or three times more than their predecessors. The reason is not surprising when considering the innovations the Air Force requested for its Advanced Tactical Fighter to be produced before the turn of the century: voice-activated controls to allow pilots to operate their weapons without having to remove their hands from the controls, technology making the plane nearly invisible to enemy radar, instrument panels that can be read even if there are nuclear flashes, and an internal oxygen-generating system that would allow the plane to operate in environments contaminated by nuclear fallout or biological weapons (Keller 1985).

24. In 1985, the Italian cruise ship *Achille Lauro* was hijacked by Palestinians in the Mediterranean. It was, indeed, an Achilles heel, the first ship hijacked in twenty-five years.

25. According to a 1986 report of the International Task Force on the Prevention of Terrorism, "the probability of nuclear terrorism is increasing" because of the vulnerability to sabotage of nuclear power plants and research reactors and the fact that many U.S. nuclear weapons, particularly the thousands of short-range devices stored throughout the world, fail to have safety devices to prevent unauthorized explosion (*New York Times* 1986).

26. There is, however, still considerable controversy over the likelihood of this "secular apocalypse" (Seitz 1986). The entire scenario is a product of computer simulations, limited scientific objectivity, pacifists' desires to dramatize the horrors of nuclear war, and the reluctance of skeptics to question the results out of fears of being labeled as hawks.

27. In 1984, to dramatize this equivalency of nuclear war with suicide, undergraduates at Brown University voted on urging the school's health service to stockpile "suicide pills" in case of a nuclear exchange (*New York Times* 1984b).

28. President Eisenhower made the decision to use atomic bombs in North Korea and Communist China, if necessary, to end the Korean War (Gwertzman 1984). To this day, nuclear arms remain in South Korea, and the United States retains the right to use them in defense of an all-out attack from the north.

29. Among those groups opposing U.S. passage were the Daughters of the American Revolution, the American Legion, the Liberty Lobby, the John Birch Society, and, until 1976, the American Bar Association (Sciolino 1984).

REFERENCES

ABC News. 1987. "The Summer of 1944." *Our World* (April 9).

Adelman, Kenneth. 1985. "Again, the Scourge of Chemical Weapons: Credible Deterrent Needed." *New York Times.* August 19, p. 19.

Alexander, Yonah, and Seymour M. Finger. 1977. *Terrorism: Interdisciplinary Perspectives.* New York: John Jay Press.

Ansberry, Clare. 1986. "In the Star Wars Era, Scientists Grow Warier about Jobs in Defense." *Wall Street Journal.* July 11, pp. 1, 7.

Archer, Dane, and Rosemary Gartner. 1976. "Violent Acts and Violent Times: A Comparative Approach to Postwar Homicide Rates." *American Sociological Review* 41(6):937–63.

Bacon, Francis. 1910. "Of the True Greatness of Kingdoms." *The Harvard Classics* III. Ed. by Charles Eliot. New York: P. F. Collier & Son.

Berger, Peter. 1977. "Languages of Murder." In Peter Berger, ed., *Facing Up to Modernity: Excursions in Society, Politics, and Religion.* New York: Basic Books, pp. 83–94.

Boyer, Paul. 1985. "The Cloud over the Culture." *New Republic.* August 12 & 19, pp. 26–31.

Broad, William. 1985. "New Atomic Weapons Are Being Designed at a Furious Pace." *New York Times.* July 16, pp. C1, C6.

Browne, Malcolm. 1985. "100 Years of Maxim's 'Killing Machine.'" *New York Times.* November 26, pp. 17, 20.

Brozan, Nadine. 1986. "Feminist Says Sexual Equality in Israel Is Illusory." *New York Times.* February 21, p. 23.

Campbell, Colin. 1985. "Line of Song Provides a Clue on Ancient Troy." *New York Times.* January 2, pp. 1, 8.

Chagnon, Napoleon. 1988. "Life Histories, Blood Revenge, and Warfare in a Tribal Population." *Science* 239:985–92.

Chavez, Lydia. 1984. "Argentina Detailing Army's 'Dirty War.'" *New York Times.* September 21, p. 3.

Dyer, Gwynne. 1985. *War.* New York: Crown.

Eringer, Robert. 1986. "Secret Agent Man." *Rolling Stone.* January 16, pp. 20–24, 41.

Farney, Dennis. 1985. "Famed Psychiatrist Analyzes the World, Finds It Needs Help." *Wall Street Journal.* December 23, pp. 1, 9.

Feron, James. 1984. "Indian Links Poverty to World Spending on Arms." *New York Times.* September 28, p. 1.

Franklin, Ben. 1987. "Veterans of Vietnam Found to Have a High Death Rate." *New York Times.* February 11, p. 8.

Freud, Sigmund. 1959. "Thoughts for the Times on War and Death." In *Collected Papers,* Vol. 4. New York: Basic Books.

Galbraith, John Kenneth. 1982. *East/West Outlook* (September). Reprinted in *New York Times,* October 14, p. 14.

Gerth, Jeff. 1985a. "Pentagon Worried over Cost of Weapons Manuals." *New York Times.* April 1, p. 11.

———. 1985b. "U.S. Weapons Makers Ring Up Healthy Profits." *New York Times.* April 9, p. 29.

Gist, Adlum. 1947. *Love and War in the Middle English Romances.* Philadelphia: University of Pennsylvania Press.

Gwertzman, Bernard. 1984. "U.S. Files Tell of '53 Policy on Using A-Bomb in Korea." *New York Times.* June 8, p. 9.

Hammer, Richard. 1971. *The Court-Martial of Lt. Calley.* New York: Coward, McCann, and Geoghegan.

Harris, Marvin. 1979. *Cultural Materialism: The Struggle for a Science of Culture.* New York: Random House.

Hearst, Norman, Thomas Newman, and Steven Hulley. 1986. "Delayed Effects of the Military Draft on Mortality." *New England Journal of Medicine.* March 6, pp. 620–23.

Herr, Michael. 1978. *Dispatches.* New York: Alfred A. Knopf.

Hoffer, Eric. 1951. *The True Believer.* New York: Harper.

Holmes, Richard. 1985. *Acts of War: The Behavior of Men in Battle.* New York: Free Press.

Isaacson, Walter. 1983. "The Winds of Reform." *Time.* March 7, pp. 12–30.

James, William. 1964. "The Moral Equivalent of War." In *War: Studies from Psychology, Sociology, Anthropology.* New York: Basic Books.

Keller, Bill. 1985. "Air Force Superplane Found Costly. *New York Times.* April 26, p. 7.

Lamm, Richard. 1987. "The Uncompetitive Society." *Dartmouth Alumni Magazine* (May):32–36.

Lifton, Robert. 1967. *Death in Life: Survivors of Hiroshima.* New York: Random House.

Lindsey, Robert. 1987. "Veterans Agency Draws Fire for Destroying Data in Suit." *New York Times.* January 9, pp. 1, 9.

Lorenz, Konrad. 1966. *On Aggression,* trans. by M. K. Wilson. New York: Harcourt.

McLuhan, Marshall. 1968. *War and Peace in the Global Village.* New York: McGraw-Hill.

McNeill, Robert. 1982. *The Pursuit of Power: Technology, Armed Force, and Society since A.D. 1000.* Chicago: University of Chicago Press.

Mansfield, Susan. 1982. *The Gestalts of War: An Inquiry into Its Origins and Meanings as a Social Institution.* New York: Dial Press.

Maverick, Maury. 1985. "A-Bomb Began Cold War." *San Antonio Express-News.* September 29, p. 3M.

Mohr, Charles. 1985. "Missile Shield Held to Raise Risk of a Nuclear War." *New York Times.* September 25, pp. 1, 13.

Moyers, Bill. 1984. "The Arming of the Earth." PBS series, *A Walk through the 20th Century with Bill Moyers* (February).

Mumford, Lewis. 1946. "Gentlemen, You Are Mad!" *Saturday Review of Literature.* March 2, pp. 5–6.

New Republic. 1984. "Bad Chemistry." May 21, pp. 7–9.

New York Times. 1982. "Big Winners in Construction of the MX." December 7, p. 29.

———. 1984a. "U.S. Share in Arms to 3d World Rose." May 14, pp. 1, 14.

———. 1984b. "Brown Students Vote on Atom War 'Suicide Pills.'" October 11, p. 10.

———. 1984c. "Transcript of the Reagan-Mondale Debate on Foreign Policy." October 22, pp. B4–B6.

———. 1985a. "Famine Foreseen in 'Nuclear Winter.'" September 13, p. 14.

———. 1985b. "A Nuclear Balance Sheet: The 2 Sides' Arsenals." October 4, p. A12.

———. 1986. "Nuclear Terrorism Is Studied." June 26, p. 6.

Newton, Verne. 1984. "Lessons of the U.S.S. Iowa." *New York Times* November 6, p. 27.

O'Boyle, Thomas. 1986. "Moscow Is Said to Plan Big Role for Tox Gas in a European Conflict." *Wall Street Journal.* June 12, pp. 1, 12.

A Report from Iron Mountain: On the Possibility and Desirability of Peace, intro. by Leonard Lewin. 1967. New York: Dial Press.

Richards, Bill, and Tim Carrington. 1986. "Controversy Grows over Pentagon's Work on Biological Agents." *Wall Street Journal.* September 17, pp. 1, 20.

Rosenberg, Tina. 1984. "Bumbling Bomb Squad." *New Republic.* December 17, pp. 18–21.

Rosenthal, James. 1985. "The Myth of the Lost POWs." *New Republic.* July 1, pp. 15–19.

San Antonio Express-News [AP]. 1980. "Navy Gunners Have Difficulty Sinking Coffin." August 30, p. 5A.

———. 1985a. "Widow Wants Husband Remembered." March 4, p. 12B.

———. 1985b. "A-bomb Bosses Eyed Poison, Too." April 19, p. 16A.

———. 1987. "Rambo Mentality Motivates Warriors." November 18, p. 5F.

Schlesinger, Arthur. 1985. "Last Shot to End the Arms Race?" *Wall Street Journal.*
    October 7, p. 22.
Sciolino, Elaine. 1984. "World Accord on Genocide: An Issue since Truman Era."
    New York Times. September 6, p. 6.
Seitz, Russell. 1986. "The Melting of 'Nuclear Winter.'" *Wall Street Journal.*
    November 5, p. 30.
Shenon, Philip. 1985. "Vietnam War Memorial to Get 300 More Names." *New York
    Times.* April 13, p. 7.
Sherry, Michael. 1981. "The Slide to Total Air War." *New Republic.* December 16,
    pp. 18–25.
Shurkin, Joel. 1988. "Modern Terrorists Are 'Anemic.'" *Stanford Observer.* February,
    p. 6.
Sivard, Ruth. 1985. *World Military and Social Expenditures 1985.* Washington, D.C.:
    World Priorities.
Smith, Timothy. 1985. "In Alabama's Woods, Frank Camper Trains Men to Repel
    Invaders." *Wall Street Journal.* August 19, pp. 1, 6.
Subak, Susan. 1984. "The Soviet Union's Nuclear Realism." *New Republic.* December
    17, p. 19.
Tolchin, Martin. 1983. "Bush Breaks Tie Again as Senate Approves Producing of
    Nerve Gas." *New York Times.* November 9, pp. 1, 9.
Toynbee, Arnold. 1950. *War and Civilization.* New York: Oxford University Press.
Weiss, Stanley. 1986. "The Complex Meaning of Ike's Famous Talk." *Wall Street
    Journal.* January 17, p. 14.
Wellborn, Stanley. 1985. "Sons of Star Wars: Fallout of a Huge Project." *U.S. News
    & World Report.* December 9, pp. 48–50.
Werth, Alexander. 1964. *Russia at War.* New York: E. P. Dutton.
Wieseltier, Leon. 1983. "The Great Nuclear Debate." *New Republic.* January 10 &
    17, pp. 7–38.
Wolfe, Tom. 1982. "Battle of the D.C. Vietnam Memorial: It's Being Called 'A Trib-
    ute to Jane Fonda.'" *San Antonio Light.* October 24, pp. 1K, 3K.

Chapter 10

Death in Popular Culture

Previous chapters have detailed a number of social processes contributing to the American death ethos. We considered, for instance, the religious and philosophical foundations of cultural death denials and how the causes of premature death have historically shifted from natural to man-made. We noted how the ethos of violence was historically spawned by the frontier and is currently being reinforced by a culture of poverty, how the controversies over capital punishment and abortion shape the politics of the day, and how a confluence of interests fuels an unrelenting drive to perfect military instruments for mass death. These sources of death-related messages are not, however, necessarily the social vehicles by which they are conveyed to the general public. More people, for example, have learned of the out-of-body experiences of the dying or of homicidal urges from the popular media than from medical or philosophical journals. Stories of death are increasingly filtered by various intermediaries and social interpreters. Here we will examine these messages and their media.

Apart from rare firsthand experiences with mortality, the death lessons of modern individuals are primarily received from television, cinema, newspapers, and the arts. No longer directly exposed to natural death (of both humans and, increasingly, large animals), people generally learn only of atypical deaths, as only they qualify as being either newsworthy or entertaining. Further, as Marshall McLuhan argued, the form of each medium brings its own message. Each peculiarly distorts the lesson as each differentially affects our cognitive habits, reshaping the traffic of symbols and experiences from which we derive meaning. "Hot" media (McLuhan 1967), such as books and records, allow for less sensory involvement and participation than is the case for "cool" media, such as television and cinema, where more senses are involved and where feeling is more likely to be interwoven with thought. The cooler the media through which cultural death themes are broadly disseminated—which has been the historical trend—the greater death's ability to control attention, to frighten, or to galvanize public opinion for some cause.

Endings in Mass Media and the Arts

There are a number of ways by which researchers can approach death's role in mass media and the arts. First, they can speculate on the cultural context stimulating the performances. Artists are a product of their times and perhaps are more sensitive than most to shifts in cultural concerns or the unfolding of social events. Second, researchers can analyze the patterns of death themes developed within various media, specifically content analyzing longitudinal patterns in who dies, how they die, where, and when, as well as the centrality of death to the entire presentation. Third, the death orientations of the artist can be studied, examining how the individual's biographical experiences, age, preoccupations, and immortality urges motivated the direction of his or her artistic expression. And finally, researchers can gauge how an audience is affected by the death messages presented, such as the studies of the collective hysteria spawned by Orson Welles's 1936 radio broadcast of "The War of the Worlds" or testing the conventional wisdom that excessive media death desensitizes the viewer to the tragedy that death actually brings.

As developed in Chapter 6, dying cultures tend to spawn unparalleled cultural creativity. In part, as Harold Innis speculates (1951), this may be a result of the weakening of social authority, producing a certain energy and spontaneity unleashed in the face of chaos. In *The Third Man,* for instance, Orson Welles observes that thirty years of warfare, terror, and bloodshed in medieval Italy produced the Renaissance, whereas five hundred years of peace and democracy in Switzerland produced the cuckoo clock. In speaking of the surge of creativity in war-ravaged Lebanon, Charles Rizk, president of Lebanon's state-run television system, reflected: "A political shock is always pregnant with cultural achievement. When simply walking down the street becomes a matter of life and death, people start to ask themselves very fundamental questions. And what is culture if not expressions of man's questioning himself about his ultimate destiny?" (Friedman 1982).

Shifts in the use and nature of thanatological themes in the arts also occur in reflection of changes occurring within the various institutional spheres of social life. Fears of ecological destruction following the first detonations of hydrogen bombs, for instance, led to the 1950s genre of science fiction movies which featured mutated creatures preying on the remnants of the human race. The moral upheavals in the United States following the Vietnam War,

Watergate, and the changing life-styles and values of the young undoubtedly contributed to the public fascination with evil, producing a receptive climate for such demonic movies as *The Exorcist* and *The Omen*. And the increasing cultural violence and homicide rates during the late 1970s and early 1980s stimulated a genre of revenge movies, such as the "Dirty Harry" and Charles Bronson series, just as the militarism of World War II produced an abundance of war valor movies.

Rare is literature in which death does not function as a central motif or plot device. For Hemingway, a writer obsessed with violence and death, it was the bullfight. In *The Dangerous Summer*, he writes:

> Any man can face death, but to bring it as close as possible while performing certain classic movements and do this again and again and again and then deal it out yourself with a sword to an animal weighing half a ton which you love is more complicated than just facing death. It is facing your performance as a creative artist each day and your necessity to function as a skillful killer. (1985, p. 141)

The various arts reflect, reinforce, and shape the death fears existent within a culture at any given time. Of creators and performers, sociologists Hans Gerth and C. Wright Mills observed: "skill groups, such as poets and novelists, specialize in fashioning and developing vocabularies for emotional states and gestures; they specialize in telling us how we feel, as well as how we should or might feel, in various situations" (1953, p. 56). To categorize their thanatological themes, one could locate a novel, television show, or song on the following continuums: death as incidental or central theme, death as tragedy or comedy, the degree of death's realism versus abstractness, and whether death serves a didactic or cathartic function for the audience.

Given the importance of the artist's role in molding a culture's orientation to dying and grief, considerable social attention is often given to how the artist approaches and manages his or her own death. Facing old age and diminishing powers, Hemingway took his own life with the blast of a rifle. Yukio Mishima, a Japanese author and Nobel Prize contender, ritually disemboweled himself before being decapitated by his chief lieutenant following the failure of his radical militarist movement. We remember Rupert Brooke not only because of his poetry on war but also because of the fact that he was himself one of the casualties of World War I. Finally, it is worth noting that of all work forms (see Chapter 7), the products of these "skill groups" that Gerth and Mills discussed perhaps give these individuals a greater chance for immortality than is the case for most. Their memories are preserved in the literature they write, the records they record, and the celluloid on which their acting talents are captured.

Finally, there is the issue of the media's impacts on the audience. As we

65

29. Maaler und Kunstverwandte.

Conrad Meyer's "Death and the Artists," from Rudolf Meyer's *Sterbespiegel* (Mirror of the Dying), printed in Zurich in 1650. Dover Pictorial Archives.

saw in Chapter 4, the sheer reporting of a suicide is correlated with subsequent increases in the rates of suicides and fatal accidents involving automobiles and aircraft. Political systems obviously believe such messages can have profound consequences: in the United States, congressional hearings have been conducted on the impacts of television and popular music on the homicidal and suicidal behaviors of children, and in England, the proeuthanasia group Exit was forbidden to publish its handbook on how to commit suicide. From the 1985 General Social Survey ($n = 1534$) of the American public conducted by the National Opinion Research Center (1986), it can be demonstrated that the average number of hours of television watched daily and the frequency of reading newspapers are significantly related to the attitudes viewers have toward such death-related issues as euthanasia, capital punishment, suicide, and abortion. In particular, even taking into account individuals' age, education, sex, and intensity of religious beliefs, with increasing hours of television watched, people are more likely to favor capital punishment and euthanasia.[1] Further, the likelihood of one supporting the right of a terminally ill patient to end his or her own life or of one endorsing the right of a woman to have an abortion upon demand increases with the frequency of newspaper reading.

This chapter's discussion is confined to the role of death in television, cinema, music, and sports. Appreciating the impossibility of exhausting the ending themes of even these media, the attempt here is merely to suggest the scope of the subject matter and the methodological strategies for approaching it.

Death and Television

The year is 1980, and you are an executive with either NBC or CBS television. Your opposition, ABC, is carrying the Olympics. What do you show in order to enhance ratings and thereby keep the costs of your commercials up? <u>Death</u>. In fact, during that Olympics week, the following programs were shown:

- *Sunday and Monday*. NBC: *Towering Inferno,* two parts. CBS: *Exorcist I* and *Exorcist II.*
- *Tuesday*. NBC: *The End* (advertised with the line, "Think of Death as a Pie in the Face from God").
- *Wednesday*. CBS: *The Escape.*
- *Thursday*. CBS: One of America's favorite coroners, *Quincy.*
- *Friday*. NBC: *Detour to Terror.*

By the age of sixteen, according to the National Institute of Mental Health, the typical American has witnessed some eighteen thousand homicides on television. These killings come in various guises, energizing the plots of conflicts between cowboys and Indians, cops and robbers, earthlings and aliens, as well as between the living and the dead. These homicides are packaged either individually, such as when the good guy outdraws and kills the outlaw, or collectively, as when an entire populated planet is destroyed by Darth Vader. Even the advertisements carry thanatological messages: there's Charlie Tuna, who desires to be hooked and cannibalized by Starkist purchasers (slightly reminiscent of a Tennessee Williams play). The trade journal *Adweek* noted that "for some arcane reason, if you're in the business of creating TV commercials, funerals are funny. So is the reading of last wills and testaments" (1984). What are the consequences of young receptive minds absorbing so many lessons in death? One fifteen-year-old youth, accused of murdering an eighty-three-year-old woman in her Miami Beach home, held the defense that he had become intoxicated with violence from watching violent television. Though the jury was not convinced, the case marked an interesting precedent and further legitimized the belief that we are all possibly subconsciously susceptible to media influences.

In considering the symbolic messages implicit within such presentations, George Gerbner claims that death "is just another invented characterization, a negative resource, a sign of fatal flaw or ineptitude, a punishment for sins or mark of tragedy" (1980, p. 66). In addition, the medium's death lessons are unwittingly "calculated to cultivate a sense of insecurity, anxiety, fear of the 'mean world' out there, and dependence on some strong protector" (p. 66). So who is most likely to kill, and who is most likely to die? In Gerbner's sample of television programs between 1969 and 1978, women and minorities were most vulnerable. In Table 10.1, we see the ratios of killers to vic-

Table 10.1 Killer/Killed Ratios for Major Characters in Television Programs between 1969 and 1978

	All characters	Males	Females
All characters	1.90	2.02	1.20
Age			
Children, adolescents	3.00	3.00	none
Young adults	2.00	2.17	1.33
Settled adults	2.07	2.13	1.60
Elderly	0.57	1.00	only victims
Social class			
Clearly upper	1.50	1.57	1.25
Mixed	2.07	2.20	1.20
Clearly lower	0.90	0.83	1.00
Race			
White	1.97	2.11	1.26
Other	1.69	1.60	none
Character type			
"Good"	2.93	3.85	0.62
Mixed	1.33	1.27	1.50
"Bad"	1.84	1.86	1.67

Source: Gerbner 1980, p. 68. From Gerbner, George, "Death in Prime Time: Notes on the Symbolic Functions of Dying in the Mass Media." The Annals. January, 1980, p. 68. Copyright © 1980 by The Annals. Reprinted by permission of Sage Publications, Inc.

tims, which Gerbner interprets to be an indicator of power. The smaller the ratio, the more likely a group is to be a victim rather than a victor. Also evident in the table, the "good" characters are more likely to be victors than the "bad," whites are more likely than nonwhites, the young are more likely than the old (the latter, whose ratio is less than 1.00, indicates a greater number of aged victims than aged aggressors—as opposed to adolescents, among whom there are three times as many killers as victims), and the upper class are more likely than the lower class. In another study, Gerbner found on prime-time television shows that scientists have the highest mortality rate of any professional group, with one in ten being killed (Blakeslee 1985). Rarely is the audience allowed any identification with these victims, and rarer still is any sign of grief following their demise. Further, those killed have a tendency to reappear on other shows—an important lesson in death denial for the young viewer.

In addition to the action programs, sit-coms, and soap operas, death is a frequent theme of the feature-magazine-format shows, the disease-of-the-month telethons, comedy (NBC's *Saturday Night Live* comes to mind), and children's cartoons (Gerbner [1980, p. 67] reported an average of five violent incidents per hour during prime time and eighteen per hour in weekend daytime children's programming). When television handles the actual deaths of public figures, Michael Arlen notes that "for the most part, . . . what it commonly does is to attend briskly and meticulously to the *famousness* of the departed, and to leave the death, and everything that humanly has to do with death, at arm's length" (1975, p. 76).

The greatest density of televised death stories is to be found on the evening news. Death is news, and it attracts viewers just as it sells newspapers. The day of the space shuttle *Challenger* explosion, the regular network evening newscasts scored a combined rating of 40 in twelve major markets, compared to a 30 rating the preceding week (*New York Times* 1986). As the medium evolved, it discovered the difference, say, between reporting one hundred air-crash fatalities and actually recording a single disaster. Editorial taste dictated whether the camera's lens was focused on the covered corpses being carried from the scene of the accident or on the human fragments intertwined in the wreckage. But technological innovation and growing public callousness toward televised death was to inflate the visual requirements. The synchronization of the Vietnam War with the development and dispersal of color television and satellite relays produced a new death experience: live war deaths during the supper hour. Certainly, the ability to capture death on a visual medium is a major accomplishment of technology, timing, and skill. The crash of the *Hindenburg* remains, after half a century, a clear and terri-

TV Mistake Turns Joy to Sadness

Scott Crull, a 12-year-old Chicago Cubs fan, was elated as his idol Bobby Murcer clobbered a home run against the Pittsburgh Pirates on nationwide television Monday night.

Murcer had telephoned Scott earlier in the day, saying he would try to hit a homer for the bed-ridden youth.

Just after the blast, ABC-TV sportscaster Keith Jackson announced the home run was hit for young Scott, who Jackson said was dying of cancer.

This was the first time the boy had heard of his condition.

Scott was placed under sedation in his home in suburban Calumet City, stunned by the knowledge that he has had cancer for at least three years and has less than two months to live.

Coder 1977. Reprinted by permission
San Antonio Light © 1977.

fying experience, with most Americans having witnessed the famous news-reel footage of the crash and heard the terror in the voice of the commentator on the spot.

Since the mid-1970s, Americans have witnessed a local newscaster committing suicide during the evening news, Los Angeles police killing members of the Symbionese Liberation Army during a 1975 shootout (carried live and commercial-free on California television stations), and the presence of television cameras perhaps inciting South African blacks to even further violence against the apartheid regime. So necessary has the staple of death become on the evening news that people object if certain deaths are not adequately covered. In 1985, Puerto Ricans complained that the American news media gave limited coverage to the mud slide that had killed five hundred of their people, "as if it had taken place in a far-off country" (Campbell 1985).[2]

The medium is not incapable of showing real death and real grief. In 1976, WGBH of Boston aired a documentary entitled *Dying*. Said producer-director Michael Roemer, "You can't learn to die as though it were a skill. People die in the way they have lived. Death becomes the expression of everything you are, and you can bring it only what you have brought to your life" (*Time* 1976). The show began with an interview of a young widow whose husband, age twenty-nine, had been diagnosed as having lymphosarcoma. She said of the day of his death: "in a strange way it was a good day. We were able to share things. I read to Mark. I gave him his last bath. Then early in the evening he kissed me and said, 'Let's call it quits, Pooh.' And he died about half an hour later." The program also revealed the wrenching aspects of death, such as for a woman in her early thirties who, feeling frustrated and angered by her husband's mortal illness, could only make him feel guilty for dying and leaving her with two sons to raise. Such shows, however, are rare. The emotions and fears they evoke are too great, their exhibition too "real" for the comfort of their escapist viewers, to garner the viewer ratings required to subsidize their production.

Death in Cinema

According to Geoffrey Gorer (1965), the American appetite for violence and perverse forms of death has produced an ethos of "pornographic death." The motif is pornographic as it involves the culture's twentieth-century prudery toward and denial of natural death. As sex becomes pornographic when divorced from its natural human emotion, which is affection, so death becomes pornographic when abstracted from its natural human emotion, which is grief (May 1973, p. 105). Perhaps nowhere is this more evident than in the cinematic medium, wherein, over time, such deaths have become increasingly vivid.

There are a number of ways to approach the evolution of pornographic death in cinema. In part, it is a function of the medium itself, which focuses on observable action and not on the subjective perspectives of individuals, which is one of the hallmarks of literature. The medium, exhibited to be larger than life and designed to be publicly viewed, must be attention-getting to hold the interest of large numbers of people, and it is death, not grief, that commands attention. To continue holding interest, cinema must constantly outdo itself, whether by producing increasingly absorbing plots (seasoned with shock or surprise), showing increasing amounts of action sequences, employing increasingly spectacular special effects, or featuring dying film stars.[3] Features achieving commercially successful chemistries of these elements spawn genres of sequels and imitations.

Another strategy, however, is to focus on the sociocultural factors shaping the public's receptivity to particular pornographic themes. A movie becomes successful at a particular point in time not only because of its technical or artistic merits but also because of its social context. Accordingly, one sociological enterprise has been to correlate cinematic themes with their sociohistorical settings. It was no coincidence, for instance, that the horror movie became a successful genre during the 1920s and early 1930s. Exploring the contests between good and evil as well as the conflict between our animal impulses and higher human traits, this cinematic motif first succeeded in the era of the *Scopes* monkey trial, a period of intellectual self-doubt and disillusionment following the atrocities of the "war to end all wars" and the time when Victorian mores were being eroded by an ethos of materialism and hedonism. In the context of prohibition, *Dr. Jekyll and Mr. Hyde* premiered, reaffirming the evil of drugs and reminding us of the beast that lurks within. In 1932, during the depths of the Depression, both *Dracula* (an immortal creature who must subsist on the blood of the living) and *Frankenstein* (a monster comprised of parts of dead bodies) were released, providing cathartic relief in ways reminiscent of Greek tragedy. The following year, perhaps to the delight of the economically oppressed, *King Kong* attacked the symbols of the establishment in New York. When society had to cope with all of the real death of World War II, these images of terror were to be employed for humor, as in *Abbott and Costello Meet Frankenstein* (PBS 1983). Following World War II, the uncertainties and fears of the nuclear legacy were symbolized by new monsters, unintended mutations produced by clumsy attempts to technologically harness this new force of death.

Another cinematic motif was the western, which used death to differentiate the good from the bad. During the 1930s and 1940s, the heroes—Roy Rogers, Gene Autry, and Red Ryder—avenged the deaths of innocents with more death. There was not much blood in these black-and-white episodes and always time for the outlaw to acknowledge his guilt before expiring (Rodabough 1980). By the late 1960s and early 1970s, however, in the context of the Vietnam War, the bloody protest movements, and the assassinations of John and Robert Kennedy and Martin Luther King, the pornographic obsession was to be fed by the gory "spaghetti westerns." Here the cowboy, now the symbol of true individualism, took it upon himself to execute evil, this time graphically and in "living" color.

Several death leitmotifs received extensive elaboration during the 1970s. One involved the theme of man controlling death: there was *Logan's Run*, in which, because of population pressures, individuals had only thirty years of life before being ritually destroyed. *Zardoz* dealt with the clash of two cultures, one a technological commune in which there was no aging process and no death, and the other a dying world populated with brutal inhabitants. The Vietnam War spawned its own celluloid explorations of war and death *(The Deer Hunter, Apocalypse Now)*, as did urban violence. In March 1979, a gang film called *The Warriors* was released by Paramount with the following ad: "These are the Armies of the Night. They are 100,000 strong. They outnumber the cops five to one. They could run New York City. Tonight they're all out to get the warriors." The film's first link to actual killing came in a Palm Springs drive-in in a racial incident involving a white group, the Family, and a black one, the Blue Coats. The following night in Oxnard, California, a scuffle broke out in the lobby following the first showing of *The Warriors*, leaving a white youth stabbed to death by a black youth. In Boston,

The "Nature Kills Man" Genre of Movies during the 1970s

Alligator, 1980

The Andromeda Strain, 1971

Ape, 1976

Attack of the Killer Tomatoes, 1977

Barracuda, 1978

The Bat People, 1974

Battle for the Planet of the Apes,
1973

The Bees, 1978

Ben, 1972

The Black Belly of the Tarantula,
1972

Bug, 1975

The Capture of Bigfoot, 1979

The Cars That Ate People, 1974

Chomps, 1979

Claws, 1977

Conquest of the Planet of the Apes,
1972

The Crimes of the Black Cat, 1972

Crocodile, 1981

Damnation Alley, 1977

Day of the Animals, 1977

Deer—Golden Antlers, 1972

Devil Dog: The Hound of Hell, 1978

*Digby—The Biggest Dog in the
World,* 1973

Dogs, 1976

Earthquake, 1974

Empire of the Ants, 1977

Fisheye, 1979

The Food of the Gods, 1976

Frogs, 1972

The Giant Spider Invasion, 1975

Godzilla on Monster Island, 1972

Godzilla vs. the Cosmic Monster,
1974

Godzilla vs. Megalon, 1973

Godzilla vs. the Smog Monster, 1971

Godzilla's Revenge, 1971

Grizzly, 1976

Jaws, 1975

Jaws 2, 1978

Killer Fish, 1979

King Kong, 1976

Kingdom of the Spiders, 1977

Kiss of the Tarantula, 1976

The Legend of Boggy Creek, 1972

The Legend of Loch Ness, 1976

Meteor, 1979

Night of the Lepus, 1972

Orca, 1977

The Pack, 1977

Piranha, 1978

Poodle, 1979

Rattlers, 1976

*The Rats Are Coming! The
Werewolves Are Here!* 1972

Return to Boggy Creek, 1978

Squirm, 1976

Sssss, 1973

The Swarm, 1978

Tentacles, 1977

Tidal Wave, 1974

Willard, 1971

From Willis 1982.

there was a nonracial event in which a member of the Dorchester gang yelled, "I want you!"—a line from the script—and a youth died of stab wounds six hours later. Then there was *Cruising,* a film focusing on a killer preying on New York homosexuals, yielding gay protests from coast to coast, fearing copycat violence. United Artists, the movie's distributor, said that theater owners could deduct extra security costs from receipts.

One additional death motif of cinema during the 1970s involved attacks on humanity by the natural order. Why during this era should people be attacked by rats, frogs, bees, sharks, meteors, earthquakes, and tidal waves? As noted in Chapter 6, there was a dramatic increase in the number of such deaths during this decade, but that probably had little effect on the cinematic expositions of the theme. Instead, perhaps people had grown tired of man-made death and had become desensitized to its terror. Further, having become fully urbanized, nature had become an unknown, its forces of destruction no longer respected when compared to our own potential for evil. In a sense, then, the motif represented a rediscovery of the natural order, bolstered by the culture's growing environmental awareness and reappreciation of ecological interdependencies.

During the decade that followed, cinema returned death to human control in an era marked by international terrorism and increasing militarization. By the mid-1980s, it was military violence that gained immense popularity, epitomized by *Rambo* and its sequels and imitations. In the original, not counting the groups of individuals who were slaughtered in more than seventy explosions, there were forty-four specific killings—one every 2.1 minutes (Powell 1985).[4] War became romanticized, and the message was that it takes violence to resolve complex problems. In addition, the fears of random, meaningless deaths were to be dramatized in the *Halloween* and *Mad Max* series of films. It has been hypothesized that these movies, attracting two disenfranchised groups (specifically, the young and those of working-class backgrounds), provided an outlet for class antagonisms, and their ambiguous endings dramatize the loss of faith in the "just world" assumption disseminated by the upper classes (Hensley and LaBeff 1986).

With the advent of video cassettes, the ability to view uncensored death in the privacy of one's home further dramatizes Gorer's notion of pornographic death. As opposed to the obscene, which produces social embarrassment and is enjoyed socially, pornography produces fantasy and is enjoyed privately. During 1985, *Faces of Death* appeared in American video rental outlets. Here actual death was displayed, with images of suicides, executions, and autopsies. The popularity of this film among teenagers—whose suicide rate was skyrocketing—prompted editorial reflection. One movie reviewer said he couldn't tell what was acting and what was real.

Death and Music

Except for simple conversation, perhaps the oldest vehicle by which to express death fears and transcendent hopes, to share stories of death and how

Home viewing in the 1980s: Pornographic death themes abound in today's video rental stores. James Bolan.

others have met it, is music. American folk music, for example, features numerous songs of death spawned by war and violence (e.g., "Mountain Meadows Massacre"), work and class oppression ("John Henry"), disease ("The TB Is Whipping Me," "Meningitis Blues"), and fatal accidents ("The Wreck of the Old 97"). Music not only reflects a culture's death ethos but possibly shapes it as well. The 1933 song "Gloomy Sunday," written by Rezso Seress[5] and lyricist Laszlo Javor, was banned from the airwaves of Budapest because of the seventeen suicides inspired by the piece. This publicity led to its import to the United States, where "The Famous Hungarian Suicide Song" ("Angels have no thought of ever returning you. . . . Would they be angry if I thought of joining you?") received three recorded versions (from bandleaders Paul Whiteman, Hal Kemp, and Harry King).

To explore some of the relationships between death and music, let us here focus on the postwar music identified with American adolescents: rock and roll.

While academicians argued about the culture's death denials, the music of the postwar baby-boomers became imbued with death, not only being a frequent theme of its songs but also the premature fate of its performers (around whom dead-rock-star cults were to emerge). According to folk-pop singer-songwriter Don McLean ("American Pie," 1972), Buddy Holly's 1959 death in an aircrash was "the day the music died." Well, yes and no. Though the death of Holly, one of the forces behind the new rock-and-roll music of the late 1950s, was a blow to the music industry, it did not end rock and roll. If anything, it sanctified the movement and gave it its dark side. An intimacy with death was to be created that eventually was reflected even in the names of its groups: the Grateful Dead, the Zombies, the Dead Kennedys, Sharon Tate's Baby, the Clash, D-Day, the Explosives, Megadeath, and Terminal Mind.

In the early years of rock, the death of a loved one was often romanticized in song (in a sense, it was rock's Victorian era): in Mark Dinning's "Teen Angel," she ran back to the stalled car to get his high school ring but was killed by the oncoming train; in "Last Kiss," "she's gone to heaven so I've got to be good, so I can see my baby when I leave this world." Denisoff (1972, p. 172) refers to these as "coffin songs," often featuring a Romeo and Juliet motif. What could be a more effective rebuff to adults' claim that it is only puppy love?

Thanks to the mass media of the 1960s, this was to be the best informed of young generations, and the youth of America were to become increasingly politicized against the situation in Vietnam. They were frustrated by their inability to vote and yet their duty to fight in an unpopular war. This led to the rise of protest music, stimulated by the 1965 release of Barry Maguire's "Eve of Destruction." Strangely, in the following year, the number one single in the United States was a song dedicated to the warriors, Barry Sadler's "The Ballad of the Green Berets." The late 1960s continued the morbid themes of the previous years. With dead soldiers being returned in body bags by the thousands and with the assassinations of Bobby Kennedy and Martin Luther King, the world seemed to be falling apart. Nothing of the establishment (which was taken to be those over age thirty) was to be believed, and in such a context the rumor of the death of Beatle Paul McCartney swept coast to coast.

Death was not only a frequent theme of the music of the time, but it also was to become the fate of many of its performers. Death came prematurely not only to Buddy Holly (age twenty-two at the time of his fatal crash) but to Elvis Presley (drug-related coronary, age forty-two), Jim Morrison (heart

attack, twenty-seven), Jimi Hendrix (drug-related, twenty-seven), Janis
Joplin (substance abuse, twenty-seven), Otis Redding (thirty-six), Keith Relf
(of the Yardbirds, electrocution from guitar, thirty-three), Jim Croce (plane
crash, thirty), Ronnie Van Zant (Lynyrd Skynyrd, plane crash), Keith Moon
(the Who, drugs), Brian Jones (Rolling Stones, drug-related drowning),
Lowell George (Little Feat, drugs), Sid Vicious (Sex Pistols, suicide), Pig Pen
(Grateful Dead), Cass Elliot (Mamas and Papas, age thirty), Minnie Ripper-
ton (cancer), Duane Allman (motorcycle accident), John Lennon (murdered, age forty),[6] Bill Haley, and Karen Carpenter. Of those musicians
appearing in the film of the 1968 Monterey Pops Concert, ten were dead by
1981. During the late 1970s and early 1980s, the posthumous releases by
these dead stars often outsold the recordings of the living.

Not only was death a theme of rock-and-roll songs and the fate of some
performers, but the audience became involved as well. Mass murderer
Charles Manson supposedly believed that the Beatles were sending him messages through the lyrics of songs from their "white album," particularly
"Helter Skelter." At Altamont Speedway near San Francisco, it proved
unfortunate to mix the Rolling Stones with the Hell's Angels motorcycle
gang, which had been hired to provide security. When a fan attempted to
gain access to the stage, he was beaten and stabbed to death by the Angels,
all in view of the movie cameras that were filming the concert movie *Gimme
Shelter*. In Cincinnati, Ohio, the crush of a crowd at a Who concert left six
trampled to death. In Pueblo, Mexico, during a 1983 performance of the
Puerto Rican group Menudo, thousands of fans stampeded toward the only
open exit after a concert, crushing three to death and injuring eighty others.

Endings in Sports

If the earth were to be visited by anthropologists from another planet, one
activity they would probably study to ascertain the cultural ethos of a given
society would be its preferred sports. Through its games, a society socializes
its younger members for their future adult roles and reinforces its cultural
values in the minds of older spectators. An alien social scientist would see
that, as in East Germany, sports can possibly be—after the political party,
the army, and the police—one of the most important social institutions, able
to galvanize entire populations and to focus their energies and attention
toward a benign end (Markham 1983). They would note that professional
games can be so important, as in the United States, that cities float bonds
and tax all residents, whether they are spectators or not, to finance huge
sports complexes.

Contests between professional sports teams are high-drama expressions of everyday life. As paintings abstract visual experience and music abstracts the auditory, so the game abstracts the structure of role relations inherent in the economic sphere of life.[7] In the sociology of sports, there are two perspectives that address this relation of sport to the cultural value systems of at least the United States. One, the thesis of sport as a microcosm of American society, directs attention to the exaggeration of cultural values in the sports institution: competition, materialism, the domination of the individual by bureaucracy, racism,[8] sexism, and the accentuation on youth (Eitzen and Sage 1978). In team sports, we are sensitized to the interdependency of individuals occupying specialized roles, within which individuals differentially age (baseball catchers, for example, aging faster than first basemen) and interact with others of differing generations. (Teams experiment with differing chemistries of experience and philosophies regarding "the aged." Football's 1977 Washington Redskins, for example, made their Super Bowl bid with a group of seasoned veterans seeking to "end at the top.") The second perspective portrays sports as a secular, quasi-religious institution which, through ritual and ceremony, "functions in disseminating and reinforcing the values regulating behavior and goal attainment and determining acceptable solutions to the problems in the secular sphere of life" (Edwards 1973, p. 90). Like religion, professional sports uses past generations as referents for the present and confers conditional immortality for its elect, through statistics and halls of fame. The dead provide benchmarks for greatness. As Pete Rose closed in on Ty Cobb's all-time record for career hits or as Hank Aaron approached Babe Ruth's career record of home runs, a rarely seen vitality was imparted to the game.

Given this centrality of sports to cultural values systems, let us turn to some of the ending lessons that come from this social medium.

Death in Sports

Death has been a constituent feature of sports since the earliest recorded times, such as in the battles between gladiators or the jousts of knights. Today we find athletes attempting to win at any cost, even death, by taking potentially lethal doses of pituitary hormones and steroids to increase their performance. In front of both live and television audiences, individuals get paid to risk death, whether by driving more than two hundred miles an hour, punching each other's skulls, or skirmishing with a bull. These risk takers often die. Taking motor racing sports in 1982 as an example, death came to six racing drivers (Gordon Smiley, Jim Hickman, Gene Richards, Riccardo Paletti, and Gilles Villeneuve), two speedway motorcyclists (Brett Anderton,

Professional Sports Halls of Fame

American Association of College Baseball Coaches Hall of Fame, 1946

Association of Sports Museums and Halls of Fame, 1972

Breeders of Peruvian Paso Horses Hall of Fame, 1975

Greater St. Louis Amateur Baseball Hall of Fame, 1973

Indianapolis Motor Speedway Hall of Fame

International Swimming Hall of Fame, 1965

Lacrosse Foundation Hall of Fame, 1959

Ladies Professional Golf Association Hall of Fame

Naismith Memorial Basketball Hall of Fame, 1959

National Association of Intercollegiate Athletics Hall of Fame, 1952

National Association of Left-Handed Golfers Hall of Fame, 1961

National Baseball Hall of Fame and Museum, 1936

National Football Foundation and Hall of Fame, 1947

National Museum of Racing and Hall of Fame, 1957

National Pigeon Association Hall of Fame

National Sportscasters and Sportswriters Hall of Fame, 1959

National Tennis Foundation and Hall of Fame

National Track and Field Hall of Fame of the U.S.A.

PGA Hall of Fame, 1940

Professional Bowling Association Hall of Fame

Professional Football Hall of Fame

Track and Field Association/USA Hall of Fame, 1968 (discontinued)

U.S. Harness Writer's Association Living Hall of Fame
   (est. by Hall of Fame of the Trotter), 1961

U.S. Hockey Hall of Fame, 1973

U.S. Soccer Federation Hall of Fame Meritorious Award, 1970

Women's International Bowling Congress, 1953

World Golf Hall of Fame

Denny Pyeatt), one road motorcycle racer (John Newbold), and three powerboat racers (Dean Chenoweth, David Mason, Micth Chip).[9]

Not only has death historically come to the contestants, but it threatens spectators as well. Following the race of their two main teams of charioteers in A.D. 532, Roman fans began rioting and tried to declare a new emperor, which led to more than thirty thousand deaths (Goleman 1985). Death still comes to the spectator: violence spawned by soccer games killed 318 Peru-

Life's last moment for Gordon Smiley as his racing car disintegrates around him during a 1982 qualification attempt at the Indianapolis Motor Speedway. The Bettmann Archive, Inc.

vian fans in 1964 and 38 British and Italian fans in 1985. In fact, so thoroughly interwoven is this relation between death and sports[10] that it is difficult even to describe the games without using the language of death: spectators yell "Kill 'em!" as the contestants enter "sudden death" play, hoping that once again their team will "murder" the opposition.

One possible reason for sport's lethality is that it is one of the few socially sanctioned outlets for violent, aggressive, and/or daring activities. In the case of personal leisure sports, Chapter 4 considered the psychological attraction of hang gliding, mountain climbing, parachuting, and hunting. The ecstasy of flirting with death led twenty-two-year-old Steven Trotter to fulfill a childhood dream in 1985 by becoming the sixth person to survive plummeting over Niagara Falls. In addition, the attraction comes from testing oneself against the ultimate challenges to the biological self, as in the pure aggression of football and boxing.

The savagery and lethality of the latter have led several states to attempt to outlaw the sport. A New Jersey investigatory commission said that boxing "has no place in a civilized culture" and "that not even the sturdiest of statutory controls will reduce the brutality of the sport to any significant degree. In addition, the commission believes that no truly viable social or economic benefits can be derived from such legal savagery" (Sullivan 1985). In 1984, the American Medical Association called for an abolition of boxing. Said the association's president, Dr. Joseph Boyle, "It seems to us an extraordinarily incongruous thing that we have a sport in which two people are literally paid to get into a ring and try to beat one another to death, or at least beat them into a state of senselessness, which can then leave them permanently brain damaged" (Sullivan 1985). The sport's violence is contagious. According to sociologist David Phillips, the national homicide rate briefly rises by an average of 12.46 percent after a nationally televised heavyweight fight, or, in actual numbers, 193 more people are killed following a bout than would have been expected by chance over a six-year period (Davidson 1983). Sports violence is also attractive. Dolf Zillman and Jennings Bryant (1986), two psychologists who have studied television's tendency to magnify violent incidents in football and hockey, found exceptionally rough plays being twice as likely to receive instant replays than those that are relatively mild, with longer attention of the camera given to those involved in the more vicious behavior.

Particularly attracted to the violent sports are those of the lower classes, those for whom fighting is one of the few sources of status and meaning (see Williams and Dunning 1984). Observed Richard L. Clutterbuck, professor and author of ten books on political violence, "they are people for whom life offers nothing, who want to have something in their life that's worth having. The only thing they can attach themselves to is their local football team" (Thomas 1985).

Retirement in Professional Sports

Though there are the actual casualties of the game, the primary thanatological lessons of professional sports involve the symbolic deaths of our working selves as described in Chapter 7. It is in the sports section of the newspaper, not the business or the news pages, that one can read of the emotions and tribulations associated with the twilights of careers.[11] In one sense, the very game can be seen as a contemporary morality play on finitude, evidenced in a *Time* editorial, "To an Athlete Growing Old": "But the athlete's half-life is so short; his decline and failure become a model of the mortality in everyone" (Morrow 1978).

Sports retirements have been subject to invidious comparisons: some are better than others, and a postmature exit can stigmatize an entire career. In contemplating his own retirement, baseball star Lou Piniella observed that "everybody wants the opportunity to leave the game on top. Some people do that and other people don't. I want to be remembered for being a good hitter, not for being a guy who played for the sake of playing and couldn't carry his weight" (Gross 1984). And the retirements of athletes provide a powerful cultural metaphor for role conclusions in general, not because they are typical (indeed, retired athletes usually move into new careers) but rather because it is within this arena that the detrimental effects of age on role performance are most apparent. For example, "Quoted in the industry newspaper Electronic Media, Donahue said, 'I don't want to be the old ballplayer who gets hit in the head with the fly ball because he didn't get off soon enough. I'd like to go out proud and successful'" (Bednarski 1983). Here we consider the lessons about conclusions appearing in professional sports and observe the potency of endings in shaping how careers are remembered.

One powerful image of the game is the aging athlete (Morrow 1978), the "old man of the game," whose longevity derives from being able to constantly develop, to survive the constant challenges of physically superior youth by being increasingly game-wise and always indispensable.[12] But bodies always give out, and with this realization the mortality play can feature reactions surprisingly akin to the so-called stages of death described by Kübler-Ross (1969). There's the inevitable depression that leads to "slumps," but further, there are the following:

- *Denial* Evidenced in the futile attempts of Muhammed Ali and Joe Lewis to return to the game and their failure to accept the finality of their careers.

- *Anger* Bruce Ogilvie, sports psychologist, describes the reaction of athletes toward their age-linked failures in the following way: "Their resentment is reflected some way toward someone. The hostility is part of the denial process, a refusal to take responsibility for what is going on in their life" (Shirley 1982).

- *Bargaining* As described by Bradley (1976), athletes made a "Faustian bargain" and eventually "live all [their] days never able to recapture the feeling of those few years of intensified youth."

- *Acceptance* The following was written of the "on-time" retirement of Sandy Koufax: "Sandy Koufax has retired from baseball. Forget the other statistics that have stamped him as one of the great pitchers in the history of the game. . . . Remember instead that he retired with honor and dignity instead of negotiating a huge 1967 contract and then quitting after a few games, as some colleagues urged him to do" (*New York Times* 1966).

For a culture searching for successful models of old age and strategies for disengagements and successions, the game's management of the fate of its older players is a powerful metaphor: voluntarily retiring "for reasons of health" is better than being involuntarily "washed out" in the preseason; mentoring is better than being in constant conflict with youth; and to end one's career with a flourish enhances one's immortality, all factors being equal, over ending "postmaturely." In a nonscientific sampling of professional sportswriters and sports aficionados, the most frequently cited example of a "good ending" was the voluntary career conclusion of football's legendary Jim Brown. Considerable publicity was given to this story and why so great an athlete would quit at the apparent peak of his career. Brown himself gave the following justification:

Let's start with pride. That's something that had a lot to do with my decision. I've seen too many examples of great athletes who stayed around just a little too long. Real great athletes. Sugar Ray Robinson, for example. Joe Louis, for example. I've heard people say, "They were great, great champions, but they stayed around just a little too long. I wish they would have retired at the peak of their careers." So pride had a lot to do with it. I think a man ought to be remembered first of all as a great champion, à la Rocky Marciano, à la Otto Graham.

But deep down inside I knew that I ought to go ahead and call it quits. I knew that this was really the year to step out. Why this year? Let's look at it this way: I had just been picked as Most Valuable Player—by the other players—and I had just won the MVP award in the Los Angeles pro game. So that was evidence that I was still a very valuable man. That was evidence that I wasn't all used up. I still had something left. I still had commodities that were valuable. Jim Brown was still "saleable"—having something valuable that other people want to buy—has a lot to do with a decision as to whether you retire at a certain time or whether you hang on a little longer to what you have. Timing, you see, is very, very important. (Sanders 1966)

Beyond the obvious aesthetics of this conclusion, there are several themes that bear striking similarity to thanatology's dimensions of an "appropriate death." As defined by Weisman (1973), an appropriate death is one that is timely, such as following the completion of an act; significant, where the death itself stands for something; good, for both the dying individual and the survivors-to-be; and wished for. Likewise, Koufax is remembered for the timeliness of his departure, whereas the postmature retirement of Willie Mays produced the following media presentation:

"It was my decision alone," Mays said, fending off any suggestion that his retirement had been forced. "I'm not ashamed of the way things have gone the last couple of months. They didn't run me out. In San Francisco, I don't think I would have played this year, the people would have run me out of the city." (*New York Times* 1973)

The significance of Roberto Clemente's accidental death during a Latin American humanitarian relief mission produced one of three exceptions to baseball's Hall of Fame induction requirement of a five-year wait period. And Roy Campenella's final years will be remembered as good for his mentoring:

There was no way of estimating Campenella's value to the team from a morale stand-point. The best way to get a glimpse of the real Campy was to see him at Vero Beach, Fla., during spring training. He never sat alone. Younger ballplayers always clustered around him and a lot of older ones did, too. Round Roy was like a mother hen with the chicks at his feet as he philosophized and talked baseball hour after hour. (Daley 1958)

Conclusion

As knowledge of death has increasingly become secondhand information, the influence of the various media that transmit the stories of death has become increasingly potent. Their potential for being used as mechanisms of social control should never be underestimated. In the Third Reich, Joseph Goebbels demonstrated their propaganda utility when perpetrating the "Big Lie," either by portraying alleged atrocities being committed against the German people in order to incite them to war or by ignoring the evils being waged by the Nazis themselves. In the political hot spots of the contemporary world, both governments and their oppositions battle for exposure before the television cameras of the world community. And to counter the perceived biases of secular humanism, churches purchase their own television networks and beam their eschatological messages to communication satellites for global dissemination.

In the United States, where media presentations are generally determined by the forces of the marketplace, a new danse macabre has evolved: pornographic death. In place of the classic religious themes, the contemporary iconography features violent death committed in the name of entertainment. Their implicit lessons, as we have seen, are often unintended. Children may think that death is reversible, avoidable, or the consequence of malevolence, while the old may believe, having witnessed a surfeit of television violence, that the outside world is too dangerous a place to venture. Nevertheless, it is the theme of premature deaths that sells newspapers and phonograph records and invigorates the plots of ratings-sensitive television programs.

By perceiving professional sports as a cultural totem for the contemporary work world, one can see abstracted at an accelerated pace the drama of every worker's encounter with time and inevitable symbolic death: the obsolescence of personal skills; the challenges between generations for upward mobility; how careers can be punctuated by fate (the critical injury or death), failure (being "washed out" in preseason competition for limited numbers of roles), or design (such as retiring a bat after completing a winning season); and the challenges to the sanctity of seniority systems by meritocracies (does the team keep the aging superstar during his "twilight years" or employ the expensive rookie who has the promising future?). Longevity remains an ideal, but so, now, does the quality of one's career conclusion.

NOTES

1. To statistically demonstrate this assertion, attitudes toward capital punishment ("Do you favor or oppose the death penalty for persons convicted of murder?") and euthanasia ("When a person has a disease that cannot be cured, do you think doctors should be allowed by law to end the patient's life by some painless means if the patient and his family request it?") were taken as dependent variables and regressed against age, education, sex, intensity of religious belief, hours of television viewed daily, and frequency of reading the newspaper. Media exposure was taken to be significant if it entered the predictive equation with a coefficient whose probability of being 0 was less than .05. In the equation predicting opinions on euthanasia, for instance, hours of television had half the explanatory power of education and age and one-quarter that of the intensity of religious belief.

2. The day of the mud slide was the same day that an Italian cruise ship, the *Achille Lauro*, was hijacked by terrorists. Puerto Ricans were upset by the fact that media focused more on the murder of one elderly, wheelchair-bound American than it did on the five hundred individuals who were citizens of a commonwealth of the United States.

3. America holds peculiar death watches for its motion-picture stars. Industry officials know very well the money to be made from the last pictures (the "swan songs") of dead or dying stars, as evidenced by the last (and often mediocre) films of Gary Cooper, Susan Hayward, Steve McQueen, and John Wayne (Polunsky 1985). If possible, the Academy of Motion Picture Arts and Sciences conducts a funeral of sorts for its stars nearing death by giving them special Oscars or holding a special award ceremony. It is worth noting the immortality celluloid brings to actors and actresses, an ideal-type illustration of work's immortality potential as described in Chapter 7. What an insight for children to realize that they can still view the activities of those now dead! Even ownership of the image of the deceased star is a matter of debate. In 1984, the California state legislature was asked to support a law giving a celebrity's estate ownership of the image for fifty years after death because of the growing celebrity look-alike industry.

4. In the sequel, dozens of Russians became victims when Rambo rescued Americans held prisoner in Southeast Asia. The Soviets countered in 1986 with their own "Rambo" in *Odinochnoye Plavaniye*, or "Solo Voyage," wherein it was Americans who were slaughtered when trying to carry out a scheme of the military-industrial complex to start a third world war (Taubman 1986).

5. Seress jumped to his death from a Budapest building in 1968.

6. Retrospectively, there was a grim irony in the 1980 killing of John Lennon, leader of the musical totem of the baby-boomers, the Beatles. Elton John (in "Clinkin") had explored the psychology of the killer in the decade that featured such attempted presidential assassins as Squeaky Fromm and Sarah Moore (who tried to kill Gerald Ford), foreshadowing John Hinkley (who wounded President Reagan) and Mark Chapman (Lennon's killer) in the 1980s. Now rock and roll would influence the pathologies of the feeble-minded, individuals seeking immortality at least through infamy.

7. Sports provides an ideal example of how different groups can read into its drama their own meaning systems. To the psychoanalyst, for example, there is the symbolic sexuality implicit in football whereby grown men, carrying an egg-shaped ball, gang tackle one another in their attempts to penetrate the others' end zone; for the work supervisor, the game generates statistics that provide near-perfect measures of role competence; for the clergyman, there is the immortality awarded for excellence (the halls of fame); and for the politician, there is the epitome of teamwork.

8. In professional team sports, minorities still are rarely allowed to occupy those central positions which determine the direction and pace of the game, such as the quarterback role in football or the pitcher in baseball.

9. But where, you may ask, is death in the number one spectator sport in America: horse racing? In June 1984, a lead-off story on the NBC evening news asked, "How did Swale die?" Swale was that year's victor in both the Kentucky Derby and the Belmont Stakes, dying mysteriously one week after winning the latter. Three formal investigations were initiated, but nothing was revealed in his autopsy. The horse had been well guarded, and foul play was considered unlikely. Blood and tissue samples were sent to two universities for further analysis. Swale was buried at his Kentucky farm alongside the remains of Triple Crown winner Gallant Fox. Horse racing has an established practice of burying the famous straw burners in the infields of their "favorite racetracks." For example, Ruffian, the filly whose demise was witnessed by millions of television viewers, was given "human treatment" and buried at the track where she met her end. Lamb Chop was the first modern thoroughbred buried at Santa Anita, it being the wish of the filly's owner that she be laid to rest where she had won the first stakes of her career. Also there are Pan Zareta, Black Gold, and Native Diver. In Native Diver's honor, a twenty-foot monument with a gigantic gold cup resting on the top was erected. On the four sides bordering the small area is the following sign: "Keep Off, Native Diver's Grave." The Kentucky Horse Park features a magnificent, larger-than-life statue of Man o' War. This, the world's only park dedicated solely to a horse, consists of more than one thousand acres, created in 1978 at the cost of 33 million dollars. Man o' War, the first thoroughbred to be embalmed, was moved from his original gravesite at Faraway Farm to the Horse Park and is now buried with some of his offspring. And then there is the death orientation of horse racing's most frequent spectator: the gambler. Dr. Robert Custer, a psychiatrist who works with problem gamblers, said: "Of the hundreds of persons I've seen, I have noted an inordinate fear of dying, . . . coupled with a constitutional need for stimulation. Gambling tends to give them a sense of being alive. When they're not gambling, they're dead—they

don't exist. Gambling is their existence. It obliterates all other fears" (*New York Times* 1983).

    10. See Goldstein (1983).

    11. A recent trend in the sociology of sports literature has been to minimize the traumas associated with ending an athletic career. Jay Coakley (1983) has demonstrated, contrary to popularly held assumptions, that such retirements do not inevitably lead to stress, identity crises, or adjustment problems. However, this tradition generally addresses the consequences of retirement and not the concluding phase of one's role career or the motivation to end well.

    12. The mean career lengths of players enshrined in baseball's Hall of Fame are almost biblical in their longevity when compared with the nonelect. Of those inducted between 1936 and 1979, Hall of Fame pitchers averaged more than sixteen years in the big leagues, and fielders averaged more than seventeen. On the other hand, the mean career length of the 6330 fielders who played in the major leagues between 1900 and 1979 was 5.11 years (computations derived from Reichler 1979).

REFERENCES

Adweek (Southwest ed.). 1984. "What's New Portfolio." November 26, p. 37.

Arlen, Michael. 1975. "The Air, the Cold, Bright Charms of Immortality." *New Yorker*. January 27, pp. 73–78.

Bednarski, P. J. 1983. "Donahue Says His Show Nearing End." *Austin American-Statesman*. August 31, p. D6.

Blakeslee, Sandra. 1985. "Scientists View Themselves in TV Hall of Mirrors." *New York Times*. May 30, p. 14.

Bradley, Bill. 1976. *Life on the Run*. New York: Time Books.

Campbell, Colin. 1985. "News Coverage of Mud Slide in Puerto Rico Is Criticized as Inadequate." *New York Times*. October 15, p. 9.

Coakley, Jay. 1983. "Leaving Competitive Sport: Retirement or Rebirth?" *Quest* 35:1–11.

Coder, Timothy. 1977. "TV Mistake Turns Joy to Sadness." *San Antonio Light*. August 10, p. 20A.

Daley, A. 1958. "End of the Road?" *New York Times*. January 29, p. 20.

Davidson, Keay. 1983. "Telecast Fights Beam Death." *San Antonio Express-News*. August 14, p. 8S.

Denisoff, R. Serge. 1972. *Sing a Song of Social Significance*. Bowling Green, Ohio: Bowling Green University Popular Press.

Edwards, Harry. 1973. *Sociology of Sport*. Homewood, Ill.: Dorsey Press.

Eitzen, D. Stanley, and George H. Sage. 1978. *Sociology of American Sport*. Dubuque, Iowa: William C. Brown.

Friedman, Thomas. 1982. "Amid Lebanon's Postwar Turmoil, Cultural Creativity Thrives." *New York Times*. May 13, p. 22.

Gerbner, George. 1980. "Death in Prime Time: Notes on the Symbolic Functions of Dying in the Mass Media." *Annals* 447:64–70.

Gerth, Hans, and C. Wright Mills. 1953. *Character and Social Structure: The Psychology of Social Institutions.* New York: Harcourt, Brace & World.

Goldstein, Jerry. 1983. *Sports Violence.* New York: Springer-Verlag.

Goleman, Daniel. 1985. "Saying Goodbye Speaks Volumes." *New York Times.* April 3, pp. 19, 20.

Gorer, Geoffrey. 1965. *Death, Grief and Mourning.* New York: Doubleday Anchor Books.

Gross, Jane. 1984. "Piniella, His Timing Off, Is Pondering Retirement." *New York Times.* March 3, p. 24.

Hemingway, Ernest. 1985. *The Dangerous Summer.* New York: Charles Scribner's Sons.

Hensley, John, and Emily LaBeff. 1986. "A Sociological Analysis of Motion Picture Violence as Class-Related Fantasy Aggression." Paper presented at the Southwest Social Science Association Meetings, San Antonio.

Innis, Harold. 1951. *The Bias of Communication.* Toronto: University of Toronto Press.

Kübler-Ross, Elisabeth. 1969. *On Death and Dying.* New York: Macmillan.

McLuhan, Marshall. 1967. *The Medium Is the Message.* New York: Random House.

Markham, James, 1983. "East German Sports: Politics Everywhere." *New York Times.* August 1, p. 29.

May, William. 1973. "The Sacral Power of Death in Contemporary Experience." In Arien Mack, ed., *Death in American Experience.* New York: Schocken Books, pp. 97–122.

Morrow, Lance. 1978. "To an Athlete Growing Old." *Time.* February 27, p. 86.

National Opinion Research Center (NORC). 1986. *General Social Surveys, 1972–1986.* Chicago: National Opinion Research Center at the University of Chicago.

New York Times. 1966. "Editorial." November 19, p. 32.

———. 1973. "'Maybe I'll Cry Tomorrow,' Says Mays." September 21, p. 27.

———. 1983. "Life and Death, Race-Track Style." September 17, p. 14.

———. 1986. "For Shuttle Coverage, a Huge Audience." January 30, p. 23.

Polunsky, Bob. 1985. "A Public Death Watch Fascinates Hollywood." *San Antonio Express-News.* September 8, p. 2H.

Powell, Stewart. 1985. "What Entertainers Are Doing to Your Kids." *U.S. News & World Report.* October 28, pp. 46–49.

PBS (Public Broadcasting System). 1983. "The Horror of It All." February 23.

Reichler, James, ed. 1979. *The Baseball Encyclopedia,* 4th ed. New York: Macmillan.

Rodabough, Tillman. 1980. "The Cycle of American Perspectives toward Death." *Journal of the American Studies Association of Texas* 11:22–27.

Sanders, Charles. 1966. "Jim Brown: 'Why I Quit Football.'" *Ebony.* December, pp. 119–26.

Shirley, Bill. 1982. "Aging Athletes: Ego, Fame and Fortune Make the Real-world Transition a Tough One." *Sunday Denver Post.* February 7, p. 28. ("Contemporary")

Sullivan, Joseph. 1985. "Jersey Panel Recommends a Ban on Boxing." *New York Times*. December 12, pp. 1, 55.

Taubman, Philip. 1986. "Soviet Hits Back with Own 'Rambo.'" *New York Times*. July 24, p. 7.

Thomas, Jo. 1985. "British Soccer Fan: Why So Warlike?" *New York Times*. May 31, p. 5.

Time. 1976. "Death Watch." May 3, p. 69.

Weisman, Avery. 1973. "Coping with Untimely Death." *Psychiatry* 36:366–78.

Williams, John, and Eric Dunning. 1984. *Hooligans Abroad: The Behavior and Control of English Fans at Continental Football Matches*. New York: Routledge Kegan Paul.

Willis, Donald. 1982. *Horror and Science Fiction Films II*. Metuchen, N.J.: Scarecrow Press.

Zillmann, Dolf, and Jennings Bryant. 1986. *Perspectives on Media Effects*. Hillsdale, N.J.: Laurence Erlbaum.

Chapter 11

Death and the Medical System

On one hospital wing, a clinically dead man is resurrected with the heart from a victim of a fatal motorcycle accident. Two floors down, a pregnant woman undergoes an abortion after learning from an amniocentesis that she carries a child with a chromosome defect. And in another wing, an eighty-four-year-old irreversibly comatose patient is kept alive with life-supporting technology. It was not many years ago that such stories were news; nowadays, they are routine procedures conducted in the culture's frontline battle against death.

In many ways, this book's analysis of the American death experience culminates with this chapter. With modernization,[1] medicine has replaced religion as the major institutional molder of cultural death fears and immortality desires (Segerberg 1974; Harrington 1977). Like religion and law, medicine is a moral enterprise that seeks to uncover and control things it considers undesirable. In recent years, for example, the medicalization of social problems has made alcoholics out of drunkards; poorly performing students who used to be called stupid are now seen as victims of learning disorders; and the disoriented senior, who used to be understood as a victim of dramatic social change, is now viewed as senile (Freidson 1970).[2] Given this shift in moral arbitration from religion to medicine, it is ironic that the caduceus—originally the staff of the Roman god Mercury, patron of thieves and outlaws, and later, in early Christendom, the sign of Satan, whose gifts included knowledge, healing, and immortality (Harrington 1970)—is now the symbol adorning every medical facility.

Medicine's roots spring from the universal tradition of the human quest for prolongevity, if not immortality. Until a century ago, however, medicine was a relatively powerless institution; physicians did almost as much to kill or harm as to cure the patient (Hartwell 1973, p. 16). But since the time of Pasteur, scientific advances in the West have come at such a pace that the

Medicine as Moral Entrepreneur:
"Extra-Marital Sex Can Be Bad for You"

Philandering is only for the strong of heart, according to a leading Philippine heart specialist.

Dr. Arturo Ardena told a convention of heart specialists recently that sex with someone other than one's spouse is dangerous for persons with heart problems.

Because it tends to elevate the blood pressure and pulse rate more than the stay-at-home variety, extra-marital sex could cause heart spasms in anyone with a heart ailment, he said. . . . For the healthy person, there is little reason for concern, although overindulgence could bring on heart disease, he said.

His conclusion: The key for heart patients, men and women, "is never indulge in extra-marital sex. . . . Be content with comfortable, predictable sex with a familiar partner."

San Francisco Chronicle 1976. Reprinted
by permission of Reuters, © 1976.

---

immortalist desires of individuals have once again been rekindled. Late-twentieth-century American medicine is as different from that of 1960 as the medicine of 1960 was from that of the Italian Renaissance.[3]

Such profound change does not occur without registering some impact on the psychologies of individuals. Instead of generating moral doubt, premature death is now perceived to be something avoidable, being caused either by an inadequate life-style—such as from smoking, poor exercise habits or diet, or, in the case of AIDS, one's sexual preferences—or by the "underconsumption of clinical care" (Illich 1975, p. 38). In fact, so extensive is the faith Americans have in the ability of medicine to conquer most forms of untimely death—reinforced by the highly publicized breakthroughs in the battles against polio, smallpox, and even such new enemies as Legionnaires' disease—that they believe that medical science will provide a cure for anything that ails them, including old age and death. Egyptian mummification has been replaced with cryonics, the preservation of bodies at temperatures approaching absolute zero; recombinant genetics research is conducted with the same intensity that medieval alchemists used to dabble for immortality; and the contemporary Gilgamesh now seeks to be cloned. The moral deaths of ancestors have been transformed into the technological deaths of the likes of Barney Clark, the first recipient of an artificial heart.

Although medicine embodies cultural hopes for immortality, it is also very much involved with the business of death. Fears of death are shifting from concern about postmortem judgment to worries about how one dies (the fear of cancer has become a clinically recognized disease unto itself) and

Table 11.1 Causes of Death, 1950–1981 Crude Death Rates
per 100,000 Persons (% of Total Deaths)

	1950	1960
Cardiovascular diseases	494.1 (51.3)	515.1 (54.0)
Heart diseases	356.8 (37.0)	369.0 (38.6)
Cerebrovascular diseases	104.0 (10.8)	108.0 (11.3)
Atherosclerosis	———	20.0 (2.1)
Malignancies	139.8 (14.5)	149.2 (15.6)
Accidents	60.6 (6.3)	52.3 (5.5)
Bronchitis, emphysema, asthma	———	9.9 (1.0)
Pneumonia, influenza	31.3 (3.2)	37.3 (3.9)
Diabetes mellitus	16.2 (1.7)	16.7 (1.7)
Liver disease, cirrhosis	9.2 (0.9)	11.3 (1.2)
Suicide	11.4 (1.2)	10.6 (1.1)
Homicide, legal intervention	5.3 (0.1)	4.7 (0.5)

[a] Rates = 1960–1981.

Source: U.S. Bureau of the Census 1972, 1984.

where one dies (the elderly fear nursing homes more than death itself). Medicine is not only the institution that manages the dying—some 80 percent of all deaths occur in hospitals and nursing homes—but it kills as well. A 1974 National Planned Parenthood Association survey found that abortions were the second most commonly performed surgery after tonsillectomies, destroying nearly 16 million fetuses in the decade from 1974 to 1984. Some of the central ethical dilemmas of our time are spawned by the medical enterprise.

The Prolongevity Revolution

The epidemic diseases that historically wreaked havoc on social systems have virtually disappeared as causes of death. In 1950, tuberculosis, diphtheria, poliomyelitis, and measles killed 2729 American children; in 1973, these diseases killed only 43. Herman Feifel observed that the

major communicable diseases such as tuberculosis, influenza, and pneumonia are being replaced by more chronic and degenerative types associated with aging, notably heart disease, cancer, and stroke. Additionally, medical headway has lengthened the average time which now elapses between the onset of a fatal illness and death. This is bringing in its wake exacerbated problems of chronic pain, fear, dependency, loss of self-esteem, and progressive dehumanization for many persons. (1977, p. 7)

1970	1981	Percent change in rates, 1950–81	Percent change in percentage of total
496.0 (52.5)	424.2 (49.2)	−14 %	− 5
362.0 (38.3)	328.7 (38.1)	− 8	+ 3
101.9 (10.8)	71.3 (8.3)	−31	−23
15.6 (1.6)	12.2 (1.4)	−39[a]	−33[a]
162.8 (17.2)	184.0 (21.3)	+32	+47
56.4 (5.9)	43.9 (5.1)	−28	−19
15.2 (1.6)	25.7 (3.0)	+160[a]	+200[a]
30.9 (3.3)	23.4 (2.7)	−25	−16
18.9 (2.0)	15.1 (1.7)	− 7	0
15.5 (1.6)	12.8 (1.5)	+39	+67
11.6 (1.2)	12.0 (1.4)	+ 5	+17
8.3 (0.9)	10.3 (1.2)	+94	+1100

As a consequence, accidents, homicides, and suicides—in other words, man-made deaths—emerged among the major causes of premature death. As evident in Table 11.1, nearly as many persons die of suicide as from diabetes, tuberculosis, or pneumonia.

The mortality revolution (Goldscheider 1971) described in Chapter 4 owes much to the medical establishment. As society learns how to better stave off heart disease, stroke, cancer, and other killers, an increasing proportion of the population are living into their eighties, nineties, and beyond.[4] In 1940, only 365,000 Americans were age eighty-five or more, a mere 0.3 percent of the total population. By 1982, the number had expanded to 2.5 million, or 1.1 percent of the population. By the end of this century, the Census Bureau predicts that this oldest age group will top 5.1 million, almost 2 percent of all Americans, with more than 100,000 centenarians. By 2050, after the postwar baby-boomers have all reached the highest age brackets, more than 16 million men and women will be age eighty-five or older, some 5.2 percent of the total population (Otten 1984).

Such increases beyond the biblical allotment of three score and ten years would seem to be the occasion for social celebration. Instead, old age has become viewed culturally as a "social problem," bringing to mind another Greek myth of immortality. In the tale of Tithonus, a beautiful young man asks Aurora, the goddess of morning, to make him immortal. She does, and he ages continuously. Finally, pitying his never-ending dissolution, she makes him into a grasshopper. Instead of making the oldest of the old into grasshoppers, the medical establishment has produced a population requiring ever greater services with advanced age, because of a multiplicity of illnesses and including the million or more nursing home residents so disabled that twenty-four-hour care is required.[5] According to geriatric psychiatrist Carl Eisdorfer, "dementing illness roughly doubles every five years after 65. About 1% show it at 65, 2.5% at 70, 5% at 75, 12% at 80, up in the 20s at 85, and 40% to 50% in the 90s" (cited in Otten 1984). In addition, the number of cancer cases may double among Americans over the next forty years as a result of the increasing incidence of cancer in old age.[6]

The costs of caring for our Tithonuses is staggering, with two-thirds of the health-care bill for those sixty-five years of age and older being paid by the federal government (Altman 1985). So great and rapidly inflating are the costs that at least one financing scheme, Medicare's hospital-insurance fund, is projected to run out of money before the end of the century. Barbara Torrey, a government economist who has studied the elderly, estimated that the government provided 51 billion dollars in payments and services to those eighty and older in 1984 and that by the year 2000, it will be paying 34.3 billion dollars more (in 1984 dollars) solely because of the increasing numbers of the very old (Otten 1984).

Not only have physicians come to control the final passage, but they have achieved considerable influence in shaping the nonmedical aspects of the final stage of the life cycle as well. If it is the contemporary old who are trailblazing a new stage of the life cycle, then it is the physician who is their trail guide. In mass-media advice columns, public seminars, and professional journals, it is the physician who informs the elderly on such nonbiological matters as retirement, friendships, finances, and leisure. The social problem and moral dilemmas of old age have become firmly medicalized.

Immortality Hopes

How many would not be here were it not for the innovations of medical science? Between 1700 and 1930, concurrent with the first scientifically based models and technologies for cure, the total death rate dropped 60 percent. But most dramatic have been the declines of this century: two-thirds of the improvement of the species' longevity since prehistoric times has occurred since 1900 (Preston 1976).[7] Infant mortality rates, for example, were cut by three-quarters between 1940 and 1984, from 47.0 deaths per 1000 live births to 10.6 per 1000, according to the National Center for Health Statistics (*New York Times* 1985c). For each decade of the twentieth

Small comfort for the victim: An advertising bulletin of the
Insurance Medicine Company promising a $500 indemnity
in the event of death due to the consumption of its products.
Circa 1890. The Bettmann Archive, Inc.

century, male life expectancies at birth have increased 3.3 years and those of
females 3.8 years. If such trends were to continue, male and female life
expectancies at birth would be 79.6 and 87.0 years, respectively, in the year
2000, and 96.0 and 106.2 years in 2050.

Though much of these decreases in mortality are the result of improved
sanitation, better nutrition, healthier life-styles, and safer work environments, the conventional wisdom holds that such improvements derive from
the skills of our cultural high priests, physicians.[8] The media have done much
to reinforce this line of thinking, as has the pace of innovations in recent
years. Immortalist hopes soared with Christiaan Barnard's first heart trans-

plant in 1967; with Barney Clark in 1982, whose diseased heart was replaced with a Jarvik-7 artificial heart; with an infant known as Baby Fae, who, in 1983, was kept alive by the heart of a baboon for three weeks following its implant at a medical center owned and operated by the Seventh-day Adventist church; with the disclosure of a new genetically engineered drug that dissolves blood clots and is nearly twice as effective as any medication previously used in halting heart attacks (Schmeck 1985a); with the approval of national guidelines for employing gene therapy with humans against a range of fatal hereditary diseases (Schmeck 1985c); and with the University of Pittsburgh's approval of an operation to replace six organs simultaneously (the liver, stomach, large and small intestines, pancreas, and spleen) in the abdomen of thirty-six-year-old Herbert Seal (*New York Times* 1985d).[9] Further, one's very right to die has come into question: in 1971, the New Jersey Supreme Court upheld a lower-court decision that hospitals may give blood transfusions to save the life of an adult patient even if it means violating the patient's religious beliefs. The court maintained that there is no constitutional right to choose to die or that individuals' religious beliefs are absolute.

Even when there is no cure, medicine is the institution of hope for the terminally ill. When all typical treatment fails, there are experimental drugs.

Whenever a proposed new drug bursts on the scene—tumor necrosis factor for cancer, HPA-23 or "Compound S" for AIDS—large numbers of the desperately ill clamor for it as if it were space on a lifeboat of the *Titanic*, buoyed by new hopes. But the hopes of researchers, tempered by scientific skepticism, may be little more than that results over a long time will yield some data that can advance the arduous quest for answers. (Chase 1985, p. 1)

Of the substances proven effective enough in animal tests to warrant human testing, only one drug in ten pays off, according to Robert Young of the National Cancer Institute (Chase 1985).

Providing Death-Transcending Options

Not only does medicine assist in the quests and hopes for immortality of the self, but it is the provider of other forms of death transcendence as well. For example, developments involving in vitro fertilization and sperm cryobanking illustrate medicine's role in assisting genetic immortality. First there was the 1978 birth of Louise Brown, a child conceived in a test tube, which raised a host of ethical and legal questions. But these were to be dwarfed six years later, when there arose a new urgency in moral clarification in the wake of technological innovation. Following the loss of their own genetic immortality with the death of their only child, and with the wife no longer able to conceive, a wealthy Los Angeles couple went to Australia's Queen Victoria Medical Center, where the only successful attempt to produce an infant from a frozen embryo had been accomplished. Mrs. Elsa Rios had a fertilized egg implanted, but she later miscarried, leaving behind two frozen embryos for possible future implants. Shortly thereafter, the couple died in a plane crash. Do orphaned test-tube embryos have the right to survive? What of their inheritance rights? And would the disposal of these embryos constitute murder? In the same year, a Parisian widow legally won the right to use the sperm her deceased husband had deposited with a sperm bank, despite the objections of the Center for the Study and Conservation of Sperm, which had argued that her spouse did not specify what was to be done with his secretions in the event of his death. Her lawyer asked the court to declare that "a deceased man has the right to breathe life into the womb of his wife and prove that love is stronger than death" (Dionne 1984).[10]

The medical establishment has also produced practitioners who claim to have scientific evidence for the survival of self after death. One physician, cardiologist Michael Sabom (1981), has attempted to scientifically substantiate the near-death experiences of patients having close brushes with death (see Chapter 12). In his random sampling, Sabom found that four out of ten had vivid memories of their "deaths." One-third remembered floating above the operating table and viewing their resuscitations; half recalled traveling through a dark tunnel toward a bright light; and all described a strong sense of reality and timelessness. Interestingly, religion, occupation, and race produced no difference in the sensations of these patients.

Medicine even puts the dead to work for the sake of the living (thereby achieving an additional form of transcendence). In the past, its professional predecessors preserved the middle finger of Galileo, the pelvic bones of Charles Lowell (now in a Boston anatomical museum), the brains of Einstein and Maj. John Powell, the bladder of Italian Spallanzani (publicly displayed in a museum in Pavia, Italy), and the hair and a tooth of George Washington. Nowadays, the skin, lungs, heart, kidneys, and other organs survive death through transplants into the living.[11] From the dead are also "harvested" corneas and bone marrow.[12]

With advances in drug therapies and medical technology, the demand for such surgical procedures (see Table 11.2) is exceeding the number of available donors. Because of inefficiencies in the health-care delivery system and the fact that it is basically the old who die, there is a shortage of organs for transplant. Approximately eight thousand Americans, for example, were waiting for kidney transplants in the mid-1980s. So limited are supplies that when the wife of a senior advisor to the king of Saudi Arabia received the kidneys of two deceased Americans in Pittsburgh—bypassing long-waiting

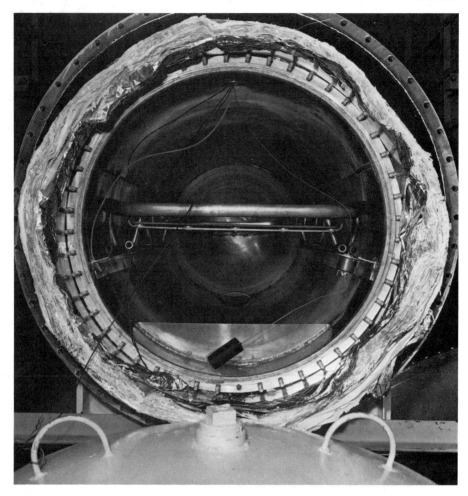

Technology for the contemporary Lazarus. The inside of a cryogenic chamber in which a fatally ill person is preserved at 195 degrees below zero (Celsius) until a cure is found. As yet no technology for successful resuscitation exists. UPI/Bettmann Newsphotos.

Americans in the transplant queue—heated debate arose concerning organ rationing (Gruson 1985). In addition, competition developed among hospitals seeking the prestige and publicity that accompany organ-transplant programs. This led to attempts by the government and private insurers to limit such procedures to large "centers of excellence," which meant those facilities having the volume that would keep prices down (Otten 1986b).

Further, cadavers inform the living about causes of death, and their supply

Table 11.2 Transplants in the United States

	1981	1982	1983	1984
Heart	62	103	172	346
Kidney	4885	5358	6112	6968
Liver	26	62	164	308
Pancreas	———	35	218	87

Source: U.S. Department of Health and Human Services, Office of Organ Transplantation (Otten 1985c). Reprinted by permission of the *Wall Street Journal,* © Dow Jones & Company, Inc. 1985.

partially determines the quality of teaching hospitals. Corpses informed researchers at Boston's Bent Bringham Hospital that physicians failed to make the correct diagnosis in one case out of every four and that 10 percent would not be cadavers had their conditions been recognized and treated correctly (Sullivan 1983). And then there are the neomorts. These are the remains of those who are brain-dead and yet with functioning organs. They are kept alive for the testing of drugs and surgical procedures, replacing prisoners, the retarded, and volunteers as experimental subjects (Medved 1984),[13] and also serve as manufacturing plants for antibodies.

There is one final twist to medicine's ability to assist in death transcendence. In the very course of curing, this institution can also induce another experience under the traditional purview of religion: rebirth or "born-again" sensations, the shedding of old, used-up selves in exchange for revitalized new ones. To first identify the phenomenology of religious born-again experiences, several individuals claiming to have had such sensations were interviewed (Patten 1984). They described their rebirths as an "awakening" to the true meaning of life, a meaning they previously did not have. One described it as realizing a "second chance"; another reported it as a "peaceful calm." When asked about how this transformation affected their attitudes toward death, each claimed to feel more comfortable and accepting of the inevitable as a consequence. Interestingly, the descriptions of such religious experiences were nearly indistinguishable from the reports of elderly members of Mended Hearts, a national organization for individuals who have experienced heart attacks and/or heart surgery.

One sixty-year-old, for example, experienced three heart attacks and underwent a triple bypass following the last. On the job when the third heart attack struck, he immediately thought of death and was so convinced that he was going to die that he wanted the ambulance to take him home instead of to the hospital. He did not want surgery, feeling certain that he would die on the operating table and "wouldn't know it," preferring instead to experience the pain and to die at home. The heart attacks were not his first close brushes with death—he had seen action in three wars—but these encounters produced much different feelings. Following the bypass, he felt so lucky to still be alive that an entirely new attitude toward life ensued. Facing the ever-present specter of death, he viewed each day as a special gift, and he sensed a greater appreciation and love for his family. Viewing his job as too pressurizing and time-consuming for what few personal benefits were gained, he immediately retired, realizing that he had accomplished much in life and no longer needed "to play the silly game of reaching for meaningless career goals. Too much effort had been invested in searching for the magical mythical mountain." Another bypass patient claimed that his proximity to death sparked the most thought-provoking situation of his life, yielding a sobering life review that included the realization that he had neglected his family and his religion. Initially feeling remorseful and worthless, after surgery he had the feeling of having "been given another chance." He, too, immediately rearranged his priorities, changing occupation to a desk job that required fewer hours and less stress, and devoting more of himself to his family and faith.

In sum, the medical establishment is now responsible for waging war against death (Harrington 1977; Segerberg 1974). The battle flag of this cultural crusade is the caduceus, and its flagships are the numerous health science centers dotting the country. According to John Bedrosian, president of the Federation of American Hospitals, "the insatiable quest for immortality fuels patients' demands for the latest in high-technology treatment that lengthens and saves lives" (*Rocky Mountain News* 1982). This issue will come up again in considering the political economy of health.

The Politics of Disease

It is interesting that hard-won medical victories lead not only to rising expectations but to further problems as well. Consider the rising expectations and social class resentments of those unable to afford artificial or transplanted hearts. Or the generational resentment of the old who hear of medical breakthroughs forecast for shortly after their probable demise. Or a public led to believe that through their contributions a cure will be found, only to find years later that little progress has been made. Such disappointments have far-reaching economic and political implications.

Certainly, it is in the political interest to avoid diseases or their cures becoming unintentionally politicized. For example, consider the hypothetical situation of fatal cases of smallpox or polio occurring within some minority group on the East Coast of the United States. Given the political responsibility and medical capacity for cure, such an outbreak would reflect a major flaw in the entire political economy, possibly leading to political disaster for those in power. Death, like life, must appear to the citizenry to be equal-opportunity. President Ford, on the other hand, trying to prevent a potentially deadly disease from infecting the older and younger segments of the population, intentionally made swine flu a political disease. Before the 1976 presidential election, Ford, in a possible attempt to improve his humanitarian image, responded to forecasts of a flu epidemic resembling that of 1918–19 and mobilized the pharmaceutical industry to inoculate America's high-risk groups. As events transpired, more individuals died from the vaccine than from the flu, which mysteriously never appeared except among a few swine handlers.

Diseases can also become political when cures fail to occur according to publicly expected timetables. Blacks, for example, see the failure in making inroads toward the eradication of sickle-cell anemia as the consequence of a racist medicopolitical enterprise that gives lower priority to minority ailments. Homosexuals have similarly perceived slow-motion efforts in the battle against AIDS because of the social stigma attached to the disease. And the elderly saw little public investment in arthritis research until children started appearing in ads requesting support. But perhaps it will be the failures in the war against cancer that will produce the greatest political fallout. It is certainly now the major scapegoat for public mortality frustrations.

In 1978, a best-seller, Samuel Epstein's *The Politics of Cancer*, portended a major cancer epidemic resulting from the proliferation of synthetic chemicals in everyday life. Although researchers have little idea about the origin of most tumors, public officials fostered the notion that nearly all cancers are induced by man-made chemicals and that these carcinogens are identifiable through lab tests. Edith Efron (1984) called this the "Big Cancer Lie," which led to an empire of federal health agencies predicated on the belief that by controlling industrial chemicals deaths would be decreased. (Nature had been thought to be relatively free of carcinogens, but now grilled hamburger, metals, oxygen, peanut butter, pepper and spices, sassafras, smoked fish, tea, and vegetable oils are all suspected agents; Marshall 1984.) Political medicine, like religion, is involved in the salvation business. And corresponding with the religious fundamentalist revival of the times, this salvation involves locating the evils associated with modernization. "In this vision, cancer is the Black Death of the twentieth century, a punishment for ill-gotten gains" (Marshall 1984).

Indeed, contrary to public expectations and the pronouncements of government officials, a growing group of distinguished analysts are finding very little progress over the past quarter-century in curing cancer. The much-ballyhooed gains in survival rates of cancer patients may be merely a statistical mirage, caused solely by changes in the definition and detection of cancers (Boffey 1984 and 1987). Between 1962 and 1982, one study showed that cancer deaths actually rose 8.7 percent, despite statistical adjustments to reflect the aging of the population (Bailar and Smith 1986). So where has the money gone? According to Ruth Sager (1977), professor of cellular genetics at Harvard Medical School and chief of the Division of Cancer Genetics at the Sidney Farber Cancer Institute, it was milked by businessmen and managers acting out of either greed or ignorance. She cites the example of some 27 million dollars in contracts awarded for developing the Frederick Cancer Center "to take advantage of the breakthrough in cancer" when it occurs.

Housing Cultural Death Fears

The medical institution not only shapes our cultural hopes for immortality but also shapes the nature of our death fears. Given the change in where we die, coupled with the secularization of our times, death fears have historically shifted from postmortem concerns (e.g., judgment, Hell, and reincarnation) to fears of the dying process. We now die because of medical, not moral, reasons;[14] a positive result on a cancer or AIDS test holds the same terror for us that not being on St. Peter's entry list at the gates to Heaven did for our ancestors. Further, for many, the quest for prolongevity has proven fatal. Susan Sontag develops in *Illness as Metaphor* that the treatment that is meant to cure often kills (1978, pp. 64–65). For example, the iatrogenic diseases caused by antibiotic and anticancer drugs include anemia, heart and kidney failure, blindness, liver and lung damage, infection, and bleeding (Hellerstein 1980). According to Dr. John Gofman, a professor emeritus of medical physics at the University of California at Berkeley, "unnecessarily high diagnostic X-ray doses are signing a cancer death warrant for 750,000 people every 30 years" (Hull 1985).

Four-fifths of the fifty-five hundred Americans who die daily do so in hospitals or nursing homes, normally while receiving some sort of medical treatment. These sites which house the concluding phase of human life have often become the scenes of depersonalization and social death. The sheer fact that these are the places where people die would be enough to give them the stigma of death, bringing fear to those admitted. But as Ralph Nader's nursing-home study (Townsend 1971) and the Autumn Hills Nursing Home trial in Texas revealed, in such places death can also be intentionally accelerated.

Death can come as a result of medical treatment. A 1970s study of hospitalized patients in California (jointly commissioned by the California Medical Association and the California Hospital Association) showed that one out of twenty admissions was injured by medical treatment and that 17 percent of these injuries were caused by legally provable negligence. Further, one out of four of these negligent injuries (or one out of five hundred hospital admissions) actually died because of the treatment they received (NBC Reports 1978; Stein 1987). Deaths from treatment also occurred in Norristown, Pennsylvania, during the first half of 1977, when labels on outlets to oxygen and nitrous oxide were found to be switched. In the six months before discovery of the mislabelings, thirty-five deaths were recorded in the new emergency room (Janson 1977).

One reason for these treatment-induced deaths is unnecessary medical intervention. How else can one explain the declines in California's mortality rates during that state's 1976 physicians' strike? In Los Angeles, for instance, the weekly death rate had averaged 19.8 deaths per 100,000 between 1971 and 1975; during the five-week-long strike, it fell to 16.2, and at the strike's conclusion it rose to 20.4 deaths per week (*Science News* 1978). Not surprisingly, the likelihood of receiving unnecessary treatment is related to one's position in the status hierarchy. A 1977 congressional investigation found surgery being performed on the needy and the near poor at twice the rate of that on the general population (Lyons 1977). The evidence of such useless surgery being performed for profit was impressive: in 1974, for example, 2.38 million unnecessary operations were conducted in the United States, costing 4 billion dollars and causing 11,900 needless deaths. This study of the House Commerce Committee calculated that nearly half of the postoperative complications and 35 percent of the deaths were preventable.

Other lethal maladies have arisen because of high-technology treatments. The excessive x-raying of children in the late 1940s and early 1950s may produce an excessive leukemia rate for this cohort as it ages. In 1985, preliminary reports surfaced that the polio vaccine given to 98 million Americans in the 1950s and 1960s may have been contaminated with a virus that possibly causes some types of brain cancer. University of Chicago Medical Center researchers also found this virus's genetic material in brain tumors of three children born to mothers who had received the vaccine (*San Antonio Express-News* 1985). And then there was the FDA recall of the Bjork-Shiley 60-Degree Convexo-Concave Heart Valve, whose failures were linked to the deaths of at least sixty-four people in 1984 (Molotsky 1985).

"Cancer" Patient Awarded $3 Million from Doctors

Two doctors who told a patient he had three months to live must pay $3.1 million for misdiagnosing his illness as cancer, then treating him with powerful drugs that may put him at risk of leukemia, a state Supreme Court jury has ruled.

Ignatius Lombardo, 56, a New York City real estate appraiser, underwent chemotherapy for 17 months, attorney Peter DeBlasio said Saturday.

"It's a shocking case," DeBlasio said. "This poor guy, he didn't have cancer, they said he did, they treated him for it, and they just about injected him with cancer. He's at great risk." . . .

Lombardo said when he was initially diagnosed as having three months to live, one brother left his job in Paris to be with him, another closed his business in Florida, and a third commuted from upstate New York several times a week.

When he was told that he did not have cancer, "I felt—there's no way to describe the feeling—it's like you're reborn."

San Antonio Express-News 1984. Reprinted by permission of The Associated Press, © 1984.

What makes medicine clearly distinct from other professions is that physicians' mistakes can kill. Observes columnist Andrew Stein (1987), "Every year hundreds of thousands of Americans die or are maimed because of the incompetence or negligence of members of the medical profession—more than were killed or wounded in any year of the Vietnam War." The passive role of patients in purchasing medical care may be ending, as evidenced in 1985 when Americans filed more than three times as many malpractice claims than they had a decade earlier, about sixteen for every one hundred physicians (Brinkley 1985a). Although various medical groups have estimated that between 5 and 15 percent of U.S. physicians are incompetent enough that they should be barred from treating patients, because of the inadequate system of medical discipline, the medical licensing boards revoked only 255 licenses in 1984—one for every 1701 practicing physicians (Brinkley 1985b). The medical license continues to entitle the physician to practice any kind of medicine, regardless of specific training in that specialty and without any future testing of competency. Despite the rapid changes in medical knowledge, only eighteen states require physicians to attend continuing education courses. In forty-two states, relicensing involves only the payment of a fee (Brinkley 1985b).

With the inability of physicians to police their own profession, other groups have devised their own monitoring systems. Because industry pays the medical bills of nearly a quarter of the U.S. population, corporations have begun to hire consultants to study their employees' insurance claims. General Motors and other major companies began evaluating the quality of care at various hospitals, including the mortality rates for different procedures, and are encouraging employees to use only the best facilities. In 1987, to assist consumers' assessments of the quality of health care, the federal government began issuing its own box scores: the mortality rates of Medicare beneficiaries in nearly six thousand hospitals. Not surprisingly, health-care marketing took advantage of these statistics to advertise the quality of particular hospitals, such as, "If you are considering heart surgery—read this: Eisenhower Medical Center had the lowest mortality in the country" (Rundle 1987).

The Political Economy of Health Care

With health care and longevity becoming citizenship rights, the federal government has invested heavily in the medical enterprise through such programs as the Veterans Administration and Medicare. Symbolizing political involvements with the quasi-religious goals of universal health and prolongevity, eleven national institutes of health, specializing in distinct fields of medical research (e.g., the National Cancer Institute, the National Institute of Neurological and Communicative Disorders and Stroke, and the National Institute on Aging), were established to spearhead society's attack on death and disease.[15] As Illich (1975, p. 28) observed, such reorganization enhances the legitimacy of both medicine and the political order while increasing professional exploitation. Equal opportunity to receive the best care available was not to be. Medicine became a big business, and, like all big businesses, it began organizing itself for profit. As a result, health costs have skyrocketed and a two-tier system of health care has emerged.

The governments of the developing countries are becoming increasingly concerned about the prospects of spending 8 percent or more of their GNP on health services, but that is exactly what has happened in the developed world. By the mid-1970s, the health-care complex had become the third largest industry in the United States (behind farming and construction) and the largest private employer. Just between 1968 and 1972, it expanded 21 percent, and by the late 1980s employed more than five million individuals. Part of its success derives from its ability to employ from all levels of the stratification hierarchy, from janitors and orderlies to secretaries, salespersons, and accountants, to physicians and administrators. Nearly one dollar of every nine spent by Americans went for health care. Each year nearly one in six, or forty million, Americans are hospitalized. The country's 1985 medical bill was 425 billion dollars, or more than 1721 dollars for every person in the country, an increase of more than 1700 percent from 1950 and double that

Table 11.3 The Cost of Health Care in the United States

	Expenditures in billions of current dollars, not adjusted for inflation	Percentage of GNP
1965	$ 41.9	5.9%
1967	51.5	6.3
1969	65.6	6.8
1971	83.5	7.6
1973	103.4	7.6
1975	132.7	8.3
1977	169.9	8.5
1979	214.7	8.6
1981	287.0	9.4
1983	357.2	10.5
1985	425.0	10.7

Source: U.S. Department of Health and Human Services (cited by Pear 1986). Copyright © 1986 by the New York Times Company. Reprinted by permission.

of 1979.[16] In 1986, the cost of medical care increased 7.7 percent, seven times the rate of the Consumer Price Index for all items (1.1 percent). Businesses that twenty years ago had agreed to pay for the medical costs of their retirees faced health-care obligations amounting to hundreds of billions of dollars. Former HEW secretary Joseph Califano Jr. estimated such medical benefit promises amount to two trillion dollars for the five hundred largest industrial companies alone, a figure that exceeds their total assets (Freudenheim 1985). Such developments occurring in a capitalist economy proved irresistible to corporate interests; health and prolongevity became commodities for sale by profit-seeking conglomerates.

By the mid-1980s, more than one of every three hospital beds was owned and operated by a chain, one of eight by a for-profit chain (Starr 1983). These profit-seeking chains now challenge the professional autonomy of physicians while usurping the control of local authorities over their own hospitals. Physicians increasingly come under their employ as often they are unable to afford the expensive, state-of-the-art high technology or the malpractice insurance premiums (some of which have been increasing by 50 percent a year and cost more than one hundred thousand dollars annually). The game of profit translates into physicians generating as many admissions and medical tests as possible for for-profit hospitals and into their minimizing these things for health-maintenance organizations (Starr 1983). The profitability lesson was obviously learned: between 1983 and 1984, the surplus revenues (income treating patients minus expenses) doubled to 2.5 billion dollars on revenue of 128.5 billion for all fifty-eight hundred U.S. hospitals. During the same period, the net income for the twelve hundred for-profit hospitals increased 44 percent (Waldholz 1985).[17] The federal government attempted to crack down on the soaring medical costs by establishing a predetermined reimbursement system for Medicare treatments of specific illnesses. An important revenue source, Medicare covers about 40 percent of all hospital patients.

In overthrowing religion as the moral arbitrator, medicine must now address the social correlates of health. But this entails confronting how patterns of death and disease are related to the economic, political, and social structures of a society (Waitzkin 1981, p. 91). Marxist critics of this institution have noted that the lesson was long in coming, that in simply treating the individual and attributing disease to personal failures, the broader social causes were not challenged. They also note the class correlates in the prolongevity quest: as fiscally pressed public hospitals are taken over by profit-seeking hospital chains, it may be the case that those without any resources will no longer be treated for little or no cost and that only the wealthy will receive top-level care. "We are regressing, moving back from the Great Society days, and reneging on our commitment to the poor," said Dr. Arnold Relman, editor of the *New England Journal of Medicine.* "Health care is being converted from a social service to an economic commodity, sold in the marketplace and distributed on the basis of who can afford to pay for it" (Tolchin 1985).

Death and the Physician

Having reviewed medicine from both cultural and social structural perspectives, we now turn to those individuals directly engaged in the battle against death. It is the physician who is ultimately responsible for diagnosis and care, the person to whom the patient entrusts body and life, the one responsible for informing seriously ill individuals of their terminality and survivors of their loved one's extinction.[18] Because of this involvement in matters of life and death, this occupation is among the most prestigious in American society. The median income of its practitioners is nearly twice that of lawyers or dentists. Having such status, it is the province of the upper classes: though the working class comprises nearly half the population, it is the source of only 12 percent of medical students.[19] And no other group is allowed to perform its business, hence the lack of paramedics and the legal prosecutions of nonphysicians practicing acupuncture and child deliveries. But it is also one of the most self-destructive of all professions: physicians commit suicide at three times the rate of the population at large; as many take their own life each year as graduate from Harvard Medical School (*Time* 1981).

This cultural high-priest status of physicians has basically arisen since World War II,[20] concurrent with their triumphs over infectious disease and their ability to legitimize and regulate their professional sovereignty.[21] Ironically, as physicians' power over life and death increased, the personal interactions between the physician and the dying deteriorated. With the evolution of such different specialties as pulmonary, cardiology, endocrinology, and radiation therapy, individual care has become impersonal. Patients find themselves at the mercy of specialists, whose examinings are not explained in everyday language. No longer is the individual viewed or treated as a whole person.[22]

Studies have found that physicians actually avoid dying patients. (Glaser and Strauss 1965; Kübler-Ross 1969).[23] One reason for this avoidance may be the basic personality structure of the physician (Schulz and Aderman 1980, p. 134). Physicians have been found to have on the average an inordinately high fear of death. A second is the idea, implicit throughout medical training, that death is evidence of failure (Rabin and Rabin 1970). The lack of medical education in the areas of dying and death is a third reason. Indeed, medical education may have a desensitizing and dehumanizing effect on students (Backer, Hannon, and Russell 1982, pp. 95–98). Fourth, because the dominant model of the medical institution—man as machine— originates from the mechanistic paradigm of Cartesian-Newtonian science (Dossey 1981, p. viii), the average physician tends to have a limited view of the factors necessary for quality of life and of the forces responsible for a death. Weisman admits, "It is our scientism that excludes human and personal elements and decides that only lesions matter in determining death. . . . Medicine forgets that man is more than a simple organism struggling to survive" (1972, p. 163). Finally, to the physician, the inability to prevent the death of a patient symbolizes powerlessness and an inability to control (Benoliel 1974, p. 221). In sum, according to Benoliel, the behaviors of doctors and nurses in the face of death may reflect "a lay response to death and points to a lack of appropriate and consistent norms for professional behavior" (1974, p. 219).

Socialization to Death

Our culture does not prepare us to cope with our own death or with the deaths of others. As Chapter 12 will develop, the dying have needs above and beyond the physical treatment of their illness, needs requiring emotional and psychological support. But how many doctors recognize these needs and emotions? What socialization do they receive for managing this most terrifying of experiences?

The necessity for some formal, structured death education at medical schools is evident when one considers the informal and unintentional lessons currently being taught. On his or her very first rounds, the medical student discovers that there are specific wards where death is to be confined. During the second year of medical school, the medical student is introduced to a cadaver.[24] Often it is the remains of an older person, possibly affecting stereotypes of those who are most likely to die and who are medicine's most frequent consumers. The medical student also observes that those who die are rapidly deindividualized: hospital personnel—like those in "primitive societies"—tie the deceaseds' hands and feet together and then wrap them in "morgue sheets" for a secret removal to the basement morgue. Eventually, the deceased becomes merely an entry on numerous bureaucratic forms: death certificate, autopsy permit, release of personal belongings form, and provisional death certificate. In sum, the student learns that death is "controllable" through medical routinization.

During the student's professional death education, he or she learns that personal feelings and attitudes are to be denied or ignored. The death of another human being is an event one must not take personally. This could be difficult, as many physicians have an above-average fear of death, often stemming from childhoods that were marked by a death or serious illness in the family (Toufexis and Castronoro 1983). Protecting themselves by a process of mastery, they become doctors. By learning how to deny one's own feelings, attitudes, and apprehensions toward dying and death, the student learns the defense of objectifying oneself and observing death from an impersonal and purely biological point of view.

While learning that death should not affect one personally, it is recognized that death does affect one professionally. There is the unspoken "but subtly perpetuated idea that the death of a patient represents a failure" (Barton 1972). Death becomes a matter that threatens professional identities. Also learned is that there exists a certain professional stigma in even having contact with death, such as being an oncologist. Finally, the specific training of physicians touches upon ethical issues as well: many patients in teaching hospitals are surgically operated on not by the surgeons they engage but rather by surgical trainees under their supervision (Rensberger 1978).

In sum, medical schools build a base of fact-oriented knowledge that will aid the student in diagnosing and treating medical textbook diseases, but this does not necessarily help the patient as a person. Training encourages the student to ignore the personal element of a patient and to treat the symptoms and the physical body; emotional status is largely ignored. This helps the physician to maintain professional distance from the patient so as not to become emotionally involved (Redding 1980). It was not until 1972 that the specific area of death education for medical students was first addressed (Liston 1975). Before this course, instituted by David Barton at Vanderbilt, medical students were on their own in dealing with dying patients. For the years 1960 to 1971, the *Cumulative Index Medicus* is devoid of articles addressing the teaching of medical students about death and dying (Liston 1975). In Dickinson's 1980 survey of medical school curriculums, he found that of 107 medical schools, only 7 had a full-term course on the subject, while 44 had a minicourse and 42 featured occasional lectures on the subject (Dickinson 1981).[25]

Managing the Death Trajectory

There is a certain irony in the controversy over whether a physician should inform a dying patient that death is imminent. Should the doctor be blunt or ambiguous in discussing the patient's prognosis? Most physicians believe that a patient should not be told he or she has only six weeks, six months, or any finite time to live (Shneidman 1973, p. 90). There are several reasons: such information may cause the patient to give up or attempt suicide; the physician may not really know how long a person has to live, and there is always the possibility of remission; and, finally, there is always the chance that a cure will be found (McCormick 1980, p. 133). Research shows that

---

 A Dictionary of Medical Death Terms

What language of death exists among hospital personnel, and how may this shape their approach to the dying?

CMO: comfort measures only

Code 90: patient utterly without hope

DAS: dead at scene (colloquially "dead as shit")

DNR: do not resuscitate, no heroic measures in the event that the patient seems about to die

DOA: dead on arrival

DRT: dead right there (where found)

Gomer: get out of my emergency room; often the old

Hanging crepe: what to tell the family of one who could either live or die

The O sign: deceased's mouth is open

The Q sign: deceased's mouth is open and tongue is hanging out

Therapeutic misadventure: an operation that kills the patient

Circling the drain: death is imminent

---

between 70 and 90 percent of physicians favor a conspiracy of silence regarding interactions with the terminally ill (Rabin and Rabin 1970).

One result of this professional silence is a new ritual of exit. It is an informational game, dealing with the knowledge of someone's forthcoming death and who tells whom about it. Consider, for example, the story of Mrs. Phillips, a seventy-three-year-old widow diagnosed with terminal stomach cancer. After exploratory surgery two weeks earlier, her family was informed of the prognosis, but she was not. Mrs. Phillips started noticing a change in her family members' behavior and began receiving many unexpected visits, such as from her grandchildren, who usually only visited during the summers. She had only seen her physician once since her surgery, and nothing had been discussed at that time. She became very suspicious and angry. According to a son, all of the family members refused to talk about "it" and did not want her informed. Finally, after three days of this, the son convinced his siblings that their mother should be told the truth, and they requested that her physician be the one to confront her.

But Mrs. Phillips knew, as do most terminally ill patients, and did not have any great difficulty accepting her fate. What she did feel was anger, anger toward both the physician and her family for withholding *her* information. "I'm entitled to any information about myself. It's only my body that has deteriorated, not my mind." She then felt a growing distance between herself and family members and experienced loneliness. She wanted so much to discuss her fate, but the family would only "talk about mundane things" or about themselves. Mrs. Phillips was not a winner in the information game of death.

Studies have consistently shown that physicians often believe that the terminally ill do not want to know about the severity of their situation, that such information would destroy all hope and thereby accelerate death. In a 1982 study of three thousand Texas physicians conducted by Drs. Bruhn, Bunce, and Scurry of the University of Texas Medical Branch at Galveston, for example, 47 percent said they try to avoid telling a patient directly that he or she is dying, and another 27 percent admitted that they avoid a dying person altogether (*San Antonio Express-News* 1982). Despite this professional silence, a majority of patients do wish to be told the truth and feel betrayed if it is withheld. Glaser and Strauss (1965) modeled this informational game in their elaborations of "awareness contexts," which take into account the combination of what each actor knows about the identity of the other and his or her own identity in the eyes of the other:

- *Closed awareness.* In this situation, though the staff knows, the dying are not informed of their impending demise—thus denying these persons the opportunity to put their affairs in order and to retain personal control over their lives until death. Instead, the dying are integrated into an established routine and institutionally managed. Their absent rights include privacy, consent to treatment, choice of place and time of death, and disposition of body after death (Castles and Murray 1979, p. 86).

- *Suspicion awareness.* This situation is a modification of the closed awareness situation, but here the patient suspects that he or she is dying and suspects that the staff is withholding this information. Often the dying are aware of changes in their interactions with family and staff and make strategic moves in attempting to elicit information from them.

- *Open awareness.* In this context, both the staff and the patient know and acknowledge the likelihood of death. Though such openness does not necessarily assist in death's acceptance, it does open the opportunity for feelings to be expressed and support to be shared.

- *Mutual pretense awareness.* This is a modification of open awareness, where the terminally ill patient, family, and staff are fully aware of the forthcoming death, but here all pretend that recovery will come. This can become a complex interaction game—potentially leading to hypocrisy, deception, and false hopes—which dying children are often forced to play.

High Technology and Medical Ethics

Technology is overwhelming the art of healing. It prolongs the dying process in sterile, alien environments. It requires the presence of paid, impersonal professionals, instead of family and friends, to conduct the modern death watch. It also produces new trade-offs for death avoidance: the implantations of artificial hearts, for example, could lead to strokes that erase all memories—in other words, continued physical existence at the cost of one's symbolic self (reminiscent of the tales of Satan's "bargains" when offering immortality for one's soul). As one elderly woman observed, "it was a whole lot easier when God made the decision" (*New York Times* 1984b).

Curiously, though science is increasingly able to predict disease and death and to prevent or delay their occurrence, it also has produced controversy over exactly what death is and over the ways in which it is to be avoided. Financial factors are joined with ethical considerations in the everyday determinations of whether respirators are disconnected, dialysis or transfusions withheld, organ transplants made, infections treated (Kleiman 1985), or experimental drugs administered to the terminally ill.[26] Heart transplants in 1985, for example, cost from $57,000 to $110,000 and liver transplants up to $238,000, with considerable subsequent expenses. With the shortage of organs for transplants, who decides who the recipient will be? And who pays?

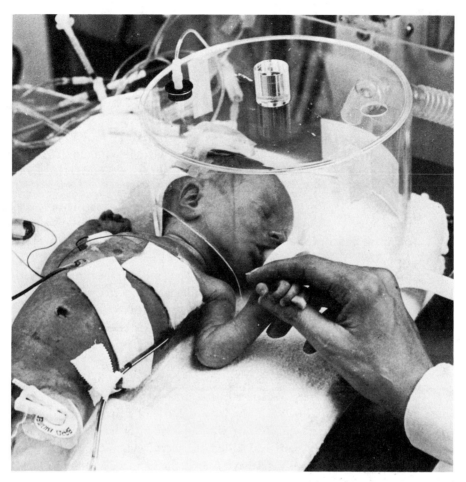

Over 500 neonatal wards treat about 150,000 premature babies every year in the United States. In the 1970s nearly all such infants died but since the 1980s nearly 80% of babies delivered during the 27th week of gestation and/or weighing two pounds survive. However, about a quarter of the survivors have serious disorders, including cerebral palsy, extremely low intelligence, and retardation. This four-pound boy, in whom doctors installed a pacemaker, sucks on a pacifier as he grips his mother's thumb. UPI/Bettmann Newsphotos.

Private health-insurance policies are broadening their coverage to include "medically necessary" transplantations, while financially strapped state governments pay (under Medicaid) for transplants given to indigents and the federal government picks up the tab for kidney and liver transplants for some children (Otten 1985c).

As scientists neared perfecting the tests for detecting the genes responsible for Huntington's disease, cystic fibrosis, and muscular dystrophy, hopes were raised for being able to similarly detect the genes predisposing one to premature heart attack, breast and colon cancer, diabetes, schizophrenia, and Alzheimer's disease. Certainly such diagnostic capabilities would allow preventive strategies to be taken by those at high risk, but what rights would employers, insurance companies, and the federal government have to this information (Bishop 1984)? Does one even tell the individual of the nature of his or her forthcoming demise? And what if medicine fails to detect a lethal gene or infirmity? The New Jersey Supreme Court ruled in 1984 that a child born with health defects could sue the physicians for the medical costs incurred when they failed to diagnose his mother's German measles during pregnancy. Attorneys for the infant contended that the child would be better off if he had never been born. Said Justice Stewart Pollock, "Such a claim would stir the passions of jurors about the nature and value of life, the fear of nonexistence and about abortion. That mix is more than the judicial system can digest." The court concluded that "the crux of the problem is that there is no rational way to measure nonexistence or to compare nonexistence with the pain and suffering of his impaired existence" (Sullivan 1984).

The fourth artificial heart recipient was a businessman who was initially identified as "the godfather of Swedish crime" (*Dallas Times Herald* 1985). A person is considered dead by Swedish law when the heart ceases beating; could Leif Stenberg escape the tax evasion charges that had been levied against him? In New York, the legal defense of a man charged with murdering an individual whose heart was subsequently transplanted into another was that the physicians had killed the victim when they removed his functioning organs. Such cases have forced the law to elaborate on exactly what death is. As of 1984, thirty-eight states recognize a person as legally dead when the brain ceases to function, even if the functioning of heart and lungs is artificially maintained (Margolick 1984). The brain, and no longer the heart, is now understood to be the vital organ and the seat of the soul.

The Baby Fae case illustrates that the strategies for avoiding death can generate ethical controversy as well. The infant was born with the fatal birth defect called hypoplastic left heart syndrome. A number of baboons were slaughtered in order to find the right-sized heart for the two-week-old infant, and one was implanted. Her progress was front-page news, and hundreds of American sent flowers, cards, and money. After the baby's death, however, moral questions set in. What right do we have to kill nature in order to preserve human life? This question became more than an academic query when the head of the operation team admitted that another infant heart had not been sought, even though the *Los Angeles Times* and other news organizations claimed that the heart of a two-month-old had been available (Altman 1984b).[27] One year after the operation, it was revealed that Baby Fae had died because the physicians had failed to match her blood type with that of the baboon (Eckholm 1985)—a standard procedure in human transplant operations—further fueling criticism that the desire for publicity and professional acclaim by the facility staff, not concern for this child of a broken and impoverished family, had motivated the experiment.

And then there are the financial considerations. People now typically pass through the death trajectory as a meteor passes through the earth's atmosphere: often the old go through a number of hospital admissions before finally expiring in one, much like the cosmic bodies skipping in the atmosphere before entering their final plunge; and as the meteor typically burns up before reaching the ground, the resources of the old are often exhausted[28]—first by the medical profession and then by the funeral industry—when the end is finally met. Care for those in a persistent vegetative state now costs about one hundred fifty thousand dollars a year (Malcolm 1985). There is a "treatment at all cost" ethic fostered by hospital and physician fears of legal retaliation, physicians' professional duty to heal, public compassion for the elderly and expectations for the curability of any ailment, the absence of standards for limiting medical treatment, and the need for return on investments for expensive medical technology (Lief 1985). About 28 percent of the nation's total Medicare budget goes to maintaining the 6 percent of Medicare patients in their last year of life, 11 percent of this total for the last forty days (Lamm 1984; Kleiman 1985). This amounts to more than one percent of the entire gross national product going toward health care for old people in their last year of life (Gartner 1988). As former Governor Richard Lamm of Colorado observed, "we spend four times as much on these patients who die as we do on other Medicare patients. . . . Technological immortality is running into fiscal reality" (1984).

The Right-to-Die and Euthanasia Controversies

On June 11, 1985, Karen Ann Quinlan died. When she lapsed into a substance-abuse coma on April 15, 1975, her case prompted a historic right-to-die court decision after her parents successfully sought to have her disconnected from a respirator. The New Jersey Supreme Court ruled that she could die "with grace and dignity." When she was disconnected on May 22, 1975, contrary to the expectations of physicians, she remained alive, in a fetal position, in what was described as a "chronic vegetative state." Quinlan came to symbolize the whole of the medical ethics–high technology controversy (Schmeck 1985b). The placement of her coffin in the aisle between the family and the press dramatized the public significance of this private event. Ten years is a staggering period to be in the limbo between life and death. She died socially less than a year after Nixon resigned the presidency and yet did not expire physically until well into Reagan's second term, when individuals were walking about with artificial hearts. Undoubtedly, had a spirit resided in such limbo for such a period within a more primitive culture, it would have tested the explanatory limits of the cultural ethos.[29]

In ways, Quinlan was able to successfully haunt our own culture. Her condition challenged definitions and understandings of death, the relative power of physicians versus family members to decide when to end heroic measures, the individual's very right to die, the role of government in ensuring the citizenship rights of life and death to its citizens,[30] and the mid-1980s legal decisions concerning active euthanasia (such as the right to terminate the feeding and watering of the brain-dead). Opponents of the right to die claimed that Quinlan's survival was proof of divine will. M. O. Turner, a member of San Antonio's Right to Life Committee, said, "They disconnected her, and God's still in charge. I think God just re-connected her." Thirty-one years of age at the time of her death from pneumonia, Quinlan weighed seventy-five pounds and was fed through a tube in her nose.

At Quinlan's funeral, Monsignor Thomas Trapasso said that he prayed her death would not "erode society's concern for the worth of human life. Our hope is that law, medicine and theology will work together, lest we become slaves to the technological imperative which says 'We can do it, therefore do it.' The three disciplines must work together, so that technology will not be seen as the means of achieving victory over death" (Schmeck 1985b).

There is a fine line between active and passive euthanasia, a line currently being tested and defined by the courts, religious groups, ethicists, and state legislatures. The decision of Quinlan's parents to allow her to die, for example, was backed by their Roman Catholic priest, who said, "Extraordinary means are not morally required to prolong life." However, a staff member of the Vatican daily *L'Osservatore Romano* disagreed, writing: "It is impossible to support the claim of the right of 'death with dignity.' A right to death does not exist. . . . Love for life, even a life reduced to a 'ruin,' drives one to protect life with every possible care" (*Time* 1975). Not only does controversy continue to exist on the matters of indirect euthanasia, but it has expanded to include such issues as the quality of life, direct euthanasia, freedom to choose death or have others choose in instances of incompetency, and whether age should be a criterion for giving or withholding treatment (Goodman 1984).

In *Death by Choice,* Daniel Maguire (1975) explores the possibility that we overestimate our moral right to kill in military settings while underestimat-

Can't We Put My Mother to Sleep?

When I was a boy, my family had a beloved bulldog. Eventually he became very old—blind, incontinent, wheezing heavily, barely able to eat or walk. We took him to the vet and, as the euphemism then had it, the vet "put Jerry to sleep."

Every few days now, I go to visit my 90-year-old mother in a nearby nursing home, more to salve my own conscience probably than to do her any meaningful service. For her, in fact, there is little I can do. She lies on her side in bed, legs drawn rigidly into a fetal position, blinks at me uncomprehendingly as I prattle on about family doings, and rarely utters a sound except a shriek of pain when the attendants turn her from one side to the other in their constant battle to heal her horrible bedsores. She must be hand-fed, and her incontinency requires a urethral catherer.

Why do we treat our aged and loved animals better than we treat our aged and loved human beings?

Otten 1985a. Reprinted by permission of the
Wall Street Journal, ©Dow Jones & Company, Inc. 1985

ing it in some medical and private contexts. Few instances of such underestimation are more apparent than in the case of William Bartling. A seventy-year-old suffering from five usually fatal diseases, including lung cancer, Bartling was refused by a Los Angeles County Superior Court judge to be freed of arm restraints so that he could turn off his respirator. The lawyer for the Glendale Adventist Medical Center argued that to turn off the respirator would violate the ethical duty to heal. Said Judge Lawrence Waddington, "The court is of the view that the law requires that the party be terminally ill. I find no case in the United States in which the person applying for injunctive relief is not in a comatose, vegetative or brain-dead state." Bartling's attorney replied, "We do not ask for this court to issue a death warrant, or for any defendant to disconnect the respirator. We ask that Mr. Bartling be put back in a position of power" (*New York Times* 1984a). Bartling appealed, but he died five months later, just twenty-three hours before his appeal was to be heard by a California appellate court. Nonetheless, deliberations were made, and the court ruled that he had the constitutional right to refuse medical treatment. The decision read: "If the right of the patient to self-determination as to his own medical treatment is to have any meaning at all, it must be paramount to the interests of the patient's hospital and doctors. The right of a competent adult patient to refuse medical treatment is a constitutionally guaranteed right which must not be abridged" (*New York Times* 1984c). "Life was so much easier," said his lawyer, "when we knew we didn't know all the answers to life's mysteries" (Malcolm 1984a).

The parameters of the right to die were further expanded in the mid-1980s to include matters of less indirect euthanasia. The New Jersey Supreme Court ruled in the matter of *Conroy* that all life-sustaining medical treatment can be withheld or withdrawn from incompetent as well as competent terminally ill nursing-home patients if that was what they wanted or would want, provided a series of "best-interest tests" was followed.[31] In this case (later upheld by a presidential commission), the court eliminated the distinction between artificial feedings (feeding tubes) and other forms of life support, such as respirators, in reversing a state superior court decision that the removal of a feeding tube from a mentally incompetent eighty-four-year-old woman constituted homicide (Sullivan 1985; Meisel 1985). In 1987, delegates of the California Bar Association approved a resolution to support legislation that would allow physicians to give a lethal dose of drugs to terminally ill patients (*New York Times* 1987).

But what if one exists in a nonterminal vegetative state, as is the condition of an estimated ten thousand Americans (Malcolm 1985; ABC News 1985)? Dramatizing this situation was the case of Paul Brophy, who by 1985 had remained in a vegetative state for more than two years in the New England Sinai Hospital. His family, eventually realizing that there was no hope for recovery, wanted to honor his wishes of never having to remain in a comatose state—a condition he knew well from his years of experience with the fire department. Said his wife to the judge, "In essence, his life is over. He has no quality of life" (Malcolm 1985). However, the hospital representatives and a court-appointed attorney representing Brophy argued that food and water were basic human rights and that it would violate professional ethics to withhold them. One attending physician said, in effect, that death was their decision and not the family's. The case boiled down to whether or not starvation would be a painful death for an unconscious man (ABC News 1985). Prolife groups were attracted to the case and accused the Brophy family of trying to commit a "Nazi murder." The judge ruled that the feeding tubes were not to be removed, nor could the family move Brophy to another facility, where perhaps their wishes would be honored. And so, at the time of this writing, both Brophy and his family remain in limbo, he between life and death (at an estimated cost of one hundred fifty thousand dollars per year) and they in legal ambiguity. According to Dr. Richard Field, a Mount Sinai physician, the longest case on record for remaining in such a state is more than thirty-seven years (ABC News 1985). In early 1986, the judicial council of the American Medical Association decided that it would be ethical for doctors to withhold "all means of life-prolonging medical treatment," including food and water, from patients in irreverisble comas even though death may not be imminent. Though having no legal standing, the opinion reflects the changing social climate toward euthanasia (Malcolm 1986). However, the withdrawal of food and water may be a barrier many are unwilling to cross. Dr. Christine Cassel, chief of internal medicine at the University of Chicago Medical School, observes the need to cut "a broad swath between letting people die because their lives have become an inconvenience to them and letting them die because their lives have become an inconvenience to us" (Otten 1986a).

Nurses or family members who take matters into their own hands—whether by disconnecting ventilators, giving lethal injections, or shooting the patient—still receive the full brunt of the law. So do those who refuse to disconnect life-support systems. In Akron, Ohio, a 1.26-million-dollar suit was brought unsuccessfully against a physician who refused to disconnect a respirator from a seventy-year-old comatose woman despite her family's wishes to do so and a court's permission allowing the disconnection (*New York Times* 1985a). If direct euthanasia should ever be legitimized, it will be only the physician who has the right to assist.

In the meantime, public opinion continues to increasingly support the right of the terminally ill to die. Pollster Louis Harris asked the following question over several time periods: "The patient who is terminally ill, with no cure in sight, ought to have the right to tell his doctor to put him out of his misery, or do you think this is wrong?" In 1973, 53 percent of the American public thought it was wrong; by 1981, Harris found 56 percent thinking that the patient does have the right. Further, Harris found in 1981 that 78 percent of Americans feel that "a patient with a terminal disease ought to be able to tell his doctor to let him die rather than to extend his life when no cure is in sight," and 73 percent favored giving the family of one "terminally ill, in a coma and not conscious, with no cure in sight" the right to tell doctors "to remove all life-support services and let the patient die" (Harris 1981). As evident in Table 11.4, the antieuthanasia position is most likely to be found among nonwhites, the most religious, the most conservative, and those with the least income and education.

Death with Dignity

In the past, the quest to give some dignity to the perhaps undignified lives of individuals produced excessive funerary expenditures among the poor, leading to Parliament passing restrictive laws concerning funeral costs in nineteenth-century Britain (see Chapter 3). Nowadays, people seek dignified conclusions to their lives by minimizing the monies expended for their terminal treatments. As Lamm noted, "a new liberation movement is forming, a movement for liberation *from* our machines when they are used not to pro-

Table 11.4 Americans' Attitudes toward Euthanasia

A 1947 survey conducted by the National Opinion Research Center (NORC) found 37 percent of Americans answered affirmatively to the question, "When a person has a disease that cannot be cured, do you think doctors should be allowed by law to end the patient's life by some pain-less means if the patient and his family request it?" In 1985, nearly forty years later, NORC found this agreement rate had increased to nearly two-thirds. A random selection of 1534 Americans were surveyed by the NORC concerning their attitudes toward a host of social issues. Below is a breakdown of how they responded to the question (derived from NORC 1986). (Results exclude the 2.9 percent of the public who either did not know or gave no answer to the question.)

	Yes	No	N
Total	65.6%	34.4%	1489
Age			
Younger than 30	74.2%	25.7%	342
30–39	75.4	24.6%	334
40–49	65.0	35.0	214
50–59	57.4	42.6	216
60 and older	54.4	45.6	380
Education			
Less than high school	53.1%	46.9%	401
High-school	70.7	29.3	776
1–4 years college	68.7	31.3	227
5 or more years college	68.2	31.8	85
Income			
Less than $6000	60.1%	39.9%	168
$6000–9999	59.3	40.7	140
$10,000–17,499	62.3	37.7	252
$17,500 and up	70.5	29.5	810
Sex			
Male	70.0%	30.0%	674
Female	61.8%	38.2%	815
Race			
White	68.3%	32.7%	1304
Nonwhite	53.5	46.5	185
Religion			
Protestant	63.1%	36.9%	924
Catholic	63.8	36.2	398
Jewish	80.6	19.4	31
None	86.1	13.9	108
Religiosity			
Weak–moderate	72.9%	27.1%	742
Strong	51.6	48.4	591
Political views			
Liberal	71.9%	28.1%	363
Moderate	69.0	31.0	545
Conservative	60.8	39.2	518

long living but to prolong dying. We have reached a point where doctors have the capability of keeping patients alive long after they have ceased to exist as thinking, feeling human beings. Do patients or their families have the right to refuse the 'benefits' of these machines?" (Lamm 1984, p. 21).

We no longer die honorable deaths. As Berger, Berger, and Kellner (1973, pp. 86, 90) noted, honor is the direct expression of status—as it implies that identity essentially derives from institutional roles—and entails prescribed standards of behavior. The dying have no status, for they have normally been socially disengaged and transformed into nonpersons. The dying have no ritual, no means by which to assert their personal worth and adequacy as role incumbents. Instead, people nowadays speak of "death with dignity": "Dignity, as against honor, always relates to the intrinsic humanity divested of all socially imposed roles or norms. It pertains to the self as such, to the individual regardless of his position in society" (Berger, Berger, and Kellner 1973, p. 89). But dignity cannot be asserted if one is totally institutionalized and has no control whatsoever over one's fate. It cannot come to those who ask, as did one terminally ill older woman, "Who owns my body, Medicare, the hospital, the state, or me?" (Lamm 1984, p. 21).

Since the 1970s, the death-with-dignity movement has produced a number of groups dedicated to enhancing the individual's control over his or her own demise, including Concern for Dying, Society for the Right to Die, the Hemlock Society, the American Society of Law and Medicine, the Hastings Center, and the Society for Health and Human Values (Malcolm 1984b). Some, like the Hemlock Society, go so far as to provide suicide strategies; more moderate groups sponsor the legalization of "living wills," which authorize the termination of unnecessary heroic measures.[32] Another outcome of this movement is hospice.

The Hospice Movement: Challenging the Medical Monopoly[35]

Old and interminably dying of cancer, she was unable to care for herself any longer. At the hospital, she was examined, x-rayed, and assigned to a bed. Intravenous therapy alone was instituted at this time; additional chemotherapy was contraindicated. Fiercely independent all of her life, she pleaded to be sent home; but, completely bedridden, she had to remain institutionalized. Her debilitation continued, intensified perhaps by the impersonal care and sometimes degrading treatment she received. Her pain, both physical and psychological, increased. Within one month, she died.

This death was unaffected by the death-with-dignity movement that has emerged during the past twenty years. Not only does a "good" death often elude the majority of the terminally ill, but there are differing perspectives regarding what actually constitutes a good death. Such ambiguity is a recent phenomenon; in the past, members of Western society remained in agreement on the definition of a successful death, even as this definition changed through the centuries (Ariès 1974). In Ariès's view, the contemporary era of tabooed death arose, in part, from the attempts of those close to the sick (and dying) person to conceal the patient's condition in order to spare his or her feelings. The patient, on the other hand, became responsible for the management of his or her stigma, taking care that the efforts of normals to ease matters for him or her were seen as effective and appreciated (Goffman 1963). This interpersonal dynamic eventually became culturally amplified, and death itself became denied in order to dampen "the disturbance and the overly strong and unbearable emotion caused by the ugliness of dying and by the very presence of death in the midst of a happy life" (Ariès 1974, p. 87). With the expulsion of death from everyday life, the subjects of death and dying became taboo, "surrounded by disapproval and shame" (Feifel 1963, p. 14). The dying are isolated by death-denying hospital staff and prevented from controlling their own lives once they are institutionalized.

This loss of control experienced by institutionalized terminally ill patients is a central motif of much thanatological research. Loss of control is seen as the loss of dignity. Dying patients' basic human rights are seen to be violated when they lack the knowledge and the power to make decisions (Levine and Scotch 1970). Patients have the right to know their condition, to choose or to reject the treatment regimen, to choose or to reject attempts to prolong their lives, and to decide fully regarding the disposal of their remains. But the fact remains that as the dying person deteriorates, others must take control of the life remaining. The possibility of Weisman's (1972, pp. 39–40) "appropriate death" therefore hinges on the relationship between the dying individual and the caregivers, which becomes problematic in the case of the elderly, who are seen to be incapable of managing their own lives anyway. In fact, according to Kastenbaum and Aisenberg (1972, p. 121), rather than being provided with appropriate environment and care, the terminally ill elderly person is more likely to be rejected as a deviant and denied control because being both old and dying is doubly stigmatizing.

Today, the inevitability of the isolated, depersonalized, technological deaths now prevalent in the United States is in question. One alternative, hospice, is beginning to revolutionize care of the terminally ill. The word *hospice* originally meant a place of shelter or rest for pilgrims and strangers. Today, the proponents of the modern hospice have redefined the word to mean a concept, not a place. It is a philosophy and a method of care—a way in which one may retain control of one's life until death. As defined by the National Hospice Organization, hospice

is a centrally administered program of palliative and supportive services which provides physical, psychological, social and spiritual care for dying persons and their families. Services are provided by a medically supervised interdisciplinary team of professionals and volunteers. Hospice services are available in both the home and in-patient settings. Home care is provided on a part-time, intermittent, regularly scheduled, and around-the-clock, on-call basis. Bereavement services are available to the family. Admission to a Hospice program of care is on the basis of patient and family need. (1982, p. 8)

Hospice, then, can be viewed as an alternative to technological death, a reaction against the physicians' total control of the final rite of passage.

Hospice Practitioners

Given the historical perspectives of the hospice movement and its structural attempts to restore "appropriate deaths," to what extent do hospice workers appreciate the revolutionary bearing and historical antecedents of their tasks?[34] To find out, in 1983, Rinaldi and Kearl (this author) examined the attitudes, opinions, and perceptions of randomly selected hospice workers from around the country.[35]

Nearly three-quarters of the respondents agreed that the growth of hospice can be directly related to the work of Kübler-Ross and that it represented a return to values important before high technology. As expressed by one informant:

For the most part, yes [hospice is a reaction against institutionalized death], and that due primarily to Kübler-Ross's work and publications in the early 1970s. But essentially I believe it is a reaction within a larger context, one indication of the "swinging of the pendulum" by industrialized nations back to the personal, the simple, the human values that technology denies.

Hospice workers further unanimously see their movement as an indication of a general change in social consciousness toward a natural acceptance of death.[36] As put by one participant, hospice "seems a move toward acceptance of death as a natural part of the life cycle in a culture which has more and more denied the reality that we are mortal." Another perceived it as "one of those historical happenings when many people in various professions (and many nonworking people as well) began to work together to take death out of the closet."

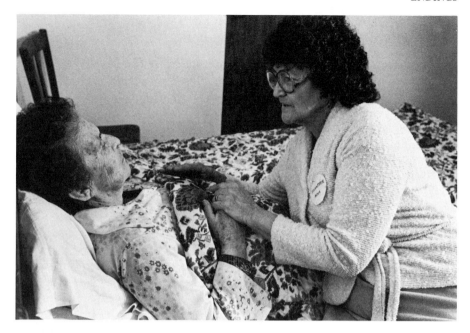

A volunteer talks with a house-bound senior citizen. Mimi Forsyth, Monkmeyer Press.

The hospice informants appreciated the revolutionary nature of their activities. Sixty-two percent agreed that "hospice is a radical departure from the medical model of care for the terminally ill." Representative of this view were the following comments:

Yes, I believe the hospice movement has come about as a reaction to the impersonal deaths that have occurred in institutional settings. For many years the dying were set aside, almost neglected, since the medical professionals felt that there was no reason to put time and caring into a person they had no hope of cure for. Society as a whole was unable to talk about, let alone deal with, the dying.

Hospital focus is on lifesaving. Death is perceived as a failure by staffs. Family often gets angry and feels betrayed at the outcome. The patient is put through every known treatment program, often at great expense and added suffering. My own interest in hospice is not so much a reaction against a geographical setting as against an atmosphere which does not allow the patient to express his real feelings about dying and living until death. Hospice fights the taboo against death.

A minority of the respondents proffered an even more radical portrayal of hospice origins. Nearly one out of three agreed that "in part, hospice can be viewed as a female-sponsored movement which developed in reaction to the male-dominated medical establishment." For some women, perhaps hospice represents a means by which they can exercise their historical role in caring for and nurturing the ill. Further, slightly fewer than one-third considered hospice as a clergy-sponsored movement. This finding indicates that hospice may represent to some the attempt of clergy to regain their historic control—lost to medicine with the advent of high technology—over the final passage and to bring spiritual values to the dying process.[37]

When respondents were asked exactly how a hospice death differs from the typical institutional experiences of patients, the theme of patient control was seen as most significant. When asked to rank the most frequently mentioned aspects from the first questionnaire, the themes of control, dignity, and quality interactions were rated most highly. However, the surrendering of control by the staff was an acknowledged difficulty for more than two-thirds of the respondents. More than 87 percent agreed that physicians had difficulty yielding control, and 81 percent agreed that traditional nurses have the same problem. The emphasis is on treatment of the patient rather than care. As one hospice worker commented:

It is best to address the issue of control in the following way: with hospice patients, the focus is on the person, the patient rather than the illness. People are not treated aggressively nor is the illness. The disposition is one of caring and comforting. The energies, therefore, are different. It takes education and orientation to help the staff see that the focus is not only the illness.

It should be noted that hospice, too, has a problem of control. After all, for example, both patients and families have been socialized to surrender control to medical authorities. In part, this is what has made the social workers' role so important; they are trained in principles of self-determination and enabling of their clients. One social worker remarked: "About 80 percent of the families do take control because of the continuing support given by me (or by the person following the case). There are times when the control has to be backed up by my presence or by an in-service or even a meeting with the administrator." And according to another, "especially for the family, the availability of a social worker can make a difference in the family's ability to function as effective caregivers."

The suitability of hospice for the elderly, who make up the vast majority of hospice patients, produced the greatest amount of disagreement. Forty-two percent agreed and 58 percent disagreed that the old "tend to be passive and accept the physician's recommendations, even if these mean separation from loved ones and prolonged suffering." Some expressed strong belief that the old are more compliant, amenable to institutional care, and possibly unable to benefit from hospice:

Actually, in many ways the concepts of talking about feelings and taking control are foreign to the elderly and more comfortable to younger people who have been raised to deal more openly with feelings, etc.

Many older patients have great respect for authority figures, especially doctors, and when institutionalized or in their offices would never think of (or are fearful of) questioning.

The old are not necessarily the favorite type of patient; 73 percent of the sample disagreed with the statement that "the older person is less demand-ing, more accepting, and easier to work with."

Despite the fact that the many hospice professionals had been socialized by the dominant medical model, which views death as stigmatizing for both the terminally ill and their caregivers, these individuals have voluntarily cho-sen to care for the dying.

Conclusion

Medicine is the institution in which culture's battle against death is ritually waged. It is here that immortality hopes are invested and the strategies for death avoidance are devised and played out. As the twentieth century has unfolded, such hopes have become routinely reinforced by the eradication of diseases, wonder drugs and organ transplants, the routinization of old age, and, most recently, recombinant genetics. Medicine has come to define the very limits of human existence, forcing some hospitals to employ philoso-phers to ponder the moral dilemmas wrought by accelerating technological breakthroughs. When new diseases threaten the lives of patrons or when cures for old killers are not found, illness becomes politicized, and massive resources are invested within the institution. But as the medical establish-ment has grown in social power and as its practitioners have come to profes-sionally monopolize its healing rituals, the costs of its services have skyrock-eted, making the quality of health care dependent on the ability to pay. Further, medicine has become the instrument by which death is culturally banished, institutionally hidden, and psychologically denied. For the dying individual, the medicalization of death has resulted in deindividuation and loss of control.

The near eradication of premature death has come at the cost of individ-uals losing control over their own slow-motion demise. This trend toward the loss of control has accelerated greatly with the prolongevity revolution and its changing quality of death, the development of technological medi-cine, and the institutionalization of the dying and the dead. With the removal of death from everyday life, families have lost the knowledge of how to care for and even how to relate to the dying person, and the fear of dying—particularly in nursing homes—has come to exceed the fear of death among those most likely to die. And those trained to cure, the health-care professionals, wanting to believe that properly applied science holds all the answers, have come to reject dying persons as evidence of their own failure.

In reaction against this tendency to stigmatize and depersonalize those about to die and to treat only the malady instead of the whole person, hospice emerged. This philosophy, dedicated to preserving the dignity of the terminally ill and the ideal of good death, concentrates on care rather than cure and encourages the dying person and his or her family to retain as much control as possible throughout the last days of life. The rapid proliferation of hospice in the United States may be an indication that a change in attitude toward death and dying is taking place.

NOTES

1. Modernization here means not only the emergence of high technology but also secularization and the concomitant breakdown of moral consensus (medicine seems to flourish where there is religious tolerance), urbanization with its attendant individualism, and the worship of science. The new cultural cathedral may well be the medical centers dotting the country. In Houston, for example, the town that brings us *the* temple of consumption, the Galleria, also brings us the Baylor Medical Center, occupied by such high priests as Dr. William DeBakey. Here, it seems, each organ of the body has its own separate facility dedicated to it.

2. Lest the moral power of this institution be questioned, consider which had the greater influence over the sexual activities of Americans: the 1983 Vatican guidelines on sex education or the AIDS epidemic? Physicians in charge of a Madison, Wisconsin, program for the control of venereal diseases in homosexual men found that men surveyed in 1982 had an average of 6.8 sexual partners in the previous thirty days. One year later, as fears of AIDs spread, that number plunged to 3.2 (Lyons 1984).

3. Such "progress" does not necessarily correlate with greater life expectancies, however. There is a certain irony to the fact that the pockets of longevity around the world (Vilcabamba, Ecuador; the Hunaz region of south-central Asia; the Caucasus Mountains) are in some of the most underdeveloped rural areas in the world. Apparently, the very contact with the stresses of modern civilization can kill.

4. From evolutionary theory, mammals are provided with their greatest resistance to harmful environmental factors during the period of their life span when they enjoy their greatest reproductive capacity. Evolution has little interest in the survival of those in the postreproductive period, and senescent animals are rarely found in a natural environmental niche.

5. Though only 6.4 percent of the seventy-five- to eighty-four-year-olds are in nursing homes, more than 21.6 percent of the eighty-five and over group reside there.

6. The probability that an individual will develop cancer in the next five years is 1 in 700 for someone aged twenty-five. But at age sixty-five, it is 1 in 44. The peak increase in cancer incidence and mortality occurs between the ages of forty-five and sixty-five, after which cancer risk levels off. Whereas cancer accounts for 30 percent of the deaths among people from the ages of sixty-five to sixty-nine, it is the cause of death in only 12 percent of those older than eighty (Altman 1984a).

7. In 1900, only 41 percent of newborn babies could be expected to reach age sixty-five. By 1973, about 73 percent of Americans were born with that expectation.

8. Instead of receiving stern moral lessons as instruction for salvation, we now witness the proliferation of health-care warnings guiding our prolongevity quests. Physicians address the mass media with warnings about the dangers of cigarettes and stress and the need for exercise. The new demons are probably as omnipresent now as they were in the past, if one believes Dr. Bruce Ames, chairman of biochemistry at the University of California at Berkeley, who claimed that natural poisons may be ten thousand times as common in the human diet as man-made pesticides. Genetic damage supposedly can be caused by alfalfa sprouts, potatoes, tomatoes, celery, herbal teas, and mushrooms (Ames 1983).

9. Even if death does come, medical technology has provided the means for at least genetic immortality with the establishment of sperm banks. For example, Robert Graham's Repository for Germinal Choice, popularly known as the Nobel Prize sperm bank, as of 1984 had seen the births of fifteen children to mothers artificially inseminated with the sperm of its genius donors. In addition, cells that have long outlived their donors are preserved, deep-frozen, in the living archives of the National Institute of General Medical Science's Human Genetic Mutant Cell Repository and the National Institute on Aging's Aging Cell Repository.

10. However, when medicine, through vasectomies, takes away one's capacities for genetic immortality, one may be healthier as a result. A 1983 study showed that half as many men with vasectomies died of cancer each year and only 60 percent as many from heart and blood vessel diseases (*San Jose Mercury News* 1983). Such findings, reminiscent of the traditional myth that death is the cost of one's procreative capacities, if believed and acted upon by the populace, could lead to depopulation. From a religious perspective, this is personal selfishness and has the same consequences as abortion.

11. The dead have even killed the living. In several cases of cornea transplants, there has been the transmission of a deadly virus that led to Creutzfeld-Jakob disease, a degenerative brain disorder (Schmeck 1977).

12. In the state of Texas, because of a little-known 1977 law, family permission no longer has to be obtained to harvest the corneas of the deceased. In Oregon, hospital officials are legally required to ask principal survivors for the organs of the deceased so they may be transplanted in another person in need (*Wall Street Journal* 1985). In 1988, the United States had twenty regional multiple tissue banks, one hundred eye banks, thirty skin banks, and more than four hundred surgical bone banks (Asinof 1988). Another medical opportunity for immortality for the dead can

be found on the obituary pages of any newspaper. One can observe in the "in lieu of flowers" obituaries that medicine is a frequent recipient of monies contributed in the name of the deceased.

13. Following the revelation of scandalous medical experiments during the 1960s, federal rules were established controlling all research involving humans, which led to, among other things, the requirement of "informed consent." Interestingly, in the case of Alzheimer's research, such consent is impossible, as, almost by definition, Alzheimer's patients cannot be informed. Further, though positive diagnosis is only possible through an autopsy, not enough are permitted by surviving families. Political concern for protecting life runs at odds with the need for medical research (Otten 1985a).

14. Victims of AIDS being the notable exception, according to some fundamentalists and conservatives.

15. Commemorative days have also been created for both medical practitioners and their patients: National Nursing Home Residents Day, National Operating Room Nurses Day, National Recovery Room Nurses Day, and National Recognition Day for Nurses.

16. The health-care industry proved during the recent recessions that it is immune to economic downturns as well. Instead of economizing, nearly 10 percent of hospitals by 1977 had turned to advertising as a means for explaining their services and high costs. The old tradition of limiting advertising (formerly banned to protect consumers from being duped) evaporated in order to save the massive infusions of public monies.

17. The search for high returns on investment also translated into medical noninvolvement with unprofitable Third World needs. For example, though a measles vaccine was introduced in the United States in 1963 (reducing the U.S. incidence of the disease by 99.9 percent by 1985), in 1984 the disease killed more than 1.5 million children in the less developed world when a dose of the vaccine cost only seven cents (Katz 1985).

18. In Texas, for example, it is unlawful to notify a family of a death until a physician has signed the death certificate. In 1970, a New York law was passed requiring physicians to issue death certificates for fetuses.

19. The proportion of entering medical students who are black declined during the 1980s, despite their increased proportion of applications. At predominantly white medical schools, the percentage of black entering students went from less than 1 percent in 1948 to 6.3 percent in 1974, then declined to 5.6 percent in 1983 (*New York Times* 1985b).

20. See Paul Starr's Pulitzer-winning *The Social Transformation of American Medicine* (1982) for a historical analysis of the professionalization of medicine.

21. According to Freidson (1970, p. 17), professionals justify their authority to control their activities, free from the restraint of others, through three claims: that unusual professional skill and knowledge are involved and that nonprofessionals are unable to either evaluate or regulate; that professionals are responsible and can be trusted to work without supervision; and that professionals can police themselves and

manage those who are incompetent or unethical. As Starr observes, "the acceptance of authority signifies 'a surrender of private judgment'" (1982, p. 10).

22. By the mid-1970s, the American Medical Association said that there were 160,509 certified specialists but only 54,000 general practitioners.

23. Such avoidance of the dying and the dead was highlighted in the midst of the AIDS epidemic. A 1987 news story reported that one-quarter of 258 doctors in training at New York hospitals did not think it unethical to refuse to treat AIDS victims, raising serious questions about the integrity of the medical profession (Prager 1987).

24. Sudnow (1967) reports that the status of internship residencies is partially determined by the number of cadavers available for study.

25. Until recently, even the subject of nuclear war was rarely broached in medical curriculums. In 1984, Praeger Publishers produced the first textbook for such courses (Sanger 1984).

26. In 1987, a federal rule took effect that allowed pharmaceutical companies to sell promising experimental drugs to the terminally ill. For the dying, such therapies may be the only source of hope. For the researchers, having willing human subjects is a necessary condition for both professional and financial rewards. Such a situation poses considerable ethical risk. Observed John Fletcher, a National Institutes of Health bioethicist, "This is one thing to keep our eyes on to see if more people end up being killed by the research, not the disease" (Budiansky 1987, p. 58).

27. The case was further stigmatized by revelations that the parents were poor and unmarried and had had brushes with the law. The father had deserted the mother one week before the birth (Wallis 1984).

28. By 1986, few couples could afford the $45,000- to $64,000-a-year costs for nursing-home care. In addition, only the Medicaid health program provides insurance for such care, but it requires its recipients to reach the poverty level in order to be qualified. Consequently, a lifetime's accumulated savings and pensions are quickly drained into the medical complex.

29. Quinlan by no means had the endurance record in such limbo. In 1977, August Muscle died after being in a coma since 1954 following a car-train accident. He had required around-the-clock nursing care for twenty-three years (*San Antonio Light* 1977).

30. Dr. Willard Gaylin, the president of the Hastings Center, which examines ethical issues in medicine, observed that the federal government has repeatedly sought to influence care given to some newborns with serious birth defects. The government has asked the courts to require treatment that parents and doctors want to forgo (Schmeck 1985b).

31. These best-interest tests include attempting to determine the patient's attitude toward the matter when competent, and, if not possible, then the family and physicians should judge whether the burdens of life with treatment outweigh the benefits of life. The severity and duration of pain should be such that the administration of life-sustaining treatment would be "inhumane" (Sullivan 1985). As of 1986, four states had laws stating that artificial feeding may not be rejected by a patient.

32. In 1976, California was the first state to pass a "living will" law. In 1977,

seven states followed suit; by the end of 1985, a total of thirty-four states had given legal status to individuals' rights not to be kept alive artificially (Otten 1985b).

33. Much of this section is an abridgment of "The Hospice Farewell: Ideological Perspectives of Its Professional Practitioners," by Anoel Rinaldi and Michael Kearl, presented to the Gerontology Society of America in San Francisco, November 1984.

34. In part, our research was inspired by a 1980 symposium, sponsored by the Bexar County Medical Society, entitled "Hospice, Science and Religion Join Hands."

35. We randomly selected 102 hospices from the National Hospice Organization's *Locator Directory of Hospice in America 1981–82*. A letter describing the study and requesting participation was addressed to the "Social Worker" at each hospice in addition to a self-addressed, stamped post card to facilitate participation. Because the social workers in a hospice have an overall perspective on hospice dynamics, they were chosen as the designated "experts" in this study. Experienced hospice administrators advised that the hospice social worker is in a position to interact with all patient-family units and all staff members. Of those initially contacted, a remarkable 69 percent agreed to participate. These hospice experts then participated in two rounds of a modified Delphi technique to describe attitudes and perspectives of individuals knowledgeable about hospice. "Delphi" is the nickname for a set of procedures developed by researchers at the Rand Corporation to elicit systematic group judgment (Dalkey 1972, p. 2). This method generally consists of three features: anonymity, controlled feedback, and a statistical group response. In a Delphi sequence, a group of experts is interrogated using a series of questionnaires which not only ask questions but also provide information to the participants about the degree of consensus and the arguments presented by the members in the earlier round of questioning. The method is most frequently used to provide technological forecasts, but it has also been used in values clarification. Participants in the final mailing numbered forty-eight. Their ages ranged from twenty-four to sixty-eight (median thirty-five); twenty-seven were social workers, ten coordinators, seven directors, and two counselors. Mean job time was 1.8 years, and mean time with hospice was 2.2 years. Of the forty-eight full-term participants, forty-six were paid staff.

36. Even though Medicare reimburses hospice care, ironies continue to abound with regard to culture being able to accept a "natural death." One story was of a female internist who was dying of abdominal cancer. A theosophist, she came to one hospice to die and requested that absolutely no care be given. However, in order to receive Medicare, she had to be given therapy.

37. Religious support of hospice is not, however, universal. There are some Protestant ministers, for example, who argue that hospice accelerates the dying process and thereby diminishes one's time to repent.

REFERENCES

ABC News. 1985. "Dad Would Want to Die." *20/20*. December 5.

Altman, Lawrence. 1984a. "Study Ties Longer Life to Higher Cancer Costs." *New York Times*. June 22, p. 12.

————. 1984b. "Baby with Baboon Heart Better; Surgeons Defend the Experiment." *New York Times*. October 30, pp. 1, 22.

————. 1985. "How Healthy Are the Oldest Old?" *New York Times*. August 27, p. 18.

Ames, Bruce. 1983. "Dietary Carcinogens and Anticarcinogens." *Science*. September 23, pp. 1256–64.

Ariès, Philippe. 1974. *Western Attitudes toward Death: From the Middle Ages to the Present*. Baltimore: Johns Hopkins University Press.

Asinof, Lynn. 1988. "Business Bulletin." *Wall Street Journal*. January 7, p. 1.

Backer, B. A., N. Hannon, and N. A. Russell. 1982. *Death and Dying: Individuals and Institutions*. New York: John Wiley.

Bailar, John III, and Elaine Smith. 1986. "Progress against Cancer?" *New England Journal of Medicine*. May 8, pp. 1226–32.

Barton, D. 1972. "The Need for Including Instruction of Death and Dying in the Medical Curriculum." *Journal of Medical Education* 47:169–75.

Benoliel, J. Q. 1974. "Anticipatory Grief in Physicians and Nurses." In B. Schoenberg et al., eds., *Anticipatory Grief*. New York: McGraw-Hill, pp. 218–28.

Berger, Peter, Brigitte Berger, and Hansfried Kellner. 1973. *The Homeless Mind: Modernization and Consciousness*. New York: Random House.

Bishop, Jerry. 1984. "Scientists Are Focusing on Genes Predisposing People to Illnesses." *Wall Street Journal*. September 12, pp. 1, 27.

Boffey, Philip. 1984. "Cancer Progress: Are the Statistics Telling the Truth?" *New York Times*. September 18, pp. 17, 20.

————. 1987. "Report to Congress Terms Gains on Cancer Overstated since '50." *New York Times*. April 16, pp. 1, 12.

Brinkley, Joel. 1985a. "A.M.A. Study Finds Big Rise in Claims for Malpractice." *New York Times*. January 17, pp. 1, 10.

————. 1985b. "U.S., Industry and Physicians Attack Medical Malpractice." *New York Times*. September 2, pp. 1, 10.

Budiansky, Stephen. 1987. "Playing Roulette with Experimental Drugs." *U.S. News & World Report*. July 13, pp. 58–59.

Castles, M. R., and R. B. Murray. 1979. *Dying in an Institution: Nurse/Patient Perspectives*. New York: Appleton-Century Crofts.

Chase, Marilyn. 1985. "To Doctor and Patient, Test of a New Drug Is Turbulent Experience." *Wall Street Journal*. September 26, pp. 1, 26.

Dalkey, N. C. 1972. *Studies in the Quality of Life: Delphi and Decision Making*. Lexington, Mass.: Lexington Books.

Dallas Times Herald. 1985. "Alive and Well, or Dead? Jarvik-7 Patient's Status Hits Heart of Debate over Swedish Law." April 15, p. 1.

Dickinson, G. E., 1981. "Death Education in U.S. Medical Schools: 1975–1980." *Journal of Medical Education* 48:577–78.

Dionne, E. J. 1984. "Paris Widow Wins Suit to Use Sperm." *New York Times*. August 2, p. 7.

Dossey, L. 1982. *Space, Time & Medicine.* Boulder, Colo.: Shambhala.

Eckholm, Erik. 1985. "Baby Death Laid to Wrong Blood." *New York Times.* October 17, p. 11.

Efron, Edith. 1984. *The Apocalyptics: Politics, Science, and the Big Cancer Lie.* New York: Simon & Schuster.

Epstein, Samuel. 1978. *The Politics of Cancer.* Jackson, Calif.: Sierra.

Feifel, Herman. 1963. "Death." In N. L. Farberow, ed., *Taboo Topics.* New York: Atherton, pp. 8–21.

————. 1977. *New Meanings of Death.* New York: McGraw-Hill.

Freidson, E. 1970. *The Profession of Medicine.* New York: Harper & Row.

Freudenheim, Milt. 1985. "Company Expenses for Retirees Soar." *New York Times.* September 9, pp. 1, 26.

Gartner, Michael. 1988. "The 'Golden Years' and Medicine: An Age-Old Challenge." *Wall Street Journal.* April 7, p. 25.

Glaser, B. G., and A. L. Strauss. 1965. *Awareness of Dying.* Chicago: Aldine.

————. 1968. *Time for Dying.* Chicago: Aldine.

Goffman, Erving. 1963. *Stigma.* Englewood Cliffs, N.J.: Prentice-Hall.

Goldscheider, C. 1971. *Population, Modernization and Social Structure.* Boston: Little, Brown.

Goodman, Walter. 1984. "Scholars Debate 'Biomedical Ethics.'" *New York Times.* June 18, p. 18.

Gruson, Lindsey. 1985. "Some Doctors Move to Bar Transplants to Foreign Patients." *New York Times.* August 10, pp. 1, 7.

Harrington, Alan. 1977. *The Immortalist.* Millbrae, Calif.: Celestial Arts.

Harris, Louis. 1981. "Terminally Ill Should Have Right to Die." Release 39, May 14.

Hartwell, R. M. 1973. "The Economic History of Medical Care." In Mark Perlman, ed., *The Economics of Health and Medical Care.* New York: John Wiley, pp. 3–20.

Hellerstein, David. 1980. "Cures That Kill." *Harper's.* December, pp. 20–24.

Hull, Jennifer. 1985. "Faulty X-Ray Devices, Untrained Operators Overdose U.S. Patients." *Wall Street Journal.* December 11, pp. 1, 27.

Illich, Ivan. 1975. "The Political Uses of Natural Death." In Peter Steinfels and Robert Veatch, eds., *Death Inside Out: The Hastings Center Report.* New York: Harper & Row, pp. 25–42.

Janson, Donald. 1977. "Deaths at Pennsylvania Hospital Laid to Mixup in Labeling Gases." *New York Times.* August 3, pp. 1, 10.

Kastenbaum, Robert, and Ruth Aisenberg. 1972. *The Psychology of Death.* New York: Springer.

Katz, Samuel. 1985. "Measles—Forgotten but Not Gone." *New England Journal of Medicine* 313(9):577–78.

Kleiman, Dena. 1985. "Changing Way of Death: Some Agonizing Choices." *New York Times.* January 14, p. 1, 11.

Kübler-Ross, Elisabeth. 1969. *On Death and Dying.* New York: Macmillan.

Lamm, Richard D. 1984. "Long Time Dying." *New Republic*. August 27, pp. 20–23.

Levine, S., and N. A. Scotch. 1970. "Dying as an Emerging Social Problem." In O. G. Brim Jr. et al., eds., *The Dying Patient*. New York: Russell Sage, pp. 211–24.

Lief, Philip D. 1985. "Is It Really a Good Idea to Prolong Dying?" *New York Times*. March 22, p. 26 (letter to ed.).

Liston, E. H. 1975. "Education on Death and Dying: A Neglected Area in the Medical Curriculum." *Omega* 6(3):193–197.

Lyons, Richard. 1977. "Surgery on Poor Is Found Higher." *New York Times*. September 1, pp. 1, 15.

———. 1984. "Sex in America: Conservative Attitudes Prevail." *New York Times*. October 4, pp. 17, 19.

McCormick, 1980. *Ethical Issues in Death and Dying*. New York: Columbia University Press.

Maguire, Daniel. 1975. *Death by Choice*. New York: Schocken Books.

Malcolm, Andrew. 1984a. "Moral Dilemmas of Mercy Killing: Technologies Require Greater Wisdom." *New York Times*. November 11, p. 10.

———. 1984b. Movement Seeks to Advance Rights of Dying." *New York Times*. December 12, pp. 1, 12.

———. 1985. "Comatose Patient's Case Tests Stopping of Food." *New York Times*. May 27, p. 8.

———. 1986. "Reassessing Care of Dying." *New York Times*. March 16, pp. 1, 13.

Margolick, David. 1984. "Court Ties Death to Brain Function." *New York Times*. October 31, pp. 1, 16.

Marshall, Eliot. 1984. "Topic of Cancer." *New Republic*. May 14, pp. 33–36.

Medved, Michael. 1984. *Hospital: The Hidden Lives of a Medical Center Staff*. New York: Pocket Books.

Meisel, Alan. 1985. "Landmark Rulings on the 'Right to Die.'" *New York Times*. March 30, p. 14 (letter to ed.).

Molotsky, Irvin. 1985. "Recall of a Heart Valve is Urged." *New York Times*. June 27, p. 13.

National Hospice Organization. 1982. *NHO President's Letter*. January/February.

National Opinion Research Center (NORC). 1986. *General Social Surveys, 1972–1986*. Chicago: National Opinion Research Center at the University of Chicago.

NBC Reports. 1978. "Medicine in America: Life, Death and Dollars." January 3.

New York Times. 1984a. "Man Must Stay on Respirator." June 23.

———. 1984b. "The Best Way to Die." September 24, p. A18.

———. 1984c. "Patient May Refuse Life-Support Care, Court on Coast Says." December 28, pp. 1, A13.

———. 1985a. "Doctor on Trial in 'Right to Die' Case." September 18, p. 10.

———. 1985b. "Proportion of Blacks in Medical School Drops." October 10, p. 13.

———. 1985c. "Infant Mortality Rate at Record Low." October 12, p. 14.

———. 1985d. "Six-Organ Transplant Cleared in Pittsburgh." October 30, p. 13.

———. 1987. "Lawyers' Group Backs Doctors' Aid in Suicide." September 23, p. 18.

Otten, Alan L. 1984. "Ever More Americans Live into 80s and 90s, Causing Big Social Problems." *Wall Street Journal.* June 30, pp. 1, 12.

———. 1985a. "Can't We Put My Mother to Sleep?" *Wall Street Journal.* June 5, p. 30.

———. 1985b. "New 'Wills' Allow People to Reject Prolonging of Life in Fatal Illness." *Wall Street Journal.* July 25, p. 33.

———. 1985c. "Rising Success in Organ Transplants Strains Hospitals and Governments." *Wall Street Journal.* September 25, p. 31.

———. 1986a. "Issue of Force-Feeding to Keep Patients Alive Enters Political Arena." *Wall Street Journal.* June 9, pp. 1, 8.

———. 1986b. "Fight Grows over Which Hospitals Should Perform Organ Transplants." *Wall Street Journal.* November 21, p. 29.

Patten, Pamela. 1984. "Comparing the 'Born Again' Experiences of the Religiously Devout with Those of Coronary Bypass Patients." Unpublished manuscript, Trinity University.

Pear, Robert. 1986. "Spending for Health Care Rose in '85 at Lowest Rate in 2 Decades." *New York Times.* July 30, p. 7.

Prager, Kenneth. 1987. "What? Physicians Won't Treat AIDS?" *New York Times.* October 23, p. 25.

Preston, S. H. 1976. *Mortality Patterns in National Populations.* New York: Academic Press.

Rabin, D. L., and L. H. Rabin. 1970. "Consequences of Death for Physicians, Nurses and Hospitals." *The Dying Patient.* New York: Russell Sage Foundation, pp. 30–40.

Redding, R. 1980. "Doctors, Dyscommunication, and Death." *Death Education* 3:371–85.

Rensberger, Boyce. 1978. "The Touchy Ethical Issue of Trainee Surgeons Operating without Consent of Patients." *New York Times.* February 6, p. B12.

Rocky Mountain News. 1982. "'Immortality' Fuels Health Cost." March 25, p. 40.

Rundle, Rhonda. 1987. "Hospitals Cite Mortality Statistics in Ads to Attract Heart Patients." *Wall Street Journal.* July 28, p.29.

Sabom, Michael. 1981. *Recollections of Death: A Medical Investigation.* New York: Harper & Row.

Sager, Ruth. 1977. "Cancer: Misdirected Attack." *New York Times.* March 24, p. 32 (letter to ed.).

San Antonio Express-News. 1982. "Study: Some Doctors Avoid Dying Patients." January 21, p. 1.

———. 1984. "'Cancer' Patient Awarded $3 Million from Doctors." February 12, p. 9A.

———. 1985. "Virus-Tainted Polio Shots Linked with Brain Cancer." April 26, p. 2A.

San Antonio Light. 1977. "Patient Finally Dies." August 10.

San Francisco Chronicle. 1976. "Extra-Marital Sex Can Be Bad for You." June 1, p. 15.

San Jose Mercury News. 1983. "Men with Vasectomies Seem Healthier, Study Shows." November 15, pp. 1A, 14A.

Sanger, David E. 1984. "Future Doctors Look at Nuclear War." *New York Times.* November 26, p. 17.

Schmeck, Harold. 1977. "A Deadly Virus Apparently Transmitted by Surgery." *New York Times.* May 9, pp. 1, 23.

———. 1985a. "Test Drug for Heart Attack Found Twice as Effective as One in Use." *New York Times,* April 4, pp. 1, 10.

———. 1985b. "Quinlan Case: It Became Symbol of Ethical Problems Inherent in New Medical Technology." *New York Times.* June 13, p. 24.

———. 1985c. "U.S. Sets Guidelines on Using Gene Transplants in Humans." *New York Times.* September 24, pp. 1, 18.

Schulz, R., and D. Aderman. 1980. "How the Medical Staff Copes with Dying Patients: A Critical Review." In R. A. Kalish, ed., *Caring Relationships: The Dying and the Bereaved.* Farmingdale, N.Y.: Baywood.

Science News. 1978. "Doctors' Strike Lowered Death Rate." October 28, p. 293.

Segerberg, Osborn. 1974. *The Immortality Factor.* New York: E. P. Dutton.

Shneidman, Edwin. 1973. *Deaths of Man.* New York: Quadrangle.

Sontag, Susan. 1978. *Illness as Metaphor.* New York: Farrar, Straus and Giroux.

Starr, Paul. 1982. *The Social Transformation of American Medicine.* New York: Basic Books.

———. 1983. "'Medicine Has Overdrawn Its Credit' in American Society." Interview by Alvin Sanoff. *U.S. News & World Report.* September 12, pp. 77–78.

Stein, Andrew. 1987. "Medical Negligence Needs a Study." *New York Times.* May 30, p. 15.

Sudnow, David. 1967. *Passing On: The Social Organization of Dying.* Englewood Cliffs, N.J.: Prentice-Hall.

Sullivan, Joseph. 1983. "Boston Autopsies Find 1 in 4 Diagnoses Wrong." *New York Times.* April 28, p. 15.

———. 1984. "Child with Birth Defects Allowed to Sue Doctors." *New York Times.* August 2, p. 22.

Sullivan, Ronald. 1985. "'Right to Die' Rule in Terminal Cases Widened in Jersey." *New York Times.* January 18, pp. 1, 10.

Time. 1975. "If Death Shall Be No More." November 3, p. 58.

———. 1981. "M.D. Suicides." February 16, p. 57.

Tolchin, Martin. 1985. "As Companies Buy Hospitals, Treatment of Poor Is Debated." *New York Times.* January 25, pp. 1, 10.

Toufexis, A., and V. Castronoro. 1983. "Turning Illness into a Way of Life." *Time.* April 18, p. 69.

Townsend, Claire. 1971. *Old Age: The Last Segregation.* New York: Bantam Books.

U.S. Bureau of the Census. 1984. *Statistical Abstract of the United States.* Washington, D.C.: Superintendent of Documents.

Waitzkin, Howard. 1981. "A Marxist View of Medicine." In Scott McNall, ed., *Political Economy: A Critique of American Society.* Glenview, Ill.: Scott, Foresman, pp. 72–108.

Waldholz, Michael. 1985. "Most Hospitals Quickly Learn to be Profitable." *Wall Street Journal.* August 28, p. 6.

Wall Street Journal. 1985. "Oregon to Require Hospitals to Ask for Transplant Organs." September 3, p. 24.

Wallis, Claudia. 1984. "Baby Fae Loses Her Battle." *Time.* November 26, pp. 88–89.

Weisman, A. D. 1972. *On Dying and Denying.* New York: Behavioral Publications.

Chapter 12

Death and the Individual:
The Social Psychology of
Dying and Surviving

Like describing how tides and storms continuously alter a coastline, the enterprise of this book so far has been to chart the broad historic currents and the contemporary social eddies shaping the American death ethos. By and large, such a pedagogical exercise threatens few—it is similar to studying hurricanes from outer space. When intellectualizing the subject of death and studying the deaths of anonymous others, we can keep it at arm's length, confining it to a realm of academic abstraction. We have merely set the stage, identifying the cultural scripts and the social props social actors find at their disposal when they are actually forced to make sense out of life and mortality.

Many are the times when it is oneself in the hurricane, one's own home that is washed away, or one's own life that is threatened. When it comes to one's own death or the death of a loved one, things become different. When a New Jersey man learned that his wife had been killed in a plane crash in Poland, he collapsed and died, an apparent victim of a heart attack. When forty-six-year-old Archie Hanlan was informed that the mild weakness in his right hand was symptomatic of a fatal malady, he felt a grief so terrible that all he could do was lean and cry against a tiled wall in the hospital laboratory. His liberated, outspoken friends became a bunch of mice in the face of death. Left basically alone for his momentous departure from life, Hanlan's send-off received only the stares of a few unrecognized shorehands from the same piers where life began (Hanlan 1979). Such are the medically orchestrated endings of life.

This chapter considers the subjective reactions people have both to their own impending deaths and to the deaths of others. Such subject matters are typically the purview of psychologists and psychiatrists, but the goal here is to note how these individual experiences of endings are socially structured. Young children, for instance, rarely fear death. They must be socialized to fear postmortem judgment, to think of another's death as being either their loss or gain, or to internalize the death-denial orientation of their culture. To make matters even more interesting sociologically, with the historical shift from public to private death (see Chapters 2 and 11), our knowledge of death and grief experiences has gone from being second- to thirdhand information. The actual experience of dying has always been a function of one's anticipations, but these anticipations have become increasingly divorced from reality. They now derive from mass-media images, lessons in church, or rumors swapped among friends. Many times we are not privy to the thoughts and fears of those most likely to die—the old—either because we are afraid to ask or because they are reluctant to share them.

Finally, we will explore the implications of death being a dualistic process, involving a dynamic interplay between the person who dies and those who survive. The quality of survivor grief is conditioned by the quality of death; conversely, the quality of death is conditioned by the reactions of the survivors-to-be.

A Life-Span Perspective on Death

Like those at the dawn of the human species, young children understand neither the inevitability of their own mortality nor its finality. Paralleling the attempts of anthropologists and historians to map the death ethos of Western culture over time, there is a sizable research tradition in psychology and psychiatry on exactly how children's concepts of death unfold developmentally. As social scientists have studied the long-term social and cultural consequences of mass epidemics and total war, psychiatrists attempt to gauge how early firsthand death encounters later affect the motivations, psychoses, and fears of adulthood.

First, there is an awareness of the collective self that is immortal. The very young cannot distinguish themselves from their environment—Mom and Dad are like appendages; the collective ethos of agrarian societies engender the mind-set that death is a natural event that does not disrupt what is important, namely one's clan or tribe. Neither do very young children or cultures distinguish the animate from the inanimate. Guided by the sense of magic to those events that one cannot control, predict, or explain, young children and ancient societies perceive death as a temporary state preceding some rebirth experience, whether it be like the arousal from sleep (Maurer 1966), the rebirth of nature as winter turns into spring (Eliade 1959), or the resurrection of the snake as it disposes of its old, dead self. Both have the tendency to believe that the dead continue to exist and can influence the affairs of the living.

Next, with the increasing individualism of a culture and with a child's emerging sense of self, there arise fears of one's own death and strategies for coping with them. The late Middle Ages produced salvation rituals and the *Ars Moriendi*, a manual on how to die; the child begins to learn the appropriate emotional responses to death. During this historical era of dramatic social change and this developmental period of early self-concepts (Alexander and Adlerstein 1958), cultures and early adolescents have greater emotionality toward and preoccupations with death. For both, initial naivety sees death coming from some external source. Death comes because of the whims of angry gods or, for the young, from the likes of the bogeyman; it can be avoided by appeasing the deities or by eluding the "Death Man" (Nagy 1948). McIntire, Angle, and Struempler (1972) found that as early as the age of five, American children cast aside their fantasies and begin to focus on organic decomposition. They also found interesting class differences in the understandings of what causes death: children of the lower social classes are more likely to cite violence, whereas those of the middle class cite disease and old age.

With time, egocentrism is followed by a period of concern for others and awareness of interdependencies. Pre-Renaissance Western man perceived himself to be at the center of the universe and the pinnacle creation of some divine plan. But then came Copernicus and Darwin, dethroning the species from the center of the cosmos, making ourselves and our world but parts interrelated with everything else. Ariès describes the concurrent emergence of bonds of affection among family members and of rituals for mourning. He claims that "the death which is feared is no longer so much the death of the self as the death of another" (1974, p. 68). Analogously, the child becomes concerned with the death of his or her parents and becomes interested in generations that preceded him or her, akin to the cult of memory.

According to Gesell and Ilg (1956), at around the age of ten there is a diminished interest in the afterlife or in any theoretical issues about death. Then, with increasing maturity, the individual goes through periods of increasing speculation and skepticism. Perhaps, as a culture, the United States has just moved beyond this phase of disinterest, as evidenced by the popularity of Kübler-Ross's books on the stages of dying and Raymond Moody's works on the out-of-body experiences of the clinically dead.

In attempting to determine a chronology for these evolving death conceptualizations, developmental psychologists have found that the stages of responses to death involve an interplay between maturity and firsthand experiences. Perhaps the same holds for cultures. As children who experience the catastrophes of war or famine may be more likely to develop a fatalistic attitude toward death (DeSpelder and Strickland 1983, p. 95), so, too, do early cultures, which must cope with the premature deaths of their members, typically feature a fatalistic ethos.[1]

With these points in mind, let us turn to the kinds of death experiences American society provides its members as they pass through time. Then, once having considered Americans' death socializations across the life span, we will elaborate on their actual experiences of dying and grief.

Childhood Lessons in Death and Immortality

> And it seems possible to further paraphrase the relation of adult integrity and infantile trust by saying that healthy children will not fear life if their elders have integrity enough not to fear death.
>
> Erickson 1963, p. 169

In the early 1800s, one way young girls were molded to fit the female role of the times was by learning needlework on samplers. In Rhode Island, one of the better-known schools was that of Mary Balch. One embroidery design that her students were to sew thousands of times was of a memorial, featuring an urn atop a tomb with a bent willow in the background. One variation included a female mourner, dressed in black, kneeling over the sepulcher. The inscriptions on the tomb were always readable, including the deceased's name, birth and death dates, and some message. One's seven-year-old daughter would have sewn such thoughts as:

> Centered in CHRIST, who
> fires the world within,
> The flesh shall know no
> pain, the soul no sin.
> E'en the terror of
> expiring breath.
> We bless the friendly
> stroke, and live-in
> death.
>
> No pang/
> Like that of bosom torn
> from /Bosom bleeding
> o'er the sacred dead.

The death education of early nineteenth-century Rhode Island girls included sewing a needlepoint sampler of a woman grieving over a crypt. Courtesy of Rhode Island Historical Society.

From a historical perspective, this all seems rather morbid, an indicator perhaps of the excesses of Romanticism at that time. And yet what will social historians make of the childhood instructions imparted by the contemporary American death ethos? Imagine yourself two hundred years from now reading the following anthropological account of a day in the life of a late-twentieth-century youth:

On a Saturday morning, little Brian Allan begins his weekly ritual. Upon dressing in his "GI Joe" uniform, he informs two "dead-tired" parents that the sun is up and then drags his plastic machine gun to the kitchen. On the shelf are his two favorite breakfast cereals, "Frankenberry" and "Count Chocula."[2] After preparing his selection, he settles down for his thanatological lessons. While eating his immortality flakes (both Frankenstein and Count Dracula were immortal—albeit flawed—creatures),[3] Brian watches his favorite cartoon, "The Roadrunner." The story line never varies: a coyote employs a number of strategies to kill (we assume to eat) a bird, only to have each attempt lethally backfire before he is once again resurrected to resume the hunt. This cartoon is followed by others bearing similar messages of violence, death, and indestructibility. When Brian's mother finally appears, her news is not good: Charlie the goldfish floats motionlessly on top of the water. Before flushing him down the drain, she reassures the distraught little boy that Charlie is in heaven and that they will replace him with another fish during their outing to the mall.

Brian plays with his dinosaurs until his mother says that it's all right to go visit his friends. With them, he spends much of the day acting out the lives and deaths of cowboys and Indians, cops and robbers, and earthlings versus aliens. Then Brian goes to the grocery store with his father to find something for dinner. Dad finally makes a selection from the host of indistinguishably packaged animals; there's not a sign of hoof, hide, feather, or fin. At the checkout counter, Brian asks about the headlines of the tabloids. The father informs him that the *Enquirer* has stories of a haunted house and a man buried alive for three days. Dinnertime conversation focuses on Halloween costume options and Brian's conflict over whether to be a devil or a ghost.[4]

After his father announces that he's "so full he could burst," Brian and his parents adjourn to watch together the "family hour" episodes of "The Six-Million-Dollar Man" and "That's Incredible." That night, the latter features a story about the seventy-five confirmed cases of spontaneous human combustion and shows the "death-defying" feat of a stuntman leaping over an oncoming automobile traveling seventy miles an hour. Finally, it's off to bed. Brian dons his "Ghostbuster" pajamas and listens as his mother reads his favorite bedtime story, "The Three Little Pigs." Finally, he says his prayers as the lights are turned off:

> Now I lay me down to sleep,
> I pray the Lord my soul to keep,
> If I should die before I wake,
> I pray the Lord my soul to take.

Although the above is a composite caricature of an American middle-class youth, it should reveal the scope of our culture's death-denial messages. On the surface, it all seems rather humorous. But are we to believe that Brian internalized these thanatological lessons as Mary Balch's students absorbed the religious consolations from their samplers? One tends to think not, but then we hear stories of children severing limbs so that they can be replaced with bionic parts; of a thirteen-year-old whose absorption in the fantasy game of "Dungeons and Dragons" supposedly led to his suicide (Brooke 1985);[5] and of a young child who told her recently widowed mother, "Don't worry, Mommie, we'll get you another one" (DeSpelder and Strickland 1983, p. 96).

In general, there has been a tendency to shield the young from "real" death, even to the extent of not involving them with funerals or allowing them to see a parent grieve. A quarter of a century ago, Geoffrey Gorer (1965) surveyed bereaved English families and found 41 percent telling their

In modern America, death lessons begin with breakfast. Two cereals feature flawed but immortal creatures: Frankenstein, a creature created from body parts, and Dracula, who subsists on the blood of the living. The other cereal contains kernels shaped like long-extinct animals. Kemp Davis.

children under the age of sixteen nothing about their parents' deaths. In half of his sample, children were simply told fairy tales: "He's gone to sleep," "She's gone to heaven," and so forth. Such denial strategies, of course, are dependent on the rarity of death, and therefore we must take into account variances in the class structure. Given that death is socially stratified (see Chapter 4), the lower one's position in the social hierarchy, the greater the probability that there will be a death in one's immediate family or friendship circle. The higher one's social class, as discovered in a 1970 survey conducted by *Psychology Today* (1970), the more likely one's childhood death lessons came from pets and such social media as books or television.[6] So secondary have these instructions become that childhood health experts have expressed concern over the psychological impact of thousands of children watching Christa McAuliffe, who was to be the first teacher in space, and six other astronauts dramatically die when the space shuttle *Challenger* blew up on "live" television. Psychologists warned that some children might experience exaggerated fears and nightmares or be unable to concentrate and that such traumatic reactions may not show up until weeks, months, or even years later (Goleman 1986).

Modern children rarely must confront the prospects of their own deaths, which is why the death of a child is so tragic.[7] As recently as 1900, youth

Boston Children Learn "Dying Isn't a Vacation"

Away from the boisterous noise in the rest of the building, hushed children listen to dirges, touch a plastic-shrouded dead frog and peer into an open coffin in a museum exhibition that teaches them about death.

The exhibition at the Children's Museum bears a warning, "This is an exhibit about death and loss," and tells children in a videotaped puppet show: "Dying isn't a vacation. It's not like going to visit your grandmother. You don't come back again."

"We have a commitment to children, to make life less threatening to them," said Janet Kamien, who developed the project with a team of advisers, including child psychologists, authors and clergymen. "Parents have a natural instinct to protect their children from the harsh realities and scary, no-no topics in life. This show provides a vehicle to talk about dying and loss."

In the exhibition, a television screen repeatedly shows a speeded-up film of maggots devouring a dead mouse. "Everything that is alive now will die, decompose and return to life," a sign says.

A film shows fighting in Lebanon and bloated, bullet-ridden bodies in the streets of El Salvador and contrasts this real death with make-believe death by showing a sneering actor shooting a cowering foe who dies in a pool of blood, but then stands up, laughs and shakes hands with the "gunman" after an off-screen voice shouts: "Cut! It's a take!"

Painted in big white letters on one wall are slang terms for death: "put to sleep," "six feet under," "belly up," "croaked."

New York Times 1984b. Copyright © 1984
by the New York Times Company. Reprinted by permission.

accounted for 53 percent of the total deaths in our society while comprising only one-third of its total population. Now those under the age of fifteen account for less than 5 percent of deaths. We assume that they will survive whatever had killed earlier generations.[8] In fact, evident in childhood is the history of the mass killers of our species: the contemporary "childhood diseases" such as chicken pox, measles, and mumps were all great killer epidemics of the past. Whereas a few centuries ago one was considered a fool if, by the teenage years, one had not saved for one's own funeral (Ariès 1962), to do so nowadays would undoubtedly lead to psychiatric care.

Perhaps the most extreme childhood confrontation with death involves the passing of a parent or sibling. Such losses can heighten one's sense of vulnerability and distrust in the environment, leading to an emotional arrest that lasts a lifetime. Birtchnell and his associates report: "A history of parental loss has been associated with psychoneurosis, suicide, alcoholism and narcotic drug addiction, schizophrenia, depressive illness, anxiety reactions, sociopathic character and criminal behavior, poor employment records, and failure in the Peace Corps" (1973, p. 41). There can also arise a sense of guilt, stemming from the quasi-magical style of thinking of early adolescence. For example, consider a seven-year-old staying with his grandmother for a summer visit. The child has a bad day and is sent to bed without dinner. Secretly, he wishes his grandmother would die in retribution. That night, she coincidentally suffers a massive stroke and dies. Such guilt, regardless of its rationality, can underlie years of self-destructive thought or behavior.

On the other hand, George Pollock, director of the Chicago Institute for Psychoanalysis, has identified hundreds of writers, artists, and philosophers for whom mourning was an adaptation that tapped creative energy. For Franklin D Roosevelt, Lincoln, Lenin, Darwin, and Tolstoy, the death of a parent seemed to spur them on to greatness (Koch 1977). Certainly, the quality and form of one's death experiences react with the quality and form of one's moral, emotional, and intellectual development. Death can spawn depression and social withdrawal, or it can invigorate, stimulating individuals to pursue new heights in their social performances.

Death and Early Adulthood: Drunk with Future Time

In American culture, early adulthood is viewed as the "best years of life" (see Chapter 6). For most this age, death is but an abstraction. During the late 1960s, for instance, David Gutmann observed: "The young people of the counter-culture now obsessively use the terms 'life' and 'death' to make political, moral, racial and even generational distinctions . . . [taking] away the horror of death by presenting it as an invention of the establishment" (1973, p. 50). When death does end the life of someone from this age group, which is a rare event, it is typically man-made (accidents—the cause of some 55 to 60 percent of college-age deaths—followed by homicides and suicides are the leading causes of death) and therefore avoidable. And as we saw in our discussions of thrill seeking (Chapter 4) and the thanatological themes of rock-and-roll music (Chapter 11), death for this age group is also something that can be flirted with.

To be so removed from the possibility of death can give one the sense of limitless opportunities with limitless time to accomplish them. As noted earlier, with the increases in expected years on this earth, there has been a concomitant prolongation of adolescence and dependency. If, as was the case only a few centuries ago, one sees that most others die before their thirtieth birthdays, why would one choose to remain in school twelve, sixteen, or more years? Or wait until one's twenties to marry? Nowadays, of course, women can plan to pursue a career and postpone a family life until their late thirties or early forties. Students can become the legendary "perpetual students," residing in graduate education programs until their thirties before seeking entry into the full-time work force. This mind-set, as if being drunk with future time, is a feeling conditioned not only by one's age but by one's social class as well. The upper classes can quite simply retard their social aging by remaining longer in educational systems (physicians, one of the prototypical illustrations of prolonged socializations, nearly all come from upper-middle-class families), remaining longer in singlehood status before first marriage, delaying their parenting roles, and having the greatest opportunity to postpone their retirements (if they desire). For some of this age group, however, the absence of pain and/or the absence of the sense of excitement with life-threatening situations has led to potentially self-destructive behavior: automobile racing, hang gliding, skiing out of control, experimenting with drugs, and risking oneself in acts of political protest. Those with the greatest amount of future time also have the least commitments to and investments in social life.

The death flirtations of those in their late teens and twenties assumed epidemic proportions during the late 1970s and the 1980s. The preceding generation had its own death form to deal with, namely the Vietnam War. Not only were tens of thousands of its members decimated by combat-related causes, but even those who denounced the war risked death, as when members of the Ohio National Guard opened fire and killed four protesters at Kent State University. But this recent generation was different. Its homicide and suicide rates increased dramatically. There was a romanticization of love and death not seen since the late 1950s and early 1960s, when the "coffin songs" (e.g., "Teen Angel" and "Last Kiss") were fashionable—popularized by another cohort of young adults who followed a generation who had to go to war. In 1984, national attention focused on teenage males who, attempting to enhance their masturbations by near asphyxiation (such as with a rope tied around their necks or a cellophane laundry bag tied around their heads), lost consciousness and died. One victim's mother called autoerotic asphyxia "history's best-kept secret," the cause of a conservatively estimated one thousand deaths a year (Brody 1984).

The social reactions following an epidemic of drug-related fatalities perhaps best dramatizes society's concern about the drug flirtations of this age group. The war on drugs was the pretext President Reagan used to justify increased American military involvements in Central America during the latter half of the 1980s. When two prominent athletes died within one week of drug overdoses—college basketball star Len Bias (who died the day after being selected as the first-round draft choice of the Boston Celtics) and professional football star Don Rogers (who died the evening before his wedding)—a national drug witch hunt was put in full gear. The polity had a new battle line against premature death and for cultural death denials. By eliminating drugs, such activism would supposedly eliminate not only users' deaths but many of those deaths caused by human error—whether of an air-traffic controller, a pilot, an ambulance driver, a nurse, or a worker in an automobile assembly line.

Death and Middle Age: The Loss of Immortality

For the American middle class, the first symptom of one's own mortality often occurs after the age of thirty-five. It may be precipitated by a serious illness or a premature heart attack. It is the time of life when the first of one's friendship circle normally dies of "natural causes," when one witnesses the routine deaths of one's parents and those of their generation of friends, when initial purchases of life insurance are made, and when one begins to read the obituaries.

Few deaths match the psychological significance of those of one's parents. Each year, 11.6 million American adults—5 percent of the population—suffer the loss of a parent (Myers 1986), making this the most common cause of bereavement. In Table 12.1, derived from a 1984 national survey of Americans eighteen years of age and older, the mortality rates of parents are summarized, broken down by age. We see, for example, that among respondents eighteen to thirty-five years of age at the time of the survey, 1.5 percent of their mothers and 4.9 percent of their fathers had died before the children had reached the age of sixteen. Of those seventy-five years and older, 3.3 percent had lost their mothers and 4.3 percent had lost their fathers before their sixteenth birthdays. We also can see the effects of the prolongevity revolution with one out of eight individuals sixty-five to seventy-four years still having a mother alive and 3.3 percent of those seventy-five and older still having a living father. But it is between the ages of fifty and sixty-four when one is most likely to experience a parent's death. For this age group, nearly two-thirds of their mothers and more than three-quarters of their fathers have died.

The middle-aged have a unique perspective on the whole of the life span by virtue of being in the position to see the flow of generations. They watch their parents' generation leave the world while their grandchildren's generation enters it. One day a middle-aged woman may tend to the needs of her incontinent, bedridden mother, and on the next day she changes the diapers

Table 12.1 Age by Which One's Parents Have Died

Age of respondent	Still alive	Died before respondent reached age 16	After respondent reached 16, more than 5 years ago	1 to 5 years ago	Died last year	Total
Respondent's Mother						
18–35	94.4%	1.5%	1.8%	2.0%	0.4%	549
36–49	80.4	0.9	11.3	5.9	1.5	337
50–64	37.9	3.2	46.8	7.7	4.4	248
65–74	12.5	3.5	77.8	5.6	0.7	144
75+	2.2	3.3	91.1	2.2	1.1	90
TOTAL	66.0%	2.0%	26.2%	4.4%	1.5%	1368
	(903)	(27)	(358)	(60)	(20)	
Respondent's Father						
18–35	83.8%	4.9%	3.8%	5.1%	2.4%	550
36–49	54.5	6.3	28.1	8.1	3.0	334
50–64	12.4	7.4	62.0	13.6	4.7	258
65–74	10.8	5.4	81.1	1.4	1.4	148
75+	3.3	4.3	90.2	1.1	1.1	92
TOTAL	50.2%	5.7%	34.6%	6.7%	2.7%	1382
	(694)	(79)	(478)	(93)	(38)	

Source: National Opinion Research Center 1985.

of her new grandchild. Nevertheless, the death of one's parents, one's first and most lasting significant others, means that one's own generation is the next to face the grim reaper and that one's own ending countdown has begun.

It is also during the middle years that the individual is typically the most engaged with the social system, and this is the time when death produces its greatest social ripple (which is, in part, the reason for the disruptiveness of AIDS). During this life stage, one holds memberships in the greatest number of groups and organizations,[9] is responsible for the needs of both the older and younger generations of family members, and—for the middle class—is at the peak of one's upward mobility in the hierarchies of work. But time is no longer infinite, and priorities must be made.

In recent decades, the attitudinal and life-style changes associated with this awareness of one's finitude have come to be referred to as the "midlife crisis" (Kearl and Hoag 1984). It is the time of life when there are the first physical symptoms of old age, such as the end of childbearing capacity with meno-

Reflections on Parents' Retirement Illustrate Fears
of Next Generation

Margaret Bruno is 34 years old. In the past 13 years, she has seen her father die and watched her mother—who now lives with her—grow frail and poor. And now Ms. Bruno is emphatic about how she intends to live out her own live.

"My father died at 50, and he had nothing—but he had never done anything either. If I'm going to go out at 50, I want to make sure I've done as much as I possibly can between now and when I'm 50. If I don't have anything for when I'm 52, I'll handle it. Somehow I'll handle it."

When asked to consider the idea of retirement, most young professionals readily acknowledge their fears about the future—and just as quickly admit their inability or unwillingness to prepare for it. Perhaps the best illustration of those fears and responses come from young adults' reflections on the condition of their parents as they enter old age.

Unlike past generations, many members of the baby-boom generation are watching their parents begin retirement comfortably. But that frustrates some young professionals, who fear that reaching the same standard over the next 30 years will be difficult if not impossible. Meanwhile, young adults whose parents are ill-prepared to retire are also worried; they fear that if they deny themselves luxuries now, they still run the risk of not being able to enjoy the good life later.

Ruffenach 1985. Reprinted by permission of the
Wall Street Journal, © Dow Jones & Company, Inc. 1985.

pause, the awareness that one's "biological peak" has passed, and the appearance of white hair. With these biological signals—possibly coupled with a parent's death—death denials are weakened. One begins to realize that time is running out and that, like Dickens's Scrooge, one has one last chance to make one's life count. It is the time when one no longer thinks in terms of how long one has lived but rather how much time is left to accomplish those dreams still remembered from early adulthood (Erikson 1963; Jacques 1965; Levinson 1977).

This particular crisis associated with the middle years has apparently resonated well with the public's lay developmental psychology, as illustrated by the popular reception given to Gail Sheehy's *Passages* and John McLeish's *The Ulyssean Adult,* the release of such movies as *Middle-Age Crazy,* the use of menopause as a plot device on television situation comedies, and the fact that the theme has received humorous (we tend to laugh at those things that make us most nervous) expressions in syndicated cartoon strips and on cocktail napkins (Kearl and Hoag 1984, p. 280).

Death and Old Age: When Time Runs Out

In old age, the individual's futurity dissolves as time runs out. With four out of five deaths in the United States occurring among those sixty-five years of age and older, death has become the province of this age group. It is the old who are most likely to think about and discuss death (Kalish and Reynolds 1976) and who are least likely to be frightened by it. But the stigma of death associated with this last phase of life has transformed what should be understood as one of the greatest social accomplishments—specifically, the near guarantee at birth of being able to live a full, complete life—into a socially problematic stage in a culture that values youth.

Old age is a time of loss: the loss of one's spouse, friends, job, health, standard of living, role as driver,[10] and future time. With many living into their eighties and nineties, it is no longer unusual even to outlive one's children in addition to one's peers.[11] For the institutionalized elderly in hospitals or long-term-care facilities, where death is all around, there are the additional losses of independence and, often, of dignity. In sum, the old now die a number of social deaths before physically expiring. Such losses produce the common experience of loneliness, grief, depression, despair, anxiety, helplessness, and rage. Without much future, old age is a time of reflection and reminiscence. This inwardness, coupled with the social and psychological disengagements often made from life, can diminish such losses as attachments to the things of this world are lessened. It is also the period when, as Butler and Lewis observe, "the sins of omission and commission for which an individual blames himself weigh even more heavily in light of approaching death" (1981, p. 37).

Old age has increasingly become the time until which many postpone putting their affairs in order and deciding on the postself to be left behind. First, there is the matter of leaving a legacy. Older family members take care to ensure that others know who is to get what after they die. Leaving a legacy is leaving a portion of oneself. It may be an object affirming one's existence on earth and within which one's memory is invested. Or the legacy may be one's story and the family folklore, now entrusted not only to relatives' memories but to the cartridges of tape recorders and VCRs as well.

Where assets are involved, it is the legal institution that controls the ritual of legacy through the instrument of the will.[12] John Stuart Mill argued: "He who had bequeathed property had mixed his labor with it during life under the expectation he could continue his power over it, even beyond the grave." Just as older individuals can control the behavior of their heirs by threatening their disinheritance, in death such regulation can continue through the oversight of the power of attorney: a grandchild may be "cut off" if he or she fails to graduate from college, a son-in-law may lose his claims to a share of the estate if he divorces the deceased's daughter, or a university may be limited in how it spends its bequest if terms for its expenditure were specified by the benefactor. If an individual fails to leave a will (an intestate death), state laws exist to dictate the distribution of the estate. In most states, for instance, a widow with two children only receives one-third to one-half of the estate; if there are no children, the parents and siblings of the deceased automatically receive as much as one-half.[13] The Illinois intestacy distribution treats half-blood relatives the same as full-blood kin (Slater 1986). To ensure that their legacies are minimally taxed and their heirs minimally hassled by probate, the old may also create tax-saving trusts and joint bank accounts (those in the deceased's name are frozen, whereas joint accounts are not).

When putting one's affairs in order, one may also leave instructions for how one's remains are to be disposed of (e.g., being cremated or leaving one's body to science), whether organs are to be donated, and the type of funeral service one desires. One may also leave a "living will," specifying the course of medical treatment when dying in the event that one is no longer conscious. In sum, there are a number of details to be attended to when "checking out" from life. With the expanding complexity and bureaucratization of life, such preparations not only have proliferated but also increasingly require the assistance of a broad range of experts.

In conclusion, thoughts of death are most frequent among those most socially marginal: children, the elderly, women, and the mentally ill (Feifel 1959). Further, the higher one's socioeconomic class, the more likely one is to be shielded from death in childhood, to be able to postpone or control the timing of one's life endings (later graduation from school, later "peaking" in one's work career, and later retirement), and to delay death itself.

Death Fears across the Life Span

To conclude this analysis of death fears and exposures across the life span, let us consider the fears engendered by the institutional forces described in the previous eight chapters. For example, to what extent do fears of nuclear war, environmental pollution, and criminal victimization differentially weigh on the minds of various age groups?

In part, such questions were inspired by one judge for the 1984–85 arts-recognition and talent-search program in writing sponsored by the National Foundation for Advancement in the Arts. She observed the recurrent motifs of suicide and nuclear war in the works submitted by some of the country's most gifted teenagers:

Again and again I came across the topic of self-induced death as the panacea for nuclear war, divorce, child abuse and the general neglect and apathy of the world toward its children; . . . that it is better to choose one's own epitaph than to be indiscriminately vaporized in a nuclear holocaust, and it is better still to kill oneself than to endure a life of programmed activities designed to keep one busy while substituting mechanical robotry for warm, spontaneous human interaction. (Flores 1984)

Similarly, Alice Powell (1986) found in her study of 628 adolescents that those most likely to worry about the nuclear threat were more competent and more informed and had less anxious personalities than their less fearful or nonfearful counterparts, regardless of their ethnic, racial, or socioeconomic origin. In addition, the more worried adolescents were more likely to come from homes in which parents held similar concerns and were more likely to discuss political matters with their children.

During the summer of 1986, the Field Institute conducted a poll of California voters about what concerned them the most. Of the twenty-six topics considered, seven dealt with issues potentially involving death. All of these fell into the top ten issues that voters felt "extremely concerned" about. As can be seen in Table 12.2, these fears are remarkably uniform across all ages of adulthood. What slight trend there is points toward an increasing concern with age: it appears that as one's time becomes increasingly scarce, one is

Table 12.2 Major Concerns of California Voters, 1986

	Total percentage extremely concerned	Percentage extremely concerned, by age			
		18–29	30–39	40–59	60+
1. Toxic wastes	74%	74%	73%	74%	77%
2. Illegal drug use	73		67	79	89
3. Crime and law enforcement	71	67	65	70	84
5. Air and water pollution	68	70	64	68	70
7. Controlling the spread of AIDS	65	62	63	64	76
9. Defense spending	59	★	★	★	73
10. Health care	59	★	★	★	71

★ Less than 60%.

Source: Field Institute 1986.

more likely to be "extremely concerned" about the lethal forces and by-products of social institutions.

The Social Psychology of Emotions

Thus far, we have briefly considered the specter of death as it is typically understood and experienced across the life cycle. This life-span model of death awareness is, of course, modified by the individual's social coordinates in the ethnic, religious, and socioeconomic topography of American society. A black child in the poorer regions of Detroit or New York City, for example, is more likely to suffer the premature deaths of siblings or parents because of the culture of violence than is the case for an upper-middle-class white youth from Minneapolis, for whom the only familial deaths often experienced before adulthood are those of great-grandparents and grandparents. But the experience of a loved one's death or the realization of one's own forthcoming demise triggers a spectrum of feelings that cannot be totally predicted from one's death socializations or from one's stage of cognitive development. Unleashed are the most profound of emotions, feelings that may alienate any bystanders and thereby exacerbate one's experiences of isolation, antipathy, and estrangement, feelings that can accelerate death itself. So significant are the emotions associated with dying and surviving that researchers have typically focused on their manifestations when describing the death experience. But emotions connote the irrational and impulsive, the beast within us (which is why successful executives must learn to control and hide any evidence of such feelings when interacting with others), challenging the explanatory schemes of human behavior.

In the social sciences, there is a theoretical conflict about whether emotions are culturally specific or universal. Charles Darwin, for instance, believed that such basic emotions as fear and anger are biologically determined universals that derive from instinct rather than from intellectual motivation. On the other hand, some social scientists assume that emotions are largely determined by social norms for emotion, or "feeling rules," and that social actors must define situations before emotions can even be experienced. Emile Durkheim, for example, wrote:

mourning is not the spontaneous expression of individual emotions. . . . [It] is more generally the case that there is no connection between the sentiments felt and the gestures made by the actors in the rite. Mourning is not a natural movement of private feelings wounded by a cruel loss; it is a duty imposed by the group. One weeps, not simply because he is sad, but because he is forced to weep. It is a ritual attitude he is forced to adopt out of respect for custom, but which is, in a large measure, independent of his affective state. . . . [It] is the social organization of the relations of kinship which has determined the respective sentiments of parents and children. (1965, pp. 442–43)

Some psychologists have gone so far as to claim that emotions precede thought, that people do not decide how they feel and then behave accordingly but rather first observe their own behaviors and then decide how they feel (e.g., "I'm crying, therefore I must be sad") (Zajonc 1980).

As is normally the case in such debates, there are undoubtedly elements of truth in both perspectives. One researcher who has linked the biological to the sociological is Paul Ekman, who found evidence that just the act of flexing facial muscles into the characteristic expressions of certain emotion, such as joy or sadness, can produce effects on the nervous system normally associated with these emotions (Ekman, Levenson, and Friesen 1983). In other words, say that you attend the funeral of a friend's grandparent whom you did not personally know. You adopt the somber expressions of those at the funeral—it would indeed be a faux paus to look happy and be cracking jokes—and perhaps soon find yourself crying. Further, there seem to be biological implications of either expressing or suppressing such feelings when they do occur. James Pennebaker (1985), for instance, showed that the sheer ability to confide in others about troubled feelings affects one's vulnerability to disease, a point to which we will return when we consider the implications of "silent grief."

Since the 1970s, research has detected a number of intriguing findings concerning the impacts of emotions on physiological processes. One tradition has been to identify links between emotions and the body's immune system. The stress of academic examinations, for instance, has been linked with declines in the production of interferon, thereby reducing one's ability to fight infection and disease (Kiecolt-Glaser et al. 1984); outbreaks of genital herpes vary inversely with feelings of depression (Kemeny 1984); and those not suppressing feelings of anger and distress have more positive immune response to serious skin cancers than those who do (Temoshok et al. 1985). Even the likelihood of death has been linked to one's emotional state. In a study of mastectomy outpatients, summarized in Table 12.3, researchers at London's King's College Hospital found a profound correlation between women's emotional response three months following their surgery and their rate of survival a decade later.

This interplay among biology, psychology, and social structure becomes complete when we consider the extent to which emotions are socially standardized. We learn of our own emotions by observing ourselves (e.g., "I am

Table 12.3 The Impact of Emotions on Cancer Incidence

Psychological response 3 months after operation	Patient status after 10 years			
	Alive, no recurrence	Alive, with cancer	Dead	Total
DENIAL. "Despite the operation, I don't believe I really ever had cancer."	50%	0	50%	10
FIGHTING SPIRIT. "I'm going to conquer this thing."	60%	10%	30%	10
STOIC ACCEPTANCE. "Keep a stiff upper lip—don't complain."	22%	3%	75%	32
HELPLESSNESS, HOPELESSNESS. "There's nothing to be done. I'm as good as dead."	20%	0	80%	5

Source: Cited in Goleman 1985b. Copyright © 1985 by the New York Times Company. Reprinted by permission.

crying, therefore I must be strongly moved by this television program") and, more importantly, by what other people observe and report to us (e.g., "You look down. Are you all right?"). Both attributions are strongly influenced by social settings and the normal emotions associated with them; the meaning of a situation to a person sets the experience and nature of emotion (Gerth and Mills 1953, pp. 54-55). In fact, only rarely in history have spontaneous individual emotions and their expression been socially approved. When they do occur, it is generally during times of great social transformation, such as during the beginning of the Renaissance or during the American and French revolutions. Normally, the emotions we carry serve as bases for both personal motivation and social control.

Grief

> Every one can master a grief but he that has it.
>
> Shakespeare, *Much Ado about Nothing*, III:ii.

We consider the sociological and biological facets of emotions as a prelude to approaching the feelings induced by the death of others. To appreciate what such losses can personally mean, let us briefly review a few tenets from the symbolic interactionist school of social psychology.

Who we are (or, at least, who we think we are) is the product of our interactions with others. The dynamic goes something like this: what we think of a person influences how we will perceive him; how we perceive him influences how we will behave toward him; and how we behave toward him ulti-

Mrs. Elizabeth Fortuin, mother of Bernard Fortuin, is comforted by a family member at the graveside. UPI/Bettmann Newsphotos.

mately influences who he becomes. Further, there are those individuals whose influence in shaping one's identity far exceeds the impact of most others. These significant others are those through whose eyes a social actor chooses to see himself or herself (because identity is largely symbolic, it is from the feedback of these individuals, and not the reflected light from a mirror, that we can even "see" ourselves), who bring out a unique and desired self. Thus, when a significant other dies, a portion of oneself likewise dies, never again to be reactivated. And, to a large extent, it is this loss of self that is mourned, which is possibly why ambivalence toward the deceased is so often experienced.[14]

Grief may well be an inherent reaction to loss, whose core experience is universal and largely unshaped by culture (Kastenbaum 1977, p. 245). Researchers since the publication of Darwin's *Expression of the Emotions in Man and Animals* have detected the possible existence of grief in the animal kingdom, especially among the primates (Konner 1982, pp. 328–29). Common grief reactions have been noted among the experiences of widowhood, divorce, separation, unemployment, and property damage following a natural disaster (Lynch 1977; McLeod 1984).[15] In Lindemann's classic study (1944) of the survivors of the Coconut Grove disaster, a 1942 Boston nightclub fire that killed 491, psychiatrists found a remarkably uniform syndrome associated with their acute grief: somatic distress, tightness of the throat, choking with shortness of breath, frequent need for sighing, an empty feeling in the stomach, lack of muscular power, and intense mental pain and depression. So novel and profound were these experiences for the victims that some feared the encroachment of insanity. For many, the phenomenon of grief can lead to a sociological equivalent of the phantom limb experiences of amputees: in one widowhood study, so strong were reunion fantasies that nearly one-fifth of the survivors hallucinated their dead spouses' presence. Most were burdened by feelings of guilt, feeling that perhaps their neglect had contributed to the deaths of their loved ones. Of sociological significance is the fact that many of Lindemann's survivors detected a loss of warmth in their relationships with others and often felt unable to initiate or maintain organized patterns of behavior. Other researchers have detected a frequent self-hatred (Clayton and Darvish 1979), with some individuals, unbeknownst to themselves, engaging in self-destructive behavior: uncalled-for acts of generosity, foolish economic deals, loss of friends or colleagues through series of stupid acts, and self-punitive behavior.[16]

Such uniformities have led some psychologists and psychiatrists to search for further similarities and to affix stages to the course of normal grief over time (Hardt 1978–79). Depending on the suddenness of the death and the relationship with the deceased, the first two to four weeks are marked by shock, numbness, and denial. The next six to eighteen months are usually the most painful. There are frequent reruns of the death, constant attempts to give the death meaning, to explain why it took place. Often the deceased is idealized beyond any semblance to actual fact; sinners become saints, and

Excerpt from a Grief Observed, by C. S. Lewis

No one ever told me that grief felt so like fear. I am not afraid, but the sensation is like being afraid. The same fluttering in the stomach, the same restlessness, the yawning. I keep on swallowing.

At other times it feels like being mildly drunk, or concussed. There is a sort of invisible blanket between the world and me. I find it hard to take in what anyone says. Or perhaps, hard to want to take it in. It is so uninteresting. Yet I want the others to be about me. I dread the moments when the house is empty. If only they would talk to one another and not to me.

There are moments, most unexpectedly, when something inside me tries to assure me that I don't really mind so much, not so very much, after all. Love is not the whole of a man's life. I was happy before I ever met H. I've plenty of what are called "resources." People get over these things. Come, I shan't do so badly. One is ashamed to listen to this voice but it seems for a little to be making out a good case. Then comes a sudden jab of red-hot memory and all this "commonsense" vanishes like an ant in the mouth of a furnace.

On the rebound one passes into tears and pathos. Maudlin tears. I almost prefer the moment of agony. These are at least clean and honest. But the bath of self-pity, the wallow, the loathsome sticky-sweet pleasure of indulging it—that disgusts me. And even while I'm doing it I know it leads me to misrepresent H. herself. Give that mood its head and in a few minutes I shall have substituted for the real woman a mere doll to be blubbered over. Thank God the memory of her is still too strong (will it always be too strong?) to let me get away with it. . . .

And no one ever told me about the laziness of grief. Except at my job—where the machine seems to run on much as usual—I loathe the slightest effort. Not only writing but even reading a letter is too much. Even shaving. What does it matter now whether my cheek is rough or smooth? They say an unhappy man wants distractions—something to take him out of himself. Only as a dog-tired man wants an extra blanket on a cold night; he'd rather lie there shivering than get up and find one. It's easy to see why the lonely become untidy; finally, dirty and disgusting. . . .

An odd by-product of my loss is that I'm aware of being an embarrassment to everyone I meet. At work, at the club, in the street, I see people, as they approach me, trying to make up their minds whether they'll "say something about it" or not. I hate it if they do, and if they don't. Some funk it altogether. R. has been avoiding me for a week. I like best the well-brought-up young men, almost boys, who walk up to me as if I were a dentist, turn very red, get it over, and then edge away to the bar as quickly as they decently can. Perhaps the bereaved ought to be isolated in special settlements like lepers.

alcoholics become teetotalers. Survivors describe this period as being an emotional roller-coaster ride, with feelings of resolution followed by further bouts of depression. After one year, an estimated 10 to 20 percent of the widowed population is still sufficiently symptomatic to be considered clinically depressed (Clayton and Darvish 1979). After eighteen to twenty-four months, there comes a period of strong self-reorganization. This gathering of strength apparently cannot be prematurely forced.

Lindemann (1944) coined the term "grief work" to describe the efforts of survivors to resolve their losses. This notion came from observing the resistance of patients to acceptance of their discomfort and distress. Grief work involves the emancipation from the bondages of the deceased, formation of new relationships (such as through replacement and substitution), and readjustment to one's new self and environment. Failure to successfully accomplish this work (as when the culture neglects to assist the individual through his or her rite of passage) can lead to "morbid grief reactions,"[17] which are characterized by distortions of normal grief and by such psychosomatic disorders as asthma, ulcerative colitis, and rheumatoid arthritis. In the extreme, such morbid grief reactions can lead to total psychological closure and the complete inability to function in one's social roles. In studying the survivors of Hiroshima, the *hibakshu* (literally, "explosion-affected person"), psychologist Robert Lifton found such prevalent symptoms as aimless behavior, psychic numbing, and the sense of existence being a weird, unreal, dreamlike state. He observed that the "survivors seem . . . to have imbibed in it [the atomic disaster] and incorporated it into their beings, including all of its elements of horror, evil, and particularly of death" (1967, p. 29). How else

---

 Man Kept Wife's Skeleton

Boston (AP)—An elderly man who was friendly to neighbors but never let them into his apartment kept the skeleton of his 86-year-old-wife in his bedroom for nine years until he died this week, authorities said Thursday.

"He always told everyone his wife died years ago, and gosh darn if it wasn't true. She was right here," said neighbor Henry Dahlbeck, 74, who lived below the couple's apartment for seven years.

Police said they found the body of 90-year-old Pandeli Demetre on Wednesday, near the skeleton of his wife, Mary P. Demetre. Her remains were lying on a bed, sheets and blankets pulled to her neck, and her wedding ring was still on a finger.

San Antonio Express-News 1984. Reprinted by
permission of the Associated Press © 1984.

---

could they go among the blue phosphorescent flames to collect the burned, mutilated remains of the dead?

Another research tradition of the possible extreme effects of grief has been to gauge the "broken heart syndrome," that is, to determine grief's impact on mortality. As far back as 1657 in London, "griefe" was one of the classifications of causes of death (Parkes 1976, p. 333). In the early 1960s, a study by Michael Young and his associates of 4486 widowers aged fifty-five and over revealed a 40 percent mortality rate increase during the first six months of bereavement (cited in Parkes 1976, p. 335). After following the lives of 1204 men and 2828 women widowed between 1963 and 1974 and matching them with married persons in terms of age, race, sex, education, cigarette smoking, age first married, and even number of pets, Knud Helsing and his associates found little evidence of increased mortality in the first few months of bereavement. But whereas a spouse's death had little eventual effect on the death rate of widows, for widowers aged forty-five to sixty-four the mortality rate was more than 60 percent higher than for married men the same age. For widowers younger than fifty-five, the death rate for those who remarried was more than 70 percent lower than for those who did not (Helsing, Szklo, and Comstock 1981). According to a 1984 study of the National Academy of Sciences, men under the age of seventy-five have an increased risk of death from accidents, cardiovascular disease, and some infectious diseases, and for six years their death rate is above average for those who do not remarry. The death risk for widows does not increase until the second year, when greater risks of cirrhosis and suicide were detected. But in general, evidence of any increases in mortality and morbidity among survivors was not clear-cut (Osterweis, Solomon, and Green 1984).

Bereavement and Mourning

> There's no analogue from the records of the past societies . . . in which a majority of the population lack common patterns or rituals to deal with crises inherent in man's biological character.
>
> Geoffey Gorer (1965, p. 63)

Despite the similarities, the anguish individuals feel following the death of others is marked by its variability. Researchers have found grief to be situationally relative, entailing interrelated psychological, sociological, and cultural processes. The experience is a function of the personality and ego integrity of the survivor, the quality of the relationship with the deceased, the predictability of the death (there is a normal timetable to our losses: first the deaths of great-grandparents and grandparents, then parents, and finally siblings, peers, and spouse), as well as the clarity of the cultural role expectations for those grieving. To disentangle individuals' subjective reactions to death from their objective cultural and social situation, psychologists make distinctions among grief, bereavement, and mourning (Kastenbaum 1981). As opposed to the emotional reactions of grief, *bereavement* is the formal status allocated to those experiencing legitimate grief, which is socially prescribed (hence the dilemmas involved in losing a live-in lover as opposed to a spouse). *Mourning,* on the other hand, entails the culturally patterned ways in which bereavement is expressed and how grief work is to be conducted (Kastenbaum 1981, pp. 217–18). Here we enter into the ways culture provides the models by which we interpret our personal subjective experiences. Our culture, for example, defines death as someone's "loss," and thus we tend to regard grief as something that is both natural and desirable (Volkart and Michael 1981, p. 177). On the other hand, Volkart and Michael note that death represents in some societies a status gain for the deceased and that mourning for one's loss would be inappropriate. Grief, then, is only one of a spectrum of emotions associated with bereavement.

By studying cultural mourning rituals, one can also gauge the relative importance of social relationships as well as observe the reaffirmations of the status hierarchy. In early Victorian England, for instance, as we saw in Chapter 2, the specified length of mourning for grandparents was nine months, compared with three months for an aunt or uncle and twelve months for parents or spouse. By the turn of the century, however, this obligation toward grandparents had declined to six months and for one's aunts and uncles to two, reflecting a diminished importance of these roles. Further, women are often more rigidly controlled by these obligations than men. In their review of seventy-three societies, Paul Rosenblatt and his associates found incredible variations in the form and intensity of mourning (Rosenblatt, Walsh, and Jackson 1976). In sixty of the societies, there were gender differences observed in crying behavior: in thirty-two, both sexes cried equally, and in twenty-eight, it was the women who cried more; in nearly one-quarter of the societies surveyed, both sexes attempted some form of self-injury, such as severing a finger at the joint, whereas in twelve societies, women were the more frequent self-mutilators.

Some bereavement problems may be occasioned not only by the severity of the loss but also by one's inability to play the bereavement role properly. In our culture, what there is of a social bereavement role concentrates on the feelings and expression of loss (Volkart and Michael 1981, p. 179). There is a neglecting to provide for the other emotions and the needs they create, such as hostility and guilt. As a result, the widow of an emotionally unfulfilling relationship may experience profound guilt when she feels relief

Mourning accouterments such as these two black bonnets, a black fan, and black-rimmed mourning stationery were formal expressions of grief expected of Victorian survivors. The mourning stationery was commonly used for a year after the loss of a child, spouse, or parent; six months after the loss of a grandparent; or two months after the loss of an aunt or uncle. Kemp Davis.

instead of sadness. If there is much latent hostility, there is the need for discharge; if guilt is strong, there is the need for release and displacement. Ira Glick and associates observe that attempting to fit one's psychological responses into an ill-fitting ritual is like putting a sore foot into a shoe two sizes too small (Glick, Weiss, and Parkes 1974).

On the other hand, one may experience profound grief but not be perceived as a legitimate occupant of the bereavement role. Employers, for example, are often not as willing to give the same time off to those losing a second cousin as they would to those experiencing the death of a parent or spouse. The loss of a pet may trigger the same reactions as if a family member had died, particularly for older individuals for whom the animal is their chief companion and major source of responsibility. James Quackenbush, a social worker who has studied the mourning of pet owners, claims that their grieving process is identical to those experiencing the death of a human loved one (*Psychology Today* 1985).

Social and Psychological Needs for Ritual
Over the past few hundred years, Western societies have witnessed the privatization of death. Whereas in the late 1940s some 70 percent of all deaths occurred at home, by the mid-1980s more than 80 percent died in institu-

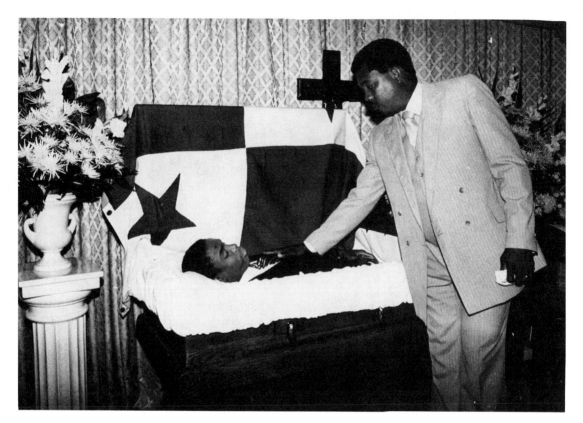

A father's last goodbye: Harold Brown rests his hand on the chest of his son, Arturo, a Boston University basketball star who died of a heart attack. The flag of Panama, their native land, is draped over the lid of the coffin. UPI/Bettmann Newsphotos.

tional settings. One now dies in private just as one bathes, defecates, or copulates in private. Concurrently, grief has likewise become privatized and bereavement underinstitutionalized as a role.

The privatization of grief is another symptom of the cultural ethos of death denial. In part, it is caused by the diminishing of solidarity bonds among the living: the community feels less involved in the death of one of its members (Ariès 1981, pp. 612–14) because of geographic mobility, the population densities of urban life, the disengaged status of many of those who die, and the anonymization and bureaucratization of social relations. It also is a consequence of the changing quality of death. When death came suddenly and unexpectedly, the burden of grief largely fell on the survivors. Such was the case for most of recorded history, when a huge proportion of deaths were premature. Nowadays, however, with the preponderance of slow-motion deaths, much of the grief work might be completed before the actual death, with the dying person left alone to his or her own resources when coping with the end. As Ariès noted, there is a historical correlation between public deaths and the existence (and clarity) of bereavement ritual.

But there remain both social and psychological needs for ritual. From society's perspective, bereaved individuals may be unable to function in their roles if they are overwhelmed by grief, incapacitated by fear and anxiety of death, or refusing to develop relationships to replace those dissolved. This problem becomes significant when we realize that every year some 8 million Americans suffer the death of a close family member (*New York Times* 1984c). For the individual, there is the need for the time and space to publicly express the feelings occasioned by loss. Without ritual, people get nervous because they don't know what to do, producing a situation that more powerful others can take advantage of.

The need for ritual for those experiencing marginally legitimate forms of bereavement has led to the rise of a number of specialized support groups. Since the 1970s, for instance, hundreds of such groups emerged for parents suffering prenatal deaths, from miscarriages early in pregnancy to stillbirths at the end.[18] In these groups, parents learn that it is common to blame themselves for the death even though they know that they have done nothing wrong, and that others find themselves calculating—even years later—what their child would be doing if still alive and hesitate to visit friends with children (Belkin 1985).

 Jewish Mourning Rules

Jewish law provides for three successive periods of mourning following the burial, each observed with increasingly less intensity. The first period is known as *shiva*, which means seven and refers to the seven-day period of mourning following the burial.

Shiva is observed for the following relations: father, mother, spouse, off-spring, siblings.

It is most proper for a family to observe the shiva together in the home where the deceased lived. . . .

Mourners do not sit on seats of normal height, but on low stools. Footstools or hassocks may serve the purpose. . . .

Mourners do not wear shoes made of leather. Slippers, canvas or rubber shoes may be worn as an alternative to stockinged feet.

Male mourners refrain from shaving and hair cutting; female mourners avoid the use of cosmetics.

Mourners may not go to work. The local rabbi should be consulted for exceptions, as there may be extenuating circumstances in individual cases.

Avoidance of pleasure: One does not bathe or shower for comfort, although it is permissible to wash for cleanliness, unless it is a matter of severe discomfort.

One may not engage in sexual relations.

One may not put on new or freshly laundered clothing.

One may not engage in Torah study, except for books or chapters dealing with laws of mourning, and books such as Job, Lamentations, and parts of Jeremiah, which speak of grief and anguish.

The second period is known as *shloshim*, which means thirty and refers to the period from the end of shiva through the thirtieth day after burial. Attending parties even where no music is played and getting married is forbidden during this period; so is shaving or cutting one's hair for the entire month. This concludes the mourning for all relatives other than mother or father.

The third period observed for a mother or father is known simply as *avelut*, mourning. It terminates at the end of twelve months from the day of death. During this period, joyous events, dinners with music, theaters, and concerts should be avoided. Kaddish is said daily by sons for eleven months of the year. After the year, it is forbidden to continue practices or restraints that openly indicate the continuation of the grief.

From Donin 1972, pp. 299–300. From To Be a Jew: A Guide to Jewish Observance in Contemporary Life, by Rabbi Hayim Halevy Donin. © 1972 by Hayem Halevy Donin. Reprinted by permission of Basic Books, Inc., Publishers.

Finally, corresponding with the impoverishment of mourning ritual has been the fading of the consoling role. We now see funeral participants immediately resuming their roles and leaving the immediate survivors with such lines as, "Call me if you need help." Except for those of the Jewish faith, most Americans do not have prescribed rules for comforting the mourner.[19] Employers typically grant only one week off for the death of a parent or spouse. For the recently bereaved, immediate support ends before grief work really begins. Gorer observed:

Giving way to grief is stigmatized as morbid, unhealthy, demoralizing—very much the same terms are used to reprobate mourning as were used to reprobate sex; and the proper action of a friend and well-wisher is felt to be distraction of a mourner from his or her grief; taking them "out of themselves" by diversions, encouraging them to seek new scenes and experiences, preventing them "living in the past." (1965, p. 113).

As a result, the bereaved are left alone to struggle in freeing themselves from their bondages with the deceased, releasing negative emotions, renewing social relationships, and rediscovering meaning in their lives.

The first chapter of this book developed the analogy of death being to social members what an atom smasher is to nuclear physicists. Only when a death occurs or the nucleus of an atom is destroyed can we appreciate how

each constituent part contributes to the whole structure. Only by experiencing grief and the mourning process can we appreciate how thoroughly
human lives are intertwined.

Widowhood: The Permanent Status of the Bereaved

Of all relationships affected by death, it is the death of a spouse that most
changes the social identity of the bereaved. Husbands become widowers, and
wives become widows. There is no comparable change in the title of parents
whose child has died, of children who lose a parent (except for "orphans,"
but that requires normally the death of both parents before late adolescence—one does not become "orphaned" at the age of twenty-five) or grandparent, or of one who loses a lifelong friend. The existence of such a title
reveals a fundamental change in one's standing in the social order. Further,
given the tendency of males to marry females younger than themselves coupled with the fact that women have a life-expectancy advantage of eight years,
widowhood carries the female stigma in a sexist society (Lopata 1971).

Widowhood is not merely a label assigned to surviving spouses, but it is a
social status as well. As is the case with all social statuses, there are normative
patterns to its timing and behavioral expectations, and these, in turn, are a
function of one's place within the sex, age, and class hierarchies. Cross-culturally, the most severe behavioral restraints are typically observed among
females, particularly those of childbearing age yet without children. The traditional Indian custom of *suttee,* for example, where the widow (never the
widower) sacrificed herself on the blazing funeral pyre of her husband, was
not expected of postmenopausal or pregnant women (Lopata 1972). So
great are the freedoms of widows in the United States that we fail to appreciate that normative standards can emerge around such issues as whether one
returns to one's family of origin or remains with the family of one's deceased
spouse (the widow can, for instance, be expected to marry or be the responsibility of a brother of her husband); whether one's residence is to be patri-
local or matrilocal; whether or not one can remarry and, if so, to whom,
when, and by whose consent; and what rights one has to the former spouse's
estate. Still, American widows are frowned upon if they begin dating a week
after the funeral or remarry a few months thereafter.

An ideal-type rite of passage for marital survivors would involve the phases
of destroying one's married self, ritually becoming able to pass from the
world of couples back to the world of singles, and finally being publicly rein-
corporated into this new world with at least the same social status one had
when married. One problem for widows in American society, for example,
is that they exist in a marital limbo, neither of the world of marrieds nor of

Giving the Widowed an Arm to Lean On

One of the saddest things about being widowed is the word "widowed."

"Perhaps a couple of better words might be 'de-spoused' or 'disspoused' or 'spouseless,'" said Fran Koch, a widow who counsels the widowed in Brooklyn. She said this facetiously, and was greeted with equal measures of laughter and groaning from the 150 other widows and widowers who had gathered in a Manhattan auditorium Saturday to share their experiences of bereavement.

"There's *nothing* wrong with the word widow," said Charlotte Potak, who has twice been widowed and has a 24-year-old son from the first marriage and an 8-year-old daughter from the second. "I don't think we should try to change the word, but try to change the public's perception of the word widow." She runs workshops for the widowed in Allentown and Bethlehem, Pa.

"The image of the widow is that of someone who is over the hill, pathetic, pitiable and dependent," said Lynn Cain, "and yet one widow out of four is under the age of 45." The 1974 book about her own experience, *Widow*, first brought the special problems of the widowed to a nationwide audience and became a rallying point for those who have pushed for more public awareness of the needs of the bereaved.

"Well as bad as the word 'widow' is, at least we have a word for it," said Lily Singer, a widow who counsels the bereaved in Westchester. "When I work with those parents who have lost a child, do you know what some of them say to me? They say, 'At least you have a word that describes your experience. But the language doesn't even give us a word to describe what we've lived through.'"

Projections from census data suggest that 75 percent of all married women will be widowed, and that they will survive their husbands by some 16 years.

the world of singles. In a couple-oriented culture, the widow—particularly the first in a friendship circle—can be perceived as threatening to her married female friends, as she represents a possible contender for the attentions of remaining males. There can occur the so-called widow-attachment syndrome, in which the bereaved claws for attachments with intimate others, ensnaring them into obligatory roles, such as having others do one's decision making. The new widow is stigmatized by her proximity to death, a depressing reminder for other women of their own eventual fates. In Helen Lopata's study (1973b), nearly four out of ten widows claimed to have a less active social life than before their spouses' deaths. And since the average age for entering this predicament is fifty-six years, one actually faces more than two decades with this status unless she remarries. But the prospects for remarriage are dim, given the rivalry of younger women and the fact that one is often not up to forging an entirely new set of understandings and common history with another male who, in all likelihood, would leave her to cope with his dying.

But the problems experienced by many of the 11 million widows in the United States are not limited to changing social relationships. In addition to the loss of friends and social isolation, researchers have located the common themes of financial stress, feelings of aloneness, and problems with other family members. Once again, such a list of difficulties is only words, encapsulated "you knows," which fail to capture the profoundness and scope of such hardships. The notion of loneliness, for example, does not convey what the absence of a spouse and constant companion for forty years means to one forever deprived of their presence. Perhaps it is because of the very fear of loneliness that many prefer a bad relationship to none at all. And what might "problems with other family members" mean? Children, for instance, may deny their widowed mother opportunities for substitute intimate relationships, demanding a nunlike status out of respect for their deceased father. The widowed person must attempt to acquire new skills and fill unaccustomed roles. These new, sometimes confusing roles are apt to be assumed with little insight and with considerable reluctance, leading to strong feelings of inadequacy and frustration (Bowlby 1980).

It may be the case that the problems cited above are more profound for widows of earlier cohorts. These are the generations of women, now old, who were relatively unaffected by the feminist movement.[20] So totally dependent are their identities on those of their spouses that when their husbands die these females lose a significant portion of their very self-concept (Carey 1977).[21] For more recent cohorts of women, on the other hand, individuals may have more anticipatory socializations for widowhood because of earlier divorces and may be less devastated by their spouses' deaths as their identities are more likely to derive from their work.[22] Coming of age in an era when the traditional sex roles underwent considerable modification, these women are no longer as dependent on their husbands' status for their own identities, and their spouses' deaths no longer necessarily entail diminished social status. In sum, the changing meanings of "wife" and "marriage" will lead to changing qualities and meanings of widowhood.

With the prolongation of life and its associated forms of slow-motion death, the very nature of widowhood has changed. Recall (Chapter 4) the example of the spouse of an Alzheimer's victim in the later stages of the disease. Because of the effects of this disease on cognition, language, and memory, the victim dies socially long before dying physiologically. "For better or for worse, till death do us part"—the seemingly simple marriage vow—entails a more demanding and challenging commitment for an increasing number of persons. Spouses who must exist with living death, who have lost the mates they once knew just as surely and permanently as if by death, are in many ways widowed. However, since the familiar body remains, society neither recognizes the Alzheimer's spouse's grief nor provides the support and comfort accorded to traditional widows whose grief is recognized. And without formal rituals for mourning, perhaps the plight of the Alzheimer's spouse is even more distressing than that of the widowed person.

It is difficult for most to appreciate the full scope of this form of widowhood. Eventually, most everyday activities become impossible for the Alzheimer's victims, who have difficulty remembering their names, selecting the clothing appropriate for the season, and knowing how to interact with others. Not only is there the burden of care, the heartbreak of having a spouse awaken next to you and ask who you are, but there is also the isolation resulting from friends being scared off either by misfounded fears of contagion or by the victim's abnormal behavior. Families' descriptions of the course of the disease portray it as a "funeral that never ends" (Aronson and Lipkowitz 1981, p. 569; see also Kapust 1982). Spouses of dementia victims commonly see themselves as "walking widows" (Steuer and Clark 1982, p. 91).

Facing One's Own End

We turn from the reactions of individuals to others' deaths to the responses of people facing their own demise. As developed earlier, it was not many generations ago that death was a public event. Even children were allowed to witness life's final moments. With the privatization of death in institutional settings, however, this event which we all must face has become a matter of secrecy and mystery. Americans must increasingly rely on the second- and thirdhand accounts of professionals to discover exactly what happens, and huge markets now exist for any information regarding what to expect. The dying are often unable to share their last sensations because so many die while in a coma or in a state of drugged semiconsciousness.

Emotional Responses to One's Death

With modernization, death fears shifted from concerns about postmortem fates to fears of the dying process. And with the cultural goal of creating the opportunities for "good" deaths being addressed through therapeutic means, it is not surprising that most contemporary accounts of the death experience come from medical and psychiatric, not religious, practitioners.

One predominant theme of these professional descriptions is grief. There are a number of similarities between this grief and that experienced when someone else dies. Benoliel (1970), for example, identified five stages of adaptation to a chronic disease: (1) shock and disbelief, during which denial is a common reaction; (2) a gradual awareness of the reality of one's changed condition, occasioning expressions of guilt and anger; (3) reorganization of relationships with other people; (4) resolution of loss through active grieving; and (5) reorganization of identity to incorporate the changes that have taken place.

A second basic professional theme is denial. Weisman (1972) proposes that there are varying degrees of death denials and that the process is never constant. He classifies these degrees of denial into three orders. First-order denial is when the dying person minimizes or denies his or her symptoms. Second-order denial occurs when the patient minimizes the implications of his or her illness. And the third order results from a basic denial of extinction. In terms of a stage model of death acceptance, Weisman claims that not all individuals pass through this final order.

Finally, the third theme of these professional accounts is fear. Lacking the language to capture the full terror, the fear of dying is instead broken down into the specific (and therapeutically describable) fears of dependency, loneliness, pain, physical disfigurement, and loss of dignity (Brim et al. 1970; Koenig 1973; Nash 1977):

- *Dependency and loss of control.* We live in a society that frowns on dependency. However, the terminally ill individual knows that he or she will slowly grow increasingly dependent on financial, medical, self-care, and emotional assistance. Such dependencies erode self-respect.

- *Isolation and loneliness.* Once an individual is identified as being a "dying patient," profound changes take place. An immediate response is to isolate the dying patient in a private room. For elderly individuals, already segregated from society, such separate placement only enhances the degree of their actual and symbolic isolation. The "terminal" label also causes medical staff, family, and friends to relate to one differently (Nash 1977). Of all age groups, loneliness is most likely to be experienced as a problem by individuals aged seventy years and older (Nash 1977). This can be partially attributed to the social value placed on the dying old. One's social value is contingent upon such factors as age, intelligence, occupation, family position, and beauty. The elderly are impoverished in many of these areas and therefore receive low social priority. Epley and McCaghy (1977) claim that this perceived moral worth of a dying individual has obvious implications for the treatment received from medical personnel, family, and friends. These investigators found that the public attitude is to avoid persons with incurable disease and that more negative attitudes are expressed toward the dying than toward the ill or healthy. Loneliness also occurs because the dying individual's family and friends (not to mention medical personnel) treat death as a taboo subject. All too often, a dying person must participate in mutual pretense games instead of being allowed to discuss overwhelming emotions. Koenig (1973) suggests that there is a degree of isolation and loneliness past which one prefers death.

- *Pain.* One facet of pain is loneliness. When experiencing significant pain, one cannot focus on anything else (Nash 1977). Each person experiences a pain that is unique and often indescribable. There is the fear that once such unbearable pain occurs, one will be denied painkilling medication. Conversely, there is concern of others that one will become too dependent on medication and will lose the sense of reality.

- *Physical disfigurement.* Severe weight loss, loss of hair, and so on are often outcomes of terminal illness or its treatment. This fear comes particularly to those placing great importance on physical appearance, such as those who think that the security of a love relationship depends on their sexual attractiveness (Koenig 1973). Physical disfigurement may also limit social interaction if the individual believes others will find him or her repulsive (Carson 1971). It is a misconception to believe that the elderly are not concerned about their appearance or about being sexually attractive to their partners.

- *Loss of dignity.* People with terminal illness are not just dying; they are also living. Dying persons have the desire for some contact with everyday life. Nash (1977) points out that the loss of the ability to relate and to love lowers one's capacity to be involved, leading to the loss of one's sense of control. A loss of control, in turn, leads to a loss of dignity. Reinforcing this dynamic is the passive role American patients normally assume. The dying individual may come to feel that he or she has no right to make decisions that concern his or her life. Nash observes that in situations rated low in opportunities for dignity, patients appear weary, isolated, apathetic, indifferent, and resigned to their coming death.

- *Fear of the unknown.* There is a host of secular and religious anxieties unleashed by the prospects of immediate death. At no other time in one's life do the existential questions that have haunted the human animal since the dawn of civilization become so poignant and personally salient.

The separate fears detailed can cause the dying individual to become withdrawn and lose interest in his or her surroundings and family. Koenig (1973) refers to this as a state of bankruptcy—a period during which there are no more important credits to be added and nothing of importance left to be taken away. However, many investigators feel that such reactions can be avoided if the patient is allowed to discuss feelings about death as well as to have control over its direction, deciding whether to aggressively prolong life with medical advances or to surrender earlier to the natural dying process (Malcolm 1986).

In reviewing the professional breakdown of these specific fears, Thomas Powers (1971) observed that it may be a form of cultural hypnosis; by focusing on the specific sensations, we can ignore their entire gestalt. Probably the best-known attempt to synthesize these subjective reactions are the works of psychiatrist Elisabeth Kübler-Ross (1969, 1970). So widely read are her descriptions of the stages of death that dying patients inform physicians and nurses of the stages they are in.

According to Kübler-Ross, when a patient is informed that he or she has a potentially terminal illness, the first reaction is normally one of shock and denial. This is the "no not me" stage, a phase typically characterized by magic, hope, disbelief, and denial—all self-protective personality functions. In addition to *denial,* there are the following stages:

- *Anger.* A stage posing considerable challenge to staffs, as patients often become hard to handle, critical and demanding, nasty and uncooperative. Kübler-Ross notes significant others can erroneously view this as an expression of ingratitude, leading to fewer and shorter visits, reinforcing the sense of isolation and abandonment. She recommends emotional venting and proposes "screaming rooms" for both patients and staff.

- *Bargaining.* A temporary truce—"Yes, it's happening to me, but . . . " For the first time, patients fully grasp what is really happening to them but often bargain for more time by promising good behavior.

- *Depression.* Mourning for past and future losses characterizes this period of grieving, silence, and withdrawal as the dying person begins separating himself or herself from all that is known and loved. Those who tell a person to "cheer up, everything will be all right" are perhaps impeding this reconciliation with the inevitable.

- *Acceptance.* One recognizes that the end is near, and it is all right. It is neither a happy nor an unhappy time, nor is it a resignation. Lyn Helton, a poet, wife, and mother who died of bone cancer at age twenty, wrote during her final days: "Dying is beautiful. Even at the ripe old age of 20. It is not easy most of the time, but there is real beauty to be found in knowing that your end is going to catch up with you faster than you expected and that you have to get all your loving and laughter and crying done as soon as you can. I am not afraid to die, not afraid of death, because I have known love."

The Kübler-Ross stage theory has been challenged for its validity (Schulz and Aderman 1974). Some have interpreted the stages to be sequentially ordered, which was not the intent. Criticism has been leveled at Kübler-Ross's methodology, which, relying more on clinical insight than on objective measurement, allows for a considerable degree of "unscientific" subjectivity. Other investigators have failed to duplicate the stages of dying

(Benoliel 1970; Garrity 1974; Schulz and Aderman 1974). Despite such crit-icisms, what should be remembered is that the stages at least provide a frame-work for understanding the coping strategies terminally ill people employ and for appreciating the dynamics occurring between the dying and the surviving.

In many ways, Kübler-Ross is a product of her times. If she was not the one to hold the proverbial candle to the cultural darkness surrounding death, someone else undoubtedly would have done so, for the silence had become deafening. In attending her talks around the country during the 1970s, this author had flashes of being at some old-time revival. The house was always packed and the audience always enthusiastic. The message was one of demodernization, saying that medicine only treats body mechanics and not spiritual repair and that we should be more like children in approaching our end—unfretful and without fear. In flirting with the marginal, Kübler-Ross walked a tightrope between religion and science, initially embraced by both but later abandoned. In late 1979, it was revealed that her close association with Jay Barham, a former sharecropper and aircraft worker who founded the Church of the Facet of Divinity, produced seances that included sexual inter-course between participants and "entities" of the spiritual world. The focus of Kübler-Ross's work turned to the afterlife, and she spoke of "spirit guides" and portrayed death as a cure-all. In 1981, she agreed to a *Playboy* magazine interview, fusing once again the themes of sex and death.

Fulfilling Emotional and Professional Attempts to Shape Good Deaths

In addition to the often negative fears and emotions, there are other sensa-tions and preoccupations triggered by the approach of death. Some of these can be quite positive and satisfying, such as the intensity, meaningfulness, and richness of life that many terminally ill persons experience. The aware-ness of one's finitude can lead to a sense of ecstasy at being freed from social constraints, an experience explored by existential philosophers (see Chapter 6). Many devote their lives to conforming to the expectations of others so as to receive their attention, and true individualism may only come at life's end. To assist in death's potential to produce such self-discoveries, psychiatrist David Spiegal of Stanford (*Human Behavior* 1978) conducts group therapy sessions for terminally ill cancer patients. To gain a sense of resolution and not waste final days with death preoccupations, he had individuals first pre-pare lists of their central properties and attributes. They then meditate on giving up each of these aspects of their identities, one by one, quality by quality. Finally, they are perhaps able to locate the essential part of themselves that remains.

With the cultural rediscovery of death and the personal and social needs for good endings, experts emerged who specialized in shaping such experiences to enhance the quality of death. Their strategies range from therapy groups to training terminally ill people to practice Eastern meditation techniques—supposedly assisting one in "letting go" at the time of death so that one's ego can merge "into the cosmic flux of the universe" (Boerstler 1986, p. 115)—to administering the psychoactive drug LSD to the dying, which supposedly enhances morale, reduces depression and pain, and collapses one's orientations toward the past and future into the now, theoretically enhancing interactions with family and environment (Grof and Halifax 1978).

 "Will Dying Become a Pleasant Experience?"
   From The Futurist *Magazine*

Someday people may actually look forward to dying.

Death will be a pleasant experience—in fact, the most pleasant of a person's life—and people will look forward to it throughout their lives.

Suicides may someday become actively encouraged. The growing cost of Social Security benefits means that the taxpayers have a major interest in encouraging people to die as soon as possible after they become eligible for Social Security benefits.

A special "buy out" program could be instituted. All persons who agree to die within a certain length of time would get additional benefits. Their dying would also be paid for. . . .

A first step toward making death more pleasant might be to legalize suicide and provide ways to assist a person whose life has lost its meaning in ending it. A person wishing a suicide license could apply to a government board. The board would consult with physicians and others whose advice might be useful in determining whether a license should be granted. Family members might also be consulted. Permission would normally be granted only to elderly persons in poor health, though exceptions could be made. . . . [If] permission is granted, the would-be suicide could get all kinds of special help from physicians and others in ending his life as pleasantly as possible. Special institutions might spring up to help people commit suicide. . . .

A person ready to die and properly licensed could get help from a thanatologist, or death specialist, who would be licensed to dispense a variety of potent drugs. Some of the drugs would be designed to kill a person painlessly; others would provide feelings of euphoria. . . . Medical research promises even better drugs than now exist to make people blissfully happy during their last days. And many things could be provided to make dying pleasant. During a "festival of dying," a dying person might have an opportunity to say farewell to friends and relatives, sharing happy memories. . . . The final act of death might include a special death feast, which could include the actual drinking of the poison that will send him into a final sleep. Ancient Romans sometimes committed suicide in a party-like atmosphere, so the future festival of death may be only reviving a past practice.

. . . People licensed for suicide might come to be thought of as "Free Souls" or "Liberated Ones."

Cornish 1986. Reprinted, with permission, from the Futurist,
published by the World Future Society,
4916 St. Elmo Ave., Bethesda, Maryland 20814.

Robert Butler (1963), observing the frequency of reminiscing behavior by those approaching death, gave clinical recognition to an equivalent of the popular accounts of drowning swimmers seeing their lives flash before their eyes. Calling this phenomenon the "life review," Butler argued that it is a "naturally occurring" and "universal process," characterized by a "progressive return of past events and conflicts to consciousness where they can be surveyed and integrated."[23] So important is this need to make sense of and to share one's life that some institutions have actually hired individuals to do little more than simply listen to the dying talk.

There is nothing new in listening to and recording the last thoughts of dying individuals. What has changed is the motive. In the past, people listened for a lesson. There existed a mythology about the veracity of endings, with the deathbed as the setting for a profound summation of the meaning of it all. In discussing the literary quality of suicide notes, a writer for the *American Mercury* (Wolf 1931) remarked: "Of all such documents, I am especially interested by the suicide notes because, when confronted by death, the American who goes through life talking a pretense usually blurts out a truth . . . the letter quoted lays bare the soul of a coward in all his shame and ignominy." In recent years, perhaps because of the changing quality of death, we hear fewer dying words. However, there is the trend of prominent people publicly speaking of their feelings toward and insights from being seriously ill. Actors dying of lung cancer make public service announcements on the evils of cigarette smoking. Lifetime achievement awards are given to the dying, who, acknowledging them, summarize the meaning of their careers. Writer Norman Cousins inspired Senator Jacob Javits, who was slowly succumbing to amyotrophic lateral sclerosis (Lou Gehrig's disease—an interesting eponym), to publicly reflect on the meaning of his existence. Javits said

Famous Last Words

Florenz Ziegfeld (1867–1932, American theatrical producer), in a delirium: "Curtain! Fast music! Lights! Ready for the last finale! Great! The show looks good. The show looks good."

Thomas Edison in a coma: "It is very beautiful over there."

Henry Ward Beecher (1813–1887, American clergyman): "Now comes the mystery."

Buddha: "Beloved, that which causes life, causes also decay and death. Never forget this; let your minds be filled with this truth. I called you to make it known to you."

George Bernard Shaw to his nurse: "Sister, you're trying to keep me alive as an old curiosity, but I'm done, I'm finished, I'm going to die."

Charles Darwin: "I am not the least afraid to die."

Oscar Wilde (dramatist, died 1900): "It would really be more than the English could stand if another century began and I were still alive. I am dying as I have lived—beyond my means."

Green 1979.

that the most important point in staying alive was "to keep my brain in order and functioning. . . . This is the essence of life" (Altman 1984).

Out-of-Body Experiences and Glimpses of the Hereafter

In one way, this entire book has been required to set the stage for the following phenomenon. We began with the proposition that "death" is a socially constructed idea and that its associated fears and hopes serve as the bases of social control and personal motivation. We next mapped the cultural and social forces contributing to this knowledge system to better understand the relationship between mental phenomena and social organization—how, for example, shifting power among the social elites (e.g., from religion to medicine) is correlated with shifts in public anxieties (e.g., from fears of postmortem fate to fears of how one dies).

One legacy of existentialism and psychology was a focusing of public attention toward the subjective aspects of life and death, producing a receptive climate for Elisabeth Kübler-Ross's reports on the experiences of dying. Concurrently, there were medical advances enabling physicians, the new high priests of death, to literally resurrect those "clinically dead." By the late 1960s, stories of what it is like to die began to circulate widely in professional quarters. In 1975, these were shared with the general public in *Life after Life*.[24] Here *Dr*. Raymond Moody reported tantalizing similarities among the reports of those having had "near-death experiences," or NDEs, as they were to be called.[25] A "typical" case Moody cites is the following:

About a year ago, I was admitted to the hospital with heart trouble, and the next morning, lying in the hospital bed, I began to have a very severe pain in my chest. I pushed the button beside the bed to call for the nurses, and they came in and started working on me. I was quite uncomfortable lying on my back so I turned over, and as I did I quit breathing and my heart stopped beating. Just then, I heard the nurses shout "Code pink! Code pink!" As they were saying this, I could feel myself moving out of my body and sliding between the mattress and the rail on the side of the bed— actually it seemed as if I went *through* the rail—on down to the floor. Then, I started rising upward, slowly. On my way up, I saw more nurses come running into the room—there must have been a dozen of them. My doctor happened to be making his rounds in the hospital so they called him and I saw him come in, too. I thought, "I wonder what he's doing here." I drifted on up past the light fixture—I saw it from the side and very distinctly—and then I stopped, floating right below the ceiling, looking down. I felt almost as though I were a piece of paper that someone had blown up to the ceiling.

I watched them reviving me from up there! My body was lying down there stretched out on the bed, in plain view, and they were all standing around it. I heard one nurse say, "Oh, my God! She's gone!" while another one leaned down to give me mouth-to-mouth resuscitation. I was looking at the back of her head while she did this. I'll never forget the way her hair looked; it was cut kind of short. Just then, I saw them roll this machine in there, and they put the shocks on my chest. When they did, I saw my whole body just jump right up off the bed, and I heard every bone in my body crack and pop. It was the most awful thing! (Moody 1975, p. 36)

The results of an early 1980s national survey indicated that as many as 8 million Americans have had such experiences (Gallup 1982).[26] An earlier study, conducted between 1959 and 1972 by Osis and Haraldsson (1977), found considerable congruity between the near-death experiences of people in the United States and in India.

Underlying his scores of interviews, Moody (1975, 1977) detected the following common themes:

- *Ineffability*. So profound and extraordinary were the experiences that the revived were unable to capture through language what they went through.
- *Witnessing one's death*. Many reported hearing staff pronouncing their deaths and even seeing the attempts at their own revival from above the heads of physicians and nurses.
- *Hearing sounds*. Immediately after death, persons heard a loud ringing or buzzing noise.

- *Tranquil feelings.* Although the experience was totally novel, for most there were accompanying feelings of peace and serenity.

- *Out-of-body experiences.* Respondents claimed that they left their bodies, being able to see them and the surroundings from a vantage point above and being able to travel almost instantaneously to distant places.[27]

- *The dark tunnel.* For some, there was a quick journey through some void or darkness, frequently likened to a dark tunnel.[28]

- *The life review.* Akin to the myth of seeing one's life flash before one's eyes, subjects reported a rapid, panoramic view of their entire biographies.

- *Interactions with dead others.* One was not alone in this new realm, often encountering deceased relatives and friends or religious figures who offered guidance to another world.

- *The light.* Often reported were sightings of a brilliant golden light, which for some was a being with whom they communicated.

- *The boundary uncrossed.* Some approached a border of no return, such as a river, mountain, or door, which they could not pass.

- *The ambivalent return.* Though many failed to remember exactly how they reentered their bodies, the return was often a letdown. For them, it was not yet time to go on; there were still things to be done.

- *Fear of sharing one's story.* So bizarre and yet so personally meaningful were these experiences that individuals were hesitant to tell others about them, fearing either personal ridicule or the diminution of their experiences.

- *A born-again outlook.* Of interest to existential philosophers and other humanist thinkers are reports that many NDEs consequently reappraised and altered their life course, felt greater confidence in dealing with life, no longer fearing death, and they had increased appreciation for the nonmaterial aspect of life.

Not everyone on the threshold of death has (or can remember) such near-death experiences, and of those who do, only a subset of the above sensations are normally encountered and with no common order to their manifestations.

Such experiences could not be ignored. Too many had endured them, convinced that they were more "real" than everyday, wide-awake consciousness. Could it be that such experiences spawned religious beliefs in the immortality and in Christ's ascent to heaven (Smith 1973)? Did they produce the primitive animistic beliefs about the soul's ability to leave the body during sleep or death ("giving up the ghost") (Ehrenwald 1974)? Are they related to the astral projections of shamans and transcendental meditators? And should such positive stories of death even be disseminated, as they may inspire suicidal behavior (Richardson 1979)?

Scientific skepticism was not about to let such experiences go unchallenged, especially when it came to accepting them as prima facie evidence of life after death. Medical researchers were quick to portray these near-death experiences as a "fantasy of death" (Blacher 1979), attributing them to hallucinations accompanying oxygen deprivation (Blacher 1979), pharmacological side effects, sensory deprivation (Comer, Madow, and Dixon 1967), or a surge of endorphins triggered shortly before death (Carr 1981). Personality disorders were viewed by psychiatrists as possible determinants of the occasion and content of such sensations, conceptualizing them to be but additional manifestations of death-denial defenses (Hunter 1967; Ehrenwald 1974).

This skepticism was to find its way into the popular literature as well. Upon the disclosures of Kübler-Ross's involvement with fornicating spirits, Ron Rosenbaum wrote in an article entitled "Turn On, Tune In, Drop Dead":

But a case can be made that intercourse with entities—okay, let's call it sex with the dead— is not an aberration but a summation, a consummation, of the whole misbegotten love affair with death that the movement [defenders of death awareness] has been promoting. . . .

Kübler-Ross herself has become the guru to a nationwide network of death 'n' dying centers called "Shanti Nilaya"; the "Conscious Dying Movement" urges us to devote our life to death awareness and also opens up a "Dying Center"; a video artist kills herself on public television and calls it "artistic suicide"; the EXIT society publishes a handy, do-it-yourself Home Suicide guide that can take its place next to other recent Home Dying and Home Burial Guides; a pop science cult emerges around the "near death experience," which makes dying sound like a lovely acid trip (turn on, tune in, drop dead); attempts at two-way traffic with the afterlife abound, including a courier service to the dead using dying patients and even phone calls from the dead; belief in reincarnation resurfaces as "past lives therapy." (1982)

As matters stand, reports of (and beliefs in) near-death experiences have the same validity status as religious portrayals of the hereafter: both are a matter of faith.

Conclusion

Having focused earlier on death from the cultural and social structural levels, this chapter considered death from the perspective of the individual. From the vantage point of the higher, more abstract levels developed earlier, one may have laughed at the movie advertisement for *The End* ("Think of death as a pie in the face from God"). But when it involves the death of a loved one or one's own medical diagnosis of a terminal malady, the topic is suddenly transformed. No longer is it something that one can stand back from and intellectualize about, but rather it becomes an issue toward which one can only respond emotionally.

Emotions comprise a facet of self that social scientists are only now beginning to appreciate and understand.[29] To suppress such primordial feelings can be damaging, both psychologically and sociologically. A child who does not grieve and mourn a parent's death may, as a consequence, later suffer neuroses and psychoses in adulthood. Gorer speculated: "If one can deny one's own grief, how much more easily can one deny the grief of others; and one possible outcome of the public denial of mourning is a great increase in public callousness" (1965, p. 113). It is the variety and intensity of emotions that social scientists have traditionally focused on in describing the experiences of dying and bereavement. From their studies there is revealed (anthropologists may claim "rediscovered") a human need for ritual as a means for coping with these feeling states. It is ritual that gives one the attention of others as well as a recipe for acting when one's reality is in disorder. Given the culture's paucity of ritual for those experiencing life's most trying times, service providers have jumped in with their own therapeutic ceremonies to address the void: morticians offer themselves as "grief experts" to the bereaved, hospice provides at least an ideology for care and attention for the terminally ill, and psychiatrists offer group counseling and controlled LSD trips for the dying.

Death and dying is a dualistic process involving both the dying and the surviving. The quality of death depends on the reactions and interactions of both. The "good" death developed in Chapter 4 involves a proper synchronization of the rites of passage of the dying and the survivors-to-be. Ideally, for the dying, the death should be anticipated, welcomed, nonstigmatizing, and following the completion of one's central social obligations and personal desires or goals. For the surviving, the death should occur neither prematurely nor postmaturely, with the affairs of the deceased in order, with their (the survivors') status at least remaining intact, and having had the opportunity to say or do with the deceased all that was desired and without any regrets. With increasing public awareness of the options, with the confinement of death to the old, and with the slow-motion nature by which most deaths arrive (whose timing and prediction is increasingly controlled by the medical institution), the possibility for "good" deaths to become the norm has never been greater. The major obstacle is society's ability to provide full, meaningful lives that allow the individual the sense of closure and completeness when the end does arrive. The problem of death remains the problem of life.

NOTES

1. One might compare European and American cohorts born between 1935 and 1941 to determine what impacts World War II had on the two populations. Considering that these individuals are now in their forties and fifties, their "social prime" in terms of social involvements and power, one wonders whether personal experience in the war has shaped their attitudes toward disarmament.

2. For those of you not familiar with these two brands, both were spinoffs of the monster craze that swept America's postwar baby-boom youth during the 1960s and 1970s. The cereal boxes are adorned with cartoon images of the horror classics: Frankenstein, the creature fashioned by a scientist from the parts of corpses, and Dracula, a foreign, aristocratic type who sleeps in a coffin by day and by night sucks the blood of the living.

3. During the mid-1980s, parents, too, received a death-defying lesson from their breakfast cereals. An advertising campaign by Kellogg's associated its All-Bran cereal with the finding that a high-fiber, low-protein diet may reduce the risk of some kinds of cancer (Molotsky 1984).

4. The thanatological lessons of Halloween are evidence of the cultural outlook to which children are socialized. Ghosts, skeletons, demons, and monsters are the traditional symbols worn by those least likely to die in our society. Despite the historical fears about and meaning of such symbols of death, children learn that such images are to be played with, mocked, and defied. And the adults play along. But the lessons of October 31 are changing with the times. Whereas a decade or two ago, in many middle-class neighborhoods, children would venture to the doors of strangers, nowadays candies are laced with poison and razor blades, and the instruction is one of mistrust.

5. This suicide by a Putnam, Connecticut, youth triggered a debate about whether the game should be allowed in the public schools during free periods. Said a spokesman for the local Christian Information Council, "Playing these games can desensitize players to murder, suicide, rape, torture, robbery, the occult or any other immoral or illegal act." Added a parent, "It is another of Satan's ploys to pollute and destroy our children's minds" (Brooke 1985).

6. There is a growing number of children's books addressing the subject of death (see Cook 1974). Some of the traditional "classics" include Margaret Brown's *The Dead Bird,* Judith Viorst's *The Tenth Good Thing about Barney,* and Sandol Warburg's *Growing Time.*

7. This decreasing likelihood of death has undoubtedly affected the nature of parent-child relationships. Not only was there the absence of the kind of emotional bonds that now hold family members together, but in the past parents simply could not invest their energies with a creature that would probably soon die. Emotional investments are conditioned by temporal expectations. On the other hand, considering the contemporary anti child ethos, perhaps it could be argued that adults used to be nicer to children because they typically had so little time to live.

8. According to a 1984 report of the National Cancer Institute, the number of deaths of children under the age of fifteen declined dramatically since World War II.

Comparing the death rates between 1965 and 1979 with the number expected at 1950 rates, the number of deaths fell 80 percent for Hodgkin's disease, 69 percent for kidney cancer, 50 percent for leukemia and bone sarcoma, 32 percent for non-Hodgkin's lymphoma, and 31 percent for all other cancers (*New York Times* 1984a).

9. According to the NORC 1984 General Social Survey, the percentage of various age groups belonging to three or more organizations breaks down as follows:

Age	Male	Female	Percentage of total	(N)
18–34	22.1%	23.6%	23.0%	(554)
35–49	29.4	34.5	32.3	(392)
50–64	41.6	22.6	30.5	(264)
65–74	31.7	15.8	21.9	(154)
75+	20.0	11.4	13.7	(94)

10. A colleague of this author was struck by the similarities between his aging mother and his sixteen-year-old son in terms of the meaningfulness of having access to an automobile. For both, having a car and the license to drive it symbolizes mobility and independence. To lose one's license in old age is to lose one of the last privileges of freedom associated with adulthood.

11. Based on his clinical experience, Gorer (1965) claims that the loss of a grown child is the most distressing and long-lasting of all griefs.

12. There is considerable variance among state laws regarding the relative legitimacy of various types of wills. In the state of Texas, for instance, there are four types of wills that can be made by any person eighteen years of age and older:

Formal self-proving will: in writing, signed by testator and two witnesses (fourteen years of age and older) in the presence of testator and a notary public

Formal will: same as formal self-proving will but does not contain the self-proving affidavit

Holographic will: written wholly in handwriting of testator and requiring the testimony of two witnesses familiar with testator's handwriting

Nuncupative will: an oral will made at time of the deceased's last illness, not valid when value of estate greater than thirty dollars "unless it can be proved by three credible witnesses that the testator called on in person to take notice or bear testimony that such is his will, or words of like import"

13. Experts recommend that individuals leave not only a will but also a letter of direction that gives instructions about where the will, insurance policies, inventory of properties, and bank accounts can be found. If there is a designation of funeral home, the type of funerary service desired, and organ donations, the will is normally not the best location to place such information, as it is often not unsealed until after the funeral.

14. Willard Gaylin, a Columbia University psychiatrist, said: "Ambivalence is most likely to lead to pathological grief when it is accompanied by a strong psychological dependence on the person who had died. If you feel you need the other person

to cope with life, then they threaten your very survival by dying, you feel abandoned" (Goleman 1985a, p.23).

15. In fact, divorce may exceed widowhood in terms of long-term emotional and physical tolls. National mortality data reveal that for those deaths attributed to psychological factors, such as suicide, the divorced fare worse than the widowed in eight of ten categories (Brody 1983). For the first time in history, a married couple is as likely to be parted by divorce as by death. More than half of American children are likely to experience the dissolution of their parents' marriage by the time they are eighteen (Weitzman 1985).

16. Curiously, despite the fact that this research tradition of studying grief was well established by the early 1940s, the government did not accumulate reliable information with regard to the civilian-survivor effects of military deaths until the mid-1950s (see Bucher 1957).

17. Our culture tends to therapeutize those symptoms it deems undesirable, and the management of grief is no exception.

18. There are an estimated six hundred thousand miscarriages each year in the United States, including stillbirths. The Centers for Disease Control in Atlanta have calculated that between 10 and 20 percent of all pregnancies end in miscarriage (Belkin 1985). Even for these types of deaths, parents still can experience a sense of loss twenty years later (Cole 1987).

19. We might note, however, the appearance of specialized sympathy cards for such situations (see Rhodes 1971; Woods and Delisle 1978; and McGee 1980).

20. Parkes and Weiss (1983, p.11), for example, found that older couples have a much sharper division of labor than younger couples. Thus, a spouse's death could be expected to be more devastating to the older survivor than would be the case where familial roles intersect or are shared, as is more often the case among more recent cohorts.

21. On the other hand, because age discrepancies between husbands and wives were greater in the past than in the present, many husbands had prepared their wives to be widows. Further, for some women of these older cohorts, widowhood has had positive effects. Perhaps for the first time in their lives, they discover out of necessity that they can balance the checkbook and compete successfully in the work force (particularly those who inherited their husbands' businesses).

22. On the other hand, Lopata (1973a) found that women with the most education were most likely to report a major change of self following the death of a spouse. For the highly educated woman, the reconstruction of self could be a more difficult process.

23. It is easy to speculate about whether such subjective experiences provided the template on which societies developed such ideas as postmortem judgments and heaven and hell.

24. Two years later, *Life after Life* was reviewed in *Reader's Digest*, perhaps *the* forum of common public knowledge, having the largest circulation of any U.S. magazine.

25. The use of the NDE abbreviation deserves mention. Such a reference implies not only the veracity of the phenomenon but also its scientific nature. Neither religion nor philosophy has concepts so "accepted" that they can be summed up in abbreviated forms in common parlance.

26. It seems that "truth" is no longer revealed in the oracle of Delphi or in the message of a prophet but rather through public opinion polls.

27. In Greyson and Stevenson's (1980) study of seventy-eight individuals having near-death experiences, three-quarters had such out-of-body experiences.

28. In the Greyson and Stevenson (1980) study, the impression of passing through a tunnellike structure was significantly more prevalent among executives and professionals than among laborers and service workers.

29. Social scientists, for example, still don't know whether the grief of a mother who has lost her oldest child is lessened if she is convinced of the existence of a wondrous afterlife or not. Nor do they know how much of grief is psychobiologically innate and how much is social-psychologically shaped. Not only are there observed emotional differences between sexes, ethnicities, cultures, and social classes, but between differing cohorts as well.

REFERENCES

Alexander, Irving, and Arthur Alderstein. 1958. "Affective Responses to the Concept of Death in a Population of Children and Early Adolescents." *Journal of Genetic Psychology* 93:167–77.

Altman, Lawrence. 1984. "150 Doctors Hear Javits Hail 'the Essence of Life.'" *New York Times*. May 11, p.12.

Ariès, Philippe. 1962. *Centuries of Childhood: A Social History of Family Life*. New York: Vintage Books.

———. 1974. *Western Attitudes toward Death: From the Middle Ages to the Present*. Baltimore and London: Johns Hopkins University Press.

———. 1981. *The Hour of Our Death*. New York: Alfred A. Knopf.

Aronson, M. K., and R. Lipkowitz. 1981. "Senile Dementia, Alzheimer's Type: The Family and the Health Care Delivery System. *Journal of the American Geriatrics Society* 29(12):568–71.

Belkin, Lisa. 1985. "Counseling and Support following Miscarriage." *New York Times*. June 6, pp.19, 20.

Benoliel, J. Q. 1970. "Talking to Patients about Death," *Nursing Forum* 9(3):255–69.

Birtchnell, John, et al. 1973. *The Effects of Early Parent Death*. New York: MSS Information.

Blacher, Richard. 1979. "To Sleep, Perchance to Dream . . . " *Journal of the American Medical Association* 242(21):2291–92.

Boerstler, Richard. 1986. "Meditation and the Dying Process." *Journal of Humanistic Psychology* 26(2):104–24.

Bowlby, John. 1980. *Attachment and Loss.* New York: Basic Books.

Brim, Orville Jr., Howard Freeman, Sol Levine, and Norman Scotch, eds. 1970. *The Dying Patient.* New York: Russell Sage Foundation.

Brody, Jane. 1983. "Divorce's Stress Exacts Long-Term Health Toll." *New York Times.* December 13, p.17.

———. 1984. "'Autoerotic Death' of Youths Causes Widening Concern." *New York Times.* March 27, p.27.

Brooke, James. 1985. "Fantasy Game Is Blamed for Suicide of Avid Young Player in Connecticut." *New York Times.* August 22, p.18.

Bucher, Rue. 1957. "Blame and Hostility in Disaster." *American Journal of Sociology* 62(5):467–75.

Butler, Robert. 1963. "The Life Review: An Interpretation of Reminiscence in the Aged." *Psychiatry* 26(1):65–76.

Butler, Robert, and Myrna Lewis. 1981. *Aging and Mental Health: Positive Psychosocial and Biomedical Approaches.* St. Louis: C. V. Mosby.

Carey, Raymond. 1977. "The Widowed: A Year Later." *Journal of Counseling Psychology* 24(2):125–31.

Carr, Daniel. 1981. "Endorphins at the Approach of Death." *Lancet.* February 14, p.390.

Carson, J. 1971. "Learning from a Dying Patient." *American Journal of Nursing* 71(2):333–34.

Clayton, Paula, and J. Darvish. 1979. "Course of Depressive Symptoms following the Stress of Bereavement." In J. E. Barrett, ed., *Stress and Mental Disorder.* New York: Raven Press, pp.121–36.

Cole, Diane. 1987. "It Might Have Been Mourning the Unborn." *Psychology Today.* July, pp.64–65.

Collins, Glen. 1984. "Giving the Widowed an Arm to Lean on." *New York Times.* April 9, p.20.

Comer, N., L. Madow, and J. Dixon. 1967. "Observations of Sensory Deprivation in a Life-Threatening Situation." *American Journal of Psychiatry* 124:164–69.

Cook, Sarah. 1974. *Children and Dying: An Exploration and Selective Bibliography.* New York: Center for Thanatology Research and Education.

Cornish, Edward. 1986. "Will Dying Become a Pleasant Experience?" *The Futurist* 20(6):2, 49.

DeSpelder, Lynne, and Albert Strickland. 1983. *The Last Dance: Encountering Death and Dying.* Palo Alto, Calif.: Mayfield.

Donin, Rabbi Hayim H. 1972. *To Be a Jew: A Guide to Jewish Observance in Contemporary Life.* New York: Basic Books.

Durkehim, Emile. 1965. *The Elementary Forms of the Religious Life* (1915), trans. by Joseph Swain. New York: Free Press.

Ehrenwald, Jan. 1974. "Out-of-the-Body Experiences and the Denial of Death." *Journal of Nervous and Mental Disease* 159(4):227–33.

Ekman, Paul, Robert Levenson, and Wallace Friesen. 1983. "Autonomic Nervous

System Activity Distinguishes among Emotions." *Science*, September 16, pp.1208–10.

Eliade, Mircea. 1959. *Cosmos and History: The Myth of the Eternal Return*. New York: Harper & Row.

Epley, R. J., and C. H. McCaghy. 1977-78. "The Stigma of Dying: Attitudes toward the Terminally Ill." *Omega* 8(4):379–91.

Erikson, Eric. 1963. *Childhood and Society*. New York: W. W. Norton.

Feifel, Herman. 1959. "Attitudes toward Death in Some Normal and Mentally Ill Populations." In Herman Feifel, ed., *The Meaning of Death*. New York: McGraw-Hill, pp.114–30.

Field Institute. 1986. "A Digest on the Degree of Public Concern about Important State Issues." *California Opinion Index* 5 (September).

Flores, Aurora. 1984. "Young Writers Have Suicide and Nuclear War on Their Minds." *New York Times*. December 28, p.22 (letter to ed.).

Gallup, George Jr. 1982. *Adventures in Immortality: A Look beyond the Threshold of Death*. New York: McGraw-Hill.

Garrity, T. F. 1974. "Psychic Death: Behavioral Types and Physiological Parallels." *Omega* 5(3):207–13.

Gerth, Hans, and C. Wright Mills. 1953. *Character and Social Structure: The Psychology of Social Institutions*. New York: Harcourt, Brace & World.

Gesell, Mark, and Frances Ilg. 1956. *The Child from Five to Ten*. New York: Harper & Row.

Glick, Ira, Robert Weiss, and C. Murray Parkes. 1974. *The First Year of Bereavement*. New York: John Wiley.

Goleman, Daniel. 1985a. "Mourning: New Studies Affirm Its Benefits." *New York Times*. February 5, pp.19, 23.

———. 1985b. "Strong Emotional Response to Disease May Bolster Patient's Immune System." *New York Times*. October 22, pp.13, 18.

———. 1986. "Disaster's Impact on Young Feared." *New York Times*. January 30, pp.1, 13.

Gorer, Geoffrey. 1965. *Death, Grief and Mourning*. New York: Doubleday Anchor Books.

Green, Jonathon, compiler. 1979. *Famous Last Words*. New York: Quick Fox.

Greyson, Bruce, and Ian Stevenson. 1980. "The Phenomenology of Near-Death Experiences." *American Journal of Psychiatry* 137(10):1193–96.

Grof, Stanislav, and Joan Halifax. 1978. *The Human Encounter with Death*. New York: E. P. Dutton.

Gutmann, David. 1973. "The Premature Gerontocracy: Themes of Aging and Death in the Youth Culture." In Arien Mack, ed., *Death in American Experience*. New York: Schocken Books, pp.50–82.

Hanlan, Archie. 1979. *Autobiography of Dying*. New York: Doubleday.

Hardt, Dale. 1978–79. "An Investigation of the Stages of Bereavement." *Omega* 9:279–85.

Helsing, Knud, Moyses Szklo, and George Comstock. 1981. "Factors Associated with Mortality after Widowhood." *American Journal of Public Health* 71(8):802–9.

Human Behavior. 1978. "Death Coping: The Lessons Can Sharpen Living." 7(5):46.

Hunter, R. C. 1967. "On the Experience of Nearly Dying." *American Journal of Psychiatry* 124(1):122–26.

Jacques, E. 1965. "Death and the Mid-life Crisis." *International Journal of Psychoanalysis* 46:502–14.

Kalish, Richard, and D. Reynolds. 1976. *Death and Ethnicity: A Psychocultural Study.* Los Angeles: University of Southern California Press.

Kapust, L. R. 1982. "Living with Dementia: The Ongoing Funeral." *Social Work in Health Care* 4(4):79–91.

Kastenbaum, Robert. 1977. *Death, Society, and Human Experience.* St. Louis: C. V. Mosby.

Kearl, Michael, and Elisabeth Hoag. 1984. "The Social Construction of the Midlife Crisis: A Case Study in the Temporalities of Identity." *Sociological Inquiry* 54(3):279–300.

Kemeny, Margaret. 1984. "Psychological and Immunological Predictors of Recurrence in the Herpes Simplex II." Paper presented at the 92nd Annual Meeting of the American Psychological Association, Toronto.

Kiecolt-Glaser, Janice, Ronald Glaser, C. Speicher, G. Penn, J. Holliday, and R. Glaser. 1984. "Psychosocial Modifiers of Immuno-competence in Medical Students." *Psychosomatic Medicine* 46(1):7–14.

Koch, Joanne. 1977. "When Children Meet Death." *Psychology Today.* August, pp.64–66, 79.

Koenig, R. 1973. "Dying versus Well-Being." *Omega* 4(3):181–95.

Konner, Melvin. 1982. *The Tangled Wing: Biological Constraints on the Human Spirit.* New York: Harper & Row.

Kübler-Ross, Elisabeth. 1969. *On Death and Dying.* New York: Macmillan.

———. 1970. "The Dying Patient's Point of View. In Orville Brim, Jr., *et al.*, eds., *The Dying Patient.* New York: Russell Sage Foundation, pp. 156–70.

Levinson, Daniel. 1977. "The Mid-Life Transition: A Period in Adult Psychological Development." *Psychiatry* 40:99–112.

Lewis, Clive S. 1963. *A Grief Observed.* Greenwich, Conn.: Seabury Press.

Lifton, Robert. 1967. *Death in Life: Survivors of Hiroshima.* New York: Random House.

Lindemann, Erich. 1944. "Symptomatology and Management of Acute Grief." *American Journal of Psychiatry* 101:141–48.

Lopata, Helena. 1971. "Widows as a Minority Group." *Gerontologist* 2:67–70.

———. 1972. "Role Changes in Widowhood: A World Perspective." In David Cowgill and Lowell Holmes, eds., *Aging and Modernization.* New York: Appleton-Century Crofts, pp.275–303.

———. 1973a. "Self-Identity in Marriage and Widowhood." *The Sociological Quarterly,* 14:407-418.

————. 1973b. *Widowhood in an American City*. Cambridge, Mass.: Schenkman.

Lynch, James. 1977. *The Broken Heart: The Medical Consequences of Loneliness*. New York: Basic Books.

McGee, Marsha. 1980–81. "Faith, Fantasy, and Flowers: A Content Analysis of the American Sympathy Card." *Omega* 11(1):25–35.

McIntire, Matilda, Carol Angle, and Lorraine Struempler. 1972. "The Concept of Death in Midwestern Children and Youth." *American Journal of Diseases of Children* 123(6):527–32.

McLeod, Beverly. 1984. "In the Wake of Disaster." *Psychology Today*. October, pp.54–57.

Malcolm, Andrew. 1986. "Fateful Choice in Fatal Illness: How Long to Live." *New York Times*. February 14, p.8.

Maurer, Adah. 1966. "Maturation of Concepts of Death." *British Journal of Medicine and Psychology* 39:35–41.

Molotsky, Irwin. 1984. "Cereal Ad Praised by an F.T.C. Aide." *New York Times*. December 5, p.11.

Moody, Raymond. 1975. *Life after Life*. Covington, Ga.: Mockingbird Books.

————. 1977. *Reflections on Life after Life*. New York: Bantam Books.

Myers, Edward. 1986. *When Parents Die*. New York: Viking.

Nagy, Maria. 1948. "The Child's Theories concerning Death." *Journal of Genetic Psychology* 73:3–27.

Nash, M. L. 1977. "Dignity of Person in the Final Phase of Life—An Exploratory Review." *Omega* 8(1):71–79.

National Opinion Research Center. 1985. *General Social Surveys, 1972–1985*. Chicago: University of Chicago.

New York Times. 1984a. "Few Children Dying of Cancer." March 26, p.11.

————. 1984b. "Boston Children Learn 'Dying Isn't a Vacation.'" August 26, p.16.

————. 1984c. "Bereavement Toll on Living Studied." September 23, p.29.

Osis, K., and E. Haraldsson. 1977. *At the Hour of Death*. New York: Avon Books.

Osterweis, Marian, Frederic Solomon, and Morris Green, eds. 1984. *Bereavement: Reactions, Consequences, and Care*. Washington, D.C.: National Academy Press.

Parkes, Colin Murray. 1976. "The Broken Heart." In Edwin Shneidman, ed., *Death: Current Perspectives*. Palo Alto, Calif.: Mayfield, pp.333–47.

Parkes, C. Murray, and R. Weiss. 1983. *Recovery from Bereavement*. New York: Basic Books.

Pennebaker, James. 1985. "Inhibition and Cognition: Toward an Understanding of Trauma and Disease." *Canadian Psychology* 26:82–95.

Powell, Alice. 1986. "Smart Kids Worry More about Nuclear War." *New York Times*. January 2, p.18. Data from Powell's forthcoming dissertation, "Adolescent Reaction to the Nuclear Threat: Variables Related to Levels of Express Nuclear War Fears."

Powers, Thomas. 1971. "Learning to Die." *Harper's Magazine*. June, p.72–80.

Psychology Today. 1970. "You and Death." August, questionnaire. pp.67–72.

———. 1985. "Gates of Heaven." August, p.65.

Rhodes, R. 1971. "Packaged Sentiment." *Harper's Magazine*. December, pp.61–66.

Richardson, Glenn. 1979. "The Life-after-Death Phenomenon." *Journal of School Health* 49(8):451–53.

Rosenbaum, Ron. 1982. "Turn On, Tune In, Drop Dead." *Harper's Magazine*. July, pp.32–42.

Rosenblatt, Paul, R. Patricia Walsh, and Douglas Jackson. 1976. *Grief and Mourning in a Cross-Cultural Perspective*. New Haven, Conn.: Human Relations Area File Press.

Ruffenach, Glenn. 1985. "Reflections on Parents' Retirement Illustrate Fears of Next Generation." *Wall Street Journal*. December 11, p.33.

San Antonio Express-News. 1984. "Man Kept Wife's Skeleton." June 22, p.2A.

Schulz, R., and D. Aderman. 1974. "Clinical Research and the Stages of Dying." *Omega* 5(2):137–43.

Slater, Karen. 1986. "Been Putting Off Making a Will? Consider the Consequences of Dying without One." *Wall Street Journal*. January 9, p.21.

Smith, Morton. 1973. *The Secret Gospel*. New York: Harper & Row.

Steuer. J. L., and E. O. Clark. 1982. "Family Support Groups within a Research Project on Dementia." *Clinical Gerontologist* 1(1):87–95.

Temoshok, Lydia, et al. 1985. "The Relationship of Psychosocial Factors to Prognostic Indicators in Cutaneous Malignant-Melanoma." *Journal of Psychosomatic Research* 29(2):139–53.

Volkart, Edmund, and Stanley Michael. 1981. "Bereavement and Mental Health." In Sandra Wilcox and Marily Sutton, eds., *Understanding Death and Dying*. Port Washington, N.Y.: Alfred Publishing, pp.175–88.

Weisman, A. D. 1972. *On Dying and Denying: A Psychiatric Study of Terminality*. New York: Behavior.

Weitzman, Lenore. 1985. *The Divorce Revolution*. New York: Free Press.

Wolf. H. 1931. "Suicide Notes." *American Mercury* 24:264–72.

Woods, Abigale, and Robert Delisle. 1978. "The Treatment of Death in Sympathy Cards." In Charles Winick, ed., *Deviance and Mass Media*. Beverly Hills, Calif.: Sage Publications, pp.95–103.

Zajonc, Robert. 1980. "Feeling and Thinking—Preferences Need No Inferences." *American Psychologist* 35(2):151–75.

Index